BETTY FRIEDAN

and the Making of
The Feminine Mystique

D0881897

A *Volume in the Series*

CULTURE, POLITICS, AND THE COLD WAR

EDITED BY
Christian G. Appy

BETTY FRIEDAN

and the Making of
The Feminine Mystique

THE AMERICAN LEFT, THE COLD WAR,
AND MODERN FEMINISM

with a New Preface by the Author

Daniel Horowitz

University of Massachusetts Press
Amherst

Library of Congress Cataloging-in-Publication Data
Horowitz, Daniel, 1938–
Betty Friedan and the making of the feminine mystique : the
American left, the cold war, and modern feminism / Daniel Horowitz.
p. cm. — (Culture, politics, and the cold war)
Includes bibliographical references and index.
ISBN 1-55849-168-6 (cloth : alk.paper) / ISBN 1-55849-276-3 (pbk. : alk. paper)
1. Friedan, Betty. 2. Feminists—United States—Bibliography.
3. Feminism—United States. 4. United States—Politics and government—20th century.
I. Title. II. Series.
HQ1413.F75H67 1998
305.42'092—dc21   98-7592
[b]   CIP

British Library Cataloguing in Publication data are available.

To

Aimée Brown Price
Monroe E. Price
Louis Wilson
friends who become family

and

Judith H. Katz and Leonard A. Katz
family who become friends

Contents

Illustrations follow pages 120 and 216

Preface to the Paperback Edition

The publication of Betty Friedan's *The Feminine Mystique* in 1963 played a pivotal role in the rebirth of feminism in the United States. This best-selling book awakened hundreds of thousands, if not millions, of women in the United States—characteristically middle-class, college-educated suburban ones—to possibilities beyond housekeeping and child rearing. It also helped launch Friedan into a position of leadership among feminists. In her book, Friedan told of how her suburban captivity led her to discover women's issues in the suburbs. This story resonated with its audience and became part of the central narrative of the popular and scholarly histories of postwar women.

Betty Friedan and the Making of "The Feminine Mystique" tells a different story, and the differences are crucial in understanding Friedan's life and the history of postwar feminism. The evidence in this book shows that Friedan's feminism had its roots not only in suburban captivity of the 1950s, as she has claimed, but also in labor radicalism of the 1940s, which she continues to deny. Admittedly, Friedan was a suburban housewife in the 1950s, but she was no ordinary suburban housewife.

The response of reviewers to what my book reveals has been varied. As expected, women's historians and those on the left, especially socialist feminists, appreciate what I have done. The evidence discovered and the connections made have helped convince them of the accuracy and importance of this reinterpretation of Friedan's life.[1] Nor is it a surprise that conservatives use my book as an occasion to call into question the legacies of Friedan, feminism, and the 1960s.[2]

What I did not anticipate is the skepticism that representatives of a younger generation of women have directed at my insistence that the

social analysis and political experiences of the Popular Front had significant bearing on the shaping and nature of Friedan's feminism. They prefer
the picture that Friedan herself offered: disconnected from her political
past, a self-actualizing individual shaped primarily by personal experiences as a suburban housewife and mother. They like Friedan's own version of her life because they advocate a feminism grounded in middle-
class experience, humanistic psychology, and a celebration of the ability of
the heroic and isolated self to discover truth that is more personal than
political or at least not political in terms set by socialist feminists. Given
how they would rather see Friedan and feminism, they dissent from the
thrust of my conclusions. Generally speaking, although they do not question the evidentiary basis of my claims, they show little interest in grappling with what I have discovered about her past in the 1940s and early
1950s. They remain deeply skeptical of my picture of Friedan's feminism
and life as influenced by what she wrote and witnessed as a labor journalist. For them, Friedan's efforts in the 1940s to fight racism, male chauvinism, and corporate power pale into insignificance. They distance themselves, feminism, and Friedan from the radical origins of her work in the
Old Left.[3]

Several months after the publication of the first edition of my book in
November 1998, the first biography of Friedan's entire life written for adult
audiences appeared. In *Betty Friedan: Her Life* (1999), the journalist Judith
Hennessee relied on extensive interviewing to provide a version of Betty
Friedan's life that differed significantly from the story I reconstructed from
archival material in Friedan's personal papers and elsewhere. If my book
focused more on the development of Friedan's idea than on events in her
personal life, the opposite was true in Hennessee's book. She devoted a
good deal of attention to the fights that Friedan had with her husband and
with other feminist leaders. She told the story of the paradoxes that explained Friedan's life. She painted a picture of Friedan as a feminist who
treated women badly and instead sought the favor and love of men.
Hennessee saw Friedan's labor union activism as preceding her feminism
rather than as closely connected with it. "During her years as a labor
reporter Betty received a complete education in women's issues, but there
was no 'click,' no moment of truth." Noting that Friedan in 1953 had
heard a speaker at a union conference say, "Women must be treated as
equal members of society, not as recipients of favors," Hennessee concluded that "the words did not resonate."[4] The emotional dimensions of a
celebrated figure's early life are always hard to determine. Yet surely some
skepticism is in order when we are told that a woman, known throughout

her life for her passionate engagement, disconnected herself from emotional involvement with issues that concerned her personally and politically.

Friedan's *Life So Far: A Memoir* (2000) largely perpetuated the version of her life that she had been offering since the 1960s, especially the relationship between what she learned as a labor journalist and the feminism she espoused beginning in the late 1950s. Well before the publication of her book, I was aware how she reacted to what I had said in my book. "He's got it so wrong, it annoys me," she remarked in December of 1998. Friedan "made it clear," a reporter remarked at the time, "that her feminism did not arise from exposure to left-wing ideologists during her reporting days." How could she learn feminism from men in the Old Left, Friedan wondered, when they "were every bit as male chauvinist as the rest of the world"?[5]

In the memoir, Friedan acknowledged her involvement in 1940s radicalism more fully than she had previously, but denied that it had had anything to do with shaping her consciousness of women's issues. Using a distinctly anti-feminist note that minimized her agency in founding the women's movement, she remarked that "it *just happened*, I would say, by some miracle of convergence of my life and history, serendipity, one thing leading to another." Implicitly denying the impact of ideas she had learned as a college student and a Popular Front journalist, she insisted "that ideology has to come from personal truth." Even though her book contained evidence of awareness of her own engagement with women's issues as a labor journalist, she still maintained that her radicalism in the 1940s did not involve any focus on women's issues, that she only discovered feminism in the late 1950s. Therefore, she asserts that there is a sharp separation between the parts of her life, with the break coming around 1957. "When I thought about politics, which I did a lot" in the late 1940s, she remarked in her memoir, "it was not about women at all."[6]

In contrast, the historical record suggests considerable continuity in her engagement with women's issues, stretching from the late 1930s until the present. This difference is critical for understanding both her life and the history of the modern women's movement in the United States. This book explores a number of explanations of why her story and mine differ. I have become convinced that in the almost forty years since it first appeared, Friedan has simply forgotten, or chosen to forget, how thorough and deep was her engagement with women's issues before she started working on *The Feminine Mystique*. Her experiences as a labor journalist played a significant role in fostering her feminism.

The differences between Friedan's story and this one are vitally important to historical understanding. They are fights over history, not over personality.[7] Friedan is one of the missing links in the history of American feminism. I have tried to restore a sense of connectedness to Friedan's life and the history of American feminism. What is at stake in understanding the origins of feminism is considerable. This is not the narrative of how one person, living outside of history, came to consciousness of women's issues. Rather, it is the story of how a participant in a social movement did so. In the 1940s the labor movement began to focus on issues of critical importance to women. As Laura Shapiro said in her essay on *Betty Friedan and the Making of "The Feminine Mystique"* in *Newsweek,* "the real roots of modern feminism" lie in "familiar issues of pay and child care raised half a century ago."[8] In contrast, in its 29 June 1998 feature story on feminism, with Friedan's picture on the cover, *Time* magazine disparaged the women's movement by saying that 1960s feminism "didn't start in the factory. It started in wood-paneled salons," then "spread to suburban living rooms," and "eventually ended up with Norma Rae," the woman in a 1979 movie who, despite overwhelming odds, organizes her co-workers in a southern factory into a union. "That trajectory," *Time* concluded, emphasizing the middle-class origins of the modern women's movement, is feminism's "biggest problem today."[9]

This book argues the contrary. It joins the work of a series of historians, including Dorothy Sue Cobble, Dennis Deslippe, Joyce Folet, Lisa Kannenberg, Gerda Lerner, Ruth Rosen, Landon Storrs, and Kate Weigand in reversing that trajectory. Feminism of the 1960s had important origins in the factories of the 1940s. Middle-class observers, such as Betty Friedan, were inspired by the passion of working-class trade union women involved in labor insurgency in the years during and immediately following World War II. McCarthyism attempted to snuff out those flames, driving the thriving feminism of the 1940s underground. That feminism, shaped in the cauldron of the 1940s, was too strong to die. Submerged in the 1950s, it reemerged during the 1960s, transmuted in varying degrees in the work of Betty Friedan and of others such as Bella Abzug, Eleanor Flexner, and Gerda Lerner. As we recover more stories of feminism on the left in the 1940s and 1950s, stories of its vitality as well as its suppression, we will be able to connect the past to the present in the lives of women in twentieth-century America.

DANIEL HOROWITZ

Northampton, Massachusetts
October 2000

Notes to Preface

Abbreviations are listed on pages 257–58.

1. See, for example, Rochelle Gatlin, "History, Memory, and McCarthyism: The Case of Betty Friedan," *SWLSA Newsletter*, winter 2000, 3–4; Mark Greiff, "She Liked to Read Books," *Boston Book Review*, March 1999, 11; Linda Kerber, "Moving beyond Stereotypes of Feminism," *Chronicle of Higher Education*, 23 April 1999, B 6–8; Ruth Milkman, "Before the Mystique," *Women's Review of Books*, June 1999, 1, 3–4; Annelise Orleck, review, *AHR* 105 (April 2000): 574–75; Katherine Osburn, review, H-NET List for Women's History, Jan. 2000; Ruth Rosen, "Untold Stories," *Dissent*, summer 1999, 111–14; June Sochen, review, *Choice*, 1999; Alan Wald, "The Costs of McCarthyism," *Against the Current*, March–April 2000, 34-38; Robert E. Weir, review, *Newsletter of the Northeast Popular Culture/American Culture Association*, Oct. 1999, 13; Allan Winkler, "Problem That Had No Name," *Times Higher Education Supplement*, 9 April 1999, 29. For an exemplary review that is both sympathetic to my work and skeptical of some of my conclusions, see Lori E. Rotskoff, "Home-Grown Radical or Home-Bound Housewife? Rethinking the Origins of 1960s Feminism through the Life and Work of Betty Friedan," *Reviews in American History* 28 (March 2000): 120–27. Wald, the only reviewer who contextualized the controversy surrounding my book, notes that Eakin and Shulevitz, cited below, attributed to me "opportunist motives and sensationalist claims that are nowhere in evidence in the book": Wald, "Costs of McCarthyism," 36.

2. Among the reviews from conservatives are anonymous, *First Things*, June–July 1999, 61; Richard J. Ellis, "The Forgotten Betty," *Times Literary Supplement*, 19 March 1999, 5–6; David Horowitz, "Feminist Fibber," *Salon Magazine*, 18 Jan. 1999. Generally these observers appreciated my work; only David Horowitz found my sympathies significantly problematic.

3. For evidence of these tendencies, most notable in the Shulevitz review, see Judith Shulevitz, "Outside Agitator," *NYTBR*, 9 May 1999, 18; Elizabeth Lasch-Quinn, review, *Wilson Quarterly*, spring 1999, 132; Emily Eakin, "The Way She Was," *Lingua Franca*, spring 1999, B 1-2, 30, 32, 38, 40–43. Once Friedan's memoir appeared, Shulevitz visited these issues again: Judith Shulevitz, "A Mother's Day Mash Note, of Sorts, to Betty Friedan," *Slate*, 9 May 2000. For evidence of Lasch-Quinn's opposition to the soical welfare policies that Friedan and other feminists have advocated, see Elizabeth Lasch-Quinn, "Mothers and Markets," *New Republic*, 6 March 2000, 37–44.

4. Judith Hennessee, *Betty Friedan: Her Life* (New York, 1999), 54.

5. Betty Friedan quoted in Linda Myers, "Friedan's Agenda." Apply Feminist Ideals of Equality, Fairness to Men, Too," *Cornell Chronicle Front Page*, 3 Dec. 1998; Myers, "Friedan's Agenda." For additional responses by Friedan to my work see Betty Friedan, *Life So Far: A Memoir* (New York, 2000), 14; Glenn Lewis, "Personal Truths Spark a Movement," *Library Journal*, 1 April 2000, 112; Elaine Woo, "Betty Friedan: Feminist Keeps a Sharp Eye on Her Movement and Her Mystique," *Los Angeles Times*, 4 June 2000.

6. Friedan, *Life So Far*, 13, 73; for evidence of her engagement with women's issues while working for the *UE News*, see Friedan, *Life So Far*, 65.

7. The principal controversy that followed the publication of Friedan's book focused on the nature of her relationship with Carl Friedan during their marriage: contrast Betty Friedan, "Battling for Women While Being Beaten at Home," *George*, May 2000, 82-87, with Carl Friedan, letter to editor, *NYT Book Review*, 16 July 2000, 4, and the material on his website, CarlFriedan.com.

8. Laura Shapiro, "The Feminist's Mistake?" *Newsweek*, 9 Nov. 1998, 72.

9. Ginia Bellafante, "Feminism: It's All About Me!" *Time*, 29 June 1998, 57.

BETTY FRIEDAN

and the Making of
The Feminine Mystique

Introduction

> In a certain sense it was almost accidental—coincidental—
> that I wrote *The Feminine Mystique,* and in another sense
> my whole life had prepared me to write that book; all the
> pieces of my own life came together for the first time in the
> writing of it.
>
> BETTY FRIEDAN, *"It Changed My Life,"* 1976

In 1951, a labor journalist with a decade's experience in left-wing movements described a trade union meeting where rank-and-file women talked
and men listened. Out of these conversations, she reported, emerged the
realization that the women were "fighters—that they refuse any longer to be
paid or treated as some inferior species by their bosses, or by any male
workers who have swallowed the bosses' thinking." The union was the
United Electrical, Radio and Machine Workers of America, commonly
known as the UE and one of the most radical American unions in the
postwar period. In 1952, that same journalist wrote a pamphlet, *UE Fights
for Women Workers,* which in 1993 the historian Lisa Kannenberg, then
unaware of the identity of its author, called "a remarkable manual for fighting wage discrimination that is, ironically, as relevant today as it was in
1952." At the time, the pamphlet helped raise the consciousness of Eleanor
Flexner, who in 1959 would publish *Century of Struggle,* the first scholarly
history of American women. In 1953–54 Flexner relied on the pamphlet
when she taught a course at the Jefferson School of Social Science in New
York on "The Woman Question." Flexner's participation in courses at the
school, she later wrote, "marked the beginning of my real involvement in
the issues of women's rights, my realization that leftist organizations—
parties, unions—were also riddled with male supremacist prejudice and discrimination." The labor journalist and pamphlet writer was Betty Friedan.[1]

Yet in 1973 Friedan remarked that until she started writing *The Feminine
Mystique* (1963) "I wasn't even conscious of the woman problem." In 1976
she commented that in the early 1950s she was "still in the embrace of the
feminine mystique." Although at one point in the 1970s she alluded, in
often vague terms, to a more radical past, even then she left the impression

1

that her landmark book emerged principally from her own captivity by the very forces it described. When she entered the limelight, Friedan was careful about her autobiographical revelations and how she connected her past to her present. Her claim that she came to political consciousness out of a disillusionment with her life as a suburban housewife was part of her reinvention of herself as she wrote and promoted *The Feminine Mystique*. When I use the term reinvention I refer to the process, which all of us carry out to a greater or lesser extent, of developing a series of narratives of our lives that are, in turn, shaped by how events and memory influence us.[2]

Friedan's version of her life, which historians and journalists readily accepted, hid from view the connection between her union activity of the 1940s and early 1950s and the feminism she articulated in the 1960s. Her story made it possible for white suburban women readers to identify with its author and thereby enhanced the book's appeal. The narrative she offered also reflected shifts in Friedan's political commitments that involved some repudiation of her radical past. Friedan's knowledge of the dangers of McCarthyism of the 1950s prompted her to minimize her work as a labor journalist. In the short term, her misery in the suburbs may have prompted her to write *The Feminine Mystique;* a longer-term perspective makes clear that the book's origins go back much farther—to her youth in Peoria, her education at Smith College, and her experiences with labor unions in the 1940s and early 1950s. Although in the end it might be possible to reconcile Friedan's and my version of her life, in important ways they diverge. An exploration of her experiences as a young radical and activist are crucial to understanding Friedan's life and the history of modern feminism.[3]

In her 1963 book, Friedan presented a powerful and influential analysis of what she called the feminine mystique, the beliefs that trapped those middle-class suburban women for whom extra income was not an economic necessity but a choice about identity and self-development. She asserted that in the aftermath of World War II, a series of factors came together to encourage women to seek fulfillment as wives and mothers and avoid pursuing careers, professionalism, or politics. This happened, she noted, even though an increasing proportion of women were working outside the home. She identified a shift from a pre-war emphasis on individuality and careers to a postwar equation of fulfillment with the role of housewife and motherhood. She accused popularizers of Freudianism, but not Freudian therapy itself, of giving a scientific gloss to old notions that "women are animals, less than human, unable to think like men, born merely to breed and serve men," when they were not busy envying or hating them. Similarly, Friedan blamed the anthropologist Margaret Mead for promoting the mystique by glorifying feminine women and emphasizing their sexual and biological responsibilities. In addition, she attempted to explain why more women were going on to college, yet many of them were choosing early marriage rather than entering the professions. Friedan pointed to "sex-directed educators" who, influenced by the set of psychological and social constraints to which she gave the name feminine mystique, worried more about personal adjustment of their students than their intellectual achievement. As a consequence, colleges and universities promoted conformity to the conventional conceptions of housewife and mother.[4]

The result of all these forces was the emergence of "the problem that has no name." The gap between what women read and experienced produced confusion and self-doubt that typified the feminine mystique. Although experts and the media told American women that housewifery and motherhood made them happy, in fact they themselves knew there were more fulfilling activities in life than cooking meals, cleaning house, and chauffeuring children to school and lessons. According to the mystique, Friedan argued, a fundamental cause of all problems for women was that they "envied men." Consequently, they found "fulfillment only in sexual passivity, male domination, and nurturing maternal love." The feminine mystique prevented women from realizing their full human potential by locking them into domestic prisons.[5]

With affluence underwriting a sense of self that no longer depended on necessity, Friedan argued, consumer culture, working through "the sexual sell," had filled the void created by women's lack of identity. She asserted that the suburban house was a "comfortable concentration camp" which fostered "passivity, softness, boredom" in American children, and unsatisfying sex and false promises of abundance through mechanized housework for their mothers. The interviews she carried out revealed that women who saw themselves as housewives and mothers were so preoccupied with their chores that their work, despite the promise of technology, expanded to fill the time they had. In contrast, Friedan admired professional, married women with children who kept their housework in perspective and got it done efficiently.[6]

If consumption, housework, and sex offered only inauthentic and unsatisfactory experiences, Friedan asserted that women achieved fulfillment principally through personal growth. The focus on housework and on a submissive sexuality had prevented women from recognizing the need for self-esteem. Rejecting a narcissistic version of self-realization, Friedan instead emphasized that people developed a healthy identity not through routine work such as that of the housewife, but through commitment to purposeful and sustained effort. In the conclusion to her book, Friedan offered

"A New Life Plan for Women." Here she called on them to pierce the feminine mystique by combining marriage and family "with the work toward a greater purpose that shapes the future." She believed that taking just any job or volunteering in the community were both traps. For her, work that led to personal growth and self-fulfillment involved several key elements. It had to require intelligence, "initiative, leadership and responsibility." It had to make a real social contribution, which, Friedan noted, usually meant there had to be financial compensation. Above all, married women with families could realize their abilities and achieve identity through "the lifelong commitment to an art or science, to politics or profession." Such determination allowed variation over the course of the life cycle: "a full-time paid job in one community, part-time in another, exercise of the professional skill in serious volunteer work or a period of study during pregnancy or early motherhood when a full-time job is not feasible."[7]

Friedan recognized that women who pursued such goals would face formidable obstacles. They would have to break out of the trap of the feminine mystique. Institutions of higher education would need to make provision for people, women especially, whose lives did not easily fit into the pattern of college completion by age twenty-two, followed directly by a career. Having acknowledged the importance of certain policy issues, Friedan ended her book by returning to what was in many ways its dominant message, urging women to break the mental chains of the feminine mystique in order to achieve greater self-realization. "The time is at hand," she wrote in the book's last sentence, "when the voices of the feminine mystique can no longer drown out the inner voice that is driving women on to become complete."[8]

As much as any book written in the middle of the twentieth century, *The Feminine Mystique* helped transform the course of America's political and social history. Historians view its publication as marking the beginning of the modern women's movement. Despite an initial printing of only three thousand copies, it eventually sold millions and millions. Though the women's liberation movement doubtlessly would have emerged without the book, *The Feminine Mystique* nonetheless defined the perspective of a generation of white middle-class women with its argument that what trapped them was sexual passivity, limited career ambitions, and identity crises. By raising the consciousness of legions of women, Friedan helped lay the groundwork for their participation in the feminist movement that emerged with increasing force in the late 1960s. How Friedan came to write the book is a complicated story, one that requires an acknowledgment of how significantly her radical past and prior engagement with women's issues influenced the book and her career. We already understand how left politics of the 1940s and 1950s shaped the civil rights movement. Friedan's life underscores the fact that the other significant social movement of the 1960s—feminism—also has important origins in the two preceding decades.[9]

The Feminine Mystique also transformed Friedan's life and her position in American history. Before 1963, she was no ordinary suburban housewife and mother, but one with a distinctive past who was struggling to make it as a writer. For more than two decades she had wrestled with the question of how an author could freely speak her mind. With the publication of The Feminine Mystique she found the voice that gained her the power to command the attention of vast audiences. After 1963, she quickly emerged as a woman who made major contributions to the resurgence of the feminist movement in America—as the founding president of National Organization for Women in 1966 and as a founding member of the National Women's Political Caucus in 1971. As a writer, speaker, organizer, and media figure Friedan helped change the lives of millions of women and men.

The primary task of this book is to offer the story of Betty Friedan's life, focusing on what enabled her to make two extraordinary contributions: to write The Feminine Mystique and then to help launch the feminist movement in the 1960s. I seek to enrich our understanding of the origins of 1960s feminism by locating one of the routes to that movement in left-wing labor union activity of the 1940s and 1950s. Placing Friedan's life in a wide range of contexts, I want to restore a sense of connectedness between her life and the worlds it illuminates. I have not written a biography in any usual sense of that word. As an intellectual historian, I am interested in where ideas come from, how they develop, and what forces shape and reshape them. However, before I proceed with my main task, I think it important to talk about how I came to write this book and what challenges I encountered along the way.

In 1963, with my wife and colleague Helen Lefkowitz Horowitz, I bought a copy of The Feminine Mystique. In the ensuing years, because Friedan's work was so important and because it continued to fascinate me, I regularly assigned it in my classes. Then in 1984 as part of a book on how Americans responded to affluence after 1940, I planned to include a chapter on Friedan's 1963 book. In 1987, I met Friedan for the first time. The previous fall, Helen had begun her work at University of Southern California (USC), serving as Professor of History and Director of the Program for the Study of Women and Men in Society. One of her colleagues was Betty Friedan, whom I interviewed in March 1987, focusing primarily on her life from her arrival at Smith College in 1938 until the publication of The Feminine Mystique twenty-five years later. As I listen to the tape recording knowing what I now know, patterns are readily apparent. She talked vaguely or briefly about experiences, such as her work as a labor journalist, that she had long ago decided not to talk about in an extensive or revealing way. Yet she also offered clues to someone who had, as I did not at the time, the knowledge, acuity, and patience to follow where they might lead. For example, when she mentioned she worked for the UE, I did not know enough to recognize the activist commitments signified by her postwar work for that union.[10]

Yet as Helen and I stood in our kitchen in Claremont while she decompressed after a hard day at the office, she often discussed how she sensed that when she was with Friedan she was in the company of someone whose life was shaped not exclusively by suburban captivity, but by left-wing social movements in the 1940s as well. As Helen watched Friedan run one of her USC "Think Tanks," a gathering of feminists from universities and from the entertainment industry, it became clear to her that Friedan resembled someone schooled in the tradition of the community organizer Saul Alinsky. Friedan was attempting to get these women to place some specific issue in a larger framework and then consider how they might solve the problem their discussion had identified. Moreover, the goal toward which she was trying to move people was often not an exclusively feminist one, but one that was shaped in part by the social democratic commitments of Popular Front politics of the 1940s—that umbrella under which a wide variety of radicals had united.

In the late 1980s, Helen discussed with Friedan the possibility of writing her authorized biography. Asked to interview Friedan for an oral history project, Helen spent a day looking at Friedan's papers, which Friedan had transferred to The Arthur and Elizabeth Schlesinger Library on the History of Women in America at Radcliffe College. In the end, Helen decided not to write a book on Friedan. She did so for a number of reasons, partly because of the dilemmas she would face as an authorized biographer, but largely because her work on a book about M. Carey Thomas, the founding dean and second president of Bryn Mawr College, had made her less than eager to write another full-scale biography.

In the late 1980s, I continued to work on the study of consumer culture. My chapter on Vance Packard grew into a book, which appeared in 1994. In the meantime, through Helen I came to know Friedan. She hosted a book party in New York to celebrate the publication of Helen's *Campus Life* (1987). A mutual friend invited us to have dinner with Friedan when she was in Northampton. Helen asked Friedan to come over to our house during Smith graduation weekend in 1992. On one occasion she offered Helen the use of her Manhattan apartment when she was away. I prevailed on

Helen's relationship with Friedan when I asked her to write a jacket blurb for my book on Packard, something she graciously agreed to do.[11]

In February 1995, I resumed my research on Friedan while on a fellowship from the National Endowment for the Humanities. At the time, I thought I was working on *The Feminine Mystique* as the focal point for a chapter on women and consumer culture. The Packard book had got me in the habit, which is hard to resist, of reconstructing my subjects' lives before proceeding to examine their ideas. I gathered much of what journalists and historians had written on Friedan and her own autobiographical statements that had appeared in print. Then I started to write a brief sketch of her life. I quickly realized, however, that I could not make sense of what I was reading because there was too much that was vague. I wondered what she did at Smith, other than studying Gestalt psychology. I was especially curious about what happened in her life from the time she left graduate school in the spring of 1943 until she began to work on *The Feminine Mystique* in the late 1950s, a period on which there was remarkably little in print.

By early March 1995, I realized I would have to go to the archival sources in order to be able to write, even briefly I still thought, about Friedan's life in the 1940s and 1950s. I began locally, a few hundred feet from my office, in the Sophia Smith Collection and the Smith College Archives. Especially compelling were the editorials in the Smith newspaper written when Friedan was editor-in-chief for a year beginning in March 1941. These editorials were anti-war until Pearl Harbor, anti-fascist, pro-labor unions, for students' rights, opposed to the college administration, and critical of the privileged lives many Smith students lived and some even flaunted.

Until this point, I had assumed that Friedan's papers at the Schlesinger Library were closed. So I wrote her on March 17, 1995, to gain permission to look at some of the material in her collection and to interview her when I came to Washington at the end of the month. In the meantime, learning that much of the material in the Schlesinger collection was open, I went there on March 22, 1995. Although it would take me a long time before all the pieces of the puzzle fell into place, that day I found papers Friedan had written in an undergraduate course on socialism and workers, an FBI report concerning her alleged activity in the early 1940s, scores of articles in the labor press in the 1940s and 1950s signed by Betty Goldstein (Friedan's maiden name), and evidence of Friedan's participation in a rent strike in the early 1950s. The significance of what I discovered gradually dawned on me. Though most women's historians have argued that 1960s feminism emerged in response to the suburban captivity of white middle-class women during the 1950s, the material in Friedan's papers suggested additional origins—antifascism, radicalism, and labor union activism of the 1940s.

A week later, I saw Friedan. She had dinner with Helen and me in Washington on March 29. Our host was someone I had known since my college days, Charles Blitzer, director of the Woodrow Wilson International Center for Scholars at the Smithsonian Institution, where Friedan was a scholar-in-residence. Before dinner Friedan told me she thought that the agreement with her authorized biographer, Ellen Chesler, precluded her from allowing anyone else to interview her in connection with a book about her life. Then, during dinner, Blitzer asked Friedan what she had done between her arrival at Smith and the publication of *The Feminine Mystique*. What Friedan said in response was a little more revealing—especially about her years at Smith—than what she usually told reporters. After dinner, the people from the next table—Gertrude Himmelfarb, Irving Kristol, Seymour Martin Lipset, and Sydnee Lipset—came over and engaged Friedan and Blitzer in cordial chat. That moment impressed upon me the importance of thinking of Friedan not only in the context of American feminism; I also became interested in comparing her writings with those of neo-conservative New York intellectuals to examine how postwar writers grappled with moral and political issues.

In April 1995 I tried to make sense of what the documents in the Schlesinger Library suggested. I soon realized that it was necessary to put aside the book chapter for a while and focus on Friedan's life, the hidden and the recently revealed. Researching and writing with a sense of excitement, I knew the story I was telling was important, one that would enrich the history of feminism and our understanding of a major figure in the postwar world. By late May I sent off a draft to *American Quarterly,* the scholarly publication of the American Studies Association. In the next months, I put together more pieces of the puzzle and began to connect my discoveries to what had happened in the lives of some of Friedan's contemporaries, especially the women's historians Gerda Lerner and Eleanor Flexner. Like Friedan, they had participated in the world of radicalism and labor union activism in the 1940s, and later emerged as key figures in the development of second-wave feminism, the women's movement that began in the 1960s, in contrast to the first wave that began in the nineteenth century. What I discovered, about Friedan and others, convinced me that my initial hunch about one of the sources of 1960s feminism was right.

When I wrote a biography of Vance Packard, I examined many issues that would emerge with this book on Friedan, especially the relationship between the 1950s and 1960s, the role of the popular social critic, and the problems faced by free-lance writers. Moreover, I had to come to terms with a number of challenges arising from my relationship to the subject of my study. At various moments, but especially early in my work, I felt I was invasive, stealing both Packard's memory and his version of his own life.

Over time, I settled down and accepted the relatively minor differences between Packard's take on his past and the story I would tell. Throughout, my encounters with Packard remained direct, cordial, and untroubled. Early on, we signed a simple agreement that gave me the nonexclusive right to use and cite his unpublished works, without giving him the right to see what I had written before publication. He cooperated with the intrusive historian without complication. He gave me free rein with his papers and eased the way for me to interview his lifelong friends.[12]

The situation with Friedan turned out to be far more complicated. In September 1995 I wrote her, asking for permission to quote from unpublished portions of her papers. I expressed a willingness to "listen to additions or clarifications" she wished to make. By carefully reading my letter, she could easily tell the drift of my argument. In response, she denied me permission to quote anything from her unpublished papers. Employing a word familiar to people scarred by McCarthyism, she believed I was drawing on her unpublished papers to use "innuendos" in describing her past. As she had done so often in print, she asserted that she had not discovered feminism until the late 1950s. Then she quoted from a letter a lawyer had written her, using his words to question the relevance of the FBI report and the paper she had written on Marxism to understanding her adult life. She also relied on the lawyer's words to state that though she was not retaining an attorney to protect the commercial value of her unpublished papers, she would show my letter to a lawyer if I did in fact infringe on her right to earn money from her intellectual property.

The same day Friedan sent me the letter, something happened to reinforce my belief in the importance of what I was doing. Friedan got up before an audience at the Smithsonian Institution in Washington, D.C., and gave a lecture in a series on the 1950s. She repeated the stories she had told before. No, she asserted, she had no awareness of women's issues before she began to work on *The Feminine Mystique;* no, she insisted, during the 1950s she had no interest in pursuing a career. What she said that evening, as well as what appeared to me as her stand against what I was doing, persuaded me of the importance of what I had found. When my *American Quarterly* article appeared in March 1996, Friedan did not return the telephone calls of reporters who contacted her for a response to what I had written. Her reaction to the article made it clear that I would get nowhere with further requests for cooperation.[13]

As I wrote this book, I puzzled over the implications of stating honestly what others, less sympathetic than I to Friedan and to her past, would surely view unfavorably. In 1996 and 1997, I discovered that beginning at least as early as 1940, Friedan knew a wide variety of radicals whom anti-communists investigated in the late 1940s and 1950s. I emphasize these connections not to paint Friedan with a red brush, but to suggest that the McCarthyite attacks on people she knew may have made her fearful of redbaiting. These attacks shaped not only her politics from the 1940s on, but also American feminism in the postwar period. The end of the Cold War makes it easier to write frankly about what some would consider fellow traveling, the tendency of those committed to fighting for social justice during the height of the Cold War to work cooperatively with members of the Communist Party. While I recognized the connections between what Friedan wrote in the 1940s and the 1960s, I also realized I was living in a world where Newt Gingrich, Pat Buchanan, and the Christian Coalition were powerful, if not consistently ascendant. So I worried that I might be revealing elements of Friedan's past that conservatives could use to discredit not only Friedan but the entire women's movement.[14]

The relationship between Friedan's life, McCarthyism, and the Popular Front is a central theme of the story I tell. Starting in 1940 and for at least a dozen years thereafter, Friedan was part of a movement best identified as Popular Front or progressive feminism. Cultural historian Michael Denning has defined the Popular Front, which he sees as ebbing and flowing for more than forty years from its beginning around 1934, as concerned with "the laboring of American culture." The Popular Front, he has argued, was "a radical social-democratic movement forged" around issues such as anti-fascism, anti-racism, civil liberties, and the CIO's industrial unionism. Borrowing from the sociologist C. Wright Mills, Denning has emphasized the role of what Mills called the "cultural apparatus"—the people who wrote, painted, directed, and researched; the unions to which they belonged; and the cultural contributions they made. Denning stresses the working-class origins of the creators and audience for Popular Front culture. Friedan's middle-class background and identity meant she was often more a sympathetic observer of radical activism than a direct participant. Still, as a student at Smith College, a supporter of labor unions, a member of the New York Newspaper Guild, and a writer for the labor press, Friedan participated in Popular Front culture at least from 1940 until 1953. Neither duped by an alien social movement nor seduced by a foreign ideology, Friedan was a home-grown radical, a phenomenon McCarthyites found it impossible to imagine.[15]

In the 1950s, critics of the Popular Front and fellow travelers adopted a one-dimensional core-periphery model which exaggerated the degree of control of the Kremlin and the Communist Party over people who they thought were passive and naive recipients of a party line. Such a perspective over-emphasizes the importance of actual party membership, as well as the influence of the party and Moscow. Rather, I would stress the varied sources of American radicalism, whose origins, power, and sophistication a focus on the party underestimates. When I use a phrase like Popular Front, I mean to describe those who battled anti-communists and were inspired by issues articulated by radicals—party members and non-party members alike.[16]

In exploring Friedan's early feminism, I seek to enrich and interrogate an important scholarly interpretation. With *The Feminine Mystique* Friedan began a long tradition among American feminists of seeing compulsory domesticity as the main consequence of 1950s McCarthyism. This emphasis, while in some ways on the mark, nonetheless threw later feminists off-track. It helped prevent them from seeing that another significant result of McCarthyism was that many left-wing feminists had to go underground in the 1950s. Left-wing feminists later emerged as second-wave feminists, some of them, like Friedan, minimizing any connection to 1940s radicalism. Others, like Lerner and Flexner, displayed considerable continuity in their commitments when, in the late 1950s and early 1960s, they paid attention, as Friedan did not in *The Feminine Mystique,* to working-class and African American women.

A news item in the spring of 1996 reminded me of what might be at stake in demonstrating the connection between 1940s radicalism, Jews, and 1960s feminism. The *Chronicle of Higher Education* reported: "Vandals drew swastikas in at least 40 library books at the University of North Carolina." Most of the books focused on "socialism, communism, and Marxism. A few dealt with Jewish and women's issues." The question arose, what if people on the right got hold of what I was writing and said, "Aha, just as we have always thought, feminism was a Communist conspiracy." But I realized that if historians worried excessively about how others could use their scholarship, they would never publish anything controversial. Moreover, any real analysis of meaningful evidence is itself a stand against attempts to suppress the truth that freedom of speech reveals.[17]

For me, all of these tricky problems raised the thorny question of how to write, after the Cold War ended, about people who had been associated with party members, publications, or positions. I knew that in the immense amount that Friedan published in the 1940s and early 1950s, some of which appeared in party-sponsored publications, she never mentioned the party or displayed a preference for the Soviet social or economic system. I have found no evidence that she sanctioned the killings of millions of people carried out by Stalinists in the USSR, approved of pro-Soviet Americans conveying national security secrets to a foreign nation, or looked favorably on the party's penchant for making dramatic and opportunistic shifts. Above all, I seek not to sensationalize but to understand her radical convictions, how they were silenced, and then transformed. The most important moral of this story is not about Friedan's association with people, movements, and positions on which some observers would look askance. Nor is my book meant to condemn her for rewriting her story for complex and not always knowable reasons. Rather, I wish to highlight the damage McCarthyism did to progressive social movements of the 1940s and early 1950s, and especially to feminism, which it forced underground but could not destroy.

In the years I worked on this book, the scholarly crosscurrents about American Communism and anti-communism have swirled with great intensity. On the one hand, some writers, especially those influenced by the revelations contained in the recently opened Soviet archives, have insisted that the infiltration and espionage of American Communists was much more serious than previously suspected. Therefore, they have argued, much of the anti-communism of the 1940s and early 1950s was actually a diverse movement and one that, far from being irrational, correctly perceived the danger of Communist impact on American life. Here they joined earlier generations of scholars who emphasized the Soviet-centered nature of American Communism and cast a highly skeptical eye on the social justice commitments of the Old Left, which they considered opportunistic at best.

On the other hand, the easing and eventual ending of U.S.–Soviet antagonism have encouraged some scholars to come forward with a more sympathetic evaluation of the impact of Communist and Old Left influence on American life. They insist on exploring the issues without concentrating on the obedience of some party members to a Soviet-directed party line. In addition, when appropriate, they identify people's organizational affiliations, not in the interest of redbaiting but of historical accuracy. These revisionists have convinced me that people joined the party for a wide range of reasons; that the boundaries between membership in the party and in radical organizations were permeable; that it is necessary to understand party membership within specific historical and social contexts; and that many idealistic people, who were not especially interested in factional issues or the USSR, joined or were sympathetic with the party. I also find persuasive the evidence scholars have provided that in the 1930s and 1940s American radicals, many of them members of, or in close proximity to, the Communist Party of the United States of America (CPUSA), sustained a genuine commitment to social justice. I agree with those who insist on demonstrating how association with American Communists changed its meaning over time. Excusing the party for its defense of the Nazi-Soviet pact in 1939, or for its rationalizations of Stalin's slaughter of millions is indefensible. In contrast, I can well appreciate how progressives would join with party members in supporting the Soviet-American alliance in World War II, or in fighting for social justice for women or African Americans.[18]

Again and again, what I discovered about Friedan's life convinced me that she emerged out of the Old Left as someone who, in response to poverty, racial discrimination, and sexism, developed a commitment to social justice for idealistic reasons. From the outset, I accepted what historians on the left had come to articulate: that the critical issue regarding most American Communists and radicals of the 1940s was not their relationship to the party but to a whole range of causes. This perspective involves shifting the focus from a Soviet and party-centered view to one that understands relationships among radicals in a more complex way.

From 1940 through the early 1950s, Friedan moved in radical circles in Northampton, Berkeley, Manhattan, Queens, and Rockland County. In these worlds Communist Party membership was less important than one's commitment to the causes of social justice and anti-fascism. There is no evidence that this feisty, fiercely independent, and volatile woman toed the party line. Friedan's politics developed within contexts where the borders between the party and a broad movement for social justice were easy to cross. Support for this position came from an important quarter when I gave a talk before a group of Smith faculty members and staff in September 1995. Afterwards, Helen K. Chinoy, a retired faculty member whose close friendship with Friedan began during World War II, stood up and congratulated me for talking openly and proudly of the importance of 1940s radicalism, including Communism, in shaping 1960s feminism. Though I was well aware that Friedan might not agree, I felt that what I was going to reveal about her life made her a more significant, heroic, and interesting figure in American history than her own story allowed. After all, I was arguing that Friedan's life, in connecting the 1960s and the Old Left, gave second-wave feminism a richer heritage, one of which both Friedan and American feminists should be proud.[19]

As a historian, the greatest challenge I have faced in writing this book has been the difficulty in gaining full access to Friedan's views. So far as I know, there is no diary or extensive correspondence that would illuminate key points in her life before the mid-1960s. Though vast sections of her papers are open, without permission from Friedan or her family key sources remain closed until the years 2029 and 2043. I refer here especially to correspondence from the 1940s and 1950s. Unable to interview her again, or to examine an interview with her that is under wraps at the Schlesinger Library, I have found it difficult to verify some facts and test some interpretations. Though I have carried out many interviews, problems remain in seeking access to history through this medium: tricks played by memory, the death of key witnesses, and the fact that some of Friedan's friends and colleagues (and even enemies) did not respond to my inquiries, or responded too cautiously to be useful. These obstacles to a wider range of sources increase the likelihood that I would make mistakes—a risk I am willing to assume.[20] These and other limitations on what I can use are especially unfortunate, given how vivid and effective a writer Friedan is. Consequently, at critical points her own voice is missing when it should be present.

All of this has thrown me back on my resources as an intellectual historian, encouraging me to examine how Friedan's ideas developed without always knowing the specific personal, editorial, and social conditions under which this took place. My narrative and analysis inevitably depend on the sources I can use. These limitations turn my story into one in which ideas and political commitments matter more than feelings, friendships, and debates carried on beyond the reach of the historian. They make it more difficult for me to write a feminist biography that connects the personal with the political.[21]

To me, Friedan's position is both understandable and puzzling. Understandable because almost no one likes to have a researcher go through her life with a fine-toothed comb and then reveal to an eager public a story that the subject will almost inevitably see as partial, distorted, and even hostile. These predictable responses are most certainly intensified by Friedan's sense that someone with whom she has had prior cordial relations has betrayed her. Puzzling, for a number of reasons. It is possible that Friedan has an explanation of her own life that, for one reason or another, I cannot fathom. When she uses key phrases such as feminism or women's question, she may understand them differently from how I do. She and I may not share the same view of cause and effect—especially between her years as a labor journalist and as a nationally known feminist. Friedan's response is also puzzling because if she truly wanted to hide her radical commitments, she would not open to researchers so much of her papers—including the paper she wrote at Smith for Professor Dorothy W. Douglas, her FBI file, and a letter to her from the editor of *New Masses*. She is to be congratulated for making the record of so much of her life accessible; but nonetheless her openness seems at odds with her unwillingness to discuss what the documents reveal. Moreover, Friedan has talked at private dinner parties about her life as a labor activist but not, so far as I can determine, shared these recollections with journalists or scholars. Her position further puzzles me because she offered clear indications of her radical past in the 1970s and then did not elaborate at any later points. Above all, it is puzzling because in the end, no matter how much one knows of the human toll of McCarthyism, her sensitivities remain mysterious.[22]

As I worked on this book, I learned that Friedan, talking in private, believed that I had redbaited her in my article on her years as a labor journalist. One time she said so in public. In a speech at American University in November 1996, she remarked that "some historian recently wrote some attack on me in which he claimed that I was only pretending to be a suburban housewife, that I was supposed to be an agent." Clearly she believed that I was calling into question the authenticity of her suburban experience and, by extension, the premise of her 1963 book. In addition, her use of the word "agent" reveals how much McCarthyism continues to inform her view of the world. She dramatically and incorrectly intimated that I had accused her of secretly working as an agent provocateur or a party agent. I recalled the one instance I had found when she had used the term agent—in 1961 when she descried how redbaiters mistook nonconformists and intellectuals for "communist agents." Her public response to what I had written underscores how sensitive she still is to historical analysis that discusses political affiliations during a period when her views might have made her subject to political repression. In fact, in my piece in *American Quarterly,* I never said she was an agent. In addition, I made clear that she was a suburban housewife, but one whose experience was marked by discontent, nonconformity, ambivalence, and very real professional achievement.[23]

Despite the obstacles I faced, I have remained committed to writing this book as I see fit. What lent my work excitement was the process of doing what I had learned to do, initially as an undergraduate and then as a graduate student: devise research strategies to discover connections, track down evidence, put together pieces of a puzzle, and then place what I discovered within wider frameworks. What sustained me throughout was the sense of creativity and discovery I experienced as I uncovered new evidence and developed a richer analysis. What I found connects the pieces of Friedan's life, explains how a wide range of her experiences enabled her to write *The Feminine Mystique,* and transforms our understanding of the roots of modern American feminism.

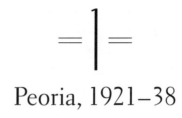

Peoria, 1921–38

Bettye Goldstein's childhood, youth, and adolescence in Peoria powerfully influenced her adult life. The social and personal dynamics of the Goldstein household shaped her sense of herself as a daughter, sister, Jew, intellect, and woman. The challenges she faced in school sharpened her eye, intensified her interest in books, honed her writing, and started to awaken her awareness of herself as a woman. The backdrop of her adolescence—a series of events in Peoria, the nation, and Europe—highlighted issues of union organizing, anti-Semitism, and anti-fascism on which she would draw later when she fully engaged with politics.

Born February 4, 1921, in Peoria's Proctor Hospital, Bettye Naomi Goldstein spent the first seventeen-and-a-half years of her life in Illinois's second largest city. During the 1920s, the city's population boomed, growing from 76,121 in 1920 to 104,969 ten years later. Located on the Illinois River, one hundred and seventy miles southwest of Chicago, Peoria was a transportation and manufacturing center, with its railroad stations and port connecting Chicago with the Mississippi River and eventually with the Gulf of Mexico. The local factories processed meat and produced cordage, washing machines, barrels, and agricultural machinery. Distilleries turned corn grown on midwestern farms into liquor, making the city the nation's largest producer of spirits. Whatever boost to the local economy came with the end of Prohibition in 1933 was tempered by the dramatic drop in sales experienced in the 1930s by Caterpillar Tractor Company, the farm equipment manufacturer whose world headquarters were in Peoria.[1]

In the 1920s and 1930s, Peoria had a varied population and an unsavory reputation. Among its inhabitants were Germans whose ancestors began to arrive in significant numbers in the 1840s, enough Jews to support two synagogues with several hundred families in each, and a sufficient number of Roman Catholics to sponsor one cathedral and more than half-a-dozen churches. Many of the city's inhabitants had moved off midwestern farms to find jobs in the city. African Americans accounted for about 3 percent of the population. In many ways, Peoria was a southern city, one where racial segregation and racism ruled. Although it had a varied cultural life, in these years Peoria was known as a raw and wide-open town. A corrupt political boss controlled a machine that, profiting from organized gambling and prostitution, thwarted any attempt to clean up local government. During World War II, Billy Rose wrote a popular song, "I Wish't I Was in Peoria," that pictured it as a backward, frontier town. "Except for Brooklyn," a reporter later noted, "no community in the United States has been slandered so elaborately as Peoria." Comedians had "vulgarized" the Illinois city, the reporter observed, "as the symbol of the rube and the boob," making its name "the companion word for 'hayseed.'" In 1978 Friedan recalled that admitting she was from Peoria "used to embarrass" her. "It was a vaudeville joke," she remarked, "the epitome of the hick town."[2]

Bettye's father, Harry Goldstein (1881–1943), had immigrated to the United States from near Kiev, and as an adult spoke English with an accent. He arrived in Peoria in his teens, soon earning a living by selling collar buttons from a street-corner stand. Over time, like many Jewish merchants of his generation, he was quite successful, rising to run Goldstein Jewelry Company, a store that sold gems, silver, and china. In 1918, with boastful aspiration it advertised itself as the "Finest Jewelry Store in the Middle West," and a family member later described it as "the Tiffany's of Peoria."[3]

Bettye's mother, Miriam Horwitz Goldstein (1898–1988), eighteen years younger than her husband, was the daughter of immigrants from Hungary. Her father had come to St. Louis as a young rabbinical student and went on to graduate from medical school. He eventually settled in Peoria, where, after returning from World War I, he served as the city's public health commissioner. Bettye's mother graduated from Peoria's Bradley College. The earlier arrival and success of Bettye's maternal grandparents meant that her mother was from a higher social position than her father. When Bettye's parents married shortly after the end of World War I, her mother was writing for the society page of a Peoria newspaper, a position Harry Goldstein insisted his wife quit so she could run the household. She raised a family that eventually included Bettye and her two younger siblings, Amy and Harry Jr. She participated in community affairs and helped her husband at the store during busy seasons. Although the family's relative affluence en-

abled Miriam Goldstein to have considerable leisure, her frequent absence
from the store, which separated her from the locus of money and power,
weakened her authority in the family.[4]

When Bettye was growing up, the Goldsteins lived in a section of the city
known as the Bluffs. From there, a contemporary guidebook noted, "residential Peoria commands a view of the clustered business district, the ser-
rated line of mills and factories along the curving river, and, far beyond the
industrial suburbs, the checkered farm fields." The family occupied a well-
appointed, comfortable, eight-room house on Farmington Road, not far
from Bradley College. The Goldstein house was not in one of the fanciest
sections of the Bluffs, though one such area, complete with enormous Victorian mansions, was about ten blocks away. At the time, their house was
suitable for a middle-class family with more aspirations than resources. It
was fully detached from neighboring houses, but there was only enough
room between houses to allow a car to pass to the garage in the back yard.
The brick exterior of the residence was more solid and plain than graceful or
decorative, with porches its most prominent feature. When Bettye was still
in grade school, her parents came close to purchasing a larger and fancier
residence, something the Depression prevented them from doing. What the
house on Farmington Road lacked in grandeur or land was offset by its
location overlooking Bradley Park, an area of more than three hundred acres
that included a pavilion, a bandstand, a pergola, playgrounds, a lake, an ice
skating rink, tennis courts, and Japanese gardens.[5]

The Goldsteins experienced both the privileges and tensions of Jews
whose relative prosperity in the 1920s was shaken by the Depression of the
next decade. The family belonged to the financially troubled North Shore
Country Club, but as Jews could not join the more restrictive, prestigious,
and financially healthy Peoria Country Club. In the 1920s, a maid cleaned
the house, a nurse took care of the children when they were young, and on
special occasions a man served as chauffeur and butler. During the summers, Miriam Goldstein took the children north to Wisconsin or Minnesota
for vacations while her husband stayed behind to work at the store. One
spring she took Bettye to Chicago to see plays. At home in Peoria, as the
maid waited on the table, Bettye's father orchestrated dinner conversations.
He made it clear that he expected the children, but especially Bettye, to
respond thoughtfully to his challenging inquiries about politics or the latest
among the many books he had read. "The serious questions about what was
going on in the world would always be directed at Betty and the frivolous
ones at me," her sister Amy later recalled with a jealousy that from her
childhood on marked her relationship with her sister. Amy hated the way
Bettye "dripped with hostility toward what she called 'my feminine wiles.'"[6]

The family belonged to Anshai Emeth Temple, a Reform congregation founded in the 1850s by German Jews, some of whom made fortunes in manufacturing, distilling, and retailing. Bettye's grandfather, mother, and father were active in the temple. A week before her confirmation in the ninth grade, Bettye told the rabbi that she did not believe in God; he responded by asking her to keep her news secret until after the ceremony. Her father admired Robert G. Ingersoll, the nationally famous agnostic who lived much of his adult life in Peoria. The decisions of Bettye's parents to go against traditional Jewish practices by naming their son after his father, by celebrating Christmas, and by joining a Reform temple rather than a less assimilationist synagogue were unusual for an immigrant like Harry Goldstein. These preferences stemmed from the skepticism of Bettye's father and the social aspirations of her mother, something underscored by her writing for the society page of the local newspaper. The family's choices about its identity also reflected the increasing secularization and acculturation of American Jews, especially outside major cities. Young Bettye's confession to her rabbi, not at all atypical for someone her age, nonetheless testified to her rebelliousness and her identity as a Jew in a cultural rather than a religious sense.[7]

Despite social pretense and aspirations, life in the Goldstein household was tumultuous. Bettye herself was given to angry outbursts, at times acting out violently. She hit a boy on the head with a hoe and tore a patch of hair from the head of a girl. Another time, a book she threw at her sister hit its target with such force that Amy had to have stitches. In 1938, a high school friend told Bettye that she was "capable of burning jealousy and strong dislikes." "Betty chased me, threw a book," Harry Jr. remembered. "She was screaming and she scared the hell out of me! Betty was volatile; she had a short fuse and could get wild when she lost her temper." Moreover, Bettye was not the only person in the house given to angry outbursts. She recalled being offended by the "phoniness" that stemmed from the contradiction between her mother's charming, even unctuous public manner and her anger in private. After Miriam Goldstein got off the phone with a friend she had just called "my dear sweet darling," she would then label her "that bitch." Mother and daughter fought, principally over whether Bettye would give in to the demands of her well-dressed, handsome, refined, and charming mother that she pay attention to her grooming and clean up her room as well. "When I grow up," Bettye stated emphatically, in a way that revealed her sense of class aspirations and entitlement, "I'm going to be rich so I can hire somebody to clean the room."[8]

More protracted and serious fights between Bettye's mother and father focused most often on money, as Miriam Goldstein's yearning for a fashionable life outran her husband's ability to provide for it during the Depression. With jewelry store sales adversely affected by the dramatic economic downturn, the family had to lay off the maid and the chauffeur/butler. Unable to stop buying on credit, Miriam Goldstein hid the bills she ran up and then compounded the debt by gambling secretly and unsuccessfully. When she told her husband what she had done, the ensuing battles "shook our house at night," recalls Friedan. Young Goldstein claimed her parents' arguments provided her initial knowledge of how the economy worked. The word Depression reminded her of how she awakened at night to her parents' bitter arguments over money. Burdened by debts, her father nonetheless hoped that an improved economy would bring more customers into the store. Bettye was more realistic. She knew his dreams would be undermined by expenses, some of them unavoidable. For example, his heart condition required that he travel during the winter to a warmer climate.[9]

Her mother's temper bothered and confused young Bettye. To outside observers, Miriam Goldstein led a charmed life. People found her attractive and well dressed. They "turned around to look at her in the street," her daughter Amy remarked. Someone who prided herself on her grooming, Miriam Goldstein "was a fashion leader and people imitated her." She engaged in the round of activities typical of a person of her position: she taught Sunday school at the temple; participated in two Jewish women's groups, Sisterhood and Hadassah; volunteered for the local Community Chest; and had the leisure to play bridge, mah-jongg, and golf, as well as ride horseback. Yet Bettye puzzled over why a woman who was so fortunate was also so angry. Nothing Bettye could do satisfied her.[10]

In contrast with how Miriam Goldstein viewed Amy, whom she considered pretty, she felt Bettye was her unattractive daughter. As a young girl, Bettye's adorable face, with large brown eyes that peered out from heavy lids, and her short "roundly filled little frame" would have made her attractive to a more loving mother. Yet Miriam Goldstein focused on the prominence of her daughter's nose, increasingly apparent during adolescence, which demonstrated that Bettye had inherited what she considered one of her husband's worst features. Although peers considered her appealing as a teenager, a reporter later noted that Bettye "wasn't an attractive girl—her long nose had already drawn the crude comments of the boys in school." Miriam belittled Bettye's appearance and ridiculed the way she dressed. If only her daughter was less unkempt, Miriam insisted, she would be more attractive. Hoping to launch her daughter as a lady, Miriam believed it was improper for her to appear, as a biographer commented, "trudging up Main Street Hill, lopsided and clumsily burdened" by the books she carried home from the library. Bettye felt her mother's constant criticism undermined her own sense of confidence.[11]

The social differences that divided her parents intensified their fights and placed young Bettye in a difficult position. Miriam Goldstein's immigrant husband, who lacked formal education, embarrassed her, something she made clear as she ordered him around. He let loose his temper, especially when his wife tried to discuss her financial troubles with him. Although eventually she came to see her father in more problematic light, Bettye apparently sided with her father, partly because he expressed so much pride in her. She remembered the pleasure of early morning walks with her father through the park. She recalled the geniality of someone who loved his family and earned the respect of people in the community. Friedan later noted that her father conveyed to her "the dreams that circumstances did not let him realize himself."[12]

Over time Friedan came to understand the relationship between her mother's situation and her own interest in women's issues. Her own feminism, she wrote in 1981, "somehow began in my mother's discontent" over being forced to quit her job when she married. Her mother's anger at her economic dependence on her husband, Friedan remarked with retrospective insight shaped by therapy and the women's movement, taught her that she had to earn her own living. Elsewhere, she talked about how she eventually saw her mother as someone with "a typical female disorder," characterized by "impotent rage," who often demeaned her husband because she had too much power inside the household and too little outside. Her mother's turn from professional career to housewife and mother forced her to channel her frustrations into an emphasis on her children's success. Once Bettye was in junior high school, Mrs. Goldstein pressured her into fulfilling her own unrealized ambitions, especially in journalism. Meanwhile, her mother's gastrointestinal disorder, colitis, made it necessary for her to stay in bed for extended periods of time, experiencing great pain that only abated when her husband's heart disease and, later, death made it necessary for her to run the store.[13]

From the outset, medical problems plagued young Bettye. Unhealthy as an infant, neither her parents nor her doctors thought she would live very long. Even though she confounded their expectations, health problems continued. During the first winters of her life, she battled respiratory illness. For three years as a very young child, she wore braces to straighten her legs. When her teeth came in badly, she had braces on them as well. At age eleven, she began to use eyeglasses. These experiences made her feel that fate meant she was both unhealthy and unattractive. The writer Amy Stone wrote in 1976 that Goldstein "grew up with the triple burden of being intelligent, unattractive and Jewish."[14]

There were, however, moments of social pleasure. As a child, Bettye participated with friends in a round of games and parties. They dressed up in their mothers' clothes and then pretended they were movie stars, royalty, or socialites. They acted as detectives who solved mysteries by exploring forbidden places and leaving secret messages. They joined the Girl Scouts. As a teenager, she attended dancing school with boys and girls, and played kissing games called Post Office or Hide-in-the-Dark. She and her friends went to roller-skating, movie, and dance parties. They played golf and bridge. In the summers they picnicked, swam, and played tennis at the country club. At overnight camp, she went horseback riding and canoeing.[15]

Yet Bettye recalled her sense of herself during her childhood as odd, terribly unhappy, and painfully alone. She would sit in a cemetery for hours, crying and composing poems as she daydreamed about having a boyfriend and being an actress. "Those were . . . such . . . painful . . . painful years," she remarked in 1970, pausing for emphasis. On the rare occasions that she dated, the boys she went out with were ones she could never develop an interest in. Like her, they were marginal, "rejects, misfits." So, when members of the congregation were saying the S'chma, a particularly important invocation, she would silently pray that a boy would come along who would like her.[16]

To battle the sense of isolation she felt, Bettye Goldstein performed in school plays, gave public speeches, experienced nature, wrote for the school paper, composed poems, and read books—especially fantasy novels that told of the adventures of children in England. Indeed, she was such a voracious reader that her friends called her "Bookworm." She was, a high school friend remembered, a "hard-working, brainy, free-thinker and fledgling writer." Another friend mentioned how Bettye "could talk your leg off on any subject." She impressed her younger brother as "the most brilliant person I've known in my life," someone whose brain, upon examination after her death, would be "bigger than Lenin's." The fact that she preferred reading books to playing with dolls worried her parents. "Five books at a time is enough!" her father insisted. "It doesn't look nice for a girl to be so bookish." Thinking something was wrong, her parents took Bettye to a therapist. Despite the reassurance they received, her father limited the number of books Bettye could borrow from the library at any one time in order to encourage her to develop more facets of her personality. Precocious, she skipped a grade in elementary school. Successful as a student, she would graduate as one of the high school valedictorians. Inspired by the accomplishments of the French

Nobel laureate Marie Curie, she dreamed of pursuing a career in science. Yet one teacher told her she could not fully realize her ambition, cautioning her to plan on being a lab technician, nurse, or receptionist. When Bettye led her friends in the Baddy Baddy Club in acting out by chewing gum loudly or coughing violently, the principal took her aside. "You've got a talent for leadership, Betty, but why do you use it to do harm? I hope you find a way to use it wisely."[17]

"When you're a Jewish girl who grows up on the right side of the tracks in the Midwest, you're marginal," Friedan commented much later. "You're IN, but you're not, and you grow up an observer." Cut off from the greater number of poor Jews, the members of her family were also excluded from the groups to which their social position and ownership of a fancy store gave them some access. Referring to the common phenomenon of five o'clock friends, Mr. Goldstein told Bettye that socially prominent Christians would simply not talk to him after business hours. Her experience as a Jew in Peoria intensified her sense of herself as an observer, a writer, and someone passionately committed to fighting to improve social conditions. Thus, she noted in 1976 that her "passion against injustice . . . originated from my feelings of the injustice of anti-Semitism."[18]

Her adolescent trials came to a head in her sophomore year, when her female peers marked her marginality by turning down her bid for membership in a sorority at Peoria High School because she was a Jew. Until adolescence, social groupings had been fluid; as often happens, in their teen years her peers became more exclusive, but in this instance their action involved an animus against Jews. Their decision, she later wrote, was part of a pattern of "covert anti-Semitism" in Peoria. Even her mother, she remarked in 1988, was a Jewish anti-Semite. Here Friedan referred to the way some parents told their children not to be too Jewish or not to dwell on evidence of anti-Semitism, something that made it impossible for mother to explain to daughter why the sorority rejected her. This rejection was painful for Bettye, keeping her away from the social world her peers enjoyed. "Believe me," she later remarked, "I would have rather been eating hamburgers at the burger place with the other boys and girls than reading poetry and looking at tombstones." For the first time she was made acutely aware of what it meant to be subject to exclusion as a Jew.[19]

The pleasure she took in writing poetry and reading books was not sufficient compensation for the lack of close relationships with siblings or friends. The shifting tides of friendship groups, the rejection by the sorority, and the fact that older boys paid attention to her female peers, but not to her, upset young Bettye. In 1938, with a seventeen-year-old's flair for the dramatic, she labeled her condition "an inferiority complex" that made her feel like "a social outcast [who] plumbed the depths of misery." She worried that because she was not sexy, she would never marry. Like some other girls in her situation, at times she hid her brightness, hoping that would make her more popular.[20]

Rejection and exclusion because she was a Jew presented a teen-age Bettye with a confusing situation. As a member of an assimilating, midwestern Jewish family, she had learned not to be too Jewish, to have some sense of the problematic and even embarrassing nature of her identity as a Jew, and to confine her Jewishness to home and the temple. "You didn't talk about it," her sister later remarked about anti-Semitism. "You had to act as if it didn't bother you and since nobody was there to say there was something wrong with these other people, you thought: 'There's something wrong with me because they don't want me.'" The sorority's rejection of Bettye stripped away the social pretense of assimilation even as it underscored the contradictions between her social privilege as someone from a well-to-do family and the limits her identity as a Jew imposed.[21]

In her two last years of high school, the isolation and sense of rejection eased considerably as Bettye, determined to be accepted, became more outgoing and lively. She held court among friends gathered at her home. She won a prize for a school essay on how the Constitution protected democracy. She recited Abraham Lincoln's Gettysburg Address at a Memorial Day celebration, after which U.S. Representative Everett Dirksen patted her on the head. She worked on the high school newspaper, one of the few activities that pleased her mother. She wrote book reviews and had her own feature under the heading "Cabbages and Kings." When the student editors turned down Goldstein's plans for a column, she and several friends launched a literary magazine they named *Tide*. As a senior, she won an award for acting as the madwoman in a high school production of *Jane Eyre*. "She was locked up and kept out of sight upstairs in the manor for all but one memorable scene when she appeared, [and] laughed maniacally," a high school friend later noted. Friedan herself evoked the image of the mad woman writer in the attic as representative of the conditions under which she wrote *The Feminine Mystique*. As two literary critics point out, *Jane Eyre* focuses on "confinement" and "rage even to madness," with its heroine becoming "the emblem of a passionate, barely disguised rebelliousness."[22]

Bettye's years in high school came at a time when Franklin D. Roosevelt and the New Deal triumphed and then stalled, fascism was surging in Europe, and social conflict made a marked appearance in Peoria. Pushed to the left by populist challenges, in the spring and summer of 1935, just before Goldstein's sophomore year in high school, Roosevelt offered the second New

Deal. The results were impressive. The National Labor Relations (Wagner) Act guaranteed workers the right to collective bargaining, the Social Security Act lay the ground for modern America's social welfare system, the Works Progress Administration placed relief workers on the federal payroll, and tax legislation contained what conservatives called "soak-the-rich" provisions. In late 1936 and early 1937, rank-and-file workers in the Congress of Industrial Organizations (CIO) led the effort for union recognition. In 1937, unions called almost five thousand strikes, gaining victories in the vast proportion of them. Yet, after Roosevelt's triumph in the 1936 election and throughout most of Goldstein's junior and senior years in high school, the New Deal seemed over, cut short by FDR's attempt to pack the Supreme Court and by the recession of 1937–38. As Alan Brinkley has shown, what ensued was a rethinking of the meaning of liberalism. In the late 1930s and early 1940s, New Dealers moved in a more conservative direction—they were less hostile to corporations and more skeptical of government capacity to reshape capitalism. Events abroad were also disturbing. In the spring of Bettye's sophomore year, Italy completed the annexation of Ethiopia, and the Spanish Civil War broke out the following summer. In the fall of her junior year, Hitler and Mussolini formed the Berlin-Rome axis, and in the spring of her senior year Hitler annexed Austria.[23]

At the same time Father Charles Coughlin, the Detroit-based radio priest, intensified his virulent anti-Semitism. Between 1933 and 1939, writes the historian Leonard Dinnerstein, "an explosion of unprecedented antisemitic fervor" permeated cities and towns across the nation. Respectable community leaders, fundamentalist Protestants, Roman Catholics stirred by Father Coughlin, and native-born fascists insisted the United States was a Christian nation. Many of them envisioned a worldwide Jewish conspiracy— sometimes of bankers and at others of Communists—that was responsible for America's economic crisis. In response, Dinnerstein has written, many American Jews turned on their heritage, tried to hide their immigrant origins, and "suffered silently or bewailed their fate."[24]

Studies of anti-Semitism in the 1930s in Indianapolis and the Twin Cities of Minneapolis and St. Paul, urban areas larger but in many ways comparable to Peoria, underscore the pervasiveness of attacks on Jews. In Minneapolis, anti-Semites, especially active between 1936 and 1938, tried to organize boycotts against Jewish businesses; painted swastikas on Jewish homes, businesses, and synagogues; and attacked Jewish youths. Protestant ministers and members of organized hate groups drew connections between radicalism, Communism, Jews, the CIO, and the New Deal. The Christian Front and Father Coughlin had a local following, especially among low- and moderate-income Roman Catholics, Lutherans, blue-collar workers, and the unemployed. As a result of all of this, the entire Jewish community felt threatened. The situation in Indianapolis seemed less ominous, though the author of an authoritative study has stated that "the difference between anti-Semitism in Minneapolis and in Indianapolis was a matter of degree." Leaders of the Jewish community in the Indiana capital used a number of strategies to counter the rise of anti-Semitism, including efforts to disassociate Jews from radical politics. They hoped this would cut the links anti-Semites made between Bolshevism and Jews. Though it is hard to determine the extent of anti-Semitism in Peoria, some things are sure. The Ku Klux Klan was active in the city in the 1920s. In the interwar years, Peoria was in the orbit of Chicago, a city where a number of important anti-Semitic organizations had their headquarters. Moreover, Peoria had an explosive mixture of people that had produced vicious outbursts in other urban centers: Jewish merchants, as well as Protestants who had migrated from farms and small towns, German-Americans, and Catholics.[25]

Peoria also had a history of conflict between workers and corporations, which erupted with considerable force during Goldstein's last two years in high school. Reactionaries in the city made the absurd claim that there were fifteen thousand Communists. In the summer between Bettye's junior and senior years, the *Peoria Journal-Transcript* discharged three members of the Newspaper Guild and then reinstated two of them a month later. Industrial conflict was especially dramatic in April 1937, which was the spring of her senior year. Organizers from the national offices of the CIO and the American Federation of Labor (AFL) mobilized workers. Corporations responded by shutting down their operations and encouraging workers sympathetic to the corporate position to form company unions.[26]

Conflict between corporations and workers commanded the attention of politically active high school students. For example, the unpublished issue of *Tide* contained an article on unions which Goldstein and her co-editors feared reactionary businessmen would have opposed. In Goldstein's junior year, a student writer described the sit-down strikes at General Motors factories in the Midwest as a struggle between property rights and human rights. Two weeks later, with the strike settled, another student wrote sympathetically of the CIO's activism. One of Goldstein's fellow students picked as the nation's most noteworthy news event the story of an April 1937 strike at the local Caterpillar factory. It was a dramatic moment: a two-day strike, a mass meeting of over five thousand workers, and an agreement between the CIO and company officials. "The C.I.O.," a student noted in an article right next to a column Goldstein wrote, "had demanded recognition and got it." A week later, another student had a hard time deciding which of two events was more important: the Supreme Court's validation of the Wagner Act, or the denunciation by the Canadian premier of the arrival of the CIO in his country as an invasion of "foreign agitators and the chaos created by them in the United States."[27]

Students in Goldstein's circle were well aware of national and international affairs, which the high school newspaper regularly tracked. In Bettye's junior year, the editors made clear their opposition to the fascist takeover of Spain. In the winter of her senior year, between the time when the United States reaffirmed its neutrality and Nazi Germany annexed Austria, she and her peers listened to a debate between an anti-war retired Marine officer and a corporal who was sympathetic to American intervention. The ensuing editorial in the school newspaper, for which Bettye wrote features, warned that war was not so far away that it could be ignored. "Now is the time to THINK about it," the author stated, "before it becomes necessary to DO something about it." A month later, two students debated the issue of America entering the war in the pages of *Tide*. One of Bettye's best friends argued against a referendum on the war. In contrast, another student supported a national vote, in order to "save America from war profiteers and from the 'inevitable war' that may cost millions of lives and billions of dollars." Politically conscious students at Peoria High School also paid attention to right-wing movements in the United States. In April 1938 a student writing in *Tide* warned of the danger of the anti-Semitism and false nationalism of the Black Legion, the Ku Klux Klan, and especially the German-American Bund.[28]

It is likely that in the conversations Goldstein's father directed, her family discussed current affairs, including the rights of unions to organize and the rise of Nazi anti-Semitism. Goldstein's high school writings, composed with wit, style, and imagination, reveal her as an adolescent with a wide range of interests, whose awareness of contemporary issues was greater than her commitment to engaging them fully or passionately. The adolescent nature of her concerns is illustrated by her fascination with the social drama of high school life. She displayed a keen eye for the rituals, fads, and codes that defined student life. Writing of her vacation in her junior year, she captured "the glamour of a Christmas Eve spent dancing in the midst of lovely beings clad in silks and satins and velvets, in formal black and white." She wrote lyrically of students enjoying themselves as they participated in winter sports. She evoked the intense feelings students experienced while working on a school play.[29]

In a series of articles she wrote with a classmate, Goldstein revealed an interest in high school politics typical of student journalists. Writing self-consciously, she and John Parkhurst portrayed themselves as trouble makers on issues concerning students' social lives. They called on students to participate more fully in school affairs. They pressed their peers to reform student politics unless they wished to give in to "a too thoughtless acceptance of the luxury of self-government." They urged the school to recognize the "fledgling orator or the harassed editor" as much as it did the football hero. Reflecting their commitment to traditional values, they asked those who wanted to uphold the school's reputation to criticize students guilty of "an appalling lack of good taste and good breeding" when they misbehaved in a school theater audience.[30]

Despite her preoccupation with school life, Bettye's eyes were also on momentous local, national, and international events. She was aware of the Spanish Civil War. In a paper she wrote in her senior year, she gave evidence of her awareness of the tumultuous happenings in Europe, especially the rise of dictatorial governments. She asked herself if what transpired in Europe could happen in America, but remained convinced that the U.S. Constitution protected the nation's future. Despite the thinness of direct evidence, she was certainly aware of the rising Nazi anti-Semitism in Europe and the virulent American anti-Semitism as forces that had implications well beyond her membership in a sorority and her family's social position. Someone who grew up in a situation remarkably similar to hers has recalled that, as a girl in high school in Omaha in the late 1930s, she learned of anti-Semitism by listening to radio reports of what was happening under Hitler's rule.[31]

Goldstein showed an early interest in anti-fascism in the first of a series of book reviews, written in the fall of her junior year just before Roosevelt's reelection. Responding to Sinclair Lewis's *It Can't Happen Here* (1935), a widely read novel about the coming of a dictatorship to the United States, she cited the novelist's allusions to Governor Huey Long of Louisiana and Father Coughlin. She warned of a "spirit of unrest" in the contemporary world that came from "war scares, depression, rearmament, mob hysteria." Lewis's book, she wrote, would cause readers to pause. "It surely 'can't happen here' and yet—" she remarked inconclusively, even as she resumed her discussion of the danger of dictatorships.[32]

In Bettye's own contribution to the unpublished issue of *Tide,* "Education for the Masses," she mixed elitism and sharp criticism in the most outspoken statement of her high school years. She mocked Americans for their boastfulness about democracy, equality, and material comforts. Again and again, she stressed the gap between the nation's aspirations and reality. She criticized public schools for the sterility of the education they offered, which she saw in their focus on memorizing, their hostility to culture and creativity, the drabness of the buildings, and the provincialism of the teachers.

From grade school through college, she argued, American students attended a series of institutions, each of them having the characteristics of an industrial plant designed to teach marketable skills rather than awaken intellectual curiosity. For her, neither college nor graduate school seemed appealing. At one, social skills were paramount, and at the other, people researched specialized and irrelevant topics. It was not formal education, Goldstein argued, but the mass media that really shaped what American youth dreamed, believed, and wore.[33]

This edition of *Tide* that never appeared gives additional evidence of what shaped Bettye's political consciousness. Fearing suppression of their free speech by the high school administration, Goldstein and her peers backed off from putting into print an issue that included several controversial pieces. Harry Goldstein had stopped his wife's writing career altogether; this was the first of many times that his daughter Bettye would face difficulty in turning her ideas, especially controversial ones, into published words.[34]

As a teenager, Goldstein also explored relationships among people from divergent social groups. The most direct experience she had along these lines came through a summer job in a settlement house in Peoria, located a mile south of her father's store. The work most certainly sharpened her impression of social conditions during the Depression. In December of her junior year, she made clear her sensitivity to the travails of a cross-class romance in contemporary America, writing in a book review about aristocratic parents who vigorously objected when their son fell in love with and married a girl from humble origins. In December of her senior year, imagining what classmates would see when they returned to Peoria High School in the distant future, she explored the diverse fates those around her might face. The cast of characters in this drama of return included a married couple on the verge of divorce, hoboes, prisoners, and members of the country club set.[35]

There is also some evidence of Bettye's awareness during her last years in high school of conflict between workers and capitalists. In her column for the school newspaper, Bettye castigated boys who with a "childish spirit" would "imitate factory workers" by staging " 'sit-down' strikes on girls' front porches. . . . Now," she remarked humorously, "somebody ought to imitate the militia." While still in high school, she drafted an outline for a play about a strike at a mill, in which, after the bosses ignored the pickets, scabs and pickets fought, prompting the police to enter the fray.[36]

Yet neither the anti-Semitism she and her family experienced nor the rise of Naziism in Germany seemed to sensitize her to broader issues of race. Like others she knew, Bettye implicitly accepted racial segregation as a given. Her high school class had only one black member. She most frequently encountered African Americans as people who did work that eased the burdens of white, middle-class life. Consequently, she was surely un-aware of the implications of her remarks in a review of a book by a white woman who served as a missionary doctor in Africa for three years. Young Goldstein, then a fifteen-year-old high school junior, wrote of the author's "entertaining" discussion of "barbarous" but "childlike and lovable" people with "savage rituals and primitive superstitions!" When they encountered Europeans, she noted, Africans gladly gave up their traditions in exchange for mass media and consumer goods.[37]

Despite her early insensitivity to racial issues, at moments during her high school years, Bettye Goldstein displayed consciousness of the choices women faced. In a sketch, she compared two female students—Bea Grass-hopper and Ada Ant. Here she relied on one of Aesop's fables that contrasted a grasshopper whose carefree attitude prevented it from preparing for the future, with an ant who worked hard to make provisions for the unexpected. Bea Grasshopper "sauntered" into class, sexily walked to her seat, and sat down. She then spent five minutes putting on her make-up, after which she flirtatiously looked at Professor Glucose and offered to sew on a button for him. Next to her sat Ada Ant, Bettye's alter ego, who approached her aca-demic tasks with intelligence, hard work, and a touch of sarcasm. The professor, Goldstein noted, scoffed at girls who were intellectually assertive. Ada got an A in the class and ended up as a secretary to a renowned re-searcher. Bea married her professor, and her admiration for him so en-hanced his own self-esteem that he received a series of promotions, even-tually gaining membership in President Roosevelt's Brain Trust. Bea "had the feminine touch!" Goldstein concluded wryly, describing a style that com-bined sex appeal and assertiveness in the cause of finding a prosperous husband who would support her comfortably as a homemaker.[38]

This satire reveals Goldstein's early sensitivity to issues in women's lives. It expresses her ambivalence about intellectual assertiveness and about her pretty and sexy peers who, like her sister, were objects of both her dislike and emulation. It makes clear her keen awareness of two alternate paths women faced. Neither of her two stock characters got very far along the road toward individual achievement. While Bea used sex appeal, domes-ticity, and adulation to enable her husband to achieve considerable profes-sional power, she gained a position of only vicarious achievement. Ada's intelligence, diligence, and lack of sex appeal landed her in a respectable career, but it was one with limited horizons. Unavailable to either woman—as it had been to Bettye's mother—was the opportunity to combine marriage and career.

Labor-capital conflict in Peoria and major events in America and Europe gave Goldstein knowledge on which she would build in college and after-wards. Yet it would be a mistake to exaggerate the direct and conscious impact of political events on Bettye during her Peoria years. Though she was aware of key social and political issues, they hardly engaged her in any sustained or deep way. Her desire to enter the mainstream of student life, her class allegiance and aspirations, and her longing for a boyfriend all con-flicted with her spirited rebelliousness. The craft of writing commanded her attention more than the passion of particular positions. As an adolescent girl, Goldstein was most concerned with personal relationships, identity, and her future. Nowhere is this clearer than in an autobiographical essay she wrote as a class assignment in the spring of her senior year in high school. Whether trying to make things seem better or reflecting how she actually felt, she made clear that she had derived a good deal of pleasure from her youth in a well-to-do house, her accomplishments, her love of books, her acting roles in plays, and her friendships with boys and girls. She admitted that she regretted never having fallen in love with a boy. She acknowledged that some of the boys she most admired treated her more like a sister than a girlfriend. She counted as her friends Jews (including two of her closest friends, who apparently were German Jews) and Gentiles. Though she em-phasized its significance, she tended to minimize the impact of her rejection by the sorority. Yet she was quite aware that her route to success in high school came not through popularity but by achievement in activities. In addition, she acknowledged how much her own situation improved in her junior year, especially as she worked on the high school newspaper and then started a literary magazine. "My whole personality changed," she recalled, "I stopped being so miserably self-conscious."[39]

As biographer Justine Blau has noted, Bettye's essay about her life shows that when she was accepted and getting her way, "her gregarious nature came to the fore." Indeed, Bettye bragged about her skills as a leader and organizer, someone able to compel others to act. In contrast, Blau continues, Goldstein felt "bitterness and insecurity . . . when her childhood friends no longer stayed in the tightly knit group she preferred."[40]

Though she had already developed an interest in psychology, in the essay Bettye defined herself as a writer and a lover of beauty. Had she the manual dexterity necessary to get through medical school, she wrote, she would have become a psychiatrist so that she could understand herself. Indeed, a few weeks before, she had told a reporter for the high school paper that "to be a writer is second only to her ambition to become a psychiatrist." Regard-less of what she did, however, she wanted eventually to write; first, she proclaimed, she had to live. Though she noted that her views shocked others, she put her politics second to her love of beauty, whose emotional power she reported finding in nature, classical music, and literature. It was a testament to her ambition that before she left Peoria she sent off an article about *Tide* to *Quill and Scroll,* the national high school journalism magazine, which it published in late 1938. At some level, in trying to reach a national audience, she made clear how ambitious she was to develop a reputation beyond Peoria.[41]

She resolved that when she grew up, things would be different from what she had known in Peoria. "If they don't like me," she wrote of her high school friends, "some day they'll learn to respect me." Foreshadowing her later desire to combine marriage and career, she said she wanted love from a man, a family, and a career. Revealing her longing for what she understood as a normal heterosexual relationship, she remarked that "I want to fall in love and be loved and be needed by someone. I want to have children." Yet she made clear that she wanted a marriage different from that of her parents. Her relationship with her mother made her resolve not to repeat what she saw as her mother's mistakes. As the daughter of an immigrant father and a second-generation mother, Bettye, though aware of social boundaries, had higher expectations of inclusion and achievement than even her assimilated mother. The man Bettye married had to be smarter than she, and someone who shared her interests. She did not want to focus solely on domestic responsibilities. She asserted, "I don't want to marry a man and keep house for him and be the mother of his children and nothing else."[42]

In 1938, her close friend Doug Palmer described her as "inordinately ambitious," someone who would "strive . . . to reach the top of the world." Bettye herself echoed this. "I want to do something with my life—to have an absorbing interest." With an adolescent flourish that also revealed the extent of her ambitions, she remarked, "I want success and fame."[43]

Bettye Goldstein at Smith College, 1938–40

AN EDUCATION IN CREATIVITY, PSYCHOLOGY—AND POLITICS

As a high school senior, it seemed to Bettye Goldstein that she had always wanted to go to Smith College, a school her maternal grandparents had prevented her own mother from attending. Frustrated about her aborted career in journalism, Miriam Goldstein was eager for Bettye not only to study at Smith and but also to edit the college newspaper. However, what her daughter accomplished at Smith involved much more than vicariously fulfilling her mother's dreams. During her undergraduate years, Bettye came into her own as she pursued interests that she would bring together in *The Feminine Mystique:* writing, progressive politics, the challenges facing women, and psychology.[1]

Courses she took, relationships she established with peers and professors, events in the United States and abroad, and her campus leadership transformed her in a number of ways. They turned her from a provincial outsider and largely apolitical rebel into an advocate of trade unions as the herald of a progressive social vision, a student exposed to feminist concerns, and a fierce questioner of the social privilege of her wealthy peers. By the time she graduated, she had become a healthy skeptic regarding the authority and rhetorical claims of those in power, a staunch opponent of fascism, and a defender of free speech. By the summer between her sophomore and junior years, the spread of fascism in Europe, as well as the culture and politics of the Smith campus, had begun to awaken her interest in radicalism. Their effects on her would only become fully apparent later, for during her first two years at Smith, as in Peoria, Bettye Goldstein focused much of her attention on studying, reading, writing, and creativity.

Located in Northampton, Massachusetts, Smith College in the late 1930s and early 1940s was an extraordinary institution. Many faculty members welcomed bright and non-conforming young women; at the same time some of their peers from socially prominent families did their best to put them in their place. President William Allan Neilson, who retired at the end of Goldstein's first year following more than two decades in office, provided the college with inspired leadership. He supported the free speech of his faculty members, pro-fascist and Marxist alike. Committed to racial justice, he served on the board of the National Association for the Advancement of Colored People (NAACP). A strong internationalist, he was an early critic of fascism. A Scot married to a German, he dedicated himself, nationally and at Smith, to rescuing refugees from Europe.[2]

Due in large measure to Neilson's vision and leadership, Smith had an exceptional faculty. In the spring of 1940, the student newspaper boasted that 14 percent of those who had recently received Guggenheim Fellowships were present or former Smith professors. At a time when there were few if any Jews teaching at other leading institutions, the Smith faculty included a considerable number of Jews. Under Neilson's leadership in the 1930s, Smith, more than any other mainline college or university, dedicated itself to hiring significant numbers of émigrés from Europe. A member of the class of 1944 remembered that there were many professors who "even in teaching ancient history, could relate it to what they had lived through" in Nazi Germany. The addition of émigrés to a faculty that included many native-born members steeped in progressive politics gave the Smith community a strongly liberal and anti-fascist cast.[3]

Smith offered its students many women professors who served as role models. In 1940, when institutions like Yale, Harvard, Amherst, and Williams admitted only men as undergraduates and had no women with regular professorial appointments, women held 63 percent of the faculty positions at Smith. Though Smith would not have a woman as president until 1975, in Goldstein's sophomore year Elizabeth Cutter Morrow moved over from the board of trustees to serve as acting president while the search for a long-term appointment of a man with academic credentials continued. A fund raiser and an author of poetry and children's stories, Morrow was the widow of the investment banker, politician, and diplomat Dwight Morrow, with whom she had several children. To the assembled students in the fall of Goldstein's sophomore year, Morrow talked of how wonderful it was that, having secured the vote, American women could pursue economic opportunity through paid work, participate in a public social life, and play sports. Her grandmother, she noted with regret, as she also made clear how long her own family had been upper class, was never able to put her work as a woman "upon the market."[4]

Yet Northampton and Smith were hardly paradise. Some of the college's most distinguished faculty members were eager to leave in order to teach in a university and live in a more cosmopolitan area. Many students found life in the small, provincial town boring. Nor was Smith distant from society's problems. Classes, including those in psychology, visited the nearby mental hospital, a series of sprawling buildings on a hill overlooking the campus that housed well over a thousand patients. Several professors and at least one undergraduate organization took students to union meetings and local factories, one of which stood within a mile of the campus. In the spring of Goldstein's first year, the president of the Smith chapter of the American Student Union (ASU) wrote an article that described the hard times and struggles affecting workers in Depression-wracked New England communities, Northampton included.[5]

Nor was Smith a feminist institution, as a later generation would understand that term. The college offered no courses in women's history, literature, or psychology. There was little explicit emphasis on Smith as a woman's college, something normally left unstated at a time when so many elite institutions were single sex. At the end of Goldstein's sophomore year, a poll revealed that the faculty were more committed than students to questioning stereotypes about women. A significantly higher percentage of professors indicated they would vote for a qualified woman for president of the United States, advocated married women working for a living even if their husbands could support them, and felt it was not "indecent" for students to wear shorts in public.[6]

Despite student conservatism on these issues, Smith promoted gender equality and awareness. Many members of the faculty encouraged students to take themselves seriously. Mary Henle, like Goldstein, was a Jew who came to Smith in the 1930s from the Midwest and majored in psychology. After going on to a distinguished academic career, Henle wrote that "nobody told us that we could not do professional work." She also noted that "outstanding women on the faculty," in psychology and in other fields, "would have given the lie to any such advice." Evidence of concern with women's issues also comes from Marian G. Champagne's *The Cauliflower Heart* (1944), a novel written by a member of the class of 1936. She pictured a heated discussion among students about the pros and cons of a women's college. Without men in the classroom, one character remarked, students could "get away from the eternal boy-girl situation and not be afraid to stretch the old mentality as far as it will go." Her focus on a student who aspired to be a medical doctor allowed her to explore a wide range of discriminatory practices and pressures ambitious women would face after graduation from Smith.[7]

Other evidence of attention to women's issues is not hard to find. In the spring of 1940, the student newspaper published a satirical piece on how Smith should offer courses to prepare students to be good wives and mothers. In the fall of 1940, an editorial writer protested Yale's Sadie Hawkins Day, when women could ask men out on dates, and threatened to lynch any Smith student found pursuing a Yale man. The literary magazine paid considerable attention to established women writers. Student leaders, who felt the faculty treated them as adults, opposed the restrictive social rules imposed by the administration on the grounds that the regulations treated them as girls. In the fall of 1938, an advertisement in the student newspaper featured settlement house pioneer Jane Addams as one of the "Great Women in History," before going on to encourage Smith students to stay in an all-female hotel in New York so they could become "successful career women."[8]

Moreover, as a women's college and especially one with a liberal tradition, Smith fostered in many of its students a concern for women's issues that was at least implicit—by enabling them to assume leadership positions and by encouraging them to take themselves, their ideas, and their ambition seriously. They could find in the classroom and in their work for student organizations a world unavailable in their hometowns. Smith was a place where girls could become young women with a sense of independence from reigning social and political norms. During the period when Goldstein headed the student newspaper, an editorial writer remarked that new students who did not know how to dress properly, "who have no facile small talk, who feel that their beliefs are at war with" those of their peers, would find a place for themselves at Smith. Among the students at Smith during Goldstein's years were women who would go on to earn major roles in academic life, publishing, the arts, religion, computer science, environmentalism, and in politics on the local, state, national, and international levels.[9]

If much in the institutional life at Smith fostered the intellectual and professional ambitions of bright young women, the student body posed problems for someone such as Goldstein. Like others who came from relatively privileged backgrounds in medium-sized midwestern cities, now she discovered the social networks, wealth, and prestige enjoyed by young women from East Coast elite families. Most Smith students were acutely aware of the way social divisions, especially those based on class and lineage, played out in campus life. Social privilege came in many forms, few of them available to Goldstein, a very rebellious, quite brainy, and somewhat awkward Jew to whom the experiences and arrogance of graduates of eastern boarding and private day schools were new. Students with the right social credentials could join secret societies, which a spring 1940 editorial denounced as "a most undesirable and adolescent display of snobbery which has absolutely no place on such a democratic campus as ours." Students arriving from private schools knew how to play sports such as field hockey that many from public schools had never even heard of. Middle-class students often envied upper-class ones for the parties and dances they attended.[10]

The student body of two thousand women was hardly a representative cross section of American society. A poll taken at the end of Goldstein's sophomore year revealed that almost a quarter of the students described themselves as upper class, with 70 percent feeling they belonged to the middle class, and only 1 percent to the lower class. According to another survey, almost 54 percent of the students' fathers were businessmen or bankers, with the remainder having largely middle-class and upper-middle-class occupations. A long list of jobs included a janitor as the only working-class representative. Most of the mothers were housewives, many of whom also did volunteer work. Under 5 percent of the students had mothers who worked for pay, and most of these did so in historically female occupations. Most parents were from mainline Protestant denominations, with about 8.5 percent each Roman Catholic and Jewish.[11]

Many of the Jewish students considered themselves outsiders. In some ways they were cast into the same role as African Americans of the 1980s and 1990s: objects of both curiosity and racism, learning to maneuver through the shoals of delicate relationships among themselves and with non-Jews, their dress and manners always subject to scrutiny. Many radicals—Jews and non-Jews alike—understood the connection between anti-Semitism and other kinds of prejudice. As a non-Jewish radical said in Champagne's novel, "the so-called Jewish problem is not something unique." Rather, she connected it with British imperialism in India, Japanese attacks on the Chinese, and violence by fascists in Italy. The powerful and greedy, she concluded, deliberately use "poverty, ignorance, fear" to divert attention "from the struggle for justice and liberty into the alley-ways of Jew-baiting and lynching and Yellow Peril scares."[12]

Northampton and Smith were overwhelmingly white environments. The town had a minuscule number of African Americans. There were only nine African American students at Smith for at least one of the years when Goldstein was there. Most of them were light skinned and from socially prominent families, including Jane White, class of 1944, whose father headed the NAACP. The administration and faculty responded to this racial imbalance by assigning books by Booker T. Washington and the Harlem Renaissance writer Countee Cullen, and by bringing to the campus prominent African Americans, including Marian Anderson and the Hampton Institute Singers.[13]

At Smith, Bettye Goldstein encountered daughters from very wealthy and pedigreed families for the first time, but as someone not on scholarship, she was also aware that some students were from backgrounds far more humble than hers. Indeed, the college had a series of three residences in which only those on scholarship lived; more than that, the college placed these houses in a hierarchy, deciding which students would live in each, according to the extent of their financial need and the resulting degree of obligation to earn money in college. These social distinctions were made visible daily, as students with the largest scholarships served food to classmates who received little or no financial aid.[14]

Although social tensions on the Smith campus did not reverberate politically until Goldstein's junior and senior years, she came to Smith at a critical moment in her family's history. Her father's illness, which grew more serious after Bettye went off to Smith, placed at risk both the social order and income stream of the household. Coming from a family that had experienced greater prosperity in the 1920s than in the 1930s, Goldstein faced the threat of downward social mobility. Growing up in a family blocked by prejudice from those above and sheltered by geographical location and social position from those below, Goldstein arrived at Smith vaguely aware of class inequality and some of the suffering it caused. Social class, experienced personally and socially, opened her eyes to new perspectives.[15]

Bettye Goldstein came to a Smith that international issues had electrified. In her first year, 1938–39, the Germans annexed Czechoslovakia and began to chip away at Poland. When she returned for her second year, Adolf Hitler and Joseph Stalin had just signed a nonaggression pact. The USSR now cooperated with the Nazis, an action that shattered the Popular Front coalition of Communists and non-Communists. On the eve of her return to college, Germany invaded Poland, and France and England declared war against Germany. In the spring of her sophomore year, Germany swept across Europe. During all these events, many students experienced Smith College as an intensely political campus, with the student newspaper, the classroom, and public lectures persistently connecting life in Northampton with events beyond the campus. Neilson's weekly talks, recalled a member of the class of 1938, helped students take their minds off "campus affairs and the local problems and [their] own personal problems," and realize that they "were a part of the world community."[16]

At no time was Neilson's sense of urgency greater than in his response to *Kristallnacht*, the night of November 9, 1938, when Germans assaulted Jews, burning their synagogues and destroying their businesses. At a mass meeting in Northampton, Neilson described Hitler's hatred of the Jews as something "so fierce that it stops at no cruelty." Neilson was forceful and clear in his call on America to remember its commitment to a "common humanity" that included Jews. At a time when few Americans, President Franklin D. Roosevelt included, were willing to open the nation's doors to victims of Nazi persecution, Neilson insisted that it was necessary to confront American anti-Semitism and then convince the nation to accept hundreds of thousands of Jewish refugees to keep them out of Hitler's reach. At Smith, Neilson built support for his vision of a society and college that welcomed Jews fleeing the Nazis. During Goldstein's first year at Smith, her housemates debated whether to aid these efforts. A group of wealthy Jews from Cincinnati remained silent, while Bettye and a few Protestants spoke up in favor of Neilson's plan for the nation and college to welcome Jews who escaped from Nazi Germany.[17]

Throughout Goldstein's career at Smith, people committed to liberal and left-wing positions dominated campus-wide public discussions. Most politically conscious students and faculty agreed on a set of core values: free speech, the liberal arts, tolerance, progress, social responsibility, social justice, community, democracy, and peace. Smith hosted a steady stream of progressive speakers. Emigrés from Germany and Italy spoke, as did people who stood in opposition to the caste system in India and in favor of the efforts of Mahatma Gandhi to overthrow it. Similarly, a significant proportion of the American speakers were on the left: the folklorist Alan Lomax, the theologian Reinhold Niebuhr, the propagandist for the USSR Anna Louise Strong, the independent radical Corliss Lamont (then the head of Friends of the Soviet Union), Labor Secretary Frances Perkins, presidential wife and social reformer Eleanor Roosevelt, and pacifist A. J. Muste.[18]

As was true elsewhere, students on the left tended to dominate student publications at Smith. They did not speak for the considerable number of undergraduates to whom ideas and political issues hardly mattered. Nor was the faculty all of one mind. One male professor did not think African Americans or women "were ever geniuses," and another was a Nazi sympathizer. More typical of faculty sentiment was Otto F. Kraushaar, a native of Iowa from whom Goldstein took two philosophy courses, who spoke for many in the Smith community when he attacked fascism and expressed more skepticism about Soviet practice than Communism's underlying principles. He promoted an ambitious liberalism that included the distrust of all absolutes, and expressed appreciation for those who sympathized with "the dispossessed and the radical champions of the underprivileged."[19]

A series of commitments differentiated liberals from radicals of the kind Goldstein was becoming. Radical students, many but not all of them Jews, realized that their very attendance at an elite college made them, as one student put it, "privileged beyond most," and obligated them to take seriously their role as citizens. Leaving issues of race to a small group of concerned Christians who went about their business quietly, radicals sustained a commitment to achieving social justice through labor unions. They asserted that large American corporations prevented the nation from living up to its ideals. More concerned than liberals with anti-Semitism, aware of the intense factionalism on the American left, grounded in Marxism, and sensitive to issues of redbaiting, they approached a wide range of issues with exceptional intensity.[20]

The anti-fascism of students on the left at Smith differed from the milder version espoused by liberals. Before and after Pearl Harbor, radicals insisted that war not be allowed to threaten democracy and social justice, foster nationalism, or tempt Americans to forget that the British were imperialists. Writing in the ASU-sponsored *Focus,* one student worried about fascism abroad and at home, especially that of Father Charles Coughlin. She was acutely aware of how those on the right alleged connections between the New Deal, Jews, and unions. Finally, she well understood how fascists advocated traditional womanhood and motherhood. Student radicals in the late 1930s and early 1940s also learned the importance of hiding specific political affiliations, which they felt were nobody's business. They knew that if they revealed their organizational commitments even to their allies, they would not be able to work together. Subordinating all else to larger and nobler causes, they felt that what mattered was one's position on specific issues and not membership in a specific group.[21]

A knowledge of student radicalism elsewhere is essential to understanding the situation at Smith. In the late 1930s, the American Youth Congress (AYC) served as the clearing house for more than sixty national youth organizations, including the ASU. The twenty-thousand-member ASU was the largest Popular Front national organization of students. After the signing of the Nazi-Soviet pact in the summer before Goldstein's sophomore year, the national student groups sharply divided, splitting Communist supporters of the agreement from non-Communist opponents. By early 1940, Communists and their sympathizers within the ASU dominated the organization. The ASU's increasing pro-Soviet orientation, as well as its anti-interventionism, pitted it against those who controlled the national office, especially the ASU Executive Secretary Joseph Lash, the Roosevelt administration, and redbaiters in Congress. When the Communists justified the USSR's invasion of Finland on November 30, 1939, it further eroded the organization's credibility as a group that spoke with moral authority against aggression.[22]

In the late 1930s and early 1940s, Smith radicals followed paths that both resembled and differed from those taken on other campuses. Surprisingly, student radicals elsewhere focused more on issues concerning women and African Americans than did the radicals at Smith. In the critical year of 1939–40, with the Communists tempering their hostility to Nazi Germany, pro-Soviet isolationism would have found few supporters on a campus so committed to anti-fascism. In the first months of 1940, Smith did experience the consequences of events within the student movement and in Europe. In February, when Bettye Goldstein was one of five assistant editors on the college newspaper, an editorial supported the "sound verbal spanking" that President Roosevelt had given to the AYC at the White House. The paper defended the AYC against congressional charges of domination by Communists, but called into question the "small minority of Communists" in the Young Communist League (YCL) who "exert an influence out of all proportion to their size." In April came the response of Vivian Rutes, a member of the class of 1942 who had been at the meeting of the AYC in Washington. She attacked the February editorial for redbaiting. Then she went on to emphasize how the AYC supported federal legislation for jobs for young people, opposed discrimination against African Americans, condemned the congressional investigation of Communist influence in the student movement, and remained committed to keeping the United States out of the war.[23]

Most Smith students and faculty were internationalists and anti-fascists who had remained cautious about American intervention in World War II. The German march across western Europe in the spring of 1940 changed the minds of many at Smith. The administration and influential members of the faculty marshalled resources to persuade students to accept intervention. The emotional exhortations of those in authority, the student newspaper remarked, had convinced Smith students to switch from the pacifism they had embraced in most of the interwar years. Then, an editorial writer noted caustically, at a time when radicals among the students remained noninterventionist, "in true 'womanly' fashion" students changed from nonintervention "to a state of teary jitters, of almost hysterical uncertainty."[24]

While students were still on campus, Acting President Morrow made clear her commitment to aid the Allies in Europe. Here she played out a complicated family drama. In a nationally broadcast radio program on May 29, 1940, she took issue with her son-in-law Charles Lindbergh, who had achieved heroic status when he flew the "Spirit of St. Louis" across the Atlantic, and whose isolationism in the 1930s involved a sympathy for Adolf Hitler. With the memory of her late husband, an avowed internationalist, on her mind, she spoke out in support of aid to the Allies, whom she saw as the first line of defense against Hitler. Her words added weight to Smith's anti-fascism and internationalism.[25]

The college's commitment to liberal values, the leadership of Neilson and Morrow, the presence on the faculty of so many who were to the left of center, and the social tensions among students posed problems for campus radicals. To a greater extent than most of their peers, they were aware of the contradictions between democratic rhetoric and a more problematic reality. As noted above, some students chafed at social restrictions imposed by the college administration that they felt were patronizing and demeaning. The visibility of scholarship students and maids who waited on their more privileged peers served as constant reminders of the inequalities at Smith and in society. The existence of secret societies reinforced social divisions on a campus where democratic rhetoric predominated. The left-liberal nature of public discourse, combined with the dynamics of social relationships, spurred radicals on to define themselves in an adversarial manner.

Bettye Goldstein arrived on the Smith campus from Peoria in the fall of 1938 in the midst of a furious hurricane, already aware of issues involving anti-Semitism, fascism, and labor unions. The charged political atmosphere of the Smith campus intensified her emerging interest in politics. Yet early on, what captivated much of her attention were issues that had fascinated her in Peoria—the pursuit of beauty and imagination, her ambition as a writer, and her interest in psychology. Composing essays and poetry for classes, she also founded, edited, and published in the student literary magazine. Courses in psychology in her first two years were critical in her intellectual development. They introduced her to faculty members important to her future. They provided her with tools to question commonly held assumptions. Professors supported her intellectual ambitions, giving her a sense of what it meant to join the community of educated women and reinforcing her commitment to make a contribution beyond marriage and the family. Finally, what she learned placed her anti-fascism on a firm intellectual foundation.

During her first two years at Smith, Bettye Goldstein's accomplishments soon marked her as a major figure on campus. Winning the Arthur Ellis Hamm Scholarship Prize for outstanding academic performance in her first year made her someone to reckon with. In her sophomore year, she was selected as a member of the much coveted Sophomore Push Committee, a group of students who helped organize events surrounding the 1940 Commencement. During her first two years, professors praised her work, using words like "excellent," "extremely intelligent," and "masterful." She later remarked that "for the first time, I wasn't a freak for having brains." No longer an outsider, she was now rewarded for what had set her apart in much of her adolescence—her intelligence, ambition, writing ability, and love of books. During college, what had begun in her last years in high school grew: at the center of a circle of friends, she became more assertive, confident, and outgoing.[26]

Yet Bettye Goldstein achieved all she did despite the fact that important aspects of her life were not going well. The initial transition from Peoria to Smith was difficult. Serious health problems quickly emerged, including a series of asthma attacks. Moreover, while at Smith Bettye found it difficult to meet young men, and to develop sustained romantic relationships with them. The problem was all the more painful since many of her classmates were dating and becoming engaged.[27]

Though friendships and her many activities enabled Bettye to overcome her loneliness, she nonetheless stood in an adversarial relationship to the dominant social groups on campus. Her friend Mary Anne Guitar recalled that Bettye often reacted negatively to peers she felt disdained her. They were everything Bettye was not—graduates of private schools, from the East, Protestant, politically conservative or disengaged, and adorned with circle pins and Peter Pan collars. If she had gone to a university with more Jews, fewer social snobs, and a far more politicized and intellectual student culture, Guitar thought, Bettye probably would not have been so determined to excel and to challenge her opponents. Loving the role of outsider, Bettye thrived best in an atmosphere where not everyone accepted her. Spirited, ambitious, and brainy, she characteristically remembered a criticism from a professor as a challenge, not a put down: "Miss Goldstein, you lack humility. You are too arrogant."[28]

One of the most marked features of Goldstein's early years at Smith was the intensification of her interest in writing, something she pursued in both her academic and extracurricular work. In her second year at college, she became a member of the campus poetry club, and her poems appeared in student publications. The poems she wrote that year, most of them composed for a course, reveal a rebellious and engaged sensibility, someone who was grappling with issues of personal identity and political commitment, but who did so with wit and a sense of irony.[29]

In some of her poems, Bettye concerned herself with various kinds of forbidden love. In one, she talked about the knowing reaction of Smith students as they saw two older women professors showing signs of affection to each other. In another, she wrote about a female college student who was in love with her married male professor and wondered how he felt about her. Yet another pondered the implications of the British philosopher Bertrand Russell's penchant for extramarital affairs at a time when his sexual activity, pacifism, and radical politics had landed him in a nasty academic freedom case at City College of New York. While the editors of the college newspaper focused on the threat to academic freedom in Russell's case,

Goldstein emphasized the issues of the sexual double standard and the contradictions of bourgeois morality.[30]

Other poems engaged political issues more directly. She thought about the implications of different roles students assumed. She wondered about the student, not unlike Bea Grasshopper, who chose domesticity and marriage to a wealthy man as protection against existential anxieties. She cast a skeptical eye on do-gooders and peace activists who seemed more interested in their own well-being than in that of the people they were ostensibly trying to help, and on those whose privileged pleasures contrasted with the horrible lives of European soldiers. Even when she acknowledged her own political struggles as a peace activist, she worried that she remained unaffected by the traumas that afflicted soldiers on the front lines. Although she opposed German fascism, she could imagine the pain and anxiety German soldiers faced as they marched across Europe. The USSR's invasion of Finland in late November 1939 spurred her to write several poems, ones in which she sympathized with the Finns, and by implication criticized the Soviets for the invasion. In October 1939, she wrote a five-line poem on the Nazi-Soviet pact, in which she wondered if Machiavelli was laughing to himself and if politicians had forgotten what they might have learned from a reading of *The Prince*. Writing at a time when the Nazi-Soviet pact had divided the left and discredited American Communists, Goldstein's response, far from dogmatic, was nuanced, ironic, and thoughtful.[31]

Goldstein revealed her political position even more fully in a long poem she wrote in the fall of 1939. Here she responded to a speech by ex-President Neilson. After mimicking his call for American youth to be idealistic, she launched into a powerful and ironic critique of what he had said. She asked if the American way of life was so wonderful that it was wise to feel morally superior. She wondered why the Soviet invasion of Finland was more deserving of censure than the German conquest of Czechoslovakia the previous spring. She attacked British imperialism in a manner that called into question that nation's sense of righteousness. Then she defended student indecisiveness toward the war by emphasizing how the Smith education, with its emphasis on skepticism, had sharpened students' minds, making it difficult for them to take an idealistic stance toward politics. This poem reveals how political issues engaged Goldstein as a sophomore, and underscores that she saw politics in generational terms. Above all, it shows that at this point in her college education she had strong political convictions but expressed them with a sense of humor. By the end of her sophomore year, she had moved beyond the awareness of national and world events that characterized her high school years. She was interested in radical circles and issues but not yet fully absorbed in them. There was a distance to go from irony to passion.[32]

While still at Smith Goldstein claimed that politics did not concern her until her junior year, but there is considerable evidence of her political engagement before that. Yet there are several distinct indications of Bettye Goldstein's independence from loyalty to established organizations and beliefs. In her sophomore year, she and her friends had struck out on their own and created *Smith College Monthly,* which competed with ASU's *Focus.* Though she shared many positions with student ASU members, Goldstein was never listed in the yearbook as a member or officer. Sharing a page with the Rutes article on the AYC was her poem, "Miami, Significant." Here she reacted to the jumble of images in the Florida resort city, where she may well have spent a vacation with her ailing father. Bettye Goldstein was still poised between creative writing and the appeal of politics. Though she was becoming politicized, her ambition and fierce independence meant that she was still keeping her distance from anyone else's social or political movement.[33]

More than any other subject, in both poems and essays Goldstein focused on problems facing authors. The issues of censorship and writing under political pressure connected her experience as a high school journalist with her knowledge of the suppression of free speech of radicals and anti-war activists, especially in World War I. They also provided the background against which she would encounter the consequences of expressing unpopular ideas during the Cold War. In poems she talked of how difficult it was to write, partly because she was a woman who was struggling to find her voice. In January of her first year at Smith, as she returned to the implications of the issue of *Tide* that remained unpublished in high school because of the anticipation of censorship, she wondered about the relationship between commitments to creativity and political action. She speculated on what would have happened if Emily Dickinson had left her house in Amherst to witness social problems, and if Virginia Woolf had chosen to struggle with social misery rather than focus so much on style. She thought about what it meant for Abraham Lincoln to write powerful prose that remained unpublished because he preferred leadership to writing. In late September 1939, she lamented the fate of European authors who, when faced with war, had to abandon the pursuit of art, or use it for political purposes.[34]

A long review of John Steinbeck's *The Grapes of Wrath* linked her interest in the novelist's creativity with her own dedication to progressive politics. Writing in *Focus,* the eighteen-year-old Goldstein answered conservative critics of the novel. Yes, she said, it was "'profane and shocking in its detail,'" as some "rabid" adversaries had suggested. However, Goldstein answered, the America Steinbeck described so truthfully was indeed profane and shocking. Ten months after James Gibson, one of the professors who most influenced her, had expressed the hope that educated people would develop what he labeled "good" propaganda, Goldstein called the novelist's achievement "very artistic propaganda" whose message was "non-political, non-dogmatic." In characterizing the novel as "a fiery document of protest and compassion," and analyzing how Steinbeck combined artistry and social commitment, she may have revealed something of her own aspirations as a writer.[35]

Bettye Goldstein's education in psychology provided her with another intellectual arena that influenced how she saw the world. Courses in the discipline sharpened her commitment to scholarship and opened up options for the future. In them, Bettye encountered ideas and ways of thinking that would shape her writing and her career. Her training in psychology provided the bridge between the issues of creativity she explored in her first two years of college and the political orientation that took full shape in her junior and senior years. Courses in the field led her to at least one radical faculty member, and provided an academic basis for her anti-fascism.[36]

   With considerable justification, Friedan later claimed that what she learned from the psychologists with whom she studied as an undergraduate was a commitment to question assumptions, a belief that ideas mattered, and an interest in seeing problems in their totality. An editorial in the student newspaper, perhaps written by Goldstein, stated it best. "To think below the surface into the true nature of a group of facts," wrote the author, is "to see interrelationships and the complexities of cause and effect, . . . to analyze assumptions, question dogma, evaluate values." Later, Friedan connected what she had learned as an undergraduate with what she wrote more than two decades later. "If I hadn't had that kind of grounding intellectually," she said, "I wouldn't have been able to pierce my way through the Freudian and sociological seemingly-perceived truths . . . established in sophisticated thought" that it was necessary to see through in order "to question the feminine mystique."[37]

   By the middle of her sophomore year, Bettye Goldstein was developing an impressive, professional mastery of the field. Her education in psychology provided a broad and rigorous training, one that offered a number of perspectives, including Freudian, social, Gestalt, behavioral, and experimental. Goldstein's lecture notes and papers in psychology for her first two years at Smith give the impression of someone whose education in the discipline was highly technical and apolitical. Even this early, however, there is some evidence that she was beginning to ponder the political implications of what she was learning. This became clear in May 1940 when she wrote a long paper for a French course that explored how Sigmund Freud's concept of narcissism illuminated the character of Emma in Gustave Flaubert's *Madame Bovary*. Goldstein insisted that Emma's situation was hardly abnormal, foreshadowing her later interest in the psychological condition of middle-class women. Perhaps thinking of her mother or her mother's friends, Goldstein remarked that in America there were many women who lived miserable and aimless lives, suffused with narcissism and unreality.[38]

The paper on *Madame Bovary* underscores a woman-centered element in Goldstein's education in psychology at Smith, for here she was using the discipline to call into question women's capitulation to debilitating conditions. She described how Emma's imitation of her father led her to develop business skills. She also emphasized that Freud demonstrated how some people could resist identification more effectively than others. Indeed, during her sophomore year, the study of psychology convinced Goldstein of the malleability of human nature. She was coming to believe in the ability of psychologists to predict behavior, control people's personalities, and generate concepts applicable to a wide range of fields. In the spring of 1940, she listened as a lecturer in a psychology course talked about how female college students struggled to establish independence from their parents, as they negotiated what it meant to be women. The lecturer emphasized the "feelings of failure" that college women experienced in dating situations, and how they often responded by becoming more masculine or feigning frailty. The lecture concluded with the recommendation that students read a book on birth control.[39]

Although Friedan in the 1970s asserted that at Smith there were "no women role models, virtually none, that combined serious work with motherhood," in fact at college she had a number of people, women included, on whom she could model herself. Goldstein took courses from two compelling role models, James Gibson and Eleanor Gibson, husband and wife and parents of two children, the first of them born in 1940. Eleanor Gibson grew up in Peoria before she came to Smith eleven years before Goldstein, married James Gibson, who was one of her undergraduate teachers, and eventually became a professor at Smith because it had no anti-nepotism rule. Goldstein also studied with other married career women with children, as well as with Harold Israel and Elsa M. Siipola, who were married to each other and without children.[40]

Many of Goldstein's teachers also played a critical role in sparking her interest in anti-fascism and the labor movement. Especially important was a year-long course in her sophomore year with James Gibson. He later recounted how the Depression had radicalized him, with Marxist socialism providing "the only general theory for social action" that he found acceptable. Searching for a mass basis of social change, he quickly developed an interest in unions. He and some of his Smith colleagues formed a local branch of the American Federation of Teachers, with Gibson serving as president of the Western Massachusetts Teachers' Federation the year before Goldstein arrived at Smith. Throughout Goldstein's years at Smith, Gibson was visibly active in fighting against fascism and for the labor movement. At the beginning of the second semester of Goldstein's first year, Gibson gave a public lecture in which he discussed the difference between bad and good propaganda, on which Goldstein drew in her discussion of Steinbeck. He criticized bad propaganda, using as examples Hitler's anti-Semitism and cosmetics advertisements that played on women's desires and diverted attention from economic problems. He contrasted this with the good propaganda of pro-union advocacy, which he urged educated people to develop in order to persuade others to fight for good causes. In the fall of Goldstein's sophomore year, Gibson published a scholarly piece on "The Aryan Myth," in which he explored the dynamics of anti-Semitism in the United States, but especially in Nazi Germany. At the same time, in *Focus* he argued that an alliance between teachers and unions would strengthen both groups and prevent fascism in America by fostering democracy.[41]

In the summer between her sophomore and junior years, Bettye Goldstein studied with Kurt Lewin at the Child Welfare Research Station at the State University of Iowa. The fact that her mentors encouraged her to attend confirmed the seriousness with which they took her potential. Her experience there sharpened her sense of the connection between psychology and anti-fascism. Though there was little explicitly political in what she studied, some of what Lewin taught, inspired by his familiarity with Nazi Germany, focused on the question of how frustration, success, and failure might affect children's aspirations. Indeed, Friedan later remarked that through her studies with Lewin she "began to understand the dynamics of the anti-Semitic Jew."[42]

Lewin served as an important bridge between the Gestalt psychology of the 1930s and the humanistic psychology that was to emerge fully in the 1950s. By the time Goldstein encountered him, he was developing a theory of dynamic psychology that emphasized the relationship between frustration, quest for success, avoidance of failure, response to authoritarianism, and changing levels of aspiration. If explorations of these issues mattered to a man who had recently emigrated from Nazi Germany and who now watched from a distance as Germany marched across France, they also concerned an impressionable nineteen-year-old college student whose life and education were teaching her about issues of anti-Semitism, authoritarianism, fascism, democracy, and "Economic Insecurity." This last phrase was the title of a paper Bettye Goldstein wrote that summer, in which she pondered Lewin's experiments in light of her own family's sense of economic insecurity and perhaps the economic insecurity of society as a whole. Wider acceptance of cooperative labor for social ends, she argued, would encourage people to shift their attention from self-aggrandizement to social service. This change, she concluded, would reduce people's personal difficulties and enhance their sense of security.[43]

When Bettye Goldstein left Smith at the end of her sophomore year, she should have done so with a great sense of accomplishment. Ambitious as a writer, she had already seen her poems and prose printed in student publications, and had launched a magazine. In her second year, she was promoted from assistant editor to news editor and became a member of the literary board of the student newspaper. She had found mentors on the faculty and friends among students. She had done exceedingly well academically, earning high grades that gained her the prize for outstanding work in her first year. Her peers had acknowledged her position as a campus leader when they selected her for Sophomore Push.[44]

When Goldstein returned to college in September, events in Europe, along with the concomitant change in the Smith political climate, presented her with a dilemma. Like most radical students at Smith, she was still an anti-war internationalist and anti-fascist. Yet she would come back to a Smith that embraced intervention, leaving her isolated. She was on the eve of a new moment in her life. When she first arrived at Smith, anti-Semitism, experienced in personal ways, was fresh on her mind. As she shifted to more public expressions of anti-Semitism, anti-fascism was becoming the bridge to her commitment to labor unions that would in turn flower into a passion for women's issues.

The Radicalization of
Bettye Goldstein, 1940–41

Sensitized to political issues in her first two years at Smith, as a junior and senior Bettye Goldstein became fully radicalized. She continued working on creative writing and her courses. Yet beginning with her junior year, politics took hold of her life. Some of what shaped her was nearby: events on campus, courses she took, editorials she wrote or supervised, and political battles she fought. Meanwhile, beyond the confines of Smith and Northampton, the world turned upside down and did so in a way that, along with events at Smith, began to transform her anti-fascism into a concern for workers.[1]

During Goldstein's junior year, Smith College continued to foster her intellectual and political development. The most significant course she took that year was Economics 319, Theories and Movements for Social Reconstruction, taught by Dorothy Wolff Douglas. Douglas provided Goldstein with perspectives that helped shape her future and develop the ideas that proved so consequential to the reemergence of American feminism. For Goldstein, Douglas was surely a striking model—Jewish, wealthy, attractive, cosmopolitan, widely read, radical, and politically engaged.

Douglas grew up in a wealthy New York German-Jewish family. As early as 1915 she was able to use her private income to support progressive causes. In that year she also married Paul H. Douglas, whose introduction to politics had come in 1911, when he was moved by the tragedy of the Triangle Shirtwaist fire in Manhattan that killed about 150 female workers. In the 1920s, while living in Chicago, the Douglases were friends of Jane Addams, the peace activist and founder of Hull House. Together they had four children before they divorced in 1930. After a career as a distinguished labor economist, Paul Douglas served as a U.S. Senator from Illinois for eighteen years beginning in 1948. Dorothy Douglas began teaching at Smith in 1924, when her husband joined the faculty at nearby Amherst College. They had moved from Chicago after she made clear to him how important it was for her to have a regular academic job, something that a nepotism rule at the University of Chicago, where he was then teaching, prevented. Though Paul Douglas soon returned to Chicago, she remained at Smith for more than a quarter of a century.[2]

In the 1920s and 1930s, Douglas made clear her commitments to women, workers, and social change. In 1920, she attacked as "ultra-reactionary" the notion that the earnings of working-class women provided "pin money." Instead, she emphasized the importance of wages that compensated women for the "inescapable burdens" they faced, including those that resulted from their participation in the household economy. In her first book, published in 1925, she stressed her support of radical social movements and academic freedom. She wrote her second book, *Child Workers in America* (1937), with her partner, Katharine Du Pre Lumpkin. An attractive and stately person, Douglas lived with her four children and Lumpkin in the Manse, one of the largest and most historically significant houses in Northampton. In their book Lumpkin and Douglas provided vivid evidence of the deplorable conditions under which children worked. They emphasized how market forces and corporations led to the exploitation of young laborers, which governmental regulation had failed to control. When they turned to the question of how to remedy this situation, they denigrated what they saw as the timid role of privileged middle-class reformers and underscored instead the historic contribution of organized and militant members of the working class.[3]

When Douglas and Lumpkin wrote the preface to the second edition of their book on child labor, completed in the month Goldstein entered Smith, the emergence of the CIO enhanced their hopes for fundamental social change. They remarked that the CIO's activity demonstrated the existence of a clear line between progressives willing to support broad measures for social reform and reactionaries who protected the status quo. During the 1930s, Douglas supported social change achieved through strong labor unions and national legislation. When she criticized moralistic reformers, she knew whereof she spoke. In 1930–31, she had chaired the Committee on Women in Industry of the League of Women Voters, where she worked tirelessly to push the League from study to action on federal legislation on behalf of the unemployed. Douglas was especially concerned about discrimination against women in the work force. There was, she reported in 1930, an "organized drive" only twenty miles south of Northampton in Springfield, Massachusetts, aimed at the "discriminatory discharge of women."[4]

Though she ended her brief stint for the League, Douglas played a very public role in radical, pro-union circles in Northampton, surrounding communities, and nationally. In May 1931, she spoke at a local meeting, arguing that "the weight of unemployment falls upon the industrial woman doubly, as worker and as member of a family." Beginning in 1932, she provided the funds that enabled Lumpkin to be research director of the Council of Industrial Studies, a project housed at Smith that sponsored pioneering works in social and economic history. As efforts to write history from the bottom up, these books would not be equaled in sophistication and method until the late 1960s.[5]

Douglas was in the forefront of a series of radical causes. She actively campaigned for striking Northampton workers, the rights of workers to organize, and the importance of federal support for unionization. In the 1930s she advocated federal social welfare programs. She protested her alma mater's decision to end its innovative Bryn Mawr Summer School for Women Workers, having concluded that administrators did so because they worried that accusations of Communist influence would adversely affect fund raising for the college. She protested a Massachusetts law that required teachers to take a loyalty oath. In the late 1930s, she lent her support to pro-Soviet causes. In the summer of 1937, she and Lumpkin traveled to the Soviet Union to study trade unions and social insurance. The following December, Douglas spoke in Northampton at a meeting of socialists on Karl Marx's *Communist Manifesto*. She was active in the American Federation of Teachers and served as vice president of the Massachusetts Council of Teachers' Unions. In the fall of 1940, Douglas launched a labor research project, with herself as chair, Lumpkin as director of research, and well-known African American scholars and labor historians on the board.[6]

Economics 319, which Bettye Goldstein took in 1940–41, was a rigorous course that emphasized labor history, utopian movements, and socialist thought. She carefully recorded what Douglas had to say about dialectical materialism, the class struggle, the role of the working class in fostering revolutionary change, and the Popular Front in western Europe. She took down Douglas's assertions about the oppressiveness of capitalism. She underlined Douglas's statement that the capitalist political system was ripe for change. She listened as Douglas talked about how, in an effort to undermine unions in the South, home-grown American fascists lumped together Jews, Communists, and the CIO as their enemies.[7]

Especially important is what Goldstein recorded when Douglas talked about the condition of women in Nazi Germany and the USSR. On Goldstein's twentieth birthday, in February 1941, Douglas mentioned what she called the "feminist movement." She talked about the "traditionalism" of the Nazis' attitude to religion, women, children, and family. According to Goldstein's notes, Douglas said the Nazis placed children at the center of family lives, celebrated motherhood, and opposed women working outside the house in professional positions (not as farmers and manual laborers). They minimized the intellectual capacity of women, emphasizing instead the importance of their feelings. In the middle of her lecture on women under Nazi rule, Douglas noted parenthetically that men who controlled women's magazines participated in this conscious ideological effort to tell women that despite their aspirations for intellectual life, in fact they were instinctual beings who belonged in the home. In contrast, Douglas said, women in the USSR experienced equality of opportunity, with their wages almost matching (and in some cases exceeding) those of men.[8]

What Douglas said of women under fascism and communism was not exceptional for the American left in the late 1930s and early 1940s. Nationally, student radicals in the 1930s paid some attention to women's issues, although questions of class and race, along with events in Europe, took precedence. As the historian Robert Cohen has written, women student activists of the day "did not possess a fully developed feminist language in which to analyze gender issues" but they "did display at least elements of a feminist sensibility." This explains why Molly Yard, a leader of the American Student Union (ASU) in the 1930s and head of the National Organization for Women decades later, said in the 1970s that "I didn't use the word feminist at that time although I was then and have always been one." As Cohen has remarked, "American student activists noted with alarm Adolf Hitler's reactionary policy toward German women, which would remove them from political life, relegating females to the home and 'the three K's— Kinder, Küche, und Kirche,'" a common refrain that referred to children, kitchen, and church.[9]

Although what Douglas said of women under fascism was familiar on the left, what makes her teaching historically significant was the presence of Bettye Goldstein, carefully taking notes and absorbing her lectures. Over twenty years later, as Betty Friedan, she would excoriate the powerful social forces in America that celebrated motherhood and a child-centered home in an attempt to keep educated women out of the work force.

With youthful enthusiasm characteristic of many in her generation, Goldstein sympathetically responded to the Marxist critique of capitalism that Douglas offered. Answering an exam question for Douglas, Goldstein argued that worsening conditions would change history, a process to which bourgeois intellectuals would lend their support. Indeed, when she responded skeptically to another exam question about the leftward movement of the French Revolution, Douglas cautioned her that the lack of qualifications "gives to your generalizations a rather sweeping and dogmatic tone."[10]

In a paper Goldstein wrote for the course, she wrestled with Jerome Davis's *Capitalism and Its Culture* (1935), a book that spelled out how capitalism affected every aspect of a nation's life. A student publication to which Goldstein contributed publicized that Davis had been involved in an academic freedom case at Yale stemming from his radicalism, especially his promotion of alliances between teachers and unions, and his presidency of the American Federation of Teachers in 1937. In his book, Davis talked about class conflict and capitalist oppression, as Douglas had in her lectures. What most marked Davis's approach was his interest in the way capitalism shaped culture. Pointing to what Americans wore and how they prayed and worked, he said of capitalism's offerings that "we breathe them in from the cradle to the grave until they are as much a part of ourselves as the very air."[11]

In her paper, Goldstein embraced the Marxist analysis Douglas and Davis presented. She remarked that the description of the United States that Davis offered made it hard for her to understand how Americans could support what she considered an evil and sick society. She wondered about the conditions under which a revolution might come about in America. In the end she concluded that capitalist propaganda was so powerful, even among workers, that the nation was nowhere near the revolutionary situation of Russia in 1917. Her position reveals just how much her politics were those of a bourgeois intellectual to whom the exercise of the mind was more important than direct political action. Indeed, Goldstein seemed of mixed mind on the role of people like herself in such a situation, recognizing as she did how difficult it was for members of the bourgeoisie to escape the constraints of their class position. Yet she concluded that it was important for writers to persist in arguing for progressive positions.[12]

Most of the courses Goldstein took in her junior year were required for her major in psychology. The greatest influence on her education in her major, she later claimed, came from Kurt Koffka. One of the founders of Gestalt, he emigrated from Germany in 1924 and spent most of his American career at Smith. In opposition to behaviorism and positivism, Koffka emphasized the wholeness of experience. As he said in 1935 in what became a landmark and rigorously scientific book, "the acquisition of true knowledge should help us to reintegrate our world which has fallen to pieces." Consequently, he emphasized the way experience was organized as a totality, a "field" composed of the interactions between the ego and the wider behavioral environment.[13]

As a junior, Goldstein took a year-long course on Gestalt psychology from Koffka. During the 1930s, Koffka worried about the fate of Jews in Germany, including his brother and mother. With a political philosophy that was more organic and elitist than democratic, one that relied on his admiration for the "fairness and tolerance" of the English people, he looked in horror at the rise of Naziism. Writing in September of 1939 about Germany, he remarked that "the Jewish situation is unbearable beyond words." When Koffka died in the fall of her senior year, Goldstein wrote the editorial eulogy that emphasized the challenge and excitement of his courses. At the time she studied with him, Bettye Goldstein acknowledged the appeal of Gestalt psychology in her course work. She appreciated its focus on large questions and its avoidance of narrow specialization. Unlike behaviorism, she asserted, Gestalt engaged questions of value.[14]

Yet even while involved in the study of psychology with Koffka and others, Goldstein's attention turned to pressing political issues. In the middle of her notes in Koffka's course, she inserted material from the lecture by James Gibson regarding good and bad propaganda. Like Kurt Lewin, whom Goldstein had studied with during the summer of 1940, Gibson was active in the left-liberal wing of the profession through his membership in the Society for the Psychological Study of Social Issues. His November 1940 talk on propaganda included information on how employers attacked union organizers as outside agitators who stirred up otherwise satisfied employees, while the workers themselves believed they were acting on their own. In the second semester, she placed in her material on Koffka's course information from what Gibson was teaching, in particular, material on "War Propaganda," Hitler's *Mein Kampf,* and racial ideology. In 1940 and 1941, Gibson was trying to join Marxism and psychology in order to explain false consciousness. How, he wondered, could people understand the limitations created by their social position and ideology? Eventually he would conclude that action enabled individuals to achieve new understandings, something Goldstein was exemplifying in her life at Smith.[15]

More and more, Bettye Goldstein was focusing on what was happening at Smith, in the nation, and in Europe. In 1940 and 1941, the main drama abroad was the Battle of Britain, in which an imperiled nation valiantly defended itself against German air strikes. Americans increasingly came to believe that stopping Germany was central to the protection of national security and the halting of fascist aggression. Anglophiles and internationalists called on the nation to aid the Allies. Until the German invasion of the USSR in the summer of 1941, the Communist Party opposed American intervention. Socialists and pacifists struggled with the question of whether resisting fascism was more important than their commitment to peace. Many of them, together with conservative isolationists, remained opposed to American intervention. By the spring of 1941, however, the move toward greater American aid for the Allies and support of intervention seemed inexorable. The administration of Franklin D. Roosevelt increasingly committed the nation to the Allied cause. On May 27, the first day of final examinations at Smith, Roosevelt declared an unlimited state of national emergency. The United States had thrown in its lot with the Allies.[16]

On college campuses, issues of war and peace swirled with great intensity. In Goldstein's junior year, most students opposed the war but supported preparedness. Editorial boards of most campus newspapers, like the one on which Goldstein served, had been selected in the spring of 1940 when antiinterventionism was still strong; the following fall they remained committed to staying out of war. On the left against the war were Youth Committee Against War (YCAW) and the American Youth Congress (AYC). On most campuses, these groups faced an uphill battle, as was clear by the failure of YCAW to mobilize students against the first peacetime draft in October 1940. With the left anti-interventionists discredited, in the fall of 1940 leadership in anti-war efforts on many campuses fell to people from a disparate variety of political positions. Campus chapters of America First sprang up, with *Yale Daily News* editor Kingman Brewster taking the lead at Yale, a university for which he later served as president. At the same time, antiisolationist groups emerged on college campuses. National coordination came from the International Student Service (ISS), headed by former ASU executive Joseph Lash and supported by Eleanor Roosevelt, with William Allan Neilson on its executive committee. By the spring of 1941, the tide had clearly turned from isolationism to interventionism on most college campuses, including Smith. The last gasps of left-wing anti-war activity on campuses were at hand, a situation that placed Bettye Goldstein in an increasingly isolated position. In February 1941, several thousand college students gathered in Washington under the auspices of the AYC to protest Lend Lease, the American plan to send military supplies to Britain. Then in April 1941 came the eighth and final national college student mobilization, which failed to revitalize left-wing campus anti-interventionist sentiment. It was a sign of the times that some students opposed the anti-war mobilizations because, they believed, they were Communist led.[17]

All of these events echoed on the Smith campus and in the life of Bettye Goldstein. Students returned in the fall of her junior year to greet a new president, Herbert J. Davis, an English born and educated scholar of English literature. With the Battle of Britain raging and the United States moving toward intervention, Davis was a visible symbol of Anglo-American friendship. Indeed, he and his wife had living with them not only their own offspring, but six of the thousands of English children sent to America to be safe from the German bombings.[18]

Student sentiment was still far from unanimous on the question of intervention. The local ASU chapter, opposing economic aid to Britain because it was an imperial nation, supported an embargo. The results of one student poll, taken in fall 1940, showed a strong preference for the Republicans, prompting a writer in the campus newspaper to comment that this provided either "proof of parental persuasion" or evidence of the trend away from "'professorial dictation.'" Yet many students were apolitical, as Smith professor Daniel Aaron realized in the spring of 1941 when he pointed to "uncomfortably large numbers of docile students who reveal neither bias nor principle."[19]

By her junior year, Bettye Goldstein had emerged as an influential, compelling, and controversial figure. She was a slim five foot, two inches, with hair down to her shoulders. Sondra Henry and Emily Taitz, who wrote a biography of Friedan, noted that "her dark, solemn eyes look out under heavy eyebrows." In pictures taken for the yearbook, they remarked, she was "usually dressed in a skirt, a white blouse under a crew-neck sweater, 'bobby' socks . . . and saddle shoes." As was true in Peoria, she was often inattentive to how she dressed, letting her Braemar sweater become disheveled and allowing a piece of her slip to remain caught in the zipper of her tweed skirt. Biographers noted that she "often felt homely and left out," especially when her friends had dates with boys. As she had done in high school, she poured her energies into her academic work. She quickly earned a reputation as "the psychology brain." More so than in Peoria, she was a major figure among her peers. As Marcia Cohen has written, she was "the throaty social conscience, who argued, always, for justice, for the poor, for the disadvantaged."[20]

Bettye Goldstein was not among the docile students Aaron had mentioned. Her work on student publications, the newspaper especially, was a key aspect in her college education and revealed the strength of her convictions. She gained invaluable experience as a journalist, activist, and leader. The editorials written when she was editor-in-chief reflect a young woman who was developing a radical politics marked by sympathy for unions and workers, an interest in issues affecting women, a sustained opposition to interventionism, and a skepticism regarding the authority and rhetorical claims of those in power. During much of her junior year, she served as news editor of the student paper and managing editor of *Smith College Monthly,* which she and her friends had fought to revive the previous spring. Under Goldstein's influence, what had begun as a literary magazine edited by Madeleine L'Engle Camp, ended up as a much more political one, controlled substantially by Goldstein and her friends.[21]

In the fall of 1940, when the first issue appeared, the Smith community was debating issues of war and peace. There still remained considerable common ground, especially on the subject of free speech. In response to the suggestion by the president of Columbia University that it might be necessary to curb academic freedom during the war, *Smith College Monthly* published a series of articles by faculty and administrators defending freedom of speech even during war. In the same issue, Goldstein and her fellow editors printed essays in which students discussed their preferences in the upcoming presidential election.[22]

In the same issue, Goldstein stated her political position most fully. In an article titled "For Defense of Democracy," she expressed concern that when the words "defense," "civilization," and "democracy" were used to justify the curtailing of freedom and justice, Americans were likely to forget the principles for which they might be called on to fight. Articulating a sense of generational conflict, she was concerned especially about the aimlessness of cynical young people in America, to whose European counterparts totalitarianism offered a sense of purpose. She passionately defended democracy and warned about the possibility of fascism coming to America. She heralded "the possibility of a better world which would make the present wrongs no longer vague but quite clear." Her position showed little resemblance to that of absolute pacifists. Nor were there clear echoes of socialism or anti-capitalism. Yet she clearly stood against unconditional American entry into World War II. At a time when American Communists, mindful of the Nazi-Soviet pact, were often more interested in opposing intervention than in fighting fascism, Goldstein coupled skepticism about intervention with anti-fascism. She insisted that any intervention by the United States must be based on vigorous support of democracy and social change.[23]

By early 1941 Goldstein was moving from an emphasis on creativity to a passionate focus on politics. "When we have something to say," she and a friend stated emphatically in February 1941, "we shall be able to say it." February was a critical month for Bettye Goldstein's contribution to important events on campus. For the first time since she came to Smith, the student newspaper reported fractious dissension on issues of war and peace. Student opinion had decisively turned toward intervention, leaving Bettye Goldstein in the kind of oppositional minority she both relished and feared. According to a poll taken in February 1941, only 6 percent of the students opposed aid to Britain, 57 percent favored prohibiting strikes in defense industries, and 74 percent approved of a peacetime draft. The administration of the college brought out its most prestigious speakers in favor of aid to Britain. Neilson returned to campus and countered the arguments of pacifists, and then called for America to aid Britain. The Davises sponsored a concert to benefit war relief for the British. Speaking at Smith, Eleanor Roosevelt lent her weight to a greater degree of intervention. She said that democracy's hope lay in youth. A day or so before, while sitting in Douglas's class, Goldstein had jotted questions to ask Roosevelt in an interview. After Roosevelt's speech, a reporter for the student newspaper, perhaps Goldstein in her capacity as news editor, asked her what she thought of student groups that opposed the war. After Roosevelt praised the interventionist International Student Service, the reporter noted, "she did not answer the question about" the American Youth Congress. Immediately following Eleanor Roosevelt's visit, and in a statement that underscored how uncertain the editors were about the war, the newspaper called into question the wisdom and tactics of members of the ASU who had attacked Roosevelt during her visit.[24]

On the same page as the story of Roosevelt's speech, there appeared an article reporting that Bettye Goldstein was traveling to Washington with eight of her Smith peers. They were attending a gathering of five thousand students sponsored by the AYC to oppose Lend Lease. Years later, Friedan claimed she went as a reporter and returned radicalized. Again minimizing the extent to which she was already politicized, she remarked in 1987 that in February 1941 she was seeking "truth for truth's sake" and "wasn't going to be involved." In fact, of course, when Goldstein went to Washington her political education was well underway. Indeed, the trip came only a few days after Douglas gave the lecture on women under fascism.[25]

In a special report to the Smith newspaper, Goldstein told about the AYC meeting. She noted the change in the response of the White House, saying that "the hostility of the administration" had not undermined the vitality of those attending. She took pains to emphasize the orderliness of the gathering, as well as its commitment to democratic processes. She stressed the heterogeneous nature of the crowd and its sympathy with oppressed peoples. Students from elite women's colleges, she noted, sat next to those who represented share-croppers and miners. The high point of one session, she wrote, came when "tumultuous" applause greeted students from India who pleaded for support in their struggle against British rule. In contrast was the mixture of silence and loud booing that greeted Joseph Lash, the former ASU activist who was now pro-Roosevelt and pro-intervention. In a letter to the editor, Frances Wilkinson, a Smith student, defended the meeting of the Youth Congress against attacks by those who believed it was "dominated by the communists." She reminded her audience of the commitment by African Americans and Jews to "fight employment discrimination" and noted that the "idealistic fire of the delegates speeches was a far cry from materialism." In contrast, a Smith faculty member who had attended the gathering in Washington and supported an Anglo-American alliance claimed that "the extreme left controlled the meetings with every trick of mass psychology; singing, music, derogatory and inflammatory speeches."[26]

Goldstein's trip to Washington and her competition for the position of editor-in-chief of the student newspaper came at about the same time that she had a major health crisis. While skiing one day, a biographer has written, "she had a savage attack" of asthma that "came on so violently it collapsed a lung." Asthma can be brought on by a combination of factors, including psychological stress, exercise, and cold air. The severe attack caused her to experience acute breathlessness and audible wheezing that was quite terrifying. Thinking her life was in danger, friends rushed her to the infirmary, which transferred her to the local hospital. Her mother arrived from Peoria to help her recover.[27]

In March 1941, Goldstein won the battle to be the editor-in-chief of the college newspaper. Putting out the paper twice a week engaged the energies of eighty students. Under her leadership, her staff aligned itself with progressive forces. The editorials immediately became more political and combative. Thus the new board's opening statement, which Goldstein probably wrote, defined progress as "learning to build a better future from the present rather than acquiring techniques for preventing change." At the same time, she remained concerned that the nation's entry into the war might mean not only death of soldiers, but also the end of the struggle for political and economic democracy and for free expression.[28]

As April approached, when peace rallies around the nation were held for the last time, Goldstein and the others in control of the newspaper kept up their campaign against American involvement in the war effort. Although they published a column by Mary Jackson, an interventionist whose father was attorney general of the United States, they acknowledged that the newspaper's editorials were not going to represent the majority views of those on campus or even those on the editorial board. In early April, the editors applauded peace rallies on American campuses as efforts to keep the nation out of war and fight for democracy at home.[29]

On April 22, Goldstein's faction on the editorial board made its case. In an editorial entitled "They Chose Peace," they appeared realistic about the dismal prospects for peace, aware that it was only a matter of time before the United States entered the war. They denied that they were "either under the influence of Moscow or . . . hopelessly idealistic," asserting that they came to the position they held independently and as the result of much deliberation. Perhaps, they wrote, democracy would be better served by extending it in the United States than by weakening it at home in order to fight a war abroad whose democratic results were uncertain. Although worried about the costs of war in human terms, they did not make their case on pacifist grounds. The editors made it clear that defeat of fascism was their primary goal and determined their position on questions of war or peace. They found the situation so complex they were unable to support the case for intervention. They doubted that America's entry into the war was the best way to fight fascism, preferring to extend democracy at home rather than to aid an imperialistic Britain.[30]

The following day, at a peace rally on the Smith campus attended by a relatively small audience of about 130 students, Goldstein spoke on academic freedom. This was an issue she well understood from her high school experience, the case of Jerome Davis at Yale, as well as from what she believed Dorothy Douglas and James Gibson might face. In her speech, she asserted that when war came, academic freedom would inevitably be limited. Although Smith might stand firm for free speech, it would be "powerless" in the face of national legislation. The next day, Douglas gave a speech warning of the danger of legislation curbing the right of unions to strike during a national emergency.[31]

Goldstein faced strong opposition to her anti-war position. In early May, the dissenting members of the editorial board called for intervention on the side of the British. This was not the only statement against the position taken by both the newspaper and the ASU. In mid-April, Janet Carlson, a member of the class of 1941 and of the interventionist Federal Union (supporters of a federation of democracies, especially the United States and Britain), denounced the ASU and unnamed members of the faculty for being "tools of Nazi-Communist propaganda." Two students, one of whom had written an earlier piece with Goldstein, responded. Carlson's letter, wrote Carolyn Clausen and Mary Newman, was "an unusually clear example of plain old-fashioned Red-baiting," characterized by "innuendo" and "malicious suspicion." If Carlson's letter was a product of a Smith education, they concluded with a sense of humor, "COME THE REVOLUTION quick!" Years before the rise of McCarthyism, Bettye Goldstein inhabited a world where she and her allies felt the force of redbaiting.[32]

For Goldstein, the stakes in her opposition to the war were considerable. In April and at later points, the editorial writers placed their concerns within a larger context. What haunted them was the spread of fascism and the prospect of America's involvement in a world war. Echoing Goldstein's "For Defense of Democracy," the editors expressed dismay at how liberals and conservatives used rhetoric to avoid truly democratic commitments. An editorial printed just before the peace rallies contrasted the image of the United States as an arsenal of democracy, with the way colleges dismissed pacifists, Communists, or others who fought to enable African Americans to participate in athletic events. Cognizant of the suppression of free speech and unpopular opinions in the Red Scare after World War I, the editors worried about the tyranny of the majority. "Sometimes a few 'strange,' 'queer' people," they wrote, "turn out to be right."[33]

Central to the insistence on a capacious meaning for democracy was the commitment to insurgent trade unionism. Although most domestic issues claimed little attention in the late 1930s and early 1940s, there was one exception. After a period of stagnation and schism in the late 1930s, in 1941 the CIO came to what one historian has called the "year of decision." Aided by the step-up in defense production that marked an end to the Depression, it moved ahead forcefully and successfully in its efforts to organize workers. The turning point came in the spring of 1941, the second semester of Goldstein's junior year. In April, as she was fully absorbing what Douglas was teaching and as the CIO was making some of its most important gains, the editors hailed labor unions as the institution in the vanguard of progressive social change. An April editorial protested the way reactionary interests, always anti-labor, were "now able to shroud their views under a patriotic veil." The paper had recently announced the forthcoming visit to Smith, sponsored by the campus Labor Group, of James Dombrowski from Highlander Folk School. In a lecture in Dorothy Douglas's class, Dombrowski told Goldstein and her peers about the work of the school. In the notes Goldstein took down from his lecture, titled "Native American Fascism," she recorded his saying that opponents of progress "beat organizers to death in Southern towns" and engaged in a "fight against Jews & Reds (C.I.O.)."[34]

As issues of war and peace energized the campus, Goldstein worried about the consequences of the intense debates. An editorial she wrote that May, entitled "We Are Aware of the War," noted that arguments took place everywhere throughout the day. "The voices grow shrill," she asserted, "and the epithets ugly—uttered in scorn, contempt, fury." She emphasized the "great tiredness" students felt. In the midst of this, she thought it inappropriate for professors, whether pro- or anti-war, to discuss contemporary political issues. She admitted that professors were expected to have opinions about the war, and that the right of free speech extended to political comments made in the classroom. What she found offensive was how such remarks abused authority, wasted time, mocked the values of a liberal arts education, and corrupted "intellectual standards," as professors used the merest pretext to "preach politics."[35]

As a response to events at Smith, her editorial worked on several levels. Like earlier pieces, it celebrated the idea of pure knowledge and an education driven by scholarship without "patriotic indoctrination in the classroom." Perhaps an editorial board sharply divided on issues of war and peace could unite on a commitment to a liberal arts education. Moreover, as someone cognizant of the repression in World War I and committed to unpopular causes and to radical professors, Goldstein could use the goals of free speech and a liberal arts education as a way of protecting fragile rights as the nation prepared for war. In addition, if the notes she took down are any indication, neither Douglas nor Koffka used their lectures as political forums in the narrow way Goldstein understood the term political, as an opportunity to offer remarks on contemporary policy issues. Aware that the interventionists were winning the battle for the hearts and minds of students, Goldstein may have resented the way liberal faculty used their prestige to bring students around to their views by making such patriotic statements in the classroom. In early May, more than one hundred faculty announced that they supported the declaration of a state of national emergency to defeat Naziism. Kurt Koffka and Otto Kraushaar signed the petition, while James Gibson and Dorothy W. Douglas did not.[36]

Bettye Goldstein's position on intervention was problematic. Now and earlier, usually only by negative example did she make clear what full support for democracy meant for America—academic freedom and the rights of workers to organize. At key moments, she evidenced more concern for the possible spread of totalitarianism in the United States than its actual advance in Europe. Though in "For Defense of Democracy" she mentioned the "bestial hordes of Nazis thirsting for our blood," the horrors of *Kristallnacht* should have struck an anti-fascist radical and a Jew as more horrible than anything American fascists had recently done in America. The April 22 editorial did not mention the Nazis or anti-Semitism specifically, focusing its attention instead on evils of the British and on the way fascism in Europe "has stifled freedom," this latter a vague and understated characterization of the evils of Nazi Germany. Also puzzling is why a Jew who so well understood the costs of anti-Semitism on a personal level did not argue that the best way to fight fascism was to work simultaneously for democratic changes at home and American military involvement abroad. After all, in the spring of 1941 Hitler was the most visibly powerful enemy of Jews and progressives. Except for principled pacificists, which she apparently was not, those who wanted to fight fascism were deciding that American intervention was necessary. Thus her anti-fascism seemed confused, as it was not coupled with an internationalism that supported forceful opposition to the most evident fascists in the world, the Nazis who increasingly controlled Europe.[37]

At the same time that all these issues were swirling in her world, women's concerns were coming to the forefront for Goldstein. In April and early May, Goldstein was involved in a series of fights with the administration that she believed had both a generational and a gendered dimension. In the fall of

1940, she had written an editorial that attacked "indignant elders" for having "indoctrinated" students with an "absolute pacifism." Now, she wrote, instead of helping students understand the complicated nature of contemporary issues, faculty attacked students for what they incorrectly saw as their "indifference, ignorance, and apathy."[38]

In addition, as young women coming into their own, Goldstein and the other editors chafed against the illogical restrictions imposed on Smith students. Just because their parents could afford the costs of a Smith education, she wrote in early May, "we automatically become members of another species of woman, a species that must be sheltered from reality." She protested "the numerous petty restrictions that hedge us in . . . and keep us sheltered in the solicitous manner of a female seminary." Her dissatisfaction with the rules rested on her sense that protection in the idyllic world of college poorly prepared young women "for the responsibility we shall soon be forced to assume." Reflecting none of the domestic ideology that she would later insist had overwhelmed her generation of women, Goldstein recognized that women in their late teens and early twenties were old enough to have families and "to work, to earn salaries and live on them."[39]

In the April issue, *Smith College Monthly* published a debate between a man from Yale and a woman from Smith on the roles of the sexes that resonated with Goldstein's experiences. Yale junior Douglas Palmer published "Woman's Place is in the Home." He conceded there was no returning to the days of the grandmothers of Smith students, when the existence of separate spheres placed women in the home and men in the world of work and politics. Yet in fact his article amply conveyed the sexist sentiments Friedan would later challenge. Although Palmer was concerned with the way working-class women's entry into the work force led to juvenile delinquency, he reserved his strongest criticism for how college education for women, especially in women's colleges like Smith, tempted too many women not to marry, or to marry but not to have children, or to have children and neglect them.

To Palmer all this meant that women were putting aside responsibilities that he believed nature destined them to fulfill. While admitting that some of them had to earn money, he objected to those women who worked because they wanted a career or were bored by housework. He called on women to "abandon this false god of Independence." He lamented the way the demands of women for a fuller life had "precipitated its full share of chaos in family standards." Believing that professional accomplishment for women neither led to their happiness nor contributed to society, Palmer urged women to value the importance of their contribution as wives and mothers. This was how women could fulfill themselves, he concluded, achieving "a happiness and satisfaction ever more profound and enduring than lies in their competition with men." Palmer's words had a special meaning for Goldstein. They came not from a stranger, but from a friend from Peoria High School with whom she had founded *Tide*, who she felt had treated her like a sister, and who had described her as "inordinately ambitious."[40]

A month later, under the title "Shades of Susan Anthony," Smith student Marcia Williams responded with wit and passion. Although she admitted that career women often neglected their families, she insisted they needed "an understanding husband" to combine career and family. She discussed the arguments of the author Pearl S. Buck, who had recently written that the discontent of middle-class American women might pave the way to America's adoption of solutions offered by a dictator. When their children were still young, Williams wrote, women should not have full-time jobs, because "a day nursery cannot be substituted for a mother's care with equal results." Yet she opposed Palmer's insistence that women limit themselves to conventional lives. Even women with young children should have some interest outside the home—in volunteer work, "in some creative field," or with a job that had flexible hours. Educated women could benefit from the leisure that the new home appliances gave them. If a college-educated woman simply stayed at home, her mind might "grow rank with new and harmful stereotypes," and the skills she developed in college might atrophy. Women who chose only home and family, she insisted, are "to be either pitied or reprimanded." Not to give women a choice, she concluded, "is to furnish a far larger group of discontented women. Think of the consequences and tremble, Mr. Palmer!"[41]

Although it is difficult to recover what the twenty-year-old Goldstein thought about Palmer's article, his words reverberated with Douglas's remarks about fascism's support of traditional roles for women. Perhaps it was Palmer's paper and Williams's response that prompted Goldstein toward the end of her junior year to reflect on where she had come from and where she was going. In an unpublished essay, she did so in a way that revealed that although she was coming into her own politically, she was still very much a late adolescent struggling with issues of identity. Once again, but now with more sharpness, she looked at her life in Peoria. She denounced the dullness of middle-class mores in her hometown. She bemoaned her family's complacency and sentimentality. She depicted her father as a kindly man angered by his wife's youth. Her portrait of her mother was searing: domineering, arrogant, and self-sacrificing, someone avaricious in her consumption of fine clothes and falsely fine culture. Goldstein spoke of her own interest in politics, the labor movement, and abstract scientific philosophy. She thought she would eventually marry, but hoped for someone who did not accept

Palmer's views of women. She looked forward to a fulfilled life that gave her some control over what she did, enabling her to pursue serious interests.[42]

By the spring of 1941, it was clear just how much the events of her junior year had radicalized the twenty-year-old Bettye Goldstein. The response of Kraushaar, one of the faculty's leading left-liberals, to one of her papers was especially revealing. Earlier, when Goldstein had taken other courses with Kraushaar, their political outlooks had not been so dissimilar. Now, with the professor favoring intervention and his increasingly radical student committed to an anti-war position, their paths were sharply diverging. In the paper, Goldstein revealed why her major was so important to her larger vision: psychology provided the basis for a progressive political ideology. She emphatically stood against a psychological determinism based on genetic inheritance and opposed what she saw as totalitarianism's attempt to make people identical rather than equal. She argued that psychology offered the possibility that people could shape their worlds and, foreshadowing ideas that would ring out two decades later, foster self-realization. At one point, she drew on Friedrich Nietzsche to argue for a vision that emphasized danger, conflict, power, and mastery. For Goldstein this did not involve hedonism; rather, she adopted the notion of a hierarchy of needs in which bodily ones were surpassed by the individual's constant striving to fulfill the human need to love, heal others, create, and have security and power.[43]

Nothing in these aspects of Goldstein's argument drew objections from Kraushaar. Rather, he took issue with her statement about the gap between the flowery promises of America's democracy and lack of any real commitment to make their realization possible. Relying on Davis's *Capitalism and Its Culture* and the two books on Middletown by Robert S. Lynd and Helen M. Lynd, Goldstein expressed doubts that there were any positive values, visions, or ideals animating American society and culture. Consequently, she claimed that Americans failed to realize that social structures limited human potential. These statements drew a skeptical response. Writing in the margin, Kraushaar asked "How can you say this in the face of the steady growth" of social reform under Presidents Woodrow Wilson and Franklin Roosevelt. "Does a thing have to be absolutely perfect," he queried, "before it can be something of its kind?" On the cover of the paper, he concluded his long response with the statement that "the nature of your reference to democracy seems to indicate that you are now in full flight from reality—and it makes me very sad."[44]

A more significant and public criticism came from Mary Ellen Chase, one of Smith's most respected faculty members. A professor of English, Chase had already gained a national reputation with the publication of more than a dozen books. At Smith, she was so revered as a teacher that students referred to her courses as "Chase" rather than by their catalogue titles. She was also a leading anglophile at Smith, with her opinion on war and peace carrying considerable weight on campus.[45]

On May 12, 1941, she attacked Goldstein's May 9 editorial, "We Are Aware of War," before the college community. Earlier that morning, one of Goldstein's friends had "pulled her out of bed, helped her grab a coat to cover her pajamas, gave her a comb to half arrange her hair, and sent her flying to John M. Green Hall," the college's largest auditorium, capable of seating the entire student body and all of the faculty. Standing on the stage in a well-tailored suit, Chase looked over the audience, seeing but not publicly acknowledging Goldstein's late arrival. Chase then defended the right of faculty to talk about the war in the classroom. However, what she said was more far ranging. Acknowledging that war "in right-minded people" bred "a splendid hatred," she encouraged students to hate more, asserting that this was an appropriate way to develop a love of what was right. She wanted students to realize that it was appropriate to hate "indifference" and to hate anything that undermined cherished American values. Yes, she admitted, without mentioning Goldstein by name, the editorial writer was correct in noting that war bred the wrong kinds of hatred. However, she concluded, war fostered "fine and noble hatreds also. And this war breeds the finest hatreds of all war."[46]

Not to be outdone, Bettye Goldstein responded in an editorial the next day. Answering Chase, she noted that students "have not yet begun to hate," although they had "learned that there can be inconsistency in the words of the old and the wise" and that it was necessary to question "the infallibility of authority." She hailed the way a "new awareness of the meaning of democracy" was affecting undergraduates. Sensing that students agreed on a set of core values but disagreed on how to realize them, she took pride in the fact that her peers could no longer be described as "indifferent, ignorant, or apathetic" on issues of war, peace, and fascism.[47]

As editor-in-chief, Goldstein may also have had a hand in answering Chase in the commencement editorial in June 1941 that was filled with foreboding. There the author expressed a sense of "the chaos and disintegration and violent changes" that marked the present and would mark the future. She saw only one ray of hope in a world that the commencement speaker had described as uncertain and bleak. Young people were finding their voices. "Becoming aware of realities in the light of values clearly realized for the first time, and strong in that new awareness," she concluded, "may make it a better world than the world of the status quo."[48]

The criticisms from Kraushaar and Chase must have gone down hard with twenty-year-old Bettye Goldstein. They threatened the acceptance she had gained at Smith that had largely eluded her in Peoria. Yet the attacks on her writings were balanced by sources of satisfaction elsewhere. Goldstein had recovered from the frightening bout with asthma. She was doing well in a series of challenging courses, earning election to Phi Beta Kappa as a junior. In James Gibson and Dorothy W. Douglas she had two mentors who taught her what it meant to combine the lives of parent, scholar, and radical activist. Along with national and world events, they had helped radicalize Goldstein even as she remained independent of dominant opinion and any organized political movement. She had found politically and personally productive ways to express her ambition and her anger. As editor-in-chief of the student newspaper, she turned it into a source of interest and controversy, and made many on campus take notice of her energy and passion. Ideas were coming together in her life—her commitments to anti-fascism and free speech, her opposition to the war, her vision of trade unions as sources of progressive social change, and her growing awareness of women's issues. She had made the crucial transition from being a believer in beauty and an ironic commentator to being a passionate writer and actor in the political arena.

= 4 =
It All Comes Together, 1941–42

ANTI-FASCISM, WOMEN WORKERS, UNIONS, WAR, AND PSYCHOLOGY

Bettye Goldstein's senior year at Smith was an appropriate culmination of an extraordinary undergraduate career. During the summer, she spent several weeks at Highlander Folk School in Tennessee, a unique center for the education of labor organizers in the South, and a place central to the lives of several generations of radicals. Back at Smith in September, she continued to develop a very strong academic record. She capped her major in psychology with an honors thesis that later appeared in a major scholarly journal, and with her election to the national honor society in the sciences, Sigma Xi. She concluded her editorship of *SCAN*, the campus newspaper, with an intense two-month stint that was as provocative as that of the preceding spring.

Once again, she found herself embroiled in controversy. She was sharply critical of students who demeaned the intelligence of women workers on campus. She campaigned for the right of campus workers to unionize. Until Pearl Harbor she remained opposed to America's entry into the war, placing a higher priority on the fight against fascism and for democracy. After Pearl Harbor, anti-fascist sentiments quickly merged with wartime mobilization efforts. Now she worked to diminish the power of wealthy, socially prominent students at Smith as she called on them to aid the war effort by cutting down on excessive expenditures. She insisted that Smith as a woman's college had a special obligation to secure for its graduates opportunities in employment equal to their talents. In short, during Bettye Goldstein's senior year everything in her life came together—passionately advocated anti-fascism, unionization, equality for women, and progressive psychology.[1]

In the summer of 1941 Goldstein continued her political education when she went, at the suggestion of Dorothy W. Douglas, to Highlander Folk

School in the Appalachian town of Monteagle, Tennessee. Its founders were native-born southerners in whom Reinhold Niebuhr at Union Theological Seminary had inspired a commitment to Christian Socialism. As writer John Egerton has noted, Highlander "departed in unorthodox and controversial ways from the prevailing dogma on labor, race, class, and other fundamental issues." Central to the school's efforts was the fight for social justice for African Americans and women. Its mission was capacious, for Highlander's leaders believed that working-class people had within themselves and their communities the resources to solve the problems they faced. People who attended the school learned how to organize picket lines and sing protest songs. During the late 1930s and early 1940s Highlander served as a training ground for CIO organizers and their supporters in their struggles in the South.[2]

Not surprisingly, reactionaries misunderstood the school's broad-based and homegrown commitments. In the late 1930s and early 1940s Highlander experienced the vicious attacks of redbaiters. Although there were continual accusations that the school was aligned with the Communist Party, FBI director J. Edgar Hoover decided that Highlander was "liberal" and "radical," but had not come under "Communistic influence." Leading New Deal and labor union representatives openly supported the school.[3]

Bettye Goldstein was making arrangements to go to Highlander when momentous events occurred in Europe: on June 23, 1941, Germany invaded the USSR. When Goldstein wrote Dombrowski about coming to Highlander later in the summer, she described her life in Peoria as quintessentially middle class, something she believed that Robert S. Lynd and Helen M. Lynd had captured in *Middletown* (1929). When asked about her work experience, in response to which most applicants would have talked about their jobs in factories, mines, or fields, Goldstein acknowledged that her labor had involved helping out in the family jewelry store at busy moments, volunteering at the settlement house in Peoria, and working on the Smith newspaper. Goldstein was drawn to Highlander, she explained, because she had recently been politicized through reading, friendships, and her activity in what she called, in words that would become common in the 1960s, "a student movement." This had earned her the reputation as a "radical" at Smith. She wanted to go to Highlander to remedy her relative ignorance about unions and workers, gaining knowledge that might be useful if she decided to have a career as a journalist and not, she left unstated, as a union activist.[4]

Beginning in late July 1941, Goldstein spent about eight weeks at Highlander. For the first two, she participated in a writers' workshop, learning from skilled practitioners how to write more effectively in a range of genres, from short stories to radio scripts to plays. The emphasis was on a documentary style that conveyed specifics in an artful manner. She also enrolled in a program designed to educate students about unions, workers, and the economy, as well as to provide practical information on how to conduct union business on the picket line and at rallies. In the second program many of the students were activists who participated directly in labor organizing in the South.[5]

Her experience at Highlander enabled her to experiment with new ways of thinking, feel how her class and regional position marginalized her, and reflect on what it meant to be an ally of workers. In two essays, one published and one not, she answered those who, frightened by its pro-labor stance, accused the school of relying on Soviet funds and of fomenting a Communist-inspired revolution. She reminded them that most Americans were laborers, people who did ordinary work. She praised the school as a place that was thoroughly American in its pursuit of justice and democracy. She stated that her political awakening came at Smith through classes she took and books she read. What she had learned prepared her "to accept the case against capitalism and its culture," she remarked, but her education, derived from books, discussions, and conjecture, stemmed from activities that "do not lead to much action." Though she claimed little knowledge of the labor movement even at Smith, she acknowledged that she supported unions because she was relying on them "to prevent Fascism."[6]

Goldstein looked back on how conditions in Peoria shaped her political consciousness. Now she had a language to talk about her perceptions in high school regarding the power of class divisions in her home town. What she wrote seems confused and conflicted, as she alternated between the snobbery fostered by her privileged position and criticism of elite privilege itself. She depicted a class-divided Peoria in the 1930s, a city where, she claimed, she had never met anyone from the vast part of the population that worked in the large factories, and where she lived among what she described as the tiny minority of families whose earnings did not come from wage work. As a youth, she wrote, she ran around with a few score of students who lived in an elite neighborhood, stayed together in classes for which the selection process linked intelligence with high social status, joined fraternities and sororities, went to dances together, dominated most extracurricular activities, and had little to do with the hundreds of students outside their social circle. Though she spoke of the pleasantness and optimism this life fostered, she also acknowledged her own adversarial position. She recalled her sharp criticism of the American educational system and her cynicism regarding the impact of the mass media. All of this, she concluded, fostered in her a skeptical approach to the world. "I began to understand," she said in words that later reverberated in *The Feminine Mystique*, "that the things you are told are devices to keep you from thinking." Consequently, she "got a reputation for being a radical."[7]

Here Goldstein did not even hint at the way being a Jew in Peoria made her feel excluded. Moreover, she exaggerated her father's closeness to the local elite. However, she described the dilemma of Jewish liberal shop-keepers like her father who wanted to get along with their well-to-do customers but still remembered what it meant to be a poor immigrant. She remarked that her father dissented from the politics of the bankers, merchants, and factory owners he encountered who celebrated the virtues of an economic system based on private property, opportunity, and beneficent employers. They denounced workers as greedy people, she reported him as observing, with "revolution and anarchy roaring [in their] heads." When union members took over factories with sit-down strikes, she reported, Peoria's elite hoped the federal government would use troops to dislodge the workers. In this situation, her parents found themselves in a difficult position—unable to express their disagreement with the conservatism of the wealthy customers on whom the health of their jewelry store depended. Her parents could not reveal their avid support for President Franklin D. Roosevelt, a man whom their clients believed was bringing socialism to America.[8]

In what she wrote at Highlander, Goldstein was both apologetically self-critical and forthrightly assertive. Now she faced real, living workers and organizers. Finding it difficult emotionally and ideologically to negotiate the worlds of Peoria, Smith, and Highlander, she remained more the intellectual than the activist, engaging in heated discussions in which she made clear her preference for abstract ideas. She was exposed to a radical, Marxist view of class that drew on the day-to-day experiences of her peers at Highlander. She admitted the limitations of her privileged background and education even as she insisted on the validity of her own experience. As in her paper for Douglas, she saw herself more as an intellectual sympathetic to workers than as an activist on their behalf.[9]

When Bettye Goldstein returned to Smith for her senior year in late September 1941, she was well aware of a transformed international situation. What continually put the campus situation into perspective was the world-wide war and power of fascism. On October 5, in a letter to her friends at Highlander, she compared the situation at Smith College with Nero fiddling while Rome burned. What she meant became clear in an editorial she wrote for the paper. Fresh from the experience at Highlander where she had sensed a more real world of struggle and conflict, she contrasted the idyllic life at Smith with the ominous events around the world. Safe in Northampton and as a woman protected from the draft, she realized that there was nothing in the comfortable world around her to foster a "realization of a world destroying itself." Though she concluded by emphasizing the importance of studying, she nonetheless recognized that she could know little "of war, poverty, of terror, of persecution." She warned that "the present prosperity" was "a false boom" and ahead lay "a depression, more terrible than the last." With a "test of democracy versus fascism" coming soon, she asked, "shall we be lovely examples of the decadence that comes at the end of things?"[10]

Goldstein was now in an increasingly difficult situation, with anti-war commitments making her more and more isolated from dominant campus opinion. Torn as she often was between her desire to be accepted and her commitment to speaking her mind, she was no longer in the mainstream at Smith. She also dissented from the position of American Communists who in June, with the German invasion of Russia, had embraced Allied intervention. In August, Roosevelt and Prime Minister Winston Churchill signed the Atlantic Charter that outlined the principles governing war and peace. In November, the United States extended Lend Lease to the USSR. On the home front that fall, the most dramatic series of events involved the increasing marginalization of United Mine Workers leader and anti-war advocate John L. Lewis, whose union conducted strikes. The war mobilization prompted a sharp anti-labor response from people concerned that the right to strike might impede the war effort. Goldstein knew the consequences labor activists faced. In October, someone from Highlander wrote her that two Mine, Mill and Smelter Union organizers, one of whom she had met in the summer, "were savagely beaten, bones fractured, teeth knocked out, and tarred to boot."[11]

Goldstein's experience at Highlander reinforced her interest in anti-Semitism, the form of social exclusion she had experienced most intensely. Early on in college, she had encountered anti-Semitism not only from Christians but also from Jews who shunned association with other Jews, experiences that reverberated with her rejection by the high school sorority and her mother's silence on the reasons for such discriminatory action. While at Highlander she had worked on "The Scapegoat," a short story that thoughtfully explored the dynamics of anti-Semitism, which she interpreted as part of a larger pattern of racism. Unusually ambitious for a twenty-year-old, in the fall of her senior year she contacted a major New York literary agency to see if she could get the story published in a national magazine. Failing in that effort, she revised and published it in *Smith College Monthly* that fall.[12]

In "The Scapegoat," she focused, as she had done in Peoria, on the personal consequences of anti-Semitism. She fully recognized the shock value of her story about Jewish and Gentile students who join together to marginalize a Jew named Shirley. They persuade themselves that they are shunning Shirley not because she is Jewish but because she is uncultivated. They avoid Shirley so that non-Jews will realize how cultivated many Jews are, and that people like Shirley are responsible for "segregation." Goldstein, still acutely aware of the pain she felt as an outsider, displayed a keen eye for the ways anti-Semitism infected Jew and non-Jew alike, and how Jews can hate themselves and other Jews. At the end of the story, she made clear her identification with Shirley, wondering how she felt as she sat in a room with Jews and Gentiles who ignored her.[13]

In papers she wrote for classes, Goldstein continued her education in literature and creative writing, with issues of creativity and self-expression joined with questions of identity and politics. She thought about the difficulties of written expression, and wondered about the relationship between writing and social action. At one point, contemplating the connection between her experiences at Highlander and at Smith, and her future, she wondered what it meant for someone interested in unions to be only an observer. She pondered her own mortality and privilege as when she heard that a train carrying Smith students returning to Northampton from a weekend at Yale hit and killed a construction worker. Elsewhere, she explored the peculiarities of her situation in Northampton. She wondered about the relationship between female students and their male professor, fantasizing that students sat naked in a classroom as they awaited his arrival. She thought about what it meant for Smith students to protect themselves from the emotional pain they might confront if they visited patients in the local mental hospital. Listening to students talk about where they would be in ten years, she was pessimistic about her own prospects, unable to envision what she might do.[14]

Her essays also revealed her preoccupation with the family dramas of her Peoria household. She portrayed a woman in Peoria who, when her husband had an affair and left town for several months, not only continued to run the household, do volunteer work, and raise children, but also successfully ran the family business. Her most poignant and revealing story told of a college student who neglected her ailing father while she was home during a vacation. As the family stood around waiting for him to die, he felt anger over his fate, his wife's spending, and his daughter's inattention. Like Bettye, who had just returned from Christmas vacation in Peoria, the fictional daughter wanted to escape this troubling situation, but wondered how she would feel when her father died.[15]

In a story entitled "Saturday Night," Goldstein offered a complicated meditation on romance. The story reflected the loneliness of a college girl without a date on a Saturday night, who felt sexual excitement as she watched a movie in which Lawrence Olivier courted Vivian Leigh. Yet the story made clear that when women had fun together they were not necessarily envious of the murmurs and laughter of dating heterosexual couples. While the narrator celebrated the intense pleasure adolescent women took in each other's company, she expressed discomfort when women's physical intimacy became too intense.[16]

Even when studying the European novel, pressing political issues were not far from Goldstein's mind. Listening to lectures, she connected what she heard to urgent issues of the day. Thus in the fall of 1941, when a professor talked about the functions of comedy, Goldstein expressed wonder at the way wealthy people stalled progressive changes in society, and she speculated on the connection between German character and Hitler's ascendancy. A long and powerful term paper on psychological issues in nineteenth-century novels brought together her interest in literature, psychology, and identity. She opposed any psychology, including Freudianism, that saw the individual psyche isolated from society. Relying on Karen Horney and Carl Jung, she placed what Freud wrote within the context of nineteenth-century European society, and emphasized the interaction between culture and personality.[17]

As editor-in-chief of the student paper, Goldstein continued to stir things up. She wrote her friends at Highlander that she hoped that her editorials would have dramatic impact, but complained that almost everyone else was rallying around the liberal position. She did not have to wait long for controversy to embroil her and the paper. Under her leadership, SCAN launched a number of campaigns. The editors took on the student government for its undemocratic practice of holding closed meetings. They fought successfully to challenge the administration's right to control what the newspaper printed. They excoriated social clubs for their secrecy, and published critiques of professors' teaching. In addition, the editorial board campaigned for the relaxation of the rules that restricted student social life. With a hint of feminism and a touch of irony, Goldstein mocked Smith students who chose to support the military by socializing with airmen at nearby Westover Field.[18]

Under Goldstein's leadership, the editors launched a campaign to link wartime sacrifice with an attack on social privilege. On November 11, after the campus had appointed "heat cops" to go around the dormitories and close windows in order to save fuel, the editors called on students to sacrifice in additional ways. They questioned the conspicuous consumption of many of the wealthier Smith students, something that had special meaning for Goldstein because of her mother's overspending and her father's jewelry store. When a campus fund drive for the needy drew an inadequate response, the editors pointed out that their peers were still spending money on horseback riding lessons and evening clothes. While elsewhere in the world young people had to make real sacrifices, the editors noted that Smith students were "asked to understand the meaning of the word sacrifice only in the trivial terms of our own allowances."[19]

In late October, *SCAN* carried a nationally syndicated column sounding a cautionary note about the choices female college students faced. Moreover, the author was significant: Marjorie Nicolson, the Dean at Smith from 1930 to 1940, who, after being passed over for the college presidency, became the first female professor on the graduate faculty at Columbia University and the first woman to be national president of Phi Beta Kappa. Nicolson said she had come to notice that female professors were much more conscientious about their work and much more personally responsible for family members (including their parents and their children) than their male counterparts. To remain creative and therefore advance in their careers, she asserted, women had to stop working so hard in their professions and at family life. In the end, although she believed individual women could succeed as well as men, she had come to "doubt whether women as a sex can ever achieve complete equality with men in world affairs." Her comments pointed in two directions. While she was urging women to become more creative in their careers, she believed that women's work ethic and moral concern for others made it unlikely that their achievements would match those of their male counterparts. Above all, what is striking is that Nicolson's analysis, appearing in the paper Goldstein was editing, prefigured many ideas that as Betty Friedan she would attack in *The Feminine Mystique*.[20]

In the fall of 1941, the editors increasingly accepted the inevitability of war even as they made it clear that they believed "fighting fascists is only one part of fighting fascism." The editorials written on Goldstein's watch reveal a young woman who believed that almost every issue—at Smith, in the nation, and abroad—involved the struggle for democracy, freedom, and social justice. As the nation mobilized, students on the left at Smith and elsewhere expressed concern that if war came, the nation would sustain its democratic commitments and minimize the pressure of militarization. Unlike most of her peers, Goldstein remained anti-war even when the local chapter of the American Student Union (ASU), with three pacifists dissenting, followed the lead of the national office and supported American aid to the Allies because Germany had invaded the USSR. In mid-October, Hans Kohn, one of the strongest and most articulate interventionists on campus, announced his support for Allied aid to the USSR, "irrespective of any judgment of the character of the Soviet government." He did so because, with the German army threatening Moscow, only Soviets seemed to stand between Hitler and world domination. A few days later, Smith President Herbert Davis signed a petition asking the Roosevelt administration to give more aid to Russia.[21]

In a speech on November 17, Davis sharply criticized the editorial position the student newspaper espoused under Goldstein's leadership. He began by announcing that if students thought they were coming to a peace meeting, as the newspaper had announced, they would not appreciate hearing what he had to say. Directing his attack even more pointedly, he remarked that when he read the student paper, he often wondered "whether words have any meaning left in them at all," with phrases "thrown about with such recklessness and triviality." Davis, who had fought with the British in World War I, went on to denounce "mass murders" that resulted from "the ruthlessness and vile inhumanity of total war" for which he held the Nazis responsible. Asking members of the Smith community to put aside their stands on specific issues, he insisted they confront one basic question: "Will you accept the Nazi idolatry and what that stands for, or will you resist?"[22]

The next day the editors of SCAN responded, making clear that they would "resist Naziism, fascism, in whatever form it appears, in German dress or Italian or backwoods American." The editorial writer, probably Goldstein herself, having answered the question Davis posed, went on to make clear how she differed from him. She found it difficult to equate the British Empire with democracy. Moreover, she remained uncertain that an Allied victory would necessarily result in a triumph over fascism, especially since a war would likely involve suppression of American freedoms. What was involved, she declared, was full recognition that fascism was "the greatest ultimate evil." A week later, as if to further underscore Goldstein's isolation, her mentor Kurt Koffka died. At the same time, students from the local ASU responded to a recent anti-interventionist speech by the socialist Norman Thomas by equating his isolationism with appeasement, a policy, they asserted, that assured Hitler's victory and threatened to undermine American democracy.[23]

Some Smith students reacted to the newspaper's reluctance to support intervention wholeheartedly by redbaiting, accusing the editorial board of being dominated by Communists. Ironically, this came at a time when the United States and the USSR were allied against a common enemy. In response, one editor denied that any members of the board belonged to the party. Yet like many college newspapers in these years, the staff of Smith's paper included some students attracted by radical politics. As Goldstein's friend Neal Gilkyson wrote in arguing against lumping Communists and Nazis together, Communism was not a "dark terror" but "a precarious scheme worked out by millions of civilized men and women." She contrasted the "vulgar ignorance and insolence" of student redbaiters with the spirit of idealism that led their adversaries to be curious about new ideas. She juxtaposed the utopianism and plausibility of Communism with the reality in the Soviet Union, which she saw as involving horrible techniques and "treatment of minorities" that was "almost as intolerable as Hitler's." Gilkyson concluded that it was possible to envision a country where Communist practice was closer to the communist ideal. Stalinist methods, she insisted, had "no integral part in the final phase of Communism." The commitment of Goldstein and her fellow editors to anti-fascism and their reluctance fully to embrace interventionism after the German invasion of the USSR makes clear their dissent from the Communist Party position. Best operating, as she often did, from an unpopular and adversarial position, at some level Bettye Goldstein relished her increasingly lonely stance against support for World War II. Yet, her position, although not uncommon among left intellectuals, was morally problematic: as others at Smith realized, the best way for someone who was Jewish, on the left, and not a pacifist to fight fascism in the fall of 1941 was to support the Allied effort to defeat Naziism without giving up the commitment to democratic values.[24]

Support for workers' rights remained central to Goldstein's sense of what democracy and anti-fascism involved. This became clear that fall when *Tatler,* the campus humor magazine with which Goldstein had long been adversarial, published an article poking fun at the maids who cleaned students' rooms and at the students who befriended them. Fearful that "they might be feeling unstrung after reading about Russia," the anonymous writer cautioned, Smith students worked hard to improve the lives of maids. "We fall in with their every mood, we dally with their every idiosyncrasy," the author cynically noted. She talked about one female worker at Smith who "had been officially pronounced a high-grade moron somewhere in her career"; another who "has monstrous buck teeth and a truly beautiful lisp" and whose "speech was absolutely incomprehensible to the uninitiated"; and a third whose absences between courses at dinner students suspected were due to her going on dates, smoking cigarettes, tossing "off a few novellettes," and perhaps sneaking a drink of liquor.[25]

Under Goldstein's leadership the student newspaper condemned the article, expressing indignation at its depiction of people as less than human. Reflecting the feelings of many Smith students who well understood both the cruelty and rudeness of the piece, the editorial asserted that the article insulted Smith, "a dignified and democratic institution." When the college administration temporarily suspended *Tatler,* Goldstein and her colleagues supported the action. Though worried about the precedent, they were concerned that national attention to the satirical article created the impression that Smith was "a school for the daughters of the idle rich" who were trivial, superficial, and snobbish. What was at issue, the writer asserted, was not so much free press as the college's good name.[26]

The fight over the *Tatler* piece made clear that everyday life at Smith was profoundly shaped by the relationship between relatively well-to-do students and the working-class women who waited on them. The social order at Smith reflected arrangements that many students understood from the homes in which they grew up. In the 1930s, two cooks and six chambermaids earned low wages working in a dormitory housing sixty students. Many of them were part of the local Roman Catholic working class, people whose parents or grandparents, and sometimes themselves, were immigrants from Ireland, Italy, Poland, and French Canada. The maids cleaned students' rooms and bathrooms, answered doorbells, and emptied ashtrays.[27]

The maids played a supporting role in upholding genteel traditions. Smith students experienced formal rituals incorporating proper manners. Assisted by scholarship students, hired help served all meals, which were seated and took place at set times. At breakfast maids took orders from each student. Dinner began with the saying of grace and concluded with the serving of coffee in a living room. During exam periods, maids prepared snacks twice a day. With both sides aware of proper etiquette, the maids called students Miss Goldstein or Miss Buckley, while the students called the adult women who waited on them Julia or Barbara. A woman who was at Smith in the 1930s, from a background somewhat similar to Goldstein's, felt considerable unease at being waited on by scholarship students and maids.[28]

On the other side of the social divide, the maids articulated their resentment against students. In the late 1940s, a chambermaid was heard to complain to her young granddaughter about some students in the dormitory where she worked, "Oh, those girls, they called me a bitch, right to my face! A bitch. A she-dog." More immediately, one maid responded to the *Tatler* article revealing considerable resentment over the student's caricature as well as the social dynamics on campus. Signing her letter "A So-called Moron," she began by saying: "Maybe we AIN'T college grads or fair socialites," but that if the *Tatler* article was the result of a college education, then the maids were "satisfied with what we are." She went on to reveal that the maids saw students as sloppy, careless, demanding, ungrateful, impolite, and at times drunk. "We'll take a furlough and see what the houses look like on our return," she continued. "Do you suppose then you could appreciate 'Maid Service'?" Immediately a group of maids organized and threatened to strike. Exactly one month later, they announced they would organize into a union.[29]

On October 21, at a critical moment in the unionization process on campus and while workers at several nearby factories were fighting for unionization, the student newspaper printed Goldstein's editorial, "The Right To Organize." Against those who "denounce unions as un-American," Goldstein responded somewhat condescendingly that union members were "as American as the funny papers they read." Their fight, she wrote, was central to the "expansion of democracy in America." With an advertisement for a dress in which students could "TWIRL AWAY AT TEA-TIME!" on the same page, she asserted that life, liberty, and the pursuit of happiness meant very different things to employers and employees. Unequal power, she argued, "has to be admitted and dealt with if democracy is to have meaning for 95% of the citizens of this country, if democracy is to continue at all in this country." On the copy of the issue she sent to Highlander, Goldstein wrote that a local union passed a resolution thanking the student newspaper and sent a copy of it to William Green, the national head of the A.F. of L.[30]

In following weeks, as the male workers prepared to vote for their own union, the student newspaper and Goldstein herself supported the unions' fight. The editors made it clear that faculty members who belonged to the teachers' union supported the workers' organizing effort. At the same time, Goldstein gave a public talk on her Highlander experience. She applauded the school for "really trying most vitally to get at the causes of economic chaos." The fear of poverty, she continued, in that part of the South gives "rise to Fascist shirt organizations, the Ku Klux Klan and 'vigilante' groups." Consequently, she argued, supporting those who fought such reactionary groups helped fight fascism.[31]

On November 13, a week after the announcement of the suspension of *Tatler*, the Smith buildings and grounds workers voted to accept the A.F. of L. as its union. This successful effort to organize workers happened in a college that had long operated as a paternalistic employer. A few days after the union voted, a *SCAN* editorial linked news of a United Mine Workers strike and the strong student sentiment that such strikes were unpatriotic. The use of the word "treason," the editorial writer reminded her peers, "is bandied about by only the most reactionary anti-labor people." She insisted on the importance of supporting the right of workers to strike in wartime as part of a democratic struggle and to counteract the power of employers to benefit from emergency conditions.[32]

These events took place on a campus where purveyors of expensive goods made constant appeals to elite students. Sharing a page with the November 14 editorial was an advertisement for fur coats with the tag-line: "SMITH COLLEGE GIRLS KNOW what makes the big difference in furs." Moreover, student support for unions was superficial. Four days later, when the newspaper reported that a union strike threatened to delay the publication of the college yearbook, the *SCAN* reporter told the story in a one-sided, anti-union manner.[33]

Goldstein bragged to her friends at Highlander and to the labor press about her activities. Immediately before the final vote to unionize, she noted with some bravado that some people believed she and her friends had played a key role in organizing the workers. Having earlier written her Highlander friends that she was thinking of helping local factory workers, she announced that she was about to talk to a union in a nearby town about her Highlander experiences. Almost two years later, she again told someone at Highlander that she helped organize workers at Smith and added, perhaps with some exaggeration, that her editorial almost got her thrown out of college. At the time, however, she was frustrated that her agitation was not piercing the consciousness of most Smith students. She remarked that they were completely unaware of anything outside their peaceful little world. She believed that everything she did came up against the sense of comfort and satisfaction her peers felt.[34]

In early December, the editors of the student newspaper found their own rights under attack as they became embroiled in another battle involving freedom of the press, conflicts among social classes, and the students' relationship with the administration. Around the time of the *Tatler* piece on maids, *SCAN* had launched a campaign to expose the influence of campus secret societies whose members came from the most elite and privileged social backgrounds. Two members of the newspaper's staff, supposedly acting without support from the editors, broke into the room of the president of one of the societies and stole documents. The administration moved against *SCAN*, forbidding it from publishing material collected in the break-in.

Goldstein led the successful effort to persuade the administration to punish individual students but not to infringe on the paper's freedom. In an editorial entitled "Declaration of Student Independence," *SCAN* called into question whether the administration had the right to suspend either *Tatler* or *SCAN*, offering a ringing defense of freedom of the press. The editors invoked language that student rebels had often used to challenge the power of a college administration, calling for a Bill of Rights that would give students power to control their social lives and their publications. In the midst of all this, life at Smith went on. The issue of *SCAN* that printed the "Declaration," announced the opening that evening of a student musical with Nancy Davis, the future Mrs. Ronald Reagan, playing "A Lady Tourist."[35]

Two days later, on December 7, 1941, when the Japanese attacked Pearl Harbor, local events suddenly seemed less significant, and Goldstein changed her anti-war stance. All but the most dedicated isolationists and pacifists agreed that the United States had to join the fray. On December 11, meeting at Smith, members of the Western Massachusetts Teachers' Federation, without using the word "war," promised their support for the effort to defend America and eliminate fascism. The group, led by Dorothy W. Douglas and James Gibson, pledged its help "to the end that all Americans, regardless of racial, religious, or economic differences" could unite against fascism "as the first step toward creating a decent world." At the same time *SCAN* published an editorial accepting America's new role loyally but soberly. While recognizing the necessity of war to defeat fascism, the editors rejected "words of lofty justification, of exalted righteousness, or horrified invective." In response to the editorial, one student remarked that members of the "pinkish pacifistic editorial board" had acknowledged the existence of the war, and were "resigning themselves to winning it."[36]

With America's entry into World War II, Goldstein's attention turned to new issues. How, she wondered, could American undergraduates, especially female ones, make positive contributions to the war effort? Goldstein and her peers were well aware that students at all-male Dartmouth and Yale were enlisting in the armed forces, experiencing air raid drills, and, by foregoing vacations and party weekends, ending the academic year early so they could go off to war. Committed to continuing their education until their war tasks became clearer, the *SCAN* editors called on their peers to sacrifice. In the meantime they labeled academic life "detached and fruitless." As they witnessed the stirring up of hatred of aliens at home and abroad, with 1,500 Yale undergraduates running through the streets of New Haven as they shouted "kill the dirty Japanese," they reminded their readers that the real enemy was fascism, not the people the Allies were fighting. They regretted that in order to fight fascism it had become necessary for Americans to kill their adversaries. Soon after Pearl Harbor, Goldstein privately sketched her own ideas about the obligations of a women's college like Smith in the war. She felt strongly that educated women should not just do the kind of busy work of the Junior League, like wrapping bandages, and hoped the college would ensure that its graduates would find professional jobs equal to their qualifications.[37]

When students returned to Smith in early January, the war and mobilization were moving into full swing. In her remaining two months as editor-in-chief of *SCAN*, Goldstein saw the American war effort as a way to ensure achievement of democratic and egalitarian social goals. In addition to her newspaper work, she was busy completing her undergraduate education in psychology and finishing her honors thesis. In the midst of all this, she supported the unionization of Smith maids.

An article published in the spring of 1942 underscored the distinctive position of radicals like Goldstein at Smith. Three leftist students, at least one of them a close friend of Goldstein, wrote that although most of their peers approved of unions, in fact they accepted them only theoretically. This outlook, they believed, betrayed both "the bias of family and social group" and "a sympathetic reaction" to the anti-labor perspective they felt dominated the media. They felt that most students believed that labor leaders were either corrupt or Communists and that wartime conditions made it vital for unions to surrender their right to strike.[38]

In the first editorial of the new year, the writer, perhaps Goldstein herself, made clear that her worst fears about the militarization of American society were coming true, with ominous consequences for women. She responded to a statement by the head of New York City's board of education that Americans had to develop programs for women that would lead to "the upbuilding of the race" by emphasizing marriage and motherhood. Restating what Douglas had said a year before and pointing to what Goldstein would say more than two decades later, the writer responded to the quotation by saying that "in Germany education for women is built around these words, 'Kinder, Küche, Kirche.'"[39]

The last editorials written while Goldstein was editor reflected her pessimism about social change. Commenting on student reluctance to make meaningful sacrifices, one writer remarked that "the serious drama becomes suddenly a great farce." Mindful of their privileged positions and retaining their commitment to the well-being of working-class women, the editorial writers placed one condition on their support of a plan for cooperative housing: that it not cause hundreds of women to lose their jobs.[40]

In the final editorial of Goldstein's reign, entitled "Epilogue of Failure," the writer, presumably Goldstein, acknowledged that many students and faculty were critical of the editorial board for their persistence in asking embarrassing questions and pressing too boldly for change. She said that "greater bitterness" came from "the realization of our own failure" to transform the Smith campus. In the annual student show, she remarked, students had portrayed the newspaper, and by implication Goldstein herself, "as a strident voice haranguing from a perpetual soap-box." After Goldstein's term as editor ended, class issues came into sharper focus when maids at the college successfully organized a union. The new editorial board did not give the story the attention Goldstein and her colleagues surely would have.[41]

During her senior year, most of Goldstein's courses were in psychology. In retrospect it is possible to draw a political message from two of her psychology papers, one on the tension between individualism and cooperation among animals, the other on the Nazi focus on race and intelligence. Yet

Goldstein herself usually left unexplored psychological and political connections, choosing instead to do work that maintained separation between
professional academic work and politics. Almost all of her psychology papers drew on what she learned from books and on her passion for addressing tough theoretical issues, not on the results of experiments or contact
with people. She wished to predict, control, and comprehend behavior more
than to establish contact or empathize with actual people, let alone get her
hands dirty by working in a laboratory with animals.[42]

In clear contrast with much of her work in psychology, beginning in her
senior year and continuing for a year after she graduated from college,
Goldstein wrote a sprawling, ambitious, and richly suggestive project in
which she struggled mightily to combine her interest in psychology with her
political commitments. Here she played off Francis H. Bartlett's *Sigmund
Freud: A Marxian Essay* (1937), which explored ways to synthesize the two
thinkers. Bartlett had laid down the challenge she took up: "the scientific
achievements of Freud," he had written, "can be further developed only if
the theoretical structure in which *they* grew up is overcome by revolutionary
criticism." She concentrated more on Freudian than Marxist theory for
several reasons, including the nature of what she was reading and the exten-
siveness of her education in psychology. Moreover, as a privileged member
of the middle class, she was more interested in the situation of people like
herself, which Freud set out to explain, than in the condition of the pro-
letariat, which Marx explored. She drew heavily on Freudian texts, including Freud's *Civilization and Its Discontents* (1930) and the work of Franz
Alexander, Anna Freud, Helene Deutsch, and Erik H. Erikson. She filled her
notes and drafts with evidence that she was working to understand basic
Freudian terms. She was also trying to work out the relationship of these
concepts to what she absorbed from classics in American social thought,
including books by John Dollard, Leonard Doob, Helen M. Lynd, Robert S.
Lynd, Thurman Arnold, William Ogburn, John Dewey, and William James.[43]

The central task of this uncompleted project was to bring together the
insights of Karl Marx and Sigmund Freud in order to create the foundation
for a social theory that would explain the relationship between the individual personality and the dynamics of social change. Goldstein was trying to
rescue Marx from the vulgar Marxists and Freud from those who insisted
that he had no relevance to social analysis. As others have done, she argued
that central to these endeavors was the recognition that Freud's concepts, far
from being universal in their applicability, emerged from the specific tem-
poral, geographical, and social context in which he worked. She pondered
the question of how the child learned about the external world. She located
the origin of resistance to social change in the way parents prohibited chil-

dren from touching their siblings' property. When generalized through social mores, this lesson, she insisted, lay the groundwork for society's most basic conflicts. Emphasizing the tension between individual needs and social restraints, she analyzed how frustration and regression originated in the way society raised people's expectations about security and material possessions and then left them unsatisfied. For Goldstein this project brought together key elements of her life: the lessons she learned from her own family's dynamics, her commitment to fundamental social change, and her interest in psychological concepts, including narcissism, the isolated ego, the gestalt, and the relationship between frustration and aggression.[44]

Goldstein capped her education in psychology with a senior honors thesis, written under the direction of Harold Israel. A shortened version appeared, under both of their names, in a scholarly journal shortly after her graduation. Its central task was to develop a critique of operationism in psychology, an approach that insisted on the importance of observable, measurable operations and minimized the role of thoughts and feelings. It offered a careful dissection of the scientific claims certain psychologists, including B. F. Skinner, made when they applied the ideas of the physicist P. W. Bridgman to psychology. With great precision and a keen analysis of conceptual issues, Goldstein criticized Skinner and others for not thinking through what it meant to apply to one field concepts developed in another. Operationism as most psychologists understood it, she warned, would result in an insignificant and impoverished discipline that relied on a litany of names and scholarship for scholarship's sake.[45]

Such impassioned statements in her thesis were rare. Compared with the short stories, poetry, political essays, and editorials she wrote, she approached her thesis in a highly technical manner—precise and on the surface not at all engaged in the issues of war and fascism. In October she wrote a Highlander friend that she was dissatisfied with the abstract quality of her thesis. Yet it is not hard to discover the larger meaning of her argument. Emigré scholars at Smith, Kohn and Koffka among them, criticized the determinisms that others used to circumscribe human freedom. In that context, Goldstein's critique of behaviorism lay the groundwork for a celebration of human possibility in a world where fascists and behaviorists wanted to place strictures on personal freedom. Indeed at one point she linked Skinner's psychology with blind nationalism.[46]

Goldstein graduated *summa cum laude* from Smith in early June. Her father did not come to her commencement, claiming his heart condition prevented him from doing so. During her years at Smith, her father's health had become more precarious and her mother had taken over the family business.

Goldstein suspected the real reason for his absence was that he felt she would be ashamed by his accent. Whatever the reason, his absence from her moment of triumph must have hurt. "Betty has the most outstanding record of any student ever matriculated at Smith," a college administrator told her mother at graduation. "Her thesis is an original contribution to the field of behavioral science. It could stand for a Ph.D."[47]

The commencement speaker was Archibald MacLeish, then Librarian of Congress. Under the Nazis, he noted, women were "first, bearers of children and, thereafter, providers of unskilled routine labor." With fascism, he continued, "women are obliged to undertake the duty of motherhood" without the honor that accompanied that role elsewhere. The National Socialists "taught the holy obligations of the wife without exercising the right of personal choice, the right of disposition of their persons, which alone makes wifehood holy." So women became maids and servants of men. Rallying his audience to oppose the Nazis, he emphasized that Americans were fighting against a nation that had made women "the indiscriminate and undiscriminating brides—of the State itself" turning necessity into a virtue by "denying to any woman, of its own or of another race, the central, essential right to be the mistress of herself." MacLeish's remarks echoed Douglas's lecture on women in Nazi Germany and *SCAN*'s 1942 editorial on the relationship between war, women, and fascism.[48]

After graduation, Goldstein headed for graduate school at Berkeley to continue her education in psychology. Throughout much of her senior year she had been undecided about her future. Having rejected the possibility of working in the union movement, she was torn between graduate school and a vaguely defined career as a journalist. Although she had urged her peers to help in the war effort by making sacrifices, rather than going to work in a factory or hospital, she headed for a Ph.D. program. There was an additional contradiction between her personal choices and her politics: an unresolved tension between her burgeoning radicalism and her longing for a romantic relationship with a man. "I was that girl with all A's and I wanted boys worse than anything," she remarked. "With all that brilliance, I saw myself becoming the old maid college teacher."[49]

Goldstein's years at Smith had given her some of the tools which in 1963 would enable her to write a book that helped reinvigorate American feminism. She had learned how a journalist investigates. She had engaged in radical politics. Through her education in psychology, she had acquired a way of looking at the world. Professors had taken her seriously, rewarding her ambition and intelligence without signaling that her gender would limit her horizon. On several fronts, she knew what it meant to fight for women's rights. She had shifted her attention from anti-Semitism to an interest in workers. To a young woman eager for commitment and action, Smith and Northampton seemed removed from the real world. When she left Smith, she dropped the "e" from her first name, perhaps a symbolic statement that she was no longer a girl from Peoria. It would take more than twenty years before she would again be at the center of things, commanding attention from a rapt audience. When sitting in the classroom junior year listening to Dorothy Douglas lecture, she wrote down the title of a 1935 autobiographical book by Anna Louise Strong that unintentionally revealed her future: *I Change Worlds: The Making of an American.*[50]

$$= 5 =$$

A Momentous Interlude

BERKELEY, 1942–43

Betty Goldstein spent the academic year 1942–43 as a graduate student in psychology at the University of California at Berkeley. It was a brief, but momentous, time for her. The transitions were by no means easy. She moved from a small New England town to a West Coast city that was part of a major metropolitan area. She went from a small women's college to a large public university with a coed undergraduate life organized around fraternities and sororities, and a faculty to whom research was often more important than teaching. In addition, America's full-scale entry into the war intensified the impact of the changes she experienced. Berkeley was at the center of the military mobilization of the academic world, although to most observers the full import of its involvement was not yet apparent.

The move from peace to war and from Smith to Berkeley meant that Goldstein was once again an outsider. While in Berkeley, she sustained her commitment to progressive politics and entered the world of Popular Front activism. But she was apparently unable to combine activism and academic work or to find the kind of leadership position and attention she had as editor of *SCAN*. Although she would long maintain an interest in psychology and continued to think about becoming a psychiatrist, during this year she ended her formal education in the discipline. As if all of these transitions were not enough, at Berkeley Goldstein experienced a series of major medical and emotional crises.

After spending some time in Peoria and working as an intern psychologist at a hospital in Westchester County, New York, Goldstein arrived in Berkeley to start the academic year. With a population of more than eighty thousand, Berkeley was a complex city. Its factory district, situated along the waterfront, employed more than five thousand workers. Its residential areas housed laborers, white-collar workers, many of whom commuted to office jobs in San Francisco, university students, faculty members, and wealthy families. Located on more than five hundred acres, the campus was in a park-like setting. There were over eleven thousand undergraduates and two thousand graduate students, just about the number of undergraduates at Smith. In 1938–39, the ratio of male to female graduate students at Berkeley was slightly over two to one. In 1942–43, with war dramatically lowering the number of men, there were just about as many women as men.[1]

Of even greater significance than the war's demographic impact was how it militarized the university. President Robert G. Sproul committed the university to aid in the national defense effort, and in January 1942, Berkeley began to benefit from large government contracts. In the hills above the main campus, the Berkeley Radiation Laboratory expanded rapidly as scientists worked to produce a uranium isotope. That summer, just as Goldstein was preparing to go to Berkeley, scientists met on campus to plan the research for development of the atomic bomb. One year to the day after Pearl Harbor, as Goldstein was nearing the end of her first semester, the War Department told the owners of Los Alamos Ranch School that they were taking over the property, which would soon become the key location in the Manhattan Project.[2]

In Berkeley, the physicist J. Robert Oppenheimer was one of the central figures at work on the bomb. Angry over the impact of the Depression on his students' careers and over the Nazi treatment of Jews (including his own relatives), from 1936 until the early 1940s he was involved in radical politics through the Teachers' Union, the fight to improve the lot of migrant workers in California, and the Republican cause in the Spanish Civil War. When he learned about the Japanese attack on Pearl Harbor, most scholars agree that he started to move away from these political commitments in order to focus on the urgent task of building a weapon that would defeat the Nazis.[3]

Before Goldstein came to Berkeley, she had worried about the adverse impact of World War II on academic life. Although no one in her position could have understood the role Berkeley was playing in what was to happen in Hiroshima in August of 1945, she could hardly have escaped noticing the evidence of the institution's commitment to an all-out war effort, even as much of it operated under a shroud of secrecy. People within Goldstein's world at Berkeley knew graduate students, in physics and other fields, who were going off to work at an undisclosed location on a project they could not discuss. They knew Oppenheimer was a charismatic figure, with radical political commitments who was now involved in a secret project.[4]

In the fall of 1942, news of the war's impact on the campus dominated the student paper. The *Daily Californian* told about the selling of war bonds, the opening of courses training students for war, and the listing of "Bears in Uniform." Its readers also learned of the decision of Smith College to host the training program for women naval officers. If she read the paper, the world reflected in the pages of the *Daily Californian* would have seemed benighted and even offensive to Goldstein. In its pages, students debated whether coeds should become majorettes. Included in the paper's listing of campus war activities were the traditional tasks for women she had objected to at Smith: wrapping bandages and knitting sweaters for soldiers. Some of the stories were blatantly sexist. "In the cause of patriotism," announced the woman who headed the Summer War Council, "pretty campus coeds will give a kiss to every University man who buys a bond next term." A fraternity announced that it was seeking "names of blonde, blue-eyed sorority pledges" so its members could choose the "Sweetheart of Sigma Chi." In February 1943, the *Daily Californian* reported how women who answered "yes" to the question "Can Woman's Place Be Evermore in the Home?" supported traditional gender roles. They argued that women's obligations were to their children, not their jobs, that few women truly wanted careers, and that women's entry into the work force during the war was temporary. In May 1943, the paper mentioned a lecturer in human relations who gave a talk about how, in the postwar world, working wives would cause problems of readjustment.[5]

Most of the writers for the *Daily Californian* were equally conservative on issues of labor and race. A September 2, 1942, editorial criticized organized labor as selfish, quoting a letter from a campus leader-turned-soldier who descried "the obstructionist tactics of money-mad unionists." Goldstein arrived in California just as a particularly controversial racial situation was coming to a head. By early August almost 120,000 Japanese Americans in the western states had been rounded up; by early November, the government had placed them in internment camps. Spurred by the racist antagonism endemic in California, the government denied the Japanese Americans their fundamental rights. In response, a reporter for the *Daily Californian* announced that Japanese American alumni were helping to "vitalize life" at relocation camps in which they were forcibly interned.[6]

Yet even in the pages of the *Daily Californian* there was some evidence of political dissent on campus. Students working under the auspices of the Joint Anti-Fascist Refugee Committee protested internment of Japanese Americans in concentration camps. The Young Communist League (YCL) provided the most visible leadership on the left at Berkeley, being more pro-Soviet and more internationalist than student radicals at Smith. On rare occasions, women's issues came to the fore in radical circles. When a campus leader remarked that a woman could not be president of the student body, the YCL publication, *Communist Campanile,* responded that this view mirrored "the Fascistic slogan that 'a woman's place is in the home,'" and was especially inappropriate since women were taking jobs as welders.[7]

Yet the YCL's efforts seemed weak. The *Communist Campanile* was a modest, even amateur affair, without the style or sophistication of *SCAN.* Especially compared with the range and energy of Goldstein's campaigns at Smith, there is strikingly little evidence, in the *Communist Campanile* or the *Daily Californian,* of more than minimal public activity on the left. On campus, the campaigns of the YCL and other radicals met with a combination of indifference and concerted hostility. The most serious threat to radical groups came from state and federal efforts to investigate and limit the freedom of speech of those on the left. State Senator Jack Tenney chaired California's Fact-Finding Committee on Un-American Activities. Radicals at Berkeley criticized the anti-communist crusade led by U.S. Representative Martin Dies, in one instance noting that American reactionaries, like German Nazis, saw Communists as the greatest evil.[8]

In spite of the difficult climate for progressive politics at Berkeley during the war, Betty Goldstein retained her leftist convictions, and her social circle included many radicals and activists. With a handful of graduate students in her department, she participated in an informal seminar that explored ways of bringing together Marxism and psychology. Ralph Gundlach was the faculty mainstay of this group. A visiting lecturer from the University of Washington, he was an admirer of Kurt Lewin and a founding member of the Society for the Psychological Study of Social Issues. Beginning in the mid-1930s, he fought for progressive causes at the university and in Seattle. When Goldstein knew him, Gundlach's scholarship addressed how to secure lasting peace, which he believed required fundamental changes in the social and economic structure. He distinguished between fascism and Soviet Communism, arguing that at least on the theoretical level the USSR was trying to build a better society. He lamented Americans' hostility to the Soviet experiment, believing that it led to misinterpretations of the Soviet purges of dissidents, the Nazi-Soviet Pact, and the USSR's invasion of Finland. He lamented that the reactionaries' disdain for Communism and the Soviets undermined progressive social policies and militant unionism. He saw America as a nation dominated by a business class that exploited labor and fostered imperialism, so much so that redbaiting was becoming common among newspaper columnists and politicians. Like Goldstein, he felt that U.S. war aims should include such grandiose goals as creating "a society where exploitation of human beings is impossible."[9]

At Berkeley in 1942–43, Gundlach was among the most radical faculty members, speaking out frequently on issues of racial and economic justice. "The most dangerous part of student propaganda," he announced in November 1942, "is the anti-Jewish stories and those that belittle our own government." In early January 1943, he emphasized how fraternities and sororities included few if any African American, Asian American, or in many instances even Jewish students. To eradicate discrimination, he asserted, it was necessary to attack its root causes, which he located in the personal and economic dynamics of competition. He believed that Americans were too inclined to blame social problems not on the economic system but on labor unions, Jews, Communists, and African Americans.[10]

Goldstein also became romantically involved with a radical, David Bohm, a physics graduate student who worked under Oppenheimer. Unsuccessful at Smith in her pursuit of a satisfying romantic relationship, Goldstein could have found in Bohm what she had long yearned for. Several years older than Goldstein, Bohm had much in common with her. He was an American Jew of eastern European ancestry. He had grown up in a small town as a brainy and lonesome boy in a household with quarreling parents. In high school, the anti-Semitism of Father Charles Coughlin had awakened his interest in politics and in fighting fascism. He was certainly as smart as Goldstein, and discussed issues with passionate intensity. They shared a commitment to figuring out how to combine academic theory and activism. The relationship opened up the possibility that at last she could resolve the tension between her radical politics and her conventional longing for an egalitarian heterosexual relationship.[11]

At Berkeley, Bohm and Goldstein also shared political commitments. Drawing on an interview with Friedan, Bohm's biographer F. David Peat has reported that "on arriving at Berkeley, Betty was amazed by the radical nature of the campus politics." Her sympathy for radical causes and her friendship with Bohm, Peat asserts, led her to join a "political study group" with him.[12]

In 1942–43 Bohm and other Oppenheimer students were working on a project to make uranium 235 usable in atomic weapons at the same time that they engaged in radical politics. Their radical activities caused them to be put under surveillance by the government security agents. Bohm's research was so secret that security officials blocked him from writing his Ph.D. thesis because that would involve public access to vitally important secrets. He joined the Communist Party in November 1942. His party unit focused on local issues and attempted to generate student protests. Bohm and some of his friends also tried to organize workers at the Radiation Laboratory into a union, the Federation of Architects, Engineers and Technicians. In 1942–43 Bohm met with Steve Nelson, the legendary radical, veteran of the Spanish Civil War, and Bay Area party official. Bohm's involvement in party activities was short-lived, but beginning in 1942 he developed an intense interest in Marxism, especially its application to theoretical physics.[13]

Goldstein's social circle included people the government was investigating to determine if scientists working on the atomic bomb were security risks. In the spring of 1943, according to the university's records, Goldstein lived at 2634 Channing Way. On April 12, 1943, a security officer of the Manhattan Project noted that two of Oppenheimer's radical students, Giovanni Rossi Lomanitz and Bohm "took a girl who lives at 2632 Channing Way to dinner. This is the address of Bernadette Doyle, Organizational Secretary of Alameda Co. Communist Party, and also the address of Wilhelmine Loughrey, close associate of Steve Nelson, Secretary of the Alameda County Branch of the Communist Party. Probably the girl was Helen Jenkins, an associate of the above women and a known Communist."[14]

Such a document, though problematic, is also suggestive. Perhaps it was merely coincidental that Goldstein lived in the same building as or next door to Doyle and Loughrey. Perhaps Betty did not know them well. Perhaps Goldstein knew Bohm but not Lomanitz or the other students of Oppenheimer who were Jewish, radical, and scientists at the Radiation Laboratory. Yet some things are more certain. There is considerable evidence, even from Goldstein's hand, that she lived at 2634 Channing Way for much of the year. It is highly likely that the security officers correctly identified Bohm and Lomanitz, whom they had been investigating fully and at times openly. In his autobiography, Nelson talked of Doyle as "a strong and determined woman," who held a leadership position in the party. Thus, it is probable that Goldstein had more than a passing familiarity with several of the people under surveillance, that on some occasions the security officers saw her but considered her identity inconsequential, and that her social world included a fair number of party members.[15]

According to Goldstein's FBI file, a document of problematic reliability but nonetheless one that has to be reckoned with, she sought affiliation with the Communist Party during her year at Berkeley. In 1944 an informant told the FBI that Goldstein went to a party office in the East Bay area, announced that she was already a member of the YCL, and sought entrance into the party itself, as well as a job writing for its paper, *The People's World*. A party official supposedly opposed her admission on the grounds that "there already were too many intellectuals in the labor movement and that she would have greater party influence by staying in her own field which is Psychology." Of course, reports such as these, sometimes the product of paid informers, must be viewed skeptically. Moreover, there are enough mistakes in Goldstein's folder to cast doubts on the Bureau's ability to get its facts straight. For example, the report noted that her mother's name was Miriam Horowitz, not Horwitz; that Bettye had lived in "Chopin" House at Smith, not Chapin; and that in 1941 she had been "in North Hill, Massachusetts at some conservatory." At a time when Goldstein was working in New York for a radical labor publication, the FBI had what it considered reliable information that she had recently been offered a job doing public relations for General Electric, then one of the nation's most anti-union corporations and one against which Goldstein battled as a labor journalist in the 1940s and early 1950s. Yet the report also contained some accurate evidence. The FBI did find out that Goldstein had actively supported campus labor unions at Smith, and it uncovered the article she had published in the Highlander magazine.[16]

In September 1944, when its informants offered "little result," the FBI concluded: "no information received indicating subject is presently active in the Communist Political Association," the wartime name of the Communist Party. Though she had taken positions at Smith that made clear she rejected the party line, her interest in the Popular Front in 1942–43 was fully consistent with her political activism. If Goldstein did in fact try to join the party, something that is not certain, she did so in her early twenties and at a particular moment in history. It was a time when the party, in an effort to defeat the fascists, returned to its inclusive Popular Front positions. Media and major political figures were applauding the USSR's bravery. Goldstein's stay in Berkeley coincided with Ambassador Joseph E. Davies's popular *Mission to Moscow* and its movie version, which ignored the horrors of Stalin's reign and celebrated the Soviet people as heroic. Because of the wartime alliance, writes the historian Richard Gid Powers, by the end of World War II, communism "seemed almost respectable." If Goldstein did seek party membership, she may have been searching for a focus for the political passions and activism for which she had found such rewarding outlets at Smith.[17]

As a graduate student, Betty Goldstein continued to excel in psychology, gaining an education from a distinguished group of scholars and winning a fellowship which would have carried her through to the Ph.D. During the year, as one of her male peers in the department later recalled, she was "quite sickly" with asthma but nonetheless "quite assertive" and "intellectually competitive"—a graduate student who, unlike many of her female counterparts, did not hold back in classroom discussions. When Goldstein arrived, her department was just beginning to feel the effect of the war, which reduced the number of professors in the department to four. In the short term, the war had a beneficial impact on Goldstein's standing. Over the course of the year, she won a series of increasingly lucrative fellowships, not only because of the high quality of her work but also because there were fewer students to compete for the awards.[18]

Goldstein studied with a range of teachers not unlike those she encountered at Smith. The department included several leftist professors who provided a model of how to combine intellectual and political commitments. It also contained women who had made conventional and unconventional choices about their lives, and several émigrés from Europe. Jean Macfarlane, who taught most of the department's offerings in clinical psychology, had helped put her husband through medical school before they divorced. She never remarried and lived with her mother. Warner Brown, along with Macfarlane and Harold E. Jones, served on the committee that was to supervise Goldstein's master's thesis. Jones worked with his wife, Mary C. Jones, on a longitudinal study of adolescents in the Oakland school system. Goldstein took a seminar on abnormal psychology from Olga Bridgman, a medical doctor who earned the department's first Ph.D. She also studied with R. Nevitt Sanford who in 1943 began to research *The Authoritarian Personality* (1950). Goldstein worked with another author of that classic book on anti-Semitism, Else Frenkel-Brunswik, who had arrived in Berkeley from Vienna in the mid-1930s. Jane Loevinger, who received her Ph.D. in 1944 and went on to a distinguished career in psychology, was both teacher and friend.[19]

While at Berkeley, Betty Goldstein continued to master Freudian theory. Much of her education along these lines came in a seminar taught by Erik H. Erikson, who had been analyzed by Anna Freud in Vienna in the late 1920s and who would emerge in the 1950s as an influential psychoanalytic thinker. In the early 1940s, Erikson was beginning to work out his ideas, some of which Goldstein noted down, on how children's play revealed that girls on the verge of adolescence focused on scenes of quiet, inner space represented by the home and family, while boys imagined exterior space filled with motion and excitement. Though it is a minor part of what she studied, there is some evidence that Goldstein wrestled with Erikson's writings on gender. Revealing the continuation of her interest in women's issues, she noted that he talked about the ability of girls to combine femininity with assertiveness.[20]

In Erikson's seminar, she continued the work she had begun at Smith. He provided her with key building blocks for her long-term project to locate Freud's writings in their economic and social realities, and to test them against what Freud actually observed. This would have the effect, she later remarked using a Marxist term, of "unreifying" his categories. As at Smith, much of her work was philosophical rather than clinical or experimental, involving a careful dissection of a problem, an analysis of words, and a critique of concepts.[21]

She continued to read widely in social theory, absorbing what John Dewey, Edward C. Tolman, Kurt Lewin, Abram Kardiner, and others had to say, but focusing especially on psychoanalytic literature. However, she now was less interested in trying to reconcile Freud and Marx. In her readings for Erikson's class, she gave particular attention to the writings of Freud, Melaine Klein, Karl Abraham, Susan Isaacs, and Otto Fenichel. She explored the psychosexual dynamics of her relationship with her parents. Although she later said that in this year she learned the anti-feminist ideas of penis envy and castration, she gave little attention to Karl Abraham's 1920 misogynist paper on the female castration complex. Rather, she was interested in Abraham's views on the effects of weaning and toilet training on personality. She took notes on his explanation of the psychodynamics of the financial relationship between husbands and wives. "Spending money," he asserted, "can represent an equivalent for a longed-for but neurotically inhibited release of libido." At a time when she may have wondered whether her mother's overspending had hastened her father's decline, she read what Abraham had written about women's extravagant spending. Abraham asserted that this "expresses hostility towards the husband, whose 'means' are taken away from him in this way," going on to note that the German word for "means" or "wealth" also referred to "sexual capacity." This drama between husband and wife, Abraham suggested, involved "an expression of the female castration complex in the sense of a revenge on the man. We see here again," he concluded, pointing to the relationship between spending, saving, and evacuation, "sadistic motives co-operating with those of anal-erotic origin."[22]

If Goldstein's work with Erikson raised questions about her parents' relationship and her own identity, with Tolman she faced different issues. He was the most renowned and influential member of the department. He had grown up in Massachusetts, the son of a successful textile manufacturer and Quaker mother. His own approach, known as "Purposive Behaviorism," opposed the mechanism and reductionism stated so forcefully in J. B. Watson's *Behavior* (1914), yet avoided introspection. When he left Harvard, Tolman initially went to Northwestern, but in 1918 moved on to Berkeley in good measure because of the trouble caused by his pacifism and his conscientious objection to World War I. At Berkeley, he introduced a rigorous psychology that relied on experiments with rats. Tolman remained a politically engaged citizen. When Goldstein was at Berkeley, his *Drives Toward War* appeared, a book that revealed his commitments to anti-Naziism, socialism, collective living, internationalism, pacifism, and to a psychology that drew on a wide range of approaches, including Freudianism and Gestalt. Friedan later remembered that as Marxists she and her peers were incredulous when Tolman spoke of the transition from economic to psychological explanations of human nature.[23]

A May 1943 research paper Goldstein wrote in a course Tolman directed reflected her feelings about graduate school. Perhaps titled in an intentionally revealing way, "Foci of Confusion in Learning Theory" involved an attempt to reconcile the work of Koffka and Tolman, who had known each other in Germany. Noting how bored she was with the paper, she remarked that she was trying to see if its reader was paying any attention. She concluded with a poem that playfully suggested how difficult it was for psychologists to be sure what rats learned. Her Smith professors had responded to her papers with extensive marginal notations. Though the professor, possibly Tolman, gave her an A and paid her high compliments, there were no marginal comments, and no response to the trap she had set.[24]

Events in Goldstein's life, and in the culture around her, also presented considerable challenges in her year at Berkeley. The key story she later told of this year, on which it is necessary to cast a skeptical eye, concerns falling in love for the first time and then facing a difficult choice. In the narrative she presented in *The Feminine Mystique* and elsewhere, Friedan related that she earned the university's most prestigious and lucrative fellowship, one that would have supported her through the completion of her doctorate. Her boyfriend (whom she explained was a physicist without giving his name) was jealous of her success. He gave her the choice of staying with him or accepting the fellowship. "Is this really what I want to be?" she asked herself as she pondered a future as a psychologist. The decision frightened her, she reported in *The Feminine Mystique*. She mentioned living "in a terror of indecision for days, unable to think of anything else." She also realized that "no question was important to me that year but love." She asked herself if she "would be choosing, irrevocably, the cold loneliness of that afternoon," if she went on to the doctorate and a professional career in psychology. And so, she turned down the fellowship "in relief."[25]

Betty Friedan has thus portrayed her year in Berkeley as one that shaped the rest of her life, a judgment true in its conclusion but not in all of its details. She used her love affair and decision to give up the fellowship to illustrate the emergence of the feminine mystique in the early years of the war and how it swept her in its wake. The year 1942–43 was certainly a time when the crosscurrents of American culture gave women conflicting signals. In 1942, Philip Wylie had argued in *Generation of Vipers* that since women had acquired the right to vote in 1920, America had witnessed corruption, degeneration, and war. "I give you Mom," Wylie wrote, laying the blame for America's demise on the way sons worshipped their mothers, "I give you the destroying mother." Wylie asserted that the United States was a matriarchy in which "the women of America raped the men." Among other things, Wylie attacked American mothers for misusing the time that new technologies had given them: playing bridge "with the stupid voracity of a hammerhead shark," worrying about spending money that their husbands struggled to earn, and mindlessly devoting themselves to volunteer work that promoted a shallow morality. Wylie did not stop there. In his early fiction, as Michael Rogin has shown, "liberated women represent the Communist threat." In the 1940s and 1950s Wylie fiercely opposed Communism and supported a build-up of the American atomic arsenal as a means of defeating both Communism and momism.[26]

As further evidence that the feminine mystique was "coming along fast," Friedan recounted an incident that occurred after she saw the theater version of *Lady in the Dark* in San Francisco. In the play, Friedan later remarked in an interview, "the magazine editor career woman repents of her ways as a result of Freudian analysis, and she leaves her job and marries the advertising deputy." Later, Friedan recalled, when she and Loevinger came back to the psychology offices after lunch, Tolman remarked "O, here come the career women," in response to which she and Loevinger cringed.[27]

Yet women were receiving conflicting messages about their role in society. In 1941, Pearl S. Buck, who had won the Nobel Prize in literature three years earlier, published *Of Men and Women*. Having returned to America after a stay in China, Buck was astonished at the situation many American women faced. What struck her was the contrast between what she felt was the exceptionally privileged position of the American woman and "all her small daily explosions, her restlessness, her irritability." Moreover, what astounded her, as it would strike Friedan two decades later, was the isolation of the American home from the world, something that had produced "a sharp and devastating loneliness." Accustomed to relying on professional women in Chinese cities, Buck could not find a female bank manager or doctor in her own country, and concluded "that woman's influence is almost totally lacking in the centers of American national life." She called on women to enter American life fully, in the professions, in politics, and in business. Until women achieved equality with men, she insisted, American democracy would be incomplete. She believed women had to learn how to assert themselves, that it was not men who were preventing them from achieving equality. She saw a connection between the struggle for women's equality and the fight against fascism.[28]

When the United States entered the war, national leaders undertook a concerted campaign to get women into the work place in greater numbers and in jobs from which they had previously been barred. Rosie the Riveter reigned, with the media, government, big business, and unions joining to tell women it was their patriotic duty to work outside the home, often in jobs few women had ever held before.[29]

Understanding the impact of Goldstein's Berkeley year is no easy task. To begin with, whether what she later called the feminine mystique was actually affecting her in 1942–43 is open to question. A reading of the play *Lady in the Dark* suggests that what it may have evoked in Goldstein had less to do with early evidence of the feminine mystique than with her own relationship with her parents. Through therapy, the hero of the play, perhaps like Goldstein herself, uncovers the key trauma of her childhood, the moment when father contrasted his daughter's unappealing looks with his wife's beauty. "I wanted to cry out: 'It's not true! It's not true! I'm like my mother!'" the daughter tells the psychoanalyst. Then she recalls her father saying "Daddy's little ugly duckling, isn't she?" and that she left the room. "I ran to the nursery and looked in the mirror," she tells her therapist. "I felt ugly and ashamed. When my mother came in I hated her because she was so beautiful!"[30]

Goldstein's decision to leave Berkeley was thus more complicated than her account of giving up a prestigious fellowship in order to placate her boyfriend and embrace the feminine mystique. As Friedan herself has acknowledged, she was disappointed with the intellectual quality of her graduate education compared with her undergraduate years. Moreover, the sharpest of her male peers and many of her professors were leaving to join the war effort. Anti-Semitism may also have played a role in her decision not to pursue a Ph.D. One of her contemporaries in the graduate program in psychology, himself a Jew with an identifiably Jewish name, has recalled that Tolman asked if he was willing to change his name so he would have a better chance of getting an academic position, since most leading universities did not hire Jews. While in California, Goldstein thought about becoming a medical doctor, an aspiration she had in high school. She may have seen psychiatry or journalism as fields where a Jewish woman could have a career.[31]

The editorials Bettye Goldstein and her Smith classmates had written in *SCAN* following Pearl Harbor revealed an impatience to be near the action. One of her reasons for leaving Berkeley, she remarked in the 1980s, was that she *"missed* the activism" she had learned to appreciate at Smith. A letter she wrote to Leon Wilson at Highlander not long after she left Berkeley bears this out. After leaving Smith, she told Wilson, she was determined to be a

psychologist or psychiatrist. At Berkeley she grew uncertain about her decision, in large measure because her chosen field seemed less compelling
given all the critically important struggles going on in the public arena. Her
decision to turn away from academic life involved overcoming her tendency
to think abstractly, so evident at Highlander. In her senior year at Smith and
her year at Berkeley, she reported, a career as an academic or intellectual,
even a politically engaged one, no longer captivated her.[32]

The consequences of her father's death also influenced her decision. On
her way home for Christmas vacation, she stopped in Chicago to visit a male
high-school friend. When she finally got to Peoria, two biographers have
reported, "her father was furious. Now he turned the full force of his familiar
temper on Betty, accusing her of being immoral" for having spent time with
a man unchaperoned. In response, Betty was shocked and angry, finding it
difficult to understand why her father had so little confidence in her. Goldstein was so outraged that she did not say good-bye to her father when she
left Peoria.[33]

From Peoria she went to a meeting of the Topological Society in Northampton. Underscoring how much confidence her mentors had in her, she
was probably the only first-year graduate student among such luminaries as
Gregory Bateson, Jerome Bruner, Jerome Frank, Horace Kallen, Kurt Lewin,
Margaret Mead, and E. C. Tolman. Then she returned to Berkeley, and on
January 11, 1943, less than a month before her twenty-second birthday, her
father died at age sixty-one.[34]

This event had tremendous importance for Goldstein, especially given
the hostility she felt toward her mother and the support for her aspirations
she had often felt coming from her father. Her asthma returned, along with
serious emotional tensions. She entered therapy with a Gestalt psychologist.
There she discovered, she reported in 1970, "deep-seated hostilities" toward
her mother that underlay her respiratory problems, hostilities "boiling inside" that "had to be released."[35]

The events in Goldstein's Berkeley year highlighted issues involving career choice and identity. Events, personal and political, seemed to conspire
to thwart her ambitions. Despite the presence on the Berkeley faculty of role
models who combined marriage and career, the dream she had since high
school seemed difficult to realize. Anti-Semitism and sexism threatened to
dash her hopes of ending up as a professor. Though the psychologists with
whom she studied at Berkeley included people who blended activism and
academics, following the road James Gibson and Dorothy W. Douglas first
suggested now seemed impossible. She wanted a career that combined intellectual analysis and political action in a way that gave meaning to her inner
life, perhaps something that a woman of her generation could not achieve.

In the political world shaped by Gundlach, Tolman, and Bohm, she was not the leader she had been a year earlier. At Berkeley, as toward the end of her career at Smith, she was closer to the radical fringe than to the mainstream of institutional life. With a war raging, the pursuit of academic psychology seemed too abstract and she found academic life boring and isolating. At a time when her own intensely personal difficulties made her study of psychology more individually relevant, the possibility of working to reconcile Marx and Freud faded.

With American entry into World War II and her ongoing commitment to fight fascism by supporting workers and combatting anti-Semitism, she preferred action to graduate study. Once again without a romantic relationship, she now made a positive choice to focus on radical issues rather than sacrifice career to heterosexual love or to sustained therapy. A 1943 article in the Peoria paper reported that Goldstein turned down the fellowship because "she decided she wanted to work in the labor movement—on the labor press."[36]

Federated Press, 1943–46

POPULAR FRONT LABOR JOURNALIST

In 1943 when she started working for Federated Press, Betty Goldstein began nine years as a Popular Front labor journalist. Her experience at Smith established high expectations for what it would mean to be involved in a social movement. Her year at Berkeley soured her on academic life but strengthened her interest in radicalism. Now, continuing what she had begun as a junior in college, she saw the trade union movement as the vanguard of progressive social activism. Through her work for this union news service, she called for justice for Jews, women, and African Americans, denounced what she saw as a conspiracy by big business to undermine progressive change, and opposed the unraveling of the U.S.-Soviet wartime alliance. Her work for Federated Press, and later for *UE News*, placed her in the most progressive and controversial reaches of the American left. As a labor journalist she thus had direct knowledge of working-class radicalism and Popular Front feminism. This enabled her to gain perspectives central to her development as an activist, intellectual, and author.

As a writer for Federated Press for three years, Goldstein covered many of the most important events in the mid-1940s. Like others on the left, she believed the years surrounding the end of World War II in 1945 were full of hope, albeit precariously so. The war had fostered a sense of national unity in which Americans worked together to defeat fascism. Especially promising were the gains African Americans, workers, and women made as a result of the mobilization. Moreover, the fight against the Axis powers had brought the United States and the USSR into what she and others hoped was a long-term alliance. The Allied victory in 1945 proved the success of American-Soviet cooperation, made possible the formation of the United Nations, and brought about the decisive defeat of the fascist government of Nazi Germany. Many American radicals believed that the Depression would return in the postwar world. By demonstrating the weakness of American capitalism, an economic downturn would provide support for their organizing efforts. In the meantime, Goldstein hoped, the dispossessed people the war had enfranchised would work together to extend their hard-won gains.

After Betty Goldstein completed her work at Berkeley in June 1943, she went to Peoria to see her family and to recover from another asthma attack. By late August she was in Manhattan looking for work. She wanted to recover from the traumatic events of the year in Berkeley. She was eager to find a man to love, who would love her in return. Her expectations were high. In high school she wrote of her ambition to have both a marriage and a career; at Smith she remarked that she wanted a husband who would support her desire to work outside the home. Now she worried that her ambition made it harder to establish a healthy relationship with a man. Indeed, during her years at Federated Press Goldstein dated many men but remained single in a world where millions of couples were rushing to the altar.[1]

Soon after she arrived in Manhattan, twenty-two-year-old Goldstein wrote Leon Wilson at Highlander to get his help finding work as a labor journalist or a researcher for a union. Responding for Wilson, Myles Horton offered Goldstein a number of suggestions, including the Manhattan office of the Federated Press. Within a few weeks Goldstein took a job as a staff writer there, serving initially from September 1943 until June 1945.[2] After a stint at Voters Research Institute, she returned to Federated Press for six months beginning in January 1946, with a weekly salary of sixty dollars. During her years as a labor journalist her asthma persisted, flaring up at moments of stress and anxiety. Moreover, at times a writing block made journalism an excruciating chore. Therapy seemed to offer a way of understanding the origins of both her respiratory illness and her writing difficulty. To pay for it, she persuaded her mother, now remarried, to use some of the money from her father's estate. Eventually her asthma diminished and her writer's block lessened, but hardly disappeared. In her early years in New York, Goldstein was enrolled in the pre-med program at New York University, so she could become a psychiatrist. Ambitious women, especially those who were Jewish and radical, had remarkably few professional opportunities in the 1940s. Psychiatry, journalism, and radicalism were among the few areas where they had some hopes of even beginning to satisfy their aspirations.[3]

Federated Press was launched at the Farmer-Labor Party convention in 1919 in Chicago by representatives of the Socialist Party, the Non-Partisan

League, and militant trade unions such as the International Workers of the World (IWW). They formed what turned out to be the most sustained effort in American history to develop a left-wing news service. Beginning in the early 1920s, Carl Haessler, a former Rhodes Scholar, led the news service. In jail during World War I for his opposition to American involvement, he led the first general strike within a military prison. By the mid-1930s, according to the historian Nelson Lichtenstein, Haessler had "moved into the Communist orbit." Yet during much of his career, another scholar has noted, he "shunned formal party allegiance, yet recognized the broad need for working-class unity and cooperation." In the 1940s, he ran the dispersed bureaus of the Federated Press from an office in Detroit. By 1946 Federated Press had about 250 subscribers across the nation, many of them union newspapers.[4]

As a reporter at Federated Press, Goldstein faced situations unfamiliar to her. In Peoria and Northampton she and her friends had started magazines from scratch or gained control of newspapers in their junior years when the seniors stepped down. Moreover, at Smith she was a journalist in an environment where young women exercised complete editorial control. Now in New York, she worked for a publication that was more difficult for her to shape. Goldstein encountered men with seniority and authority who had been on the local scene before she arrived. Final editorial decisions were made in a different office by men with whom she had no contact. As women involved in the 1960s civil rights movement would discover, institutions committed to democracy and social justice for all, women included, sometimes fell short of their goals. Mim Kelber, who worked closely with Goldstein in the mid-1940s, has remarked that the men involved in radical journalism, though committed to advancement of women, often engaged in sexual politics and in other ways demonstrated that they did not appreciate the contributions women made.[5]

While working for Federated Press, Goldstein learned to negotiate dramatically divergent worlds, albeit ones within a small geographical compass. She lived on Waverly Place in Greenwich Village, just west of New York University. She shared an apartment with recent graduates from Smith and Vassar, including friends from well-to-do and conservative backgrounds such as Priscilla Buckley, the sister of William F. Buckley Jr. If key elements of her private life—her friends and romantic life—were conventional, her work with Federated Press placed Goldstein in a world of radicals, union activists, and strong-minded professional women. Like the headquarters of many unions, the New York offices of the press were within walking distance of where she lived. The picture editor was Jean Roisman, the wife of

Leonard Boudin, the lawyer who in the postwar period would provide counsel in landmark civil liberties cases. The editor was Marc Stone, brother of the radical journalist I. F. Stone. The news editor was Miriam Kolkin who later, as Mim Kelber, would emerge as an activist on issues of women's rights and peace. The woman really responsible for putting out the paper was Jule Seibel. Among those who occasionally wrote for Federated Press were the long-time activist Scott Nearing and the radical historian Philip Foner. Women writers found a home at offices of the Federated Press across the nation. Jessie Lloyd O'Connor, heir to the *Chicago Tribune* fortune and the granddaughter of Henry Demarest Lloyd, worked for the press beginning in 1928. Virginia Gardner, after being fired in 1940 by the *Chicago Tribune* for her activity with the Newspaper Guild, went on to a career as a labor journalist and author, at the Washington office of the press and later with *New Masses* and *Daily Worker.* Despite its commitment to sexual equality, in the 1940s the New York Newspaper Guild held a series of beauty contests, featuring the contestants on the front page of the union publication. A 1946 story announced the winner of the Miss Page One competition. "The judges, like horseplayers," remarked a reporter, "racked their brains trying to pick a winner out of 42 thoroughbreds" and in the end selected a "blonde curvaceous one."[6]

In her years at Federated Press Goldstein involved herself in the tumultuous politics of labor journalism and the New York Newspaper Guild. This union of journalists was a principal organization that enabled white-collar workers to participate in Popular Front culture. Within weeks of her arrival at Federated Press, she joined more than three dozen colleagues in the labor press to protest what they "considered a Star Chamber Dies Committee Technique" in an investigation of the New York office by the international executive board of the Guild, apparently over the handling of local contract negotiations.[7]

At Federated Press, Goldstein was a dramatic figure. According to a 1983 fictional account by Mike Krich, the man she later called her "first love," Betty had in these years "a prodigious fluency" and a "racing intelligence." Robert Schrank, then a party member and union organizer, recalled that in 1944 a twenty-three-year-old Betty Goldstein taught him how to write for and edit a union paper. When he entered the offices of the Federated Press one day that year, he was introduced to her, "feet up on the desk, her pink panties unashamedly visible." In the same room was Katherine Beecher, from the family of both Catharine Beecher, the mid-nineteenth-century feminist, and Harriet Beecher Stowe, author of *Uncle Tom's Cabin.* Katherine, he was told, was "still trying to free the slaves, wage slaves that is." Underscoring the sexism of the men in this world of radicals committed to equality, one of Schrank's male friends said "watch out for these girls. They're really hot to trot," to which Beecher responded "Don't you wish."[8]

Goldstein impressed Schrank with her knowledge of the labor movement and current in-fighting in specific unions. Goldstein, he recalled, who "spoke in a rapid staccato" and "came across as a tough but friendly Jewish mother," impressed him with her seriousness. "What," she asked, "are the major issues bothering the members?" When he balked at the prospect of writing an editorial, Goldstein responded with "Bullshit," and then offered advice that, as Schrank's reconstruction makes clear, drew on the ability she had developed at Smith and Highlander to write vivid prose: "You listen to me. If you can speak and express yourself the way you do, then writing is simply a mechanical problem. So what I want you to do is close your eyes, imagine you're in a bar, at a union meeting, or talking to some guys at a plant. Someone asks a question like 'what's the union need a paper for anyway?' Now you have to answer. What would you say?" After he had followed Goldstein's suggestions and the two produced a draft, she pulled it out of her typewriter and handed it to him. "This is what you said. What do you think?" After he made a few changes, she looked at him. "Robert," she said, mixing approbation and advice, "you're a writer if you will always remember to write as though you're speaking to an audience. Make believe you're on a street corner or in a union meeting explaining a contract, a grievance or telling a joke after dinner. Imagine your audience. Listen to your inner voice and write it down. Believe me it will work."[9]

At Federated Press, Betty Goldstein wrote articles that revealed not only her ability to capture a dramatic moment but also showed considerable continuity with the ideology she had developed at Smith and Berkeley. Her work reflected a journalism of observation and specificity. She never pretended that she was one of the workers. Instead, her voice was that of the observer who spoke sympathetically about the struggles of the dispossessed. As a writer, Goldstein was not concerned with theoretical issues surrounding the nature of historical materialism or with a comparison of the United States with the USSR. Rather, she saw words as essential to raising people's consciousness and spurring them to collective action. She focused on specific issues that people faced in their daily lives, caused by wrongdoing in high places and remediable by a coalition of progressive activists. Instead of offering a lecture on the distinction Marxists made between use value and market value, she used a specific example, remarking that with prices of art and antiques escalating, the wealthy "have the tough problem of how to get rid of their extra millions." Rather than discussing class conflict as an abstract principle, she contrasted the fight by big business executives to keep wages down with shopping sprees "like nothing the country had ever seen." Rather than campaigning for racial justice as a vague ideal, she contrasted the conditions at a "dilapidated, unsanitary fire-trap" of a school for black children with the "eight big classrooms, a lunchroom, library and playground" reserved for whites.[10]

In the period before the end of World War II in August 1945, Goldstein focused on a wide range of issues of interest to workers and their progressive allies. She devoted considerable attention to women's situations. In a regular column called "Wartime Living," she mixed practical suggestions and political analysis. She cautioned shoppers not to expect bargains at "white sales" during January. "OK, girls—there's going to be elastic again in girdles, brassiers, garters, and underwear," she announced as she informed her audience that the government was releasing synthetic materials. She told readers that the government had raised the ceiling on the price of butter even as producers campaigned for an end to price controls and rationing because, as the American Dairy Association spokesman asserted, such measures were "out of keeping with the American way of doing business." She made clear her opposition to a regressive sales tax and her support for a progressive income tax. She applauded the government's effort to keep inflation in check. Under the headline "A Woman's Place Is Where?" Goldstein in 1944 applauded the efforts of the CIO to include women on their community councils. There, she wrote, they could fight black market racketeers, struggle to keep rents low, and "provide child care facilities for working mothers."[11]

Goldstein sustained an interest in women's issues that found expression outside her "Wartime Living" column. Shortly after she started writing for Federated Press she wrote an article on Elizabeth Hawes's *Why Women Cry, or Wenches with Wrenches* (1943). The paths that Hawes and Goldstein took to labor radicalism and progressive feminism were remarkably similar in some respects, different in others. Hawes came from a wealthy family, and her upper-class mother was active in the suffrage movement. After graduating from Vassar in 1925, where she first learned about socialism in economics classes, Hawes quickly emerged as a major and unconventional fashion designer and entrepreneur. During the 1930s, a series of events— including the Spanish Civil War, the rise of fascism, and the Moscow trials— impelled her to leave the fashion world. In the 1930s and 1940s, she developed an interest in cooperative child-rearing, an issue she focused upon as a mother, a wife whose husband resented her success, and a citizen. From 1940 to 1942, she wrote "News for Living" for the radical newspaper *PM*, a column similar to Goldstein's "Wartime Living." Michael Denning has characterized Hawes's column as "a cross between the traditional women's page of newspapers and the consumer activism of the Popular Front." During World War II, she took a job as an unskilled factory worker, where she learned first-hand about sex discrimination, racism, and anti-feminism among women. In 1944 she moved to Detroit where she wrote articles for the *Detroit Free Press* on racism, anti-Semitism, and fascism, and worked in the education department of the United Automobile Workers.[12]

In her *Why Women Cry*, Hawes drew on her experiences as a factory worker and mother. She denounced "as bad as a Ku Klux Klanner" the women who advocated an Equal Rights Amendment that would undermine protective legislation for women. She also criticized women's magazines for not treating their readers seriously, recounting one instance of an editor who forced an author to cut material because "the readers of her magazine had twelve year old minds." Her own preference was for cross-class and cross-gender cooperative efforts to build a better society, based on a combination of industrial feminism, cooperative living, child care, and clothing reform. She warned American men that they faced a "revolution [that] is likely to be brewing in your own kitchen" as women experienced the double burden of housework and factory work. Millions of women, she asserted, no longer believing their only place was in the home, wanted to combine career and family. "It is an exhausting and bitter struggle to care for a house, for one's husband and children," Hawes noted, "and at the same time try and do another job." She paid special attention to married women who worked outside the home, calling their situation "wretched." Believing that the life of servants was "little better than that of slaves," Hawes called on help from professionals and from husbands, something that would avoid "turning the wife into a servant." Moreover, she believed that a fundamental reshaping of housework would stave off fascism in America by averting "the Hitlerian routine of children-kitchen-church for the next generation of Common American women and do away with economic slavery for their husbands." In the last sentence of her book, she proudly announced "that females, as well as males, are human beings."[13]

Goldstein began her discussion of Hawes's book with a dramatic statement. "Men," Goldstein wrote, "there's a revolution cooking in your own kitchens—revolutions of the forgotten female, who is finally waking up to the fact that she can produce other things besides babies." Goldstein then told of how much Hawes had learned from working in the factory. Hawes realized that every woman should, as Goldstein put it, "have the chance to work outside her own home." She credited Hawes with realizing that housekeeping was solitary and boring, made more burdensome when women also worked in factories. She reported sympathetically on Hawes's call on unions to fight for better child care and housing, and concluded with a quote from

Hawes that combined a hope and a threat. "Men must work along with us in the solution of our basic home problems," Hawes had written, "or there will, in the end, be no homes worth mentioning in the U.S.A."[14]

At several other points during the war, Goldstein articulated a clearly feminist position. Several weeks after starting at Federated Press, she hailed the increasing number of women joining unions, the lessening of "prejudice against women's holding office in unions," and the more frequent inclusion of "equal pay provisions" in labor contracts. In a November 1943 story on the coal industry, she focused on the connection between the sexist display of women's bodies, class perspectives, and the greed of American business. To demonstrate how well off mine workers were, she explained, company executives staged a fashion show in Manhattan, parading "15 gorgeous glamour girls" who they pretended were " 'typical mine town girls.' " In fact, Goldstein's reporting revealed, they were daughters of executives, well-paid foremen, and mine owners. In July 1944, as she opposed the way Republicans were cynically using Claire Booth Luce to bolster their false claims of sympathy for women, she celebrated women's wartime political power, writing "the hand that rocks the cradle rules the nation."[15]

One of Goldstein's most significant articles on women during the war appeared at the end of her second month at Federated Press. It centered on an interview with UE official Ruth Young, a forceful advocate for women's rights in the union movement. Under the headline "Pretty Posters Won't Stop Turnover of Women in Industry," Goldstein noted Young's belief that the government could not keep women from leaving their jobs "merely by pinning up thousands of glamorous posters designed to lure more women into" factories. Neither women, unions, nor management, Young said, could solve problems of escalating prices or inadequate child care that were made even more difficult by the fact that "women still have two jobs to do." Federal government action, Goldstein reported, was needed to ameliorate the difficulties working women faced. At the end of the article, she quoted Young as saying that "women can do any job in the union, if they have the chance, anything from negotiating a contract to directing a political action program." Young "ought to know," Goldstein continued. "She does quite a few of those jobs herself."[16]

In articles she wrote at Federated Press before the war ended, Goldstein articulated progressive positions on other issues as well. She advocated a strong internationalism, revealing how fully the war had turned her from an anti-war anti-fascist to an anti-fascist supporter of the Allies. In 1943, she and a colleague hailed Vice President Henry Wallace's fight for an internationalist and broadly democratic postwar American foreign policy. In the same year she wrote several articles celebrating American-Soviet wartime alliance. She supported the emerging world institutions such as the United Nations and the World Bank.[17]

As she had done as editor-in-chief of *SCAN*, Goldstein criticized reactionary forces that she believed were working secretly to undermine progressive social change. In numerous articles, she exposed the racism of those who attacked or discriminated against Jews and African Americans. She protested the investigations by anti-communists into what they considered subversive activities. She worked with Miriam Kolkin and the radical activist Harvey O'Connor on a story about the plans of American fascists for their postwar resurgence. In November 1943, she wrote of the attempt by the National Association of Manufacturers (NAM), bankers, and corporate executives to develop plans that would enhance profits, diminish the power of unions, reverse the New Deal, and allow business to operate as it pleased. "Big business' blueprint for the postwar world," she remarked,

> is no longer a military secret. Wall Street bankers, industrial executives and local chamber of commerce bigwigs are engaged in a great publicity campaign to sell the American people on their particular postwar plan.
>
> Typical is the 4-point plan to "provide the necessary incentives to preserve and rebuild our free enterprise system" proposed recently to the Economic Club of Detroit by Chairman Alfred P. Sloan of General Motors Corp.

Goldstein then listed Sloan's four recommendations: that the federal government turn over to large corporations billions of dollars worth of "wartime industrial plant and equipment"; that the government "be nice in the future about taxing profits"; that "power must be taken away from organized labor"; and that once Washington had "fulfilled its responsibility to business," it return to a laissez-faire policy.[18]

A month later, she provided further evidence of the reactionary plans of big business as she told of a meeting in New York:

> If the Natl. Assn. of Manufacturers succeeds in carrying out the full program adopted at its 48th convention here, organized labor will be wiped out, the New Deal will be destroyed—even the war may be lost. It was as raw as that.
>
> The convention made clear that big business has one war aim, one peace aim: to make more profits for big business. The Roosevelt administration, the New Deal and organized labor, big business has decided, are the chief dampers on unlimited profits. They must therefore be destroyed. Wartime business for profits-as-usual is no longer enough for the leaders of American industry. They want political power.[19]

Like many home-grown radicals, Goldstein found additional evidence of a conspiracy of reactionary forces. In early 1944, with a journalistic scoop that grew out of her investigative reporting, she exposed Peace Now as a home-grown fascist organization that was trying to undermine the cooperation between the United States and the Soviet Union. A month later, again relying on her investigative skills, she revealed the secret plans of the White Collar League. "In an expensive office building in the heart of New York's great financial district," she wrote:

> a group of mystery men with unknown sources of big money are drawing up the blueprints for a new anti-labor, possibly native fascist, political organization, designed to split the nation's 15 million white collar workers away from organized labor and the win-the-war forces behind Pres. Roosevelt.
>
> The organization will be called the White Collar League. It will appear openly in the near future in an inexpensive headquarters as a struggling outfit of a few independent "little people" working in the interests of the whole white collar group. With the secret backing of powerful figures in the financial world, it may be an important link in the American fascists' chain.

Five months later, she denounced "stooge" employees and "subversive groups" who cooperated with company bosses and local Republicans as they followed the dictates of the KKK and Coughlinites. Playing "Hitler's game in America," they threatened both to slow the war effort and to undermine the training of African American workers for increased levels of responsibility. In these stories about the postwar plans of reactionaries, Goldstein chronicled conspiracies that, whatever pretense they had of broad social support, wealthy corporate sponsors led.[20]

In opposition, Goldstein envisioned progressive forces working together to block the reactionaries' plans. She hailed the effort of organized labor, the NAACP, the National Lawyers' Guild, the League of Women's Shoppers, and the Women's Trade Union League to fight for progressive taxation. She revealed the discrimination against Mexican Americans and Japanese Americans. She reported on the deplorable conditions under which migrant workers lived. She heralded the opening of the Jefferson School of Social Science in Manhattan as "a people's university for adults of all ages and all walks of life." The Jefferson School, Marvin Gettleman has recently remarked, "was established unofficially by the U.S. Communist Party as an expression of its view that Marxism was a legitimate doctrine neglected by conventional schools." In a September 1943 article on a small town in New York, she honored the efforts of African American children and their parents, supported by the NAACP and the ACLU, to fight against segregated and patently unequal education. A month later, she reviewed Roi Ottley's *New World A-Coming*. Ottley, an African American, was a CIO official whose book appeared just before race riots broke out in Harlem. As in earlier pieces, she ended her review with a quotation from the author that was both hopeful and ominous: "In spite of selfish interests," Ottley wrote, invoking Henry Wallace's notion of a people's war, "a new world is a-coming with the sweep and fury of the Resurrection." As the 1944 presidential election approached, she expressed optimism about organized labor's unity in the fight to win the war and gains for workers. This was, she asserted, the kind of coalition that could effectively counter House Committee on Un-American Activities (HUAC). She also hailed the CIO's commitment to end racial discrimination in factories.[21]

When President Franklin D. Roosevelt died in April 1945, a twenty-four-year-old Goldstein movingly wrote of the sadness factory workers felt at his passing. Only a few years earlier she had dissented from Roosevelt's treatment of the American Youth Congress, but now she understood his importance as a leader in the war against fascism. "It was near the end of the day," she wrote:

> The news came to the workers beside their machines in the war plants, through the din of riveting hammers in the aircraft factories and shipyards, passed by word of mouth to the day shift on the way home—Pres. Roosevelt is dead.
> They didn't believe it at first. There was a moment of absolute stunned silence. And then in the plants it was confirmed over the public address systems. For several minutes not a sound was heard. And then quietly America's production soldiers took up their work.

Union members, she commented, knew that they had lost the man "under whom American workers were given the right to organize." Goldstein's wording here was significant, betraying her middle-class approach to unions. A person who fully credited the workers' struggle would have seen the unions' triumph not as a gift of a patrician politician but the hard-earned result of years of collective action.[22]

Marked by Roosevelt's death and the Allies' victory, 1945 signaled the end of an era. Between the end of the war in August 1945 and her departure from Federated Press the next summer, Goldstein continued to articulate left-wing positions. With the national emergency over, she grew concerned about how powerful reactionary forces would intensify their efforts to undermine the progressive social changes of the New Deal and World War II. At moments, she was hopeful. She worked on several stories about plans for a national health program. She celebrated union support for the right of African Americans to vote in southern primaries, following a Supreme Court decision that made their participation more possible.[23]

In January 1946 she evoked a sense of optimism as she described the protests by union members in Bloomfield, New Jersey:

> This whole town was with the United Electrical Radio & Machine Workers (CIO) strikers Jan. 15 as they marched 5,000 strong from the Westinghouse and General Electric picket lines to the old Town Green where townsmen of Bloomfield have drilled in every war since the American Revolution.

The mayor, the merchants, the American Legion, even the police came to wish the workers well in this new war for a living wage, for a better way of life for the people of the town and the nation.

The spirit of the strikers was high though they had been up since dawn when they threw their great lines around the two plants, four deep a mile long— marching as if they'd done it all their lives, although most of them had never been on a picket line before.

With such widespread community support, she wrote elsewhere in 1946, the effort to undercut unions might be an undertaking "bigger than industry bargained for." Several typical Popular Front themes mark her article on the Bloomfield strike. She placed the protestors within an American tradition going as far back as 1776. She conveyed the sense of a unified front that included even the American Legion and the police. She acknowledged a connection between the goals of the strikers and wishes of all Americans. Finally, she emphasized the innocent freshness of the strikers' experience.[24]

Among the things that made Goldstein hopeful right after the war was her belief that women were a central part of the progressive coalition determined to prevent corporations from reversing wartime gains. In the article on Bloomfield, she noted that a majority of the union members were female, "old women with shawls over their heads" marching alongside "bobby soxers wearing slacks under their coats against the cold." Elsewhere, she depicted the wife in a union family as more savvy than her husband. The wife, understanding the relationship between the household economy and the economic system, could figure out how large corporations took advantage of the consumer.[25]

Additional evidence of Goldstein's optimism about social change and women's rights came in May 1946, when she worked on a story about the formation of the Congress of American Women. This organization of progressive women was the American branch of the Women's International Democratic Federation (WIDF), a pro-Soviet and anti-fascist group that came to have tens of millions of women members in forty-one nations. In 1946, the national offices of the Congress were at 144 Bleeker Street, a few blocks from Goldstein's apartment on Waverly Place. This article, which Goldstein and others worked on, criticized middle-class women who prided themselves on their distance from working-class women. In contrast, the authors praised European women who had joined together across class lines to fight fascism. The founders of the Congress, they noted, were determined to launch an American organization that would fight to control inflation, combat racism aimed at Jews and African Americans, eliminate the poll tax, provide for child care, support equal pay for equal work, and oppose the hardening of lines between wartime allies. The article reported that Gene

Weltfish, the anthropologist who headed the Congress, hoped "the real cause of women [would] be taken up by the working class rather than the middle and upper classes that have always had a monopoly on women's clubs." The article concluded with an announcement of the "first working conference" of the Congress of American Women.[26]

Yet more often than not, Goldstein was pessimistic about the prospects for progressive social change in the postwar world. She attacked HUAC's suppression of freedom of the press. She worried that labor unions would purge Communists from their ranks. Although she hoped that labor unions would serve as the most important bulwarks against such outbursts, she grew increasingly concerned about the growth of pro-fascist sentiments and of discrimination against Jews, Roman Catholics, and African Americans. In 1945 and 1946, Goldstein drew attention to what she saw as a rising tide of anti-Semitism. She well understood the connection between hostility directed against Jews and blacks. In a May 1945 series on "Hitler's Face in America," she chronicled the resurgence of attacks against both groups. She told of the burning of a cross at a housing project where African Americans lived, the defilement of a synagogue with swastikas, and a mob's attack on a Jewish merchant.[27]

The incidents of violent race hatred Goldstein covered came at the same time that she perceived the increasingly conservative direction of American politics. In the spring of 1946, she reported the anger of some unions at President Harry S. Truman's labor policy. In January of that year, she wrote a comprehensive piece detailing the fight between corporations and their employees. "On one side stood workers" and their representatives, she announced, fighting on picket lines and in the halls of Congress to "insure full employment, to preserve price control against inflation, for social security, better housing and medical care for all." Arrayed against them were large corporations who were "greedy for more" than the huge profits and government aid they had won. They wanted to roll back labor's wartime gains, repeal New Deal labor legislation, and "go back to the open shop days of mass unemployment and hunger," as they hoarded "profits by producing less for fewer people." A month later, she carefully tracked the campaign of corporate leaders to reverse labor's wartime victories. In one article, she pieced together the elements of a corporate conspiracy to undermine unions. She wrote of secret meetings at a New York hotel where executives and labor relations specialists from more than ten major corporations decided to force unions to strike. Complete with Goldstein's byline, this story was reprinted by a number of publications, including the *Daily Worker*, the official newspaper of the Communist Party.[28]

In most of the articles Goldstein wrote during her final months at Federated Press, she focused on international issues. With the news of atomic bombs, worldwide famine, the Holocaust, and the deterioration of the U.S.-Soviet relationship very much on her mind, she made clear her hope that America in the postwar world would adopt a progressive foreign policy. News of what the Nazis had done to Jews during the war sparked her concerns over the resurgence of fascism abroad. Goldstein responded early to news of the revelations of the slaughter of Jews in German concentration camps. In late April 1945, after the liberation of Buchenwald, she worked on a story on the concentration camps, celebrating the survival and resistance of inmates who had left-wing politics. She and her colleagues painted a picture of the horrendous conditions camp prisoners faced, mentioning torture, human skin being turned into lampshades, and crematoria used for extermination. In February 1945, she and Kolkin praised the effort of Jewish writers, artists, and scientists, aided by unions, to indict the Nazis "for their systematic mass murder of more than five million Jews" that, inspired by "spurious racial doctrines," had occurred "in gas chambers, by ax, by starvation, tortured, raped, wiped out by unheard-of atrocities."[29]

Because Goldstein also worried that tensions between America and the Soviet Union were early signs of the Cold War, she hoped for a postwar world order built on the continuation of Soviet-American friendship. In March, less than two weeks after Winston Churchill had delivered his speech in which he coined the phrase "iron curtain," Goldstein and Kolkin wrote a story that reported favorably on a protest against Churchill's fostering of hostilities between the United States and the USSR. Two days later, she hailed Wallace's efforts to rally Americans around a decreased commitment to the Anglo-American coalition and to develop in its stead a greater understanding of Soviet actions. This, she wrote, would diminish American enthusiasm for a war against the USSR. A few days later, she discussed how interest in oil led the British to support an anti-democratic government in Iran at the same time that she cast a skeptical eye on news of Russian military presence there. In the spring of 1946, she expressed concern that America's support of fascist governments abroad would lead to the deterioration of Soviet-American relations.[30]

In addition to worrying about the worsening of Soviet-American relations, in the period immediately following the war Goldstein also addressed the dangers that starvation and atomic power posed to peace. In May 1946, she wrote two stories on world hunger. Contrasting the abundance of food in the United States with the scarcity of food in other parts of the world, she insisted that America had "the major arsenal" to remedy the situation. She feared that American policy makers were going to "use food as a political weapon to put down the new democratic people's governments arising from the ashes of Fascism in Europe and Asia." Turning to the dangers of uncontrolled atomic power, she interviewed the son-in-law of Madame Curie, an atomic scientist and the husband of a French leader of WIDF, who had come to America, as she put it, to fight "the political battle to make a world safe from the atomic energy he helped release."[31]

She also focused on the dangers of military control of atomic energy. In one article, she and Miriam Kolkin asserted that most atomic scientists believed there was no way any nation could defend itself against the Bomb. America, they insisted, possessed no major secrets about how to develop a bomb, and other nations would have the capacity to wage atomic warfare in two to five years. Therefore, they wrote, it was in America's national security interest to place atomic energy under civilian and international control. Her articles appeared when opposition was growing to the May-Johnson bill, which advocated military control, in contrast with the civilian authority eventually sanctioned in the McMahon Act, better known as the Atomic Energy Act of 1946. Goldstein was also writing just before the appearance of the Acheson-Lilienthal *Report on the International Control of Atomic Energy,* about which I. F. Stone would soon write skeptically in *The Nation.* Accompanying Goldstein's articles was an appeal by the head of the Federation of American Scientists for labor to support civilian control.[32]

Like many of Goldstein's Federated Press articles on America's role in world affairs, her writings on atomic weaponry anticipated the arguments C. Wright Mills later articulated in *The Power Elite* (1956). She described intersecting elites operating secretly as they made fundamental decisions such as whether to drop the atomic bomb, a secrecy that undermined democratic processes. With some validity, Goldstein told of a plot that military leaders and isolationists were using to prepare for a war against the Soviets. Referring to "the smokescreen of the Canadian spy scare," she described the case of a clerk who defected to Canada, allegedly with information on Soviet espionage. She went on to tell of the hatching of a "conspiracy" that would deprive Americans of the benefits of the peaceful use of atomic energy and threaten world peace as well. At the same time, she reported, powerful forces in the U.S. government had strengthened espionage laws in what she saw as an attempt to discredit scientists in their fight for civilian control. Waiting in the wings were major corporations that actually had access to atomic secrets. In opposition, she wrote, stood J. Robert Oppenheimer, Harold Ickes, and Henry Wallace, who fought for civilian control. At the close, Goldstein asked rhetorically if Americans would "let the atom bomb be used by the U.S. to blow up chances of world peace or will they demand that science's greatest discovery be used for the benefit of all mankind?"[33]

Thus, on a wide range of issues Goldstein articulated a Popular Front position in her work at Federated Press. From a relatively privileged background, she was always the middle-class writer interested in the struggles of those whose suffering she could only imagine. She wrote in dramatic, accessible prose that people without much formal education could understand. She hailed the efforts of ordinary Americans to form coalitions in order to fight for progressive causes. Yet she saw powerful forces at work undermining the gains that women, workers, and African Americans had made during the war. She blamed reactionary, anti-communist forces for unraveling the wartime coalition of the United States and the USSR.

The conditions under which Goldstein ended her work with Federated Press are at once complicated and significant. In May 1946, during her second stint at the publication, she said she had lost her job eleven months earlier to the man she had replaced during the war. The reappearance of men from wartime service was indeed a major issue among New York journalists, with the New York Newspaper Guild paying sympathetic attention to the problems of veterans who now tried to reclaim their jobs, often from women.[34]

Goldstein had to give up her position, once and perhaps twice, to James Peck. Contrary to Goldstein's later claim to have been "bumped" from her position "by a returning veteran," Peck was hardly a soldier returning from military service, but he was nonetheless a veteran of many battles. Peck had a long and distinguished career as an activist. Born into a wealthy family and educated at Choate and Harvard, he had been a union organizer in the 1930s. A member of the War Resisters' League and an important advocate of direct political action, he tried to reclaim his job at the press when he returned from spending more than two years in the Federal Correctional Institution at Danbury for refusing to serve in the military during what he considered a capitalists' war. Linking American racism and German Nazism, he had led a four-and-one-half-month strike of fellow prisoners that successfully desegregated the dining facilities, the first time Jim Crow arrangements had been overturned in the American prison system. The fight over whether Peck had a right to reclaim his job and displace Goldstein became a significant issue at Federated Press. At stake were both seniority issues and the question of whether hiring Peck was a problem, given his opposition to a war that most in the union movement supported.[35]

While Peck's return was the proximate cause of Goldstein's loss of her job at Federated Press, the troubles the news service faced served as vitally important background. After the war, major changes roiled the world of labor journalism. Unions took more control of their media, and in the process changed the distributors of news from instruments useful in consciousness raising and organizing to ones that served the needs of a large bureaucratic organization that was consolidating its power. As a consequence, the labor press lost its independence. This process had ideological implications. In the late 1940s and 1950s, Federated Press came under increasing but unjustifiable attack as a front for the Communist Party. In fact, Federated Press prided itself on the wide range of political positions represented among its writers. Fearful of its independence and radicalism, powerful unions took steps to curb its influence, sometimes by stopping their subscriptions. In these battles, Walter Reuther and the UAW had a special role, one that in part grew out of friction between Reuther and Haessler that went back at least as far as the early 1940s. On March 27, 1946, Reuther had narrowly won the presidency of the UAW but lost, by a significant margin, control of the union's executive board. Reuther publicly declared his commitment to limit the influence of Communists in the union, something he did not then have the political clout to do. Because Federated Press needed subscriptions from the UAW and often sided with Reuther's opponents, Haessler had to make sure his news service paid minimal attention to factionalism in the UAW and to Reuther's attacks on Communists. When Reuther gained control of the UAW later in 1946, he ended its relationship with Federated Press, thus depriving the press of substantial revenues.[36]

These events in Detroit shaped the circumstances of Goldstein's departure from Federated Press. In early May 1946 Haessler, worried about UAW support, warned Kolkin that her job was in jeopardy because of what he called her "opinionated refusal to listen to advice [that] might lead FP into dangerous channels." Haessler felt Kolkin was giving aid and comfort to the enemies by emphasizing, as did the mainstream press, divisions in union leadership and Reuther's attack on Communists. Haessler warned that for major newspapers in big cities "such trivia are red meat for unionbusting." Moreover, Haessler made it clear that the competing and less radical Labor Press Association would take advantage of any mistakes Federated Press made.[37]

Combined with Peck's challenge, the struggle between Reuther and Haessler made the situation at the New York office tense. The fights between Marc Stone and Goldstein were especially bitter. At a meeting of the New York bureau he said, according to Goldstein, that there was "no danger of our going too far to right—danger of going overboard on left." In a like vein, in 1946 Goldstein reported that those in charge of Federated Press, trying to make the service acceptable to *Fortune* and the mainline newspapers, were worried about "letting Betty's radical enthusiasm run away with her."[38]

Goldstein believed part of the difficulty was that her stories were both widely read and too radical. Labor and radical newspapers from around the nation printed what she wrote, a fact that the New York office of Federated Press carefully tracked. In response to her story on hunger and the political uses of food, Stone supposedly asked her, "why didn't you use your imagination on something our conservative papers will like?" Those in control of Federated Press, she reported at the time, objected to several pieces she had prided herself on publishing in the spring of 1946: a story of union members picketing Winston Churchill when he appeared at the United Nations; one on international politics of oil in Iran; another on Nazi scientists in Franco's Spain; and one alleging GE's suppression of an invention. Goldstein reported that the piece especially offensive to Stone and Haessler was the one in which she suggested the conspiracy to give the military control of atomic power. On her copy of the article, someone circled the strong language that may well have offended people less radical than Goldstein: "military clique," "devastate the U.S.," and "stiffen espionage laws."[39]

In May 1946, Goldstein filed a grievance with the Newspaper Guild of New York in which she said that those in control of Federated Press were trying to get rid of her, even though she believed they had no good reason to do so. This effort had begun, she asserted, several months earlier when Stone returned from the war. He was trying to get Goldstein to leave, because she was, in words Stone allegedly used, "being built up too much in the labor press." The staff had already turned down Stone's request to demote Kolkin as news editor and hire a replacement, presumably a man, a rearrangement that would have left no room for Goldstein. Backed by Haessler, Goldstein claimed, Stone hurled angry words and small objects at Kolkin and her in an attempt to convince them to resign.

In May, the situation came to a head. Instead of allowing Goldstein to replace Kolkin as customarily happened when she was away on assignment, Stone took over the position of news editor and stopped giving Goldstein assignments. When he refused to send Goldstein to cover a story on which she had done initial work and instead hired a male free-lancer, she confronted him, demanding to know why he had blocked her reporting. "Because I would not send you to cover a dog fight. Personally," Goldstein reported Stone as saying, "I have no use for you whatsoever." Two days later, Goldstein read a letter to the staff from Haessler that made it clear, she believed, that the staff had lost its recourse to democratic procedures. When Stone found Goldstein reading the letter, he told her, "why don't you wise up. You had better start hunting for another job, because your days here are certainly numbered."[40]

Thus Goldstein lost her job for a number of reasons. Conflicts between strong personalities were too much to contain in a small office. Peck's claims on his job not only raised the issue of seniority but also what it meant to honor the guild's commitment to a radical who had resisted the war that almost all other radicals believed was justified on anti-fascist grounds. In addition, sexism played some role in her loss of a job. Stone, not comfortable with female colleagues, seemed intent on replacing women who had run the bureau during the war with men who sought postwar employment. For a woman to submit to the union a workplace grievance against a superior at a left-wing newspaper meant facing the kinds of contradictions feminists in movements committed to progressive causes have frequently encountered.[41]

The issues surrounding her departure were ideological in other ways. The anti-communism of national unions, the UAW especially, placed in jeopardy those like Goldstein who wanted Federated Press to emphasize radical causes, many of them not directly related to union issues. Federated Press and the New York Newspaper Guild were in the vanguard of the fights against fascism, anti-Semitism, and racism directed against African Americans. Within the New York Guild periodically there were titanic struggles over the issue of Communist influence, with party members and their Popular Front allies combatting anti-communists. At a time when left and right were fighting within the New York Newspaper Guild and those in authority at Federated Press were trying to protect the newspaper service from anti-communist unions, Goldstein's radicalism posed serious problems. Goldstein's battle with those in control of Federated Press came at a time when some unions, and especially the UE, were engaged in militant strikes against corporations. Other labor leaders wanted to distance themselves from the militancy advocated by its journalistic supporters, Betty Goldstein among them. As had been true at Peoria High School and Smith College, Goldstein was once again in danger of losing her ability to put her radicalism into print.[42]

tye Naomi Goldstein as a child in Peoria, c. 25. Reproduced courtesy of Schlesinger Library, Idcliffe College.

Miriam Horwitz Goldstein, Bettye's mother. Reproduced courtesy of Schlesinger Library, Radcliffe College.

rry Goldstein, Bettye's father. Reproduced cour- y of Schlesinger Library, Radcliffe College.

Goldstein Jewelry Co., 111 South Adams, Peoria, Illinois, c. 1920. Reproduced courtesy of Peoria Historical Society, Bradley University Library.

96

Bettye Goldstein at high school radio station, with Paul Jordan, Doug Palmer, and MacFarland, spring 1938. Reproduced courtesy of Schlesinger Library, Radcliffe College.

First row, third from left: Bettye Goldstein, high school journalist and member of Quill and Scroll, honorary journalism society, spring 1938. Reproduced courtesy of Schlesinger Library, Radcliffe College.

QUILL AND SCROLL

SMITH College Associated NEWS

MARCH 14, 1941
NORTHAMPTON, MASS.

REPRESENTED FOR NATIONAL ADVERTISING BY
National Advertising Service, Inc.
College Publishers' Representative
420 MADISON AVE.   NEW YORK, N. Y.
CHICAGO · BOSTON · LOS ANGELES · SAN FRANCISCO

Subscriptions for the college year, $3.00 in Northampton; $3.50 out of town. Subscriptions should be sent to Barbara Stevenson, Dawes House; business communications other than subscriptions should be addressed to Suzanne Cook, Wilder House.
Issued semi-weekly, entered as second class matter. Application for change of name and frequency pending.

EDITOR-IN-CHIEF—Bettye Goldstein. Telephone 409 after April 1.
ASSOCIATE Editor—June Rhode.
MANAGING EDITORS—Anne Grilk, Nancy Stix.
NEWS EDITOR—Janet Brown.
COPY EDITOR—Margaret Comstock.
FEATURE EDITORS—Virginia Drew, Mary Hodge.
ASSISTANT EDITORS—Priscilla Buckley, Anne Draper, Elizabeth Fowler, Sarah Gavin, Joan Griffiths, Jean Newburger.
SPORTS EDITOR—Gloria Heath.
REPORTERS—Marjorie Bernstein, Gwendolen Brandt, Aloise Buckley, Ruth Chalmers, Mary Chapman, Cynthia Dalrymple, Elizabeth Eldert, Ann Goodrich, Martha Gregory, Betty Heilbrun, Amanda Hilles, Constance Headley, Anne Kingsley, Urmila Kokatnur, Barbara Krieger, Joan Maxwell, Dorothy Pritchard, Ellen Safford, Marion Sherman, Mary-Mae Whitnah.
COLUMNISTS—Neal Gilkyson, Mary Jackson.
CRITICS—Art, Florence Swenson; Music, Doris Broder, Nancy E. Lowe, Ann Wheeler; Drama, Marjorie Allen.
CARTOONISTS—Mary Cudahy, Martha Titus.
PROOFREADERS—Ellen Saville, chairman, Barbara Pettee, Margery Hall, Barbara Hopkins, Winifred Hunt, Elizabeth Mead, Elizabeth Power, Jean Wehmeyer.
BUSINESS MANAGER—Suzanne Cook.
ASSISTANTS—Catherine Gerdes, Edwina Golding, Mary Lou Kane, Katharine Kerr, Madeline McWhirrey, Carroll Mentzendorff, Eleanor Miles, Jane Oman, Virginia Uhlman.
ADVERTISING MANAGER—Virginia Gibbs.
ASSISTANTS—Elizabeth Burgess, Elizabeth Gale, Marcia Gillies, Marion Grinberg, Georgiana Harris, Marjorie Kiefer, Patricia Mend, Ruth Van Ness, Sylvia Rosenberg, Elizabeth Stock.
CIRCULATION MANAGER—Barbara Stevenson.
ASSISTANTS—Lorraine Caldwell, Ann Millspaugh, Charlotte Milstein, Margaret Rush, Leslie Stober.

THIS IS WHAT WE BELIEVE . . . .

We take over a college newspaper in the spring of 1941 with a conception of the function a student newspaper can fulfill in this time, a conception resting explicitly on certain values which we present now as the principles upon which we shall act editorially during the coming year. We believe that these values are important; we believe that they are endangered; we believe that a newspaper can defend these values by producing an awareness of them and of the dangers which threaten their existence.

There is first the value of democracy, and of freedom within that democracy—freedom of speech and thought, academic freedom for us as students and for our professors. There is the value of intellectual integrity, of pure knowledge and the quest for truth, of the idea untinged by emotion—the value of culture and of a liberal arts education which perpetuates that culture. Today that value is questioned. There is the value of peace in a world of war, and there is the necessity of seeing that war realistically, with perspective, of retaining the ability to analyze contemporary events with the mind, and impersonally. There is the value of the individual, in a world where that value is being minimized. Finally there is the value of progress, and for us that must mean learning to build a better future from the present rather than acquiring techniques for preventing change, for adhering to outworn traditions, for remoulding the present to conform to an idealized past.

We value democracy; we conceive of our newspaper as an essential element in the democratization of Smith student government. That which prevents the potentialities of truly democratic self-government from being realized here is in great part the ignorance and indifference of the majority of the students as to the nature and value of self-government, the powers that are theirs or could be theirs. The secrecy with which such student government as there is here is carried out, the frequent presentation of new measures as fait accompli, the inertia with which suggestions are met—these also prevent the true experience of democratic self-government. And we feel that this experience, in a world where too many have neither known nor prized democracy, is necessary if democracy is to be preserved. If it is possible that human beings can govern themselves, can choose their own leaders, and we think this is possible, then self-government should be a part of their education. We agree with the majority of Smith students that there should be no patriotic indoctrination in the classroom. Far better as a training for democracy is practice in democracy. And perhaps at this time such practice is even more important for us as women than ever before, for all over the world the right to participate in government is being taken from women. The Smith woman can go out and be a force in her community; the ideas she receives here, the life she leads here will determine what sort of a force she will be. If she is to be a force for the maintenance and extension of democracy, she must actively participate in democracy here. SCAN will be working with a new and progressive student government. The new head of student government has expressed a hope that next year it be responsive to the changing demands and interests of the student body; through SCAN those demands can become articulate, those changing interests can be reflected with speed and accuracy.

We have spoken of the value of academic freedom. So far that freedom has not been threatened at Smith, although in many other colleges in this country it has been curtailed. We do not know how long Smith will remain unaffected by events occurring more and more frequently elsewhere in the academic world. We hope it will never be necessary to fight for the preservation of academic freedom here.

As for the values of intellectual integrity, of knowledge, of education itself—for the preservation of these we shall use all the means at our disposal, for we do not believe that the function of education should prepare one to meet with acquiescence an inevitable wave of the future. Rather we believe that education has still the function of handing down the best that man has thought and written and done, of instilling habits of critical analysis, of intelligent independent thought.

There is also the value of peace, and perhaps the future holds only frus-

tration and futility for those who cry out against war. But at least we can question still the motives of war, we can look beneath the surface and re-tain historical perspective. And here again we can demand the maintenance of intellectual integrity, when so much is being done to make us stop thinking and feel and act.

And there is the value of progress. SCAN has been criticized for questioning traditions and established institutions. SCAN has been accused of desiring change for change's sake. We do not desire change for change's sake, but progress means change, the realization of ideals means change, and criticism in the light of ideals implies and demands change.

A newspaper is a weapon of power—it can train strong light on darkness; it can dispel ignorance; it can prevent indifference and apathy. It can ask—and its questions usually demand answers. It can reflect what happens in a community, and if it reflects truthfully, the awareness it brings can be a bulwark against dangers. And it can work positively for the ideals of the community.

We recognize the power that is ours. We hope that we shall use it always with integrity.

J. RHODE AND B. GOLDSTEIN

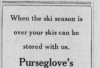

Bettye Goldstein and June Rhode, announcing Goldstein's selection as editor-in-chief and Rhode's as associate editor of *Smith College Associated News,* March 14, 1941; the page also includes Goldstein's first editorial, "This Is What We Believe . . . " and an advertisement for *Gone with the Wind,* based on novel of Margaret Mitchell, who had been a student at Smith College two decades before Goldstein. Reproduced courtesy of Smith College Archives, Smith College.

Chapin House, Smith College, probably late 1940s. Reproduced courtesy of Smith College Archives, Smith College.

Living room, Chapin House, Smith College, probably 1920s, where Bettye Goldstein lived all four years as an undergraduate. Photo by Eric Stahlberg. Reproduced courtesy of Smith College Archives, Smith College.

Professor Dorothy W. Douglas, her husband, Professor Paul H. Douglas, and their four children, c. 1926. Reproduced courtesy of Smith College Archives, Smith College.

SMITH College Associated NEWS

Vol. XXXVI. No. 38   (Z305)   NORTHAMPTON, MASS., FRIDAY, APRIL 25, 1941   Single copy, five cents

Reverend L. T. Pennington Of Boston Will Speak On Plan For Federal Union

Church Peace Union Member; Sponsored By Federalists To Talk in Graham Hall

GROUP PICKS OFFICERS

The Reverend Leslie T. Penning-ton, of Boston, will speak on "The Plan for a Federal Union," Tuesday, April 29, at 8:00 p.m. in Graham Hall. Mr. Pennington is minister of the First Church (Unitarian) in Cambridge; he graduated from Earlham College and from Harvard Divinity School. A member of the Board of Trustees of the Church Peace Union, Carnegie Foundation, and of the Board of Directors of the Massachusetts Committee of Federal Union, Inc., he has done considerable speaking on Federal Union.

Mr. Pennington will be at Smith under the auspices of the college Federal Union group.

At a meeting Wednesday, April 23, the group was reorganized, and new officers were elected for the coming year. Madelon Berns, 1942 is the new president; Margaret Wood, 1942 treasurer; and Jane Bedell, 1943, secretary. Plans were made to receive Reverend Leslie T. Pennington.

Federal Union is a comparatively new organization at Smith. Its first business meeting was held in February, and a study program has met twice since then. At the second of these meetings, the group voted to donate a copy of Clarence Streit's newest book to the library. Federal Union activity on campus is supported by Miss Chase, Kohn, Mr. Kotschnig, and many other members of the faculty; in the United States by such notables as Robert Sherwood, André Maurois, Dorothy Thompson, and Clare Boothe.

Breed To Provide Humor On Indoor Ivy Day Program

Emily Schweppe, chairman of Indoor Ivy Day, has announced that Izzy Breed has been chosen to give humorous Ivy Day speech this year.

Peggy Breed has had literary experience as director of the Special Editors' Rally Day Show and as editor of the book of student writings prepared so far. Morrow on her birthday last year by the student body. She is also the senior class historian, and has served this past year as president of Ellen Emerson House. An Avon pin recipient, she has been active in basketball, hockey, and lacrosse.

In the Indoor Ivy Day program, Saturday, May 15, is to follow in the regular tradition. After the outdoor Ivy Day ceremony, seniors will march into J. M. Greene Hall, class officers leading the line. The greeting will follow by the class president, Nancy Jay Song, and the reception address by Anton, the Glee Club will sing the Ivy Day song, and the traditional follow. (The speaker will be announced later.) After a piano interlude the exercises will be concluded with the presentation of the humorous speech.

"Country Stories" Returned At Last

Elections for vice-president and secretary were held in the House of Representatives last night. Nina Chandler, 1942, was elected vice-president, and Barbara Dawley, 1943, received the office of secretary.

The Browsing Room of the library was reopened at 7 o'clock p.m., Wednesday, April 23, when Mitford's *Country Stories*, which had been missing since two days before Spring Vacation, was returned.

Miss Dunham says that this is the longest time the Browsing Room has ever been kept closed for an offense of this sort. She is of the opinion that this incident may lead to revival of the rule that students may not bring their own books into the Browsing Room, on the assumption that some student might have carried the book off with her own without realizing it.

When Miss Dunham, thinking the book permanently lost, wrote to Barnes and Noble for another copy, she was informed that it was out of print. She then wrote them to advertise for the lost book at the Smith Library's expense. Since the book has been returned, this order will be cancelled, but all advertising already done will be paid for.

The Student Council, taking action on the situation on April 22, had appointed Margaret Stewart, Chairman of Judicial Board, to speak to President Davis to see if, contrary to usual procedure, the Browsing Room might be opened before the book was returned.

Miss Dunham stated: "This year has been the worst, as far as losses are concerned, that I can recall. Only the force of public opinion can rectify the situation."

Mrs. Douglas Speaks About Danger of Anti-Strike Bills

"It is unwise to precipitate any one of the anti-strike bills, as they would only cause greater difficulties," said Mrs. Douglas yesterday, speaking on Strikes in Defense Industries. England, who is already at war, has not informed the students that she had no control over the matter. They be-guiled Miss Anderson to accompany them to Baldwin House for a two-hour chat on the subject. Miss Anderson said that the blue columns would bring out the blue in the bricks and expressed her surprise that young girls could be so conventional. Baldwinites think the blue color will make the house intolerably gloomy, also the porch furniture has been recently painted green, which, they fear, will not add to the general attractiveness.

The occupants of Baldwin are not overjoyed at the thought of the only objectors to the project. Harpers Method, which has premises across the street, may petition for the restoration of the original color.

PEACE DAY RALLY

New Members Appointed To Aid With Curriculum

Neal Gilkyson, 1942, newly-appointed head of Curriculum Committee has announced the new members of the committee: from the Class of 1942, Anne Grilk, Lawrence House, Elizabeth Roberts, Capen House, Margaret Helm, Chapin House; from the Class of 1943, Hyla Stuntz, Lawrence House, Barbara Webster, Wilder House, Clair Morris, Tyler House; from the Class of 1944, Penelope Fuller, Wallace House, Barbara Lemmon, Dickinson House, Mary Kaser, Martha Wilson.

In a statement about the functions of the committee Neal Gilkyson said: "Curriculum Committee is still unsettled, so we are ready to try anything. We want lots of creative ideas from the college at large, as well as complaints. All the members of the committee want to be put to work by the students, so we'll listen to anything."

Curriculum Committee gets under-way this Friday evening with its first meeting. It hopes to organize some kind of more informal information on freshman courses to be sent to the sub-freshman over the summer, besides the official college catalogue.

Blue Columns, Green Chairs Stir Wrath of Baldwinites

Last Friday the students of Baldwin House were startled to find the dormers and columns of the house being painted blue, under the guiding eye of Miss Anderson, assistant professor of landscape architecture. Enfessor of landscape architecture raged, they rushed to Mrs. Scales, who

New Grass Cops Chosen Duties Steadily Increase

Ruth Cutler, 1941, head of Grass Cops, announces that nine student, one junior and eight freshmen, have been selected as Grass Cops. They are: Margaret Helm, 1942, Josephine Clapp, Ann Cornell, Jane Deacon, Cathleen Duran, Joan Eager, Susan Rabenold, Alice Smith, and Anne Whittlesey, of the Class of 1944.

The Grass Cops with tin stars and whistles first began to function in 1921 in response to the wish of President Neilson that the campus be more orderly. During the same year that cops also began to function, for Student Council had ordained that no student was to go below Beckmann's without a hat. The hat cops have passed out of existence, but the Grass Cops are still at work, and it is in part due to them that Smith College has maintained its tradition of a good looking campus.

The duties of the present organization have become somewhat increased. They must also watch out for unauthorized bathing, for bicycles without lights, and stand at the chapel doors on Wednesdays.

Mr. Hankins Speaks at Rally Tells of Subtle Propaganda

"The President in reopening the Red Sea" has made possible "the creation of an incident," said Mr. Hankins, professor of sociology at Smith College when he spoke to a joint peace meeting of approximately 1,000 Radcliffe and Harvard students, last Wednesday, April 23.

"Remember the Lusitania," he added, asserting that the American people were being subjected to a barrage of "subtle propaganda". He said that they are "beginning to realize that they are being badly fooled."

His remarks brought a chorus of hisses from a small group of "interventionist" students carrying placards reading "convoys now", "war is hell—Hitler's worse", and "hang together or hang separately".

The peace group carried posters reading "No A.E.F." "No suckers for War", and cut classes to attend the rally.

Effect Of Warfare On U. S. Discussed

Peace Commission Conducts Outdoor Peace Day Meeting Led by Susan Lobenstine

SIX STUDENT SPEAKERS

The effect of a state of active warfare on the United States of America was discussed by six student speakers at an open-air mass-meeting on Burton Green last Wednesday.

The meeting was opened by Susan Lobenstine, 1942, chairman of the Joint Peace Commission, who explained the tradition of National Peace Day and Smith's participation in it. She was followed by Elizabeth Roberts, 1942, chairman of the committee in charge of Peace Day and of the Peace Day program, who introduced the speakers.

Marion Ingersoll, 1942, the first speaker, explained the platform of the Joint Peace Commission — Peace, Democracy, Humanity. She stated that although a demonstration for peace may seem untimely at this particular moment, peace has today a more positive and constructive meaning than ever before.

Mary Newman, 1941, described the war in Europe as an "advent in a world revolution" whose eventual result would be a complete change in the world system as we know it today. American participation in the war would vitally endanger our political democracy.

Virginia Momand, 1944, speaking on "Milestones in the Race Towards War," traced the steps from September, 1940, when Roosevelt said: "We will not participate in foreign wars ... except in case of attack," till April, 1941, when we are poised on the brink of war. She stated that if we are in a growing, and intelligent democracy. Academically it is impossible to think in terms of white and black, and thus in a state of war academic liberty must, in the nature of things, be curtailed. Speaking specifically of Smith College, she quoted from President Davis's inauguration speech in which he promised educational liberty, but stated that in a time of war, the head of one institution would be powerless against the United States legislation.

Carolyn Clausen, 1941, the final speaker, delivered an address on "Peace...

(Continued on page 4, column 2)

Meeting in front of building at Highlander Folk School. Bettye Goldstein attended worksho[p] at Highlander in the summer between her junior and senior years at Smith, at a time when th[e] building was standing but well before the date of this picture. Reproduced courtesy of Sta[te] Historical Society of Wisconsin. [Negative number WHi (X3) 43722, Lot 4260 #865]

Bettye Goldstein and members of the staff of *Smith College Associated News*, 1941–42. *Left [to] right:* Anne Grilk, Marion Sherman, Nancy Stix, June Rhode, Bettye Goldstein, Virginia Gibb[s,] Suzanne Cook, Barbara Stevenson, and (*standing*) Margaret Comstock. Reproduced courte[sy] of Smith College Archives, Smith College.

...ttye Goldstein, *summa cum laude*, ...i Beta Kappa, campus activist, ...aduation picture for Smith College, ...42. Reproduced courtesy of ...hlesinger Library, Radcliffe College.

...udents, including men in military ...iforms, gather outside buildings ... campus of University of Califor-...a at Berkeley during World War II. ...tty Goldstein was a graduate stu-...nt in psychology at Berkeley in ...42–43. Reproduced courtesy of ...niversity Archives, The Bancroft ...brary, University of California, Ber-...ley. [UARC PIC 4:113j]

Betty Friedan in canoe, 1947. Reproduced courtesy of Schlesinger Library, Radcliffe College.

Carl Friedan and Betty Friedan, c. 1947. Reproduced courtesy of Schlesinger Library, Radcliffe College.

Betty Goldstein, deep in thought at typewriter, probably late 1940s. Reproduced courtesy of Schlesinger Library, Radcliffe College.

UE News, 1946–52

WORKERS, WOMEN, AND McCARTHYISM

In July 1946, when she was twenty-five, Betty Goldstein began six years as a writer for the *UE News*. When she married in 1947, she became Betty Friedan in private life, even though she continued to use Goldstein as a writer as late as 1952. While at *UE News*, she married, gave birth to her first son, became pregnant with her second, and moved out of Manhattan to Parkway Village, a suburb in Queens. In these years, her relationship with her mother, sister, and brother remained problematic. "I became very estranged from my mother," she later remarked about the years after her father's death, "very critical of her. Part of it was normal growing up, becoming aware of one's own self. But I had to do it more than most." If much in her private life changed, key aspects of her public life stayed the same: she remained a labor journalist and continued her interest in Popular Front feminism.[1]

UE News was the official publication of the United Electrical, Radio and Machine Workers of America, a radical union in the forefront of the fight for social justice for African American and women workers. Her journalism for the UE came at a momentous time. Early in 1946, as part of a widespread wave of strikes by the labor movement in general, the UE shut down all Westinghouse and GE factories in the United States and Canada. As a result, these corporations shifted their policy regarding the UE from one of relative tolerance to hostility. This change, combined with the arrival of the Cold War, meant that Goldstein began at *UE News* precisely when the union faced the most severe attack in its history. She witnessed the impact of McCarthyism on the lives of progressive people and social movements, including Popular Front feminism. Her experiences at the UE—with McCarthyism and with the fight for social justice for working women—were crucial to her future as a feminist writer and leader.[2]

Friedan wrote in 1976 that during her years at the UE, she and her friends considered themselves in "the vanguard of the working-class revolution"; they participated in "Marxist discussion groups," attended political rallies, and felt "only contempt for dreary bourgeois capitalists" such as their fathers. These were the years when she was "very political, very involved, consciously radical" about African Americans, workers, the threat of war, anti-communism, and "Communist splits and schisms." One person who knew her well in these years has remarked that she stayed away from divisive ideological battles; what mattered to her, he said, were positions on specific issues. As she had done at Federated Press, she continued to fight for universal health care, government-sponsored child care for working mothers, as well as justice for working-class and minority women.[3]

In the years following World War II, events at home and abroad provided the background against which Friedan started a family and continued as a journalist. The labor movement, especially among its more radical members in the CIO, saw enhanced union power as inseparable from a broad agenda of progressive social change that included full participation in the society for a broad range of groups. Nelson Lichtenstein and Robert Korstad have demonstrated that in the 1940s union members and radicals, including Communists, hailed the possibility of fundamental social change. A war-induced economic boom had made it possible for many, especially millions of women and African Americans who entered the work force and CIO unions, to move from homes and farms into factories where they had more highly skilled, better paying jobs than ever before. Federal agencies developed commitments to social advancement, writing into law provisions that guaranteed African Americans full political participation in union affairs.[4]

As described in the preceding chapter, a series of watershed events dashed such high hopes and undermined the Popular Front coalition. The explosion of atomic bombs on Hiroshima and Nagasaki in August 1945 made clear the lethal possibility of the work of Berkeley physicists whom Friedan had known. Beginning in 1945, the revelations that Nazi anti-Semitism had resulted in the slaughter of millions of Jews, which Friedan had publicized at Federated Press, both terrified and mobilized American Jews. And, as she knew from firsthand experience, the return of veterans threatened the gains that African Americans and women had made in the job market. Friedan also understood how the years of relative prosperity promoted the development of suburbs and the expansion of consumer culture, both of which weakened older patterns of participatory politics, fundamentally altered class and ethnic relationships, and helped erode the militancy of labor unions.

In addition to these occurrences, there were other signs that the hopes for progressive social reconstruction through political action would not materialize. Inflation drove real wages down to their 1942 level. Harry S. Truman, who became president in April 1945, proved more centrist than Franklin D. Roosevelt. In September 1946, he removed Henry A. Wallace from the cabinet for taking too soft a line against the USSR. Returning veterans recently elected to Congress, most prominently Richard M. Nixon and Joseph R. McCarthy, went on the attack, linking the CIO and the Communist Party. For many, the final turning point came in 1948 with the poor showing of Progressive Party presidential nominee Wallace. Only hindsight makes clear how the radicalism of the late 1940s and early 1950s served as the seedbed of both civil rights and women's liberation in the 1960s.[5]

The Cold War devastated the worlds Friedan inhabited as a labor journalist. In the immediate postwar period, Soviet-American animosity, the early signs of which she had lamented while at Federated Press, became marked. By 1947, the die was cast. Those who shaped American foreign policy and public opinion envisioned a titanic struggle between freedom-loving Americans and expansive, totalitarian Soviets. Codified in the twin 1947 policies of the Truman Doctrine and the Marshall Plan, America's stance met with a decisive Soviet response. Soon after World War II ended, the USSR tightened its grip on Eastern Europe, which resulted in turn in the establishment of the North Atlantic Treaty Organization in 1949.[6]

The implications of the Cold War for life in America were grave. American anti-communism, alive in the 1930s and early 1940s, intensified after the war's end. Anti-communist sentiments were spurred by several factors, including Soviet expansion in Eastern Europe, the revelations in 1947 that atomic spies operated in the United States, the triumph of the Communists under Mao's leadership in China in 1949, and the Soviet explosion of an atomic bomb in the same year. In March 1947 Truman launched a program to screen federal employees in order to uncover evidence of possible disloyalty. The outbreak of the Korean War on June 25, 1950, intensified the hunt. In September, Congress passed the Internal Security Act, which required members of the party and of front organizations to register with the Department of Justice. More ominously, it enabled the federal government to intern Communists by declaring a national emergency.

A whole series of government investigations resulted in the dismissal of employees and the destruction of people's futures, without procedures to protect civil liberties that the Constitution supposedly guaranteed. What the Truman administration began, HUAC, the FBI, and McCarthy expanded. By the early 1950s the pattern was familiar: accusations, innuendos, guilt by association, naming names. For those who were not subject to its power, it is difficult to imagine the force and recklessness of McCarthyism in the late 1940s and 1950s. It ruined the lives of many Communists, ex-Communists, suspected Communists, fellow travelers, and Popular Front participants. People committed suicide, went into exile abroad or underground at home. Blacklisted writers were denied the ability to earn a living, though some of them found a friend under whose name they could publish. Investigators, authorized and unauthorized, haunted and pursued people they suspected of subversive or disloyal behavior—recording what they read or wrote, with whom they associated, and what organizations they joined.[7]

In response to McCarthyism, and to the impact of mass media, suburbs, and prosperity, a wave of conformity swept across much of the nation. Containment referred not only to American policy toward the USSR but also to what happened to aspirations at home. The results for women were especially unfortunate. Even though increasing numbers of them entered the work force, the Cold War linked anti-communism and the dampening of women's ambitions. The connection between women, anti-communism, and conformity appeared in many forums but, given Friedan's history, none more interesting than the graduation speech delivered at Smith College on June 6, 1955, by Adlai E. Stevenson, the once and future Democratic candidate for the presidency. "I want merely to tell you young ladies," he said to graduating seniors, including his future daughter-in-law, that there was much they could do "in a great historic crisis" America faced by assuming "the humble role of housewife—which," he added, "statistically, is what most of you are going to be whether you like the idea or not just now—and you'll like it!" With men dedicating themselves to specialized bureaucratic work in a nation engaged in a fight against a Soviet Union that suppressed individualism, it fell to women to restore value, integrity, and wholeness to American life. They could do this best by encouraging their children to be creative individualists. "History's pendulum," Stevenson remarked, referring to the title of Arthur M. Schlesinger Jr.'s liberal anti-communist 1949 book, "has swung dangerously far away from the individual, and you may, indeed you must, help to restore it to the vital center of its arc."[8]

In the years Friedan worked for *UE News,* women's issues burned brightly until, in most quarters, McCarthyism snuffed them out. Many aspects of feminism flourished right after the war. Friedan herself was one of many Popular Front leftists concerned with women's issues; more specifically, like Betty Millard from Barnard, Elizabeth Hawes from Vassar, and Sylvia Cohen Scribner from Smith, she was a Seven Sisters progressive, a feminist who had graduated from an elite women's college. Other types of feminism thrived among women workers, in industrial and service jobs, inside and outside of unions, both influenced by and independent of the Popular Front. Dorothy Sue Cobble, Nancy Gabin, and other historians have explored the richness of the activism of working women in the 1940s and 1950s. They experienced more fully than Friedan the force of racial and sexual discrimination, and dealt with the challenge of combining employment with the obligations of motherhood and domesticity earlier than their suburban counterparts from the 1950s on. Moreover, their stories illustrate that feminism had varied meanings in the period, but also that the flowering of a feminist consciousness in many instances occurred independent of the Popular Front and the Old Left.[9]

Like other social activists, women had reason in 1945 for cautious optimism. As discussed earlier, the Depression, New Deal legislation, and World War II had helped give them a more powerful position in government and the economy. At war's end they comprised a higher proportion of the labor force, 36 percent, than ever before. Almost three million were union members, with the strikes right after the war adding another half a million. During the war the National War Labor Board, responding to complaints by women in unions, including UE, had put its stamp of approval on the principle of equal pay for equal work.

Though the war's end meant that this decision was not implemented, in the immediate postwar period the struggle for justice for women seemed to be advancing. The federal Women's Bureau helped coordinate the efforts of women in unions to press their causes, including the fight for equal pay legislation. With the support of their unions, working-class women rejected the approach of largely elite, comfortable, and conservative advocates of the Equal Rights Amendment, and instead worked for equal pay for equal work, paid maternity leaves, higher minimum wages, and equal employment opportunities.[10]

Friedan was not the only person whose work on women's issues connected labor radicalism in the 1940s and feminism in the 1960s, though her 1963 book made her the most visible and influential one. Eleanor Flexner, who in 1959 published *Century of Struggle,* the first scholarly history of American women and a virtual bible for 1960s feminists, is another figure whose career links radicalism beginning in the 1930s with post-1960 feminism. In 1983 Flexner sent boxes of her papers to the Schlesinger Library. They contained copies of articles she wrote for the *Daily Worker,* evidence of her involvement with the Communist Party, a syllabus from a course she taught on "The Woman Question" at the Jefferson School in 1953–54, and data on her efforts to organize African American women into unions. This material, she said, showed "where some of the roots of the present lib movement came from—in my case, + that of many others—a phase in our development in the '30–40–50's, most of which I shed in the process of maturing, insofar as they reflected 'Marxist' thought." Then she added, "a biographer could also pursue the trail of a short-lived leftist organization, the Congress of American Women."[11]

The Congress of American Women, whose 1946 formation Friedan had helped announce in Federated Press, was the most important Popular Front organization of progressive women. It was the American branch of the Women's International Democratic Federation (WIDF). Among its most important leaders in the United States were women with strong left and historic feminist credentials. Nora Stanton Blatch Barney, active in the Congress, was a granddaughter of Elizabeth Cady Stanton and the daughter of Harriot Blatch. In 1946, Susan B. Anthony II, the grandniece of her namesake, wrote the Congress' "Report of the Commission on the Status of Women." Elizabeth Gurley Flynn, one of a dozen vice presidents, was a high ranking American official of the Communist Party, someone whose career was sparked by earlier involvement in the IWW. Claudia Jones, an African American, was a Harlem Party leader of the Congress. Goldstein knew the husband of Congress member Harriet Magil and probably Harriet herself. Dorothy Douglas, who taught Friedan about Marxism in 1940–41 at Smith, was a member of the Advisory Committee of the Congress. Ruth Young, the UE leader whom Friedan had interviewed in 1943, was another vice president. In the 1940s Gerda Lerner taught women's history under the auspices of the Los Angeles chapter of the Congress; in the 1960s she would emerge as a leading historian of American feminism. Eleanor Flexner did office work for the Congress and briefly chaired its editorial board. "With a sense of women's history rare for its time," writes the historian Amy Swerdlow (and a friend of Friedan's in the 1950s), the Congress "identified itself with women's democratic struggles in America," invoking the stories of Anne Hutchinson, the Lowell Mill girls, Sojourner Truth, Susan B. Anthony, and immigrant working women of the early twentieth century.[12]

Within twelve months of its founding, Congress leaders claimed a membership of a quarter million women in America's major industrial cities. Congress members set out to build a cross-class and racially integrated coalition of those who were fighting for peace and social justice. "More than any other feminist organization before or since," writes Swerdlow, who also acknowledges the difficulties in matching deeds with hopes, the Congress "made racial equality a central plank in its program and incorporated African American women in its leadership." Its members fought for price controls, tenant rights, equal pay, and government-sponsored day care, an end to lynching and racial discrimination, national health insurance, a central role for women in unions, and respectful representations of women in the media. In opposition to the Equal Rights Amendment, Congress members supported a more ambitious approach embodied in its Women's Status Bill, which combined protective legislation and the elimination of discrimination.[13]

Early on, membership and leadership of the Congress included women of varied political persuasions. Among its active members were Communists, as well as non-Communists who initially had no problem with the presence of Communists at a time when the party was legal and not yet discredited: wealthy women, suffrage leaders, prominent actresses and businesswomen, leading social scientists, and representatives of major Jewish organizations. Moreover, the male-dominated party leadership never gave the Congress its wholehearted support and Congress members developed feminist positions more fully and forcefully than the party itself. As time went on the persecution of the Congress resulted in a self-fulfilling phenomenon as redbaiters drove frightened liberals away from the Congress and strengthened the resolve and power of party members and others who remained.

In the world of progressive and labor feminism familiar to Friedan in the late 1940s and early 1950s, including the Congress of American Women, women's issues were widely debated, providing key concepts, language, and tools of analysis that would shape what she wrote in *The Feminine Mystique*. The historian Kathleen A. Weigand has captured the full range of these arguments among progressive feminists. Nowhere was the nature of these discussions clearer than in the 1948–49 essays of Millard, a writer for *New Masses* and Anthony's successor as chair of the Commission on the Status of Women of the Congress. Her two articles were designed to commemorate the one-hundredth anniversary of both the Seneca Falls Convention and the publication of the Communist Manifesto. She displayed a full sense of American women's history, stressing how women—within the Abolitionist, labor, and women's rights movements—had fought for their own liberation. There was nothing exceptional in much of what Millard wrote, especially her reliance on the Marxist analysis of Friedrich Engels and her celebration of the gains women had made in the USSR.[14]

What was remarkable was her expansive, probing exploration of women's situation. Millard paid special attention to how African Americans and women engaged in the same struggle for equality. Rape, she asserted, had its parallels in racist attacks on African Americans and Jews. She acknowledged that there was a difference between what women and Jews experienced. Women as women had not "been murdered by the millions in death camps." Moreover, she wrote, with considerable naïveté, that "in most countries, wife-beating is no longer good form." Millard recognized at least one critical difference between what African Americans and women faced. Unlike African Americans who were "isolated in ghettos," women "live in intimate daily relationships with the 'superior' sex, a relationship," she noted, "infinitely complex and entangled with biological, economic and social factors." Millard took issue with those who felt women had won their fight for equality. She wrote that even male chauvinism affected "many otherwise progressive men" who "cling to their vested interest in male superiority." In making her case, she pointed to "a quieter, more veiled kind of lynching" directed against women. Housewives, she asserted, "are doomed to circumscribed, petty lives, to the stultification of whatever abilities and interests, outside of motherhood, they may have had."[15]

She also emphasized the discrimination that wage-earning women faced. With the war over and employers wanting to justify paying women less by treating their employment as temporary, she noted, propagandists now told women that their place was "in the Küche with the Kinder." The full range of "economics, religion, customs, taboos" imposed "conflicting roles and wishes on women." She looked forward to a time when motherhood was no longer exhausting, "when it will no longer be necessary for any woman to refer to herself as merely 'a housewife.'"[16]

Like other feminists on the left in the period, Millard explored how a wide range of forces—not just economic ones—kept women subjugated. Focusing on psychological factors, she wondered out loud about what discrimination against women did to their sense of themselves. She examined how some women internalized a sense of inferiority and dependence. She sharply criticized Ferdinand Lundberg and Marynia Farnham's *Modern Woman: The Lost Sex* (1947) for using Freudian concepts such as penis envy and the female castration complex to undermine women's aspirations. (She might also have pointed out how Lundberg and Farnham had disparaged feminism by linking it to the Soviet Union. They asserted that "the political agents of the Kremlin abroad continue to beat the feminist drums in full awareness of its disruptive influence among the potential enemies of the Soviet Union." Specifically, they cited the WIDF as a group that would "probably continue to promote the theories of feminism and what it can of neurotic disorder.")[17]

In pursuing non-economic forms of oppression, Millard analyzed how language—such as the generalized use of the word man or the equation of "a four-letter word relating to sex" with aggression—reinforced patterns of exploitation and fostered in girls and women a sense of inferiority. She also explored how the world's most influential religions helped to subordinate women. To counter the powers arrayed against them, Millard asserted, women "must continue to be a major force in their own liberation" but they could "move ahead only in common action with the working class," in a way shaped by "Marxist understanding" and the union movement. At home, men and women had to share household chores. In the political arena, women had to fight for price control, fair rents, "the rights of the doubly-oppressed Negro women," day care centers, protective legislation, and equal pay. In the end, Millard linked these specifics with her larger goal of a socialism that would end exploitation and "make it possible for women to achieve real equality."[18]

Like Millard, Elizabeth Hawes was a Popular Front feminist. In addition to her book *Why Women Cry* (1943), which Friedan had hailed as signaling a revolution starting in American kitchens, in 1946 she published *Hurry Up Please*. In this book, which was well known in Friedan's world and echoed many of Friedan's experiences in the UE, Hawes recounted her own work with the United Automobile Workers (UAW). As a union organizer Hawes learned firsthand about sex discrimination, sexual harassment, racism, and anti-communism in the UAW. Like Friedan, she found Walter Reuther's leadership timid. "If one believed in getting the union work done," Hawes wrote, staking out her political position amidst tension in the UAW between party members and anti-communists, "one preferred the Communists to the Red-Baiters." Hawes made it clear that she preferred what she called "Common Communists," who like many party members active in the UE focused on practical issues, to "Catechismic Communists," who were always dragging in ideological and international issues. Like Friedan, Hawes rejected the plans of the National Association of Manufacturers (NAM) and other "capitalist-fascists" for postwar America. Moreover, Hawes announced her own preference for socialism.[19]

As her biographer has noted, in *Anything But Love* (1948), "fifteen years before Friedan's *The Feminine Mystique,* Hawes was debunking some basic American myths: the Happy Housewife and Greater Consumption as the Answer to Everything." Hawes examined how the media, especially the women's magazines and advertisers, prescribed the way women should lead their lives. Hawes intended her book as a critique of Philip Wylie's *Generation of Vipers* (1942) and Lundberg and Farnham's *Modern Woman: The Lost Sex.* Her research revealed the imposing challenges women faced. The media advised adolescent girls to aspire to standards of beauty and decorum they could not possibly attain. Because they were in such a prosperous nation where most people lived comfortably, magazines and advertisements insisted, women entered the work force principally to meet men; after age twenty-three, all women except actresses could stop working outside the home because, with their husbands supporting them, they could best achieve fulfillment through home, children, and marriage. Once married, writers in the mass media insisted, the essential task of the woman was to accumulate a full range of household goods through which she would achieve happiness. If a woman grew unhappy, it was her own fault and something remedied by redoubling her energy on the home. Hawes noted a major change when women were thirty-five, roughly the age of Friedan when she began to work on *The Feminine Mystique*. No longer important as a consumer, a married woman could quietly reverse all the rules she had lived by, even to the point of seeing the "family as a biological vice and a psychological crime."[20]

What Millard and Hawes wrote, as Weigand has demonstrated, other Popular Front feminists restated and elaborated on. Anti-fascists, they castigated reactionaries at home and abroad for advocating what Flynn in April 1947 called "Hitler's 3 K's For Woman," which she saw echoed in Lundberg and Farnham's book. Flexner looked at the relationship between anti-feminism and the fascism that led to the extermination of Jews by the Nazis. Popular Front feminists considered the special problems faced by African American and Latina women at the same time that they explored the relationship between class and race in an oppressive system. Over time, they adopted the position that all women, not just those who were working class, were oppressed. Consequently they stressed the importance of women coming together on the basis of common gender experiences. Struggling with the thorny issues of the dynamics of sexism in public and private realms, they focused on the connection between larger structural changes and their personal relationships. They countered the power of what they called "male chauvinism," even when it appeared among radical men.[21]

Progressive feminists explored the dynamics of discrimination against women in a variety of settings, including the family and work place. The debates over sex discrimination and what Flexner at the time called "male supremacist ideology" reverberated in a number of major unions and in the Communist Party. Feminists worked to remove sexist language and photographs from party publications, especially in its coverage of beauty contests and its columns of household hints. They emphasized the role of dress, literature, movies, and language in promoting a sense of women's inferiority. For several years beginning in 1952, as Weigand has shown, they participated "in the earliest American movement towards natural childbirth practices that empowered women and encouraged the participation of husbands." As Friedan did throughout her feminist career, Popular Front feminists asserted that the liberation of women would come through the democratization of household work and government-sponsored child care, which would ease the burdens that had fallen so heavily on women's shoulders.[22]

The call for easing the burden of housewives was a common refrain. In a 1947 poem titled "Occupation: Housewife," published in *New Masses*, a magazine in which articles by Friedan had recently appeared, Eve Merriam talked about how her dreams went down the kitchen drain and how her efforts to keep her home spotless evoked in her feelings of anguish and despair. In the same year, Vivian Howard wrote an article for *New Masses* that criticized the women's magazines for glorifying the work housewives had to do. She concluded her article on a skeptical note. "I'm glad that I have found these real answers to real problems," she noted ironically, "right alongside of those splendiferous ads for washing machines, canned soups, linoleum, silverware, and refrigerators." Yet though they understood the double burden carried by women who worked inside and outside the home, the primary hope of progressive feminists for women's liberation was through their entry into the paid work force.[23]

It is important not to exaggerate the receptivity of the Communist Party and the Old Left to women's issues. Feminists continually encountered male chauvinism in the party. As a woman wrote to *The Worker* in 1946, her husband "could give an excellent lecture on the necessity to emancipate women," but would never help his wife at home with housekeeping, cooking, and child care. Many party members, men especially, took culturally conservative positions on the role of women, seeing them as sentimental mothers rather than as people fully capable of intellectual and political activity. Communist publications frequently contained banal love stories as well as advice on food preparation and the use of cosmetics. As the historian Rosalyn Baxandall demonstrates, Communist theoreticians considered women's rights a bourgeois concern. In a male-dominated organization where feminist voices were heard principally at the grass roots level, Weigand has noted, women's issues were often submerged within larger discussions of class, workers, the factory, and oppression. Although the party was willing to recognize the need for African Americans to organize as a group, at key moments it did not feel the women's situation was significant enough to encourage them to organize in separate units around issues of importance to them. Though in 1943 half of the party members were women, they occupied few positions of power in the party. After World War II ended some party leaders told women to make way for men in the factories by returning to their domestic roles. Even Elizabeth Gurley Flynn asserted, according to Baxandall, that NAM "took women more seriously" than CPUSA.[24]

Several months after Goldstein began working at *UE News*, Fred Zeserson, another labor reporter and a long-time friend of Carl Friedan, introduced her to the man she would soon marry. She met Carl around the time she moved to a bare-bones basement apartment on West 86th Street on Manhattan's Upper West Side. Carl was handsome, funny, Jewish, charming, and sociable. He had returned from the war in Europe where he had organized dramatic productions for the troops. Back in the United States, he set out on a career in theater, staging summer stock and experimental productions. In June 1947, nine months after their first date, Carl and Betty married in a civil ceremony in City Hall. Several months later, at the urging of Carl's mother, a rabbi presided over a Jewish ceremony in Boston. The wedding announcement told of the marriage of Carl Fried̲man and Betty Goldstein. Perhaps out of a desire to make his name sound less Jewish, albeit not unambiguously so, Carl had already dropped the "m," but used it on the wedding announcement directed to his parents' friends.[25]

Betty Friedan, age twenty-six at the time, entered the marriage with both hope and trepidation. She had what she later called a "pathological fear of being alone." While still at Smith, before a *McCall's* editor coined the word, she wrote that "marriage means togetherness." Since she was a child, she longed to develop a sense of wholeness through a heterosexual union, a desire intensified by watching many of her friends marry. Carl, she recalled, "made her feel not alone." As Friedan later wrote, "he brought me an apple and told me jokes which made me laugh." Whatever he brought to the romance and marriage, Carl was hardly the husband Friedan had long imagined. He did not share her dream of an egalitarian marriage, her aspirations to combine career and family, or her political passions. Her conventional longings, never in abeyance but always in tension with her radicalism, once again played themselves out, this time bolstered by the postwar resurgence of what she later called the feminine mystique.[26]

Friedan began her work for *UE News* with optimism. While postwar developments were dampening nationwide hopes for radical social change, in the UE, the flame stayed bright for a while. Then McCarthyism, combined with her disillusionment with radical movements, dimmed Friedan's hopes as well. At least as early as 1943, when she wrote the article about Ruth Young, Friedan was well aware of the UE's commitments to the advancement of working women. At Federated Press, she had done several other stories on the UE. In August 1945, even before she began to work at the *UE News*, she placed in her files an article published there entitled "Reactionary Propaganda Exposed: Survey Discovers—Women Must Work!" The story revealed that the overwhelming majority of women in the UE wanted to keep on working in factories after the war. Moreover, her job with the UE kept her well within the New York world of left-wing journalism. For example, in the summer of 1947 Betty and Carl shared a house with the families of James Aronson and Cedric Belfrage, who were key figures in the founding the next year of the *National Guardian*. At day's end, they all sat on the porch and discussed what would soon emerge as the most influential radical newspaper of the period and one at the center of the resistance to the Cold War.[27]

In the 1940s, according to historian Ronald Schatz, the UE was "the largest Communist-led institution of any kind in the United States." In his authoritative book on the CIO, the historian Robert Zieger states the UE was "the only effectively led large pro-Soviet affiliate" of the CIO in the postwar years. Though members of the CPUSA held important leadership positions at the UE, the percentage of people in the UE rank and file who were party members as well was not very high. Moreover, as Zieger has remarked, "the line between party members and allied activists was unclear." As UE historians Ronald L. Filippelli and Mark D. McColloch have demonstrated, the relationship between the UE and the Communist Party was not always smooth, with their representatives often working at cross purposes on key issues. Secrecy, tactical considerations, and shifts in national and international politics all influenced whether a person sympathetic to the CPUSA and, more generally, to the issues it fought for would actually join the party. Yet to many observers, the fight over Communist influence in unions like the UE involved compelling issues. "To be a Communist, or even to be a consistent ally and defender of Communists," Zieger writes, "was to link yourself to Stalinism. It meant that you either denied Soviet crimes that killed and imprisoned millions or you justified them." As the UE activist and labor historian David Montgomery has pointed out, the worst years of McCarthyite attacks on civil liberties in the United States—1949 to 1952—coincided with a period when the USSR's leaders were themselves using trumped up charges to clamp down on dissidents.[28]

In the immediate postwar period, Zieger has written, the UE, like other Communist-led unions, made "positive responses to the distinctive problems of minority and female workers." As Gerald Zahavi has demonstrated for Schenectady, party members in the UE pressed their fight against what they called "white chauvinism" and "male chauvinism," or what later generations would call racism and sexism. The situation of blacks was especially precarious. Wartime conditions had significantly increased the numbers of African Americans in the UE. Laid off disproportionately during the 1948–49 recession because of the seniority system that many saw as having racist implications, African Americans assumed a significant burden of the costs of postwar conversion. The UE established local Fair Employment Practices Committees and addressed racial discrimination by pressing issues in contract negotiations. Party members adopted a more radical position that had limited influence on the UE. Torn by internal divisions, challenged by African American members who were angry over the existence of racism in the union and the party, and threatened by a rising tide of anti-communism in the nation, the party called on its supporters in the labor movement to fight for racial justice. In 1949–50, in an effort to reverse patterns of racial discrimination, party activists advocated the automatic granting of several years of seniority to all African Americans as compensation for their years of exclusion from the electrical industry. In the end, fearful white workers opposed any change in the seniority system. Caught up in a fight against anti-communists, union officials associated with the Communist Party did not press the case for special seniority rights for African Americans.[29]

Against considerable resistance from within the union, as the historian Lisa Kannenberg and others have shown, the UE also worked to improve the conditions of working-class women, in part by countering a seniority system that gave advantage to men. During World War II, the UE had a "strong ideological commitment to gender equality," according to historian Ruth Milkman. After the war, women in the union lost much of what they recently gained even, ironically, in the factories of GE and Westinghouse that produced home appliances and electronics for which women were the primary consumers. The situation in the UE varied considerably, depending in large part on local dynamics. Yet in important cases, many men associated with the UE, including many union staff members, had no commitment to protect women's newly won gains. UE members fought over issues such as the rights to seniority claimed by returning vets; the competing interests of married and single women; and the opposition between social activists and traditionalists who represented the white, working-class, often Roman Catholic men. Yet if some activists pioneered in articulating what we might call affirmative action for African Americans, before and during World War II, like women in a wide range of unions and within the Women's Bureau, they also advocated what a later generation would label comparable worth.[30]

A number of Friedan's experiences, including her work for the UE, clarify her identity as a Popular Front feminist, shaped her political development and contributed in crucial ways to her post-1960 outlook. When in 1976 she spoke of participating in the late 1940s in the "dangerous politics of the world revolution whose vanguard we used to fancy ourselves," she came as close as she could to acknowledging her proximity to and identification with the party-oriented left. At least from 1940 until 1953 she inhabited a world where Communists and their sympathizers held influential positions, where she witnessed redbaiting, and where she encountered the ideology of American Communists, especially in their Popular Front appeals.[31]

Specific political affiliation was not important; what was critical was commitment to a broad range of issues within the framework of a fight for social justice. As Flexner said of her own work beginning in the 1930s, left-wing movements welcomed "an enormous latitude of opinions and under a very broad umbrella." The end of the Cold War makes it possible to look at the left in the 1940s without the agendas of an earlier era. What impresses now is the rich variety of Friedan's associates during the 1940s and early 1950s: pacifists, socialists, union activists, party members, and fighters for justice for African Americans and women. Friedan's writings for the UE from 1946 to 1952 reveal that, unlike her earlier work at Federated Press, in print she now rarely if ever focused on the Soviet Union or on American-Soviet relations. While at *UE News,* Popular Front ideology continued to shape the way she viewed American society and politics.[32]

As a member of the staff of the *UE News,* Friedan worked at the union's national office located in a large town house at 11 East 51st Street, facing the north side of St. Patrick's Cathedral. A man known as the Granite King had built the mansion, which members of the Astor family later owned. The site was symbolically charged, combining a thumbing of the nose not only at the robber barons but also at the Roman Catholic Church. As a writer in *New Masses* noted in 1946, "the building might symbolically appear to some as a slender outpost of the people against the time when all the Granite Kings are dethroned, and all the costly handiwork of plain men and women is wrested from the few and reverts to the many." Tommy Wright, editor of the *UE News* from its founding until his retirement in 1967, headed the staff. In the early 1930s, he had lost his job at the *Schenectady Gazette* after he tried to organize a local branch of the Newspaper Guild. One of the reporters was Katherine Beecher, who was married to Wright and whom Friedan had known at Federated Press. Another writer was James Lerner, whose father was a socialist and a worker and who himself had to leave college because of the Depression. A member of the Lincoln Brigade in the Spanish Civil War and active in the peace movement in the 1930s, Lerner began more than forty years of work on the editorial board of the *UE News* in 1940, six years before Friedan joined the staff.[33]

Friedan's work for the UE underscored the central contradiction in her class position and helps explain the political trajectory of her life. In 1976, in the same sentence in which she said she considered herself "part of the vanguard of the working-class revolution," she wrote how she and her friends spent their salaries "on clothes at Bergdorf's, replacing our college Braemar sweaters with black cashmere and Gucci gloves, on sale." Unlike many of the union officials and writers with whom she worked and all of the workers about whom she wrote, Betty Friedan had no familial connection to the labor movement. At times, women on the picket line looked skeptically at the well-dressed Friedan. Writer Milton Meltzer, who knew Friedan in these years, remarks that the UE "liked her reporting, though they could see she had never worked in a factory but was a middle-class woman." She was aware that she learned more as a reporter than from firsthand experience as a worker or activist. She did not discover the force of corporate and state power through long hours in a noisy factory or on the receiving end of a police officer's nightstick. Yet Meltzer makes clear that "she began to understand, to feel what a worker's life was like."[34]

As at Federated Press, at the UE Friedan was a dramatic figure. "She bubbled over with energy," Meltzer has written, "talked in spurts, rarely finishing a sentence, her mind racing so fast the words couldn't keep up with it." She covered the picket lines on which strikers marched, the bargaining sessions of labor and management, the impact of strikes on workers and their families. "What are your skills?" she would ask an electrical worker in a factory. "What pay do you earn? Is it enough to take care of yourself and your family?" She commented that "It was no nine-to-five job, but a cause. Our pay was never more," she accurately noted, "than what the workers on the line got." Praising heroic workers who struggled against great odds as they fought monopolies (and probably expressing her expectations for herself), Friedan extolled the skills of a writer "who is able to describe with sincerity and passion the hopes, the struggle and the romance of the working people who make up most of America."[35]

The articles Friedan and others published in the *UE News* in the late 1940s and early 1950s open a world unfamiliar to those who think that in this period Americans heard only hosannas to democratic capitalism and American exceptionalism. The villains of the publication were Truman, Hubert H. Humphrey, Nixon, Walter Reuther, HUAC, and American capitalists. The heroes included Wallace, Roosevelt, and union leaders who fought to protect the rights and lives of working people. Above all, the paper celebrated ordinary workers, including women and African Americans, who found themselves engaged in a class struggle against greedy corporations and opportunistic politicians.

At *UE News*, as a middle-class woman covering the struggles of the working class, Friedan continued to articulate a progressive position on a wide range of issues. In one of her first pieces, she used a review of Howard Fast's *The American* to hold out the hope that the CIO had given "the people . . . a power of their own to match that of their bosses." As she had done at the Federated Press, she pointed to concerted efforts, led by big corporations under the leadership of NAM, "riding high in the knowledge that they now control U.S. government policy," to increase profits, exploit labor, and break labor unions. In 1951, she published a piece in *March of Labor* in which she criticized those leaders of the AFL and CIO who agreed to stabilize incomes during the Korean War, as they called for "'equality of sacrifice'" and appeared to Friedan to agree that America faced a "'problem of excess purchasing power.'" To prove her point, Friedan contrasted the extravagant expenditures of the wealthy (for example, an "heiress to an armaments fortune bought $6,000 worth of southern resort clothes in one hour in a swanky Fifth Avenue dress-shop") with a family of a Westinghouse worker who could afford neither fresh vegetables nor new clothes. Friedan also told of how valiant union members helped build political coalitions to fight congressional and corporate efforts to roll back gains workers made during the New Deal and World War II.[36]

As a writer for the UE News Friedan took a consistently radical stance on issues. Covering the founding meeting of the Progressive Party in Philadelphia in 1948 for the UE News, she hailed the event as one that highlighted how Wallace and his followers differed from the political mainstream. She pointed out how many of the delegates were workers, women, and African Americans. Elsewhere she exposed the existence of racism and discrimination, especially when directed against Jews and African Americans. In September 1947, she descried "the morality of one bill of rights for people whose skin is white and another for those with black skin, one kind of jobs for whites and another for black; streets to live on, schools, hotels, polling places, places to fish and camp—open to all Americans who can pay the price or pass the examination—except to Americans whose skin is black." In November 1947, she reviewed the movie "Gentleman's Agreement," which dealt with the issue of anti-Semitism among respectable people. She asserted that prejudice suffused American society, from the wealthy, to Jews themselves, and to union workers and officials as well. She excoriated "racial discrimination as a festering sore under the surface of democracy." She reminded her readers of the movie's message that racism was un-American and something they had to fight in their own lives in order to counter "the reactionary pattern that is fascism."[37]

Friedan articulated progressive positions on other issues. In 1947, she reported on a HUAC investigation into Communist influence in Hollywood. She used the case of a "storm-trooper with a southern accent" who harassed the playwright Bertholt Brecht to draw parallels between America in the 1940s and Nazi Germany in the 1930s. She made clear that powerful forces, led by HUAC and supported by big business, were redbaiting. Using Brecht's case as an example, she lamented that someone who had fled Nazi Germany in order to gain freedom to speak was now facing precisely such restrictions. She revealed how competing unions, HUAC, NAM, and supporters of the Taft-Hartley act were using every tactic they could to destroy the UE.[38]

In her years at the UE, she and Carl Friedan started their family and moved out of Manhattan. In late 1948, just before the defeat of Wallace, she took a maternity leave from her editorial work on the *UE News* to have Daniel, the first of three children. Soon Carl, Betty, and their son moved to a four-and-one-half-room garden apartment in Parkway Village, Queens, a distinctively cosmopolitan community full of other young married couples with children, where the Friedans lived from 1950 to 1956. After a maternity leave of almost a year, with only six weeks paid and cut short by a month to accommodate someone else's vacation schedule, Friedan resumed her career in 1949 using most of her earnings to pay for child care.[39]

Throughout her years at the *UE News* and while her personal life was changing so significantly, Friedan continued to participate in discussions on women's issues, including systematic corporate discrimination against women. She went to factories to interview working women she wrote about, including African Americans and Latinas. In February 1947 she stated that what she reported about the prices housewives paid was "based not on statistics or wishful thinking but day-to-day experience in the grocery store with a limited amount of money to spend and a constant number of mouths to feed." Moreover, for the people around Friedan and doubtlessly for Friedan herself, the fight for justice for women was inseparable from the more general struggle to secure rights for African Americans and workers. As she had done at the Federated Press, at the *UE News* she reported on how working women struggled as producers and consumers to make sure their families had enough to live on. She began one article with a statement from a Latina: "Sometimes I think women need a union even more than men because the boss tries to take advantage of women more, but it's got to be a union that really fights for women the same as men." In 1951, she announced the enthusiastic response of union women to the UE's determination to fight for its female members as part of its opposition to "job discrimination against women."[40]

Friedan's focus on working women culminated in her writing *UE Fights for Women Workers,* published by the UE in June 1952. She began the thirty-nine-page pamphlet by identifying the contradiction in industry's treatment of women as consumers and as producers. She noted that in their advertisements, electrical manufacturers glorified "the American woman—in her gleaming GE kitchen, at her Westinghouse laundromat, before her Sylvania television set. Nothing," she announced insightfully, "is too good for her—unless" she worked for the corporations that produced these very goods.[41]

The central theme of the piece was how, in an effort to improve the pay and conditions of working women, the UE fought valiantly against greedy corporations that sought to increase their profits by exploiting women.

Friedan discussed the landmark 1945 National War Labor Board decision on sex-based wage discrimination in favor of the UE. She touched on other issues as well. Remarking that *"fighting the exploitation of women is men's business too,"* she emphasized how discriminatory practices corporations used against women hurt men as well by exerting downward pressure on wages of all workers. To support the call for equal pay for equal work and to fight discrimination against women, she countered stereotypes justifying lower pay for women: that they were physically weaker, entered the work force only temporarily, had no families to support, and worked only for pin money. She highlighted the "even more shocking" situation African American women faced, having to deal with the "double bars" of being female and African American. Friedan set forth a program that was, Kannenberg has noted, "a prescription for a gender-blind workplace."[42]

Friedan's interest in working women did not end with the publication of this pamphlet. For a brief period after she left the *UE News*, she worked as a free-lance labor journalist. In 1953, she authored another pamphlet for the UE, *Women Fight For a Better Life! UE Picture Story of Women's Role in American History.* Here she used photographs and texts to provide the social, economic, and political dimensions of the story of how over the centuries American women had fought against discrimination and for peace, justice, and equality. She paid special attention to the role of African American women (who encountered "double discrimination"), working-class women, middle-class reformers, and unions. She emphasized the "double task of housework as well as shop work" that female factory workers undertook. "Faced with growing monopoly strength of the corporations," she noted, women joined unions to fight for their rights as they campaigned for improved working conditions, higher wages, and child care.[43]

In May 1953, Friedan carefully tracked and probably participated in a UE-sponsored conference on women's issues. There she followed discussions of the importance of men sharing household duties with their wives. She also heard of the efforts of profit-hungry corporations to control the working class by emphasizing divisions between whites and African Americans as well as between men and women. She again learned of the union's advocacy of federal legislation to lower military expenditures and support programs for child care, maternity benefits, and equal pay.[44]

In fundamental ways, Friedan's association with the labor movement gave her a thorough education in issues concerning women's work and sexual discrimination. Her years at Federated Press and the *UE News* served as a bridge between what she had learned about women at Smith—from Dorothy Douglas and from the organizing maids—and what she would write about in *The Feminine Mystique.* Because the UE remained committed in principle to gender equality, Friedan's years there may well have provided a positive inspiration.

Yet Friedan's work as a labor journalist also taught her about the power of male chauvinism. The historian Nancy Palmer has explored how, during the postwar period, the UE's commitment to gender equality became harder to sustain when the union faced threats from the International Union of Electrical, Radio and Machine Workers (IUE), corporations, and HUAC. Management, in an effort to win the loyalty of male workers, grew less sympathetic to women's concerns. Especially after the war, corporations evoked the image of woman as lesbian and prostitute in order to undermine the grievances of women workers. GE, for example, in an effort to reverse the gains women had made, appealed to male workers by linking masculinity with loyalty and cooperation. Despite or because of the wartime gains of women in the work force, corporations and unions emphasized how women were illegitimately crossing the boundaries into the male world. During and immediately after the war, at a time when almost forty percent of the UE members were women, many visual and verbal representations of workers underscored the maleness of the typical laborer and held up for admiration white, heterosexual, and feminine versions of womanhood.[45]

HUAC also used a gendered language as it conflated women, homosexuality, Communism, and progressive politics. Witnesses before HUAC often pictured strong women as betrayers, with union men too weak to stop their disloyal behavior. The move to circumscribe women's power and advancement, Palmer has argued, did not come solely from corporations and government. Women in the UE on the local level often faced difficulties when they articulated their grievances but were told, in the name of solidarity, not to rock the boat. When women applied to become union organizers, union officials sometimes responded by limiting the scope of women's activity, insisting on the centrality of maleness in the definition of labor solidarity. As a result, union women learned the limitations they faced when trying to redefine what it meant to be a woman and union activist. Women who were married, had children, and hoped to become union organizers encountered resistance from union men as they struggled to combine work and family.

However positive the UE experience was for her, Friedan also concluded from her union work that radical organizations could not live up to their vision of a just and egalitarian society. A feminist who knew Friedan well in the 1950s recently remarked that half a century later she still suffered the pain of disappointment with the failure of the social movements of the 1940s that had held such promise for her. Indeed, in the mid-1950s, Friedan privately acknowledged her own disillusionment with the inability of the left, including Communists, to develop an adequate response on women's issues. She believed that the *Daily Worker's* special section devoted to women's issues was hardly an improvement over what publications such as *Ladies' Home Journal* offered. Active in radical organizations that articulated a vision of a just and egalitarian society, she believed she experienced discrimination firsthand. At both the Federated Press and the *UE News,* she lost her jobs to men who had more seniority, a policy question that the UE had struggled with since at least the early 1940s. Her disappointment was neither the first nor the last: in the women's movements during the mid-nineteenth century and the 1960s, women's hopes for gender justice were raised and then dashed.[46]

The conditions under which Friedan left Federated Press and *UE News,* although not entirely clear, nonetheless profoundly shaped her views on how to achieve justice for women. Her accounts of these events offer hints of what she understood firsthand, the persistence of male chauvinism. Friedan later claimed that she lost her job at the UE when she was pregnant with Jonathan, her second child, because the union failed to honor its commitment to maternity leaves. She claimed that when she went to her unit of the Newspaper Guild, she was told, "It's your fault for getting pregnant."[47]

There are, however, other versions of the incident. In 1956, Friedan said she had left full-time employment because it was too difficult to combine it with the obligations that came with the birth of Jonathan in 1952. In the 1980s, after telling readers that her mother had quit her job as an editor of the society page for a Peoria newspaper, Friedan said she felt "almost relieved when I was fired" in 1952. What actually happened is complicated and not entirely clear. With a second child on the way and a preschooler at home, issues of mothering and child care, along with the powerful cultural messages about maternal obligations, made it difficult for even the most politically resolute women to sustain activism and careers. Two unions were involved, the Guild, which she claims did not protect her, and the UE, her employer with the pregnancy leave policy, which she believes did not live up to its obligations.[48]

By the early 1950s, with McCarthyism having dramatically reduced the membership of the UE, the union had to cut its staff. Union leaders laid off the two women—Friedan and Beecher. On the face of it, and to someone concerned with patterns of sex discrimination, letting the two women go and keeping the two men seems a clear act of discrimination. Perhaps it was. In the case of Beecher, the situation was complicated. Because Wright and Beecher were married and Wright had seniority, union leaders felt it would be wrong to protect Beecher's job. That meant that the choice was between Friedan and Lerner. Someone familiar with the situation has written that Friedan "offered to quit" so Lerner, a man with seniority, could remain at the

UE News. At an internal hearing before Ernest Thompson, an African American who was head of the UE's Fair Practice Committee, the UE's director of research Nathan Spero objected to Friedan's being let go, arguing that she was the lone woman left on the paper's staff.[49]

If Friedan lost her job at the UE because of her pregnancy, then her work on the UE pamphlet had a special and timely poignancy. Her experience with unions provided both a positive inspiration and a negative spur to her feminism. She was indebted to the UE for major contributions to her education regarding gender equity, sex discrimination, and other women's issues. Well before the publication of *The Feminine Mystique,* her involvement in unions taught her a great deal about the problems women faced. Friedan's commitment to women's rights, her disillusionment with unions, the contradictions of her own class position, her longings to be in the mainstream, and McCarthyism were key factors in her shifting, over time, from Popular Front feminism that focused on working-class women to middle-class suburban feminism.[50]

Above all, Friedan's union experience underscores an important and neglected aspect of postwar history. Focusing on men, scholars have seen disillusionment with radicalism in general and with Communism specifically as a result of major public events such as the Nazi-Soviet Pact, the Moscow Trials, or the revelations of Stalin's atrocities. For women, disillusionment emerged in different contexts. Many were mothers struggling to establish their careers with little support from their husbands or from institutions, including radical organizations. Consequently they were more vulnerable than men. It was, above all, the failure of the left to match promises with deeds that made some feminists recognize the inadequacies of radicalism. Their disillusionment was usually linked not to public events such as a Stalinist treaty or Nikita Khrushchev's denunciation of Stalin, but to more personal moments such as the denial of a leadership position to a woman, or the failure of radical men to support childbirth and parenting. It is possible to call into question the specific details of Friedan's stories of the loss of her jobs at Federated Press and *UE News.* Yet it is nonetheless clear that she identified a real problem experienced by many feminists of her generation—male chauvinism among men ideologically committed to equality.

The conditions surrounding Friedan's departure from the *UE News* had considerable implications for her future. At the UE she knew the way progressives, including radicals, African Americans, and union women, contended with the traditional base of the UE—white, ethnic men. She lost her job at a time when the UE suffered a steep decline in membership as a result of McCarthyism. In response, precisely when Friedan lost her job, the national leadership of the UE committed itself to special initiatives on issues concerning African Americans and women.[51]

In this situation, Friedan may have had highly charged personal feelings of betrayal, and on many levels: by the working-class women who were going over to the IUE, the CIO union competing with the UE, and by the leaders of the UE whose egalitarian ideology did not prevent her from losing her job when she was pregnant. Moreover, Friedan was disappointed as she watched workers, in whom she had put so much faith, engage in what seemed to her a chase after consumer goods and aspiration to social mobility. In her *UE News* articles she had commended the desire of workers and their families for a higher standard of living, but she had always placed that dream within the context of a larger social transformation. Eventually she came to feel that workers who wanted consumer goods had given up their larger dream. "The working class wanted those pressure cookers, too," she remarked in 1976, as she articulated a feeling some other radicals in the union movement felt.[52]

Such a statement reveals her uninterrogated sense of class privilege and the limits of her commitment to being in the vanguard of the revolution. Her disappointment or sense of betrayal belies her claim to have understood the lives of those whom she celebrated as a journalist. Her reaction recalls what she had learned at Smith from James Gibson on the value of propaganda. In addition, her belief that workers were so readily participating in the postwar consumer boom exaggerates the extent to which they actually did so. In a widely read 1957 article, Harvey Swados, whom Friedan knew when she was working on her 1963 book, warned about the tendency of "articulate middle-class intellectuals" to subscribe to what he called "The Myth of the Happy Worker." The myth, said Swados, perpetuated the benighted notion that the common worker produced and consumed like his more fortunate white-collar counterparts. This view, he asserted, relied not on firsthand experience but on "contempt for people, based perhaps on self-contempt and on a feeling among intellectuals that the worker has let them down." Friedan's turn away from the working class resembles the way C. Wright Mills, whom she also knew in the late 1950s, turned away from the "labor metaphysic" that made Marxist radicals persist in thinking that the working class was "the most important agency" of a revolution against capitalism.[53]

When she left her position at the *UE News* in 1952, Betty Friedan would never again have a long-term paid job with an organization. It was a rough time for her. The loss of her job threatened the household's economy. Carl, in an effort to increase and stabilize the family's income, eventually switched from running a theater to starting his own public relations and advertising firm. With the birth in 1952 of Jonathan, issues of child care and an egalitarian household became urgent. As we shall see in a later chapter, at this point she grew doubtful about her abilities as a writer and thrashed about over issues of identity and career.[54]

Friedan's writings on women, never her only concern from 1943 to 1952, bracketed her work on union issues. She was hardly a lone woman struggling in the dark for a language to describe the conditions women faced. Rather, her writings for Federated Press, the *UE News*, and later for middle-class audiences, provide evidence of her participation in the discussions among progressive feminists of the "woman problem." Her pamphlets for the UE reiterated themes—the historic struggles of women, the aspirations of female workers, and the dangers of sex discrimination—that other Popular Front and labor feminists had debated. Friedan knew of some of these discussions in Old Left publications. One of the articles she wrote at Federated Press had appeared in the *Daily Worker*, and she made clear that she had tracked its coverage of women. In 1945–46, Friedan published two articles in *New Masses*, where important feminist pieces appeared. Its editor, Abe Magil, referring to her as Betty in a letter, said how highly Howard Fast thought of what she had published there under a pseudonym. Magil, according to a historian, was "a top party leader." Friedan was also familiar with *Jewish Life*, where Flexner had published an article on Jewish women. In the course she taught at the Jefferson School Flexner relied on Friedan's *UE Fights for Women*, as well as on her pamphlet on women's history. Whether Flexner knew Friedan and was referring to her as one of the "many others" she mentioned in her 1983 letter about the roots of women's liberation remains unclear.[55]

Pieces Friedan wrote for Federated Press and the *UE News* (and even later, for community and mass circulation publications) focused on many issues raised in circles of progressive women: rent strikes, protests against escalating prices, discrimination against women, cooperative living arrangements, natural childbirth, the father's responsibility for child care and housekeeping, and the heroic participation of women in historic movements for social change. Intellectually inclined, a participant in Marxist discussions, concerned with women's issues, Friedan between 1943 and 1952 may well have participated in discussion groups that wrestled with these issues.

In some important instances, the evidence is more conclusive. We know, for example, that Friedan was knowledgeable about the Congress of American Women and at least one book by Hawes. She knew Ruth Young, the key feminist in the UE leadership. In addition, under a 1949 byline that used her married name, Friedan published an article in the *National Guardian* on Dr. Annette Rubinstein, a candidate for the state assembly from Manhattan on the American Labor Party ticket and at the time a member of the Communist Party interested in women's issues. Friedan reported Rubinstein's fight for justice for Jews, Puerto Ricans, and African Americans, as well as her advocacy of government provision of housing, child care, and schools. "You can't build schools with bayonets," she quoted Rubinstein as saying, "you can't build homes with atom bombs."[56]

The discussions among Popular Front feminists shaped her, as did attacks by McCarthyites against people and social movements familiar to her. The tragedy of anti-communism was that it so devastated the American left that it traumatized individuals and in the process fostered a break in historical consciousness. Her life's experiences placed her within complex networks of people whom anti-communism affected deeply and dramatically. In any reasonable world, Friedan would have been too small a player in the realm of labor journalism and radicalism for investigators to have noticed. Yet the United States of the late 1940s and early 1950s was not a place where reason reigned. Anti-communists targeted even liberal women's organizations. The attacks on groups such as the American Association of University Women, writes the historian Susan Levine, "gave voice to a strong antifeminist sentiment" that emerged "particularly when the dissenters were women who stepped out of the domestic sphere."[57]

Friedan frequently wrote about McCarthyite investigations. Congressional committees had investigated people she knew. As a Jew she was intensely aware of the way reactionaries linked anti-Semitism and anti-radicalism. Friedan had reason to worry that redbaiting, guilt by association, innuendo, and the denial of due process might affect her as it had so many people around her. People and institutions she had known well at every stage of her adult life were subject to attack. Her passion for social justice connected her with specific targets of the anti-communist crusade. Indeed, she lost her jobs at both Federated Press and the *UE News* for reasons related to anti-communism. In the first instance, labor militancy and anti-communism caused her bosses to worry about protecting their right flank. In the second, the dramatic decrease in UE membership, caused largely by anti-communist repression, resulted in the downsizing of the paper's staff.[58]

In 1953 Friedan remarked that a congressional investigating committee might eventually summon virtually any of her Smith professors because they talked so often in courses about alternative isms, including communism. They encouraged students to understand alternatives to the American system, nurture a healthy skepticism, and develop a sympathetic understanding for the American system of government. Among all those who taught her at Smith, Douglas was the most prominent subject of attack. She had left Smith in 1951, under conditions that are by no means clear, going on to teach elsewhere. In 1953, she published *Transitional Economic Systems: The Polish-Czech Example,* a scholarly and sympathetic account of how these two nations undertook "the evolution towards socialism of the Communist type." The accusation that she had been a member of the party came from a number of sources, including a faculty member at Smith and Grace Lumpkin, the sister of Douglas's partner Katharine. Grace, who was involved in party affairs, followed the lead of her hero, Whittaker Chambers, who was in turn the chief accuser of Alger Hiss. Members of HUAC claimed they had evidence that Douglas had made substantial financial contributions to the party between 1936 and 1939. When asked about these activities, Douglas invoked her constitutional protection under the Fifth Amendment. Aware of the possibility that she was prepared to provide potentially damaging information about her ex-husband, then a U.S. Senator, the committee did not allow her to submit a statement.[59]

There were other connections between Friedan's world at Smith and the anti-communist crusade. Her mentor, James Gibson, was an outspoken defender of academic freedom. In 1949, he left Smith for Cornell at the same time that he moved away from social science research: both decisions were shaped by the FBI's investigations of his political activities, and more generally by McCarthyism. As head of the Academic Freedom Committee of the Society for the Psychological Study of Social Issues, Gibson coordinated the defense of psychologists under attack. In 1951, he lost his security clearance in a manner that underscores the denial of due process and the recklessness of unsubstantiated charges.[60]

On the other side, in 1951, William F. Buckley Jr., whose two sisters Friedan had known at Smith, wrote *God and Man at Yale: The Superstitions of Academic Freedom,* and four years later launched *National Review;* both were key anti-communist publications. Moreover, his sister Aloise led the effort in 1954 to persuade Smith alumnae to stop their contributions until the college dismissed faculty members she considered subversive. In response, Friedan and some classmates drafted a letter to Smith alumnae, calling on them to oppose this attack on freedom of speech at their alma mater. Ronald Reagan, married in 1952 to Nancy Davis, Smith class of 1943, emerged in the late 1940s as Hollywood's most important anti-communist. From 1954 until 1962, he was a spokesman for General Electric, one of the major corporate opponents of the UE. He hosted a GE television program, and at one point starred in a play as an FBI agent who infiltrated Communist-front organizations. "The most dramatic part of my pitch, however, was the account of the attempted takeover of the industry by the Communists," he wrote later, referring to the UE's organizing efforts.[61]

In the 1950s, Highlander Folk School, which Friedan had attended in the summer of 1941, was a persistent target of redbaiters because of its important role in a wide range of protest causes, including the civil rights movement in the 1950s. Rosa Parks attended one of its desegregation workshops in 1955, which enhanced her understanding of what it meant to refuse to abide by segregationist rules on a Montgomery bus that fall. On Labor Day weekend of 1957, Martin Luther King Jr. helped celebrate the school's twenty-fifth anniversary. White supremacists undertook a campaign that eventually led to the school's temporary closure. As part of the effort in October, the Georgia Commission on Education issued a publication called *Highlander Folk School: Communist Training School,* and then plastered billboards with King's picture over the caption "Martin Luther King at Communist Training School."[62]

People Friedan knew in Berkeley also played major roles in the McCarthy period. In 1951 federal agents arrested Bernadette Doyle, Friedan's neighbor at Berkeley, accusing her and others of having conspired to work on the violent overthrow of the U.S. government. Several of Friedan's mentors were significant figures in the battle for academic freedom in universities in the postwar period. In 1949 at the University of Washington, Ralph Gundlach lost his tenure in what the historian Ellen Schrecker has called "the first important academic freedom case of the Cold War." News of Gundlach's firing spread across the nation, sparking a debate in the national media over the question of whether Communists deserved to be protected by academic freedom. James Gibson played a key role in Gundlach's defense. After leaving academe, Gundlach moved to New York, where he became a therapist in private practice. Continuing to fight for what he considered lost causes, in 1952 he joined with other social psychologists in filing a brief when Julius and Ethel Rosenberg appealed to the Supreme Court.[63]

Other psychologists with whom Friedan had studied at Berkeley responded forcefully to the attacks on universities. Beginning in 1949, E. C. Tolman led the opposition to the oath that the State of California insisted professors sign as proof of their loyalty to America and lack of connection to the Communist Party. Nevitt Sanford, whose *Authoritarian Personality* had recently appeared, also refused to sign the oath, claiming it moved America farther along the road to totalitarianism. The Regents dismissed Tolman, Sanford, and four other members of the psychology department. Erik Erikson resigned. The *Los Angeles Times* claimed that "Communists, on or off the faculty, have cooked up a first class fuss over the 'academic freedom' issue." Added L. M. Giannini, a regent and the president of the Bank of

America, "I want to organize twentieth century vigilantes, who will unearth Communists and Communism in all their sordid aspects." As he had done for Gundlach, Gibson worked to support the academic freedom of Tolman and his colleagues.[64]

Suspecting connections between party members and atomic espionage, in September 1949 HUAC held hearings in an attempt to find spies who had worked on the atomic bomb at Berkeley's Radiation Laboratory in 1942–43. In November 1947, writing in the *UE News*, Friedan had ridiculed HUAC tactics. Her words demonstrate that she had at least an inkling of what David Bohm, her boyfriend at Berkeley, would encounter. In addition, her writing suggests that she may have suspected that her relationship with Bohm could get her into trouble. She mentioned how the committee used what she called "an 'atom bomb plot'" in one of its investigations. "A scientist who allegedly knew a woman," she wrote, perhaps in an oblique reference to her relationship with Bohm, "who allegedly knew a man who allegedly had been seen with some movie people was alleged to have approached" a Berkeley professor "to get some information Russia wanted" from Oppenheimer.[65]

Bohm's closeness to Oppenheimer and Steve Nelson, his participation in radical circles, his involvement in the attempt to organize a union at the Radiation Laboratory, and his work on atomic research aroused the suspicions of the authorities. With Richard M. Nixon asking some of the questions, Bohm appeared before HUAC in 1949 and invoked the Fifth Amendment. Bohm also said he had no knowledge of any spy activity and was always loyal to the United States. In 1950 a federal grand jury indicted him for contempt, and Princeton barred him from coming on campus, later refusing to reappoint him to his position in the physics department. Bohm's case received prominent coverage in the *New York Times*. Although he was acquitted and was not, in fact, involved in espionage, his academic career in the United States was over. He went first to Brazil, then to Israel, and finally to England, never to return permanently to the United States. He eventually emerged as an internationally recognized New Age philosopher of science.[66]

Like those Friedan knew at Smith, Highlander, and Berkeley, people from her New York life were also targets of attacks. While living in Parkway Village, she drafted a poem that referred to community members whom congressional committees had investigated. Belfrage and Aronson, with whom Friedan shared a summer house in 1947, produced important books on the fight to defend freedom of the press from McCarthyite attack. They knew of what they spoke. In 1955, the government deported Belfrage, the English-born editor of the *National Guardian* and a member of the party for a brief period in 1937. Aronson had lost his position as editor of the

New York Newspaper Guild's *Frontpage* because of "conservatives' spurious charges that the paper had become a 'Kremlin Agent' through its support of militant unionism."[67]

The New York Newspaper Guild was subject to continued attack. In 1947 congressional testimony, the leadership of the national Guild claimed that Communists controlled the New York local. By 1948, anti-communists had dislodged their opponents from key positions in the New York union, undermining the Guild's support for a wide range of progressive commitments. In 1955, the Senate Internal Security Subcommittee launched an investigation into what it considered subversive journalism, focusing much of its attention on members of the New York Guild. Some witnesses named people who soon lost their jobs.[68]

Other investigations took aim at journalists from the Federated Press. In 1953, Senator McCarthy called Harvey O'Connor, with whom Friedan had worked on a 1944 article at the labor news service, to testify on his politics. With the CIO distancing itself from militant unions and making itself more respectable in face of the threat of witch hunts, Federated Press lost many of its subscribers. Weakened, it ceased publication in 1956, a victim of McCarthyism.[69]

Women in unions and housewives' leagues knew that their hard-won gains of the early and mid-1940s were tenuous and reversible. By the late 1940s, their worst fears were realized. McCarthyism had a chilling effect on women's activism, drying up middle-class support for trade unions, especially militant ones, turning most unions against radical activity by women, and scaring many in the rank and file away from commitment to progressive causes. It is hardly surprising that the government focused its energy on driving the Congress of American Women out of existence. In 1948 the government placed it on the Attorney General's list of subversive organizations, and in 1949 HUAC carried out an investigation. In its 1949 report, HUAC, using typical redbaiting language, claimed the Congress of American Women was "just another Communist hoax specifically designed to ensnare idealistically minded but politically gullible women" and "a specialized arm of Soviet political warfare in the current 'peace' campaign to disarm and demobilize the United States and democratic nations generally, in order to render them hapless in the face of the Communist drive for world conquest." In 1950 the Justice Department ordered the Congress to register as a foreign agent. With its power already diminished by the departure of women who objected to Soviet expansion into their homelands in Eastern Europe and by liberals who were anti-communists or worried about redbaiting, in the late 1940s the Congress became increasingly pro-Soviet and focused its energies on opposition to the intensification of the Cold War. It disappeared from the American scene in 1950 and, until recently, from historical memory.[70]

As much as any institution in America, the UE was the target of persistent attacks and investigations. Beginning in 1946, Friedan witnessed the efforts by federal agencies, congressional committees, major corporations, the Roman Catholic Church, and the CIO to break the radical leadership of the UE. Friedan actually covered some of HUAC's hearings into Communist influence in UE for the *UE News*. The Taft-Hartley Act of 1947 required union officers to sign an anti-communist affidavit if they wished to do business with the National Labor Relations Board. This encouraged other unions to challenge the UE, whose leaders refused to sign. Internecine fights took place within the UE, part of a longer-term battle between radicals and anti-communists in its ranks. One anti-communist, long active in the union, spoke of how a Communist minority "seized control of the national office, the executive board, the paid staff, the union newspaper and some district councils and locals." Before long, the UE was greatly weakened; in 1949, the CIO kicked it out of its ranks, in part because the UE supported Wallace at a time when the CIO stuck with the Democratic Party. The newly formed and CIO-backed IUE recruited many of its members. Membership in UE, numbering more than 600,000 in 1946, fell to 200,000 in 1953 and to 70,000 four years later.[71]

Many in the UE who were associated with the party went underground, knowing full well that governments and corporations hired turncoats, spies, and informers to get the goods on them. The transformation of Ruth Young's life under McCarthyism was especially fraught with meaning for Friedan, since she had written about Young early in her career as a labor journalist. Young, a Communist since 1937 and the daughter of a Communist, was the first woman member of the UE's executive committee and was active in the Congress of American Women. In 1950 Young married Leo Jandreau, a French Canadian tool-and-die worker who was a key official in the Schenectady UE. Around the same time, he ended more than a dozen years of membership in the party, and Ruth Young Jandreau severed her ties to both the UE and the party. She converted to Unitarianism and moved dramatically away from her radicalism. "It was nice to find a guy," she said decades later, "who would say, you can stay home" so she could raise a child. In 1954, several days before Senator McCarthy's committee opened hearings in Schenectady, Jandreau bolted from the UE and joined its CIO-sponsored counterpart. The UE leadership claimed that he had struck a deal; in one bold move his reputation changed from someone accused of disloyalty for infiltrating defense plans to a patriotic anti-communist.[72]

Nothing better illustrates the stakes surrounding McCarthyism than the treatment of articles Friedan wrote for *Jewish Life: A Progressive Monthly*. This publication, noted a scholar, was "in the orbit of the Communist Party" until 1956. Although it apologized for Soviet anti-Semitism, in many ways the periodical fought for admirable causes. In its pages, writers explored the relationship between Jewish life and progressive politics. They celebrated the resistance of Jews in the Warsaw ghetto uprising. They emphasized the connections between discrimination aimed at African Americans and Jews. Moreover, *Jewish Life* published some of the period's strongest attacks on anti-Semitism.[73]

In the winter of 1952–53, Friedan apparently wrote a series of articles for *Jewish Life*. They were somewhat more radical than those she had produced for the *UE News*, in part because her subject was the International Ladies' Garment Workers' Union (ILGWU), whose commitment to women workers and progressive politics was no match for the UE's. Indeed, she may have wanted to criticize the ILGWU precisely because it was allied with a union that was the UE's nemesis. She noted the unfairness of wealthy women wearing clothes that working-class women labored to produce. She told a story of rising profits and declining wages in a union that had, she argued, taken a conciliatory position with employers. *Jewish Life* published three articles in this series. The fourth was to appear in the July issue. On June 19, 1953, Ethel and Julius Rosenberg were executed in the electric chair, convicted of passing atomic secrets to the USSR. They had turned down an offer of clemency in exchange for naming names. The editors did not print Friedan's final piece, devoting the issue instead to questions surrounding the execution of the Rosenbergs, especially the connection between anti-Semitism and McCarthyism.[74]

In no position to be accused of spying, Friedan was unlikely to share the fate of the Rosenbergs. Nonetheless, she had ample cause to join others in shuddering and mourning. At least as early as her Smith years, she had heard redbaiters link radicals, the CIO, and Jews—accusations that her own experiences, as well as those of Douglas, Bohm, and others reinforced. Moreover, her romantic and political involvement with Bohm at a time when he was working on the bomb may have heightened her response to the execution of the Rosenbergs.

Indeed, around the time of the executions, Friedan drafted a scenario for a poem or play about the Rosenberg case. Though the handwriting is difficult to read, the thrust of what she wrote is clear. Her notes are reminiscent of the plays developed in the Federal Theatre Project of the 1930s, politically didactic dramas that captured a key moment and tried to raise the consciousness of the audience. Her words were raw, passionate, and intense. She sketched out scenes and characters: a jaded reporter remained aloof from the tragedy; a housewife apparently summoned the determination to speak her mind; a Jew felt marginalized and fearful; and a background chorus cheered on the executioners. Friedan imagined herself in the jail while she tried to find some way their sentences could be commuted and their lives spared. Toward the end, Friedan considered ways of arousing the public to angry opposition to the execution.[75]

Perhaps one of the reasons Friedan was relieved to quit the world of radical labor journalism was that it was getting too hot there. She might have felt she could take cover in a more feminine and less feminist place. With McCarthyism, Friedan was once again in danger of losing her voice. Now, she would begin to learn how to speak differently, a process that would eventually lead to *The Feminine Mystique*.

The Personal Is Political,
1947–63

In the late 1960s, insurgent feminists discovered that the personal was political, that what they did in their private lives was inseparable from what they faced in the public realm. In consciousness-raising groups, they explored the gendered dimensions of their relationships with their friends, lovers, family members, co-workers, and bosses. Through her own experiences in the 1940s, 1950s, and early 1960s, Friedan learned many of the lessons that a later generation absorbed. Reacting to the terror of anti-communism, redbaiting, and naming names, she sought a safer haven in the suburbs.[1]

As it turned out, however, her own experience with marriage, family, children, and suburban life hardly matched the conformity and happiness depicted in the mass media. Her whole range of experiences in the suburbs, beginning in 1950 when Friedan was twenty-nine years old, taught her the connection between the personal and the political. During her suburban exile, Friedan shifted the focus of her writing to middle-class women, and moderated her radicalism even as she continued to draw on what she had learned as a labor journalist. In the end, there remained for her a disjuncture between what she did and how she felt, something her therapy in the mid-1950s highlighted. As a housewife and writer in the 1950s, Friedan, often alone and without full awareness of what she was doing, struggled against the artificial separation of the personal and political. In the 1960s, having generalized her concerns in *The Feminine Mystique,* she led a collective effort to bring these two realms together.

Mass media images of domestic bliss turned out to provide an inaccurate picture of life in the Friedan household. To be sure, the Friedans, married in

1947, produced three talented and interesting children: Daniel in 1948, Jonathan in 1952, and Emily in 1956. Yet as someone who since childhood had dreamed she might realize the promise of romantic love and an egalitarian marriage, she was disappointed. Her asthma persisted, resurfacing at times of stress. A *summa cum laude* graduate of Smith, she had ended up with someone who had not finished college at Massachusetts State. Though on the left, Carl was not really politically compelled. He tended to look skeptically at the passionate political commitments of Betty and her friends.[2]

According to Betty, the root cause of many of their disagreements was their financial situation. With the budget always stretched, she felt Carl's income was both erratic and low. In contrast, one of her husband's best friends later claimed that Carl made more money than Betty and that the marital disagreements were rooted in personality struggles, with two strong-willed people fighting for independence. Carl himself countered Betty's stories. After interviewing him in the early 1970s, a reporter wrote that he "reserves special anger for the projected image that Betty lived a shackled, humdrum housewife experience and wrote *The Feminine Mystique* as a catharsis." Carl went on to insist that Betty "was in the world during the whole marriage, either full time or free lance" and that her dissatisfaction was "congenital." He claimed that he gave her emotional and financial support, (including a full-time maid), which helped make it possible for her to write the book. Betty, he remembered, "seldom was a wife and a mother."[3]

Whatever the truth, the problems in the marriage exacerbated her loneliness. According to Betty, "Carl's vision of a wife was one who stayed home and cooked and played with the children. And one who didn't compete. I was not that wife." Early on, tensions increased, with fights breaking out from time to time. Before long, violence marked their relationship. A reporter later noted that their marriage was "stormy almost from its beginning and would end in violence." They fought in private and in public. Once, the reporter continued, "Carl threw a bowl full of sugar in his wife's face. He carries an oversized and scarred knuckle on his left ring-finger from stopping a mirror thrown by Betty." Another reporter described the marriage as "a sadomasochistic free-for-all." Perhaps part of "The Problem That Has No Name" was the way that violence made vivid the marital conflicts over issues of personality and power. In typical domestic violence, which this was apparently not, men use physical force to punish, silence, and isolate women; in the Friedans' case, each partner gave as well as took.[4]

Betty's relationship with Carl was formative. Feeling that he was a desirable catch, and given her conventional longings, on some level she took pleasure from the badge of social respectability that came with being a wife and mother. Yet she often felt that he was not sympathetic to her aspirations for a career, an intellectual life, a democratic marriage, and political engagement. As a result, Betty's sense of entrapment by the feminine mystique referred not only to the temptations of domesticity, but also to her struggle to transform the terms of her relationship to her husband, something she declined to write about. Moreover, her relationship with Carl reflected her failure to achieve her lifelong goal of combining career and marriage and of attaining happiness in a sustained relationship, hopes that were genuine but unrealized. A whole series of forces combined to raise her expectations to a point where they were impossible to meet: her longing for a way to overcome her loneliness, her drive to rectify in her own life the problems her parents could not resolve in theirs, and the culture's insistence on the power of romantic love between a man and a woman. She desperately wanted to avoid repeating her mother's patterns of manipulative dependency, and also to avoid becoming economically dependent on Carl, whose reliability she doubted. Her yearnings underscore the persistence of her cultural conservatism, something that enhanced the temptations of the feminine mystique at the same time that it limited her ability to challenge the status quo.

In 1950 the Friedans moved to Parkway Village, where they remained until 1956. This residential development was part of the explosive growth of the northeastern section of Queens in the postwar period. Built right after World War II for United Nations personnel, the forty-acre complex housed about two thousand people from over fifty countries—an extraordinarily cosmopolitan mix, including diplomats, African Americans, and American Jews. The Friedans lived in one of the two hundred units allocated to families of American veterans of World War II.[5]

An hour-long bus and subway ride from Manhattan, Parkway Village was suburban in character. Except for the variety of people who lived there and the international goods stocked in its markets, two reporters noted in 1950, it looked "much like any other small suburb" in the United States with its stores clustered in its town center and its "tree-seamed street winding around two-storied red brick houses, newly painted white doors shining behind tall colonial columns, and large French windows opening out into back-yard lawns." This unique development, the reporters concluded, offered "living proof" that the goals the United Nations strove to achieve on a larger scale "can work out on Main Street."[6]

Though quarters became cramped as Daniel grew up and Jonathan entered the world, Friedan found Parkway Village's garden apartments much to her liking. She relished the camaraderie of other young marrieds, had access to Manhattan by public transportation, and involved herself in the community. At Parkway Village, she experienced for the first of many times what it was like to rely on cooperative arrangements: with several other couples the Friedans established a babysitting pool, planned a yearly Passover Seder, and rented a summer house.[7]

As editor of the *Parkway Villager* for two years beginning with the February 1952 issue, as a community activist, and as an author of stories about the community, Friedan gained valuable experience. She continued her education, begun at Smith College and Highlander Folk School, in how to generate support for her causes by working with committees, sending out press releases, and helping to organize meetings. Living in a suburban community, she turned her attention away from workers. With the *Parkway Villager*, she composed her first stories about middle-class women and their families. In her writings, she promoted the value of a cooperative, racially integrated international community, and one to which women contributed across national lines. In other ways, she articulated a vision with feminist themes: of women committed to pursuing careers and of husbands and wives who worked to build democratic households for their families. Her name appeared on the *Parkway Villager* masthead as "Betty Friedan," not Betty Goldstein or Mrs. Carl Friedan.[8]

She assumed the editorship at a critical moment. In June 1952, the banks that held the mortgage on the apartment complex announced a steep rise in the rents. Months of negotiations and protest ensued. The battle between the tenants and banks was fierce. The banks wielded the power that the law and their mortgages gave them. In response, the tenants organized efforts to withhold rent, held public meetings, and sponsored at least one mass rally. They formed a citizens committee that gained support from leading political figures. They pictured Parkway Village as a model of what the UN was trying to build on a world scale—a democratic community where people of all races, religions, nationalities, and colors lived together in harmony. They proudly announced that the generation that grew up in the Village would do so without prejudice. They made clear that higher rents would force many of the families to leave, with non-Caucasians facing discrimination that would make it difficult for them to find new places to live. Toward the end of the year, the banks threatened to evict tenants who refused to sign new leases at higher rents just before a temporary stay was granted at Christmas time. Before long, the disagreement quieted down and most of the tenants pursued plans to move into a complex of cooperative apartments elsewhere, where the Friedans seriously considered buying as well.[9]

In the version of the unfolding drama offered by the *New York Times*, men assumed the leadership role within the community of tenants. The only time American women appeared in the stories came when reporters interviewed housewives about their reaction to letters giving occupants the choice of paying higher rents or moving. Yet within the Village the story was different. Though women doubtlessly experienced sexism as they sought to make their voices heard, to a considerable extent they assumed major leadership positions. Friedan took an active role in the rent protest. At critical moments, she served on the executive committee of the Parkway Village Community Association. A woman chaired the rent committee in the spring of 1952, with Friedan serving as a member and as head of the publicity committee.[10]

In many ways, Friedan's political life in Parkway Village was an extension, rather than a repudiation, of her radical political activity. In her study of suburban politics in Queens in these years, the historian Sylvie Murray has made clear that in nearby communities, and doubtlessly in Parkway Village as well, citizens heatedly debated questions of patriotism and free speech, as redbaiters accused Communists of infiltrating community organizations, including the schools. Progressive residents in Queens fought hard to sustain racially integrated neighborhoods. Especially where significant numbers of Jews lived side by side with African Americans, left-wing suburbanites celebrated the cultural pluralism of communities that struggled to maintain diversity.[11]

Friedan's education in the economics and politics of housing came through her participation in the battle against the banks. As they vigorously debated the role of government and private enterprise in providing housing, citizens of Queens argued over the legacy of the New Deal. Rent strikes in New York and elsewhere were common in the period, taking place in virtually every major garden apartment development in Queens. Indeed, in 1949, an early episode of *The Goldbergs*, a nationally televised show about working-class Jews who lived in the Bronx, depicted a rent strike by tenants who protested against a landlord's refusal to make repairs.[12]

Murray has provided convincing evidence that contradicts the widely held view of 1950s suburban citizenry as passive and apolitical. Rather, she demonstrates, what characterized the work of political activists was "their sense of themselves as citizens, their allegiance to the local community, their concern for national and international affairs, and, most importantly, the integration of collective and political actions in the very fabric of suburban domesticity." She has depicted communities where participatory democracy, emerging from political discussions and action, suffused the lives of men and women as they went about their daily routines in their homes, neighborhoods, stores, and community organizations. Activists were fiercely loyal to their communities, continuously invoking what Murray has called "the symbolic power of an imagined harmonious and organic community."[13]

In the political battles in Queens, women played a critical role. As Murray has shown, their activity "was often concealed behind the public celebration of male leadership." Yet women participated actively in these community struggles—circulating petitions, sending out material to officials and the media, and showing up at public meetings in full force. They ascribed their power not to their roles as mothers but as informed citizens and experts. They refused to cast their political activity in gendered terms, reflecting their effort to confront male authority—in their households and communities, to say nothing of the banks and City Hall. As Murray has amply demonstrated, it is possible to see these women's efforts as part of women's political activism that contradicts the picture of an apolitical female citizenry.[14]

For a brief period Friedan transformed *Parkway Villager* from a chatty source of community news into an activist publication. Before and after the protest, the paper focused on accidents that injured children, recipes that women shared, and social events that all participated in. However, in one of the first issues she edited, the headlines boldly announced "Rents Going Down All Over Queens—Except Here!" and "Villagers Mobilizing to Fight Rent Increases." As editor of a small paper that appeared less than a dozen times a year, Friedan may well have written the articles that pictured a heroic community committed to achieving social justice by fighting greedy bankers. Investigations carried out by the paper, an article writer noted in May 1952, proved that "this exorbitant rent increase" was "taking advantage of the non-white international residents whose only alternative is discriminatory housing." The mortgage holders, stated another article, "are evidently trying to profiteer at the expense of their international and American tenants who wish to live in an unsegregated community." During her tenure as editor, in February 1954 the community newspaper featured a profile of Roy Wilkins, the second in command at the NAACP and a resident of Parkway Village. The article illustrated that Village residents remained committed to "interracial living," thereby proving to real estate agents and banks that the presence of African Americans did not threaten housing values. Speaking in the first person plural, the author talked of an evening at the Wilkins home "when racial problems were frankly debated," with the guests agreeing that the situation in America was improving, "only at too slow a pace, especially in the South."[15]

Other things Friedan wrote or edited in the *Parkway Villager* make clear how progressive were her commitments. In February 1952, the *Parkway Villager* featured families in which the wives expected to return to a career before too long. In the meantime, they benefited from the husband's help with the child rearing and housework. A February 1953 article portrayed a Village resident named Mary Albright as a woman who in the dozen years since her marriage had found plenty to do: hold down a series of jobs, have two children, help launch a nursery school, lead a successful rent strike, and develop a flourishing free-lance career. Among the things that enabled her to accomplish so much, the author wrote, was the "mutual respect" she and her husband had for one another "as independent people." Even in the midst of the rent strike, they were able to differ "heatedly with each other in public *not* like married people having a family argument, but like objective and respected opponents." Indeed, the story revealed that Albright was one of the women who created the community association, having heard a conversation among male residents who were discussing the seemingly intractable "loneliness of their wives."[16]

When Friedan was editor, the *Parkway Villager* highlighted other examples of democratic households including that of Djalal Abdoh, the head of the association and Iran's Deputy Representative to the UN. Coming from a country where fathers were patriarchs, the May 1952 article explained, he had learned from his young daughters that in the United States dads had to listen to their children and help with household chores. This theme was echoed in the *Parkway Villager*'s October 1953 portrait of Mrs. Paz Mendez, a resident from the Philippines who had raised six children and enjoyed a major career as an author and university educator. "American women," the author wrote, "who find it difficult to combine a career with even one or two children" could learn from Mrs. Mendez, who got her children and diplomat husband to do much of the housework.[17]

In some of her work on the *Parkway Villager* Friedan published material that touched on issues germane to the Cold War. The article on Abdoh critiqued the 1950s celebration of America's virtues. The writer quoted Abdoh as saying that peace would not come to the world until powerful nations surrendered their "ideas of the colonial way of life." Abdoh denied that the world faced a problem of "democracy versus communism," asserting instead that the struggle was between colonial powers and insurgent nationalists. At a time when America was becoming increasingly reliant on Iranian oil, he asserted that world peace and prosperity would come only when the "natural resources of some countries" were no longer "exploited for the benefit of others."[18]

In some instances, the articles in the *Villager* during Friedan's editorship focused on politics in the United States. This was the case in April 1952, when the newspaper profiled Richard Carter, a reporter for the *Daily Compass* (the successor to the radical newspaper *PM*) who earlier had served as an organizer for the New York Newspaper Guild. He had recently won the prestigious George Polk Memorial Award for articles that exposed corruption on the waterfront. In the process, the author stated, Carter "named names." There is no reason to think that either the author or Betty Friedan (who may be one and the same) treated this issue of naming names as an anti-communist would. Rather, the story praised an investigative reporter who courageously told the truth and exposed social injustice. Indeed, the author mentioned that for his next story Carter "went into Ku Klux Klan territory to expose new facts behind the wave of bombings and murders of Negroes in Florida."[19]

Friedan's concern with Cold War issues became apparent in the 1952 end-of-the-year issue of *Parkway Villager,* for which she wrote a long poem about the events of the year past. In a cleansed version, it saw its way into print. Between draft and publication, a colleague convinced her not to include certain lines from her original draft because they were too hard-hitting and political. Among the passages eliminated were ones that celebrated revenge against the landlords. In addition, Friedan had to let go of phrases that attacked those who hysterically questioned the loyalty of peace advocates. She also offered support to those whom congressional committees had blacklisted.[20]

Friedan drew on her experiences in Parkway Village in writing free-lance articles but had trouble publishing them. As in the *Parkway Villager* and in mass-circulation magazines, here too she employed a cosmopolitan and feminist cast as she focused on women's issues. For American women to work effectively with visitors from abroad, she argued in one article, they had to overcome their feelings that they were from a superior country. In "They Found Out 'Americans Aren't So Awful, After All!'" she countered the view of Americans as people who could not get along with foreigners. She wrote of how residents from diverse backgrounds lived peacefully together, with the commitment to being good neighbors overcoming prejudice. As Murray has demonstrated, Friedan emphasized how women from the United States and Canada revealed to the foreign visitors, male and female alike, the benefits of a grassroots democracy led by women. In addition, Friedan talked of how women from abroad felt sorry for their American counterparts, whose lives were severely restricted by their obligations as homemakers and mothers. Women from overseas preferred to rely on servants rather than on the machines that were supposed to save women's labor. Another drafted but unpublished article, entitled "Everyday Diplomats," observed that women from around the world were able to form friendly working relationships more effectively than the men involved in well-financed international programs.[21]

Though Friedan has acknowledged the pleasures of Parkway Village, she has characterized this as the period when she experienced the feminine mystique most intensely, a time when she learned that motherhood replaced career and politics. When her work for the *UE News* ended and she was pregnant with Jonathan, for several months she turned her back on her dream of becoming a writer. Instead she focused on housewifely chores. The result was that, mired in overwhelming feelings of helplessness, she lost her sense of her self as she embraced what she soon learned from a therapist was a false dichotomy of being a woman or exercising her mind. She told of taking classes on how to be a good mother and a good cook. She read the section of *Baby and Child Care* in which Dr. Benjamin Spock told mothers of small children not to work outside the home. She felt guilty, she later wrote, because Spock had told her she was doing the wrong thing. She learned that it was *"pushy"* of her to have career ambitions. She came to understand that "at home, you *were* necessary, you were important, you were the boss," feelings for which the feminine mystique provided the justification. What made these messages convincing was the contrast between reassuring domesticity and the intimidating aspects of her life as a labor journalist. In 1976, Friedan contrasted the small pleasures of do-it-yourself tasks and community activism on the local level with the frightening radical politics in which she participated.[22]

Psychotherapy enabled Friedan to explore the personal nature of her political journey. When she was in her mid-thirties, with the help of therapy that began in 1952 or 1953, she broke through the feminine mystique, something she accomplished well before leaving Parkway Village in 1956. Friedan's therapeutically derived narrative in an early draft of *The Feminine Mystique* provides another explanation of why she came to understand her past in a way that minimized the importance of her ten years as a Popular Front feminist. When, just as the 1950s ended, Friedan discussed her therapy, she did so in scattered paragraphs and with prose that is vague and elusive. In the 1940s and early 1950s, many progressive feminists had opposed therapy because it sought explanations in the personal situation of an individual and not in material social conditions. Friedan, interested since childhood in what psychology would reveal about her life, now learned things that connected the personal and the political at the same time that she minimized the importance of her own radical politics.[23]

In therapy, she reported, she experienced a kind of death and rebirth, emerging as someone with a new and different sense of her life. She now realized that her Smith experience was fundamentally formative. At moments, she felt it was responsible for her frustration. Yet overall she learned that at Smith she had formed an identity, gained values, and obtained an education that she knew were crucial in enabling her to survive in the suburbs. As an undergraduate, she had sharpened her ability to persuade people to see the world the way she did. In the process she had developed an obligation to use her mind for social good. She appreciated once again her education in psychology and now renewed her desire to pursue a career in the field. Friedan's recovery of her lost self convinced her that psychology and education, not labor activity, were what really mattered to her.[24]

At her own peril, she now concluded, she had abandoned what she had learned at Smith. As someone who had studied in 1940 with Kurt Lewin, she drew on his research concerning the importance of frustration to personal growth. She came to think of the years from 1943 to 1952 as what she called a "moratorium," a word she borrowed from Erik Erikson. She deeply regretted having left graduate school and given up her aspirations to become a psychologist. She now understood her ten years of work in the union movement as a period when she departed from the central trajectory of her life, an unintended diversion from her most sustaining intellectual passion. She came to feel that she submerged important parts of her identity—her passionate commitment to intellectual work that would enable her to be an independent person. Although she might not have done things differently, she felt badly that she had proceeded so haphazardly since 1943. She came to regret that through her experiences with labor journalism, the search for someone to love, and housewifery, she had refused to accept responsibility for who she was and what she was doing. Questioning her earlier commitments to radical absolutes, she now understood politics and social change in more uncertain and ambiguous ways.

In this unpublished autobiographical fragment, Friedan barely mentioned her ten years of work for Federated Press and the *UE News*. When she did so, she wrote in the most elliptical of terms. Discussing the interlude of her confused and misguided years as a labor journalist, she remarked that she had allowed what she called "the large organization" to tell her what to do and think. Ironically, her use of these words to describe the union movement generally or the UE specifically points in two problematic but opposite directions. On the one hand, to some the phrase could mean the Communist Party. On the other hand, these words appear to be an admission that she was the female equivalent of an organization man who had allowed a large corporation to dictate the terms of his life.[25]

In this early draft of her book, she made clear that she had succeeded in breaking through the feminine mystique. She regretted that as a free-lance writer, she had to write in ways that made it necessary for her to surrender to commercial pressures. She described her relationship to the feminine mystique in contradictory ways. Sometimes, she saw herself as its captive. Yet at other times, she denied that it had ever trapped her, claiming that she had been able to reject its pressures. She realized retrospectively that the suburban moratorium had enabled her, and others, to achieve a kind of gestalt, a sense of integrated wholeness. Her suburban experience, she recognized, had led to positive personal growth. Writing the book enabled her to tell women of the importance of self-realization, psychological insight, careers, and planning. Gaining a better understanding of herself enabled her to find ways of successfully meeting her obligation to society. Above all, she realized that her salvation and sense of satisfaction came through disciplined albeit often painful work.

Here and elsewhere, Friedan made clear that despite all these changes and reevaluations, there was continuity in her ideology. She knew she still believed in values that people had articulated before she was born, and to which she herself had developed a commitment by the time she graduated from college. In such statements she may have been referring to the traditions of social democratic or Marxist thought she learned at Smith. Although she had come to feel differently about herself as a labor journalist, she did not want to turn away from all that she had done in those years. She acknowledged her continued dedication to the values that undergirded the institutions for which she had worked in the late 1940s and early 1950s, by which she appears to have meant the labor movement or the UE. In a separate document, a draft of a story that is as elusive as the autobiographical fragments in early versions of *The Feminine Mystique*, Friedan described how someone like herself, a bright and promising women's college graduate, had struggled to come to terms with the vision of her life that a figure who resembled Dorothy Douglas conveyed.[26]

Friedan's reconsideration of her life solved some problems but created others. It enabled her to move on past traumatic events—from losing her job at the UE in 1952 while she was pregnant to the execution of the Rosenbergs in 1953. She now interpreted her years at Smith as a steady path toward a career in her undergraduate major, significantly omitting her efforts at Smith to integrate Freud and Marx, psychology and social action, the self and society. In the mid-1950s, she healed herself but did so at the price of creating a rupture in her sense of where she had been and where she was going. She recovered her identity but lost or hid from view crucial elements of her past. The interpretation of her life that grew out of her therapy involved the gendered story of how she relinquished her ambitions in the public realm for the more private realm of a psychologist who helped individuals. She diminished her sense of what she had struggled to achieve politically and opted instead for a feminized vision of change through personalized self-fulfillment.[27]

Moreover, Friedan's reconsideration of her life occurred at a time when external events were prompting others to reconsider their commitments as well. Rather than witnessing an economic depression that radicals had predicted, Friedan saw the most sustained period of prosperity in American history, in which many unions and workers benefited. The Cold War intensified and the horrors of Stalinism became more widely acknowledged. In August 1947, the USSR put down a revolt in Hungary. Six months later, Stalin violently suppressed dissent in Czechoslovakia. Resistance ended when Jan Masaryk, whom Friedan had interviewed in 1946, died, whether by suicide or assassination remains unclear. After 1948 anti-Semitism in the Soviet Union increased: in 1952 the Stalinist regime executed two dozen Jewish intellectuals. At home, McCarthyism continued to circumscribe dissent. The social welfare programs of the New Deal were codified but not extended. These were not events that gave most radicals the courage to go on fighting. In 1949, in the widely read *The God that Failed,* a group of prominent writers discussed how anti-fascism turned them into fellow travelers and then how they became disillusioned with Communism. In somewhat vague terms, in 1976 Friedan talked about how "disillusioning" it was "to see what was happening in trade unions, and in Czechoslovakia and the Soviet Union." By the early 1950s, she had come to realize that with workers chasing after consumer goods and McCarthyism on the rampage, the feminine mystique replaced "larger visions of making the whole world over." The mid-1950s was a time when social and behavioral scientists did their best to explain away radicalism, ascribing it to acting out that was both psychological and social.[28]

Is it possible to reconcile what Friedan concluded from her therapy with all of the evidence from her work as an activist and writer, that she sustained her commitments, even as she shifted from Popular Front to suburban feminism? The answer to the discrepancy between Friedan's version and much of the evidence lies in how a series of experiences in 1952–53 combined to trap her: the birth of her second child, the loss of her job at the *UE News,* the end of the rent strike, her short-lived decision to give up her career as a writer, and the execution of Ethel and Julius Rosenberg. These events followed on the heels of a series of momentous stories of 1948–49: the poor showing of Henry A. Wallace in 1948, along with the Congressional investigations of David Bohm and the Congress of American Women a year later. These contexts help explain the difference between what Friedan wrote and how she felt. Her essays on egalitarian households and democratic communities of women were as much expressions of her hopes and her ideology as they were of what she could achieve, given the nature of her marriage to Carl. Though she may have been under the sway of the feminine mystique briefly, her sense of being trapped was enormously powerful. What complicated this situation was how anti-feminism and McCarthyism dovetailed to make her feel trapped. She could legitimately talk about the conspiracy to deprive women of their sense of themselves. Only at her own peril could she talk about (and perhaps admit to herself) the war against radicals generally and progressive feminists particularly. Consequently, when Friedan mentioned the increasing force of the feminine mystique, at some level she also had in mind the onslaught of McCarthyism.

Recognizing the difference between how she felt and what she did thus helps make intelligible what she learned in therapy. What was important to her was not being a Popular Front feminist or combining career and family life. Rather, what mattered was how she felt about what she had done. In that sense, she may not have been so much obfuscating a past as offering an intensely personal story of what it felt like to be a suburban woman who struggled to find her way and then tell others how they could find theirs. Only when she came to a new understanding of herself did she have the confidence to speak with authority in a way that made what she experienced relevant politically and personally to millions of her peers, even as she turned on her past.

With the break-up of Parkway Village, a third child on the way, and her free-lance career launched, by early 1956 Friedan determined to move on. Later that year, the Friedans left Parkway Village for suburban Rockland County. While living in Queens they had often spent weekends trying to find a suburban development with an authentic sense of community. The Friedans explored with other families the possibility of creating a communal group of homes north of New York City. They may have been inspired by Paul Good-man and Percival Goodman's *Communitas* (1947), which offered a searching critique of the narrow range of choices suburban affluence underwrote in postwar America and provided a utopian alternative. After the birth of Emily in May 1956, the Friedans accepted a more individualistic solution, but still not an entirely conventional one, when they moved to distinctive communities in suburban New York. Their new location marked a transformation in Betty Friedan's attitude toward class and racial conflict.[29]

The Friedans moved first to a stone barn in Sneden's Landing, on the west side of the Hudson River in Rockland County, New York, just above the New Jersey border. In mid-1957, when Betty was thirty-six, they settled in an Italianate 1868 Victorian house, also on the west side of the river, in Grand View-on-Hudson, New York. With the help of the GI Bill and about $2,500 Friedan inherited from her father, the Friedans paid $25,000 for their house. At that time, only 4 percent of the residences in Rockland County sold for that figure or more. The house had eleven rooms, three bathrooms, and many elegant details such as marble fireplaces, French doors, and arched windows. It stood on an acre of land overlooking the river; on the hill above the house was a large, spring-fed natural pool.[30]

Grand View-on-Hudson, a village with a population of 349 in 1959, was a distinctive community. Among its residents were Jews, Roman Catholics, and Protestants. Just under two miles long and no more than a thousand feet wide, it stretched along one street, River Road. Hills to the west and the river to the east protected the community on two sides. Once the location of a handful of grand estates, the residents lived in newer homes as well as former mansions and their converted outbuildings—carriage houses, gardeners' cottages, and garages. Although a few of the men worked as skilled craftsmen, most of them were corporate executives, architects, teachers, engineers, lawyers, actors, writers, and local merchants. Most of the women in Grand View-on-Hudson worked as writers, engineers, social workers, actresses, doctors, teachers, and artists. One woman had been an organizer for the New York Newspaper Guild. Not far from the Friedans was a small apartment complex run by a Hindu philosopher from India, which a resident in 1962 described as a "madcap confusing bohemia."[31]

The Friedans' migration to the suburbs was part of the great postwar movement of the parents of baby boomers. Indeed, they left Parkway Village for Rockland County in the same year that the television figures Molly and Jake Goldberg moved from an apartment in the Bronx to a suburban house on Long Island, in a town the script writers named Haverville. When the fictional Goldbergs made this switch, the network changed the name of the show from an ethnically clear *The Goldbergs* to a more vaguely ethnic *Molly*. To be sure, much separated the Goldbergs from the Friedans, especially since the television characters were working class and embedded in an ethnic community defined by ties to kin. "Instead of rent strikes and collective action," the historian George Lipsitz wrote of the television show, in words that have some relevance to the Friedans' lives, "comic premises in 'Molly' emerged from the relative isolation and alienation of the suburban setting." Now, wrote Lipsitz, the Goldbergs' lives were ruled by shopping, paying off debts, fixing up the house, and taking care of the children. On the television and in life, he has argued, suburban America was a place where people could obliterate their pasts and transform their identities. Life in the suburbs enabled Americans to repress their collective memory of the 1930s and 1940s, a period marked for them, as it was for Betty Friedan, by economic dislocation and exposure to the struggles of working-class Americans.[32]

When the Friedans moved to Rockland County, it was just beginning to experience the changes that resulted from the opening a few months earlier of the Tappan Zee Bridge, which spanned the Hudson River, and from the construction of the Palisades Interstate Parkway, which connected the county with Manhattan via the George Washington Bridge. Compared with Westchester and Nassau Counties in New York and Bergen County in New Jersey, Rockland lacked efficient means of public transportation to Manhattan and vast stretches of easily developed land, making it a less likely candidate for mass-scale suburban development.[33]

In 1955, A. C. Spectorsky, who wrote on American mores, discussed Rockland County in his popular book, *The Exurbanites*. According to Spectorsky, several things made exurbanites unique. As displaced urbanites, they felt exiled, never fully permitting themselves to accommodate to their new neighborhoods. Always in the background as hip people in the know, they felt some superiority to the mass of people who consumed what they produced for they were "singularly commercial merchant[s] of dreams for the rest of the nation." Assuming that these symbol manipulators were all men, Spectorsky drew a dismal and mean-spirited picture of the exurban housewife. Compared with their sisters in the cities and suburbs, they were more geographically separated from their husbands and from their neighbors. Spectorsky characterized these women, married to men driven by fears and insecurities, as bored and impatient, with a special envy for women who still had careers. In casting his hostile eye on exurban wives, Spectorsky agreed with the judgment of psychiatrist Helene Deutsch, in calling them "active-masculine" women, who were "competitive, inclined to jealousy and suspicion (very often with reason), and aggressive." Yet Spectorsky also made clear that for some exurban women "boredom and impatience continue to grow until" they select "a sphere of activity, an outlet for emotional energy"—in some instances escapes but in other instances involvement in the schools, politics, and community. Then, as if to reassure his readers that such pursuits were not pathological, Spectorsky noted that many of the women with serious outside interests were "quite happy and happily mated."[34]

In the early 1950s, the county contained several population groups. Members of long-settled families worked on local farms and in local businesses and professions. In addition, there were authors, artists, and theater people who had moved in during the 1930s and were "long past their salad days"—Katharine Cornell, Helen Hayes, Ben Hecht, Aaron Copland, Carson McCullers, Hortense Calisher, all of whom, like the Friedans, lived along the Hudson River. There were commuters who had to travel about an hour to reach Manhattan. The county also included members of a professional middle class who worked in the suburbs—employees of Rockland State Hospital, Columbia University's Lamont Geological Observatory, or the young doctors, professors, and scientists who started out in the federal housing project at Shanks Village. The county was home to a considerable number of Jews, with one synagogue in Nyack and five located in Spring Valley, seven miles to the west. More numerous than any of these groups were the families of those who worked in the local paper mill and chemical factories. Although housewives in the county outnumbered women who worked outside the home, slightly over a third of the employees of the two largest manufacturing plants were female, and women made up just under one-third of the employed work force.[35]

In moving to Rockland County, Betty Friedan remained connected to political activists, nonconformists, and radicals. A year before they moved, Spectorsky described Sneden's Landing as a community of artists and writers whose "fetish is non-conformity, individuality, originality." Sneden's Landing, Grand View-on-Hudson, and the towns nearby were places to which a number of radicals, many of them Jewish, moved when they left the city. During the 1950s in Rockland, Friedan knew several whose work fundamentally shaped American radicalism of the 1950s and 1960s, among them Herbert Gutman, Harvey Swados, and C. Wright Mills. Gutman was a historian who, beginning in the 1960s, played a pioneering role in developing the new social and labor history. His 1963 article on the history of community support for insurgent trade union activity sounded very much like what Friedan had written for Federated Press in a 1946 story. In *On the Line* (1957) Swados vividly portrayed the impact of assembly-line work on the lives of nine laborers, something he himself had experienced as a factory worker, as late as 1956. Mills, Swados's close friend and someone Friedan also knew, lived in Rockland County and taught sociology at Columbia. In his 1948 *The New Men of Power: America's Labor Leaders,* he expressed concern that unions were losing their critical edge as they increasingly resembled other large organizations. In 1951 he published *White Collar: The American Middle Classes,* which focused on the transition from the old to the new middle classes that was reshaping the county in which he lived as well as much of America. His 1956 *The Power Elite* provided a model for radical social scientists and a bible for the New Left in the 1960s.[36]

Local issues of race and class were also apparent to Betty Friedan. Indeed, the place where she chose to live served as a marker of her class and racial privilege. Having fought to sustain Parkway Village as a racially integrated community, she now resided in a village where no African Americans lived— but one not far away from a town where struggles over racial discrimination occurred. She doubtlessly knew that African Americans and progressive whites were still fighting a losing battle to sustain nearby Shanks Village as a racially integrated project. Although only 5 percent of the county's population was non-white, most of these citizens were African Americans and many of them lived in the towns that stood at either end of River Road— Nyack and Piermont. Friedan's children went to schools with substantial numbers of African American and working-class children. Moreover, since Friedan shopped and went to the post office in Nyack (about two miles from her home) and read the newspaper published there, she was well aware of the explosive racial situation in that town in the late 1950s and early 1960s. In these years, an increasingly large proportion of Nyack's population was African American, having reached almost 20 percent by 1957. Beginning in the late 1950s, African Americans protested the use of blackface in local minstrel shows, as well as discrimination in housing, employment, recreational facilities, and schools. In 1959, Frances Batson, a local leader of the black community, proclaimed that "Rockland County is prejudiced." She made that remark in the context of a protracted and bitter fight over urban renewal in the community. To make way for parking in order to attract white shoppers to their stores, local merchants wanted to clean up what they saw as slums by enforcing zoning laws or tearing down rental units where African Americans lived. In opposition, African Americans and their allies wanted the town to seek federal aid for housing for African Americans. In early 1963, when Friedan published *The Feminine Mystique,* African Americans in Nyack, made more militant by the stalling of white leaders, staged successful sit-ins.[37]

The move to Rockland County did not end Friedan's experience with Manhattan. She often traveled there to meet with her literary agent and to do research at the New York Public Library. In addition, she taught writing courses at New York University in 1958–59 and at the New School for Social Research in 1959. In 1958, she worked on an NBC television documentary "With Love We Live," based on her 1957 article with the same title.[38]

If to some extent in Parkway Village she had succumbed to the feminine mystique, in Rockland County she had the strength to be eccentric and resist the odious aspects of suburban identity. Now she understood how it was possible to live the life of the mother and wife that her own mother had been unable to achieve without sacrificing her sense of herself. Betty Friedan threw herself into the tasks of redoing the house, raising the children, preparing meals, and participating in the local PTA.[39]

People who knew her well in these years—and sometimes Friedan herself—emphasize that she was hardly a captive of the suburban conformity she described in her 1963 book. Indeed Friedan has often pictured herself in the years in Rockland County as a freak, an outsider, someone lonely in the provinces—a description that evoked her experiences as a girl in Peoria. Friedan's life in Rockland County does not reflect the image of the 1950s as a period of suburban conformity. "She wore extreme clothes," a reporter later noted. As an agnostic Jew many of whose Jewish friends had become Unitarians, she arranged a Bar Mitzvah celebration for Daniel. The mothers of her children's classmates banned her own children from car pools because Betty preferred sending them to school in a taxi.[40]

Yet as successful as she had become in resisting the feminine mystique, her life in Grand View-on-Hudson was hardly tension free. There, a reporter noted, her "horror of provincialism turned into an abhorrence of suburbia." Friedan later portrayed herself as an active but remote member of her community, someone who felt "freakish having a career, worried that she was neglecting her children." Bored writing articles for women's magazines, she commented in the 1970s, she missed what life in Manhattan had offered, especially the chance for political and intellectual involvement. She remained concerned that she was not living up to her potential, that the domestic life was making her less of a person. In her retrospective presentation of herself in these years, she describes a woman torn by role conflicts. "I chauffeured, and did the P.T.A. and buffet dinners, and hid, like secret drinking in the morning, the book I was writing when my suburban neighbors came for coffee."[41]

Betty Friedan's own response to the questionnaire she devised for the Smith College class of 1942 presents a balanced picture of her sense of herself and her household in the spring of 1957, one very different from what she offered in hindsight. She reported that the family income fluctuated between $15,000 and more than $20,000, when the average household income of her classmates was just below $15,000. Of that total, she brought in between $4,000 and $8,000 a year, much of which went to cover her work expenses. In Parkway Village she had been able to rely on both a housekeeper and cooperative arrangements for child care (including a nursery school and a baby-sitting pool); she opted for a more uniformly individualistic solution. She had household help for three-and-one-half to four days a week. Had she been able to find the right person, she would have employed a full-time housekeeper. She made clear that the most difficult challenge she faced was finding the time that would enable her to combine commitments at home with her desire to use her mind. Although honest about the very real problems in marriage and career, on the whole her response was realistic but upbeat. She believed that as a woman she was achieving a greater ability to integrate her sense of herself, to achieve a gestalt. She came across as a woman who was very ambitious about her career, which she was still unsure would be as an author or psychologist.[42]

Over time, she had come to have fewer dreams about what could be accomplished politically, though she noted that she was more interested in politics than she had been at Smith. She frankly acknowledged what had tempered her idealism—everything from the obligations that came with family life, to her not wanting to imitate Joan of Arc, to her acceptance of complexity, to her turning away from abstract ideology, and to the general tenor of the age. To the extent that she conformed, she announced that she did so only in superficial ways. Yet she also emphasized what made her different from the average suburban housewife—she worked for the Democratic Party, preferred writing to motherhood, and resisted prejudice against Jews, African Americans, and Asians.[43]

At about the time Friedan provided this assessment, shortly after moving to Rockland County, she found an appropriate outlet for her energies and talents. Her creation and leadership of Intellectual Resources Pool, which she directed from 1958 to 1964 (the name changed in 1960 to Community Resources Pool), accomplished a number of goals. Her work on the pool began in one of those moments that mixed private and public. Soon after the Friedans moved to Rockland County, Betty worried that Daniel, who later as a mathematician won a MacArthur "genius" award, was bored in school. His teachers criticized him for solving math problems in his head rather than on paper. In the spring of 1957, as she was working on a story about new scientific discoveries at the nearby Lamont Observatory, Friedan realized that she could enrich her son's education by having him come into contact with one of the scientists who worked there. That fall, as Betty and Carl joined the fight to increase school funding, she began to consider developing a program to help not just her son but others as well.[44]

This program began with the idea of providing her oldest child with the intellectual challenges Friedan herself had lacked in Peoria. With Friedan's inspiration and leadership, the pool worked with teachers and administrators to enrich the curriculum by bringing into the schools artists, scientists, professors, and writers who lived in the area. Outside the school hours, it set up mentoring relationships between students and professionals. Under the pool's auspices, Friedan also established adult education offerings. By the early 1960s the programs for school children increasingly focused on controversial issues such as the role of racial and religious prejudice in zoning laws, urban renewal, nuclear testing, and the emerging nations of Africa and Asia. Friedan's work on the pool put her in frequent contact with people who were at the forefront of their fields. Among the people whom Friedan knew through their participation in the pool were journalists such as Roger Angell and Hazel Hertzberg; radical professors such as Gutman, Mills, and Swados; distinguished academics such as architectural historian James Fitch, philosopher Charles Frankel, and family sociologist William J. Goode; and

Rockland County residents involved in progressive politics and opposed to HUAC's redbaiting.[45]

The pool rested on commitments to enhance the creativity and identity of teenagers at the same time that it encouraged them to avoid the twin traps of a peer culture that relied on conformity, or a rebellion that tempted them to follow the example (and apparent resignation) of the Beat generation. The pool enabled her to insure that children, including her own, received an education that emphasized experimentation and hard work. Through her efforts she gained experience building and leading a complex and far-flung organization, writing grant proposals, chairing meetings, administering a budget, establishing support groups, generating press releases, and overcoming political resistance. For the first time since she left Smith, Friedan established herself as a leader at the center of an intellectual community. With this project she increased the income she brought into the household, opened up new possibilities for free-lance stories, and earned national and international attention from science educators, newspapers, the National Education Association, and the Voice of America.[46]

Friedan's work on the pool enabled her to engage critical issues of the Cold War. She entered the debate that raged nationally over the shortcomings of American public education. Her work made it possible for her to answer McCarthyites by proudly proclaiming the importance of intellectuals and ideas in American life. Her efforts rested on an insistence on the importance of identity in an age of conformity, ideas then common among social critics and social and behavioral scientists. In discussing conformity, Friedan was not only echoing the animus of 1950s social critics against mass society, but also suggesting how McCarthyism suppressed left-wing perspectives. In emphasizing identity, she drew on the notion of the individual identity crisis that Erikson developed in *Childhood and Society* (1950). Finally, through her work on the pool Friedan pondered the fate of middle-class American women—teenagers who were struggling with issues of adolescence, suburban volunteers who were committed to revitalizing their communities, and those like herself who wanted to sustain an intellectual and public life in the suburbs.

Friedan convinced the small Rockland Foundation to support the launching of the Intellectual Resources Pool in the fall of 1958. Those involved in the planning stages readily acknowledged her leadership, calling her Dean of the Faculty and giving her the title of chairman of the governing committee. For several years beginning in 1960, the New World Foundation, created by Anita McCormick Blaine and committed to supporting progressive causes such as world government and urban education, awarded the pool grants that included pay for Friedan's part-time work as project director. Under these grants, Friedan directed the establishment of a pilot program in South Orangetown, a school district with a more diverse population than much of Rockland County. Among the students participating were a significant percentage from working-class homes.[47]

Though her own situation, as well as that of her son, inspired her work on the pool, the October 1957 launching by the Russians of *Sputnik*, the world's first space vehicle, provided a critical context for Friedan's efforts. The USSR's achievement upset those who had used Cold War language to celebrate the virtues and uniqueness of America. *Sputnik* sparked debates about the deficiencies of American education, with the former Harvard President James B. Conant using *The American High School Today* (1959) to criticize the nation for falling behind the Soviets in science, math, and languages. Congress responded by linking the Cold War and social programs when in 1958 it passed the National Defense Education Act, a bill that sought to strengthen education in the sciences and foreign languages in colleges and universities.

Although conceived before the launching of *Sputnik*, the pool gained some of its power from the national debate on the crisis in education. Right away Friedan realized the connection between what she was doing and events across the nation. In the fall of 1957 she wondered why American science and education were not more creative, a deficiency that allowed the Russian scientists to surpass their American counterparts. One of the answers she offered consisted of several phrases to which contemporary social critics David Riesman, Vance Packard, and William H. Whyte Jr. had given considerable currency: suburban conformity, the lonely crowd, and organization man. Right after *Sputnik*, Friedan and the organizers of the pool held a meeting for adults with the agenda, "America's New Frontier Is Intellectual." People flocked to the symposium in numbers far greater than anyone expected. Before John F. Kennedy announced his New Frontier, in the fall of 1959 Friedan's program promised that it would "help a younger generation meet the challenge of our new intellectual frontiers." As stated in the announcement for a lecture series for adults on "The Individual and His Work," in an age of conformity it was important to "reaffirm the values of the individual."[48]

Explicit in Friedan's thinking was that the pool, with its emphasis on the centrality of intellectual life, offered a critique of the anti-intellectualism fostered by McCarthy and others in the 1950s. When she first conceived of the ideas that led to the formation of the pool, she stressed the word "intellectual" with considerable self-consciousness. At a time when reactionaries criticized presidential candidate Adlai E. Stevenson for being an "egg head," Friedan was wondering how thoughtful people, especially suburbanites without the benefit of institutions such as universities, could sustain intellectual life.[49]

The concept of identity was critical to Friedan's work on the pool. However, she did not use the word "identity" the way advocates of identity politics would in the 1970s and after, to denote a specific sense of self rooted in race, ethnicity, gender, or sexual preference. Rather, Friedan meant the word in its 1950s psychological meaning, to suggest how people, by struggling against the pressures of conformity and mass culture, exacerbated by both McCarthyism and the media, defined themselves by summoning the courage to stand against the dominant culture. As she said in 1963, reflecting on her condition and that of her children, the people who started the pool "felt that it was becoming increasingly difficult for children growing up in an American suburb or city, to find their own identity, to find the work to which they could commit themselves and thereby realize their human potential." She continued by arguing that the pool was also important because it helped people commit themselves "to an important problem of society," by becoming scientists, writers, architects, or lawyers. In late 1959, Friedan drafted an article called "the Intellectual Pied Pipers," on which she worked for the next year or so but was never able to publish. Here she focused on adolescents who struggled with the issue of identity, never able to decide what they wanted to do in any concerted way. She presented persuasive evidence that participation in the pool helped teenagers resist peer pressure.[50]

For Friedan, the question of identity had different implications for men and women. The pool enabled her to think about the situation that girls and women faced in American suburbs. Here Friedan moved on several levels at once. Having grown up in Peoria as a girl who felt the pains of being bright and unusual, and having given birth to a daughter in 1956, she was sensitive to the situation in which many female adolescents found themselves in Rockland County. As she interviewed girls who had benefited from the pool's activities, she paid particular attention to those who developed the courage to refuse to join a sorority, who were subject to derisive attacks for being brainy and offbeat, and who were afraid to speak up in class. At one point, she proudly noticed that junior high school girls joined boys in a science project. She took great pride when she learned that her project enabled girls to strengthen their sense of themselves, resist peer pressure, develop ambitions for a career, or in other ways take themselves more seriously.[51]

Friedan's programs were part of an effort, carried on across the nation, to reinvigorate American education. They challenged rote learning and answered the charges of those who were calling into question the approach of progressive educators inspired by John Dewey. In their emphasis on interdisciplinary learning, experimentation, and learning by doing, those who worked on the pool were in the vanguard of efforts in the 1960s to develop alternative educational systems. Indeed, one of the people with whom Friedan worked most closely on the pool, the Brooklyn College economist Carl Nordstrom, in 1961 published the first of a series of books on educational reform. In the series, Nordstrom and his colleagues explored many of the issues Friedan had been pondering through her work on the pool. They examined how the culture of American high schools worked "to stifle enthusiasm, to undermine fortitude, and to discourage the development of self-mastery on the part of students." Nordstrom worked with Edgar Z. Friedenberg, who between 1959 and 1965 emerged as one of the nation's leading and certainly its most adversarial critic of the educational system. In his *Vanishing Adolescent,* for which he acknowledged Nordstrom's help, Friedenberg expressed concern for the declining importance of meaningful relationships between teenagers and adults, something Friedan was then working to address. The book focused on the cultural and social forces that impeded what he, like Friedan, saw as the central challenge facing adolescents: the *"task of self-definition,"* something that could be achieved by increasing their sense of "intellectual competence" and by helping them learn that they were effective as writers and scientists.[52]

When he published *Coming of Age in America* in 1965, Friedenberg listed Nordstrom as his "co-investigator." In this widely read analysis of American public high schools, as in Friedan's unpublished work, Friedenberg explored how peer pressure and institutional restraints made it difficult for teenagers to develop an autonomous sense of self. Unlike Friedan, he paid remarkably little attention to the special situation of adolescent girls, despite the evidence he had on the subject.[53]

As Friedan thought about the impact of the pool on teenagers, she was harshly critical of members of the Beat generation, those precursors of the 1960s counter-culture who in the mid- and late-1950s had come to symbolize rebellion against conformity by wearing black, reciting Allen Ginsberg's *Howl* (1956), and reading Jack Kerouac's *On the Road* (1957). Here Friedan was anticipating the arguments Paul Goodman developed in *Growing Up Absurd* (1960), which focused on the problems young people had in developing an authentic sense of self within the confines of a society dominated by large organizations. Sharing Friedan's training in Gestalt psychology, Goodman emphasized the importance of personal growth toward "the most elementary objective opportunities and worth-while goals," marked by creativity and community. With society making the achievement of identity so difficult, he concluded, young people were disaffected. Like Friedan, Goodman found the solution the Beats offered unsatisfactory, since he recoiled at their resignation and parochialism. The quest of the Beats for "heightened experiences," he argued, was unsatisfactory, since this made it unlikely that they would pursue "the things that constitute seasoned experience." Yet in one very important respect, Goodman's analysis differed from the one Friedan was working to articulate. For Goodman, the disaffected were all males. It was they who, lacking the opportunity for worthwhile work, could not develop an authentic identity. He explained that he focused intentionally on boys and men because for him the problem of identity and meaning were "primarily" male problems. "A girl's career," he noted, "does not have to be self-justifying, for she will have children, which is absolutely self-justifying, like any other natural or creative act."[54]

Friedan's work on the pool sharpened her sense of the possibilities that adult women faced in suburbia. Though men dominated numerically in the governance of the pool and the teaching under its auspices, a considerable number of women were involved as board members, supporters, and mentors. Yet early on, Friedan recognized what was at stake. In the fall of 1957, she wrote several years later, she recognized the elemental condition of life in the suburbs: men liked to take control but, because they were away during the day, only women actually accomplished anything. At least by implication, she looked with some skepticism on women whose volunteer work rarely went beyond the mundane or who lacked a commitment to social change. Instead, she cast her lot with women who were committed to professional and sustained action, preferences that would shape what she wrote in *The Feminine Mystique*. Thus, when she gathered fifteen women in her living room in Grand View-on-Hudson to get the project off the ground, she realized that in the suburbs the real leaders among women found each other and then made time to get things done between the rounds of suburban chores. Yet she also noticed that these women often did not really understand the importance of the work they were doing. Soon Friedan found a way of addressing some of these issues publicly. In the fall of 1959 she moderated a panel discussion on "Women and Work," which featured the writer and teacher Hazel Hertzberg, a female psychoanalyst, and a housewife. She was discovering that there was a suburban audience for the discussion of women's issues.[55]

The pool caused Friedan to think about women's issues as they reflected her own situation. In the fall of 1957, when she listed groups who might want to be involved in the pool, she included women who sustained intellectual interests. Her work on the pool also gave her the courage to present herself as a professional woman. Listed as "Mrs. Carl Friedan, Chairman," in the pool brochure in the fall of 1958, a year later her name appeared as "Chairman—Betty Friedan, writer," a statement of her independence that took some courage and perhaps a sense of defiance. Indeed, a 1960 *New York Times* story about the pool identified her as "Mrs. Betty Friedan, a writer." When she described her career in grant proposals, though she did not mention her work for Federated Press or the *UE News*, she identified herself primarily as someone who since 1944 had been a writer on suburban issues. These were important statements about who she was; she remarked, in language that fully conveyed the dynamics of her own life, that by helping the young discover their identity, adult participants had developed a better sense of themselves and their commitments. Reading an article by Christopher Jencks in 1962, she marked a passage on the relationship between career and selfhood. "The man who has no occupation," Jencks had written in gendered language that Friedan would soon challenge but which she at the time used, "or who moves rapidly from one to another, may become a man without an identity."[56]

In June 1961, the pool faced its most serious crisis and one with significant echoes from Friedan's past. From time to time, Friedan and her colleagues had heard rumors that some people in Rockland County felt that, as she wrote in a report to the New World Foundation, the pool was "communistic" and the foundation "subversive." The project had raised some eyebrows in the community. Some of the old-timers, suspicious of artists, writers, intellectuals, and newcomers, cast doubts on the value of the pool's efforts. Hostility escalated when rumors circulated that the pool was bankrolled by the USSR with money channeled through the dangerous-sounding New World Foundation. The attack on the efforts of Friedan and her colleagues was ominous, connected as it was with a nationwide effort of the John Birch Society to ferret out progressive efforts, especially in the schools.[57]

Rumors intensified during the 1960–61 school year. In early June 1961, the Subversive Activities Committee of the Rockland County American Legion sponsored a talk by a speaker who charged that local Communists, whose names he claimed were well known but whom no one had bothered to finger, had selected the local high schools as one of the "prime targets" of their activities. Under the auspices of the pool, some critics said, students were being taught sexual immorality, subversion, and atheism. The New World Foundation, redbaiters asserted, was on the Attorney General's list of subversive organizations. Communists, they alleged, were active in the program. Well aware of how many Jews were involved in the pool and how much they had fought against efforts to blur the line between church and state by introducing religion into the schools, Friedan understood the anti-Semitic dimension of these attacks. At a school board meeting in late June 1961, called to consider the future of the pool's cooperation with the schools, the crisis erupted, with the meeting going on until early in the morning. Led by people Friedan had reason to believe were members of the John Birch Society, the attack became vicious, with accusations of Communist influence. The charge of the use of "Marxist dialectics" made one mother say to Friedan, "This is the way Adolph Hitler started." In the end, the school board voted to continue the program. In her report to the foundation, and perhaps in more public settings, Friedan forcefully answered the redbaiters. She insisted that it was impossible to foster excellence among children when people attacked those who were non-conformists, intellectuals, or suspected of Communist affiliation.[58]

Social scientists at the time understood that fights like that over the pool involved a new politics based on status anxieties, highly charged symbolic issues, and a sense of rootlessness. Like Friedan, in the mid-1950s they rejected social class as an explanation for such conflicts. In a 1955 book titled *The New American Right*, a group of academics explored how a resurgent conservatism expressed an anger, an anti-intellectualism, a desire to enforce conformity, and sense of conspiracy. The New Right, wrote Daniel Bell in 1955, relied on "a compulsive moral fervor" as it equated Communism with sin. The New Right rested on what the historian Richard Hofstadter, drawing on *The Authoritarian Personality*, called pseudo conservatism—"a profound if largely unconscious hatred of our society." This morally charged perspective grew out of the 1930s, Bell wrote, when the rise of Fascism caused liberals in control of cultural life to "look at the Communist with some sympathy," someone whom they saw as "ultimately, philosophically wrong, but still as a respectable member of the community."[59]

As Mills had predicted in *White Collar,* the old middle class, its social base undermined by a series of momentous social and economic changes, harkened back to an older American way of life and set of values. People like Friedan, representatives of the new middle class, would take heart from his prediction that "whatever occasional victories" conservatives won, their victories, going "against the main drift of a new society," proved "to be illusory or temporary."[60]

In the late 1950s and early 1960s, Friedan hoped that her work on the pool might lead to funding from the Ford Foundation and to her publication of a series of articles in prominent magazines. Although these proved to be dead ends, in working on the pool over more than six years, Friedan accomplished several goals that helped put her in a position to write *The Feminine Mystique*. Like her earlier efforts for *Parkway Villager,* her work for the pool drew her attention to the problems middle-class women faced in the suburbs. As she did elsewhere, in what she wrote for the pool she developed a positive picture of what suburban women could accomplish. Indeed, she herself was a powerful example of a suburban woman with children who carved out for herself a professional career of considerable significance. Moreover, her work on the pool gave her an idea of what adult education could accomplish, strengthened her sense of the importance of pioneering community activism, and helped undergird her consciousness of issues facing women.[61]

Whatever the crosscurrents of Friedan's life in the suburbs, several things are nonetheless abundantly clear. In both Parkway Village and Rockland County, she found ways to transform the places where she lived from private enclaves to cooperative communities. As a community activist in Queens and while living in Grand View-on-Hudson, she fought to validate women's roles as political and social figures at a time when dominant forces in the society worked so powerfully in the opposite direction. In both Parkway Village and Rockland County, her desire to fit into the mainstream and to earn acceptance by people whose judgment she valued bumped up against the complications of reality. Moreover, like other radicals in the 1950s, as well as some after 1968, she surrendered her hopes for a major social reorganization and focused instead on what she could do on the local level.

To a considerable extent, her experience in Parkway Village and Rockland County provided a basis for what she would write in *The Feminine Mystique*. She had learned to manage a complicated life. She had shifted her attention from working-class and African American women to middle-class and white ones. She had developed an antipathy to volunteer activities that were limited in scope, preferring instead women's professional efforts that sought to change society. Above all, she was giving extended consideration to the problems middle-class women faced in the suburbs. It was during her years in the suburbs that she emerged as a successful free-lance writer. In her articles for women's and family magazines, Friedan offered a critique of suburban America. As a writer and public figure she was finding her voice, although she encountered obstacles along the way. In both published and unpublished articles, she focused on women, often emphasizing their assertiveness, sense of community, and ambition for careers.

Free-lance Writer, 1952–63

Betty Goldstein was the labor journalist whose work ended in 1953. Betty Friedan was the free-lance writer whose career began the year before, though the fruits of her efforts would not begin to appear in print until 1955. The change in name not only announced her married state but also safely separated her from a past that McCarthyism made dangerous to reveal. Failing to gain employment with magazines published by Time Inc., she developed a career as a free lancer. She drafted or considered stories that directly challenged the celebratory picture of America as a homogeneous society. She also wrote but could not publish an attack on McCarthyism. Even when she began to break into print, she had to eliminate discussions of nonwhites and social class as well as tone down treatments of assertive women. Those who controlled the marketplace—advertisers, editors, and literary agents—taught her that if she wanted to make it as a free-lance writer, she would have to trim her political sails and write in a more reassuring way, and limit her subject matter to middle-class suburban women. Since high school, Friedan had worried about what it meant to write but not publish, a fear McCarthyism and her own difficulty as an author intensified.[1]

Getting into print in mass-circulation magazines was in many ways bittersweet. Now she was being published and widely read but at the cost of not always being able to write as she pleased. Only with the publication of *The Feminine Mystique* would she believe she had found her own voice. Yet even then what she had learned as a free-lance writer affected what she wrote. Even though there was a major shift in her perspective and commitments, some of what she did as a labor journalist and Popular Front feminist reverberated in her free-lance pieces. Now she was writing not as an observer of lives very different from her own but as a witness of lives and issues that she knew firsthand.

The articles Friedan placed in mass-circulation magazines were not naive celebrations of the pleasures of suburbia. Rather, she offered a critique, albeit a muted one, of the stereotyping and conformity of suburban life in the 1950s. If her experience with Cold War magazine culture hardly fulfilled the high hopes that Smith College, World War II, and labor radicalism inspired, neither did it make her as complicit as she later claimed in the culture that her 1963 book descried. In fact, her experience as a free-lance writer reinforced some of the lessons she learned as a labor journalist not only about women who fought and organized but also about men and corporations who resisted.[2]

As an author of articles for mass-circulation women's and family magazines, Friedan entered a world that shaped the career and writings of many who emerged as major American social critics. A number of other widely read authors of the 1960s and 1970s had careers as magazine writers, including Vance Packard, Charles Silberman, Alvin Toffler, and William H. Whyte Jr. In the 1950s, as now, it was not easy for a free lancer to make a living by writing for mass-circulation magazines. Advertisers exercised a good deal of control over what went into print. Beginning in the mid-1950s, with television competing for advertising dollars, once vital magazines faced downsizing or, in some cases, extinction. For many writers, this made income erratic at best. At the top of the heap, in-house authors or others who were in demand could earn a significant income, though changing fashions and media competition threatened even them. People like Friedan had to hustle continually as they thought up story ideas, tried to second-guess a fickle market, and negotiated with agents and editors.[3]

In the postwar world, periodicals such as *Ladies' Home Journal, McCall's, Mademoiselle,* and *Redbook* served a key role in teaching millions of mostly white, middle-class, suburban women how to live their lives. With some justification, critics and historians have argued that these publications fostered a conformist ideology. The advertisements, fiction, and human interest stories, they have noted, reinforced the notion that men were in charge of the public sphere while women dominated the private sphere. They depicted a world where women could achieve happiness as dedicated consumers, committed mothers, and loyal wives. In *The Feminine Mystique* Friedan stated that as an author for these magazines she had helped create "the picture of the modern American housewife." She detailed how the magazines pictured American women as "frivolous, almost childlike; fluffy and feminine; passive; gaily content in a world of bedroom and kitchen, sex, babies and home."[4]

Historians have convincingly challenged the way Friedan and others characterized mass-circulation magazines of the 1950s, especially their portrayal of women. Joanne Meyerowitz, having conducted a systematic analysis of non-fiction articles in widely read periodicals, has cast doubts on Friedan's assertion that such articles fostered the worst kind of Cold War ideology by emphasizing domesticity and togetherness. Meyerowitz questioned Friedan's version of the repressive mass culture of the magazine world. The articles she investigated, a wider sample than Friedan examined, revealed that "domestic ideals co-existed in ongoing tension with an ethos of individual achievement that celebrated nondomestic activity, individual striving, public service and public success." Meyerowitz has proven that many pieces in mass-circulation magazines actually "expressed overt admiration for women whose individual striving moved them beyond the home," in the process supporting women's work outside the home and women's activity in politics. Meyerowitz has enabled us to see that these magazines, even though they simultaneously advocated domesticity and femininity, also portrayed women as independent, creative, and nonconformist. Moreover, she has correctly demonstrated that Friedan's work, "remarkably rooted in postwar culture," had resonance for contemporaries precisely because it both relied on and reformulated what others had stated. Finally, she has suggested that Friedan's vision of an anti-feminist domestic and public environment, which historians have accepted, distorts the postwar scene by minimizing alternative visions available at the time.[5]

Exploring additional dimensions of the same world, the historian Eva Moskowitz has questioned Friedan's condemnation of women's magazines for emphasizing the image of the happy housewife. After examining articles in the women's magazines with the largest circulation in the postwar era, Moskowitz concluded that "far from imagining the home as a haven," they "rendered it as a deadly battlefield on which women lost their happiness, if not their minds." She has pointed to the many articles that, exploring the psychological tensions women experienced, emphasized how difficult it was for women to gain satisfaction through domesticity and marriage. Even anti-feminists, Moskowitz has shown, stressed how hard it was to achieve domestic bliss. Thus, in her 1949 article "Occupation: Housewife," Dorothy Thompson described the emptiness that women felt when they responded to the census form. To be sure, the authors of 1950s articles did not anticipate the structural changes in families and occupations that feminists would later call for. Instead they suggested that the solution would come through "therapeutic principles of psychological change." Thus writers promoted adjustment to domestic ideals at the same time that they praised the goals of self-fulfillment. What Moskowitz calls a psychological "discourse of discontent" in women's magazines underscores the continuity she sees between what appeared in 1950s periodicals and what feminists discovered in the 1960s. Consequently, she has quite properly called into question the notion that feminists, including Friedan, suddenly discovered women's unhappiness about which the magazines had supposedly been silent.[6]

Friedan learned how to become a free-lance writer from several sources. At Highlander in the summer of 1941, she had learned how to write for a wide audience, even going so far as to contact a Manhattan literary agency to see if she could break into print in a national market. As a labor journalist she had published several pieces for publications other than Federated Press or the *UE News*. At Parkway Village, many of the people she knew worked as free-lance writers. While living there in 1952, she read a manuscript of an article that told "astonishing success stories" of people who launched part-time careers, including free-lance writers. In Rockland County and through her membership in the Society of Magazine Writers, she gained from friends and colleagues invaluable clues about what topics and approaches editors were looking for. In Rockland County Friedan knew at least two other free lancers, Jhan Robbins and June Robbins, who in 1960 had published in *Redbook* an article titled "Why Young Mothers Feel Trapped." Here they explored how American women of all social classes felt profoundly confined in the "squirrel cage" of the suburban home or urban apartment. Finally, in 1958 and 1959 Friedan advised others how to develop publishable articles when she taught writing courses at New York University and the New School for Social Research.[7]

In addition, her 1961 article on free lancing appeared in a book called *Prose by Professionals*. In "How to Find and Develop Article Ideas," Friedan frankly acknowledged the problems she faced trying to combine being a suburban mother and a writer. Unable to write at home and with no library adequate to her purposes nearby, she journeyed into Manhattan and worked at her husband's office. She used income earned from publishing to hire household help. She also told how she learned from studying formulas, but emphasized that she did not want to do formulaic writing. Rather, she talked about working on topics that truly excited her. "The act of intellectual creation," she noted, "can be as real and personal and exciting as childbirth." It was possible to convey truth and reality, she continued, only if they originated in and actually became the author's intensely individual experience. "You have to see it yourself, before you can make the reader really see it," wrote the woman who would state in *The Feminine Mystique* that she was a typical suburban housewife. At the time Friedan also acknowledged her ambition to write on intellectual subjects. In an unpublished piece written around 1959, she bragged that she had increasingly abandoned standard approaches and instead experimented with how she might get across complicated academic ideas in ways that the general reader could understand.[8]

Typical of articles in mass-market magazines she wrote for, Friedan's pieces, published between 1955 and the early 1960s, revealed a woman preoccupied by finding authentic community life and successfully combining motherhood and marriage. She discussed how to sustain a productive career as she herself moved from city to suburb and left a job in an organization to become a free-lance writer. Challenging the image of Cold War domestic perfection, she critiqued suburban life by drawing a dismal picture of those who conformed. She offered alternatives to conventional choices, and explored the strength of cooperative communities. She wrote profiles of American women that stood in opposition to the picture of the happy, suburban housewife who turned her back on a career in order to find satisfaction at home. What she drafted but could not publish was even stronger, featuring racially integrated communities, liberated women, and men who battled against conformity. An examination of Friedan's magazine pieces adds weight to the conclusions of Meyerowitz and Moskowitz. At the same time it draws attention to the forces that stood between a writer's intentions and a published article.[9]

A central theme of Friedan's magazine articles from the 1950s was the ambition of independent women who achieved excellence in a career and raised a family. This was her dream, a kind of gestalt that integrated everything into a whole life. Emphasizing the importance of community-based child care and grass-roots organizing, one of Friedan's stories shows the connection between her work as a labor journalist and the feminism she later articulated. In a piece that appeared in *Parents' Magazine* in 1957, "Day Camp in the Driveways," Friedan described a group of women in a suburban housing project who successfully organized day care for their children, disproving experts, most of them male, who told them they had taken on an impossible task. Indeed, they learned from experience that, rather than relying on professionals, they should trust their own instincts. Perhaps reflecting Friedan's notion of a truly democratic organization, the women proved that they could work cooperatively without replicating a hierarchical model. They eventually developed a program that served as a pilot for a cross-class summer opportunity for city children.[10]

Another article, published in *Cosmopolitan* in 1956, profiled Marjorie Steele Hartford, the wife of the supermarket heir Huntington Hartford, who, despite her wealth, pursued a professional career in acting. Unlike the

wealthy women Friedan had castigated as a labor journ
ford lived a simple life; she not only raised her childre
joyous hard work of an actress to give her own life a
husband's fortune, Friedan noted, could not buy his wi.
and performing contracts she earned with her ability and
had a marriage where the wife's concerns mattered. Marjon
cared more for her equity card than for her expensive je
elements in her past—her family's ownership of a jewelry store and her
membership in the Newspaper Guild—Friedan was alluding to aspects of
her own past that led her to reject the feminine mystique. Even so, when
she came to write *The Feminine Mystique,* she insisted that "when you
wrote about an actress for a woman's magazine, you wrote about her as a
housewife."[11]

In the fall of 1955, Friedan published an article entitled "The Gal Who
Defied Dior" about Claire McCardell, "a small-town American girl" who
became an internationally known fashion designer by developing practical
and comfortable clothes for ordinary women to wear at home and at work.
She was innovative, gutsy, persistent—and married. Friedan's piece played
the home-grown American stylist off against the fashion monger of Paris.
Another article—reminiscent of what Friedan had known at Smith when her
mother achieved independence when her father was ill—described a woman
in a small New Hampshire town who, after her husband's death, successfully
took over publication of the local newspaper her husband had edited, and
still managed to raise five children.[12]

Friedan also described women accomplishing important tasks as they
took on traditionally feminine civic roles, implicitly undercutting the powerful image of the ideal suburban housewife. One article recounted how a
group of women of her generation, working through organizations such as
the League of Women Voters, transformed Peoria by destroying the political
machine, curbing gambling and prostitution, and improving the schools.
What drove them, Friedan noted, was a belief in their own power to bring
about change. On the one hand, Friedan's peers had elected a woman to the
city council for the first time in its history. Yet their roles were well within
the confines established elsewhere by generations of women reformers. The
city's governing board relied on the woman on the city council to apply her
housekeeping skills to City Hall, removing grime and spittoons. In addition,
the local AAUW campaigned to improve the schools.[13]

In an article titled "I Went Back to Work," published in *Charm* in April
1955, Friedan touched on some of the issues she later claimed to have only
discovered when she began to work on her book in 1957, but her approach
to these issues differed markedly from her later work. In this article, she

ned that she returned to work after the birth of her first child "both
m economic necessity and from personal choice." Initially, she confessed,
she had so much contempt for housework that she did not bother to do it
well. Though she recognized the importance of being a good mother, she
boasted, that task was not what she called her " 'real' life."

Friedan wrote that early on, she had pitied suburban housewives who led
boring lives while their husbands and women like herself did interesting
work. Over time, she had stopped feeling that she was better than housewives. She felt she had adjusted to motherhood more effectively because
she had not surrendered the pleasures she derived from her work. She felt
guilt not about going back to work, but about "feelings of inadequacy as a
mother." Over time she understood her young son needed a close relationship with her, but that she did not have to lavish attention on him all the
time. Needing to be away from home during the day to work, Friedan
eventually solved the problem of child care by hiring a woman who truly
loved her son. Eventually Friedan came to realize that it was possible to
handle multiple roles successfully. She had no regrets about her decision or
apparently about her privileged position. She believed her child and family
were better off, and acknowledged that her "whole life had always been
geared around creative, intellectual work" and "a professional career."[14]

The theme of independent women also emerged in an unpublished piece
in which she attacked McCarthyism. She wrote "Was Their Education Un-
American?" soon after her Smith classmates filled out a questionnaire at
their tenth reunion in 1952, five years before the questionnaire that Friedan
claimed was critical in first awakening her feminism in 1957. Friedan
couched her remarks about the survey as an answer to McCarthyism. The
experience of her classmates proved that when intelligent women received
an education under conditions of academic freedom, their resulting political independence justified the very academic freedom that McCarthy was
threatening. She acknowledged that her Smith classmates had read radical
books and studied with professors upon whom redbaiters would have
looked with suspicion. Her survey revealed that a significant proportion of
Smith graduates were engaged citizens who voted Republican but resisted
conformity and provided leadership to their communities, working in political campaigns, serving on community boards, and fighting to improve race
relations.[15]

Only one article celebrated motherhood and called women's pursuit of
careers into question in a fairly unambiguous manner. In an "as told to Betty
Friedan" piece, the actress Julie Harris recalled how, when she was growing
up, her career aspirations made her *"think that women who did nothing but
have babies were stupid creatures."* Then when she was rehearsing the part of

Joan of Arc, she learned she was pregnant. She hoped for a boy because she believed girls faced difficult situations. So she turned down the role of Joan of Arc to prepare for the delivery of her child by natural childbirth, encouraged by her husband but warned by her doctor she probably could not stand the pain involved. At the same time, she considered giving up her career ambitions and devoting herself to motherhood. When the pain of childbirth came, Harris toughed it out like a professional, rejecting the pain killers. When she came out from the anaesthetic administered after her son was born, she felt greater joy and a greater sense of being alive than she had experienced as an actress on Broadway. Harris insisted on breast-feeding the baby, despite the objections of both her doctor and her baby nurse. Indeed, she let the nurse go after a week, taking great pleasure in her husband's eagerness to share in the baby's care.

After a few months, Harris resumed studying for her role as Joan of Arc. What enabled her to play the role of such a great heroine, she asserted, was the confidence she achieved with the birth of her son. In the end, the lesson seemed more domestic. Now she was willing to bring a daughter into the world—she would "tell her being a mother is the most courageous, difficult profession. It's easier to be a good actress than a good mother." In the final paragraph Harris brought home her point: acting offered "only glimpses of creation. Motherhood is the experience of pure creation itself."[16]

To the extent that Friedan, in the Harris article, stated a conventional position on motherhood and career, she did so because of pressure from the editor. Indeed, when *Reader's Digest* published the piece, it left out the material on acting and focused on childbirth. Even so, the article vividly celebrated the heroics of natural childbirth, which in the 1950s contravened male medical expertise. Friedan herself believed strongly in natural childbirth but had to have her third child by Caesarian. In affirming the creativity of motherhood and placing a lesser emphasis on the appeal of a high-powered acting career, the article did not celebrate passive female motherhood or attack women for pursuing careers.[17]

Though many of Friedan's articles depicted middle-class married women as feisty and independent, she highlighted examples, both positive and negative, of cooperative, fulfilling, middle-class marriages. One article on suburban life examined how families with strong but absent fathers and homemaker mothers undermined the self-esteem of teenage girls. Drawing on the expertise of a local social worker, Friedan told the story of several sexually promiscuous teenagers from well-to-do Westchester County families who were acting out a larger drama. The article concentrated on the case of a girl named Phyllis whose sexual activity was motivated by her feelings of loneliness and lack of popularity. The social worker explored with the parents why their daughter might have negative feelings about being a girl. They discovered that the daughter was reacting against the fact that her father, trying to provide all of the material advantages he missed as a child, worked so hard that he had little time for her. Although he managed to find the time to acknowledge his son's achievements, the father considered it unmanly to reach out to his daughter. It emerged that the mother undermined her daughter in a different way. Although people in her community admired her for keeping a beautiful home and having a happy marriage, she now revealed her disappointment in having given up a promising singing career to advance her husband's profession. Instead of acknowledging that she needed fulfillment outside the home, she had tried to live vicariously through her daughter. Once the mother realized this, she resumed her career as a singer and a community worker. This situation echoed the experience of Friedan's mother, and its resolution enabled Friedan, in a figurative way, to make her own mother's life right. In the end, the mother was able to support her daughter who in turn no longer had to act out with boys to get back at her parents.[18]

In contrast to this example, Friedan also wrote about non-conformist married couples. In another "as told to Betty Friedan" piece she narrated the story of two people who met as mental patients in a residential treatment facility. She demonstrated how the couple achieved enough self-understanding and confidence to re-enter the world and get married. The story ended with an ironic play on the suburban dream: a picture of the two former mental patients living in the suburbs. The wife remarked that her husband had "put on 20 pounds on my cooking, . . . I have quit work. We are active in our church, Little League, community theater. Our house is full of friends."[19]

In *Mademoiselle* in 1955, Friedan sang the praises of a married couple, Smith- and Amherst-educated, whose lives departed from the model of the domesticated suburban housewife and organization man. Fred and Kiki Sherman had started off conventionally, until Fred rebelled against the monotony of office work. They purchased a small, deserted island off the south shore of Long Island, fifty miles from New York City, and with determination and hard work, they developed successful businesses there. "Kiki shares her husband's life in a way that few American women have since pioneer days," Friedan wrote in typical women's magazine jargon, but conveying a message that went against her later picture of such magazines as seedbeds of the feminine mystique. Friedan noted that after five years of raising children and doing physical labor under adverse conditions, Kiki "decided maybe there could be such a thing as sharing *too* much of a man's life." Yet Friedan also pointed out how the wife participated in many traditionally male activities, including fishing for food and helping in building their house.[20]

Another theme of Friedan's articles was the search for cooperative suburban communities, something she took a great personal interest in. While the Friedans were living in Parkway Village and looking at experimental suburban communities to which they might move, they came across Hickory Hill in Rockland County, a successfully cooperative subdivision. Here thirty-two families had worked hard to produce a community that provided "all the security, the rich and easy give-and-take of a big old-fashioned family." Their community objectives reflected Friedan's own commitments: to break down the isolation of the individual household, work cooperatively to build houses and take care of children, avoid making distinctions based on social status, and humanely treat children who did not fit standard definitions of normality. At times, Friedan remarked, "it would have been hard to tell which children belonged to which parents." Another article recounted the struggle of a group of Manhattanites to build a cooperative community in South Norwalk, Connecticut. Friedan celebrated the victory of volunteers over professional skeptics, and the advantages of communally owned land and the give-and-take of cooperative decision-making.[21]

By the late 1950s, Friedan was achieving success as a writer. She was able to sell articles, which were reprinted in the United States and abroad. She usually worked close to home and often focused on people she had known in her earlier life. For some articles she traveled a good distance, in one case writing a piece on corporate sponsorship of an adult education program for men in St. Louis. She approvingly discussed the benefits of continuing liberal arts education for male executives, a program she later advocated for women, modeled on the GI Bill. She praised the program for giving American businessmen breadth and vision. Indeed, she ended the article with a quote from Alexis de Tocqueville, the nineteenth-century French observer of American life. Celebrants of American uniqueness in the 1950s used de Tocqueville to hail the nation's uniqueness, but Friedan called on him to make a sharp criticism. Echoing her attitudes as a labor journalist, Friedan informed her readers of de Tocqueville's belief that society's rulers should "set less value on the work, and more value on the workman."[22]

Friedan's most successful article came from an idea suggested by the mother of one of her children's playmates, a scientist at Lamont Geological Observatory, not far from Friedan's home. The result was her September 1958 *Harper's Magazine* piece, "The Coming Ice Age," a scientific detective story about two scientists figuring out why the melting of Arctic ice might cause another Ice Age. It appeared as the cover story in *Harper's*, a highly respected general-interest magazine. It was widely reprinted, in *Reader's Digest,* in an anthology on the best articles in *Harper's* history, and in magazines around the world. In response, an editor at W. W. Norton called Friedan to see if she might expand the piece into a book. Not interested in science writing, she told him, "if I'm ever going to write a book, it's going to be about my own work!"[23]

Despite her successes as a free-lance writer, she faced serious obstacles. Her fights with Carl caught her in a painful spiral. To be more independent she needed to earn more money, but to earn more money she needed a more supportive husband and the money to buy freedom. Her income from writing articles was unpredictable, a situation exacerbated by the pressure she was under to help support the household and justify the expenses for child care. By 1957, she had three children to take care of and a large house as well. In addition, Friedan did not feel comfortable in the suburbs, where no local institutions provided a supportive environment.

There were other challenges. Some of the difficulty in publishing articles was political. Getting "Was Their Education UnAmerican?" published when Senator Joseph R. McCarthy was at the height of his power proved impossible. In 1955, her agent suggested that Friedan write about the racial integration of a New Jersey suburb, a lead she did not follow. Although the Intellectual Resources Pool provided her with contacts and story ideas, from 1957 on, her writings on it came to nought. By the spring of 1961, more than a dozen publications had rejected her article on the pool. At times writing was laboriously slow. Though she has claimed that before long she stopped writing articles on speculation, her files contain dozens of unpublished articles in various stages of completion. She carried out extensive research and wrote as many as ten drafts. In some instances, articles were accepted and then rejected, often because magazines went out of business as television diminished their advertising revenues. Sometimes more than three years elapsed from first idea to publication. Eager for financial independence, Friedan nonetheless failed in her effort to turn articles into a movie or television series.[24]

Like other journalists, at times Friedan encountered skepticism and hostility from academics. When a scientist from the observatory saw a draft of her story on the Ice Age, he claimed that it contained many errors and criticized its treatment as "flippant, sensational, suitable perhaps for an article about a person in the entertainment world, but entirely unsuitable for the presentation of a scientific theory." Friedan responded to a friend that the real issue was the low opinion these scientists had of popular magazines and the authors who wrote for them.[25]

Even when she was published, she often could not convey what was on her mind. In an early version of the article on Hickory Hill, Friedan was searching for ways to connect what she had found in the community with the writings of Erich Fromm and Rollo May regarding people's search for meaning. Missing from the published version was her observation that women were more effective than men in repairing and painting walls. In another instance she used the techniques New Journalists would employ in the 1960s to explore a topic that was too controversial for family magazines to handle in the way she wanted. Her article on sexually promiscuous teenagers ended up as an exploration of how parents and social workers worked with a girl to stop her from acting out sexually, but it originated as a series of highly personal and vivid narratives from Phyllis and her mother about questions of sexuality and identity that Friedan had wanted to incorporate into her story.[26]

More often, however, the problem was that she was challenging the Cold War consensus. She knew the difficulties from her own experience. She had been present when editors told Thurgood Marshall, then an NAACP lawyer who worked on landmark desegregation cases, they would not print stories about desegregation. In a draft of the article on South Norwalk, she mentioned the community's rejection of restrictive covenants that would prevent non-whites or Jews from owning land in the development. Indeed, Friedan made clear that several African American families, a Japanese American teacher, and a Chinese woman were among the residents. She also described how women from less integrated suburban areas looked skeptically at an integrated neighborhood. At one point, someone remarked that the community "is like a little UN." Her husband responded "No, it's a little America." A sea of whiteness erased these issues from the printed version; all that remained was mention of "people with the widest range of cultural differences," for which varied occupations were offered as evidence. Something similar happened with "New Hampshire Love Story," the article about the woman who took over her husband's newspaper after his death. In early drafts Friedan hailed her efforts to improve society by starting a local branch of the League of Woman Voters, helping to elect the only woman mayor in New England, fighting for fair treatment of her mentally retarded daughter, exposing slum conditions, and working hard to end racial and religious prejudice. None of these crucial details appeared in the published article.[27]

There were telling differences in the draft and final version of the article on Peoria as well. Pre-publication, she was writing with a passion, experimenting, as the New Journalists of the 1960s would, with ways of forcefully injecting her own voice into the piece. In the draft, Friedan gave equal prominence to her high school classmates John Parkhurst and Harriet Parkhurst (who was also her Smith classmate). The published article did not mention Harriet by name and did not mention her key role as investigator and grass-roots organizer at a time when she had four children. Moreover, the draft demonstrated that Peoria was a place with a lively political culture. This liveliness was missing from the article. Also absent was Friedan's contrast of the ideological, Washington-based McCarthyism with the responsible, practical, non-ideological politics that made Peoria an all-American city.[28]

The most telling example of how magazine editors shaped Friedan's work emerges from a comparison, which the historian Sylvie Murray has convincingly explored, between the drafted and printed version of "Day Camp in the Driveways." In the draft version, Alice Barsky, one of the mothers who organized the camp, remarked how strong her back was "for lugging kids and groceries, and how thick my skin before my hands start bleeding from detergent." Barsky did not believe that "a bunch of ignorant housewives" could pull off this project. Indeed, she confessed that she "ran to Spock everytime the kid cried, and checked with Gesell before saying yes or no." As they went about the process of signing up parents and getting equipment, Barsky told Friedan she felt "absolutely liberated." Barsky made clear that women working together could resist their husbands' criticisms. Friedan showed how a cooperative community of women developed as they stood outside the local supermarket and talked about how to proceed. Learning what they had accomplished over the course of three summers, Friedan concluded in the draft that she was witnessing the emergence of "this new breed of Jill," as they called themselves in a musical comedy they staged. In one scene, the mother turned over household responsibilities to her husband and rushed out of the apartment to go to a meeting. Her daughter asked "Where's Mommy going?" Her father answered "She's going to be president," to which the daughter responded quizzically "Of the United States?" "Could be," the father answered, "could be."[29]

As Murray has shown, key elements were missing from the published version. By omitting reference to the occupations of the ex-GIs and to how much they had to spend to move to the development, Murray writes, the published version turned "lower-middle class families into generic, classless families." The published version significantly toned down the feminist implications of the drafts, eliminating, for example, Barsky's exhilaration at being "absolutely liberated" and the celebration of "this new breed of Jill." In drafts Friedan expressed even more skepticism about male expertise than in the published version. In addition, the drafts forcefully depicted women who had become aware of their ability to get things done, and spoke more emphatically of the women's empowerment as they relied on each other to accomplish their goal. What took the place of women's self-assertion, Murray has pointed out, was a do-it-yourself story for parents. The final version did not contain the father's statement that his wife might become president of the United States. In the story, Murray has effectively argued, Friedan "portrayed this reliance on volunteering as the trend of the future." As Friedan herself wrote in the draft, these women were a new breed on the suburban frontier who were learning how to take things in their own hands and solve problems.[30]

Like her peers among magazine writers, Friedan often encountered the tension between what she wanted to say and what editors were willing to publish. She was not in a position to resist their pressure to eliminate material that was too serious, techniques that were too innovative, or perspectives that were too politically sensitive. As a result, what appeared in print under her name explored less fully than she wanted issues of race, class, and gender.[31]

Her difficulties in publishing controversial articles about women, Friedan has often remarked, led her to write *The Feminine Mystique*. Beginning in 1957, she wrote articles based on a survey of her Smith classmates as they prepared for their fifteenth college reunion. Intent on attacking the findings of Ferdinand Lundberg and Marynia Farnham in *The Modern Woman: The Lost Sex* (1947), she hoped the survey would disprove the notion that quality education made women frustrated. To develop material for an article that would show that a college education helped married women to lead productive lives, she asked her classmates to respond to her questionnaire about their experiences.[32]

As she read over the answers, she later claimed, she discovered what she would call "The Problem That Has No Name," the deep-seated and confused dissatisfaction her classmates felt but could not fully articulate. Despite what Friedan later called "underground efforts of female editors," the men in control at *McCall's* rejected the article they had originally commissioned. *Ladies' Home Journal* rewrote it in a way that changed its meaning into the opposite of what Friedan had argued. An editor for *Redbook* informed Friedan's literary agent that Friedan had "gone off her rocker," having written an article with which "only the most neurotic housewife could identify." At a meeting of the Society of Magazine Writers, Friedan heard Vance Packard explain that he had decided to write *The Hidden Persuaders* when *Reader's Digest* turned down a controversial piece on advertising. Friedan returned to the editor at Norton and received a contract for what would eventually emerge as *The Feminine Mystique*.[33]

Yet Friedan was able to publish articles that drew on material and arguments that would appear in *The Feminine Mystique*. Writing in the *Smith Alumnae Quarterly* in 1961, she played off a recent article in *Newsweek* that warned of the damage that educated women who were "just housewives" inflicted on themselves, their husbands, and their children. Friedan depicted the lives of her classmates in mostly positive terms, making clear that they did not lead boring, frustrated, materialistic lives. Those of her respondents who did not work for a living reported that they achieved sexual fulfillment and enjoyed motherhood, but that they struggled with their roles as women, learned that they could not live vicariously through their families, and did not find their role as housewives "totally fulfilling." As in her piece following the tenth anniversary, Friedan emphasized her peers' accomplishments in their communities, building support for mental health clinics and theaters, fighting for school desegregation, and participating in local politics. With their children growing up, they were taking on new responsibilities. In some cases, this meant doing as professionals what they had long done as volunteers: turning grass-roots political activity into a law career, or work as a museum docent into a career in art history. Invoking the philosophy behind the Intellectual Resources Pool, she told the new generation that "America's new frontier is intellectual." As the historian Susan Ware has pointed out in response to the more negative picture of the lives of her classmates in *The Feminine Mystique*, "if Friedan had stuck with her original interpretation of the Smith questionnaires" set forth in this article, she would have painted a more accurate picture of what middle-class American women faced in the 1950s.[34]

While Friedan painted a largely positive picture of her Smith classmates in the Smith alumnae magazine, a year earlier, writing in *Good Housekeeping*, she presented very different conclusions. Here, in keeping with the genre of women's magazines, she stressed the negative but ended on a hopeful note. Under the title "I say: Women are *people* too!" Friedan wrote that American women fought alone to deal with the "strange stirring" inside them that they could not articulate. They faced a formidable set of forces arrayed against them, with experts telling them that they should celebrate their femininity and deny their ambitions for careers and intellectual lives. Yet, she concluded, "A great tidal wave of married women" were taking jobs, not just to help with household expenses but as part of what they wanted to do, connected as it was with their "search for self-fulfillment." Now, Friedan hoped, women would at last be able to use their education and freedom. "Who knows," she asked rhetorically, "what women can be when they finally are free to become themselves?"[35]

Friedan later commented that the response to her *Good Housekeeping* article convinced her that the problem she had defined, hardly confined to graduates of elite institutions, was pervasive. The reaction was indeed intense. A woman from Texas criticized Friedan's attack on housework. "At home," she responded, "I'm my own boss." Yet most of those who sent letters found what Friedan had written eye-opening. A woman from Georgia remarked that she was one of those women who "keeps her hands, but not her mind, in the dishpan." From Sunnyside, New York, a woman wrote that the article had helped her to overcome her loneliness. "Now that I know I am not alone," she commented, "the future seems brighter." From Connecticut came a letter from a woman who reported that she cried when she read the article, which confirmed her decision to go on to become a medical doctor. A woman from Manhattan was grateful to Friedan for telling her she did not have to rely on her husband's labor to maintain her femininity. "I don't want an easy life built on somebody's sweat," she remarked. "I want to be treated as *somebody* in my own right—because I am." From Pennsylvania a woman wrote that Friedan's article made her realize that she was not childish and unrealistic in wanting something more than a husband and child. "But now," she concluded, "the really difficult job is mine—that of finding *me*."[36]

The response from readers spurred Friedan on to finish her book, but she also wanted to capitalize on the success of the *Good Housekeeping* article by convincing the magazine to hire her to write a regular column. In October of 1960 she made her proposal. She complimented the editors for beginning to treat women as more than housewives and mothers, and not as people whose problems could be solved through psychotherapy. Friedan wanted to avoid the usual formula of advice columns written in response to letters in which women asked for help. Rather, she wanted to offer serious and thoughtful responses that went beyond women's traditional roles and addressed the spiritual and religious dimensions of their lives. In the sample column Friedan provided, she made it clear that her approach would not be political; rather, she would bring to bear on women's quandaries the kinds of questions that psychologists, philosophers, and theologians were asking. She emphasized that there was more to women's lives than the pleasures of domesticity that the media told them were pleasurable. Responding to a sample letter from a woman who felt there was something missing in her life, Friedan encouraged her to ask herself about the meaning of her life beyond what she achieved through her children and husband. Friedan saw the issues as vaguely psychological and existential, stressing the quest for a more self-fulfilled life. She called on women to move beyond domesticity by having a more capacious sense of the future. Just as men debated the national purpose, she asserted, it was time for women to expand their horizons.[37]

Writing articles for mass-circulation magazines posed challenges very different from what Friedan had faced as a labor journalist. Though still under the thumb of editors, mostly male, who controlled what she wrote, now she also had to suppress her political convictions. Still, she did manage to get into print a series of articles that were mildly critical of Cold War conformity. The emphasis on independent middle-class women with careers grew out of her personal experience as a Popular Front feminist at the same time that it departed from the perspective she had written about as a labor journalist. Writing for magazines such as *Redbook* prepared her for *The Feminine Mystique*. Through her writing, and by her own experience, she had learned about married women's lives in American suburbs. By 1960, she was emphasizing ways in which middle-class women could resist limiting their own perspectives. Her approach was not political, as 1940s union activists or 1960s feminists understood the term. Nonetheless, at least implicitly she articulated middle-class women's discontents as profoundly sociological, something that sprang from the specifics of their situation in America and that could be remedied by changes in family and work.

= 10 =

The Development of
The Feminine Mystique,
1957–63

It has become commonplace to see the publication of Betty Friedan's *The Feminine Mystique* in 1963 as a major turning point in the history of modern American feminism and, more generally, in the history of the postwar period. And with good reason, for her book was a key factor in the revival of the women's movement and in the transformation of the nation's awareness of the challenges middle-class suburban women faced. *The Feminine Mystique* helped millions of women comprehend, and then change, the conditions of their lives. The book took already familiar ideas, made them easily accessible, and gave them a forceful immediacy. It explored issues that others had articulated but failed to connect with women's experiences—the meaning of American history, the nature of alienated labor, the existence of the identity crisis, the threat of atomic warfare, the implications of Nazi anti-Semitism, the use of psychology as cultural criticism, and the dynamics of sexuality. By extending to women many of the ideas about the implications of affluence that widely read male authors had developed for white, middle-class men, Friedan's book not only stood as an important endpoint in the development of 1950s social criticism but also translated that tradition into feminist terms. In addition, the book raises questions about the trajectory of Friedan's ideology, specifically about the relationship between her labor radicalism of the 1940s and early 1950s and her feminism in the 1960s.

To connect a book to a life is no easy matter. Although Friedan herself has emphasized the importance of the questionnaires her Smith classmates filled out during the spring of 1957, when she was thirty-six years old, she also acknowledged in 1976 that in writing *The Feminine Mystique* "all the pieces of my own life came together for the first time." Here she was on the mark. It is impossible for someone to have come out of nowhere, and in so short a time, to the deep understanding of women's lives that Friedan offered in 1963. Experiences from her childhood in Peoria, her analysis of the Smith questionnaire, and all points in between, helped shape the 1963 book.[1]

In Peoria Friedan began the journey so critical to the history of American feminism. There she first pondered the question of what hindered and fostered the aspirations of women. In addition, in that Illinois city anti-Semitism and labor's struggles first provided her with the material that would ignite her sense of social justice. At Smith College young Bettye Goldstein encountered social democratic and radical ideologies, as well as psychological perspectives, as she shifted the focus of her passion for progressive social change from anti-Semitism to anti-fascism, and then to the labor movement. From the defense of the maids in 1940 it was only a short step to her articulation in 1943 of a belief that working-class women were "fighters—that they refuse any longer to be paid or treated as some inferior species" by men. Labor union activity and participation in Popular Front feminism in the 1940s and early 1950s provided the bridge over which she moved from the working class to women as the repository of her hopes, as well as some of the material from which she would fashion her feminism in *The Feminine Mystique*.[2]

Popular Front feminism—represented by the unionism of the CIO and the probing discussions around the Congress of American Women—deepened and broadened Friedan's commitments. Reading people like Elizabeth Hawes and writing for Federated Press and *UE News* gave Friedan sustained familiarity with issues such as protests over the impact of rising prices on households, the discontent of housewives with domestic work, the history of women in America, the dynamics of sex discrimination, the negative force of male chauvinism, and the possibility that the cultural apparatus of a capitalist society might suppress women's aspirations for better lives.

The discussions of women's issues in Old Left circles beginning in the 1940s and Friedan's 1963 book had a good deal in common. They both offered wide-ranging treatments of the forces arrayed against women—the media, education, and professional expertise. Progressive women in the 1940s and Friedan in 1963 explored the alienating nature of housework. They showed an awareness of male chauvinism but ultimately lay the blame at the door of capitalism. They saw *Modern Woman: The Lost Sex* as the text that helped launch the anti-feminist attack. They fought the fascist emphasis on Küche, Kinder, and Kirche.

Yet despite these similarities, the differences between Popular Front feminism and *The Feminine Mystique* were considerable. In articulating a middle-class, suburban feminism, Friedan both drew on and repudiated her

Popular Front feminism. What happened in Friedan's life between 1953, when she last published an article on working women in the labor press, and 1963, when her book on suburban women appeared, fundamentally shaped *The Feminine Mystique*. Over time, a series of events undermined Friedan's hopes that male-led radical social movements would fight for women with the consistency and dedication she felt necessary. Disillusioned and chastened by the male chauvinism in unions but also by the Bomb, the Holocaust, the Cold War, and McCarthyism, she turned elsewhere. Her therapy in the mid-1950s enabled her to rethink her past and envision her future.

Always a writer who worked with the situations and material close at hand, in the early 1950s Friedan began to apply what she learned about working-class women in progressive feminist discussions of the 1940s to the situation that middle-class women faced in suburbs. Living in Parkway Village and Rockland County at the same time she was writing for the *Parkway Villager* and mass-circulation magazines, Friedan had begun to describe how middle-class and wealthy women worked against great odds to achieve and grow. What she wrote about democratic households and cooperative communities, as well as her long-held dream of the satisfactions that romance and marriage would provide, reflected her high hopes for what life in the suburbs might bring. Although she felt that in the mid-1950s she successfully broke through the strictures of the feminine mystique she would describe in her 1963 book, the problems with her marriage and suburban life fostered in her a disillusionment different from but in many ways more profound than what she had experienced with the sexual politics of the Popular Front.

If all these experiences provided a general background out of which her 1963 book emerged, the more proximate origins of *The Feminine Mystique* lay in what she focused on during her career as a free-lance writer. She well understood the connection between the magazine articles she began to publish in the mid-1950s and her 1963 book. In addition, a critical impetus to her book was her response to McCarthyism. When she drew on her 1952 survey of her classmates to write "Was Their Education UnAmerican?" she first gave evidence of pondering the relationship between her Smith education, the struggle for civil liberties, and what it meant for women to thrive as thinkers and public figures in the suburbs. Then in her work on Intellectual Resources Pool, which began about the same time that she looked over those fateful questionnaires, Friedan paid sustained attention to the question of what it meant for middle-class women to develop an identity in American suburbs, including an identity as intellectuals. She asked these questions at a time when the whole culture, but especially anti-communists, seemed to be conspiring to suppress not only the vitality of intellectual life for which free speech was so important but also the aspirations of educated women to achieve a full sense of themselves. With her book, she reassured her own generation that their education mattered at the same time that she warned contemporary college students to take themselves more seriously.[3]

The Feminine Mystique took Friedan an unexpected five plus years to complete. She was writing under conditions that were difficult at best and neither Carl nor her editor at W. W. Norton thought she would ever finish. The material was painful, and through her engagement with it, Friedan was rethinking her position on a range of issues. She was a wife with a commuting husband and a mother of three. By the end of 1957, Daniel was nine, Jonathan was five, and Emily was one. Her ten-year-old marriage to Carl was less than ideal, and in 1962 it took a turn for the worse. Carl complained to friends that when he came home at the end of the day, "that bitch" was busily writing her book on the dining-room table instead of preparing the meal in the kitchen. Carl often did not come home at night. Though his own career may not have been going well, he felt Betty was wasting her time. Her friends whispered that instead of ending the marriage she was writing about it.[4] In addition, during almost the entire time she was working on the book she was also running the pool and trying to publish articles in magazines. She had to travel for material—within the greater New York area for interviews, and to the New York Public Library where she took extensive notes on what she read. Without a secretary to type early drafts, let alone a photocopy machine or word processor, writing as many as a dozen drafts was laborious, tiring, and time consuming. In early 1961, having turned in half the manuscript to her publisher, she expected the book to be published before the year's end. But her agent, Marie Rodell, wrote back to an impatient Friedan that the manuscript was so long it would not have the impact Friedan desired. Not surprisingly, she was optimistic at some moments, discouraged at others.[5]

To support her arguments, Friedan carried out wide-ranging research in women's magazines and the writings of social and behavioral scientists. She interviewed experts, professional women, and suburban housewives. She examined the short stories and human interest features in widely read women's magazines. Though Friedan made clear her reliance on such sources, there were some books that she read but acknowledged minimally or not at all. For example, she examined works by existentialists, and though their ideas influenced her writing, especially on the issue of how people could shape their identities, she did not fully make clear her indebtedness. Friedan also returned to Thorstein Veblen's *Theory of the Leisure Class* (1899),

which she had read at Smith, now absorbing his iconoclastic social criticism, which demystified the dynamics of women's subjugation, especially
the ways domestic ideology kept middle-class women from working outside
the home.[6]

She also carefully followed the arguments in Simone de Beauvoir's *The
Second Sex* (1953), but mentioned only its "insights into French women."
Beauvoir had explored how class and patriarchy shaped women's lives. She
provided what was, for the time, a sympathetic account of the situation
lesbians faced. She fully recognized women's participation in the work force
and the frustrations of domestic life. She offered a telling analysis of the
power dynamics in marriage. Linking the personal and political, she discussed a "liberation" of women that would be "collective." Friedan's reading
notes of Beauvoir's book reveal her great interest in Beauvoir's existentialism, including her linking of productivity and transcendence. In addition,
she derived from Beauvoir a keen sense of how language, power, economic
conditions, and sexuality divided men and women.[7]

What she read in Beauvoir and Veblen, as well as what she understood
from her own situation and her reading of American women's history, also
found confirmation in Friedrich Engels's essay of 1884, "The Origin of the
Family, Private Property and the State." Around 1959, she copied the following passage from a collection of the writings of Engels and Karl Marx:

> we see already that the emancipation of women and their equality with men are
> impossible and must remain so as long as women are excluded from socially
> productive work and restricted to housework, which is private. The emancipa-
> tion of women becomes possible only when women are enabled to take part in
> production on a large, social scale, and when domestic duties require their
> attention only to a minor degree.

Here Friedan relied on Engels for support of the central thesis of her book,
that women would achieve emancipation only when they entered the paid
work force. Like feminists who preceded and followed her, she agreed with
Engels's classic statement of women's condition. Her reliance on Engels
strongly suggests that even in the late 1950s Marxism continued to inform
her outlook. There is, however, one difference between what she read and
what she wrote down. After Engels's words "when women are enabled to
take part," Friedan added, in parentheses, her own words: "along with men."
This was a significant addition, expressing both her experience as a Popular Front feminist and her hope for the cooperation of men in women's
liberation.[8]

The fact that she read Engels makes clear that Friedan and her editor had
to make difficult decisions on what to leave out and include, a process that
involved the questions of how much of her radical past to reveal, and how

political and feminist the book would be. She also had to decide how to give it shock value and personal immediacy that would intensify its impact.

The magazine editors who in 1962 looked at articles derived from Friedan's book chapters raised questions about the scope, tone, and originality of her work. Some of their comments prefigured the anti-feminist diatribes that came with the book's publication in 1963. The editors at *Reporter* found Friedan's chapters "too shrill and humorless." A male editor from *Redbook* turned down one excerpt from the book, saying it was "heavy going," and another for expressing "a rather strident" perspective. "Put us down as a group of smug or evil males," remarked an editor of *Antioch Review,* who found that Friedan's chapter "The Sexual Sell" "contributes little to understanding or solution of the problems it raises." Friedan's article, he concluded, was "dubious sociology which attempts to answer too much with too little." Others questioned Friedan's originality. An editor at *American Scholar* found nothing especially new in what she had to say about Freud. A male editor of the journal of the National Education Association remarked that though an excerpt from the book pretended to present new material, in fact it had "the ring of past history." He illustrated his point by correctly noting that educators concerned about higher education for women had "already gone far beyond" what Friedan discussed. These responses gave Friedan a sense of the tough choices she had to make with the book, even as they intensified her sense of the importance of her message.[9]

Friedan faced the problem of positioning her book in what she and her editors saw as an increasingly crowded field of writings on middle-class women. Although we tend to see *The Feminine Mystique* as a book that stands by itself, Friedan and her publisher were aware that others had already articulated many of the book's concerns. When a vice president of W. W. Norton wrote Pearl S. Buck to solicit a jacket blurb, he remarked that "one of our problems is that much is being written these days about the plight (or whatever it is) of the educated American woman; therefore, this one will have to fight its way out of a thicket." He may have been thinking of F. Ivan Nye and Lois W. Hoffman's *The Employed Mother in America* (1963), of Morton M. Hunt's *Her Infinite Variety: The American Woman as Lover, Mate or Rival* (1962), of Helen Gurley Brown's *Sex and the Single Girl* (1962), or of the abundant discussion by educators and social critics regarding the frustrations of suburban women to which Friedan herself was responding. Friedan also had to decide whether to emphasize the deliberations of the Presidential Commission on the Status of Women, whose work, underway in 1961, would result in a report that, like Friedan's book, appeared in 1963.[10]

There were additional indications that Friedan was racing against the clock. While the book gave some the impression of a powerful and unshakable feminine mystique, Friedan herself acknowledged in the book that around 1960 the media began to pay attention to the discontents of middle-class American women. There is plenty of evidence that Friedan's readers, from professional women to housewives, found what she had to say either familiar or less than shocking. Some of those who reviewed the book found nothing particularly new or dramatic in it. Similarly, although some women who wrote Friedan indicated that they found an intense revelatory power in her words, others said they were tired of negative writings that, they believed, belabored the women's situation.[11]

If what Friedan wrote was hardly new to so many, then why did the book have such an impact? We can begin to answer that question by examining the ways she reworked familiar themes to give them a special urgency, especially for middle-class white women. Nowhere was this clearer than on the issue of women's work. Especially striking is the contrast between her animus against the toil of housewives and volunteers and her strong preference for women entering the paid work force, a dichotomy a friend warned her not to fall back on. Here Friedan was advocating what she had learned from labor radicals who urged women to get paying jobs and to work cooperatively with men. Friedan recast the terms of a long-standing debate between men and women so that it would appeal to middle-class readers. In her discussion of housework, for example, she offered only scattered hints about the reluctance of husbands to help with household chores. At one moment, she mentioned "the active resentment of husbands" of career women, while elsewhere she praised cooperative husbands. Neither perspective enabled her to discuss openly or fully what she felt about her marriage, the sexual politics of marriage, and the attempts by women, herself included, to set things right. As a labor journalist she had talked of oppressive factory work for working-class women; in *The Feminine Mystique,* alienated labor involved the unrecompensed efforts by white, middle-class women to keep their suburban homes spotless. One reader picked up on what it might mean, in both trivial and profound ways, to apply a Marxist analysis to suburban women. In 1963, the woman wrote to Friedan that the book made her wish to rush into streets and cry "To arms, sisters! You have nothing to lose but your vacuum cleaners."[12]

Friedan also cast her discussion of sexuality in terms that would appeal to conventional, middle-class, heterosexual suburban women. She promised that emancipation from the tensions of the feminine mystique would insure that women intensified their enjoyment of sex. Her statement that the "dirty word *career* has too many celibate connotations" underscored her preference for marriage. She hinted at the dangers of lesbianism when she discussed the sexual role models she had known in Peoria and at Smith. She contrasted "old-maid" teachers and women who cut their "hair like a man" with "the warm center of life" she claimed she experienced in her parents' home. She was concerned that some mothers' misdirected sexual energies turned boys into homosexuals. She warned that for an increasing number of sons, the consequence of the feminine mystique was that "parasitical" mothers would cause homosexuality to spread "like a murky smog over the American scene." Friedan's homophobia was standard for the period and reflects the antipathy to homosexuality widely shared in Popular Front circles. Her emphasis on feminized men and masculinized women echoed stereotypes widely held in the 1950s. What makes her perspective especially troubling is that it came at a time when reactionaries were hounding gays and lesbians out of government jobs on the assumption that "sexual perversion" had weakened their moral character, making them more likely to breach national security due to blackmail.[13]

Friedan also made the history of women palatable to her audience. Although most scholars believe that 1960s feminism began without a sense of connection to the past, Friedan had long been aware of women's historic struggles, as many of her earlier writings make clear. Friedan not only talked of passion and "revolution" but connected women's struggles with those of African Americans and union members. Yet her version of the past highlighted women who were educated, physically attractive, and socially respectable. Friedan went to considerable lengths to connect historic feminism not with the stereotypical man-haters or "neurotic victims of penis envy who wanted to be men" but with married women who, she noted repeatedly, were "dainty," "pretty," and "lovely." Unlike her writings for Federated Press and the *UE News*, which pointed out how millions of American women had to work hard in order to support a family economy under adverse situations, *The Feminine Mystique* described women's search for identity and personal growth, not the fight against discrimination or exploitation. While immigrant, African American, and union women were the subject of her 1953 *Women Fight For a Better Life! UE Picture Story of Women's Role in American History,* in *The Feminine Mystique* she remarked that female factory workers "could not take the lead" and that "most of the leading feminists" were from the middle class. In contrast, Eleanor Flexner's *Century of Struggle* (1959), on which Friedan relied in writing *The Feminine Mystique,* included extensive discussions of the social movements of African Americans, radicals, and union women.[14]

Friedan also connected the conditions women faced with two of the great events that haunted her, as they did many members of her generation. At several points, she used the horrors of the Bomb to drive home her point.

She contrasted domesticity with a world trembling "on the brink of technological holocaust." She also chided women in the anti-nuclear Women's Strike for Peace who claimed that once the testing of atomic weapons ended, they would be glad to stay home and take care of their children. Yet for someone who exaggerated her own role as a housewife, it is ironic that Friedan criticized the professional artist who headed that movement for saying she was "just a housewife."[15]

More problematic was Friedan's exploration of the parallels between the Nazi death camps and suburban homes as "comfortable concentration camps," an analogy that exaggerated what suburban women faced and belittled the fate of victims of Naziism. This was the first time since 1946 that she had mentioned the Holocaust in print. Although in the end she acknowledged that such an analogy broke down, Friedan nonetheless spent several pages exploring the similarities. Just before her book appeared, two other Jewish writers, Stanley Elkins and Erving Goffman, had applied the Holocaust comparison to two institutions where a more compelling case could be made: slavery and a mental hospital. Similarly problematic was Friedan's omission of the anti-Semitism that drove the Nazis to murder millions of Jews. Like many Jews of her generation, Friedan hoped for a society in which anti-Semitism and race prejudice more generally would be wiped out. Therefore, in her book she strove for a race-neutral picture, in the process both trivializing and universalizing the experience of Jews.[16]

While the concentration camp analogy grew out of her youthful anti-fascism, she gave no hint of how her early experiences with anti-Semitism had started her on the road to a passionate progressivism. There is a final reason that may explain why Friedan did not want to make explicit any connection between the situation Jews and women faced. Historically and in her own experience, there was a close connection between anti-Semitism and anti-radicalism. Yet despite the fact that feminist groups such as the Congress of American Women had a disproportionate share of Jews among their members and leaders, in public discussions anti-Semitism and anti-feminism had run along largely separate paths. On some level Friedan may have realized that it was best to use the discussion of the concentration camps to raise the consciousness of a wide range of readers without linking Naziism with anti-Semitism or feminism with Jews. Though the concentration camp analogy was careless and exaggerated, it nonetheless dramatically conveyed to Friedan's readers the horrible and dehumanized feeling of women who were trapped in their homes.[17]

Another distinctive aspect of *The Feminine Mystique* was Friedan's use, and gendering, of contemporary psychology. She took what humanistic and ego psychologists had written about men, and occasionally about women, and turned it to feminist purposes. Drawing on studies by A. H. Maslow in the late 1930s, Friedan noted that the greater a woman's sense of dominance and self-esteem, the fuller her sexual satisfaction and "the more her concern was directed outward to other people and to problems of the world." Despite this earlier research, by the 1950s the feminine mystique had influenced even Maslow, Friedan noted, encouraging him to believe women would achieve self-actualization primarily as wives and mothers. Maslow and others held such notions despite evidence from the Kinsey report that persuaded Friedan of a link between women's emancipation and their greater capacity for sexual fulfillment. However, Friedan hardly wished to rest her case for women's enhanced self-esteem on the likelihood of more and better orgasms. She rejected a narcissistic version of self-fulfillment. Drawing on the writings of David Riesman, Erik Erikson, and Olive Schreiner, and on the experience of frontier women, Friedan argued that people developed a healthy identity not through housekeeping, but through commitment to purposeful and sustained effort "which reaches beyond biology, beyond the narrow walls of home, to help shape the future."[18]

Along with others, Friedan was exploring how to ground a cultural and social critique by rethinking the contributions of Sigmund Freud and Karl Marx, an enterprise that first captivated her in the early 1940s as an undergraduate. What Herbert Marcuse achieved in *Eros and Civilization: A Philosophical Inquiry into Freud* (1955), Friedan did almost a decade later, responding to the Cold War by minimizing her debt to Marx even as she relied on him. Central to her solutions to women's problems was her emphasis on personal growth, self-determination, and human potential. Here Friedan was participating in one of the major postwar cultural and intellectual movements, the application of psychological and therapeutic approaches to public policy and social issues. In the process, she recovered the lessons of her undergraduate and graduate studies, joining others such as Paul Goodman, Riesman, Margaret Mead, Erikson, Rollo May, Maslow, and Erich Fromm in using humanistic psychology and neo-Freudianism as the basis for a powerful cultural critique at a time when other formulations were politically discredited.[19]

Like others, Friedan offered what the historian Ellen Herman has called a "postmaterial agenda" which employed psychological concepts to undergird feminism. Here Friedan was responding to the way writers—including Philip Wylie, Edward Strecker, Ferdinand Lundberg, and Marynia Farnham—used psychology to suggest that only the acceptance of domesticity would cure female frustrations. Friedan's contribution was to turn the argument around, asserting that women's misery came from the attempt to keep them in place. Psychology, rather than convincing women to adjust and conform, could be used to foster their personal growth and fuller embrace of non-domestic roles. Other observers suggested the troublesome nature of male identity in the 1950s; Friedan gave this theme a twist. She both recognized the problems posed by feminized men and masculinized women and went on to promise that the liberation of women would strengthen male and female identity alike. Friedan took from other writers an analysis that blamed the problems of diminished masculine identity on life in the suburbs, jobs in large organizations, and consumer culture; she then turned this explanation into an argument for women's liberation.[20]

This last achievement reminds us that Friedan's accomplishment in *The Feminine Mystique* was to take concerns that popular social critics had articulated and translate them into feminist terms. Remembering the origins of Friedan's 1963 book demonstrates how journalists of the 1950s served as social critics who helped shape the consciousness of the next decade. A reader at W. W. Norton remarked that what she was writing, although "overstated at almost every point," was "really not more exaggerated than" William H. Whyte Jr.'s *The Organization Man* (1955). He went on to add that Friedan's "credentials" were "at least as good as Whyte's." In 1959, when she signed a contract with an advance of one thousand dollars, Friedan remarked that people at W. W. Norton thought her book might have influence comparable to that of Whyte's *The Organization Man,* Vance Packard's *The Status Seekers* (1959), and James B. Conant's *The American High School Today* (1959). To that list she might have added other influential commentaries on 1950s suburban life, including Sloan Wilson's *Man in the Gray Flannel Suit* (1955), Richard Gordon, Katherine Gordon, and Max Gunther's *The Split-Level Trap* (1961), John Keats's *The Crack in the Picture Window* (1956), A. C. Spectorsky's *The Exurbanites* (1955) and, to a lesser extent, C. Wright Mills's *White Collar* and John Kenneth Galbraith's *The Affluent Society.*[21]

What Friedan's book shared with these best-sellers accounts to some extent for her shift away from her earlier political positions. Friedan adapted what they had written about suburban, middle-class men to their female counterparts. Like them, Friedan's was a crossover book, one that combined the seriousness and research of social and behavioral sciences with a lively and accessible style that grew out of Friedan's almost three decades as a journalist. Although not published until 1963, Friedan's book clearly had its origins in the 1950s. Once *The Feminine Mystique* had been credited with helping to launch the women's movement, observers tended to understand it in the context of its results rather than in the context in which it arose.

Friedan's emphasis on identity rested on an assumption, shared by other widely read social critics of her generation, that America's main challenge was affluence, not poverty. Consequently, the problematic group was white, middle-class suburban people, not inner-city African Americans or rural poor whites. Though her research for the book was limited exclusively to privileged women, she could have interviewed the working-class, African American, and Latina women she had access to during her years as a labor journalist. To be sure, at a time when the civil rights movement was gaining national attention, Friedan made clear at several points in her book that the same forces underlying the feminine mystique worked to segregate "able American Negroes from the opportunity to realize their full abilities in the mainstream of American life."[22]

Yet overall she offered little sense that millions of Americans, herself included, had to work in order to make ends meet or to support a family economy under intense pressure from an escalating standard of living. Friedan adopted the theory of consumer culture that more goods and services provided the middle class with false satisfactions at the same time that it distracted them from solving the more authentic problems of love, work, and politics. The fact that her early working title was "The Togetherness Woman" and that she was working on a play about suburban conformity helps make it clear how closely connected her work was with issues central to the 1950s. As a consequence of her focus on identity and the plight of middle-class women, she never faced the question of which women would take care of the children when white, middle-class suburban housewives turned into ambitious, self-fulfilling professionals. Though articulating sympathy for the plight of African Americans, hers was a decidedly lily-white book. Given the nature of her marriage, moreover, it is revealing that she did not hint at the problem of violence in middle-class households. Nor, as others have noted, did she seem to have much sympathy for working-class and middle-class women who, fighting to make ends meet, were not fortunate enough to worry about self-realization and fulfilling careers.[23]

In other ways, *The Feminine Mystique* was a book that simultaneously reflected 1950s issues and reconfigured them by placing suburban women, rather than men, at the center. Friedan's male counterparts urged American men to challenge conformity by going against the grain and seeking personal autonomy. As those writers had done, Friedan held a mirror up to Americans, giving them a shock of recognition that combined personal insight and social analysis. Like Riesman, Whyte, and Packard, Friedan psychologized social problems, considering lack of identity rather than social structure as the principal impediments to a fully realized self. Though Mills went farther in identifying the scope and power of elites who operated undemocratically, Friedan nonetheless hinted at the existence of a male power elite that systematically suppressed women. Her emphasis on self-realization rather than on actual social experiences echoed Riesman's analysis of problems of autonomy, Whyte's strategy on how to cheat on personality tests in order to maintain a modicum of psychological independence, and Packard's focus on countering status seeking by returning to an earlier type of individualism. Like Riesman, Galbraith, Packard, and others, Friedan defined the good life not in terms of more material possessions and commercial services but in the language of personal growth and, in Friedan's case, a vaguely articulated commitment to solve social problems. She followed others by writing a book that was longer on analysis designed to shock readers than on public policies that provided solutions.

If some of the shortcomings of *The Feminine Mystique* came from Friedan's reworking of a familiar genre, others stemmed from changes that materially altered Friedan's original conception of the book. Had Friedan written the book she started out to or was clearly capable of, she would have focused more fully on the issues of power, racism, systematic oppression of women, and politics that some critics have accused her of neglecting. In the end, omissions and changes in emphasis made the book very different from what it might have been.[24]

The responses of Friedan's Smith classmates to the 1957 questionnaire, which she claimed shocked her, were more positive than her startled reaction would suggest. One of the women who worked with her on the survey noted, "By our own estimate, most of us are mentally healthy." Though there was some evidence of entrapment in the feminine mystique, most of those who responded found their marriages satisfying and claimed to be experiencing the best time of their lives. Those who did not work outside the home stated that they did not want to, or were waiting until the children were older. Most of her peers did not buy into the suburban dream of feminine fulfillment. When asked what problems they faced as women, many indicated that they struggled to meet all the demands on them and showed some impatience with the burdens of motherhood and homemaking. Many expressed dissatisfaction that they were not able to use their minds more effectively. They were active politically and in ways that challenged the conformity of the Eisenhower years. As volunteers, they took on important and innovative tasks and many found these challenges as satisfying as professional work.

Friedan had seen her task as disproving those who believed that it was unwise to educate women. Indeed that was the conclusion to which the questionnaire drove her. Friedan was trying to tell Smith students of the late

1950s that higher education, rather than making women frustrated, gave them the sense of themselves that made it possible for them to overcome the frustrations of the feminine mystique. Her own generation, she believed, had proven this. Thus, at the outset, work on the book provided her with an opportunity to counter McCarthyites and other skeptics who denigrated education for women and, more generally, tried to undermine free speech.[25]

As a consequence of this generally positive evidence, early on Friedan planned a chapter called "A Key to the Trap" that made clear the positive if realistic conclusions of the survey. Here, she argued that she and her classmates had by and large succeeded in breaking through the feminine mystique. In the end, Friedan radically reduced this summary and included it as a small part of her final chapter.[26]

In other ways, from first to final draft, Friedan turned what was a realistic and even positive assessment of what middle-class women faced into a mostly negative one. These changes made her book less balanced, but more powerful. In 1972, the historian William Chafe demonstrated that Friedan had misinterpreted the 1950s. The debate on women's situation in that decade was more complicated, and in many instances less anti-feminist than Friedan suggested. On this topic, as on others, Friedan reported only the negative aspects of what her research revealed. For example, she told only one part of the story that she began to track on a visit to her alma mater. In the spring of 1957, as Friedan well knew, Dorothy Rabin, the editor of the campus newspaper, who later as Dorothy R. Ross emerged as one of the nation's most sophisticated historians of American thought, had campaigned against the intellectual and political disengagement of contemporary Smith students. Friedan lectured students at Smith on the importance of taking ideas seriously. Her report of this trip was entirely negative, omitting that one Smith student had written that American women, eager to combine marriage and career, were increasingly committed "to challenge the male monopoly in the business world and community life" rather than confine themselves to the separate sphere in order to focus on preparing meals and taking care of children.[27]

In other ways Friedan's largely negative conclusions contravened her original conception of the book. At the outset, she planned to emphasize how suburban women had shattered the feminine mystique and achieved a gestalt in their lives that enabled them to integrate all the components. Friedan had initially planned, but dropped, a chapter on exemplary women who had broken through the mystique and successfully combined marriage and career. Similarly, in her unpublished writing on the Intellectual Resources Pool she observed how teenage girls successfully resolved questions of identity, while in the book her assessment had turned negative. As a result of these changes, the book's dominant view was of women being overcome by, rather than overcoming, the feminine mystique. Although Friedan scattered success stories throughout her book, its main thrust, and the way most people read it, was of frustration and thwarted possibility. Had Friedan more than minimally recognized the widely reported deliberations of the Presidential Commission on the Status of Women, she would have acknowledged that her views were not unique, and come to less gloomy conclusions.[28]

Besides the shift from the positive and nuanced tone to a mainly negative one, the other major change in the book involved the watering down of Friedan's politics. The published book contained only hints of her political vision. In drafts, she made clear that she saw "feminism" not just as something that existed in the past but as a movement to be revived that would center on the power of self-realization. In unpublished sections, she denounced established women leaders as Aunt Toms. In early drafts, she used emphatic language to describe the measures she supported to bring about changes for women. She called for a program of national legislation to help women resume their educations. Stressing the urgency for and precedents of such efforts, she drew parallels to the GI Bill in the past and civil rights proposals in the present. The GI Bill had disadvantaged women in the 1940s, and perhaps Friedan was also concerned that civil rights legislation might disregard the interests of women, as it had during Reconstruction. Women too, Friedan argued, deserved special legislation. Indeed, with the civil rights movement gaining steam as she wrote, on some level Friedan was trying to draw parallels between the problems of women and African Americans.[29]

An examination of early drafts also makes clear the dynamics of Friedan's inattention to race, class, and working women, as well as her hostility to volunteerism. In focusing only on middle-class women, Friedan was following and making even less adversarial the genre of social criticism on which she patterned her own work. In opposition to all that she knew as a labor journalist, she apparently believed that America had become a middle-class society, an assumption widely articulated by many contemporary social scientists. Some writers on whom Friedan modeled her work had indeed pushed the boundaries of the genre. For example, in *Status Seekers* Packard had included a chapter on anti-Semitism and made his readers acutely aware of the dynamics of social class in America.[30]

The way Friedan minimized race as a factor in women's history and in contemporary society is striking. As she was developing the book, Fred Zeserson, who had introduced her to Carl and who had himself fought to integrate African Americans into Stuyvesant Town, a housing development in Manhattan, questioned her choice of subjects. He asked her why she was placing so much emphasis on women when she should have focused on what he regarded as the most pressing American problems—poverty among and discrimination against African Americans. In early drafts, Friedan emphasized how prejudice against Jews and African Americans had parallels in the hostility to women. Her failure to follow up on this theme is all the more notable given her personal knowledge of the difficulties black women faced. Ironically, and as if to underscore how much more serious were the obstacles facing educated African American women, in the mid-1950s Friedan had employed as a typist an African American woman named Pauli Murray who had a law degree from Howard University. Since they apparently did not meet until the mid-1960s, Friedan probably knew about neither her race nor her education. Murray, who had been a civil rights activist in the 1940s and emerged in the mid-1960s as a major force in the women's movement, supported herself until 1956 by doing typing for authors, including Friedan.[31]

In her discussion of what options women faced, Friedan narrowed the scope of what she might have said. In her attempt to emphasize the horrors of household work and to appeal to middle-class women who did not have jobs outside the home, Friedan paid minimal attention to and greatly underestimated the importance of women, even middle-class ones, who had paid employment. Friedan's neglect of working women was partly due to the audience she was trying to reach. In addition, she avoided discussing the plight of middle-class working women because a specific notion of professionalism was so important to her personally and because it was in the professional ranks that women's work force participation had taken a dramatic down turn from the 1920s. Her personal experience and her embrace of professionalism also help account for Friedan's negative view of women's volunteering efforts. In early drafts Friedan made clear her preference for innovative work and community leadership by volunteers, such as she had done for the pool. Distasteful to her was volunteer work that was routine and seemed to involve nothing more than busyness. Moreover, in unpublished writing Friedan focused on the gendered aspect of volunteer work. Men went off to the city to do important work, she believed, while most of the women who remained behind kept themselves busy with meaningless community tasks. Such an evaluation overestimated the creativity of the work done by organization men at the same time that it demeaned the work that many women volunteers accomplished.[32]

The most striking omission from the published version was the lack of discussion of how her radical past shaped her analysis. Early on, she drafted a very brief section on how some on the left, including those involved with the *Daily Worker* and the Communist Party, ineffectively responded to women's concerns. At the same time, she speculated on the relationship between the anti-communist crusade and the arrival of the feminine mystique. She also asserted that people on the left had developed intellectual strategies for denying women's problems.[33]

Perhaps her disillusionment caused her to minimize the importance of the left to American feminism in the 1940s. When she wrote about the death of feminism after 1920, she claimed that progressive women in the 1940s had no substantial concern for women's rights because they believed "they had all been won." By insisting that the postwar period failed to produce any larger vision for women, she ignored the efforts of working-class and Popular Front feminists in labor unions and in the Congress of American Women. When she assessed the anti-female statements in *Modern Women: The Lost Sex*, a book that served as a standard whipping boy for progressive feminists in the 1940s, she did not mention its anti-communism and anti-radicalism. When she hinted at the reluctance of husbands to help with housework, she did not draw on her own work on cooperative households. Nor did she speak, as she did in some early material for the book, of a kind of guerilla warfare women waged against their husbands in order to get them to help out at home. Perhaps her desire to avoid the tricky politics of male chauvinism within the suburban home prompted her to exclude a chapter she originally planned on husbands in suburbia. Indeed, at one point an editor warned her that her emphasis on the feminine mystique would find a problematic audience among husbands.[34]

Once the book appeared, at least one observer, Gerda Lerner, raised crucial questions about what Friedan emphasized and neglected. Lerner was active in the trade union movement and in the Congress of American Women during the 1940s and in the feminist movement during the 1960s. After the mid-1960s she emerged as one of the nation's leading historians of women. In February 1963 Lerner wrote Friedan, congratulating her for writing a "splendid book." Yet Lerner made clear her "one reservation" about Friedan's approach: her focus on "the problems of middle class, college-educated women." Lerner emphasized how "working women, especially Negro women" suffered not only from the feminine mystique, but also from "the more pressing disadvantages of economic discrimination." She asserted that "by their desperate need, by their numbers, by their organizational experience (if trade union members), working women are most important in reaching *institutional* solutions to the problems of women."[35]

Despite Friedan's attempts to obfuscate her radicalism, in the book there was evidence of two autobiographical narratives. One was that of the ex-radical; the other, of the trapped suburban housewife. Nowhere in the book was this first influence clearer than in the pivotal chapter of her more radical story, titled "The Sexual Sell," where she sought to explain the forces that powered the feminine mystique. What, she asked, undermined the power of feminism and fueled the retreat of women into the privatism of the suburban home? Friedan first toyed with arguments stemming from her days at the *UE News* where she had revealed a conspiracy by the National Association of Manufacturers to undermine progressive forces in the postwar world. Given that women were mainly responsible for shopping, she argued, "somehow, somewhere, someone must have figured out that women will buy more things if they are kept in the underused, nameless-yearning, energy-to-get-rid-of state of being housewives." In showing how corporations used marketing strategies to transform the suburban wife into a person who sought fulfillment as she baked a cake or polished a floor, she relied on the work of Ernest Dichter. He had used motivational research to generate advertisements that he hoped would give American women a sense of identity, self-realization, and sexual pleasure through consumer culture. Friedan pulled no punches as she explored the dangerous immorality of what Dichter was doing. He and his colleagues, she wrote, "are guilty of persuading housewives to stay at home, mesmerized in front of a television set, their nonsexual human needs unnamed, unsatisfied, drained by the sexual sell into the buying of things." By equating satisfaction with consumer goods, market researchers had locked millions of women into the home and prevented them from achieving a more genuine happiness that could involve growth and self-development.

Having hinted at the possibility of a conspiracy to oppress women, Friedan then shifted, concluding that she "had no idea how it happened. Decision-making in industry," she wrote, contradicting her earlier attacks on NAM, "is not as simple, as rational, as those who believe the conspiratorial theories of history would have it."[36]

Having examined a range of strategies corporations adopted to keep women in their place, Friedan concluded her consideration of the sexual sell by using rhetorical strategies that offered vague hints of larger issues. She suggested that America was a "sick society," one not willing to confront its problems or see its purposes in terms commensurate with the ambitions of its citizens, including women. Like the young radicals who wrote the Port Huron Statement for SDS in 1962, Friedan seemed unable to utter the word "capitalism." Though C. Wright Mills in *The Power Elite* (1956) went farther in exploring how elites operated undemocratically, Friedan nonetheless provided the evidence for a more radical, feminist analysis.[37]

Hints of a radical perspective, and of her drawing back from its implications, came through most clearly in her discussion of the forces arrayed against women. Throughout her book, although she had the evidence to do so, Friedan stopped short of declaring that men—as fathers, husbands, editors, psychologists, educators, corporate heads, and advertising executives—had coordinated the postwar counterrevolution against women. She could not develop this possibility for several reasons. Any process of deradicalization she had undergone made her hedge her discussion of a capitalist conspiracy. In addition, as a labor radical in the 1940s Friedan had consistently argued for coalitions of men and women to fight for social justice. In *The Feminine Mystique,* she laid the blame not with husbands, but with the gender-free culprit of "society." More immediately, she may have felt that more than hinting at a male conspiracy in her book would have undermined its impact by offending middle-class women who, although uneasy about their lives, were not about to embrace an all-out assault on patriarchal capitalism. Perhaps guessing at how far she might push an audience whose consciousness she wished to raise, she decided to temper her position. Nonetheless, the consequence of these decisions was that she avoided the implications of her earlier radicalism and focused on white, privileged suburban women.[38]

Consistently throughout the book, Friedan saw the problems that women faced caused not by externally imposed factors, but by limitations on their own ability to grow and reach their potential as human beings. Rejecting the notion of "an economic conspiracy directed against women," Friedan ascribed the promotion of the feminine mystique to a vaguer and unintended process, "our general confusion lately of means with ends; just something that happened to women when the business of producing and selling and investing in business for profit—which is merely the way our economy is organized to serve man's needs efficiently—began to be confused with the purpose of our nation, the end of life itself." At this point, Friedan seemed unable to insist that capitalists or men intentionally created the feminine mystique. It was, rather, simply an unpleasant and unnecessary by-product of an otherwise efficient system.[39]

This narrative, with its radical hints often undercut, emerged elsewhere in the book. "After the loneliness of war and the unspeakableness of the bomb," Friedan remarked, Americans retreated to the comfort of their homes and families. This statement explained the appeal of the feminine mystique. Yet it also runs counter to her own experience in the war even as it reminds us of her physical proximity in Berkeley to critical decisions to develop the atomic bomb. She hinted at the link between anti-female, anti-black and anti-union stereotypes. She also talked of the feminist movement, in the past, as revolutionary. The embrace by feminists of "the revolution's necessity," she wrote, originated in, and was "a passionate repudiation of, the degrading realities of woman's life, the helpless subservience behind the gentle decorum that made women objects of such thinly veiled contempt to men that they even felt contempt for themselves. Evidently, the contempt and self-contempt were harder to get rid of than the conditions which caused them." Without acknowledging where she first heard the argument, she discussed how the phrase "Kinder, Küche, and Kirche" reminded her of the connection between Naziism and the feminine mystique. Not mentioning her own experience, Friedan discussed the transformative power of women's experience in World War II. She acknowledged the "devastating" effects of sex discrimination in employment that drove women "embittered from their chosen fields" when returning veterans got jobs they should have had, although she also wrote that middle-class women who experienced such discrimination would not take such a case to the Newspaper Guild.[40]

Although others would date the counterrevolution against women to the 1920s or 1930s, Friedan focused on the late 1940s, a period linked in her own experience with a time when cold warriors undermined the left and, more specifically, the UE's fight for justice for women. She marked 1949 as the turning point, the year of David Bohm's congressional testimony following the defeat of Henry A. Wallace's Progressive Party. This dating underscored how closely she linked McCarthyism and the arrival of the feminine mystique.[41]

There were other hints of Friedan's radical past. With *The Feminine Mystique* Friedan completed, and transformed, what she had begun at Smith: the joining of psychology (now humanistic rather than Freudian) with a watered-down Marxism, now focused on middle-class women. Moreover, it is possible to understand the notion of a feminine mystique as an example of false consciousness, the way that mystification prevented women from seeing their real interests. Again and again, Friedan intimated that people fulfilled themselves by pursuing "a human purpose larger than themselves." She insisted that it was important to recognize that there were still battles for women to fight in the United States. Drawing on her UE experience, Friedan also briefly mentioned the importance of enabling married women with children to compete by providing maternity leaves and professional child care. At one point, without mentioning herself, she talked of "women born after 1920," who, no longer fighting for feminist causes because all the rights had been secured, were "still concerned with human rights and freedom—for Negroes, for oppressed workers, for victims of Franco's Spain and Hitler's Germany."[42]

Unlike many of the books of popular social criticism, *The Feminine Mystique* lacked a critique of the USSR or a celebration of Cold War America. Of course, it is possible to read her celebration of personal growth and self-

"10 WOMEN anywhere CAN START anything," Congress of American Women, probably December 1947. In 1946 Betty Goldstein worked on an article for Federated Press announcing the formation of the Congress of American Women. Photo by Barne Stein, © N.Y. Post Corp. Reproduced courtesy of Sophia Smith Collection, Smith College.

10 WOMEN
anywhere
CAN START
anything

CONGRESS OF AMERICAN WOMEN
114 BLEECKER ST., NEW YORK 12, N. Y. · GRamercy 7-5918
New Address

over of *UE Fights for Women Workers*, 1952, written by Betty Friedan. Reproduced courtesy Schlesinger Library, Radcliffe College.

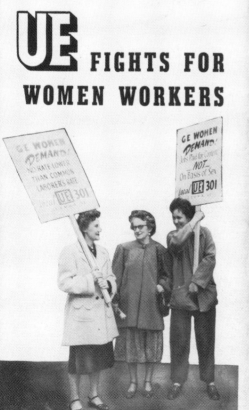

Betty Friedan, c. 1952, holding Jonathan at birthday party for Daniel, with Carl Friedan helping out. Reproduced courtesy of Schlesinger Library, Radcliffe College.

Betty Friedan in the kitchen in her home in Parkway Village, N.Y., with Daniel and Jonathan, c. 1953. Reproduced courtesy of Schlesinger Library, Radcliffe College.

Women relaxing in Parkway Village, while children from Colombia, China, and the United States play in wading pool, c. 1955. Reproduced courtesy of Schlesinger Library, Radcliffe College.

Children at Parkway Village at International Festival, c. 1955. Reproduced courtesy of Schlesinger Library, Radcliffe College.

THE HAPPY FAMILIES OF HICKORY HILL

In this new kind of community, every child insists he has "31 uncles, 31 aunts and dozens of cousins." He does, too

BY BETTY FRIEDAN
Photography by Ike Vern

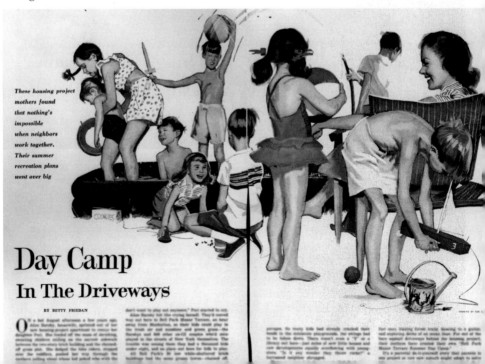

Betty Friedan, "The Happy Fa[mi]lies of Hickory Hill," *Redbook,* [] 1956, 39. Photographs by Ike V[] In this article Friedan pictu[] a community whose memb[] worked to break down the iso[]tion of the nuclear family. Rep[]duced courtesy of Schlesin[] Library, Radcliffe College.

Betty Friedan, "Day Camp in the Driveways," *Parents' Magazine*, May 1957, 36–37. Drawing by []Levering. From draft, to text, to illustration, the story increasingly pictured the figures as ideali[] assimilated, middle-class Americans. Reproduced courtesy of Schlesinger Library, Radc[] College.

These housing project mothers found that nothing's impossible when neighbors work together. Their summer recreation plans went over big

Day Camp In The Driveways

BY BETTY FRIEDAN

Friedan house in Grand View-on-Hudson, Rockland County, N.Y., where Betty Friedan worked on *The Feminine Mystique*. Reproduced courtesy of Schlesinger Library, Radcliffe College.

Betty Friedan, with men involved in Intellectual Resources Pool, Rockland County, N.Y., c. 1961. *From left to right:* Friedan; Eino S. Michelson, superintendent of schools, South Orangetown Central School District No. 1; Arnold Rist; James Fitch, president, Rockland Foundation; Anthony Barone, principal, Tappan Zee High School. Reproduced courtesy of Schlesinger Library, Radcliffe College.

WHAT KIND OF WOMAN ARE YOU?

FRANTIC COOK?

Chauffeur?

Smothered Mother?

TOO INVOLVED?

Restless?

Interesting?

𝔍𝔫𝔣𝔬𝔯𝔪𝔢𝔡?

Responsible Parent?

Motivated?

Satisfied?

BETTY FRIEDAN
author, "THE FEMININE MYSTIQUE"

Betty Friedan will help you decide when she speaks on

"A NEW IMAGE OF WOMAN"

Attend Temple Emanu-El Sisterhood

DONOR LUNCHEON

Tuesday, October 29, 1963

Sherry - 11:30 a.m.   Luncheon - 12:15 p.m.

Announcement of an appearance by Betty Friedan at a Sisterhood lunch at Temple Emanu-E
Dallas, Texas, 1963. Photo by Pellegrini. Reproduced courtesy of Schlesinger Library, Radclif
College.

etty Friedan and Emily Friedan, 1965. Reproduced courtesy of chlesinger Library, Radcliffe College.

etty Friedan, flanked by some of e founding members of National Organization for Women, 1966. *rom left to right:* Dorothy Haener, ster Joel Read, Anna Hedgeman, etty Friedan, Inez Casiano, Rich-'d Graham, and Inka O'Han-han. Reproduced courtesy of chlesinger Library, Radcliffe ollege.

y Friedan showing a women's al to Pope Paul VI, 1973. Re-uced courtesy of Schlesinger ary, Radcliffe College.

Betty Friedan with a copy of *The Feminine Mystique* and *It Changed My Life* o[n] table, c. 1980. Photo © Lynn Gilber[t.] Reproduced courtesy of Schlesinger L[i]brary, Radcliffe College.

Betty Friedan and other leaders of the women's movement march in Houston at the opening [of] the First National Women's Conference, November 1977. *Left to right:* Billie Jean King, Susa[n] B. Anthony (grandniece of the pioneer feminist), Bella Abzug, Sylvia Ortiz, Peggy Kokerno[t,] Michelle Cearcy, and Friedan. © Diana Mara Henry, 1978.

realization as a counter to Soviet totalitarianism, though one suspects that the call for women to express themselves on public issues was a code for the politics she could not openly express. Yet she used the authority of Dr. Spock to suggest the possibility that Soviet women were better off than their American counterparts. Indeed, Friedan's use of the concentration camp analogy connects with the anti-fascism that she had articulated at Smith College and with her knowledge of the evacuation of Japanese Americans into camps during her Berkeley year.[43]

Yet even though a retrospective reading can uncover these hints of radicalism, it is clear that in writing *The Feminine Mystique* Friedan took pains to hide her own radical heritage, something quite understandable given her background and her knowledge of what had happened to others with a past like hers. Whether a deliberate, strategic choice or an unconscious decision, Friedan created a second narrative in order to avoid revelations about her radical past and to project a believable persona with which her readers could identify. The second narrative, which provided the basis for and strengthened the impact of *The Feminine Mystique,* suggested that Friedan herself experienced uncertainty, blocked career mobility, and an identity crisis as a suburban housewife and mother in the 1950s. With this story, Friedan committed the historical mistake about which she knew better from her own life and those whose lives she covered: the assumption that after World War II the majority of American woman returned to domesticity.[44]

In place of her radical past, Friedan created one marked by captivity in the feminine mystique. In the first paragraph, she remarked that she realized something was wrong in women's lives when she "sensed it first as a question mark in my own life, as a wife and mother of three small children, half-guiltily, and therefore half-heartedly, almost in spite of myself, using my abilities and education in work that took me away from home." Toward the end of the paragraph, when she referred to "a strange discrepancy between the reality of our lives as women and the image to which we were trying to conform," she made readers feel she experienced the feminine mystique just as keenly as many in her audience did.[45]

Scattered throughout the book were other confessions of her entrapment: her willingness to give up a promising career as a psychologist to placate a boyfriend who was jealous of her success, her work as a journalist without a clear sense of where she was going, her participation as a free-lance writer in creating the image of the happy housewife, her ability to understand the lives of trapped suburban women because she "lived according to the feminine mystique as a suburban housewife." Using the first-person plural at one point, she wrote that "all of us went back to the warm brightness of home," describing how her generation pulled away from difficult issues. "There was a kind of personal retreat, even on the part of the most farsighted, the most spirited," Friedan wrote, in what was at best an incomplete description of her own experience. "We lowered our eyes from the horizon, and steadily contemplated our own navels."[46]

Friedan's depiction of herself in the mainstream instead of as part of the progressive minority was partially true, but partially a reinvention. Friedan knew that in writing *The Feminine Mystique*, she drew on a wide range of her own experiences. Her skills as a journalist, which she had begun to develop as a teenager, helped her to communicate with a wide audience. Her identity as a Jew and an outsider gave her a distinctive perspective on American and suburban life. Her years at Smith boosted her confidence and enhanced her political education. Her life as a wife and mother sensitized her to the conflicts millions of others experienced but could not articulate. Her education as a psychologist led her to understand the gestalt, the wholeness of a situation, and to advocate self-fulfillment based on humanistic psychology. Her image of herself as the frustrated housewife enabled her to talk about alienation and discrimination in a new setting and in less radical terms. Above all, her work as a labor journalist and activist provided her with the intellectual depth, ideological commitments, and practical experiences crucial to her emergence as a leading feminist in the 1960s.

Friedan was not alone in experiencing what it meant to have a radical past and eventually end up living in the suburbs, cut off from the realities of urban industrial life that once gave radicalism its palpability. The trajectory of her career reflects the shift of media attention from working-class, ethnically charged cultural representations to largely suburban, middle-class, and deracinated ones. Moreover, the widening division between the working class and the urban poor brought issues of race to the surface in ways that made some of Friedan's analysis outdated. At a time when unions (although not the UE) accommodated themselves to the Cold War consensus and Mills was noting the key role for university students and intellectuals in progressive politics, Friedan was arguing that middle- and upper-middle-class white women would replace workers in the vanguard of American social protest. In 1951, Mills had asserted that "the new middle classes are up for sale; whoever seems respectable enough, strong enough, can probably have them. So far," he concluded in the last sentence of *White Collar*, "nobody has made a serious bid." While Mills pointed to writers, intellectuals, and university students, Friedan pointed to women. While Mills saw the new middle classes as "politically voiceless," Friedan gave them a voice and once again took a male-gendered social criticism and turned it into a woman-centered one.[47]

Yet all my efforts to contextualize the book and understand how it might have been different only begin the task of explaining why it had such an enormous impact. In the end what is clear is that Friedan's emphasis on the importance to women of education, psychotherapy, and intellectual life hit the right chords. On so many levels, writing the book was an intensely personal experience for Friedan. Her goal was to get her readers to feel what she had experienced—self-realization and discovery through therapy that led her to recover or experience for the first time the importance of self-esteem, ideas, and education. The emphasis on developing a life plan stemmed from her understanding of what she had failed to do after 1943. The book's resonance with her own life gave it immense power for its readers as well. To fulfill her goal, Friedan successfully accomplished a series of difficult tasks. She had to undermine the authority of most of the principal centers of power that might compete in the world of educated women with her vision. Never someone who loved housekeeping, she was able to tell others what it meant to treat such an obligation as a chore rather than a sacred and infinitely expandable honor. Her denunciation of women's magazines recapitulated her understanding of the culture of capitalism she had studied at Smith and expiated her guilt for having given into market pressures when, she believed, she contributed to the feminine mystique in family magazines. Friedan felt it especially important to dethrone Margaret Mead, the most authoritative woman writer who claimed the mantle of scientific legitimacy. Indeed, Friedan had a special fascination for and animus against women writers she considered traitors to their sisters, especially Mead, Helene Deutsch, and Marynia Farnham. Like other women who wrote formulaic articles for women's magazines, Mead, Friedan had reason to feel, had betrayed the commitments her gendered perspective had initially inspired in her.[48]

Friedan needed to topple the "sex-directed educators" who she believed had destroyed the possibility of political and intellectual engagement she had experienced at Smith, a process she felt began during her years there. She had to question the legitimacy of orthodox Freudians, as she was trying to do as early as 1940, while underscoring the benefits of therapy and self-discovery that she herself had experienced beginning in her Berkeley years. Her exploration of the power of the sexual sell relied on a cleansed Marxism to enable women to understand how the consumer culture of a capitalist order had duped them.[49]

With that ground cleared away, she could develop her positive vision. Of central importance was an emphasis on therapy and education that resonated with her and her readers. Her obliteration of her earlier feminist past, and her suggestion that she came to self-understanding in the suburbs, convinced her audience (and eventually Friedan herself) of the authenticity of her experience at the same time that it claimed that therapeutically derived truths matter. In that way, Friedan's revision of her past and her "rebirth" in the mid-1950s made sense to her personally if not always to those who knew her history. Her discussions of the relationships between mothers and daughters resonated with a generation of middle-class women who, like Friedan, were coming to terms with their disappointments with their aging mothers and their hopes for their young daughters. The emphasis on psychology underscored her guilt about departing from her own initial career path even as it enabled her to suggest to her readers the explosive possibility of an unbound human potential. Above all, her statement that "even the best psychoanalyst can only give her the courage to listen to her own voice" bespoke her own experience even as it gave her listeners confidence that they too could recover a sense of themselves from their powers within.[50]

In therapy Friedan had emerged with a new sense of herself. In early drafts of *The Feminine Mystique,* Friedan communicated this in several ways. She talked about the process of discovery and rebirth. She used that self-understanding to show how other women, including her classmates, had effectively broken through the feminine mystique. Over time, however, the drafts gave way to a more one-dimensional story, of herself and her generation of women who had become trapped. Eventually, closer to a time when the book was in final form—or even later when she was able to gauge the reaction to the book—she must have felt compelled to stick by the story fixed in print. Despite the more complex version she had once believed, she insisted that she and her peers had succumbed to the feminine mystique.

By offering psychological insights, Friedan enabled her readers to analyze their own situations. She mixed personal testimony with psychological concepts to give readers tools that they could use to help themselves. With its dramatic interviews and stories of frustration, self-knowledge, and recovery, the book thus provided its audience with what Friedan had benefited from, therapeutic insight. The incorporation of firsthand personal narratives also brought to fruition a kind of journalism Friedan had been struggling to give birth to since the mid-1950s and that the New Journalists of the 1960s would develop into an art form. These approaches enabled her to convey the drama of the lives of American women. The stories were convincing because they were narratives of conversion, her own and that of her readers. After all, she portrayed herself as someone who, once trapped by and complicit in the creation of the feminine mystique, had now seen the light. With examples of how small groups of women could suddenly come to a common understanding, she offered readers what women in consciousness-raising groups of the late 1960s and after would profit from—self-knowledge obtained in the company of women. If the stories of women who suffered under the feminine mystique enabled women to understand what they felt but could not easily articulate, the stories of triumph gave them models to emulate.[51]

The power and limitations of her book came from her insistence that the feminine mystique was a mental construct and as such something women could change with equally powerful ideas. As the historian Donald Meyer has pointed out, Friedan argued that women could discover the answers in themselves and not through religious, economic, political, or social change. If they had the wrong ideas, all they needed was the right ones, which her book provided. Since the feminine mystique as a series of myths rested on the scientific claims of its proponents, she marshalled equally authoritative scientific evidence to expose and contradict what mystique makers celebrated. Yet hers was also the authoritative voice of the expert who knew better. What made her book different from those of Riesman, Whyte, and Packard was her sense of personal urgency, and her presentations of authentic voices. Old Left journalism, her experiments with new forms, her long-held feminism, and her personal experiences made it possible for her to write a book that changed her readers' lives.[52]

No institutional solutions, she insisted, with one exception: education. Friedan's emphasis on education, like that on therapy, had immense appeal to a generation that had moved to the suburbs and put contentious political issues aside. *The Feminine Mystique* itself was like an adult education course that reminded women of what it meant to wrestle with ideas. An intensely intellectual book, it displayed the agility of her mind, her powers as a researcher, and her ability to make difficult ideas easy to understand. At last, Friedan had achieved, for herself and her readers, what she first experienced at Smith and only dreamt about when she first moved to Rockland County: proof that a suburban woman could be engaged with ideas. Her critique of those who wasted their education evoked her guilt about abandoning psychology as a career, and celebrated her rediscovery of the field at the same time that it served as a jeremiad for her contemporaries as well as for the silent generation whose passivity she lamented. She had to couple education and a new life plan, a combination she felt she had abandoned when she left graduate school, thereby submerging her authentic sense of self. This was a powerful message for a generation of women who had interrupted or put aside their education when they married and gave birth to baby boomers.[53]

Though Friedan did not spend much time spelling out what a feminist future might involve, there were enough hints that enabled her to make sense of her past and sketch out a future for her readers. Her discussion of women's history enabled her and her readers to rest assured that feminism had always relied (and perhaps by implication might rely in the future) on white, middle-class, and physically attractive women. Her call for "a drastic reshaping of the cultural image of femininity" that would enable women to reach their full identity suggested, as did conversations among progressive women in the 1940s, how changes in the media might enhance women's power. With her analysis of the way the feminine mystique had forced women out of politics she held out the hope that a routing of these forces might help women enter the political arena. Her hints at a legislative agenda that included child care made clear to women that there was a connection between social welfare policy and their urgent needs. Friedan reassured her readers that strong women not only had better sex lives but were also psychologically freer.[54]

Her discussion of what it meant for a woman to be liberated from the feminine mystique read remarkably like some of the descriptions she offered in the early draft of what she had gone through. Toward the end of the book Friedan talked of the strong women who overcame obstacles to personal growth. Many of them, she noted, were driven to achieve by "childhood rejection, by an ugly-duckling adolescence." In describing how she and others had fought to fulfill their human potential, she used a word Erikson had used, "moratorium," to describe what she called "a strange breath-holding interval before the larva breaks out of the shell into maturity." They successfully countered the resistance of their husbands and of women they knew. Without really understanding what they were doing, they developed a successful life plan that combined career and children. They fought against the prescriptions of the mass media. They sustained their commitments to their long-held values. They successfully met the challenges they faced and then went on to new tasks. They developed a commitment to act in the public world. Through all these processes, they fostered a sense of their own identity. They achieved what Friedan had first understood at Smith, a gestalt, a sense of wholeness. Although she did not admit it in the book, in drafts she made clear that this was how she had come to understand herself.[55]

With the publication of *The Feminine Mystique,* a forty-two-year-old Friedan, for the first time since she left Smith College in June 1942, found herself in a position to be the leader of a network of talented women. As a graduate student, labor journalist, suburban volunteer and housewife, and free-lance writer, she had been in a world where men called the shots. With the book's publication, that long moratorium was over. "I did not set out consciously to start a revolution," Friedan insisted. At some level she hoped to take advantage of the social conditions that would enable her to lead a resurgence of feminist activism. In that leadership and political engagement, she would utilize more fully the varieties of feminism, however transformed, she had learned since she left Peoria.[56]

=11=

1963 to the Present

The Feminine Mystique has had a commanding impact on historical scholarship, cultural memory, and American feminism. The book's reception also transformed Betty Friedan's own life. It exacerbated strains in her relationship with Carl and eventually helped give her the courage to divorce him. It established her role as a writer. Above all, it helped launch her second career as an activist.

This intellectual biography complicates Friedan's assertions about women in 1950s suburbs. More importantly, it challenges her claim that her own feminism emerged principally from her experiences as a trapped housewife and the chronology of American feminism that stems from such a claim. A reconstruction of her life gives added impetus to the ongoing reconsideration of issues of memory, periodization, historical consciousness, and continuity. Her life, and those of some of her contemporaries, make clear that, whatever its fate as a movement, in the 1940s and 1950s feminism as a series of commitments was not as "dormant" and "vanished" as assumed. Her career helps illuminate a more complex picture of the history of the women's movement and demonstrates major continuities, as well as some discontinuities, between Popular Front radicalism and 1960s feminisms. If Rosa Parks refused to take a seat at the back of a segregated bus not simply because her feet hurt, then Friedan did not write *The Feminine Mystique* simply because she was an unhappy housewife.[1]

Soon after the publication of *The Feminine Mystique*, Betty Friedan's personal life began to change. In 1964 Carl, Betty, Daniel, Jonathan, and Emily Friedan moved from their house in Grand View-on-Hudson, New York, to an apartment in the legendary Dakota, on the Upper West Side of Manhattan, the neighborhood where Carl and Betty had first lived together right after World War II. Betty Friedan's notoriety and success heightened the tensions in her marriage. What she achieved apparently made Carl feel uncomfortable about being known as Mr. Betty Friedan and enabled her to move on. In May 1969, twenty-two years after they married, they divorced. The split was bitter, with accusations flung back and forth for years to come. Betty Friedan later remarked that in 1963 divorce "paralyzed me with terror in the security of my own suburban dream house." What she feared above all, she remarked, was being alone.[2]

Several years after their divorce, Carl married a younger, blonde, and classically attractive woman. He contrasted Betty with his new wife who, he said, was "no intellectual, thank God" but "makes chicken soup, and that's love." He continued, "Betty? She hates men. Let's face it, they all do—all those activists in the women's lib movement," revealing the angry scars from his marriage and his own version of the lavender menace. "My thesis is, treat them as equals, but, by God, never marry them. I'm talking about these gung ho, tobacco-chewing types. Fifty to 60 per cent are lesbians, either overt or otherwise." A reporter stated that Carl Friedan "reserves special anger for the projected image that Betty lived a shackled, humdrum housewife existence and wrote *The Feminine Mystique* as a catharsis." He claimed that "she had time to write it because she lived in a mansion on the Hudson River, had a full-time maid and was completely supported by me." Skepticism is in order about such statements, carefully calculated to extend the fight from the bedroom and divorce court to the press. Whether meant in financial or emotional terms, Carl Friedan's claim that he "completely supported" Betty Friedan is dubious. Still there is more than a germ of truth in his claim that Betty was not fully trapped in the feminine mystique.[3]

After the divorce, much changed in Betty Friedan's life. As a part of the settlement, she had to give up the apartment in the Dakota; she moved to an apartment in a brownstone on West 93rd Street and later to one near Lincoln Center. Beginning in the early 1970s, with friends she called her "extended family" she spent summers on Long Island in what she referred to as a "commune." In the year the Friedans divorced, Daniel turned twenty-one, Jonathan seventeen, and Emily thirteen. All three children flourished and went on to lead productive lives: Daniel as a physicist, Jonathan as an engineer, and Emily as a pediatrician. Jonathan and Emily married and gave Betty the pleasures of being a grandmother several times over. In 1978, she bought her own house in Sag Harbor, where friends and family visited during the summer. Other changes marked her life in the 1970s and beyond: her romantic relationships with a series of men, her growing interest in

Judaism and Israel beginning in the 1970s, her rapprochement with her brother, her acceptance in Peoria, and the death of her mother in 1988.[4]

By making her the most widely known American feminist, *The Feminine Mystique* underwrote Friedan's emergence as a major spokesperson for the women's movement. Her book awakened hundreds of thousands, if not millions, of women to what they had long felt but been unable to articulate— the way the mystique of suburban womanhood smothered aspirations for a more fulfilling life. The reception of the book gave Friedan an audience eager to hear what she had to say, ready to have her words rouse them to action. Her appearance on radio, television, and the lecture circuit helped turn her into a speaker who played a major role in creating some of the conditions for a revival of feminism.

As had happened before in American history, what set the stage for feminism's rebirth was a combination of labor union advocacy and the struggle for full citizenship for African Americans. In 1961 John F. Kennedy appointed the President's Commission on the Status of Women, with Eleanor Roosevelt as chair until her death in 1962, and Esther Peterson as executive vice chair. Peterson's union experience went back to the 1930s when she taught at the Bryn Mawr Summer School for Women Workers in Industry. In that decade she was also a labor organizer for the American Federation of Teachers in Massachusetts. There she came into conflict with Dorothy W. Douglas, who advocated a broader and more radical agenda than Peterson. In 1961, at the time of her appointment to the commission, as assistant secretary of labor and head of the Women's Bureau, Peterson was the highest ranking woman in the Kennedy administration. She was committed to advancing the agendas of key women with government experience and of those in the labor movement interested in women's issues.[5]

The civil rights movement that began in the 1950s and flourished in the 1960s helped women realize that they too could seek redress of their grievances. The addition of the word "sex" to Title VII of the Civil Rights Act of 1964, whose central purpose most politicians understood as supporting the aspirations of African Americans but whose additional importance key women in Congress well understood, provided the legal basis for challenges to sex discrimination in the work place. Women activists and politicians grew increasingly dissatisfied with the lack of enforcement by the Equal Employment Opportunity Commission. The turning point came in June 1966 at the meeting in Washington of the National Conference of State Commissions on the Status of Women, which Friedan attended. At the time the federal government was stalling in its implementation of Title VII as it pertained to women. At the meeting, government officials made clear they would talk but not act. A coalition of women—in federal agencies, state commissions, the media, and labor unions—determined to create a civil rights organization to work for women's interests.

Many had urged Friedan, as the best-known speaker on women's issues and someone unconstrained by organizational ties, to take the lead. She never said flatly no, responding instead, "I'm an author. I'm not an organization person." It is likely that Friedan sought and relished a leadership position. At a lunch, a small group of women, Friedan included, determined to launch National Organization for Women (NOW). Friedan wrote down the key words, pledging to have the new organization lead in the effort "to take the actions needed to bring women into the mainstream of American society, now, full equality for women, in fully equal partnership with men." Intentionally, NOW stood for National Organization *for* Women, instead of the gender-exclusive alternative of an all-female organization chosen previously by the Women Strike for Peace and in the future by radical feminists. Friedan was elected as the first president of NOW. Once again she moved from writer to activist. NOW's formation was announced at a press conference on November 21, 1966, after the first meeting in October. According to Lisa Hammel, the reporter for the *New York Times* whose article appeared on the women's page, no one "actually got up and cried: 'Women of the world unite! You have nothing to lose but your chains.'" That was, however, Hammel noted, "the prevailing sentiment" in the room.[6]

NOW's 1966 Statement of Purpose, whose ideas and language were largely Friedan's, reflected the ideology of the organization's many founders and the particularities of her own experiences. A number of things distinguished Friedan's draft of the document from the version NOW adopted. As in *The Feminine Mystique,* Friedan's focus was almost exclusively on middle-class, white suburban women for whom professional work was a possibility. When she talked about the obstacles African American women faced, she gave little evidence of what she had learned as a Popular Front feminist. Instead she made clear her belief that the discrimination black women faced was based on sex rather than race. Friedan showed considerable interest in the parallels between the civil rights and the women's movement: she both feared "Aunt Toms" and worried that the emergence of Black Power signaled the possibility that women might embrace separatism. Consistent with her experience as a labor radical, in the draft Friedan wrote of a day when, women having achieved equality, NOW would disband so that its supporters could join the fight for social justice for all members of society.

Whatever the reasons for the differences between draft and final versions, the statement NOW adopted echoed issues with which Friedan had long wrestled. The final version included a focus on African American and working-class women absent from the draft, an approach that connected this document to her work as a labor journalist. The mention of the "double discrimination" African Americans faced—absent from the draft—recalls what Friedan wrote in her pamphlet *UE Fights for Women Workers*.

Both the draft and the official version recalled Friedan's long-standing commitments. Unlike *The Feminine Mystique*, but like Friedan's labor radicalism, they both opposed solutions to women's problems that were individualistic and psychological. NOW's insistence on an end to job discrimination and the linking of women's issues with "many broader questions of social justice" were consistent with the idea of a broad-based struggle by Popular Front feminists. Both versions acknowledged, as had Friedan in the early drafts of her 1963 book, that NOW's inspiration arose from the struggle by African Americans for civil rights, as well as the urgency and need for a national program for child care and for women's education. Both documents called for women to enter "the mainstream" of American life, a statement that reflected Friedan's deep yearnings as well as her disappointment with the achievements of labor. As she once made clear when she added the words "along with men" to Friedrich Engels's "The Origin of the Family, Private Property and the State," she believed in the centrality of men's participation alongside women. Recalling statements made when she lived in Parkway Village, she called in 1966 for "a different concept of marriage, an equitable sharing of the responsibilities of home and children and of the economic burden of their support." Once she had reacted angrily to the portrayal of women in the *Daily Worker* and in women's magazines; in the 1966 statement she called for changes in "the false image of women now prevalent in the mass media."[7]

The first task NOW leaders took on was to fight job discrimination against women. Soon they added to their agenda equitable marriage and divorce laws, provision for equal treatment of female athletes, and fair portrayal of women in textbooks and on television. It is difficult for later generations to appreciate what the founders of NOW were up against—the institutionalization of sexism in every corner of American society. Anti-women jokes were permissible, sexist language was common, and adequate provisions for child care were rare. Financial institutions denied women credit in their own name, women's perspectives in academic life were absent, and many professional schools did not admit women. Most employers did not grant women training, job promotion, and equal pay for equal work. Those in control of media and politics, far from acknowledging what women encountered, in fact worked to make their situation more difficult.

Faced with these obstacles, Friedan in the mid-1960s began rounds of tireless petitioning, picketing, speaking, writing, and campaigning. Her articulateness, passion, and notoriety made people listen and then act. She finally developed a constituency. Early victories were important. With others she successfully challenged the way employment advertisements in newspapers made clear that the better jobs were reserved for men. NOW successfully won the inclusion of sex as a category in the government's affirmative action guidelines. Friedan urged the government to enforce existing laws against sex discrimination and pass new ones as well. She sat in at restaurants and clubs that did not allow women to enter. She urged political parties to include planks favorable to women in their platforms.

Before 1966, Friedan had been an organizer and activist as well as an author. When she worked on the Smith newspaper, in the labor movement, on the rent strike in Parkway Village, and on the Intellectual Resources Pool, Friedan had extensive experience raising money, generating publicity, organizing meetings, and building support for progressive causes. Moreover, her dramatic style and sensitivity to what the media needed to develop stories were key factors in her leadership. As Milton Meltzer has written, she gave the media what they wanted, "the star image, an individual they can focus on, the one who projects the ideas of a whole movement." However, her style, passion, and ideas also exposed her to ridicule, bomb threats, and hostility from anti-feminists. Soon after the publication of her book in 1963 and more intensely with her emergence as a political figure, men and women accused her of destroying marriage, undermining femininity, and attacking the family. As a person who felt she spoke for ordinary middle-class women and who knew the rough-and-tumble politics of the 1940s, these attacks stung. In one later instance, someone wrote her a letter threatening to bomb her and stating that she and Gloria Steinem had updated the Communist Manifesto. In another case she received a threatening letter that accused the women's movement of using "Jewish International Communist ideas to destroy America."[8]

Yet Friedan persisted in her campaigns for the liberation of women. Speaking in her recognizable manner, she made a difference. "So distinctive," remarked a reporter about her voice, "it sounded like tires on a gravel driveway." One of her colleagues captured her energy:

> She sweeps through meetings, telephone calls, dinners and speeches with frantic bursts of energy as if each day might be her last. Everything is in motion, not just her words, which come so fast she seems to ignore the necessity of breathing. Her hands gesticulate, wave, flail. Her eyes are deep, dark, charged, and violent as her language. Her nose is long, her hair, despite patient attention

at the beauty parlor, often askew. Nothing fits the accepted model of beauty. Yet she exerts a powerful, haunting attractiveness—that special combustion that lights up a few rare individuals interacting with their audience.

Her style of leadership, however, had its costs as well as its advantages. As early NOW activist Jacqui Ceballos said later, "Betty's greatest strength— her aggressiveness—is also her greatest weakness." Similarly, biographers Sondra Henry and Emily Taitz remarked that by the mid-1960s, despite the importance of her accomplishments, Friedan's "brusque manner, impatience with others, and easy irritability would constantly drive people away." As Friedan herself acknowledged, "I am nasty, I'm bitchy, I get mad, but by God I'm absorbed in what I'm doing."[9]

Eventually, her manner, tactics, and commitments embroiled her in controversy in the women's movement. From childhood on, she had been most productive as an outsider. As her college friend Mary Ann Guitar noted, if Friedan ever felt completely welcome, she would have to destroy this illusion. Friedan's life after 1963 raised the question of what a habitually adversarial person does when she finds herself central to a group's struggles. The answer was that she fought for what she believed and did so in ways that soon outraged allies and enemies alike. In 1967, she pushed NOW to support the Equal Rights Amendment (ERA). Popular Front women in the 1940s had opposed the ERA because they feared it would undermine protective legislation so important to working-class women. In 1967 some women involved in the labor movement departed from NOW, which they had helped found. They did so because, though they believed in the ERA, their unions opposed it, a situation that would eventually change. Friedan's endorsement of abortion rights in the late 1960s drove some Catholic women from NOW and ended the possibility of rapprochement with the Woman's Party, the veterans of the long battle for the ERA.[10]

Friedan left the presidency of NOW in 1970, largely because the organization mandated a maximum term of four years. At the time it had about three thousand members. The organization and movement she led had the reputation, not always deserved, of being a white, middle-class one. Evidence of a more diverse organization is readily available. Aileen Hernandez, an African American woman, succeeded Friedan as president of NOW; between 1951 and 1959 she had been an organizer and educator for the International Ladies' Garment Workers' Union. Yet a number of factors, but most notably what Friedan had written in her 1963 book, gave the women's movement she represented a predominantly white, middle-class cast and a reputation as a place where African American and working-class women, as well as their concerns, were not taken seriously. Many black women believed that the attack on sex discrimination would help white women more than the African American men and women who had been so central in initiating the rights revolution. Working-class women believed Friedan's emphasis on personal self-realization and fulfilling professional jobs underscored her own privileged position.[11]

Following her presidency at NOW, Friedan initially was able to maintain her position as leader. She did so by playing the key role in launching the nationwide Women's Strike for Equality on August 26, 1970, the fiftieth anniversary of the Nineteenth Amendment that gave women a constitutional guarantee of the right to the vote. The marchers called for abortion on demand, full provision of day care, and equal opportunities for women in education and employment. The protest, which attracted tens of thousands of women around the nation, gave the women's movement visibility in the media and a sense of exhilaration among its members. At the time, it was the largest demonstration for women's rights ever held in the United States. Moreover, it dramatically boosted NOW's membership, which by the mid-1980s had grown to a quarter of a million. In many ways this protest was the high point of Friedan's career as an activist.[12]

Soon after, however, her situation in the women's movement became precarious. In the late 1960s, many women, most of them younger and more radical than Friedan, discovered feminism. Tensions grew between Friedan and other leading feminists, and shifting issues left her on shaky ground. The key moment came with a second march in Manhattan, in December 1970. One cause of friction was the clash of personalities and ambitions, but ideology also played a significant role. Friedan had seen the purpose of NOW and feminism as enabling women to take their place in the American mainstream. People such as African American lawyer Flo Kennedy, activist Ti-Grace Atkinson, writer Kate Millett, as well as African Americans working for civil rights, socialist feminists fighting against racism, sexism, and war, and radical feminists attacking the patriarchy, wanted a fundamental restructuring of society that placed feminism at the center. While Friedan and other liberals hoped women would assume powerful positions in the United States, other feminists criticized the hierarchical notions about power and institutional arrangements underlying such a goal.

The war in Vietnam, urban riots, the shift from civil rights to Black Power, and the assassinations of Malcolm X, Robert F. Kennedy, and Martin Luther King Jr. reflected the tensions in American society. Simultaneously, conflicts in the women's movement came to a head. The issue that proved most divisive was sexual politics. As an Old Leftist and sometimes new liberal, Friedan felt that sexual matters were private. Wanting a broad-based movement that would appeal to what she called the mainstream, she feared that linking feminism and lesbianism would diminish the support of the kind of people she had grown up with in Peoria and then, in writing her book, had come to feel she both understood and spoke for. Consequently, she had insisted on excluding lesbian issues from NOW's agenda.[13]

She and her opponents had contrasting views of the movement. In 1970 a leaflet written by radical feminists stated: "It is not one woman's sexual experience that is under attack—it is the freedom of all women to openly state values that fundamentally challenge the basic structure of patriarchy. . . . They can call us lesbians until such time as there is no stigma attached to women loving women. SISTERHOOD IS POWERFUL!" At the December 1970 protest, some of the organizers planned for all participants to wear lavender arm bands, either as a statement of their sexual identity or a symbol of their solidarity. Friedan refused to wear such an arm band. She was furious at being upstaged, and at the link between feminism and lesbianism. "Men," she insisted, "are not the enemy." In 1969 she had asserted that the younger generation "only need a little more experience to understand that the gut issues of this revolution involve employment and education and new social institutions and not sexual fantasy." In 1970, she remarked that "sexual politics is highly dangerous and diversionary, and may even provide good soil for fascist, demagogic appeals based on hatred." Rather than focus on "self-pity and hatred," she advised, women, "in coalition with students, Blacks and intellectuals can build real change in society." Though during the 1970s, in the interest of unity necessary to support the ERA, Friedan tried to put aside her differences with radical feminists, the breach was never healed.[14]

Friedan faced a further challenge in the early 1970s in the struggles over the direction of the National Women's Political Caucus, an organization that sought to increase the number of women in politics and to draw the attention of politicians to women's issues. Along with Bella Abzug, Shirley Chisholm (the first African American woman elected to Congress), and Steinem, Friedan played a key role in this group. Friedan wanted to support women seeking office regardless of their views on specific issues; Abzug and Steinem insisted on helping only those committed to progressive social change. Work on this project widened the breach between Friedan, who wanted to make sure Midwestern Republican women were welcome, and those who wanted to build a coalition that centered on young, poor, minority, and radical women. At the Democratic convention in 1972, things came to a head when Steinem and Abzug outmaneuvered Friedan politically. Although in the early 1970s Friedan's power in the women's movement was waning, she successfully worked to see one of her dreams realized. From

1972 to 1974, she served as vice president of National Association to Repeal Abortion Laws; the Supreme Court decision on Roe v. Wade in 1973 made abortion legal.

After the early 1970s, Friedan never again provided leadership of the women's movement from a base in a major national organization. By the early 1970s, Justine Blau has noted, she "lost touch with many of the women she had worked with in NOW's early days." Yet in many quarters she was the representative feminist, lecturing widely at home and abroad. Over the next decades, she held academic positions at several universities. She received a number of honorary degrees, including one in 1975 from Smith College. She served as a founder and director of the First Women's Bank and as a director of the NOW Legal Defense and Education Fund.[15]

Although after the early 1970s Friedan continued as an activist, in many ways it was as a speaker and writer that she sustained her place in American public life. She claimed she had always been more skilled at inspiring and provoking than at sustained organizing. Lecturing and publishing served several purposes. They made it possible for her to earn a living. They kept her in the public eye in ways that maintained her position as one of the nation's leading authorities on women's issues. Finally, they enabled her to answer her critics.[16]

One of her most vituperative attacks came in 1973, in her *New York Times Magazine* article entitled "Up from the Kitchen Floor." She announced that around 1970, women who preached "man-hating sex/class warfare" threatened to take control of NOW, driving out all women who wanted to combine equality with loving relationships with their husbands and children. Those intent on disrupting the women's movement, she continued, "were the ones continually trying to push lesbianism or hatred of men." They did so, she claimed, with the encouragement of and even training by the FBI and the CIA. Those who were "pushing lesbianism" in NOW, she remarked, invoking her own experiences with political repression in the 1950s, "were creating a sexual red herring that would divide the movement and lead ultimately to sexual McCarthyism." At the same time, Friedan distanced herself from her past when she criticized feminists like Steinem for creating "a false analogy with obsolete or irrelevant ideologies of class warfare or race separatism." Ironically, these were the very issues that had shaped Friedan's first contemplation of "the woman question."[17]

A number of feminists responded to her charges, but none was historically more interesting than that of Mim Kelber, Friedan's co-worker at Federated Press. She descried Friedan's presumptuousness in speaking for all women. She called into question the way Friedan, "a self-described Joan of Arc" capable of "solipsism on such a vast scale," believed that so much of what she did was crucial in initiating changes in the lives of so many people worldwide, except, Kelber noted, for lesbianism, which "she views as a C.I.A.-inspired plot." She attacked Friedan's assumption that in 1963 the feminine mystique held all women in its grasp. After all, she noted, some had read *The Second Sex* and "figured out things for ourselves." She reminded Friedan that before her book many American women did not consider themselves freaks, as Friedan claimed was true about herself and others. After all, Kelber added, millions of them were working for a living. Without revealing she knew from personal experience that Friedan was misrepresenting her past, Kelber nonetheless made clear that Friedan had misconstrued history.[18]

Despite much opposition from feminists, Friedan's writing was eagerly published by the women's magazines that had once denied her a platform. As was true throughout her life, her articles were a complicated mixture of what she wanted to say, what she was willing to say in order to get published, and what those who controlled the media allowed her to say. She regularly contributed essays to the *New York Times*. From 1971 to 1973 she wrote "Betty Friedan's Notebook" as a column for *McCall's*, a women's magazine that had earlier commissioned and then rejected her articles based on *The Feminine Mystique*.

The articles in *McCall's* had important roots in Friedan's past. She had long worked to counter what the media published about women. In the "Wartime Living" columns for Federated Press, she developed a politically charged advice column. During the 1950s, she critiqued the *Daily Worker* for being no better in its treatment of women than mass-circulation women's magazines. In her own articles for women's and family magazines, she had countered Cold War conformist visions of women's lives. In 1960 she proposed to *Good Housekeeping* a column that would be serious and philosophical. In *The Feminine Mystique* she attacked mass-circulation magazines for their narrow definition of what mattered to women.

What she wrote in *McCall's* stood in sharp contrast to her most ambitious earlier efforts and to *Ms.,* the feminist publication launched by Steinem and others in 1971. Friedan positioned herself in the mainstream as part of a conscious effort to reach millions of middle-class women with a moderate feminist perspective. She commented on "clothes, food, home decor, entertaining, hairdos, kids and even happiness with men—which," she noted, "'women's lib' ignored." Some of what she said was serious and probing; some was trite and conventionally feminine. Occasionally, what she said was both nasty and political. At a July 1972 press conference announcing an article in a forthcoming issue of *McCall's*, she denounced her detractors in the women's movement, including Abzug and Steinem, as "female chauvinist boors." She accused Steinem of fostering "a female chauvinism that makes a woman apologize for loving her husband and children." The result, Friedan claimed, was that her opponents were "corrupting our movement for equality and inviting a backlash that endangers the very real gains we have won these past few years." With these words and in her August article, Friedan, responding to the victory of Steinem and Abzug at the Democratic convention, violated the understanding among feminists that they not attack one another in public.[19]

In *The Second Stage,* published in 1981 and revised in 1986, Friedan tried to align herself with centrist American politics. To her left, she saw radical feminists who, she argued, focused on separatism and single issues, making possible the resurgence of anti-feminism. She dissented from what she saw as the way lesbians and others promoted a culture of victimization among women. "Obsession with rape," she argued, "even offering Band-Aids to its victims, is a kind of wallowing in that victim state, that impotent rage, that sterile polarization." The focus by radical feminists on men as the enemy, she believed, violated "basic human needs for intimacy, sex, generation." Responding on the other side to the rise of conservative opposition to the women's movement, she criticized Ronald Reagan for what she saw as fascism with a friendly face and, along with anti-feminists, for fostering the backlash against the women's movement.[20]

In *The Second Stage* Friedan was reacting to several issues. With failure of the ERA, the women's movement stalled. A younger generation of women discovered that their attempts to be superwomen conflicted with their desire to have children and families. Friedan now called for a second stage in the women's movement. During the first stage, she argued, women had focused on single issues and false dichotomies. The shift in the second stage from either/or to both/and would make possible the resolution of left and right, male and female, work and family, volunteerism and professionalism. Consequently, she insisted, men and women had to join forces and counter the "feminist denial of the importance of family, of women's own needs to give and get love and nurture, tender loving care." She believed feminists had seen the heterosexual family as incompatible with the women's movement. Instead she insisted that the problem was in sex roles that men and women together could modify as they fought to bring about a fundamental change in human, not just women's, rights. Trying to recapture the family issue from conservative opponents of abortion and to align herself with

Middle Americans, she envisioned a new phase of feminism that would place families at the center. The failure, she asserted, was in "our own extreme of reaction against that wife-mother role: that devotional dependence on men and nurture of children and housewife service which has been and still is the source of power and identity, purpose and self-worth and economic security for so many women."[21]

With *The Second Stage*, Friedan recapitulated her political journey. In much of what she wrote she invoked her long-standing desire for heterosexual love and an affectionate family. Casting herself as a centrist involved a rejection of some parts of *The Feminine Mystique* regarding the life of the suburban housewife. Yet some of her later book also harked back to her years as a Popular Front feminist even as it underwrote her dual perspective—social democrat along with concessions to the anti-feminists. Her statement that sexual politics was a "pseudo-radical cop-out" reflected the experience of a seasoned social democrat who feared identity politics. Thus she called on those who focused on "pornography and other sexual diversions" to face instead "the real obscenity of poverty." She made clear her preference for a restructuring of the economic and social system. As she had done in the 1940s and 1950s, she called for provisions for child care and cooperative living. Her experiences of the 1940s and 1950s came through in her explanation of historical change driven by economic forces; in her picture of "a crumbling, unpredictable economy"; and in her discussion of sexual politics as a "red herring" that reactionaries used to defeat women and "distract people generally from their economic-political exploitation." Her call for women and men to work together reverberated with her dashed hopes from the 1940s and her addition of words to what Engels had written. Friedan's politics seemed confused. Some of what she wrote placed her among liberals; other things, among conservatives. Yet *The Second Stage* nonetheless offered an analysis of the relationship between women and consumer culture that was more radical than her 1963 book and echoed many of the themes in her writings as a labor journalist.[22]

With *The Fountain of Age* (1993), Friedan tried to do for middle-class older Americans what she had accomplished for suburban women thirty years earlier. She explored the mystique of aging. She discussed how the elderly gained strength from their experience. She called on her readers to explore new patterns of working and loving. Turning away from problems, she preferred instead to present retirement as a period of new opportunities. The words *African American, poverty, social class* did not appear in the index; the book did not really explore how adverse social conditions influenced people's experience with getting older, preventing millions of them from enjoying the opportunities Friedan described. As she did in *The Feminine Mystique,* in *The Fountain of Age* she described uncharted territory opening up for self-development, her own included. As she remarked in the last sentence, "I have never felt so free."[23]

Beginning in the early 1960s with the writing of *The Feminine Mystique,* Friedan worked and reworked the narrative of her life. What she has revealed of the years before her graduation from college in 1942 has been both largely accurate and selectively incomplete. She has correctly emphasized the shaping influence of the anti-Semitism she experienced in Peoria when her peers rejected her bid for membership in a sorority. She has accurately stressed the importance of some aspects of her education at Smith College, especially her training in Gestalt psychology. Yet she has not acknowledged in print or in public talks the exposure she had in Peoria to news of union activism and public anti-Semitism, the political education she obtained at Smith College, what she learned from Douglas and James Gibson, her work at Smith for unions, her opposition to American involvement in World War II until Pearl Harbor, or her experiences at Highlander Folk School.[24]

The period on which this book sheds the most new light begins with her move to Berkeley in 1942 and ends with the publication of *The Feminine Mystique.* From early drafts of *The Feminine Mystique* to the present Friedan has offered the commonly accepted version of her life in these years, one that is most familiar because it appeared in her widely read 1963 book. She has described this as a time when the feminine mystique increasingly trapped her. She has frequently mentioned the decision to turn down the fellowship in Berkeley as a pivotal moment in her life. She has given very different versions of this story, but in none of them did she explore the impact of her father's death, identify David Bohm as her boyfriend, or reveal the nature of her political and intellectual involvement with the Popular Front. Rather, she has emphasized how her experience at Berkeley reflected her own victimization by the feminine mystique.[25]

In public, with a few exceptions, Friedan has avoided, denied, minimized, or obscured her progressive political convictions of the 1940s and 1950s, especially on women's issues. She has rarely, if ever, publicly named Federated Press or the *UE News* as publications she worked for, or revealed her authorship of the 1952 pamphlet on sex discrimination against working women. Nor has she talked about the distinctive nature of the suburbs in which she lived beginning in 1950, the range of people she worked with on the Intellectual Resources Pool, or how she saw this innovative program as an answer to McCarthyism. She has not noted that she had to excise references to class and race in what she wrote for popular magazines in the 1950s, or the way she questioned the Cold War consensus in the published versions. When discussing *The Feminine Mystique*, Friedan has not mentioned how, from first draft to final product, she changed its tone and narrowed its focus. Finally, she has offered only the vaguest hints at the connection between her book and her earlier experiences with Marxism or progressive feminism. These omissions from her story have enabled Friedan to insist that until 1957 she had little or no knowledge of women's issues. As late as November 1995, she reiterated key elements of her story, especially her denial that she had any interest in women's issues before 1957.[26]

Consequently, a biographical note published in 1961 said that she "moved from academic psychology to applied social science research and finally to newspaper reporting." Similarly, the dust jacket copy for *The Feminine Mystique* noted that following her departure from Berkeley, Friedan did some "applied social-science research" and free-lance writing for magazines. Elsewhere, Friedan stated that in the 1940s "for conscious or unconscious reasons," she worked at "the usual kinds of boring jobs that lead nowhere." In 1973, she remarked that because Smith fostered in her a poor sense of the real world, she "just dabbled around with the kinds of jobs" most graduates of prestigious women's colleges got, "the editorial, research, journalism sort of thing."[27]

In contrast, Friedan has often discussed how the nature of her personal life—her marriage to Carl, the birth of her three children, and her move to the suburbs—made her feel trapped. She could not have written *The Feminine Mystique*, she has accurately remarked, had she not spent so many years in the suburbs as a housewife. As she wrote in her 1963 book, "I married, had children, lived according to the feminine mystique as a suburban housewife." On occasion she acknowledged her role in creating and directing school enrichment and adult education programs. More frequently she portrayed herself as an active but remote member of the community. In an oft-repeated story whose punch line has varied, Friedan recounted her response to the census form. In the space where it asked for her occupation, she put down "housewife" but remained guilty, hesitant, and conflicted about such a designation, on some occasions pausing and then adding "writer."[28]

Friedan laced *The Feminine Mystique* with suggestions of how much she shared with her fellow housewives. She suggested that she experienced the feminine mystique as keenly and in the same way as her readers. Using the first-person plural, she wrote that "all of us went back into the warm brightness of home" and "lowered our eyes from the horizon, and steadily contemplated our own navels." Friedan asserted that she discovered the importance of women's issues only when, in 1957, she read over the responses her college classmates made to the questionnaire.[29]

The actual story of Friedan's contribution as activist and free-lance writer is more complicated, heroic, and interesting than she has usually let on. Friedan correctly emphasized the authenticity and challenges of her experiences as a suburban housewife. However, her suburban exile took place in specific and in many ways unique circumstances. The extent to which she fully, or for more than a brief period, embraced the feminine mystique is open to question. In critical ways her difficulties did not stem from the dilemmas she described in her book: lack of career and ambition, a securely affluent household, and absence of a political sensibility. On the contrary, she was ambitious, important to the household economy, and politically engaged. During much of the two decades beginning in 1943, Friedan was participating in left-wing union activity, writing articles that ran counter to Cold War ideology, and living in a cosmopolitan, racially integrated community. Not many 1950s suburban housewives read Engels's argument for the liberation of women or developed an internationally recognized program that involved several of that decade's key radicals.[30]

In 1974, Friedan revealed much about her radical past in an article in *New York* magazine, reprinted two years later in a different version in *"It Changed My Life": Writings on the Women's Movement*. Her dramatic revelations, which neither she, nor any journalist, nor historian followed up on, occurred at a point when such truth-telling was welcome. Friedan came forth when, with the UE's nemesis Richard Nixon in disgrace over Watergate, anti-communism was discredited. Saying what she did, Friedan answered radical critics of her white, middle-class version of feminism by demonstrating how radical she herself had been on a wide range of issues, including class and race.[31]

Here Friedan suggested some of what she had omitted from earlier versions of her life. She mentioned briefly and vaguely that as a "reporter for the labor press" she "learned to pierce through the fog of words and even of psychology to the grubby economic underside of American reality." She wrote of how in the mid-1940s she and her friends considered themselves in "the vanguard of the working-class revolution," participated in "Marxist discussion groups," attended political rallies, and felt "only contempt" for their capitalist fathers. Without getting much more specific, Friedan noted that right after the war she was "very political, very involved, consciously radical. Not about women, for heaven's sake!" but about African Americans, workers, the threat of war, HUAC, McCarthyism, anti-communism, and "Communist splits and schisms." Friedan also recounted her first experience with another problem for which she claimed she had no name, sex discrimination. She recalled one incident, whose implications she said she only understood much later, when she was covering a strike as a union reporter and realized that not only the corporation but the union discriminated against women.[32]

Here Friedan placed her own story within the context of dramas shared by a whole generation. She linked the quest for security in the suburbs with the emphasis on security in major national and international events, especially the anti-communist crusade that was beginning to sweep across America. She hinted at the way disillusion with politics made motherhood more attractive. Accomplishing practical, specific tasks around the house and in local politics, she wrote, was more reassuring "than the schizophrenic and even dangerous politics of the world revolution whose vanguard we used to fancy ourselves." By 1949, she remarked in the 1976 article, she had learned that with the working class eager to participate in the affluent society, the likelihood of a "revolution" was rapidly disappearing. She found what happened in unions and behind the Iron Curtain "disillusioning, to say the least." Before the 1950s began, she insisted, McCarthyism, the heating up of the Cold War, the possibility of "fascism" coming to America, as well as "the reality of U.S. imperial, corporate wealth and power," meant that people "who used to have large visions of making the whole world over" became "uncomfortable with the Old Left rhetoric of revolution." In this context, what the feminine mystique did, Friedan argued retrospectively, was to make it "easier for a woman to retreat smugly" and with a good conscience. She described her own transformation from left-wing journalist to suburban housewife as the result of disillusionment with the left more than a response to McCarthyism on the right, emphasizing as she did that "the myth of the Communist menace was mostly an excuse for red-baiting." The pressure she emphasized was a generalized cultural one to conform rather than a highly political one to fear.[33]

Yet even at her most candid moments in the mid-1970s, she obscured much of her remarkable history. For example, in contrast to how Robert Schrank pictured her at Federated Press, she portrayed herself as a naive apprentice, surrounded by male journalists who "were avuncular to my innocence." Nor did she specify that she worked for Federated Press or the *UE News*. More significantly, she denied that in the late 1940s she had any curiosity about women's issues. She underplayed any consciousness of the difficulties women faced. She described her efforts to call a meeting in protest of her firing as "the first personal stirring of my own feminism," then adding tentatively, "I guess."[34]

Even when in 1976 Friedan suggested the more interesting and accurate version of her career, she distracted the reader from what she had revealed. She began and ended this autobiographical piece with images of domestic life. What framed the passing references to Marxist discussion groups was a description of how she and her friends read fashion magazines and spent much of their earnings on elegant clothes. The plot line of the article concerned her conversion to the feminine mystique. She learned that private concerns took the place of career and politics. She portrayed herself in the late 1940s as a woman who embraced domesticity, motherhood, and housework, even as she admitted that not everything she did at the time resulted from the feminine mystique. Friedan acknowledged her conflicting feelings about her new roles. When she left full-time employment, she was almost relieved. The guilt about working and prospect of a dead-end job made her eager, she remarked, "to embrace the feminine mystique." She claimed that two events of 1948—the unsuccessful campaign of Henry Wallace and the birth of her first child—made her suddenly lose interest in political activity. By and large, after the mid-1970s Friedan did not repeat what she said in 1976 or reveal more about her radical past.[35]

It is difficult to think of any comparable figure of the mid-twentieth century about whom so little is known concerning the formative years of her life or about whom available information is so inaccurate. Friedan did not fully reveal her past, and with the exception of authors of three biographies for children, writers have not looked at her narratives skeptically. Rather, they have tended to equate her autobiographical statements with history. Once Friedan became famous, journalists, authors of standard reference works, and historians simply repeated the narrative of her life offered in *The Feminine Mystique* and elsewhere. They adopted wholesale the story that Friedan had no familiarity with women's issues before 1957 and that, consequently, her suburban captivity was responsible for what she wrote in her vastly influential book. Though they occasionally gave evidence for an alternative script, even the new information Friedan offered in 1976 did not dislodge the accepted understanding of her political trajectory. Two examples will suffice. In 1995 *The Cambridge Dictionary of American Biography* incorrectly remarked that after Friedan married in 1947, "for almost the next 20 years [she] lived the life of a conventional suburban housewife/ mother." Similarly, in 1991 the historian of feminism Donald Meyer skipped over Friedan's years as a labor journalist and wrote that as someone who "embraced motherhood and housewifery eagerly," she was "the exemplary victim of the feminine mystique." Soon after her marriage, he wrote in a way that obliterated almost a decade of her life, she "found herself a housewife, in the suburbs of Rockland County, with three children."[36]

The question remains as to why Friedan's version of her life differs so significantly from the one this book constructs from the historical evidence. Understanding the relationship between her narrative of suburban captivity and the wide range of her actual experiences is important precisely because the tension between these two forces critically shaped what she wrote in *The Feminine Mystique*. Why did Friedan, who had spent so much energy advocating political solutions in the 1940s and early 1950s, focus in her book largely on adult education and self-realization and turn social problems into psychological ones? How did a woman who had fought to improve the lives of African Americans, Latinas, and working-class women end up writing a book that saw the problems of America in terms of affluent, suburban white women?[37]

Several factors explain the nature of the life story she developed. Having been so enmeshed in the Popular Front, she had reason to fear that revealing her past might expose her and the feminist movement to vicious McCarthyite attacks. She emphasized her experiences as a suburban, middle-class housewife because she was eager to heighten her book's impact, to insure her reputation in the women's movement as a person who understood her sisters in the mainstream, and to assure herself and others that she yearned for a conventional life. After the early 1950s, she articulated a politics that was in many ways less radical (or radical in different ways) than what she articulated in the previous decade. Finally, in the mid-1950s in therapy she developed an understanding of her past that enabled her to question the authenticity of her years as a labor radical.

Friedan had reason to worry that her involvement in radical politics for at least a dozen years beginning in 1940 meant that a full rendering of her life after 1960 was dangerous, given McCarthyism's power in memory and reality. In the 1950s and early 1960s, as a woman whose career was not yet on firm ground, she had much to lose. When she emerged in the limelight in 1963, the issue of Communist affiliation was central to the deliberations in SANE, SDS, and the civil rights movement. In the early 1960s, HUAC was still holding hearings, the United States was pursuing an anti-communist war in Vietnam, and J. Edgar Hoover's FBI was wiretapping Martin Luther King Jr., ostensibly to protect the nation against Communist influence. Moreover, for Friedan there may have been more immediately relevant parallels. In the late 1940s and early 1950s the government's harassment of the Congress of American Women had devastated burgeoning Popular Front feminism. In 1962 HUAC's investigations of Communist influence in

Women Strike for Peace served as a reminder of what had once happened and might happen again. Had Friedan revealed all in the mid-1960s, she would have undercut her book's impact, subjected herself to palpable dangers, and jeopardized the women's movement.[38]

Consequently, she may have realized that in order to launch a new feminist movement, she had to start with a clean state, excising any reference to her earlier life. One moment is especially telling. In September of 1960, a male host of a television show interviewed Friedan after she had published "I say: Women are *people* too!" in *Good Housekeeping*. At a time when the civil rights movement had begun to emerge in the South, he asked Friedan what women could do "concretely" if they found the role of wife and mother suffocating. Might they talk with each other about their experiences, he asked, before he went on to raise the possibility of getting "a movement going." Friedan did not pick up on his suggestion, responding instead with vague statements such as "just face it" and "and then begin to act on it, go out in the world." Despite such a statement, in the early 1960s Friedan was observing closely the civil rights movement and was aware of the parallels between discrimination against women as a group and that against African Americans. After reading James Baldwin's *The Fire Next Time* in 1962, she applied the anger he expressed as a black to what she felt as a woman. After she completed *The Feminine Mystique,* she tentatively titled her next book "Jane Crow," to designate the unfinished task of fighting sex discrimination. Friedan knew there were other, more concrete steps women could take. Years before she had taken them herself and encouraged others to do so. Instinctively or self-consciously she judged the moment too early or too risky.[39]

Yet even though McCarthyism makes her political moderation understandable, what she left out of her book is nonetheless significant. If McCarthyism prompted her to hide elements of her past from view, it also made it difficult for her to acknowledge directly her debt to the Old Left, perhaps out of a fear that she might betray a problematic or martyred cause. Red-baiting, still very much alive in the early 1960s, caused her to be vague about her radical past, and in the process she deprived her readers and the women's movement of the depth and wisdom that historical consciousness provides.[40]

The Bomb, along with the devastation inflicted by Hitler and Stalin, may have had the impact on Friedan that the feminist Dorothy Dinnerstein in 1976 argued for other women of her generation. These events, Dinnerstein has written, undermined hopes for a moral universe. They impressed on Friedan's contemporaries the power of irrationality and the folly of large-scale social projects that relied on the sanctions of planning and science, impelling many of her peers to switch their attention from bold and even utopian projects to local, practical, and personal ones. With the loss of ambitious public dreams, many women sought meaning and purpose in the domestic realm. Numbed by world-shattering events, the radicals of the 1930s and 1940s found it difficult if not impossible to communicate to a younger generation, in an articulate and forceful way, both the dreams they had once had and the horrors that shattered them.[41]

What relevance do Dinnerstein's observations have for Friedan? Someone in a position to know is Amy Swerdlow, a friend of Friedan's in Parkway Village in the 1950s and later, as a student of Gerda Lerner's, a scholar of women's postwar activism. In explaining the nature of women's political stances in the 1950s, Swerdlow has pointed to "the privatization and de-politicization that pushed former liberals and radicals" of the 1940s away from national politics. She has written tellingly of how they were "disillusioned with Stalinism and traumatized by McCarthyism. They were fearful and suspicious of anything that could lead to Red baiting, with its disastrous economic, political, and social consequences." In addition, she has argued, "educated white women with political ambitions were driven out of politics by the ridicule and calumny heaped upon so-called masculine women by the promoters of the new family ideology." In 1976 Friedan emphasized the impact of McCarthyism when she mentioned the "unconscious political retreat" to homes in the suburbs that many radicals of her generation made. Moreover, she wrote appreciatively of the pleasures of homemaking and local politics that were more comforting than what she saw as the crazy and frightening political activism she and others had engaged in. Similarly, in 1997 Friedan remarked on how many people in her generation, having "bought dreams called socialism, communism, or liberalism," later "recoiled from larger ideologies and their authoritarian dictates" when they "discovered the unspeakable atrocities of Adolf Hitler's Holocaust and Joseph Stalin's Gulag."[42]

Thus Friedan may well have understood the threat of McCarthyism within the larger contexts of world events of the 1940s. Indeed it is not too much to say that when she claimed the feminine mystique had been sweeping across America for two decades beginning in the mid-1940s, she had in mind something additional. The feminine mystique may also have been a coded phrase for what else was capturing America—the fear of atomic war, Cold War suspicion, and, most immediately, McCarthyism. Yet however much malaise and resignation might have affected her, viewed over the long term it is clear that her reaction to these portentous events was a mixture of determination and dissimulation.

As important as these public events were in shaping both her life and her

1963 book, at some level Friedan also engaged in an effort to heighten the impact of *The Feminine Mystique.* To make her book more dramatic and appealing, she reinvented herself. Instead of emphasizing continuities in her life, she told the story of her discoveries in captivity in order to appeal to white, middle-class women. Although we understand Friedan as an activist, during much of her life she saw herself as a writer. From her teenage years on, she had developed a keen understanding of her readers and of a variety of genres. Especially for the ten years beginning in 1953, Friedan thought of herself primarily as a professional journalist looking out for the story that would increase her income, make her career, and express her passions. Three children to educate and an upper-middle-class life to support, as well as conflicts with her husband over issues of breadwinning, help explain why she shaped the book in the hopes of generating income. She cast *The Feminine Mystique,* and her situation in the world it described, as part of an effort to enhance the book's popularity and impact.

The approach Friedan took in the book also came from changes in her politics that stemmed in part from her yearning to be in the mainstream. Ever since she was an adolescent, she longed for one version of a conventional life—a reciprocal, heterosexual relationship, a loving marriage, and a significant career. Throughout her adult life, she evoked the special insight she had that came from her having had a "Middle American background." In some ways the gendered pattern to the narrative she developed stemmed from her desire to be accepted as her version of a normal American. Thus, she minimized her participation in the public world that is often defined as male and exaggerated her involvement with the private arenas usually identified as female. A forceful and ambitious woman, she adopted feminized conventions that made it difficult to discuss the role that anger, ambition, excitement, and power played in her life. Even in the 1940s when she talked about her education as a radical, she portrayed herself as innocent and her political involvement as accidental. After 1963, when she discussed her life in the 1940s and 1950s, she constructed a narrative that emphasized how things happened to her and not how she determined to shape events. Again and again, she made her emergence as a powerful leader, along with 1960s feminism more generally, appear a result of happenstance. Social movements and their leaders do not, however, come out of nowhere. They have histories that powerfully shape their destinies, something that Friedan's participation in both Popular Front feminism of the 1940s and feminism of the 1960s so strongly emphasize.[43]

There is still another explanation for her narrative of her life and the focus of her book—her move away from her Popular Front positions after 1952. To some extent, she wrote *The Feminine Mystique* the way she did because after the early 1950s she had largely left behind her commitment to the working class, African Americans, and labor radicalism. Having participated in social movements that did not live up to her expectations, in *The Feminine Mystique,* whether consciously or not, she was trying to mobilize middle-class readers and thus prove to the men on the left that they had mistakenly abandoned or compromised women's issues in the 1940s and early 1950s. As she reconsidered her past in the mid-1950s, she acknowledged her own disillusionment with the failure of the left, including Communists, to develop an adequate response on women's issues. Friedan shifted her attention from one set of issues to another. In the process she tempered or abandoned much of her radicalism, especially on issues of race and class. Given the contradictions and ambivalences in her class position, it was not difficult to execute such a move. Her distinctive and in some ways privileged social position—the Bluffs of Peoria, merchant's daughter, Smith College, Grand View-on-Hudson—played an important role in the change in her focus from working class to middle class, from African Americans to whites, and from radicalism to reform.[44]

One final explanation of the origins of Friedan's revised story acknowledges the extent to which during the mid-1950s she experienced a sense of rebirth that changed how she understood her life. This factor makes it possible to comprehend how her story and the one this book tells might be reconciled. One story focuses on how she felt, the other on what written documents reveal. A feisty nature and a radical past does not preclude a sense of being trapped by the feminine mystique. It is not hard to imagine how a woman—with three children, shaky household finances, a problematic marriage, complicated dimensions of her class and ethnic positions, and disillusioning experiences with sexism in a professedly egalitarian social movement—could have fallen into a trap so woven into the 1950s culture that even a rebellious person could not wholly escape. What is at issue is the process by which a person who has experienced traumatic and dangerous situations reconstructs her sense of her self.[45]

In the mid-1950s, through therapy Friedan came to understand that the self who had been a labor journalist for ten years was not authentic. The result was that the years from 1943 to 1952 seemed a somewhat regrettable and disconnected interlude, a period when she was not in control of her life and for which she was not in some ways responsible. The way Friedan has conveyed a sense of division in her life, with a sharp break in the mid-1950s, may suggest powerful reasons why she wanted to separate herself emotionally and politically from her past, in the process claiming that her feminism began when she looked at the questionnaires her Smith classmates had filled out. Given the power of this therapeutically derived narrative, the emphases she gave to her past involved not deceit but her sense of how much she had changed.

In the end, however, the task of the historian is not only to be sympathetic but also to develop a story in a way that makes connections that someone who lived the life might miss or see differently. In the end, Friedan's story remains personally compelling but open to question. She has never been a person who keeps her distance from controversy. Since her adolescence, she was a woman with passionate commitments. She may have felt that her radicalism involved nothing more than dabbling and that she had no genuine interest in women's issues. Although that is not what the documents reveal, her statements speak to what she came to feel about her years as a labor journalist. There was a sea change between her outlook as a Popular Front feminist and as a suburban advocate of women's perspectives. She felt like a different person, and thus emerged a sense of discontinuity in her life. Nonetheless, while she envisioned a break, continuity is not hard to discover. In the end, Friedan's story of the trajectory of her life is enough to tempt anyone to embrace post-modernism. Its emphasis on contradictions, omissions, narrative disruptions, unstable texts, as well as on the tendency of texts to work against themselves, makes more understandable Friedan's story of her life.

All of these explanations help make Friedan's narrative intelligible. Why Friedan did not tell her full story between the early 1970s and the present stems in part from the factors already discussed, but from other issues as well. Some of the explanation lies with her ongoing commitment to accomplish urgent tasks as an author and political figure. Perhaps she hoped to write a memoir that would have the impact of her 1963 book. In addition, she knew that the shadow of anti-communism haunted the women's movement: in the late 1960s and early 1970s, NOW debated whether to welcome Marxist feminists from the Socialist Workers Party and the Young Socialist Alliance, with many NOW members fearing infiltration. In 1972, Friedan remarked that she opposed efforts in NOW to condemn radicals such as members of the Socialist Workers Party, "Radical Lesbians and square old Communists."[46]

Over time, Friedan developed a significant investment in her story. Her claims that she understood and represented middle-class women rested on her self-identification as a woman from Middle America's Peoria and on her assertion that *The Feminine Mystique* originated in her experience as a suburban housewife. Such statements gave her a certain leverage when she faced more radical feminists who attacked her for her homophobia and for her focus on white middle-class, suburban women. Moreover, new revelations she might offer would require that she justify the earlier and most famous version of her life recounted in *The Feminine Mystique*. They might also subject her to attack from those to her left and her right. She is not the only person to have reinvented herself and then convinced herself, in an unconscious way, of the truth in the story she created.

Understanding how Friedan came to write *The Feminine Mystique* provides a more connected sense of the history of American feminism. The women's movement, most historians agree, emerged in the 1960s from two sources: white, professional, and well-educated liberals, including Friedan, who, along with union activists, relied on a Washington-based approach as they called for national legislation; and a diverse group of younger women, shaped by the civil rights movement, who worked from the grass roots to develop a more adversarial insurgency. While this distinction clarifies important differences between the two stands, it overlooks the fact that although the people in Friedan's world may have been professionals, liberals, and Washington-oriented, many of them came to those positions from years shaped by labor insurgency, direct experience with working-class and minority women, and local organizing.[47]

A new understanding of Friedan's life emphasizes the remaking of progressive forces in America, the process by which a focus on women and the professional middle and upper-middle classes supplemented and in some ways replaced workers and unions. An examination of *The Feminine Mystique* reminds us of important shifts in the ideology of the left: from an earlier economic analysis based on Marxism to one developed in the 1950s that also rested on humanistic psychology; and from a focus on the impact of conditions of production on the working class to an emphasis on the effect of consumption on the middle class.

Yet to write a history of the postwar women's movement by focusing on middle-class activists such as Friedan is to give undue emphasis to the chronology that includes the death of feminism in the 1950s and its birth a decade later. This most common narrative on the revival of feminism neglects the very considerable participation by African American women in the grass-roots civil rights movement beginning in the 1950s, well before the publication of *The Feminine Mystique*. Similarly, Dorothy Sue Cobble has argued persuasively that feminism among working-class women, especially in the union movement, flourished in the postwar period and did not disappear in the 1950s. There was, she has demonstrated, no feminine mystique for these women; rather, though they did not call themselves feminists, they persisted in articulating and fighting for gender and class equity. Their vision was different from that of middle-class women. Union women, steeped in a tradition of class allegiance, voiced a communal vision of women advancing together; they sought power, security, and dignity as a group and not self-realization or social mobility as individuals. Understanding all of this helps us overcome the class and racial bias that informs the usual chronology of postwar feminism. What Esther Peterson did when she served as midwife to 1960s feminism was not, in the words of Cynthia Harrison, to "create a new agenda" but to encourage "the implementation of the program that labor women had long supported: equal pay legislation and a national commission on women."[48]

This reconsideration of Friedan's life emphasizes the importance of the 1940s radicalism in the history of American feminism. Because so much scholarship and popular understanding have focused on the 1930s, the 1950s, and the 1960s, we have insufficiently examined the period right after World War II, when women like Friedan had such high hopes for the transformation of society. At the same time, the continuities between Friedan's labor union activity and her 1960s feminism underscore the importance of what George Lipsitz has called "collective memory," the way the experiences of the immediate postwar period later reemerged in unexpected places. Her life makes clear how important were World War II, unions, and the fight during the 1940s for justice for women and African Americans in setting the stage for the reemergence of protests in the 1960s. To some extent, what shaped Friedan's perspective influenced millions of others as well: the Depression-spawned skepticism about the benefits of capitalism, the upheaval in the lives of African Americans and women in the war, and the combination of hope and disappointment in the postwar conversion, and then the onset of the Cold War.[49]

Friedan's life suggests that she served as a crucial link between generations of advocates for women's advancement. Placing Friedan's story in context reminds us that what is missing from the intellectual history of the 1950s and from all lists of New York Jewish intellectuals is what Ellen DuBois has called "left feminism," something Eleanor Flexner, Friedan, and Lerner represented. Irving Howe and others have made us aware of the troubled conversations between men from the Old and New Lefts. As he wrote in 1965, because "a generation is missing in the life of American radicalism," there was "an inordinate difficulty in communication between" younger and older radicals. Remarkable for their absence are frank discussions among Old and New Left women, one consequence of which is that most 1960s feminists had little or no inkling of what their progenitors, even those among them, had learned and experienced. With her emphasis on self-fulfillment, her work with C. Wright Mills and Carl Nordstrom, her experimentation with new forms of journalism, and her gendered anticipation of the writings of Paul Goodman, Friedan's career underscores how important she is as a link between the Old and New Left.[50]

By enriching our sense of the origins of what happened after 1960, this revision of Friedan's past sheds light on the history of women and second-wave feminism. Friedan's story suggests that, at least as far as she and some others are concerned, what we have seen as liberal feminism had radical origins. To be sure, few of the women who read *The Feminine Mystique* understood the history it contained; even fewer shared Friedan's experience with Popular Front feminism. Nonetheless, her life underscores the importance of a reconsideration of the nature of the breach between the proponents of women's rights in the early 1960s and the late 1960s advocates of women's liberation, especially socialist feminists. In the late 1960s, insurgent feminists discovered in consciousness-raising groups that the personal was political, that what they did in their private lives was closely connected to what they faced in the public realm. Through her own experiences in the 1940s, 1950s, and early 1960s Friedan learned lessons similar to the ones a later generation uncovered.

A fuller narrative of Betty Friedan's life, especially what she wrote and did in the 1940s and 1950s, makes clear, at least as far as she is concerned, that one of the sources of 1960s feminism was Popular Front radicalism of the 1940s and disappointment with that radicalism. Although some scholars have argued for a connection between protest movements of the 1940s and the 1960s, most historians believe that 1960s feminism emerged without a sense of connection to earlier social movements that included women among their concerns. Friedan's life provides evidence of such continuity by suggesting a specific and important connection between working women's struggle for justice in the 1940s and the feminism of the 1960s. Moreover, this book gives feminism and Friedan, both long under attack for a lack of interest in working-class and African American women, a pre-1963 past of which they should be proud.[51]

Friedan was not the only woman whose life connected 1940s progressive politics with 1960s feminism, though her 1963 book made her one of the most visible and influential ones. Flexner and Lerner also focused on women's and labor issues in the earlier decade and then had immense influence on the feminism of later generations. Kelber, who had worked with Goldstein at Federated Press, remained more consistent than Friedan in her commitment to a combination of trade unionism and feminism. Bella Abzug, Kelber's close friend from college days, began her political education at age twelve as a Zionist, shifting the focus of her passions in the late 1930s to anti-fascism. After graduating from law school, in the 1940s she began to provide legal counsel to workers, African Americans, tenants, and those threatened with loss of their civil liberties. In the 1960s and 1970s, beginning with her activity in Women Strike for Peace, Abzug emerged as a major figure in national politics and the women's movement. Milton Meltzer, who knew Friedan when they were both labor journalists, emerged in the 1960s as an author of books on women, Jews, African Americans, workers, and dissenters that post-1963 feminists read to their children. The African American playwright Lorraine Hansberry, author of *Raisin in the Sun*, acknowledged her debt to 1950s discussions of the "woman question," especially as they focused on working-class and African American women.[52]

Moreover, many of the women involved in the Labor Department's Women's Bureau, in the President's Commission on the Status on Women, in the founding of NOW, and in the burgeoning feminist movement of the 1960s and 1970s had deep roots in earlier social movements. Katherine P. Ellickson, Catherine East, Kathryn F. Clarenbach, Aileen Hernandez, Esther Peterson, Pauli Murray, Dorothy Haener, Mary D. Keyserling, Dorothy Kenyon, Florence H. Luscomb, and others brought to these tasks a wonderfully complex set of experiences with earlier progressive movements. One or more of them began with the fight for women's suffrage before World War I, participated in the struggle for gender equity in unions in the 1930s and 1940s, campaigned for civil rights for African Americans in the 1940s and 1950s, worked on the Wallace campaign in 1948, and involved themselves in the advocacy of civil liberties in the 1950s. Similarly, a study directed by Gerda Lerner of midwestern women who participated in the women's movement in the 1960s revealed the rich experiences of white and African American women in progressive causes in the 1940s and 1950s, including a focus on union, civil rights, and women's issues.[53]

Once we recover the stories of the middle-class activists across the nation, as well as the lives of working-class and African American women, the importance of the 1940s in the history of American feminism will be clearer. Kathleen Weigand and others have convincingly demonstrated the continuity between women's fights for social justice in the Old Left and the emergence of feminism in the 1960s. Leila J. Rupp and Verta Taylor note the importance of the complex coalition and histories of the people who came together at the Third Annual National Conference of Commissions on the Status of Women in 1966 and decided to form NOW. Among the key players, in addition to Friedan, were members of the President's Commission and state commissions, federal government officials with long-standing commitments to women's issues, Woman's Party activists, but especially, they note, women from labor unions.[54]

These groups comprise what Friedan later called "the seething underground of women in the Government, the press and the labor unions."

African American activist Pauli Murray, referring to women involved during the 1940s and 1950s in what she later called "women's issues," said they had been "involved in isolated, very often ineffectual protests. It wasn't that we weren't aware, but it was that we had no instrument, no consciousness. And among ourselves we would gripe and so this is why I say I was standing on the corner waiting." This vivid image captures both the sense of long preparation and of happenstance among women of Friedan's generation during the 1950s. They started a movement without realizing what they shared in their histories.[55]

It is important to establish an accurate story of Friedan's life because it enables us to see the complicated relationship among the parts of her past. Beginning in the late 1960s, many feminists rejected Friedan's formulations, castigating her and second-wave feminism as reactionary. In seeing *The Feminine Mystique* as a book weakened by its focus on white, middle-class, college-educated women, critics are on the mark. Yet Friedan had not afforded them an opportunity to appreciate how her feminism emerged in good measure from her own involvement in the struggle for justice for working-class, black, and Latina women.[56]

The question of continuity and change in Friedan's politics poses complicated issues. It is difficult to untangle positions and adopt meaningful labels, especially for the formative, turbulent, and rapidly changing years from 1967 to 1971. Eventually, additional historical research may help clarify the situation. Still, some statements are in order. Participants and scholars have cast Friedan in negative terms, sometimes as a reactionary but more often as a liberal, a negative word in feminist quarters after 1967. There is much truth in such a description: witness her attacks on lesbians; her resistance to broadening the women's movement to focus on poor, young, radical, and minority women; her celebration of conventionality in what she wrote for *McCall's* in the 1970s; her emphasis on family values in *The Second Stage;* and her lack of focus in *Fountain of Age* on class and race.

However, the situation is more complicated. It is hard to separate out the tactical, ideological, and stylistic dimensions of her positions. Especially in the dozen or so years after the mid-1960s, political labels had unstable meanings. Moreover, the traumas of the 1940s and early 1950s made it difficult for an older generation to speak to a younger one. Above all, it was hard for almost anyone, especially those offended by Friedan's anger and her sense of ownership of the women's movement, to understand how radical was the vision of a society that rested on opposition to sex discrimination in the economy, especially when what shaped such a vision was the combination of personal and ideological experiences of this Popular Front feminist.

All this helps explain her characterization of lesbian feminism as "pseudo-radicalism" and helps us realize that Friedan and NOW during her presidency had a more radical impulse than their detractors assumed.[57]

In the mid-1950s, Friedan did experience some political disillusionment but, as her therapy-connected autobiographical statements make clear, she did not reject the underlying values in which she had long believed. Before the mid-1950s and after 1963, Friedan focused on how to achieve fundamental social change through politics. Proof of the relevance of her experience as a progressive feminist in the 1940s comes from, among other sources, her statement in the late 1960s to a male radical. "You'd better read your Marx again," Friedan remarked, revealing her awareness of a connection between Marxism and feminism. "The only ones who can tell women how and where to run their revolution are women themselves."[58]

Others will assume the task of rethinking Friedan's post-1963 career in light of new evidence, but several comments are possible. An important question is whether Friedan's abandonment of her earlier radicalism and focus on working-class and African American women was a rhetorical strategy to promote the success of The Feminine Mystique or part of a longer-term deradicalization. Until her personal papers are fully open and extensive interviewing is carried out, and perhaps not even then, we may not know for sure the dynamics of this shift. In some ways, The Feminine Mystique marked a brief interlude in Friedan's longer term political commitments. In the early 1950s, the UE agenda involved many of the commitments that Friedan would return to in the mid-1960s: the opposition to government infiltration of social movements, the end of racial and gender segregation and discrimination, commitment to comprehensive social welfare legislation, and opposition to excessive military spending and unjust wars. The UE and Friedan (post-1963) shared much that The Feminine Mystique lacked, including a commitment to a coalition that involved unions, men, and, somewhat more unevenly, African Americans. To be sure, her aims, language, ideology, and the subjects of her agitation shifted between 1953 and the mid-1960s. Yet in important ways, she remained on the left throughout most of her life, in terms of the spectrum of American politics but not of American feminism. Full equality for women, she wrote in 1973, "will restructure all our institutions."[59]

Unlike many of her contemporaries among New York Jewish intellectuals, her departure from radical commitments did not result in her becoming a conservative. This group, whose numbers were small but whose influence was large, shared much with Friedan, especially the experience as Jews who engaged issues of social justice in the late 1930s and 1940s. Many of the most prominent women among New York intellectuals—Mary McCarthy,

Hannah Arendt, Midge Decter, Gertrude Himmelfarb—eventually became neo-conservatives. For male and female New York Jewish intellectuals, the central issues were support of Israel, the opposition to social entitlements, and the defense of Western culture. Generally speaking, they distanced themselves from the women's movement and neglected issues of gender. To some extent, Friedan shared with the more left-leaning neo-conservatives a mixture of cultural conservatism and social democratic politics. Although later than her peers, she too grew concerned with the rise of anti-Zionism and anti-Semitism among progressives at home and abroad. Moreover, her opposition to an ethic of victimization had parallels among those more commonly classified as New York Jewish intellectuals. Yet Friedan sustained commitments that separated her from those peers. She never saw the war in Vietnam as a lost opportunity for heroism and assertion of America's self-interest. As a feminist and social democrat, she consistently believed that society should do more, not less, to help the disadvantaged even if that meant a lessened emphasis on national defense.[60]

Friedan's experiences in the Popular Front activism of the 1940s and early 1950s help explain but do not excuse her animosity to lesbians and her accusations that lesbian infiltration into the women's movement was a CIA-inspired plot. Whatever their origins in her personal experiences and in partisan battles in the women's movement, in complicated and negative ways such remarks connect Friedan's later life with her early experiences with redbaiting, government suppression of radicalism, the dangers of factionalism, and class-based coalition politics. To Friedan, but not to everyone rooted in 1940s radicalism, identity and sexual politics that came into vogue in the late 1960s were anathema. Emphasizing sexual orientation conflicted with her long-standing dream of men and women working together to achieve common goals.

Final proof of the continuity in Friedan's life comes from her support for the revival of a strong and more insurgent union movement. In October 1996, she spoke at a conference that brought together intellectuals and labor leaders. "I have a pretty good historic Geiger counter," she noted, referring to what she sensed in the mid-1960s and using a metaphor that suggested something more dangerous than beneficent. "That counter is clicking again," she remarked as she articulated her hope for a revived labor movement aided by the commitment of intellectuals. What excited her about the new labor insurgency was the possibility, she asserted, of "a movement for social justice, a movement to transcend separate interests, the special interests, even the very good interests of identity politics that have been at the cutting edge of democratic progress." She called for a new vision, one that moved, as she said in a 1997 book, "beyond feminism, beyond sexual politics, beyond identity politics altogether." In her 1996 talk, she stressed that downsizing, especially its impact on men, as well as the "obscenely" greater amount of wealth the rich were accumulating, prompted her to call for women, men, African Americans, and homosexuals to put aside their differences and unite. She harkened back to fifty years earlier when, she noted, labor fought for a shorter work week that would provide more jobs. She denounced "the corporate culture of greed," and lamented that men and women with young children could not "make ends meet." What she wanted was greater democracy that would, she asserted, "revitalize our vision of the common good, a humane vision that places the highest priority on people's lives and not on the stock market index and the corporate bottom line."[61]

Friedan said essentially the same things as a labor journalist in the 1940s and early 1950s: corporate greed was destroying America, and only through a united front could progressive forces bring about a world where human values mattered more than pecuniary ones. Beginning with anti-Semitism in the 1930s, she shifted to labor activism in the 1940s. Then she changed her focus to women's issues, initially as they arose in the labor movement and then in a decidedly middle-class context. Now seventy-five, Friedan once again asserted that a coalition inspired by the labor movement held out promise for a better America.

Notes

Abbreviations

AHR   *American Historical Review*
AQ   *American Quarterly*
BF-SLRC   Betty Friedan Papers, Schlesinger Library, Radcliffe College, Cambridge, Massachusetts, Box number followed by carton number. Unless otherwise noted, the references are to collection 71-62 . . . 81-M23.
BG-SHSW   Betty Goldstein folder, Highlander Research and Education Center Papers, State Historical Society of Wisconsin, Madison, Wisconsin
CASC   College Archives, Smith College, Northampton, Massachusetts
CC   *Communist Campanile*
DC   *Daily Californian*
DHG   *Daily Hampshire Gazette,* Northampton, Massachusetts
EF-SLRC   Eleanor Flexner Papers, Schlesinger Library, Radcliffe College, Cambridge, Massachusetts
FP   *Federated Press*
HS-UMass Harvey Swados Papers, Special Collections and Archives, W. E. B. DuBois Library, University of Massachusetts Amherst
HUA   Harvard University Archives, Cambridge, Massachusetts
JAH   *Journal of American History*
JG-CU   James Gibson Papers, Rare and Manuscript Collections, Carl A. Kroch Library, Cornell University, Ithaca, New York
JL   *Jewish Life*
LWV-LC   League of Women Voters Papers, Manuscripts Division, Library of Congress, Washington, D.C.
NG-WSU   Newspaper Guild Collection, Archives of Labor and Urban Affairs, Wayne State University, Detroit, Michigan
NYHT   *New York Herald Tribune*
NYNG-NY   Papers of the New York Newspaper Guild, Robert F. Wagner Labor Archives, Tamiment Institute Library, Elmer Holmes Bobst Library, New York University, New York, New York
NYT   *New York Times*
NYTM   *New York Times Magazine*
PHSC-BU   Peoria Historical Society Collection, Bradley University Library, Peoria, Illinois

PO   *Peoria Opinion*
PV   *Parkway Villager*
SAQ   *Smith Alumnae Quarterly*
SCAN   *Smith College Associated News*
SCM   *Smith College Monthly*
SCW   *Smith College Weekly*
SSCSC   Sophia Smith Collection, Smith College, Northampton, Massachusetts
TL-NYU   Tamiment Institute Library, Elmer Holmes Bobst Library, New York University,
          New York, New York
UEN   *UE News*
WWN-CU   W. W. Norton Papers, Rare Books and Manuscripts, Butler Library, Columbia
          University, New York, New York

Introduction

1. Betty Goldstein, "UE Drive on Wage, Job Discrimination Wins Cheers from Women Members," *UEN*, 16 April 1951, 6; Lisa Kannenberg, "The Impact of the Cold War on Women's Trade Union Activism: The UE Experience," *Labor History* 34 (spring–summer 1993): 318; Eleanor Flexner, interview by Jacqueline Van Voris, Northampton, Mass., 16 Oct. 1982, 70–71, EF-SLRC. See also [Eleanor Flexner], "The Woman Question," syllabus for course at Jefferson School of Social Science, 1953–54, 1, 2, 5. For information on Flexner, see Ellen C. DuBois, "Eleanor Flexner and the History of American Feminism," *Gender and History* 3 (spring 1991): 81–90; Ellen Fitzpatrick, foreword to Eleanor Flexner and Ellen Fitzpatrick, *Century of Struggle: The Women's Rights Movement in the United States,* enlarged (Cambridge, Mass., 1996), ix–xxvii; Leila J. Rupp, "Eleanor Flexner's *Century of Struggle*: Women's History and the Women's Movement," *National Women's Studies Association Journal* 4 (summer 1992): 157–69. On the Jefferson School, see Marvin E. Gettleman, "The New York Workers School, 1923–1944: Communist Education in American Society," in *New Studies in the Politics and Culture of U.S. Communism,* ed. Michael E. Brown et al. (New York, 1993), 261–80; Marvin E. Gettleman, "Jefferson School of Social Science," *Encyclopedia of the American Left,* ed. Mari Jo Buhle, Paul Buhle, and Dan Georgakas (New York, 1990), 389–90; Daniel F. Ring, "Two Cultures: Libraries, the Unions, and the 'Case' of the Jefferson School of Social Science," *Journal of Library History* 20 (1985): 287–88; Annette T. Rubinstein, "David Goldway," *Science and Society* 54 (winter 1990–91): 386–89. On the UE, see Ronald W. Schatz, *The Electrical Workers: A History of Labor at General Electric and Westinghouse, 1923–60* (Urbana, 1983).

2. Betty Friedan, "Up From the Kitchen Floor," *NYTM,* 4 March 1973, 8; Betty Friedan, *"It Changed My Life": Writings on the Women's Movement,* 1985 edition (New York, 1976), 304.

3. For a discussion of the meanings of feminism, see Nancy F. Cott, *The Grounding of Modern Feminism* (New Haven, 1987), 4–5; Nancy F. Cott, "What's in a Name? The Limits of 'Social Feminism'; or, Expanding the Vocabulary of Women's History," *JAH* 76 (Dec. 1989): 809–29. I use the phrase McCarthyism even though what it represented began before the ascension to power of Senator Joseph R. McCarthy and persisted after his death; on this problem of terminology, see Nora Sayre, *Previous Convictions: A Journey through the 1950s* (New Brunswick, N.J., 1995), 8.

4. The quotes are from Betty Friedan, *Feminine Mystique* (New York, 1963), 54, 137, 150; see also 156, 171. Among the many commentaries on Friedan's book are Rachel Bowlby, " 'The Problem With No Name': Rereading Friedan's *The Feminine Mystique,*" *Feminist Review* 27 (Sept. 1987): 61–75; Zillah R. Eisenstein, *The Radical Future of Liberal Feminism* (New York, 1981), 177–200; Donald Meyer, "Betty Friedan," in *Portraits of American Women: From Settlement to the Present,* ed. G. J. Barker-Benfield and Catherine Clinton (New York, 1991), 599–615; Jean B. Elshtain, *Public Man, Private Woman: Women in Social and Political Thought* (Princeton, 1981), 249–55.

5. The quotes are from Friedan, *Feminine Mystique,* 15, 43; see also 26, 77.

6. The quotes are from ibid., 206, 282; see also 237, 240. Scholars have confirmed Friedan's judgment about housework: see Susan Strasser, *Never Done: A History of American Housework* (New York, 1982); Ruth S. Cowan, *More Work for Mother: The Ironies of Household Technology from the Open Hearth to the Microwave* (New York, 1983).

7. The quotes are from Friedan, *Feminine Mystique*, 338, 366, 344–48; see also 334–37.

8. The quotes are from ibid., 378; see also 372, 374, 375.

9. The sales figures come from Meyer, "Friedan," 602.

10. Betty Friedan, interview by Daniel Horowitz, Santa Monica, Calif., 18 March 1987.

11. Daniel Horowitz, *Vance Packard and American Social Criticism* (Chapel Hill, 1994).

12. For a recent article on the difficulties biographers face with uncooperative subjects, see Janny Scott, "For Writers, a Love-Hate Story: Living People Are Awfully Uncooperative, Biographers Say," *NYT*, 6 Oct. 1996, 37, 46. For the moving story of how an investigative reporter and son both reveals and comes to terms with his parents' participation in the Old Left in the early 1940s, see Carl Bernstein, *Loyalties: A Son's Memoir* (New York, 1989).

13. Daniel Horowitz to Betty Friedan, 6 Sept. 1995, author's possession; Betty Friedan to Daniel Horowitz, 6 Nov. 1995, author's possession. Rachel C. Ledford to Daniel Horowitz, 6 Nov. 1995, author's possession, summarizes Friedan's talk at the Smithsonian Institution, Washington, D.C., that evening. In response to my article in *American Quarterly*, the spring 1996 issue of the newsletter of Veteran Feminists of America, the organization representing feminists of Friedan's generation, called my article "stunning." For the article, see Daniel Horowitz, "Rethinking Betty Friedan and *The Feminine Mystique*: Labor Union Radicalism and Feminism in Cold War America," *AQ* 40 (March 1996): 1–42.

14. On the meaning of fellow traveling, see David Caute, *The Fellow-Travellers: Intellectual Friends of Communism*, rev. ed. (New Haven, 1988).

15. Michael Denning uses the phrase "Popular Front feminism" and Kathleen Weigand, "progressive women": Michael Denning, *The Cultural Front: The Laboring of American Culture in the Twentieth Century* (London, 1996), 136; Kathleen A. Weigand, "Vanguards of Women's Liberation: The Old Left and the Continuity of the Women's Movement in the United States, 1945–1970s" (Ph.D. diss., Ohio State University, 1995), 27. The other quotes from Denning, *Cultural Front*, are on xvi, xviii; see also xix, 9, 38.

16. In this discussion, I am relying on Denning, *Cultural Front*, xviii, 5.

17. "Hundreds in N.C. Protest Vandalism in Library," *Chronicle of Higher Education*, 5 April 1996, A6.

18. The writings on the history of the Communist Party cover a wide range of perspectives. Irving Howe and Lewis Coser, *The American Communist Party: A Critical History, 1919–1957* (Boston, 1957) provides a good place to begin, as does Joseph R. Starobin, *American Communism in Crisis, 1943–1957* (Cambridge, Mass., 1972). Harvey Klehr, John Earl Haynes, and Fridrikh Igorevich Firsov, *The Secret World of American Communism* (New Haven, 1995) rely on recently available documents from Soviet archives to argue that some major American Communists spied for the USSR or helped others carry out espionage; see also Klehr, Haynes, and Kyrill M. Anderson, *The Soviet World of American Communism* (New Haven, 1998). On the other hand, for a picture that emphasizes the variety, passion, and ordinariness of the lives of American Communists, see Vivian Gornick, *The Romance of American Communism* (New York, 1977). For an attack on the revisionism, see Theodore Draper, "American Communism Revisited," *New York Review of Books*, 9 May and 30 May 1985. Although Theodore Draper has been the principal protagonist against the new trends in the history of American Communism, the contrast is clearest between John E. Haynes, *Red Scare or Red Menace? American Communism and Anticommunism in the Cold War Era* (Chicago, 1996) and Brown et al., *New Studies in the Politics and Culture of U.S. Communism* (New York, 1993). Among the other books that grapple with the implications of the end of the Cold War for American history are: Dorothy Healey and Maurice Isserman, *Dorothy Healey Remembers: A Life in the American Communist Party* (New York, 1990); Tom Engelhardt, *The End of Victory Culture: Cold War America and the*

Disillusioning of a Generation (New York, 1995); Klehr, Haynes, and Firsov, *Secret World of American Communism;* Van Gosse, *Where the Boys Are: Cuba, Cold War America, and the Making of a New Left* (London, 1993); Elaine T. May, *Homeward Bound: American Families in the Cold War Era* (New York, 1988). In "Search for a Method: Recent Histories of American Communism," *Radical History Review* 61 (winter 1995): 166–74, Alan Wald provides a prob-ing discussion of the issues involved in writing a history of the Old Left. Wald's *In Writing From the Left: New Essays on Radical Culture and Politics* (London, 1994) explores the continuities in literary traditions within the Old and New Lefts. For a discussion of fellow travelers that challenges us to write their history in a more nuanced way, see Dave Roediger, foreword to *Harvey and Jessie: A Couple of Radicals,* by Jessie Lloyd O'Connor, Harvey O'Connor, and Susan M. Bowler (Philadelphia, 1988), ix–xii.

19. Helen K. Chinoy, comments at the Smith College Club, Northampton, Mass., 28 Sept. 1995. Bernstein, *Loyalties,* 17, notes that although "respectability and rehabilitation" usually elude those who were party members, "it is honorable and, in some circles, even heroic to have been on the left in the perilous epoch just past."

20. In the chapters that follow, through word choice or direct discussion, I indicate the degree of certainty of my conclusions. Among the closed sections of her papers that might have been of some use are BF-SLRC, 2: 131–34; and BF-SLRC, 86-M12—93-M146, 3: 89–93.

21. On issues in writing feminist biography, see Sara Alpern, Joyce Antler, Elisabeth I. Perry, and Ingrid W. Scobie, eds., *The Challenge of Feminist Biography: Writing the Lives of Modern American Women* (Urbana, 1992); Carolyn G. Heilbrun, *Writing a Woman's Life* (New York, 1988).

22. It is possible that even though she had experience with women's issues in the 1940s, Friedan associates terms like feminism or the woman question with the limited and even conservative meaning they had in the 1940s through their association with the Woman's Party, whose advocacy of the Equal Rights Amendment labor activists opposed. For her discussions at dinner parties, I am relying on Sarah S. Boasberg, conversation with author, Northampton, Mass., 2 May 1996.

23. Daniel Horowitz, telephone conversation with Amy Swerdlow, 17 July 1996; Nelson Lichtenstein, e-mail message to author, 9 Oct. 1996; Margaret Whitehead, e-mail messages to author, 10 Feb. 1997 and 13 Feb. 1997; Betty Friedan, "Feminism in the 1960s," speech at American University, 4 Nov. 1996, broadcast on C-SPAN; unidentified source quoted in [Betty Friedan], "The Community Resources Pool: A Pilot Project in the Enrichment of Public Education," report for 1960–61, 46, BF-SLRC, 9: 358.

1. Peoria, 1921–38

1. John M. Sumansky, "Peoria: The Growth and Development of a River Town," in *The Middle-Size Cities of Illinois: Their People, Politics, and Quality of Life,* ed. Daniel M. Johnson and Rebecca M. Veach (Springfield, Ill., 1980), 126–27; Federal Writers' Project, Works Proj-ect Administration, *Illinois: A Descriptive and Historical Guide* (Chicago, 1939), 356–61; Jerry Klein, *Peoria!* (Peoria, 1985), 88. For additional information on Peoria, see the collections of PHSC-BU. George W. May, *Students' History of Peoria County, Illinois* (Galesburg, Ill., 1968), 273, exaggerates the extent to which Peoria escaped the consequences of the Depression.

Throughout this chapter, I use Bettye Goldstein, the name she herself used in these years, except when I am mentioning the Betty Friedan who talked about her years in Peoria. Accord-ing to one biographer, she was born Elizabeth Naomi Goldstein: Justine Blau, *Betty Friedan* (New York, 1990), 21. Betty Friedan has used several names over the course of her life: Bettye Goldstein until she graduated from college; Betty Goldstein until she married and as a writer, until she made the switch from labor journalism to free-lance writer; Betty Friedman briefly at the time of her marriage; and Betty Friedan, soon thereafter and, beginning in the mid-1950s, as a writer.

For biographical information, I am relying, in addition to the archival material cited below, on Blau, *Friedan,* 21–26; Marcia Cohen, *The Sisterhood: The True Story of the Women Who Changed the World* (New York, 1988), 25, 54–62; Betty Friedan, interview by Jacqueline Van Voris, New York, N.Y., 17 and 19 April 1973, CASC; Betty Friedan, *"It Changed My Life": Writings on the Women's Movement,* 1985 edition (New York, 1976), 5–7; David Halberstam, *The Fifties* (New York, 1993), 592; Lisa Hammel, "The 'Grandmother' of Women's Lib," *NYT,* 19 Nov. 1971, 52; Sondra Henry and Emily Taitz, *Betty Friedan: Fighter for Women's Rights* (Hillside, N.J., 1990), 9–20; Milton Meltzer, *Betty Friedan: A Voice for Women's Rights* (New York, 1985), 1–13; Jennifer Moses, "She's Changed Our Lives: A Profile of Betty Friedan," *Present Tense,* May–June 1988, 30; Lyn Tornabene, "The Liberation of Betty Friedan," *McCall's,* May 1971, 137; Paul Wilkes, "Mother Superior to Women's Lib," *NYTM,* 29 Nov. 1970, 27, 29, 140; Kathleen Wilson, "Betty (Naomi) Friedan," *Contemporary Authors,* New Revision Series 45 (New York, 1995): 133–36.

2. The quotes are from Elise Morrow, "Peoria," *Saturday Evening Post,* 12 Feb. 1949, 20; Betty Friedan, "Betty Friedan and the Women's Movement: Finally, They Play in Peoria," *Minneapolis Tribune,* 24 Nov. 1978, 1C. Other information on the city comes from Sumansky, "Peoria," 124, 127, 128, 137; Klein, *Peoria,* 240; John B. Martin, "The Town That Reformed," *Saturday Evening Post,* 1 Oct. 1955, 26, 27, 107, 108; Billy Rose, "I Wish't I Was in Peoria," quoted in Sumansky, "Peoria," 137. In 1937, the Orthodox Synagogue had about 250 members: Sam Hodes, "History of the Jewish People of Peoria," unpublished paper, 17 May 1937, 33, PHSC-BU. On Peoria as a southern city, see May, *Students' History,* 102–3. For evidence of the pursuit of high culture in Peoria, see Evabeth Miller, "Cultural Trends in Peoria," paper read before Peoria Historical Society, 18 Feb. 1952, PHSC-BU.

3. The quotes are from *Leshnick's 1918 Directory,* 1414, copy in author's possession; Harry Goldstein Jr., conversation with Daniel Horowitz, Los Angeles, Calif., spring 1988. For additional information on Harry Goldstein, see "H. M. Goldstein Taken By Death," clipping from Peoria newspaper, 12 Jan. 1943, author's possession; Amy Stone, "Friedan at 55," *Lilith,* fall 1976, 11. For the first appearance of Harry M. Goldstein in the city directory: *Peoria City Directory* (Peoria, 1899), 249; Edward L. Richter, ed., *Peoria of To-Day with Peoria Blue Book Directory, 1915* (Chicago, 1915), 136. Several sources date his arrival in Peoria earlier: see, for example, "Goldstein's Going Out of Business" clipping from *Peoria Journal,* 29 April 1953, PHSC-BU; "H. M. Goldstein Taken by Death"; Meltzer, *Friedan,* 3. For the shift from pedlar to store merchant in Johnstown, Pennsylvania, see Ewa Morawska, *Insecure Prosperity: Small-Town Jews in Industrial America, 1890–1940* (Princeton, 1996), 53–54. Although Johnstown is quite different from Peoria, this book helps illuminate life in the Jewish community where Goldstein grew up. On the assimilation of Jewish women, see Paula E. Hyman, *Gender and Assimilation in Modern Jewish History* (Seattle, 1995).

4. "Memorial Service Set for Mother of Betty Friedan," *Peoria Journal Star,* 10 June 1988; birth certificate for Miriam [Marian on my copy of the certificate] Leah Horwitz, copy in author's possession; Meltzer, *Friedan,* 3–4; Moses, "She's Changed," 31; Henry and Taitz, *Friedan,* 9–10. Bettye Goldstein, "Through a Glass Darkly," paper for high school class, 3 April 1938, 2–3, BF-SLRC, 1: 248 makes it clear that Amy and Harry Jr. were a year-and-a-half and five years younger than Betty, respectively. On the role of women in Jewish mercantile families, see Morawska, *Insecure Prosperity,* 62–66 and 100–102.

5. Federal Writers' Project, *Illinois,* 357; see also Goldstein, "Glass Darkly," 2. The address was then 105 Farmington Road, changing in 1956 to 1711 and more recently to 1011. For the move in 1924 from 112 West Arcadia, see *Peoria City Directory* (Peoria, 1921), 630 and (Peoria, 1924), 469. On Bradley Park, see Monica Vest Wheeler, *The Grandest View: A History of the Peoria Park District* (Peoria, 1994), 42–48.

6. Amy Goldstein Adams, quoted in Cohen, *Sisterhood,* 55; Amy Goldstein and Bettye Goldstein, quoted in Cohen, *Sisterhood,* 60. See also Cohen, *Sisterhood,* 55; Meltzer, *Friedan,* 4; Henry and Taitz, *Friedan,* 11; Goldstein, "Glass Darkly," 2, 13. In Friedan, "Friedan and the Women's Movement," 2C, she said her family could not join the country club and Goldstein, "Glass Darkly," 9, states that her family did belong to North Shore. "North Shore Club Is Sold,"

Peoria Star, 7 Sept. 1936, makes it clear that this club, in financial trouble during the Depression, was not in a position to be very exclusive. For information on clubs, I am relying on Sam Hodes, telephone conversation with Daniel Horowitz, 8 Feb. 1998.

7. "Anshai Emeth Temple," part of unpublished manuscript, 436–77, PHSC-BU; Klein, *Peoria,* 240; Moses, "She's Changed," 30; Judith E. Endelman, *The Jewish Community of Indianapolis: 1849 to the Present* (Bloomington, 1984), 157; Goldstein, "Glass Darkly," 5. For information on the Jewish community in Peoria, I am relying on "Peoria Jewish Community Had Its Start Over 100 Years Ago," *Peoria Journal Star,* 23 Jan. 1955, copy in author's possession; Susan Weinberg, "Peoria's Religious Record," *Illinois History,* March 1970, 140; "The Jewish Community of Peoria," *The Reform Advocate,* 30 Jan. 1909, 766–81; Hodes, "Jewish People of Peoria." On her father's admiration for Ingersoll, see Bettye Goldstein, "B.G.," four-page typewritten paper, late April or May 1941, 2, BF-SLRC, 6: 276.

8. The quotes are from Doug [Palmer] to Bettye Goldstein, letter in her copy of the high school yearbook, *Crest,* 9 June 1938, following 60, BF-SLRC, 1: 247v; Harry Goldstein Jr., quoted in Cohen, *Sisterhood,* 58; Friedan and Miriam Goldstein, quoted in Cohen, *Sisterhood,* 60; Friedan, quoted in Cohen, *Sisterhood,* 58. See also Henry and Taitz, *Friedan,* 13; Goldstein, "Glass Darkly," 2.

9. The quote is from Betty Friedan, *The Second Stage* (New York, 1981), 93; see also Cohen, *Sisterhood,* 59; Bettye Goldstein, "Learning the Score," *"We Know the Score": Highlander Folk School* (fall term, 1941), 22, BF-SLRC, 6: 274; Meltzer, *Friedan,* 10. For evidence of the heavy mortgages the Goldsteins carried in the 1930s, see records in the Peoria Real Estate Mortgage Books, copies in author's possession. On the relationship between standards of living and assimilation, Morawska, *Insecure Prosperity,* 114; on the precariousness of Jewish merchants in the 1930s, ibid., 124.

10. Amy Goldstein Adams, quoted in Cohen, *Sisterhood,* 58; see also Meltzer, *Friedan,* 12; Henry and Taitz, *Friedan,* 14; Friedan, *Changed My Life,* 6.

11. The quotes are from Cohen, *Sisterhood,* 56; Wilkes, "Mother Superior," 27; Cohen, *Sisterhood,* 55; other information comes from Cohen, *Sisterhood,* 56, 58; Blau, *Friedan,* 22. For evidence of her attractiveness, see Cohen, *Sisterhood,* 61.

12. The quote is from Friedan, *Changed My Life,* 235. Other information comes from Meltzer, *Friedan,* 12; Tornabene, "Liberation," 137; Henry and Taitz, *Friedan,* 11, 14. Over time, Friedan came to see her father in a different light. For her agony over how her relationship with her father shaped her ambitions and sense of herself, see Betty Friedan, "A Kind of Destruction, The Worst, For a Woman," c. 1955, BF-SLRC, 13: 487.

13. The quotes are from Friedan, *Second Stage,* 93; Betty Friedan, quoted in Wilkes, "Mother Superior," 29; see also Friedan, quoted in Cohen, *Sisterhood,* 59; Hammel, "Grandmother," 52; Friedan, Van Voris interview, 1.

14. The quote is from Stone, "Friedan at 55," 11; for Bettye's feelings about herself, see Goldstein, "Glass Darkly," 1.

15. Blau, *Friedan,* 23; Henry and Taitz, *Friedan,* 15; Goldstein, "Glass Darkly," 14.

16. The quotes are from Friedan, quoted in Wilkes, "Mother Superior," 29, with the ellipses in the original. Other information comes from Blau, *Friedan,* 23; Henry and Taitz, *Friedan,* 15–16; Goldstein, "Glass Darkly," 14, 21; Meltzer, *Friedan,* 9. On her recollection of the pain of her childhood, see Friedan, quoted in Meltzer, *Friedan,* 9; Friedan, Van Voris interview, 2. The cemetery scene is from Cohen, *Sisterhood,* 57. For the story of her secret prayer, see Betty Friedan, "Autobiography—Betty Friedan," c. 1975, 9, BF-SLRC, 1: 63, quoted in Joyce Antler, *The Journey Home: Jewish American Women and the American Century* (New York, 1996), 262.

In what she wrote and said after 1963, Friedan portrayed much of her childhood and adolescence as miserable. It is no easy task for the historian to reconstruct this part of her past. The difficulties are especially daunting when it comes to Bettye Goldstein's pre-college years, because we have few written materials and must rely a great deal on memory to reconstruct people's experiences. The principal evidence from the period itself is a twenty-three-page paper Goldstein handed in as a class assignment in the spring of her senior year of high school

[Goldstein, "Glass Darkly"], the articles she wrote for student publications in high school, and some pieces she composed while in college.

Relying on documents such as these is not without problems. The paper Bettye wrote in high school is a rich source, yet it is shaped by the circumstances that govern what a seventeen-year-old girl, even if she knew and fully understood her feelings, would write for a classroom assignment that her teacher would see. Though she wrote openly of her social life at school, she was guarded about her situation at home. Knowing she was ending her education in Peoria and about to begin her college years at Smith, she nostalgically looked back on her youth. The articles Bettye wrote in high school are numerous and telling, even though genre conventions shape what she said and how she said it. Later experiences shaped the pieces she wrote while in college about her life in high school. The historian must move carefully between the contemporary sources and the more recent reminiscences, which are made problematic by the tricks of memory and Friedan's fame.

Some caution about Friedan's adult version of her years in Peoria is in order. Some of her Peoria friends have difficulty accepting her picture of herself as lonely and unhappy in her high school years and the emphasis she placed on the anti-Semitism she claimed she experienced on the personal level (see the statements, drawn from interviews of Friedan's contemporaries, in Henry and Taitz, *Friedan*, 17, and Cohen, *Sisterhood*, 56. See also, Mary Walton, "Once More to the Ramparts," *Chicago Tribune Magazine*, 25 Oct. 1981, 13). Indeed the paper she wrote at the end of her senior year in high school reveals someone much less lonely and unpopular than Friedan has pictured herself in retrospect. Although I think more attention needs to be placed on how public issues surrounding labor unions and anti-Semitism shaped her consciousness in high school, by and large I have accepted Friedan's picture of her childhood and much of her youth, especially the emphasis on her loneliness. Her contemporaries had little if any idea of the seriousness of the tensions in the household. Girls like Bettye Goldstein learned how to hide the sadness they experienced as adolescents.

17. The quotes are from John Parkhurst, "Peoria's Betty Friedan: An Extraordinary Woman," *North Peoria Observer*, 22 Feb. 1984, clipping in author's possession; unidentified high school friend, quoted in Cohen, *Sisterhood*, 61; Harry Goldstein Jr., quoted in Cohen, *Sisterhood*, 57; Harry Goldstein, quoted in Meltzer, *Friedan*, 8; school principal, quoted in Meltzer, *Friedan*, 7. Other information is from Hammel, "Grandmother," 52; Cohen, *Sisterhood*, 56–57; Wilkes, "Mother Superior," 29; Goldstein, "Glass Darkly," 4; Meltzer, *Friedan*, 9–10; Henry and Taitz, *Friedan*, 17. Goldstein was one of six valedictorians: "Six Tie for First in Senior Class," *PO*, 27 May 1938, 1. According to Henry and Taitz, *Friedan*, 15, in junior high school Friedan wrote for the school paper, *The Reflector*, copies of which I have not been able to locate.

18. The quotes are from Friedan, quoted in "Betty Friedan," *Current Biography Yearbook, 1970*, ed. Charles Moritz (New York, 1971), 146; Friedan, quoted in Stone, "Friedan at 55," 11. See also, Friedan, quoted in Wilkes, "Mother Superior," 140; Meltzer, *Friedan*, 8; Henry and Taitz, *Friedan*, 15; Betty Friedan, quoted in "Jewish Roots: An Interview with Betty Friedan," *Tikkun*, Jan.–Feb. 1988, 25–26; Betty Friedan, "Women and Jews: The Quest for Selfhood," *Congress Monthly*, Feb.–March 1985, 8; Moses, "She's Changed," 30; Friedan, *Changed My Life*, 6.

19. The quotes are from Friedan, "Jewish Roots," 25; Betty Friedan, quoted in Moses, "She's Changed," 30. See also Henry and Taitz, *Friedan*, 15; Wilkes, "Mother Superior," 29, 140. At the time, Friedan seems to have dated the rejection by sororities in the fall of 1935, at the beginning of her sophomore year: Goldstein, "Glass Darkly," 8; Meltzer, *Friedan*, 1 gives the same date.

20. The quote is from Goldstein, "Glass Darkly," 8–9; see also Henry and Taitz, *Friedan*, 16.

21. Amy Goldstein Adams, quoted in Cohen, *Sisterhood*, 56.

22. The quotes are from Parkhurst, "Friedan"; Sandra M. Gilbert and Susan Gubar, *The Madwoman in the Attic: The Woman Writer and the Nineteenth-Century Literary Imagination* (New Haven, 1979), 336–37. Other information is from Betty Friedan, "The ERA—Does It

Play In Peoria," *NYTM*, 19 Nov. 1978, 38–39, 130–31, 133, 136–39. Henry and Taitz, *Friedan*, 17; "Participants in Memorial Day Program," 1938 clipping from unidentified Peoria newspaper, author's possession; "Bettye Goldstein Wins Second Place in Heyl Essay Contest," *PO*, 20 May 1938, 1. The paper on the Constitution appears, with a slightly different title than that offered in the newspaper article, as "How Will the Check and Balance System of the Constitution Safeguard the Union," c. May 1938, BF-SLRC, 1: 149. Both Henry and Taitz, *Friedan*, 19, and Meltzer, *Friedan*, 10, talk of a paper she wrote in high school entitled "Why I Am Proud to be an American," for which they say she won an essay contest. I have not been able to find a copy of the paper and it is possible that these authors are referring to the one on the Constitution. In her telling of the story of the founding of the magazine, the roles of boys and girls do not stay constant: Bettye Goldstein, "Tide Literary Magazine Successfully Launched," *Quill and Scroll*, Oct.–Nov. 1938, 9–10; Goldstein, "B.G.," 3; Goldstein, "Glass Darkly," 15. To date the play, I am relying on "Jane Eyre," theater program, 9–10 Nov. 1937, BF-SLRC, 1: 249.

23. On the shift of New Dealers, see Alan Brinkley, *The End of Reform: New Deal Liberalism in Recession and War* (New York, 1995).

24. Leonard Dinnerstein, *Antisemitism in America* (New York, 1994), 105–49, with the quotes on 105, 124.

25. Michael G. Rapp, "An Historical Overview of Anti-Semitism in Minnesota, 1920–1960, With Particular Emphasis on Minneapolis and St. Paul" (Ph.D. diss., University of Minnesota, 1977), 41, 47, 49, 50, 53, 54, 56, 60–61, 67, 70, 72, 78, 82, 83, 88–89, 90, 93, 146, 166. Endelman, *Indianapolis*, 173–77, with the quote on 171; in Indianapolis, Endelman points out, a small group of Jews, including Communists, supported radical causes. An examination of the Peoria newspapers on randomly selected dates in the late 1930s and of the vertical files in the Peoria Public Library failed to turn up evidence of anti-Semitic incidents. On the presence of the Klan in Peoria, May, *Students' History*, 245, 268; on the importance of Chicago organizations, see Rapp, "Historical Overview," 62.

26. May, *Students' History*, 191–93, 264, 277; "Peoria Drops Public Ads From Paper in Guild Fight," *NYT*, 27 Aug. 1936, 22; "Peoria Dispute Is Settled," *NYT*, 24 Sept. 1936, 11.

27. The quotes are from Marian Sands, "Caterpillar's Brief Strike Rates Top Position in News of the Nation," *PO*, 16 April 1937, 8; Tom Belden, "Premier Hepburn, His Canadian Talk on C.I.O. Most Spectacular News," *PO*, 23 April 1937, 8. Other information comes from Goldstein, "Issue That Never Came Out," 2; Lola Zeman, "Efforts to Oust 'Sit-Downers' Called Outstanding News-of-the-Week," *PO*, 5 Feb. 1937, page unknown; Jack Riehm, "General Motors Settlement Important," *PO*, 19 Feb. 1937, page unknown. On Peoria as world headquarters for Caterpillar, see Sumansky, "Peoria," 127. Though formal acknowledgment of the CIO as the exclusive bargaining agent for Caterpillar workers would not come until 1942, the corporation had recognized the CIO's existence as an organization that could speak for workers: researcher Jennifer Hootman to author, late August 1996, author's possession; *Caterpillar Annual Report to Stockholders and Employees for the Year Ending December 31 1942*, 13–14. For reasons that are hard to understand, the local papers, unlike the high school one, paid relatively little attention to the Caterpillar dispute and focused instead on conflicts at other local factories: *Peoria Journal-Transcript*, 13 April 1937 through 20 April 1937.

28. The quotes are from "War, for Instance," *PO*, 4 Feb. 1938, 8; John Parkhurst and Stewart Bland, "War Referendum," *Tide*, March 1938, 6–7. On the student paper's coverage of political issues, see the following articles in *PO*: Bernard Wrigley, "Central Grad Interviews John Whitaker; 'War Soon,'" 24 April 1936, 2; "Study Reasons for War," 29 May 1936, 5; "First Tri-s Meet of Season Held; Welcome Leader," 18 Sept. 1936, 4; Jim Rindfuss, "Foreign News To be Topic Of Column," 18 Sept. 1936, 2; Paul Herschel, "Peorian Writes to Herschel About Chinese Advancement," 23 Dec. 1936, 2; Paul Herschel, "German Writes Herschel after Queer Error; Relates Feelings of People Toward Hitler," 15 Jan. 1937, 2. For the situation in Spain, see "Spain, the Loser Again," reprinted in *PO*, 15 Jan. 1937, 8. The warning about the rise of anti-Semitism and nationalism is in Charles Hogan, "Keep Hitler in Europe," *Tide*, April 1938, 10–11.

29. The quote is from Bettye Goldstein, "Cabbages and Kings," *PO*, 8 Jan. 1937, 8; additional information is in ibid., 23 April 1937, 8; 21 May 1937, 8; 5 Feb. 1937, 8; 12 Feb. 1937, 8.

30. The quotes are in Goldstein and Parkhurst, "Lost—Pride of Ownership," 8; [Goldstein and Parkhurst], "Honor System Discussed," *PO*, 8 Oct. 1937, 8; [Goldstein and Parkhurst], "Rude Audience Detracts From Successful Play," *PO*, 19 Nov. 1937, 8. See also, Goldstein, "Glass Darkly," 15; [Goldstein and Parkhurst], "What Do You Think About Social Hours?" *PO*, 10 Dec. 1937, 8. Goldstein, "Glass Darkly," 15 states that beginning in the fall of 1937 she wrote a regular feature about the high school with John Parkhurst. The first one had a byline: Bettye Goldstein and John Parkhurst, "Lost—Pride of Ownership: Student Council Discussed; Faculty, Students Challenged," *PO*, 24 Sept. 1937, 8. I am assuming that Goldstein and Parkhurst wrote many of the ensuing articles from Sept. to Dec. 1937; Goldstein, "Glass Darkly," 15 identifies the subjects of some of the ones they wrote.

31. On the awareness of the Spanish Civil War, see Friedan, "Jewish Roots," 25; she believed that she learned about this by reading Ernest Hemingway, but before she left Peoria his writings on Spain were not in places she was likely to find. *For Whom the Bell Tolls* appeared in 1940. On her response to the rise of dictators, see Goldstein, "Check and Balance System." For the parallel with a contemporary in Omaha, see Daniel Horowitz, telephone conversation with Beth Smith, 20 May 1996; Smith grew up in a situation similar to that of Goldstein: her ancestors were Russian Jews and she graduated from high school in Omaha in 1939 before going off to Wellesley College. On awareness of Coughlin and his Peoria supporters, see Hodes, Conversation.

32. Bettye Goldstein, "Long, Coughlin, Roosevelt in 'It Can't Happen Here,' " *PO*, 18 Sept. 1936, 8. For coverage of Father Coughlin in the local newspapers during Bettye Goldstein's senior year in high school, see, for example, "Fr. Coughlin to Start New Radio Series," *Peoria Star*, 7 Dec. 1937, 9; "Coughlin Goes Back on Radio," *Peoria Journal-Transcript*, 7 Dec. 1937, 2; "New Archbishop Censures Coughlin For Radio Speech," *Peoria Journal-Transcript*, 8 Oct. 1937, 3; "Coughlin Suddenly Cancels Series of Radio Broadcasts," *Peoria Star*, 10 Oct. 1937, 1.

33. [Bettye Goldstein], "Education for the Masses," unpublished typewritten essay, probably Jan. or Feb. 1938, BF-SLRC, 6: 276. In Goldstein, "Learning the Score," 23, she said she wrote this piece when she was sixteen, which would place it before her seventeenth birthday on 4 Feb. 1938.

34. Bettye Goldstein, "The Issue That Never Came Out," unpublished paper, dated 5 Jan. 1938, 1–2, BF-SLRC, 6: 262. Internal evidence suggests that the actual date of this paper is 5 Jan. 1939. Friedan probably forgot to change the year when she arrived back at Smith early in January of her first year at college.

35. For her summer work at Neighborhood House, see Bettye Goldstein to James Dombrowski, 18 June 1941, BG-SHSW, 13: 17; on Neighborhood House, see Mary P. Wright, *The History of Neighborhood House* (Peoria, 1992). On the story of a cross-class relationship, see Bettye Goldstein, " 'Kings of Beacon Hill' Romantic Tale of Aristocrats Vs. Commoners," *PO*, 3 Dec. 1936, 8. For the discussion of the return to the high school, see Bettye Goldstein, "Thoughts of a Senior on New Year's Eve," *PO*, 24 Dec. 1937, page unknown.

36. The quotes are from Bettye Goldstein, "Cabbages and Kings," *PO*, 19 March 1937, 8; for the play, see [Bettye Goldstein], one-page handwritten script for play, BF-SLRC, 1: 251. There is no date on this document but I have concluded that she composed the script in her junior or senior year of high school. I came to this conclusion for several reasons. The document has Friedan's home address and the only time she was there for an extended period after leaving for Smith in the fall of 1938 was in the summer of 1943. In addition, the handwriting is less mature than that of her college years. Finally, at the end of the script, Friedan provided time for student comment, making it clear to me that she wrote this in the context of a high school class.

37. Bettye Goldstein, "Jungles and Chinese Reveal Secrets, Native Lore in Two Exciting Books," *PO*, 2 Oct. 1936, 8. On the African American in her class, see Friedan, "Does It Play in Peoria?" 131.

38. Bettye Goldstein, "Cabbages and Kings: 'The Grasshopper and the Ant'—A Fable," *PO*, 9 April 1937, 8. The original fable is "The Ant and the Grasshopper," *Folk-Lore and Fable: Aesop, Grimm, Andersen*, ed. Charles W. Eliot (New York, 1909), 25. On her sense of herself as lacking sex appeal, see Goldstein, "Glass Darkly," 9; Goldstein, quoted in Blau, *Friedan*, 24. For another example of her awareness of issues women face, see Bettye Goldstein, "Limericks," 8 Feb. 1938, BF-SLRC, 1: 249.

39. Betty Friedan, quoted in Cohen, *Sisterhood*, 61. The other statements rely on Goldstein, "Glass Darkly," 8–15, 21. For her attention to style, see, for example, Bettye Goldstein, "I Am Paper," *Tide*, May 1938, 13–14; for her awareness of herself as a writer, see Goldstein, "Glass Darkly," 22.

40. Blau, *Friedan*, 24. For her claims about her ability as a leader, see Friedan, quoted in Blau, *Friedan*, 24.

41. The quote is from "Senior Faces of '38: Bettye Goldstein," *PO*, 11 March 1938, page unknown; these statements also rely on Goldstein, "Glass Darkly," 1, 15, 18, 20, 23; Goldstein, "Tide Literary Magazine."

42. The quotes are from Goldstein, quoted in Wilkes, "Mother Superior," 27; Goldstein, "Glass Darkly," 23. The statements rely on Friedan, quoted in Meltzer, *Friedan*, 2; Friedan, quoted in Henry and Taitz, *Friedan*, 19. On her awareness of alternative routes to popularity, see Goldstein, "Glass Darkly," 13.

43. [Palmer] to Goldstein; Goldstein, "Glass Darkly," 23.

2. Bettye Goldstein at Smith College, 1938–40

1. Bettye Goldstein, "Through a Glass Darkly," paper for high school class, 3 April 1938, 18, BF-SLRC, 1: 248; Betty Friedan, *"It Changed My Life: Writings on the Women's Movement*, 1985 edition (New York, 1976), 6. For her years at Smith, see Justine Blau, *Betty Friedan* (New York, 1990), 26–29; Marcia Cohen, *The Sisterhood: The True Story of the Women Who Changed the World* (New York, 1988), 62–63; David Halberstam, *The Fifties* (New York, 1993), 592; Sondra Henry and Emily Taitz, *Betty Friedan: Fighter for Women's Rights* (Hillside, N.J., 1990), 21–29; Milton Meltzer, *Betty Friedan: A Voice for Women's Rights* (New York, 1985), 14–20; Lyn Tornabene, "The Liberation of Betty Friedan," *McCall's*, May 1971, 138; Paul Wilkes, "Mother Superior to Women's Lib," *NYTM*, 29 Nov. 1970, 140; Betty Friedan, interview by Daniel Horowitz, Santa Monica, Calif., 18 March 1987; Betty Friedan, interview by Jacqueline Van Voris, New York, N.Y., 17 April 1973, CASC. Cohen, *Sisterhood*, 63, Meltzer, *Friedan*, 18–20, and Wilkes, "Mother Superior," 140, draw pictures of Friedan as a college rebel but to the best of my knowledge, the full nature of the politics of that rebellion has remained unknown.

2. Margaret F. Thorp, *Neilson of Smith* (New York, 1956), 337–40; Marjorie Nicolson, "William Allan Neilson," *Dictionary of American Biography*, supplement 4 (New York, 1974): 624–25.

3. The quote is from Kathleen Bell, interview in Jacqueline Van Voris, ed., *College: A Smith Mosaic* ([Northampton], 1975), 130. See also "Smith Faculty Boasts 8 Guggenheim Fellows," *SCW*, 17 April 1940, 6. On the importance of the connection between Smith's commitments and anti-fascism, see Grace M. Golub, "A Pledge to Democracy," *Opinion*, Dec. 1938, 4. For the role of refugee intellectuals in the Popular Front, see Michael Denning, *The Cultural Front: The Laboring of American Culture in the Twentieth Century* (London, 1996), 11.

4. Elizabeth Cutter Morrow, speech to Smith students, 18 Oct. 1939, 2, Elizabeth Cutter Morrow Papers, CASC, 32: 446. Aside from the person who held a chair specially designated for a woman, there was no tenured woman on the Faculty of Arts and Sciences at Harvard until 1956, and the second tenured appointment came in 1970: see "Tenured Women as of 1991" and "Women, Tenured @ Harvard," Reference, Vertical File: HUA. At Williams there were probably two Jews and no women on the faculty in 1938–42 and it was not until 1966 that a woman earned tenure: Sylvia K. Brown, communication to author, fall 1996. At Amherst in 1938–42, there were no women on the faculty: Daria D'Arienzo, communication to author,

fall 1996. In the early 1940s, there was no Jew in a senior position at Yale College: Dan A. Oren, *Joining the Club: A History of Jews At Yale* (New Haven, 1985), 116. At Oberlin, of 164 faculty members in the late 1930s and early 1940s, 3 can be identified as Jews; in addition there were 34 women on the faculty, only 3 of them full professors: Ken Grossi, e-mail to author, 3 Nov. 1996. At Swarthmore, the data on Jews on the faculty in this period is not readily available, though Swarthmore had a record approaching Smith's on refugee intellectuals; in 1938–39, 24 percent of the faculty were women, including some at a senior rank: Mary Ellen Chijioke to author, 26 Nov. 1996. For the role of Jews on American faculties and in American intellectual life, see David A. Hollinger, *Science, Jews, and Secular Culture: Studies in Mid-Twentieth-Century American Intellectual History* (Princeton, 1996).

5. On faculty dissatisfaction, see Molly Harrower, *Kurt Koffka: An Unwitting Self-Portrait* (Gainesville, Fla., 1983), 185–87. On the controversial departure in 1938 of Bertha Richardson, a faculty member at the Smith School of Social Work, see Penina Migdal Glazer and Miriam Slater, *Unequal Colleagues: The Entrance of Women into the Professions, 1890–1940* (New Brunswick, N.J., 1987), 194–99. "Social Cooperation," *SCAN*, 17 Oct. 1941, 2, gives a vivid description of how boring Northampton could be on a Saturday night in the period. On student awareness of the mental hospital, see Marian G. Champagne, *The Cauliflower Heart* (New York, 1944), 78. On student knowledge of factories and economic conditions, see "A.S.U. Plans Include Election, Rally, Factory Tours, Store," *SCW*, 12 Oct. 1938, 1; Ruth Henschel, "Dum Tacent, Clamant," *Focus*, May 1939, 10–13. For the FBI files on the ASU at Smith, see copies in author's possession. With the issue of 11 Oct. 1940, the newspaper began to publish twice a week and changed its name from *Smith College Weekly* to *SCAN*, which stood for *Smith College Associated News*.

6. "'Gallup' Poll of Smith," *SCW*, 19 June 1940, 12.

7. Mary Henle, "Mary Henle," *Models of Achievement: Reflections of Eminent Women in Psychology*, ed. Agnes N. O'Connell and Nancy F. Russo (New York, 1983), 222; Champagne, *Cauliflower Heart*, 36–38. On female role models, see also Betty Hannah Hoffman, Smith class of 1939, interview in Van Voris, *College*, 106. On Smith's fostering students' ambitions, see Lois Harkrider Stair, interview in ibid., 134; Ellen-Fairbanks Diggs Bodman, interview in ibid., 138. For evidence that some female faculty members discouraged their students, see Elizabeth von Klemperer, interview by Daniel Horowitz, Northampton, Mass., 17 June 1996.

8. "Hopeless Suggestions for Smith Curriculum," *SCW*, 10 April 1940, 6; "The Case of the Introverted Male," *SCAN*, 29 Oct. 1940, 2; *SCM*, Nov. 1942 issue (the first issue of *SCM* did not appear until October 1940); "Education: Intellectual Integrity," *SCW*, 6 Dec. 1940, 2; Advertisement for Barbizon Hotel, *SCW*, 5 Oct. 1938, 6.

9. "To the Individual," *SCAN*, 30 Sept. 1941, 2. See Van Voris, *College*, 105–39, for interviews of women who graduated from Smith in the late 1930s and early 1940s who later achieved prominence.

10. The quote is from "Are Secret Societies Necessary?" *SCW*, 10 April 1940, 2. For the sensitivity of students to social distinction, see, for example, von Klemperer, interview, 17 June 1996; Janet Kedney (class of 1944) to her family, 30 Oct. 1943, CASC; Champagne, *Cauliflower Heart*, 54, 56, 87; Jean Sovatkin Picker, Anne Thomson Waller, Marguerite Kiley Gray, interviews in Van Voris, *College*, 115, 116, 121. To get a sense of the nature of student life, including the dynamics of social relationships, see letters of Janet Firth, CASC; Janet Kedney, 24 Sept. 1941; Margaret McClumpha to her mother, 27 May 1941, CASC.

11. The first poll is "'Gallup'"; about 5 percent of both groups said they did not know to what class they belonged. The second one is "Freshman Statistics Noted; Eleven Religions Represented," *SCAN*, 7 Oct. 1941, 1, 5; this was a survey of the 574 students who entered in the fall of 1941: for that number, see Florence Snow, letter to editor, *SCAN*, 30 Sept. 1941, 2. According to a 30 Oct. 1996 e-mail from Margery Sly, then the Smith College archivist, the profile of Goldstein's class was roughly similar: over half of the almost six hundred students who at one time or another were members of the class of 1942 identified their fathers as lawyers, bankers, brokers, doctors, dentists, engineers, insurance executives, manufacturers,

or sales managers; another fifty to one hundred were teachers, professors, clergymen, or architects. Only one father was identified in each of the following occupations: fireman, mail carrier, chauffeur for Smith College, hosiery knitter, and janitor. Eleven percent of the students in the class identified themselves as Jews, with a considerable percentage reporting that one or both parents were born in Russia or elsewhere in Europe.

12. Champagne, *Cauliflower Heart*, 105; see also, *Cauliflower Heart*, 54–55, 57, 59, 62, 64, 92, 94–95, 104–5.

13. Margery Sly, communication with author, provided information on African American students. On Otelia Cromwell, see Van Voris, *College*, 111–12; on efforts to bring an African American presence to campus, see Champagne, *Cauliflower Heart*, 52.

14. von Klemperer, interview, 17 June 1996.

15. To date the increasing seriousness of the illness of Harry Goldstein, I am relying on "H. M. Goldstein Taken by Death," clipping from Peoria newspaper, 12 Jan. 1943, author's possession.

16. The quote is from Anne Dalrymple Hull, interview in Van Voris, *College*, 105. After the Nazi-Soviet Pact, when Friedan was only a reporter, the editors of the paper advocated an end to isolationism: "Repeal!" *SCW*, 4 Oct. 1939, 2.

17. William A. Neilson, speech to Northampton mass meeting, 1 Dec. [1938], 1–8, Neilson Papers, CASC, 36: 756; Betty Friedan, quoted in "Jewish Roots: An Interview with Betty Friedan," *Tikkun*, Jan.–Feb. 1988, 26.

18. To capture the tenor of political discussions on the Smith campus, see, for example, Golub, "Pledge," 4–5; "Foreword," *Focus*, March 1939, 3; editorials, ibid., 4–5; "William Allan Neilson: Liberal Educator," ibid., 8–10; Nancy Leask, "Music under National Socialism," ibid., 19–20; Ruth Henschel, "Spain's Courage," ibid., 32–34; Rose Lubschez, "Science and Democracy," *Opinion*, March 1939, 3–4; Hans Kohn, "Empires and Armaments," *Focus*, May 1939, 3–6; "Our Answer, Herr Hitler," ibid., 8–9; "Of Age," ibid., 9; Lucile Hunt, "The Last Days of Austria," ibid., 25–26; "If I Were Twenty-one," ibid., October 1940, 6–7.

19. On the professor who minimized how much African Americans and women could achieve, see Adelaide Cromwell Gulliver, interview in Van Voris, *College*, 112; for reference to "a bona fide Nazi" on the faculty, see Louise Robinson Swainbank, interview in ibid., 108; Otto F. Kraushaar, "The Ordeal of the Present," *Focus*, March 1939, 17–18; Otto Kraushaar, "Behind The Scenes of the Proletarian Revolution," *SCM*, Feb. 1941, 19–20, with the quote on 20. For Kraushaar, see the following clippings in Faculty: Individuals, CASC, 42: 942—"Prof. Kraushaar Tells of Needs Coming After War," *DHG*, 3 March 1941; "Prof Otto Kraushaar Addresses Forum," *Springfield Union*, 4 Jan. 1939; "Smith College," *Springfield Republican*, 23 Oct. 1941; "Kraushaar Finds War Is Outcome of Old Struggle," unidentified paper, 31 Jan. 1942.

20. The quote is from "For Freshmen Only," *Focus*, Nov. 1939, 10. Champagne, *Cauliflower Heart*, especially 89–109, 176–79, 208–14, 226–28, has a vivid picture of radical politics among students at Smith. For information on the group which focused on race, see "Interrace Commission Sponsors Forum Here," *SCAN*, 11 Feb. 1941, 1.

21. Henschel, "Dum Tacent," 10–13; Ruth Henschel, "The American Student Union," *Opinion*, Dec. 1938, 9–10; "Keeping Out Of The War," *Focus*, Nov. 1939, 8–9; Kathleen Trager, "Luce-Warm To Fascism," *SCM*, Spring 1942, 10–11; "The Next Five Years," *Focus*, Nov. 1939, 21–25. The observations on how radicals projected their politics rely on Robert Cohen, telephone conversation with author, 3 July 1997. For the sponsorship of the ASU, see the announcement in *Focus*, March 1939, 4.

22. In this and the following paragraphs I am relying on Robert Cohen, *When the Old Left Was Young: Student Radicals and America's First Mass Student Movement, 1929–1941* (New York, 1993), 278–311, for the story of the fights within the ASU and AYC and on college campuses in 1939–40. See also, Daniel Bell, "Y.C.L. Puts Skids Under Joe Lash As Student Union Leader Deviates" [n.d.], Joseph P. Lash Papers, Franklin D. Roosevelt Library, Hyde Park, N.Y., quoted in Cohen, *When the Old Left*, 295; Franklin D. Roosevelt, speech to Ameri-

can Youth Congress, 11 Feb. 1940, *NYT*, Feb. 1940, 44. For a perceptive discussion of the difference between the ASU at Vassar and the University of Chicago in the mid-1930s, see Katharine Graham, *Personal History* (New York, 1997), 83

23. The quotes are from "President's Blast at Youth Congress," *SCW*, 14 Feb. 1940, 2; for the response, see Vivian Rutes, "Public Opinion," *SCW*, 10 April 1940, 2; for another defense of *AYC*, see Ruth Henschel, "Why Mass Meetings?" *SCW*, 17 April 1940, 2. For discussion of women's issues in the student left in the late 1930s, see Cohen, *When the Old Left*, 270–71.

24. "Youth—Its Dilemma," *SCW*, 26 Sept. 1940, 2. For an earlier interventionist editorial, see "Repeal!"

25. Speech of Elizabeth C Morrow, NBC-Blue Network, 29 May 1940, Elizabeth C. Morrow Papers, *CASC*, 32: 445.

26. "Bettye Goldstein, Margery Hall Win Scholarship Prize," *SCW*, 11 Oct. 1939, 7. For the response to her work, see Margaret C. Deakers, comment on paper for English 18b, 14 March 1939. BF-SLRC, 6: 262; unidentified professor, comment on Bettye Goldstein, "Flaubert, The Psychologist," paper for French 14, 12 May 1940, BF-SLRC, 6: 281; James Gibson, comment on Bettye Goldstein, "Conditioning and the Thorndikian Response," paper for James Gibson on Psychology 31b, 3 Jan. 1940, BF-SLRC, 6: 290. For her increasing sense of confidence, see Betty Friedan, quoted in Wilkes, "Mother Superior," 140; Friedan, interview in Van Voris, *College*, 118–19; Henry and Taitz, *Friedan*, 23, 27; Friedan, *Changed My life*, 6. During her years at Smith, Friedan lived in Chapin House, near the center of campus.

27. Meltzer, *Friedan*, 19–20; Henry and Taitz, *Friedan*, 24–26, 29.

28. Mary Anne Guitar, interview by Jacqueline Van Voris, Northampton, Mass., 8 Nov. 1973, 31–33, transcript, CASC. On the response of a faculty member to her, see Friedan, quoting Howard R. Patch, Van Voris, *College*, 119.

29. On her membership in the poetry club, see *Smith College Yearbook 1940* (1940), 146.

30. [Bettye Goldstein], "Smith Portraits. No. 10," poem, [1939–40], BF-SLRC, 6: 277; [Bettye Goldstein], "Smith Portraits. No. 8," poem, [1939–40], BF-SLRC, 6: 277; [Bettye Goldstein], "The Bertrand Russell Case—A Commentary," poem, 8 April 1940, BF-SLRC, 6: 278; "'I Wholly Disapprove Of What You Say—And Will Defend To The Death Your Right To Say It,'" *SCW*, 10 April 1940, 2; Frank H. Hankins, letter to editor, *SCW*, 17 April 1940, 2. For background on the Russell case, see Stephen Leberstein, "Purging the Profs: The Rapp Coudert Committee in New York, 1940–1942," in *New Studies in the Politics and Culture of U.S. Communism*, ed. Michael E. Brown et al. (New York, 1993), 91–122. I locate these poems in her sophomore year because it was in both semesters of that year that she took English 24, Verse Writing, and began to publish her poetry.

31. [Bettye Goldstein], "Smith Portraits, Domestic," poem, [1939–40], BF-SLRC, 6: 277; [Bettye Goldstein], "Gratitude," poem, [1939–40], BF-SLRC, 6: 278; [Bettye Goldstein], "Smith Portraits. No. 7," poem, [1939–40], BF-SLRC, 6: 277; [Bettye Goldstein], "From Egocentricity," poem, [1939–40], BF-SLRC, 6: 277; Bettye Goldstein, "Poems for the Present: Statement," *Opinion*, March 1940, 5; [Bettye Goldstein], "Requiem for a German Soldier (with apologies to R.L.S.)," poem, 16 April 1940, BF-SLRC, 6: 279; [Bettye Goldstein], "Said a Soldier of Finland," poem, [1939–40], BF-SLRC, 6: 279; [Bettye Goldstein], "To the Wyrd of Finland," poem, [1939–40], BF-SLRC, 6: 279; [Bettye Goldstein], "Soldier of Finland," poem, [1939–40], BF-SLRC, 6: 279; [Bettye Goldstein], "On the Alliance of Russia and Germany," poem, [1939–40], 22 Oct. 1939, BF-SLRC, 6: 278. Goldstein wrote on Machiavelli at the same time that another of her courses focused on him: syllabus for Philosophy 323a, fall term 1939, BF-SLRC, 6: 285. For her contemporaneous notes on the parallels between Hitler and Machiavelli, see Bettye Goldstein, lecture notes in Philosophy 322a, on "Theory of Nation State: Machiavelli," [late Oct. 1939], BF-SLRC, 6: 285.

32. [Bettye Goldstein], "Smith Portraits. No. 4. Speaker for the Negative (after President Neilson's speech)," poem, [1939–40], BF-SLRC, 6: 277.

33. Bettye Goldstein, "B.G.," four-page typewritten paper, late April or May 1941, BF-SLRC, 6: 276; Bettye Goldstein, "Miami, Significant," *SCW,* 10 April 1940, 2.

34. Bettye Goldstein, "Fragments," *Focus,* Nov. 1939, 7; Bettye Goldstein, "Proposal," *Focus,* Nov. 1939, 11; Bettye Goldstein, "Epigrams," *Opinion,* Dec. 1939, 10; [Bettye Goldstein], "Epitaph," poem, [1939–40], BF-SLRC, 6: 278; Bettye Goldstein, "The Issue That Never Came Out," 5 Jan. [1939], 5–6, BF-SLRC, 6: 262; [Bettye Goldstein], "The Writers of Europe—1939," 2 Oct. 1939, BF-SLRC, 6: 278. Two of her poems in this series also appeared in a Williams College magazine: Bettye Goldstein, "Epigrams," *Sketch,* May 1940, 44.

35. Bettye Goldstein, review of John Steinbeck, *The Grapes of Wrath, Focus,* Nov. 1939, 29–31; James Gibson, "Educated People Should Give Aid to Good Propaganda," unidentified newspaper, 11 Jan. 1939, in his folder, Faculty: Individuals, collection 42, CASC. In Champagne, *Cauliflower Heart,* 148, a character talks about fighting with words because reactionaries controlled the media.

36. On the importance of her education in psychology, see Friedan, Horowitz interview.

37. The quotes are from "Permanence at Smith," *SCAN,* 20 Feb. 1942, 2; Friedan, Horowitz interview. See also, Friedan, Van Voris interview, 20; Friedan, Horowitz interview; Friedan, in Van Voris, *College,* 119. At the time of the February 20 editorial, Goldstein was the editor of the student newspaper.

38. On her education in psychology, see Goldstein, "Conditioning and the Thorndikian Response"; Bettye Goldstein, class notes for Psychology 31, BF-SLRC, 6: 291 and 292; Bettye Goldstein, "The Relation of Organization in Perception to Number of Phenomenal Elements," 15 April 1940, BF-SLRC, 7: 299. For her reaction to a standardized test, see Bettye Goldstein, response to "Attitude-Interest Analysis Test" by Lewis M. Terman and Catharine Cox Miles, [spring 1940], BF-SLRC, 6: 288. On the *Madame Bovary* paper, see Goldstein, "Flaubert," 22.

39. The quote is from unidentified class lecturer, quoted in Bettye Goldstein, "Problems of College Girls," lecture notes in Psychology 23b, second semester 1940, BF-SLRC, 6: 288. Other material is in Goldstein, "Flaubert," 8, 22 and Sigmund Freud, quoted in ibid., 10, fn. 19; check mark next to a reference to Karen Horney's discussion of the psychology of women in *New Ways of Psychoanalysis* (New York, 1939) in [Bettye Goldstein], notation on "Reading List," Psychology 23b, second semester 1940, BF-SLRC, 6: 288; Bettye Goldstein, one page of handwritten notes, Psychology 23b, second semester 1940, BF-SLRC, 6: 288; Goldstein, "Conditioning," 38.

40. The quote is from Friedan, in Van Voris, *College,* 119. On Eleanor Gibson, see material in her folder in Faculty: Individuals, collection 42, CASC; "Eleanor Jack Gibson," *Biographical Dictionary of Psychology,* ed. Leonard Zusne (Westport, Conn., 1984), 104–7; Gwendolyn Stevens and Sheldon Gardner, "Eleanor Jack Gibson," *The Women of Psychology* (Cambridge, Mass., 1982), 2: 119–26. For information on Siipola, see material in her folder, Faculty: Individuals, collection 42, CASC. For information on Israel, I am relying on Faculty: Individuals, collection 42, CASC; Harrower, *Koffka,* 312.

41. The quote is from James J. Gibson, "James J. Gibson," in *A History of Psychology in Autobiography,* ed. Edwin G. Boring and Gardner Lindzey (New York, 1967), 5: 134–35. For additional information on the Gibsons, see the following clippings on Gibson's talks in his faculty file: Gibson, "Educated People"; "To Discuss 'Anti-Labor Propaganda' at C.L.U.," *DHG,* 9 Jan. 1939. See also, "Propaganda Is Discussed by Prof. Gibson," unidentified paper, 11 Oct. 1940; Eleanor J. Gibson, "Eleanor J. Gibson," *A History of Psychology in Autobiography,* ed. Gardner Lindzey (San Francisco, 1980), 7: 239–71; c.v. of James J. Gibson in his faculty file; Edward S. Reed, *James J. Gibson and the Psychology of Perception* (New Haven, 1988); James J. Gibson, "Why A Union For Teachers?" *Focus,* Nov. 1939, 3–7; James J. Gibson, "The Aryan Myth," *Journal of Educational Sociology* 13 (Nov. 1939): 164–71. For a later paper that talks of the political education Goldstein and her peers received, see Betty Friedan, "Was Their Education UnAmerican?" unpublished article, written soon after the summer of 1952, 2–3, BF-SLRC, 11: 415.

42. The quote is from Friedan, "Jewish Roots," 26. For her response to Lewin's course, see Bettye Goldstein, "Lewin Course in Child Psych," BF-SLRC, 1: 252. Friedan has recalled that she took the course with Koffka in her sophomore year and that Koffka introduced her to Lewin. Koffka spent that year in Oxford and someone else may have been the intermediary: Friedan, Horowitz interview; Friedan, in Van Voris, *College*, 118. On Koffka's year in Oxford, see Harrower, *Koffka*, 185–248. That summer she also studied with Tamara Dembo; for information on her, see Gwendolyn Stevens and Sheldon Gardner, "Tamara Dembo," *The Women of Psychology* (Cambridge, Mass., 1982), 2: 174.

43. Betty Goldstein, "Economic Insecurity," handwritten notes, probably summer of 1940, BF-SLRC, 1: 251; these notes are undated and their contents convince me that she wrote them during or shortly after the course at Iowa. On Lewin, see Nordby and Hall, *Guide to Psychologists*, 110–15; "Kurt Lewin," *Biographical Dictionary*, ed. Zusne, 259–60; Kurt Lewin, Tamara Dembo, Leon Festinger, and Pauline S. Sears, "Level of Aspiration," in *Personality and the Behavior Disorders: A Handbook Based on Experimental and Clinical Research*, ed. J. McV. Hunt (New York, 1944), 1: 333–78; Kurt Lewin, Ronald Lippitt, and Ralph K. White, "Patterns of Aggressive Behavior in Experimentally Created 'Social Climates,'" *Journal of Social Psychology*, *S.P.S.S.I. Bulletin*, 1939, 271; Roger Barker, Tamara Dembo, and Kurt Lewin, "Frustration and Regression: An Experiment with Young Children," *Studies in Topological and Vector Psychology II* (Iowa City, 1941), 18: 208–16. Though the study relied on Sigmund Freud's notion of regression, it did not pursue Freud's gendered analysis.

44. On her positions on the newspaper, see the mastheads, *SCW*, 14 Feb. 1940, 2 and 10 April 1940, 2.

3. The Radicalization of Bettye Goldstein, 1940–41

1. On how she explained her political development at Smith, see Betty Friedan, interview in Jacqueline Van Voris, ed., *College: A Smith Mosaic* ([Northampton], 1975), 119. For the story of another woman's radicalization at Smith, see Natalie Z. Davis, "A Life of Learning," American Council of Learned Societies, *Occasional Papers*, no. 39 ([New York], 1997), 4–6.

2. Paul H. Douglas, *In the Fullness of Time: The Memoirs of Paul H. Douglas* (New York, 1972), 31–36, 46–49, 59, 69–70; Edward L. Schapsmeier and Frederick H. Schapsmeier, "Paul H. Douglas: From Pacifist to Soldier-Citizen," *Journal of the Illinois State Historical Society* 67 (June 1974): 307–23; Edward L. Schapsmeier, "Dirksen and Douglas of Illinois: The Pragmatist and the Professor as Contemporaries in the United States Senate," *Illinois Historical Journal* 83 (summer 1990): 74–84; "In Memoriam: Paul H. Douglas (1892–1976)," *Journal of Political Economy* 87 (Oct. 1979): 913–14; Albert Rees, "Douglas on Wages and the Supply of Labor," ibid., 915–22.

3. Dorothy W. Douglas, "The Cost of Living for Working Women: A Criticism of Current Theories," *Quarterly Journal of Economics* 34 (Feb. 1920): 226, 259; Dorothy W. Douglas, *Guillaume De Greef: The Social Theory of an Early Syndicalist* (New York, 1925), 8, 15–17, 20. On Lumpkin, see Jacquelyn D. Hall, "Open Secrets: Memory, Imagination, and the Refashioning of Southern Identity," *AQ* 50 (March 1998): 110–24; Jacquelyn D. Hall, *Katharine Du Pre Lumpkin and the Refashioning of Southern Identity* (forthcoming, 1999). Other information comes from clipping from *DHG*, 25 July 1940, in Douglas, Faculty: Individuals, collection 42, CASC; Katharine D. Lumpkin and Dorothy W. Douglas, *Child Workers in America* (New York, 1937), 180, 246, 247, 253, 267–68, 272–74, 276, 292.

4. The quotes are from Dorothy W. Douglas to Mrs. William J. Carson, 13 Dec. 1930, series II, 260: 395, LWV-LC; see also, Dorothy W. Douglas to Mrs. Lois Rantoul, 13 Dec. 1930, series II, 260: 395, LWV-LC. For additional evidence of her activity with the League, see material in LVW-LC, including Dorothy W. Douglas to Miss Rockwood, 30 Jan. 1931, series II, box 260: folder titled "Women in Industry, Comm. On"; Dorothy W. Douglas, memo to executive committee, [early Feb. 1931], series II, box 260, folder titled "Women in Industry, Comm.

On"; Dorothy W. Douglas to members of the Committee on Women in Industry, 8 April 1931, series II, 252: 338. On their book, see Lumpkin and Douglas, "Preface to the Second Edition," dated 23 September 1938, *Child Workers in America* (New York, 1937), xi–xii.

5. Dorothy W. Douglas, quoted in "Smith Professor Speaks," clipping from *DHG*, 15 May 1931, Faculty: Individuals.

6. Material on Douglas in Faculty: Individuals: "Labor Organization Formed; Mrs. D. W. Douglas On Board," *SCAN*, 11 Oct. 1940, 3. On her pro-Soviet activities, see articles from *Daily Worker* cited in U.S. Congress, House of Representatives, Committee on Un-American Activities, *Report on the Congress of American Women* (Washington, D.C., 1949), 83. Congressional investigators alleged that in the late 1930s Douglas was making substantial contributions to the CPUSA: *Communist Methods of Infiltration (Education)*, Hearings Before Committee on Un-American Activities, House of Representatives, 83d Cong., 1st sess. (Washington, D.C., 1953), 157.

7. These statements rely on Dorothy W. Douglas, quoted in Bettye Goldstein, handwritten notes for Economics 319, 1940–41, BF-SLRC, 1: 257 and 6: 258. These notes are in rough chronological order but are often undated and always unnumbered.

8. Douglas, in Goldstein, notes for Economic 319, 4 Feb. [1941]; Douglas, in Goldstein, notes for Economics 319, some time during or after late April 1941, BF-SLRC, 6: 258. In the year-long course, Douglas concentrated her concern about the impact of Naziism on the consequences for workers and unions primarily and women secondarily; she paid little if any attention to the impact on Jews. On the position of women under National Socialism, see Clifford Kirkpatrick, *Nazi Germany: Its Women and Family Life* (Indianapolis, 1938); Claudia Koonz, *Mothers in the Fatherland: Women, The Family, and Nazi Politics* (New York, 1987). For Friedan's return to the issue of the connection between anti-Semitism and anti-feminism, see Betty Friedan "Anti-Semitism as a Political Tool: Its Congruence with Anti-Feminism," type-script of speech, probably late 1980s, 40–4, BF-SLRC, 86-M12 . . . 93 M 146, 10: 359. Robert Cohen, *When the Old Left Was Young: Student Radicals and America's First Mass Student Movement, 1929–1941* (New York, 1993), 270.

9. Cohen, *When the Old Left Was Young,* 270–71; Molly Yard, from memorial tribute to Joseph Lash, in *Joseph P. Lash* (New York, 1987), 40, quoted in Cohen, *When the Old Left Was Young,* 271.

10. Bettye Goldstein, exam essay, Economics 319, 20 Nov. [1940], BF-SLRC, 1: 257; Dorothy W. Douglas, handwritten comments on Bettye Goldstein's exam booklet in Economics 319, BF-SLRC, 6: 259.

11. Although he does not mention Davis, Paul Buhle, *Marxism in the United States: Remapping the History of the American Left* (London, 1987), 155–83, discusses the emergence of a critique of culture among American Marxists in the interwar years. On Davis, see Ellen W. Schrecker, *No Ivory Tower: McCarthyism and the Universities* (New York, 1986), 67–68; "Democracy in Education—Education in Democracy," *Focus*, March 1939, 6; "Davis Attacks Yale for Views on Report," *NYT*, 3 June 1937, 12; Jerome Davis, *Capitalism and Its Culture* (New York, 1935), 249–50.

12. Bettye Goldstein, "Discussion of Reading Period Material," paper for Economics 319, 18 Jan. 1941, 1, 2, 3, 4, 8, BF-SLRC, 1: 257. See also her two other papers for the course: "Questions on *Communist Manifesto*" and "Questions on Imperialism," ibid.

13. On Psychology 33, see BF-SLRC, 6: 293 and 7: 294. On Gestalt in Germany, see Mitchell G. Ash, *Gestalt Psychology in German Culture, 1890–1967: Holism and the Quest for Objectivity* (Cambridge, U.K., 1995). On Koffka, see K. Koffka, *Principles of Gestalt Psychology* (New York, 1935), 9. On Koffka and Gestalt psychology, see "Kurt Koffka," *Biographical Dictionary of Psychology,* ed. Leonard Zusne (Westport, Conn., 1984), 230–31; K. Koffka, "Gestalt," *Encyclopedia of the Social Sciences* (New York, 1931), 6: 642–46; Vernon J. Nordby and Calvin S. Hall, *A Guide to Psychologists and Their Concepts* (San Francisco, 1974), 57–62; R. Arnheim, "Gestalt Psychology," in Raymond J. Corsini, ed., *Encyclopedia of Psychology,* 2d ed. (New York, 1994): 2: 69–71.

14. On her course work, see Bettye Goldstein, lecture notes for Psychology 36, 1940–41, BF-SLRC, 7: 300; *Bulletin of Smith College: Catalogue Issue,* series 35 (Jan. 1941): 180–81. On the importance of this course to her, see Betty Friedan, interview by Daniel Horowitz, Santa Monica, Calif., 18 March 1987; on Koffka's appeal to smart students, see James J. Gibson, "James J. Gibson," *A History of Psychology in Autobiography,* ed. Edwin G. Boring and Gardner Lindzey (New York, 1967), 5: 130–31; for a discussion of Koffka's "dictatorial" teaching, see Eleanor J. Gibson, "Eleanor J. Gibson," *A History of Psychology in Autobiography,* ed. Gardner Lindzey (San Francisco, 1980), 7: 243. On Koffka's mother as a Jew by birth but a Protestant by identification, see Ash, *Gestalt Psychology,* 108. The statements on Koffka rely on Molly Harrower, *Kurt Koffka: An Unwitting Self-Portrait* (Gainesville, Fla., 1983), an edited set of letters between Koffka and Harrower; see especially, 16, 94, 165–84; the quotes are in letters from Koffka to Harrower, 19 June 1940 [182] and 9 Sept. 1938 [169]. For another example of his concerns with what was happening in Germany, see Harrower, *Koffka,* 183–84. On Goldstein's reaction to Koffka, see "Kurt Koffka," *SCAN,* 25 Nov. 1941, 2; I identify Goldstein as the author because of her prominence on the editorial board of the newspaper and the importance of Koffka in her life; Bettye Goldstein, answer on an exam question, Psychology 36, 1940–41, BF-SLRC, 7: 300.

15. My best guess is that Goldstein was attending some of the lectures in Psychology 25 by James Gibson: Bettye Goldstein, lecture notes for Psychology 33, probably late February and March 1941, BF-SLRC, 7: 294. In his course, Gibson focused on the issue of how to develop effective propaganda for desirable goals: James Gibson, syllabus for Psychology 25, fall term 1940, BF-SLRC, 6: 289. On Gibson, see James Gibson, quoted in Bettye Goldstein, lecture notes from Psychology 24, 9 Nov. 1940, BF-SLRC, 7: 300; Edward S. Reed, *James J. Gibson and the Psychology of Perception* (New Haven, 1988), 65. At one point in the late spring, Goldstein did something she rarely did while sitting in a class, this time in a course taught by Harold Israel. She entered into her academic notes words she was writing for the student newspaper. She drafted a paragraph that, with some revision, soon appeared in *SCAN,* the campus newspaper, as an introduction to the editorial board's minority and interventionist position on America's role in the war in Europe, to which she objected: compare Bettye Goldstein, draft of "Editor's Note," BF-SLRC, 7: 294 with "Editor's Note," *SCAN,* 2 May 1941, 2.

16. Lawrence S. Wittner, *Rebels Against War: The American Peace Movement, 1941–1960* (New York, 1969), 15–32. For the position of the CPUSA in this period, see Maurice Isserman, *Which Side Were You On? The American Communist Party during the Second World War* (Middletown, Conn., 1982), 83–126.

17. Cohen, *When the Old Left Was Young,* 311–17, 416–17 n. 115; "Aid For War Prisoners Given by War Fund," *SCAN,* 31 Oct. 1941, 1; Margaret F. Thorp, *Neilson of Smith* (New York, 1956), 345.

18. "Youth—Its Dilemma," *SCW,* 26 Sept. 1940, 2; "Herbert J. Davis Undertakes Duties As Fourth President of College," *SCW,* 26 Sept. 1940, 1.

19. "Smith ASU Makes Resolution To Work For American Peace," *SCAN,* 12 Nov. 1940, 1, 3; Joy Clark, letter to editor, *SCAN,* 22 Nov. 1940, 2. On the state of political opinion on campus, see "Wendell L. Willkie Wins Campus Favor In Wednesday's Student-Faculty Poll," *SCAN,* 25 Oct. 1940, 1; "Parental Persuasion," *SCAN,* 29 Oct. 1940, 2; Daniel Aaron, "A View of the Times," *SCM,* May 1941, 2. For another estimate of student sentiment, see "Fifth Column in the University," *SCAN,* 13 December 1940, 2; for the position of one of the sisters of William F. Buckley Jr., see Aloise Buckley, "I'd Vote for Willkie," *Focus,* Oct. 1940, 6–7.

20. The quotes are from Sondra Henry and Emily Taitz, *Betty Friedan: Fighter for Women's Rights* (Hillside, N.J., 1990), 23–24; unidentified students, quoted in Marcia Cohen, *The Sisterhood: The True Story of the Women Who Changed the World* (New York, 1988), 63; other material comes from Paul Wilkes, "Mother Superior to Women's Lib," *NYTM,* 29 Nov. 1970, 140.

21. Bettye Goldstein was managing editor of the *Smith College Monthly* from its reemergence in October 1940 until March 1941; for the April 1941 issue, she was on the editorial board. "Campus Literati Engage in Stormy Discussion Over Monthly Magazine," *SCW,* 19 June

1940, 1, 3. For Goldstein's role in the founding of the magazine, see Friedan, interview in Van Voris, ed., *College*, 119.

22. "Academic Freedom—A Symposium," *SCM*, Oct. 1940, 1–4, 18–20; "If I Were Twenty-one . . . ," *SCM*, Oct. 1940, 6–8. For the caution of the editorial boards in October, when Goldstein was news editor of the student paper and when campuses around the nation were witnessing mobilization against the war, see "A New Newspaper," *SCAN*, 11 Oct. 1940, 2.

23. Bettye Goldstein, "For Defense of Democracy," *SCM*, Oct. 1940, 11, 12, 28, with the quote on 12. For editorials in which Goldstein may have had a hand, see "Cure for Youth?" "Trend Toward Change," and "An Answer," *SCM*, Dec. 1940: 1. To capture the tenor of campus debates, see also, "Dubious Methods of the A.S.U.," *SCAN*, 11 Feb. 1941, 2; Alice Kahn, letter to editor, *SCAN*, 11 Feb. 1941, 2; Marion Ingersoll, letter to editor, *SCAN*, 14 Feb. 1941, 2.

24. Mary Newman and Bettye Goldstein, "Words and Meaning," *SCM*, Feb. 1941, 25. See the 11 Feb. 1941 issue of *SCAN* for the presentation of various positions. Some of what follows relies on unsigned editorials that appeared under Friedan's editorship, which can be found in *SCAN* from 14 March 1941 to 10 March 1942, p. 2. Although members of the editorial board held a wide range of opinions, I am assuming that as editor-in-chief Friedan had a significant role in shaping editorials. The February issue of *Smith College Monthly*, in whose production Goldstein played a key role, continued its sponsorship of forums that gave voice to a variety of positions in the American student movement: *SCM*, Feb. 1941. Editorials Goldstein wrote defended traditional liberal commitments: freedom of speech, writing as "an intellectual occupation," and liberal arts education: Newman and Goldstein, "Words," 5; B.G. [Bettye Goldstein] and M.N. [Mary Newman], "Affirmation," *SCM*, Feb. 1941, 1. "Polls Show 36% Would War For Britain, 22% Have Never Frequented Rahar's," *SCAN*, 18 Feb. 1941, 1, 3. For a poll carried out by James Gibson's class in social psychology that revealed strong opposition among Smith students to intervention, see "Poll Reveals Student Opinion On War; 67% Would Vote Against Intervention," *SCAN*, 2 May 1941, 1. "Mr. Neilson Pleads For Aid to England," *SCAN*, 25 Feb. 1941, 1; "Davises To Sponsor War Relief Concert," *SCAN*, 28 Feb. 1941, 1; "Mrs. Franklin D. Roosevelt Addresses Political Forum On Youth's Responsibility To Future Of Democracy," *SCAN*, 7 Feb. 1941, 1–4. For Goldstein's interview questions for Mrs. Roosevelt, see Bettye Goldstein, "Mrs. Roosevelt Interview," handwritten notes for Economics 319, first week of February 1941; "Dubious Methods."

25. Friedan, Horowitz interview.

26. [Bettye Goldstein], "Youth Confers On Peace, Democracy At Town Meeting Held in Washington," *SCAN*, 11 Feb. 1941, 1, 4, 6. I have identified Goldstein as the author for two reasons: in my 1987 interview with her, she told me she went as a reporter. In addition, of those going to Washington for the meeting, she is the only one who was also on the *SCAN* staff: compare the lists on the masthead, *SCAN*, 14 Feb. 1941, 2, and in the "Youth Organizations To Meet In Washington This Weekend," *SCAN*, 7 Feb. 1941, 1. Francis Wilkinson, letter to the editor, *SCAN*, 11 Feb. 1941, 2. This is really Frances Wilkinson. Walter Kotschnig, paraphrased in "Youth Congress Left Partisan, Kotschnig Says in Interview," *SCAN*, 14 Feb. 1941, 1. For his support of Federal Union, see "Reverend L. T. Pennington Of Boston Will Speak On Plan For Federal Union," *SCAN*, 25 April 1941, 1.

27. Milton Meltzer, *Betty Friedan: A Voice for Women's Rights* (New York, 1985), 19–20; see also Henry and Taitz, *Friedan*, 26. Justine Blau, *Betty Friedan* (New York, 1990), 26, and Cohen, *Sisterhood*, 62, locate the medical emergency in her sophomore year.

28. Meltzer, *Friedan*, 18–19; "This Is What We Believe . . . ," *SCAN*, 14 March 1941, 2. I am assuming Goldstein's authorship because this was one of the few editorials that was clipped and placed in her papers: BF-SLRC, 7: 310. In this instance only, two copies of the editorial appear, one of them with her name written in pencil.

29. "Minority Matters," *SCAN*, 8 April 1941, 2; Mary Jackson, "Pounds and Possibilities," *SCAN*, 8 April 1941, 2; "Peace Day," *SCM*, April 1941, 1.

30. "They Choose Peace," *SCAN*, 22 April 1941, 2. For a statement of support of peace

protests by the editors of *SCM* in April 1941, when Goldstein was still on the editorial board but no longer managing editor, see, "Peace Day." Meltzer, *Friedan*, 18, identifies as Goldstein's an editorial condemning Hitler's invasion of western Europe and warning that unless dictators were stopped, they would take over America; however, I have not been able to locate such an editorial in the late spring of 1940 or fall 1940.

31. I base the estimate of the size of the crowd on an examination of the picture in *SCAN*, 25 April 1941, 1; Bettye Goldstein, quoted in "Effect Of Warfare On U.S. Discussed," *SCAN*, 25 April 1941, 1; "Mrs. Douglas Speaks About Danger of Anti-Strike Bills," *SCAN*, 25 April 1941, 1.

32. "The Case for Intervention," *SCAN*, 2 May 1941, 2; Janet Carlson, letter to editor, *SCAN*, 15 April 1941, 2; "Dr. Pennington Advocates Union of Democracies Now," *SCAN*, 2 May 1941, 1; Carolyn Clausen and Mary Newman, letter to the editor, *SCAN*, 18 April 1941, 2. For the reply, see Janet Carlson, letter to editor, *SCAN*, 22 April 1941, 3, 4.

33. "Minority Matters."

34. The quotes are from "Education in Emergency," *SCAN*, 15 April 1941, 2; James Dombrowski, quoted in Bettye Goldstein, handwritten lecture notes on James Dombrowski, "Native American Fascism," mid-April 1941, BF-SLRC, 6: 258. Other information is in Bettye Goldstein, application to Highlander Folk School, late June 1941, BG-SHSW, general correspondence, 13: 17; "Labor Group Will Sponsor Talk by James Dombrowski," *SCAN*, 11 April 1941, 1. For a report on his speech, see "Religion, Labor In The South Discussed by Mr. Dombrowski," *SCAN*, 18 April 1941, 4; Robert H. Zieger, *The CIO, 1935–1955* (Chapel Hill, 1995), 111–40.

35. Evelyn Hyman Chase, *Feminist Convert: A Portrait of Mary Ellen Chase* (Santa Barbara, 1988), 121, attributes the editorial to Goldstein. "We Are Aware of the War," *SCAN*, 9 May 1941, 2.

36. "This Is What We Believe"; "Education in Emergency"; "100 Faculty Indorse Active War Policy," *SCAN*, 2 May 1941, 1, 4.

37. Goldstein, "Defense," 11; "They Choose Peace."

38. [Bettye Goldstein], " . . . Then We Are Ignorant," editorial from *SCW*, reprinted in *The Intercollegian* 58 (Nov. 1940): 34; this appeared, with somewhat different content, as "Youth— Its Dilemma." On Bettye Goldstein, "Registration Form," for writer's workshop, BF-SLRC, 6: 274, she indicated that something she wrote had appeared in this publication of the Student Christian Movement; this editorial, consistent with other things she wrote in her sophomore year, is the only item I could locate in *The Intercollegian* that is likely to have been written by her. For the fights over the war as a battle between generations elsewhere, see Cohen, *When the Old Left Was Young*, 313.

39. "Let the Laughter Cease," *SCAN*, 6 May 1941, 2. For a statement about the threats of the campus idyll, see [Bettye Goldstein], "They Are Not Pleased," *SCAN*, 18 April 1941. I am assuming Goldstein wrote this because there is a copy clipped from the newspaper and glued on a paper with "Bettye Goldstein" written at the top, in BF-SLRC, 7: 310.

40. Douglas Palmer, "Woman's Place is in the Home," *SCM*, April 1941, 6, 19–21, with the quotes on 21, 6, 21; Doug [Palmer] to Bettye Goldstein, letter in her copy of the Peoria High School yearbook, *Crest*, 9 June 1938, following 60, BF-SLRC, 1: 247v.

41. Marcia Williams, "Shades of Susan Anthony," *SCM*, 28 May 1941, 10, 20–21, with quotes on 10, 20, 21.

42. Bettye Goldstein, "B.G.," four-page typewritten paper, late April or May 1941, BF-SLRC, 6: 276.

43. Bettye Goldstein, "Psychological Aspects of Ethical Theory," paper for Philosophy 22, 25 April 1941, 5, 7, 9, 10, BF-SLRC, 6: 284. For more information on the course, see the material, including Goldstein's lecture notes, for Philosophy 22, 1940–41, BF-SLRC, 6: 284.

44. Goldstein, "Psychological Aspects," 6–7. For her discussion of the impact of the Middletown studies on her, see Betty Friedan, "The ERA—Does It Play In Peoria," *Peoria Journal Star,*

3 Dec. 1978, page unknown. Otto Kraushaar, marginal notes in response to Goldstein, "Psychological Aspects," 6–7; Kraushaar, comments on the front page of Goldstein, "Psychological Aspects."

45. Chase supported the cooperation of North Atlantic democracies that Clarence K. Streit had proposed in his immensely popular book *Union Now,* an alliance that excluded Germany and remained skeptical about the inclusion of the USSR: Clarence K. Streit, *Union Now: A Proposal for a Federal Union of the Democracies of the North Atlantic* (New York, 1940), 111. For Chase's support of the Federal Union, see "Pennington Of Boston Will Speak."

46. For information on Chase and her speech attacking what Bettye Goldstein had written, I am relying on Evelyn Hyman Chase, "Mary Ellen Chase and the Incipient Feminist Movement," *SAQ,* summer 1987, 17–21; Chase, *Feminist,* 121–23. Mary Ellen Chase, Chapel speech of 12 May 1941, quoted in "Mary E. Chase Defends War Talk In Class Rooms," *SCAN,* 13 May 1941, 1, 4, with quotes on 1, 4. For reaction to Chase's speech, including a letter by fourteen students in defense of Goldstein's editorial, see Edith Schoenfeld et al., letter to editor, *SCAN,* 13 May 1941, 2, 3; Rita B. Packer, letter to editor, *SCAN,* 13 May 1941, 3. For Chase's appreciation of Goldstein, see Mary Ellen Chase to an unidentified friend, [early 1942], quoted in Chase, "Chase," 20.

47. [Bettye Goldstein], "A Year of Change and Unrest," *SCAN,* 13 May 1941, 2. I am assuming Goldstein's authorship because this was one of the few editorials that was clipped and placed in her papers: BF-SLRC, 7: 311.

48. "Commencement, 1941," *SCAN,* 17 June 1941, 2.

4. It All Comes Together, 1941–42

1. On the issue of the shift from anti-fascism to mobilization, see Michael Denning, *The Cultural Front: The Laboring of American Culture in the Twentieth Century* (London, 1996), 11.

2. John Egerton, *Speak Now Against the Day: The Generation Before the Civil Rights Movement in the South* (New York, 1994), 158. For information on Highlander, I am relying on John M. Glen, *Highlander: No Ordinary School, 1932–1962* (Lexington, Ky., 1988), 47–69; Egerton, *Speak Now,* 158–62; Robin D. G. Kelley, *Hammer and Hoe: Alabama Communists During the Great Depression* (Chapel Hill, 1990), 120, 122, 146, 150–51. For her own evaluation of this experience, see Bettye Goldstein to "Everybody" at Highlander, 5 Oct. 1941, BG-SHSW.

3. J. Edgar Hoover, quoted in John M. Glen, e-mail to author, 27 March 1997. On the support for the school, see Glen, *Highlander,* 47–69. In the 1930s, leading figures at Highlander, including James Dombrowski, who spoke at Smith in the spring of 1941, were members of the Revolutionary Policy Council, a radical wing of the Socialist Party, that was willing, as most socialists were not, to form alliances with Communists: Kelley, *Hammer and Hoe,* 120. For the experiences of a Smith student in the South, see Sarah Jane Holtzberg, "To Live and Die in Dixie," *Focus,* March 1939, 10–14.

4. Bettye Goldstein to James Dombrowski, 18 June 1941, BG-SHSW; Bettye Goldstein, application to Highlander Folk School, [June 1941], BG-SHSW.

5. On the documentary style, see Bettye Goldstein, "Documentary writing," handwritten paragraph, [summer 1941], BF-SLRC, 6: 274. For information on those involved in the program, I am relying on John M. Glen, letter to author, 7 April 1995, author's possession; *The Highlander Fling,* July 1941, BF-SLRC, 6: 274. Leon Wilson directed the writers' program. The instructors included Mary Lapsley, Charles W. Ferguson, Herman C. Nixon, and Lealon N. Jones. In addition, a number of people spoke to the students in Goldstein's workshop, including William H. McDaniel. For information of her fellow students, see [Bettye Goldstein], "Writers From All Fields Gather At Unique Highlander Workshop," *Chattanooga Times,* 4 Aug. 1941, Highlander Papers, SHSW, 63: 6; above the article a staff member from Highlander noted that Bettye Goldstein was the author. Additional information on the participants in the workshop is in Bettye Friedan, three-page, untitled, typewritten paper, BF-SLRC, 6: 275. For articles by the participants in the fall program, see *"We Know the Score": Highlander Folk*

School, fall term, 1941, BF-SLRC, 6: 274. I have not been able to locate any living peers from her stay at Highlander, but I have heard from the widow of one. For 1939 and 1940 (but not 1941), the workshops were jointly sponsored by Highlander and the Communist-led League of American Writers: Glen, *Highlander,* 47–69. Glen has indicated that in 1941 Highlander was the sole sponsor of the workshop: Glen, letter to author. For information on what and when she studied, see Highlander Folk School, "Summer Term—Six Weeks," pamphlet, BF-SLRC, 6: 274. There were almost two weeks between the two courses: see Goldstein to Dombrowski, 18 June 1941, Leon Wilson to Bettye Goldstein, 23 June 1941, James Dombrowski to Bettye Goldstein, 25 June 1941, Bettye Goldstein to James Dombrowski, 3 July 1941, James Dombrowski to Bettye Goldstein, 7 July 1941, and Maria Stenzel to Betty Goldstein, 3 Oct. 1941, BG-SHSW.

6. Bettye Goldstein, "Highlander Folk School—American Future," paper, [summer 1941], BF-SLRC, 6: 274; Bettye Goldstein, "Learning the Score," *"We Know the Score": Highlander Folk School,* fall term, 1941, 22–24, with the quotes on 23, BF-SLRC, 6: 274.

7. Goldstein, "Learning the Score," 22–23.

8. Ibid., 24.

9. On her preference for abstractions, see Bettye Goldstein to Leon [Wilson], 25 August 1943, BG-SHSW.

10. Her vivid analogy is in Goldstein to "Everybody." The quotes are from [Bettye Goldstein], "No Change in Emphasis," *SCAN,* 26 Sept. 1941, 2. The language and ideas in the editorial suggest that Goldstein was the author.

11. Unidentified writer [probably Maria Stenzel] to Bettye Goldstein, 10 Oct. 1941, BF-SHSW. For my guess as to authorship, I am relying on Bettye Goldstein to Maria [Stenzel], 12 Oct. 1941, BF-SHSW. On the situation unions faced, see Robert H. Zieger, *The CIO, 1935–1955* (Chapel Hill, 1995), 136.

12. On her experiences with anti-Semitism at Smith, see Sondra Henry and Emily Taitz, *Betty Friedan: Fighter for Women's Rights* (Hillside, N.J., 1990), 22. For evidence that she began work on "The Scapegoat" at Highlander, see Bettye Goldstein to Zilphia [Horton] et al., 13 Nov. 1941, BG-SHSW. Goldstein to "Everybody" mentions her contacting the Curtis Brown agency. Probably unbeknownst to her, Federated Press, a labor paper for which she would work from 1943 to 1946, published a piece of hers on a CIO union in September 1941: Bettye Goldstein, "Clerks Tell Students How They Doubled Their Pay," *FP,* 3 Sept. 1941. Soon after graduating from Smith, she delivered a talk at the synagogue in Peoria, entitled "On Affirming One's Jewishness." Here she cast a skeptical eye on Jews who minimized their identity as Jews and instead turned anti-Semitism against themselves: Amy Stone, "Friedan at 55," *Lilith,* fall 1976, 12.

13. Bettye Goldstein, "The Scapegoat," *SCM,* Oct. 1941, 5, 26, 27, with the quote on 5. For her discussions of the paper, see Goldstein to "Everybody"; Goldstein to Zilphia et al.; Goldstein turned the paper in, for English 328, on 1 Oct. 1941: Bettye Goldstein, "The Scapegoat," paper, BF-SLRC, 6: 271.

14. Bettye Goldstein, "Faithfully Squeezed, Faithfully Drawn," paper, probably fall 1941, BF-SLRC, 6: 265; Bettye Goldstein, "Articles," probably fall 1941, BF-SLRC, 6: 263; Bettye Goldstein, "Sunday Afternoon," paper, written for English 328, fall term 1941, BF-SLRC, 6: 269; Bettye Goldstein, "Ten O'Clock Class," paper, written for English 328, fall term 1941, BF-SLRC, 6: 272; [Bettye Goldstein], two-page, typewritten, untitled story, probably written for English 328, probably fall 1941, 1–2, BF-SLRC, 6: 273.

15. Bettye Goldstein, "And Grey With Pearls," paper, written for English 328, fall 1941, BF-SLRC, 6: 267; Bettye Goldstein, "Create My Child of Spleen, *King Lear,*" paper, written for English 328, 4 January 1942, BF-SLRC, 6: 270.

16. Bettye Goldstein, "Saturday Night," *SCM,* Jan.–Feb. 1942, 9–10.

17. Bettye Goldstein, lecture notes for English 334, probably mid-October 1941, BF-SLRC, 6: 260v; for her discussion of how novels revealed the dynamics of class relationships, see [Bettye Goldstein], "Forsytes and Buddenbrooks—Symbols of an Unique Class and its De-

cline," paper written for English 334, winter 1941–42, BF-SLRC, 6: 260v; Bettye Goldstein, "The Isolated Ego: A Consistent Inconsistency in Representative Novels of the Nineteenth Century," paper written for English 334, 11 May 1942, BF-SLRC, 6: 266.

18. Goldstein to "Everybody"; "Behind a Closed Door," *SCAN*, 3 Oct. 1941, 2 (this is one of the editorials that was clipped and placed in her file: BF-SLRC, 7: 310, as was another on the same subject: "Answer No Answer," *SCAN*, 7 Oct. 1941, 2); "Declaration of Student Independence," *SCAN*, 5 Dec. 1941, 1–2; "SCAN Protests Against Censorship; Administrative Board Revokes Decision," *SCAN*, 5 Dec. 1941, 1; "Review of Philosophy Courses," *SCAN*, 10 March 1942, 2; "A Few Hours More," *SCAN*, 10 Oct. 1941, 2; Goldstein to "Everybody." For a subsequent letter from some men at Westover Field, encouraging Smith students to entertain them and help make them feel at home, see letter to "Girls" from "The Boys at Westover Field," *SCAN*, 14 Oct. 1941, 2.

19. "We Cannot Refuse," *SCAN*, 11 Nov. 1941, 2. On the heat cops, see letter from a member of the class of 1943, *SCAN*, 17 Oct. 1941, 2.

20. Adelaine Kerr, and Marjorie Nicolson quoted in same, " 'Women Work Over Conscientiously,' States Miss Nicolson, Former Dean," *SCAN*, 24 Oct. 1941, 2. For a discussion of the choice of Davis over Nicolson, see Betty Friedan, *The Feminine Mystique* (New York, 1963), 158–59.

21. "War Against Fascism," *SCAN*, 24 Oct. 1941, 2; Nancy Torres, "The American Student Union," *Focus*, Feb. 1941, 14–15, 35–36; "A.S.U. Announces New Policy; Supports Full Aid For Allies," *SCAN*, 3 Oct. 1941, 1; for an assessment of student opinion on the war, see "Results of the *SCAN* Poll," *SCAN*, 11 Nov. 1941, 1; Hans Kohn, "The Soviet Union at War," *SCAN*, 17 Oct. 1941, 2; "President Davis Signs Petition Asking Further Aid To Russia," *SCAN*, 21 Oct. 1941, 2.

22. Herbert J. Davis, speech of Nov. 17, quoted in "President Davis In Protest Meeting Condemns Mass Murders of Nazism," *SCAN*, 18 Nov. 1941, 1, 5, 6, with the quotes on 1.

23. "In Answer to Mr. Davis," *SCAN*, 18 Nov. 1941, 2; "Kurt Koffka," *SCAN*, 25 Nov. 1941, 2; Smith Chapter of The American Student Union, letter to the editor, *SCAN*, 25 Nov. 1941, 2.

24. The quotes are from Neal Gilkyson, "The Gallery," *SCAN*, 21 Oct. 1941, 32, and 31 Oct. 1941, 2; the accusations appear in J.N., "The Red Menace," *SCAN*, 14 Oct. 1941, 2. Compared wih campus politics elsewhere, after the Nazi-Soviet pact the student movement at Smith was more active and radical. On the national context see Robert Cohen, *When The Old Left Was Young: Student Radicals and America's First Mass Student Movement, 1929–1941* (New York, 1993), especially 279–321. Friedan's position appears to differ significantly from that taken by leading groups of women's peace activists, which, more committed to neutrality and international cooperation, were not as anti-fascist and pro-labor as Friedan: see Harriet H. Alonso, *Peace as a Women's Issue: A History of the U.S. Movement for World Peace and Women's Rights* (Syracuse, 1993), 137–43. Goldstein's stance, hardly an unusual one, was articulated by writers from a variety of perspectives, including Socialists and Trotskyists. Her position was close to that in John Dewey, *Freedom and Culture* (New York, 1939), especially 172–76, where he linked his opposition to war and intervention with his support of democracy. Although there is evidence that Goldstein read other works by Dewey, I cannot trace her views on the war to him. She may also have been influenced by Robert S. Lynd, *Knowledge for What? The Place of Social Science in American Culture* (Princeton, 1939). Finally, she may have been reacting against the arguments of interventionists, even some of those on the left, who asserted that curtailing democracy at home might be necessary to defeat totalitarians abroad.

25. Anon., "Maids We Have Known and Loved," *Tatler*, Oct. 1941, 9, 21, with the quotes on 9, 21.

26. For *SCAN*'s response to the article, see "In the Name of the College," *SCAN*, 4 Nov. 1941, 2; for another response to this controversy, see Susan Lobenstein et al., letter to the editor, *SCAN*, 4 Nov. 1941, 2. For the response to the punishment of the magazine, see "The Tatler Suspension," *SCAN*, 7 Nov. 1941, 2. For the apology of those involved in *Tatler* and the claim

that what they did was a "well-intended caricature," see Ruth Mehrtens to Laura Scales, *SCAN*, 4 Nov. 1941, 1.

27. Margery Sly, communication to author, provided information about wages in the early 1930s, from the warden's office records; the discussion in this and the following paragraph relies on Elizabeth von Klemperer, interview by Daniel Horowitz, Northampton, Mass., 19 Aug. 1996.

28. Miriam B. Horowitz, telephone conversation with Daniel Horowitz, 11 Sept. 1996.

29. Julia L. Dunn, quoted in Patricia C. Smith, "Grandma Went to Smith, All Right, but She Went from Nine to Five: A Memoir," in *Working-Class Women in the Academy: Laborers in the Knowledge Factory*, ed. Michelle M. Tokarczyk and Elizabeth A. Fay (Amherst, 1993), 129; "A So-called Moron," letter to the editor, *SCAN*, 4 Nov. 1941, 4; "Maids at Smith Threaten Strike After Criticism," *DHG*, 3 Nov. 1941, 1; "Smith Maids Propose Union; Temporary Officers Elected," *SCAN*, 12 Dec. 1941, 4; "Domestic Employees to Elect Collective Bargaining Agent," *SCAN*, 17 March 1942, 3; "Maids Vote to Join Union; A.F. of L. Bargaining Agent," *SCAN*, 7 April 1942, 1. It is possible that a student journalist wrote "A So-called Moron."

30. "College Employees Wish To Organize; Ask Charter To Join A.F. of L. Union," *SCAN*, 21 Oct. 1941, gives a sense of the friendly relationship between the workers and the reporter from *SCAN*; "The Right to Organize" and Filene's advertisement, *SCAN*, 21 Oct. 1941, 2; Bettye Goldstein, handwritten note on copy of 21 Oct. 1941 issue of *SCAN*, BF-SHSW. On her authorship of this editorial, see Goldstein to Zilphia et al.

31. For the reporting on the efforts, see "College Employees Wish To Organize" and "Mr. King States Employees' Duties," *SCAN*, 21 Oct. 1941, 1; "Employees Of College Will Not Strike Unless Other Methods Unsuccessful," *SCAN*, 24 Oct. 1941, 1; "Mr. King's Men Weigh Union Proposal; Majority Back Plan, Reporter Learns," *SCAN*, 24 Oct. 1941, 1, 4; "Mr. Butler Clarifies Position Of Organized Labor at Smith," *SCAN*, 5 Dec. 1941, 4; on faculty support for the effort, see "Employees Continue Union Organization," *SCAN*, 28 Oct. 1941, 1; for Goldstein's talk, "Labor Education Described By Smith Summer Workers," *SCAN*, 28 Oct. 1941, 4.

32. "Labor Vote," *SCAN*, 14 Nov. 1941, 1; "Comment," *SCAN*, 14 Nov. 1941, 2.

33. Advertisement for Hollander Furs, *SCAN*, 14 Nov. 1941, 2; "Delar Strike Will Not Hinder Arrival of Yearbook Pictures," *SCAN*, 18 Nov. 1941, 1; David Lieberman, lawyer for the union, letter to editor, *SCAN*, 5 Dec. 1941, 2, 4.

34. Goldstein to Zilphia et al.; "Betty Goldstein, Local Girl, Makes Good in New York," clipping from Peoria newspaper, probably 10 Dec. 1943 issue of *Labor Temple News*, BF-SLRC, 1: 86; Goldstein to "Everybody"; Goldstein to [Wilson]. Here she also mentioned that her editorials won a National Intercollegiate Journalism Prize. Milton Meltzer, *Betty Friedan: A Voice for Women's Rights* (New York, 1985), 19, says that the president "threatened to expel" the *SCAN* reporters who uncovered wrongdoing by members of the secret society.

35. "Declaration of Student Independence," 1, 2; "SCAN Protests Against Censorship," 1, 3; "Bander-Log Will Open Tonight At Northampton High," *SCAN*, 5 Dec. 1941, 1.

36. For a letter from a student that in response mixed the trivial and the grave, see Ruth D. Honaman, letter to her parents, 9 Dec. 1941, class of 1944, CASC; on the response of left professors, see Resolution of the Western Massachusetts Teachers' Federation, reprinted in *SCAN*, 16 Dec. 1941, 1; the editorial is "We Cannot Rejoice," *SCAN*, 9 Dec. 1941, 2; the response of a student is Margaret McClumpha to her parents, 13 Dec. 1941, class of 1944, CASC. Although Friedan later described herself as a pacifist in her Smith years, it would be more accurate to think of her as someone whose commitment to anti-fascism was primary, more important than her opposition to war: Betty Friedan, interview by Daniel Horowitz, Santa Monica, Calif., 18 March 1987.

37. "Dartmouth Omits Carnival, Vacations, As Men's Colleges Organize For War," *SCAN*, 16 Dec. 1941, 1; "Our Duty Now," *SCAN*, 12 Dec. 1941, 2 [for the "detached" quotation]; "Enemies of War," *SCAN*, 16 Dec. 1941, 2 [for the "dirty" quotation]; [Bettye Goldstein], "[illegible] Women's College in War," three-page handwritten statement, probably early 1941, BF-SLRC, 7: 303.

38. Patricia Maloney, Kathleen Trager, and Mary Anne Guitar, "What Price Enlightenment?" *SCM*, Spring 1942, 4–6.

39. "Smith in the War," including quote from unnamed New York educator, *SCAN*, 9 Jan. 1942, 2. For a compelling defense of the importance of liberal arts for women, see "Permanence at Smith," *SCAN*, 20 Feb. 1942, 2.

40. "Consider the Roses," *SCAN*, 6 Feb. 1942, 2; "Campus Cooperatives," *SCAN*, 24 Feb. 1942, 2. The letters to the editor column in these days was filled with debates over sacrifice. To sample this discussion, see the letters in *SCAN*, 13 Feb. 1942, 2; "No Sacrifice," *SCAN*, 13 Jan. 1942, 2; "Step Toward the Future," *SCAN*, 3 Feb. 1942, 2.

41. "Epilogue of Failure," *SCAN*, 10 March 1942, 2. For a statement by the editors of *SCAN* that faculty and students, as well as the administration, should have a say in labor relations at the college, see "The Proposed Revision," *SCAN*, 17 Feb. 1942, 2. For evidence of student awareness of the issues surrounding the unionization of the maids, see Ruth Honaman, letter to her parents, [May 1942], CASC.

42. Bettye Goldstein, "A Comparative Study of Social Groups in Animals," paper, written for Psychology 34b, May 1942, BF-SLRC, 7: 296; Bettye Goldstein, "A Critical Evaluation of the Testing of Intelligence," paper, 19 Jan. 1942, BF-SLRC, 7: 302. For her interest in predicting and controlling, see Goldstein, "Critical Evaluation," 33. The only evidence I can find from her undergraduate days of psychology as a path to her involvement with people came when she was learning how to administer and interpret Rorschach tests: BF-SLRC, 7: 297; and a paper she wrote on an experiment she seems to have performed, probably for James Gibson: Bettye Goldstein, "An Experimental Investigation of Locomotion in a Quasi-Physical Field," dated 1941, JG-CU, 14/23/1832, 2–27.

43. Francis A. Bartlett, *Sigmund Freud: A Marxian Essay* (London, 1938), 27; on Bartlett's career, see Benjamin Harris, "The Benjamin Rush Society and Marxist Psychiatry in the United States, 1944–1951," *History of Psychiatry* 6 (1995): 312–14. Friedan later asserted that at Smith she began to accept the Freudian view about women, castration, and penis envy: Betty Friedan, interview by Jacqueline Van Voris, 20, 17 April 1973, New York, N.Y., CASC. An exhaustive examination of her vast and often difficult-to-read lecture notes may turn up basis for such a claim but a less thorough look provides little support for a conclusion that at Smith she learned the key elements of an anti-feminist Freudianism. Indeed, there is evidence to the contrary—in what she said in her paper on Flaubert, cited above, in her reading of Karen Horney, and in the extensive proof of her awareness of women's issues in these years. Bartlett, *Freud*, the book that was central to her exploration of the relationship of Marx and Freud, paid no attention to penis envy among girls and the chapter on "The Castration Complex" focused only on boys. As Bartlett did for a number of topics, in Horney's discussion of penis envy in *New Ways of Psychoanalysis* (New York, 1939), she insisted that what Freud saw as universal was cultural and far from constant.

My own examination of the relevant passages of Goldstein's papers reveals little if any attention to penis envy and considerable attention to other elements of infantile sexuality, especially orality and anality. For evidence that she was interested in the meaning of her mother's colitis, see [Bettye Goldstein], notes on Franz Alexander's writings on colitis, BF-SLRC, 7: 305. At some level, in reading Freudian psychology, she was also thinking about her relationship to her father: see, in this same section of her papers, a story about her relationship to her father, four pages, handwritten draft, on light green paper, BF-SLRC, 7: 303.

44. Bettye Goldstein, "Social Learning: A Reformulation of Freudian Concepts," Jan. 1942; this is the title and date that appears on a handwritten essay, over sixty pages long, BF-SLRC, 7: 305, that provides the most organized statement of her ideas. My best guess is that she began to work on this project, under the direction of James Gibson, both in a fall term Proseminar (Psychology 35a) and in a year-long Advanced Studies (Psychology 39), probably also under Gibson's direction. The note cards and drafts on this project are in BF-SLRC, 6: 289, 7: 303, and 7: 305. These files contain evidence that she continued to work on this in her year at Berkeley. For the central ideas, see Goldstein, "Social Learning," [31] and [45–60].

45. Bettye Goldstein, "Operationism in Psychology," honors thesis, April 1942, 72, BF-SLRC, 7: 304. For the published version, see H. Israel and B. Goldstein, "Operationism in Psychology," *Psychological Review* 51 (May 1944): 177–88; for correspondence about revision of her thesis, see BF-SLRC, 49: 1782.

46. On her dissatisfaction with the thesis, see Goldstein to Maria; on Kohn, see Hans Kohn, "Empires and Armaments," *Focus*, May 1939, 3; for information on him, see Aaron Berman, "One World: Wartime Visions of Nationalism and the Postwar World," 1996, copy in author's possession; for her critique of Skinner, see Goldstein, "Operationism in Psychology," honors thesis, 2. Ellen Herman, *The Romance of American Psychology: Political Culture in the Age of Experts* (Berkeley, 1995) explores the political uses of psychology beginning in the late 1930s.

47. Meltzer, *Friedan,* 19–20; Henry and Taitz, *Friedan,* 24–26, 29; unnamed Smith administrator quoted in Marcia Cohen, *The Sisterhood: The True Story of the Women Who Changed the World* (New York, 1988), 62.

48. Archibald MacLeish, quoted in "Archibald MacLeish Addresses Seniors At 64th Smith College Commencement," *SCAN,* 9 June 1942, 2. On MacLeish, see Richard H. Pells, *Radical Visions and American Dreams: Culture and Social Thought in the Depression Years* (New York, 1973), 314; Signi Lenea Falk, *Archibald MacLeish* (New York, 1965), especially 100–101.

49. Betty Friedan, quoted in Justine Blau, *Betty Friedan* (New York, 1990), 29. On her uncertainty about her future, see Goldstein to Maria; Friedan, *Feminine Mystique,* 69; Paul Wilkes, "Mother Superior to Women's Lib," *NYTM,* 29 November 1970, 140.

50. For the editorials with the theme of restlessness, see "We Cannot Rejoice"; "Our Duty Now"; "Campus Cooperatives"; "No Change in Emphasis"; on her reaction to Strong, Bettye Goldstein, handwritten notes for Economics 319, on a page titled "Reading Period," probably December 1940, BF-SLRC, 1: 257.

5. A Momentous Interlude

1. Verne A. Stadtman, comp. and ed., *The Centennial Record of the University of California* (Berkeley, 1968), 222; Federal Writers' Project, *California: A Guide to the Golden State* (New York, 1939), 180–82. For correspondence about her summer 1942 internship at Grasslands Hospital, Valhalla, N.Y., see the material in BF-SLRC, 8: 319.

2. Verne A. Stadtman, *The University of California, 1868–1968* (New York, 1970), 305–18.

3. On Oppenheimer in Berkeley, see Richard Rhodes, *The Making of the Atomic Bomb* (New York, 1986), 443–47; Peter Goodchild, *J. Robert Oppenheimer: Shatterer of Worlds* (Boston, 1981), 25–40.

4. On her Smith peers' concern about the militarization of academic life, see ASU's Charter of Student Rights and Responsibilities, quoted in Nancy Torres, "The American Student Union," *SCM,* Feb. 1941, 14; for awareness in her Berkeley cohort of events there, Max Levin, interview by Daniel Horowitz, Santa Cruz, Calif., 29 June 1996.

5. *DC,* 1 Sept. 1942; "25 University Women to Take Officers' Course At Smith College for Women's Naval Reserve," *DC,* 16 Oct. 1942, 2; "Smith College Inaugurates War Minors," *DC,* 26 Jan. 1943, 3; "Majorettes, Co-ed Yell Leaders? Campus Opinion Evenly Split," *DC,* 16 Sept. 1942, 1; "Those Majorettes," *DC,* 18 Sept. 1942, 4; *DC,* 10 Nov. 1942, 4; Sophia Kent, quoted in "Kisses Ok'd: Bond Stunt," *DC,* 25 Sept. 1942, 1; "Sigma Chis to Choose," *DC,* 26 Oct. 1942, 1; "Can Woman's Place Be Evermore in the Home," *DC,* 15 Feb. 1943, 4; Rona Stone, reporting on lecture by Noel Keys, "Working Wives May Cause Readjustment Problems," *DC,* 20 May 1943, 2.

6. Unidentified former student quoted in "Editorial," *DC,* 2 Sept. 1942, 4; "Ex-University Students Help Vitalize Life at Tanforan," *DC,* 22 Sept. 1942, 4. On the relocation of Japanese Americans, see Roger Daniels, *Concentration Camps, North America: Japanese in the United States and Canada During World War II* (Malabar, Fla., 1981), especially 97 and 105.

7. The quote is from "Campus Suffragettes," *CC,* 28 Feb. 1943, 2. Other material comes from Mary Ogg, "A Conflict of Values," *DC,* 12 March 1943, 8; Mary Ogg, "Share the Wealth,"

DC, 24 Feb. 1943, 8; Mary Murray, "Racial Prejudice," *DC,* 11 Nov. 1942, 4; letter to editor from Clara Pinsky, Anne Lengyel, and Estelle Bruck, *DC,* 15 April 1943, 4; Vicki Landish, president of Lincoln Steffens Branch of the Young Communist League, "Allied Charter Would Let People Decide," *DC,* 12 March 1943, 4; "Communist Rally," *DC,* 27 April 1943, 4; Max Weiss, *Youth Serves the Nation* (New York, 1942), 18, 22, 26–27, 34, 39, 41; Dave Grant, *Attack Now! Knock Out Hitler in '42* (New York, 1942); "Remember Pearl Harbor," *CC,* 7 Dec. 1942, 1; "Voice of the President," 14 Sept. 1942, 1; "We Make Our Bow," *CC,* 19 Nov. 1942, 1; "Join YCL Now," *CC,* 23 March 1943, 1; "Government Cracks Nut," *CC,* 14 Sept. 1942, 1; "Something Cooking?" *CC,* 7 Dec. 1942, 2; "Only a Crackpot?" *CC,* 7 Dec. 1942, 2; "3 Important Bills," *CC,* 18 Jan. 1943, 2; "Mobilize the Curriculum!" *CC,* 28 Feb. 1943, 1, 2; "War and Education," *CC,* 19 Nov. 1942, 2; "Liberal Arts in Action," *CC,* 6 April 1943, 1. In early 1942, the Communist Party newspaper accepted restriction of the liberties of the Japanese Americans as an unfortunate but necessary part of a program for national security: Daniels, *Concentration Camps,* 79.

8. On the newspaper's treatment of radical activity, compare "Communist Rally," *DC,* 27 April 1943, 4, with the lack of coverage after the rally in the issue of 30 April 1943; for evidence of the controversy over free speech and textbooks, see editorial and letters, *DC,* 14 April 1943, 4. On the response of radicals to investigations, see letter from "One of the Masses, W.P. '45," *DC,* 27 Jan. 1943, 8. On the anti-communist crusade in California, see Ingrid Scobie, "Jack B. Tenney and the 'Parasitic Menace': Anti-Communist Legislation in California, 1940–1949," *Pacific Historical Review* 43 (May 1957): 188–211.

9. On her friendship with radicals and participation in the informal seminar, Levin interview; Max Levin, telephone conversation with Daniel Horowitz, 16 Sept. 1995. In 1942–43, Levin, who participated in this discussion group, was finishing his Ph.D. in the Department of Psychology at Berkeley. In this year, his wife, Dorothy Levin, was a member of the YCL. For evidence of Goldstein's friendship with the Levins, see mention of them, in Betty Friedan, lecture notes for Psychology 1A, BF-SLRC, 8: 322. On Gundlach, Jane Sanders, *Cold War on the Campus: Academic Freedom at the University of Washington, 1946–64* (Seattle, 1975), 7, 47, 55–56; Ralph Gundlach, "The Psychological Bases for Permanent Peace," *The Journal of Social Psychology, S.P.S.S.I. Bulletin* 16 (1942): 297–334, with the quote on 331.

10. Ralph Gundlach, quoted in Marion McAvoy, "Psychology Professor Traces Spread of Local War Rumors," *DC,* 6 Nov. 1942, 1; the anti-Semitism probably involved blaming Jews for causing the war as well as rumors that they avoided military service because they were unpatriotic. On these themes in general, see Leonard Dinnerstein, *Antisemitism in America* (New York, 1994), 135–37; Ralph H. Gundlach, "College Education Eventually Inadequate to Combat Bias," *DC,* 7 Jan. 1943, 4. For his attack on the link between race and imperialism, see Ralph Gundlach, quoted in "When Do You Think the War Will Terminate?" *DC,* 14 Jan. 1943, 4.

11. F. David Peat, *Infinite Potential: The Life and Times of David Bohm* (Reading, Mass., 1997), 49; on Bohm's passion for ideas and politics, see David Peat, e-mail to author, 18 July 1997.

12. Peat, *Infinite Potential,* 49. As she had done when she applied to Highlander or described her political transformation at Smith, Friedan minimized her prior political education, later telling Bohm's biographer that when she arrived in Berkeley she was "fresh and naive." See Betty Friedan, 18 Sept. 1993 interview with F. David Peat, quoted in Peat, *Infinite Potential,* 49.

13. On the secrecy over Bohm's thesis, see Peat, *Infinite Potential,* 64. The information about Bohm's political activity is from Ellen W. Schrecker, *No Ivory Tower: McCarthyism and the Universities* (New York, 1986), 135–38; Peat, *Infinite Potential,* 58–64. On Nelson's vague discussion of his relationship with Oppenheimer's students, see Steve Nelson, James R. Barrett, and Rob Ruck, *Steve Nelson: American Radical* (Pittsburgh, 1981), 268–69.

14. Investigative report on Giovanni Rossi Lomanitz, Manhattan Project Security Records, Record Group 77MED, Box 100, National Archives, College Park, Md. Number 2632 Channing Way, now a parking lot, in 1943 was a duplex or small apartment building: Gregg Herken, e-mail to author, 6 June 1997.

15. The quote is in Nelson, Barrett, and Ruck, *Nelson,* 256. 2634 Channing Way was the address to which the university sent mail on 9 Nov. 1942, 21 Jan. 1943, 27 March 1943, and 31 March 1943: correspondence in BF-SLRC, 8: 320; Goldstein also wrote her address as 2634 Channing Way on a "Guest" card for the West Coast Division of the Rorschach Institute, Guest card, BF-SLRC, 6: 274.

16. FBI reports on Betty Goldstein, various dates in 1944, file no. 100–17456, BF-SLRC, 1: 67. Penn Kimball, *The File* (San Diego, 1983) explores the problematic nature of the material in his own FBI file.

17. The quotes are from FBI reports on Goldstein; Richard G. Powers, *Not Without Honor: The History of American Anticommunism* (New York, 1995), 156. On *Mission to Moscow,* see John P. Diggins, *The Proud Decades: America in War and Peace, 1941–1960* (New York, 1988), 161. When the CIA was monitoring women activists in the early 1970s, though an investigator circled Friedan's maiden name in a newspaper article, the agency seems not to have looked into the FBI files to make the connection: markings on newspaper clipping, BF-SLRC, 1: 23.

18. The quote is from Levin, phone conversation. For information on the department and its personnel, see Joan D. Grold, "A History of the University of California Psychology Department at Berkeley," typewritten paper, 1961, copy in the Education/Psychology Library, University of California, Berkeley; Jean W. Macfarlane, "Psychology," in Stadtman, *Centennial,* 99–100; University of California at Berkeley, *General Catalogue . . . 1942–43* (Berkeley, 1942), 417–23. On the fellowships, see the correspondence from university administrators in BF-SLRC, 8: 320. On the advantage she gained from the departure of male students, see Clarence W. Brown to Bettye Goldstein, 7 March 1942, BF-SLRC, 8: 320.

19. For statements on what courses Goldstein took, I am relying on material in BF-SLRC, 7: 298, 305; 8: 321–26. Unlike what is available for the Smith years, for the period in Berkeley the material in BF-SLRC is relatively thin. The lecture notes are briefer and less complete. In addition, there are few finished papers that Goldstein wrote. On her professors, see Ernest R. Hilgard, *Psychology in America: A Historical Survey* (San Diego, 1987), 367, 543–45; Don Brown, e-mail to author, 7 Oct. 1996; Levin, interview; Daniel J. Levinson, "Else Frenkel-Brunswik," *International Encyclopedia of the Social Sciences* (New York, 1968), 5: 559–62; Betty Friedan, "Accomplishments," manuscript, c. 1959, 1, BF-SLRC, 1: 62.

20. Notebook titled "Freud and Abnormal Seminars" on the outside cover and "Seminars-Psychoanalysis & Abnormal" on the inside cover; Erik Erikson, quoted in Betty Goldstein, handwritten lecture notes for Psychology 214J, spring semester, 1943, 16, BF-SLRC, 8: 323; Erik Erikson, quoted in Betty Goldstein, handwritten lecture notes for Psychology 165c, 98, BF-SLRC, 8: 324; Betty Goldstein, handwritten reading notes for Psychology 165c, BF-SLRC, 8: 323. For Erikson's years at Berkeley, see Robert Coles, *Erik H. Erikson: The Growth of His Work* (Boston, 1970), especially 43–59. Among Friedan's many statements that she studied with Erikson at Berkeley, see Betty Friedan, *"It Changed My Life": Writings on the Women's Movement,* 1985 edition (New York, 1976), 6. For evidence of her interest in Erikson's work, see BF-SLRC, 8: 322, 8: 323; Betty Goldstein, "Erikson Seminar," several pages of handwritten notes, probably Psychology 214J, contained in the notebook for a course on Experimental Psychology taught by Nevitt Sanford, BF-SLRC, 8: 326. According to Larry Friedman, Goldstein's friend Jane Loevinger was Erikson's research assistant in the early 1940s.

21. The quote is from Betty Friedan, interview by Daniel Horowitz, Santa Monica, Calif., 18 March 1987. In her Berkeley year, Friedan later claimed, she was beginning to question both Marx and Freud, Marx because he had a "blind spot" about women and no sense of the importance of individual growth: Friedan, Horowitz interview. In Betty Friedan, interview by Jacqueline Van Voris, 11, 20, New York, N.Y., 17 April 1973, CASC, Friedan discussed her Freudian education at Smith and Berkeley. Without giving the name of the author and title, she referred to Francis H. Bartlett, *Sigmund Freud: A Marxian Essay* (London, 1939). For her notes from a class by Erikson that hysteria was a product of Victorian society and, by implication, not something universal for women, see Betty Goldstein, "Experimental Dynamic Psychology (Sanford)," 75, BF-SLRC, 8: 326. On her plan for her master's thesis,

see "Certificate of Candidacy for Degree of Master of Arts," 3 March 1943, BF-SLRC, 8: 320. For evidence that she continued to work on this at Berkeley, see BF-SLRC, 6: 289, 7: 303, and 7: 305. For the philosophical nature of her work, see Betty Goldstein, "The Relationship Between Needs and Their Expression in Phantasy and Behavior: A Problem in the Interpretation of Protective Material," paper written for Psychology 214, 31 May 1943, BF-SLRC, 8: 325.

22. The quotes are from Karl Abraham, *Selected Papers of Karl Abraham* (London, 1927), 387; evidence of her interest in these issues is in Goldstein, reading notes for Psychology 214J, a card titled "Parsimony & Extravagance." Other information can be found in Abraham, *Papers*, 338; Goldstein, lecture notes for Psychology 214J; Goldstein, reading notes for Psychology 214J. Goldstein, lecture notes, Psychology 214J, 27, did refer to the pages containing the essay on female castration complex but she placed multiple stars in her reading notes near Abraham, *Selected Papers*, 259–60 (on the timing of weaning) and 374 (on narcissism and toilet training); see also reading notes on Freud's discussion of maleness and femaleness.

23. Betty Friedan, rough draft of a chapter for *The Feminine Mystique*, 433, BF-SLRC, 16: 583. On Tolman, see Grold, "History," 4–14; Hilgard, *Psychology*, 206–8; Levin, interview; Edward C. Tolman, *Drives Toward War* (New York, 1942). Tolman's book grew, in part, out of his participation in a seminar led by two San Francisco psychoanalysts: Hilgard, *Psychology*, 208. For a critical review of the book see Mary Ogg, "Here's A Bizarre Post-War Utopia Based on Psychological Precepts," *DC*, 6 Nov. 1942, 6. In her senior thesis at Smith, Goldstein had missed the breadth and nuance of Tolman's approach: Bettye Goldstein, "Operationism in Psychology," honors thesis, April 1942, 37, BF-SLRC, 7: 304.

24. Betty Goldstein, "Foci of Confusion in Learning Theory," typewritten paper for Psychology 213, May 1943, 1, 13, BF-SLRC, 7: 302; instructor's comments on Goldstein, "Foci of Confusion," cover page. One sign of her boredom and sense of distraction was how little she wrote down from lectures, especially when compared with what she recorded at Smith. Tolman directed this research course, Psychology 213: University of California at Berkeley, *General Catalogue . . . 1942–43*, 423. For additional evidence of Tolman's influence on Goldstein's education, see Betty Goldstein, lecture notes for Psychology 1A; Friedan, "Accomplishments," 1; Betty Friedan, *The Feminine Mystique* (New York, 1963), 12.

25. Friedan, *Feminine Mystique*, 70; see also, Goldstein, quoted in Justine Blau, *Betty Friedan* (New York, 1990), 27. For a similar version, see Wilkes, "Mother Superior," 140. By 1988, Friedan asserted that this story, which was "merely an anecdote," had made her "into a cliché": Betty Friedan, quoted in Marcia Cohen, *The Sisterhood: The True Story of the Women Who Changed the World* (New York, 1988), 63–64. Paul Wilkes ("Mother Superior to Women's Lib," *NYTM*, 29 Nov. 1970, 140) and Marilyn French ("The Emancipation of Betty Friedan," *Esquire* 100 [Dec. 1983]: 510) identify this boyfriend as a physicist. In an interview carried out by Bohm's biographer, Friedan acknowledged her romantic relationship with him but did not identify him as the man in her often-told story: Peat, *Infinite Potential*, 49. Wilkes, "Mother Superior," 140, notes how carefully Friedan guarded the name of her boyfriend, whose identity Peat was the first to reveal.

26. Philip Wylie, *Generation of Vipers* (New York, 1942), 189, 203; Wylie, *Generation of Vipers*, quoted in Michael P. Rogin, *Ronald Reagan, the Movie and Other Episodes in Political Demonology* (Berkeley, 1987), 242; Rogin, *Reagan*, 243–44.

27. Friedan, Horowitz interview; E. C. Tolman, quoted in Friedan, Horowitz interview. The show opened its four weeks of performances in San Francisco in late April 1943: " 'Lady in the Dark Closes,' " *NYT*, 19 April 1943, 22.

28. Pearl S. Buck, *Of Men and Women* (New York, 1941), 86, 43, 16; see also 5, 15, 35, 43–44, 46–47, 49, 94–96; for discussions of this book, see Glenna Matthews, *'Just a Housewife': The Rise and Fall of Domesticity in America* (New York, 1987), 199–200; Peter Conn, *Pearl S. Buck: A Cultural Biography* (Cambridge, U.K., 1996), 246–48.

29. See Sherna B. Gluck, *Rosie the Riveter Revisited: Women, the War and Social Change* (Boston, 1987).

30. Moss Hart, *Lady in the Dark* (New York, 1941), 137–40. Ira Gershwin wrote the lyrics and Kurt Weill, the music. With more justification, someone looking for evidence of the arrival of the feminine mystique could point to the 1944 movie version. For a summary of it, see Carolyn Galerstein, *Working Women on the Hollywood Screen: A Filmography* (New York, 1989), 36; for a discussion of some of the differences between the movie and the play, see Jeanine Basinger, *A Woman's View: How Hollywood Spoke to Women, 1930–1960* (New York, 1993), 100–105. For Goldstein's notes about the psychological literature on the intense feelings girls had for their mothers and fathers, see BF-SLRC, 8: 323.

31. On her disappointment with the situation at Berkeley, Friedan, Van Voris interview, 3–4; on Tolman's advice about name changes, see Levin, interview; for evidence of Goldstein's continuing interest in medical school, see material in BF-SLRC, 8: 322, 8: 323; for a different interpretation, see Sondra Henry and Emily Taitz, *Friedan: Fighter for Women's Rights* (Hillside, N.J., 1990), 34.

32. Friedan, Horowitz interview; Betty Goldstein to Leon [Wilson], 25 Aug. 1943, BF-SHSW.

33. Henry and Taitz, *Friedan*, 31.

34. "Topology Meeting and Greeting 1942/3"; "List of names and addresses of people interested in getting reprints," BF-SLRC, 49: 1781; "H. M. Goldstein Taken By Death," clipping from Peoria newspaper, 12 Jan. 1943, author's possession. On December 23, 1942, Harry M. Goldstein signed his final will, leaving everything to his wife: "Last Will and Testament of Harry M. Goldstein," dated 23 Dec. 1942, copy in author's possession.

35. Friedan quoted in Wilkes, "Mother Superior," 141. Other information is available in A. M. Krich, *Sweethearts: A Novel* (New York, 1983), 204; Betty Friedan, "Autobiography— Betty Friedan," c. 1975, 13, BF-SLRC, 1: 63; Lyn Tornabene, "The Liberation of Betty Friedan," *McCall's*, May 1971, 138. Cohen, *Sisterhood*, 64, suggests that Friedan first entered therapy after she left Berkeley. Henry and Taitz, *Friedan*, 29, locate the asthma attack linked with her panic over her future in September 1942.

36. Betty Goldstein, "Betty Goldstein, Local Girl, Makes Good in New York," clipping from Peoria newspaper, probably 10 Dec. 1943 issue of *Labor Temple News*, BF-SLRC, 1: 86. Milton Meltzer, *Betty Friedan: A Voice for Women's Rights* (New York, 1985), 21, provides explanations for Friedan's decision that do not rely on the standard story.

6. Federated Press, 1943–46

1. "B.G.," four-page typewritten paper, late April or May 1941, BF-SLRC, 6: 276, quoted in Sondra Henry and Emily Taitz, *Betty Friedan: Fighter for Women's Rights* (Hillside, N.J., 1990), 42; Henry and Taitz, *Friedan*, 34; A. M. Krich, *Sweethearts: A Novel* (New York, 1983), 204. She also worked briefly as a reporter on the *Peoria Evening Star*: Betty Friedan, Application for employment at Time Inc., 1 July 1951, BF-SLRC, 1: 61. For information on this period in her life, see Justine Blau, *Betty Friedan* (New York, 1990), 31–39; Marcia Cohen, *The Sisterhood: The True Story of the Women Who Changed the World* (New York, 1988), 66–71; Betty Friedan, *"It Changed My Life": Writings on the Women's Movement*, 1985 edition (New York, 1976), 8–16; Betty Friedan, biographical information in BF-SLRC, 1: 61; Henry and Taitz, *Friedan*, 37–47; Milton Meltzer, *Betty Friedan: A Voice for Women's Rights* (New York, 1985), 25–30; Lyn Tornabene, "The Liberation of Betty Friedan," *McCall's*, May 1971, 138; Paul Wilkes, "Mother Superior to Women's Lib," *NYTM*, 29 Nov. 1970, 141.

2. For a perceptive treatment of Friedan's work for Federated Press, see Blau, *Friedan*, 31. The Rare Books and Manuscript Collection at Columbia University has the records of the Federated Press, which consist solely of a complete run of the published stories.

3. Betty Goldstein to Leon [Wilson], 25 Aug. 1943, BF-SHSW; Myles [Horton] to Betty Goldstein, 16 Sept. 1943, BF-SHSW; Friedan, Application; Henry and Taitz, *Friedan*, 33–35; Cohen, *Sisterhood*, 64. On Friedan's fight with her mother over her father's estate, see Henry and Taitz, *Friedan*, 34–35. On her planning to go to medical school, see Betty Friedan,

"Autobiography—Betty Friedan," c. 1975, 16, BF-SLRC, 1: 63. On her job application for Time, Inc. Goldstein originally wrote that she first left Federated Press in June of 1945 but she crossed out June and replaced it with April. She also changed the date when she started her job there in 1943 but it is impossible to read what appeared before she wrote "October" over another month. However, in a 1946 letter she dated her hiring in September 1943 and her initial departure in June 1945. Similarly, on the application, she dated her second stint at the press from April to July 1946, but in the 1946 letter she indicated that she resumed working there in January. See Betty Goldstein to Grievance Committee of Newspaper Guild of New York, 23 May 1946, BF-SLRC, 8: 330. She began her work as a reporter at a weekly salary of thirty dollars, a figure that rose to fifty dollars in 1944: Friedan, Application. I have not been able to find out anything about Voters Research Institute, which may be a general and not a specific name. Meltzer, Friedan, 21, says Goldstein found the job at Federated Press at the suggestion of an editor in New York. Early in her stay in Manhattan, she was living at 17 Grove Street. In 1943 or 1944 Goldstein may have been seeking work on a progressive national student magazine, New Threshold: [Betty Goldstein], "Memorandum in re contents July issue New Threshold," spring 1943 or 1944, BF-SLRC, 8: 329.

4. Doug Reynolds, "Federated Press," Encyclopedia of the American Left, ed. Mari Jo Buhle, Paul Buhle, and Dan Georgakas (New York, 1990), 225–27; Nelson Lichtenstein, The Most Dangerous Man in Detroit: Walter Reuther and the Fate of American Labor (New York, 1995), 94. On Haessler, see Stephen J. Haessler, "Carl Haessler and the Federated Press: Essays on the History of American Labor Journalism" (M.A. thesis, University of Wisconsin-Madison, 1977). Jessie Lloyd O'Connor, Harvey O'Connor, and Susan M. Bowler, Harvey and Jessie: A Couple of Radicals (Philadelphia, 1988), 51, provides a vivid sense of work at the Federated Press in New York and Pittsburgh from the 1920s to the 1950s.

5. Mim Kelber, telephone interview with Daniel Horowitz, 16 Sept. 1995.

6. Friedan, Changed My Life, 8–9; Ellen Chesler, conversation, New York, 6 Jan. 1997; in 1944 Federated Press moved from 30 Irving Place to 25 Astor Place; Fred Zeserson, telephone conversation with Daniel Horowitz, 22 June 1996; Bella Abzug, with Mim Kelber, Gender Gap: Bella Abzug's Guide to Political Power for American Women (Boston, 1984); Kelber, interview, 16 Sept. 1995; Scott Nearing, "Economic Trends," FP, 13 Nov. 1944; Philip Foner, "Workers Sought Relief in 1873—Got It In 1935," FP, 26 April 1945; Reynolds, "Federated Press," 226; Virginia Gardner, The Rosenberg Story (New York, 1954), 5. On depictions of women, see Jo Cappola, "Meet Miss Page One," Frontpage, Dec. 1946, 1. In these years the publication of the New York Newspaper Guild was variously titled Guildpaper and Frontpage.

7. The quote is from Irving Mallon et al., telegram to Milton Murray et al., Investigation Commission, American Newspaper Guild, 26 Nov. 1943, NG-WSU, box 63, folder 13; see also "Local Unit Assails National News Guild," NYT, 20 Nov. 1943, 17. On the importance of the guild to the Popular Front, see Michael Denning, The Cultural Front: The Laboring of American Culture in the Twentieth Century (London, 1996), 14. To capture the intensity of the fights within the guild, see "General files (left-wing opposition), 1941–49," NYNG-NY. Penn Kimball, The File (San Diego, 1983), provides some information regarding the internal politics in the New York Guild in 1946, including the tension between different ideological factions. It is likely that Goldstein wrote and even spoke in the guild's radio series broadcast on WLIB, "The News and What to Do About It." She may well have written a radio script on the poll tax in which she criticized members of Congress who used the defense of southern white womanhood as a smokescreen to cover the disenfranchisement of African Americans: "The Poll Tax Must Go!," radio script, 16 April [1944], BF-SLRC, 8: 332. More certain is her authorship and participation in a broadcast on 7 May 1944 that hailed the federal government's seizure of Montgomery Ward because the anti-union stance of the mass merchandiser threatened the wartime labor-management peace: on top of the front page, "B," presumably standing for Betty, identifies her as the author and one of the voices on radio: "The News and What to Do About It," 1, 13, 16, 7 May 1944, BF-SLRC, 8: 332.

8. Betty Friedan, comments at service for Aron Krich, 20 July 1995, in Aron 'Mike' Krich

(n.p., [1995]), 8, copy in author's possession; Krich, *Sweethearts,* 204; Robert Schrank, "Notes from the Twentieth Century" (1995), manuscript (copy in author's possession), including quotes from Howard Friedman and an otherwise unidentified Mike, 241–42. Schrank identified this person as the future Betty Friedan but mistakenly gave her the maiden name of Goldsmith.

9. Schrank, "Notes," 242–44.

10. Betty Goldstein, "The Rich Certainly Have Their Troubles," *FP,* 15 Oct. 1943; Betty Goldstein, "Can't Raise Wages, But $5,000 is Nothing for a Mink Coat," *FP,* 20 Dec. 1943; see also Goldstein, "Rich Certainly Have Their Troubles"; Betty Goldstein, "Wartime Living: Dept. of Advertising Boners," *FP,* 5 June 1944; Betty Goldstein "Wartime Living: Store Window Sells the Woman's Vote," *FP,* 31 July 1944; Betty Goldstein, "Negro Pupils Segregated; Parents Strike; Issue Headed for the Courts," *FP,* 15 Sept. 1943. In thinking about her journalism, I have drawn on Van Gosse, "'To Organize in Every Neighborhood, in Every Home': The Gender Politics of American Communists Between the Wars," *Radical History Review* 50 (spring 1991): 109–41, and Michael Denning, *Cultural Front.* In discussing Goldstein's work for Federated Press, I am relying on articles signed by her (with full name or initials), as well as on those for which her initials appear at the bottom of the story. The custom at Federated Press was to list the initials, at the bottom of the page, of those who worked on the story.

11. Owen M. Richards, quoted in Betty Goldstein, "Butter Up, But Buttermen Still Bitter," *FP,* 20 Dec. 1943; Betty Goldstein, "Government Aid for the Figure," *FP,* 1 Nov. 1943; see also Betty Goldstein, "Don't Count on White Sales" and "Happy New Year OPA," *FP,* 20 Dec. 1943; Betty Goldstein, "Look Out for a Sales Tax," *FP,* 13 Sept. 1943; Betty Goldstein, "Wartime Living," *FP,* 6 Dec. 1943. See also BG-RT, "Thomas Demands Child Care Centers, Other Aids for Women Workers," *FP,* 25 Oct. 1943; Betty Goldstein, "Unions Aid Small Business Fight for Rent Control," *FP,* 16 Feb. 1945; BG-RT, "CIO Women Tell Congress Where They Stand," *FP,* 27 Sept. 1943. On the larger context, see May Jacobs, "'How About Some Meat?': The Office of Price Administration, Consumption Politics, and State Building from the Bottom Up, 1941–1946," *JAH* 54 (Dec. 1997): 910–41.

12. Denning, *Cultural Front,* 147; this summary of her life relies on Bettina Berch, *Radical By Design: The Life and Style of Elizabeth Hawes* (New York, 1988).

13. Elizabeth Hawes, *Why Women Cry, or Wenches With Wrenches* (New York, 1943), 22, 157, xi, xiii, xv, viii, 212, 221.

14. Betty Goldstein, "Girl Worker Finds Revolt Cooking In U.S. Kitchens," *Fisher Eye Opener* (Cleveland), undated; Elizabeth Hawes, quoted in same; for the Federated Press version, see Betty Goldstein, "'Wench With Wrench' on Trail of Male, Worker-Writer Says," *FP,* 24 Nov. 1943.

15. BG-RT, untitled story, *FP,* 30 Sept. 1943; Betty Goldstein, "Miners' Wives Wear Silver Foxes So Say Coal Bosses," *Pacific Coast Shipyard Worker* (San Pedro, Calif.), 25 Nov. 1943; Betty Goldstein, "Wartime Living: Women, Take Over—," *FP,* 17 July 1944. For her concern that with the war effort winding down women would leave the work force, see Betty Goldstein, "Wartime Living: Women Needed on the Job," *FP,* 28 Aug. 1944.

16. Betty Goldstein, "Pretty Posters Won't Stop Turnover of Women in Industry," *FP,* 26 Oct. 1943; Ruth Young quoted in same. See also AS-BG-MK [Miriam Kolkin], "Shipyards Refuse To Hire Women Despite Manpower Crisis," *FP,* 17 Jan. 1945.

17. On her support for Wallace, see BG-RT, "People's Peace Must Guarantee Security of Common Man—Wallace," *FP,* 13 Sept. 1943; see also BG-DS, "Up Peacetime Production 40% for Jobs and Abundance, Wallace Says," *FP,* 28 Oct. 1943. For her position on Soviet-American relations, see Betty Goldstein, "Green and Thomas Hail Soviet Union As Nation Greets USSR," *Utah Labor News,* 19 Nov. 1943, 1; BG-MK, "Unions Join in June 22 'Salute To Russia' Rallies," *FP,* 23 June 1944; BG-RT, "Soviet Organ Says Hopkins 'Long War' Statement Plays into Nazi Hands," *FP,* 15 Oct. 1943; BG-RT, "Citrine's Stand Slows Victory, Soviet Says," *FP,* 24 Sept. 1943; BG-RT, "TWU Convention Demands Labor Unity, European Invasion, FDR Fourth Term," *FP,* 26 Oct. 1943. For her internationalism, see BG-AL, "Old League A Debating

Society—New One Built For Action," *FP,* 19 April 1945; Betty Goldstein, "International Business Conference Opposes Government Role," *Dubuque Leader,* 24 Nov. 1944; BG-MK, "World Finance Dictators Oppose Bretton Woods," *FP,* 4 April 1945.

18. On her anti-racism, see BG-RT, "Official Report Charges Christian Front Behind Anti-Jewish Outbreaks in New York," *FP,* 11 Jan. 1944; BG-RT, "NFCL Demands Probe of Nationwide Pro-Fascist Links," *FP,* 6 Jan. 1944; BG-RT, "Native Fascist Group Will Protect Gentiles For $100," *FP,* 28 Feb. 1944; BG-RT, "New York City Probes Anti-Jewish Outbreaks," *FP,* 30 Dec. 1943; BG-RT, "Chicago Negroes Opening Campaign for Jobs on Transit Lines," *FP,* 24 Sept. 1943; BG-RT, "Christian Fascists Celebrate Coughlin Birthday," *FP,* 29 Oct. 1943; BG-RT, "Jewish Graves Despoiled in Fascist Outbreak," *FP,* 29 Oct. 1943; BG-RT, "Unions Form Group for Anti-Discrimination Legislation," *FP,* 22 Oct. 1943; BG-RT, "PM Expose of Anti-Semitic Outbreaks Brings Boston Probe," *FP,* 20 Oct. 1943; BG-RT, "Negro Parents Fined $10 Each for Keeping Children Out of Jimcrow School," *FP,* 1 Oct. 1943; BG-RT, "Alton Levy Released," *FP,* 15 Nov. 1943. For her praise of union support for keeping Palestine open to Jews, see BG-DS, "All Labor Asks Palestine as Haven for Jews," *FP,* 8 Nov. 1943. For her opposition to anti-communist investigations, see BG-MK, "Dies Report 'Fifth Column Drivel'—Robinson," *FP,* 29 March 1944; RHR-MADF-BG-AL, "California Little Dies Committee Drags Out Old GOP Red Herrings," *FP,* 24 April 1945. See also BG-RT, "Equity Refuses to Expel Robeson," *FP,* 12 Jan. 1944. Her work with Harvey O'Connor and Kolkin is HOC-BG-MK, "Silver Shirt Leader Tells American Fascism's Postwar Plans," *FP,* 14 Nov. 1944. The November 1943 article is Betty Goldstein, "Big Business Getting Desperate, Promising Postwar Jobs," *FP,* 19 Nov. 1943. See also Betty Goldstein, "Monied Interests Are the Real Fascists Here, Seldes Says in New Book," *FP,* 7 Dec. 1943.

19. Betty Goldstein, "NAM Convention Pro-War—For War on Labor, New Deal, Roosevelt," *FP,* 14 Dec. 1943. For the larger story, see Elizabeth A. Fones-Wolf, *Selling Free Enterprise: The Business Assault on Labor and Liberalism, 1945–60* (Urbana, 1994); Howell J. Harris, *The Right to Manage: Industrial Relations Policies of American Business in the 1940s* (Madison, Wisc., 1982).

20. Betty Goldstein, "Peace Now, Treason in Pious Garb," *FP,* 16 Feb. 1944; Bessie Simon, quoted in same; Betty Goldstein, "Well-Healed 'White Collar League' Seen as Disguised Native Fascist Threat," *FP,* 16 March 1944; Betty Goldstein, "Philly Transit Tieup Union-Busting Move By Company and Stooge Outfit," *FP,* 3 Aug. 1944.

21. For her articles on African Americans, see Betty Goldstein "Sales Tax Drive Can Be Defeated Only By Labor Political Action," *Arkansas Labor Journal,* 22 Oct. 1943; BG-MK, "NAACP To Contest Barring of Negroes From Polls in South," *FP,* 9 May 1944; BG-MK, "Freedom Rally Says Unity of All Races Can Bring New World," *FP,* 28 June 1944; BG-MK, "Jimcrow Shipyard Locals Sabotage War Effort, Negroes Charge," *FP,* 22 June 1944; Betty Goldstein, "Jazz World Stars Barnstorm For FDR and Victory," *FP,* 6 Oct. 1944; Betty Goldstein, "Fiery Champion of Negro People to Sit in Congress," *FP,* 21 Dec. 1944; BG-MK, "FEPC To Probe Anti-Negro Hiring of 62 Cincinnati Firms," *FP,* 12 Jan. 1945; BG-MK, "FEPC Hearing Brings Huge United Demonstration," *FP,* 21 Feb. 1945. For her interest in Mexican Americans, see BG-MK, "9 of 12 Sleepy Lagoon Frameup Victims Win Parole," *FP,* 13 June 1944; CM-BG, "Bill Outlawing Discrimination Passes Texas Senate," *FP,* 18 May 1945. For her discussion of racism against Japanese Americans, see MADF-BG, "Outside Influences Seen Responsible for Longshore Japanese-America Incident," *FP,* 21 May 1945. For her interest in the plight of migrant workers, see BG-MK, "Report Uncovers 'Depression' Conditions of Farm Migrant Workers," *FP,* 17 Jan. 1945. On the Jefferson School, see Betty Goldstein, "Workers Flock to Newly Opened Jefferson School," *FP,* 22 March 1944; Marvin E. Gettleman, "Jefferson School of Social Science," *Encyclopedia of the American Left,* 389. See also Benjamin Harris, "The Benjamin Rush Society and Marxist Psychiatry in the United States, 1944–1951," *History of Psychiatry,* 6 (1995): 317–31. On unequal education, see Goldstein, "Negro Pupils Segregated." On Ottley, see Betty Goldstein, "'Negro Problem' a Straw Man, Ottley Says in His New Book," *Shipyard Worker* (Camden, N.J.), 15 Oct. 1943; Ottley, quoted in same. On her hope for

a progressive coalition, see Betty Goldstein, "Unity on the March," *Iowa Farmer-Labor Press* (Council Bluffs), 27 April 1944. On the CIO's commitments, see Goldstein, "Philly Transit."

22. Betty Goldstein, "Workers Mourn for Roosevelt—Their Greatest Friend," *FP,* 16 April 1945; Lizabeth Cohen, *Making a New Deal: Industrial Workers in Chicago, 1919–1939* (Cambridge, U.K., 1990).

23. On a national health plan, see Susan Alexander [signed at bottom by NSA-BG-MK], "Battle Opens for National Health Program," *FP,* 2 April 1946; see also BG-MK, "New Union-Backed Health Plan for Nation Announced," *FP,* 29 Nov. 1944; BG-MK, "South's Case History Shows Need for Federal Health System," *FP,* 4 June 1945; R. H. Rhoda [signed at bottom by RHR-BG-MK], "AFL, CIO United in Compulsory Health Insurance Bill," *FP,* 31 Jan. 1945. On the enfranchisement of African Americans, see BG, "Labor, Negroes Sweep Out Reactionaries in Southern Primaries," *FP,* 9 May 1946.

24. Betty Goldstein, "UE Strikers Fighting for Us, Say People of Bloomfield," *FP,* 16 Jan. 1946; Betty Goldstein, "The People Versus Industrial Greed," *FP,* 22 Jan. 1946.

25. Goldstein, "UE Strikers"; Betty Goldstein, "Post War Living: 'Are They Putting Something Over on Us?' Mrs. Jones Wonders," *FP,* 23 Jan. 1946.

26. Susan Alexander [signed at the bottom by NSA-BG-MS], "Congress of American Women," *FP,* 14 May 1946. For the address of the Congress, see "Greetings Fellow Members," Congress of American Women, *Bulletin,* June 1947, 2. Susan Alexander was a fictious name: Mim Kelber, telephone interview with Daniel Horowitz, 7 Feb. 1998.

27. BG-MK, "Free Press On Stand at Wood-Rankin Probe," *FP,* 8 April 1946; BG-MK, "Demand to Oust Communist Leader Refused by AFL Union," *FP,* 24 Jan. 1946; BG-MS, "Steelworkers Adopt Policy, Rejecting 'Purges, Witch-Hunts,' " *FP,* 16 May 1946; BG-MK, "New York School Board Whitewashes Fascist Teacher," *FP,* 28 Feb. 1946; MK-BG-AL, "Two Navy Yard Unionists Fired for Protesting Anti-Semitic Leaflets," *FP,* 27 April 1945; BG-MK, "KKK Terror Probed in California," *FP,* 12 April 1946; Betty Goldstein, "Expose School Quotas Barring Minority Groups," *FP,* 9 Feb. 1945; BG-MK "New Southern Party Uses Hitler Slogans," *FP,* 20 Feb. 1945; BG-MK, "Start Legal Action to Dissolve New York KKK," *FP,* 30 April 1946; Jack Morrison [signed at bottom by JM-BG-AL], "Christian Americans, U.S. Union Buster Defend Nazi Atrocities," *FP,* 27 April 1945; BG-MK, "Warns Against Postwar Revival of Ku Klux Klan," *FP,* 11 April 1945; GH-BK, "Upholders of 'White Supremacy' Defeat Anti-Polltax Bills in Alabama," *FP,* 21 May 1945; BG-MK, "Housing Parley Urges People's Pressure on Congress," *FP,* 18 March 1946; BG, "Labor, Negroes Sweep Out Reactionaries in Southern Primaries," *FP,* 9 May 1946; BG, "Fiery Cross Burns Over Negro Housing Project Site in New Jersey," *FP,* 21 May 1945; RH-BG "Synagogue in Oregon Defiled With Nazi Signs," *FP,* 21 May 1945; BG, "Ohio Mob Attacks Jewish Merchant With Hitler Methods," *FP,* 21 May 1945; BG, "Anonymous Source of Race Hate Tracts Uncovered in Illinois Probe," *FP,* 21 April 1945. For her story on age discrimination, a subject to which she would later return, see HR-BG, "UAW Authorizes Chrysler Strike to Bar Firing for Age," *FP,* 25 April 1946.

28. Betty Goldstein, "Truman Is 'No. 1 Strikebreaker,' Rail Unionists Say," *FP,* 27 May 1946; Goldstein, "People Versus Industrial Greed"; Betty Goldstein, "Details of Big Business Anti-Labor Conspiracy Uncovered," *FP,* 11 Feb. 1946; Betty Goldstein, "Reveal Details of Secret Anti-Union Parleys of Trust Heads at Waldorf," *Daily Worker,* 14 Feb. 1946, 5.

29. For evidence of her concern for the resurgence of fascism in Europe, see Betty Goldstein, "I. G. Farben Postwar Cartel Exposed in Standard Oil Suit," *FP,* 7 June 1945. For her work on articles about the camps, see Herbert A. Klein [signed on bottom by HAK-BG-AL], "Political Activity Saved Labor Men From Insanity in SS Camps," *FP,* 26 April 1945; this article relied on a story by Peter Furst in *Stars and Stripes* and reminded its authors of Anna Seghers's novel about a camp, *Seventh Cross* (1942); BG-MK, "Inaugurate Black Book of Crimes Against Jews," *FP,* 16 Feb. 1945. For the initial response of Americans to the camps, see Robert H. Abzug, *Inside the Vicious Heart: Americans and the Liberation of the Nazi Concentration Camps* (New York, 1985). Deborah E. Lipstadt, *Beyond Belief: The American Press and the Coming of the Holocaust, 1933–1945* (New York, 1986), analyzes the response of reporters from major

metropolitan newspapers; for the spring of 1945, see especially 250–78; on the ability of writers, including some on the left, to break through the clouds of skepticism, see 275. For the coverage in the *Daily Worker,* see "12 Allied Nations Pledge to Avenge Nazi Murder of Jews," 18 Dec. 1942, 1–2; Sam Brown, "Nazis Slaughter All Estonia Jews," 29 July 1942, 1, 4. Mark J. Greif, "The American Transformation of the Holocaust, 1945–1965" (B.A. honors thesis, Harvard College, 1997), focuses on later responses, including Friedan's.

30. For the article on Churchill, see BG-MK, "'Go Home,' CIO Pickets Tell Churchill," *FP,* 18 March 1946. On Wallace and American-Soviet relations, see BG-MK, "U.S. Will Lose All by War With Russia, Wallace Warns," *FP,* 20 March 1946; for some of the same themes, see Betty Goldstein, "The People Must Carry on for FDR, Mrs. Roosevelt Says," *FP,* 2 April 1946, an article based on Goldstein's interview. For the situation in Iran, see BG-MK, "Fight for Oil Behind Iranian Dispute," *FP,* 25 March 1946. For her concerns in the spring of 1946, see Betty Goldstein, "Report on Spain Shows UN Can Be Force Against Fascism, Lange Says," *FP,* 4 June 1946; Betty Goldstein, "Newspapers' First Job Is To Fight Fascism, Says Noted Soviet Writer," *FP,* 3 May 1946; Betty Goldstein, "Czech Minister In Warning to Labor," *FP,* 8 June 1946. For other expressions of concern about the souring on U.S.-USSR relations, see Betty Goldstein "Russia Left Out of NAM, C. of C. Plans for World Trade Conference," *FP,* 21 July 1944; HP-BG-AL, "Southern Labor Paper Hits U.S. Stand on Argentina, Poland," *FP,* 17 May 1945; MK-BG-AL, "Russian Labor Leader Makes Hit With Hardboiled American Newsmen," *FP,* 7 May 1945; BG-MK, "U.S. Will Lose All By War With Russia, Wallace Warns," *FP,* 20 March 1946; BG-MK, "Truman Path Leads to War, NMU Council Says," *FP,* 2 April 1946; MK-BG-AL, "U.S. Union Leader Urges Seating of Poland at San Francisco," *FP,* 30 April 1945; BG-MK, "Minneapolis AFL Warns of Danger in Anti-Russian Propaganda," *FP,* 24 May 1945.

31. On her concern over hunger, see Betty Goldstein, "Famine Stalks the World," *FP,* 28 May 1946; Betty Goldstein, "The Facts on Food as a Political Weapon," *FP,* 28 May 1946. For a later argument for civil defense against atomic bombs that relied on compliant housewives to defend the nation, see Philip Wylie, *Tomorrow!* (New York, 1954). On atomic warfare, see BG-MK, "Brand Franco Spain Atomic Threat to World Peace," *FP,* 11 April 1946. For her denial that a UE strike hampered atomic research, see BG-MK, "UE Calls Company Research Delay Claim False," *FP,* 13 March 1946. See also, BG-MS, "Majority of Americans Want Manufacture of Atomic Bombs Banned Even in U.S.," *FP,* 16 May 1946. On members of the Curie family, see Betty Goldstein, "Joliot-Curie—A Pioneer of the Atom Age," *FP,* 13 June 1946. For Irene Joliot-Curie's role in WIDF, see U.S. Congress, House of Representatives, Committee on Un-American Activities, *Report on the Congress of American Women* (Washington, D.C., 1949), 4; untitled announcement of reception for Mme. Irene Joliot-Curie, in Congress of American Women, *Bulletin,* Oct. 1946, 2.

32. BG-MK, "Why Scientists Urge Civilian and World Control of Atomic Energy," *FP,* 8 March 1946. On responses to the threat of atomic warfare, see Paul Boyer, *By the Bomb's Early Light: American Thought and Culture at the Dawn of the Atomic Age* (New York, 1985), 51–54; Margot A. Henrikson, *Dr. Strangelove's America: Society and Culture in the Atomic Age* (Berkeley, 1997); I. F. Stone, "Atomic Pie in the Sky," *Nation,* 4 April 1946, 390–91. On the security and diplomatic issues surrounding atomic weaponry, see Gregg Herken, *The Winning Weapon: The Atomic Bomb in the Cold War, 1945–1950* (New York, 1981). On the efforts of scientists, many of whom had worked on the bomb, to secure international control of atomic energy, see Alice K. Smith, *A Peril and A Hope: The Scientists' Movement in America: 1945–47* (Chicago, 1965). It is possible that Friedan's friendship with David Bohm helped provide her with the information and inspiration for her discussion of the dangers of the military use of atomic energy.

33. Betty Goldstein, "Plot for Army Control of Atomic Energy Would Endanger World Peace," *FP,* 8 March 1946.

34. As best I can, I have tried to untangle the relationship between Peck's return and Goldstein's dismissal. See Goldstein to Grievance Committee; Friedan, *Changed My Life,* 9; Kelber, interview, 16 Sept. 1995; James Peck to Carl Haessler, 14 March 1946, Federated Press,

Grievances, 1945–46, TNG Local 3, Shop Files 1935–50, NYNG-NY. For additional information on this controversy see Betty Goldstein to Jack Ryan, 22 May 1946, Federated Press,
Grievances, 1945–46, TNG Local 3, Shop Files, 1935–50, NYNG-NY. On the issue of soldiers
back from the war, see, for example, Edward C. Schneider, "Veteran's Corner," *Guildpaper,*
28 May 1946, 3, 8.

35. Friedan, *Changed My Life,* 9; obituary for James Peck, *NYT,* 13 July 1993, B7; James
Peck, "A Note on Direct Action," *Politics* 3 (Jan. 1946): 21–22; James Tracy, *Direct Action:
Radical Pacifism from the Union Eight to the Chicago Seven* (Chicago, 1996) 37, 55, 68, 99;
Penina M. Glazer, "A Decade of Transition: A Study of Radical Journals of the 1940s" (Ph.D.
diss., Rutgers University, 1970), 64–66; Kelber, interview, 16 Sept. 1995; Alexander L. Crosby
to Carl Haessler, 30 June 1943, Federated Press, Grievances 1945–46, TNG Local 3, Shop
Files 1935–50, NYNG-NY.

36. Stephen Haessler, "Carl Haessler," 226–28, 265–68, 280–83, 289, 293–96; Nelson
Lichtenstein, e-mail to author, 14 March 1997; Lichtenstein, *Most Dangerous Man,* 248–57.

37. Carl [Haessler] to Miriam [Koklin], 2 May 1946, BF-SLRC, 8: 330; see also Kelber,
interview, 16 Sept. 1995.

38. [Betty Goldstein], statement on the situation at Federated Press, spring 1946, possibly
29 April 1946, BF-SLRC, 8: 330; Marc Stone, quoted in [Betty Goldstein], statement; Stone,
quoted and paraphrased in [Betty Goldstein], statement.

39. For clippings of her articles, see BF-SLRC, 8: 331 (oversize); Stone, quoted in [Gold-
stein], statement on FP; markings on Betty Goldstein, "Plot," BF-SLRC, 8: 329; Goldstein,
statement on FP. Her superiors also objected to an article she wrote in April 1946 on betatron,
a new development, similar to the cyclotron: BG-MS-MK, "GE Suppression of Invention
Aiding Cancer Cure Revealed," *FP,* 5 April 1946; on the brief *New York Times* coverage of the
betatron, see " 'Baby' X-Ray Device Developed," *NYT,* 14 April 1947, 37. Stone also objected to
BG-MK, "LEA Bill Will Cripple All Unions, Musicians Warn," *FP,* 17 April 1946. Goldstein
noted that about four dozen union papers printed her story on atomic power, even though it
was not, strictly speaking, a labor story: [Betty Goldstein], handwritten note, late spring 1946:
BF-SLRC, 8: 330; [Goldstein], statement on FP.

40. Marc Stone, quoted in Goldstein to Grievance Committee; Goldstein to Grievance
Committee.

41. For evidence of personality conflicts see [Carl Haessler] to Jack Ryan, 20 Aug. 1945; Al
[Fred G. Larke?] to Carl [Haessler], 1 July 1945, Negotiations, 1944–45, TNG Local 3, Shop
Files, 1935–50, Federated Press, NYNG-NY.

42. On the situation in the guild, see Robert G. Picard, "Anticommunism in the New York
Newspaper Guild," in *With Just Cause: Unionization of the American Journalist* (Lanham, Md.,
1991), ed. Walter M. Brasch, 277–92; Daniel Leab, telephone conversation with Daniel Horowitz, 9 July 1996; Denning, *Cultural Front,* 90; Sol Jacobson, "The Fourth Estate: A Study of
the American Newspaper Guild" (Ph.D. diss., New School for Social Research, 1960).

7. *UE News,* 1946–52

1. Betty Friedan, quoted in Justine Blau, *Betty Friedan* (New York, 1990), 29. To date the
change in employment, see Betty Friedan, Application for Employment at Time Inc., 1 July
1951, BF-SLRC, 1: 61.

2. For the change in corporate strategy, see Ronald W. Schatz, *The Electrical Workers: A
History of Labor at General Electric and Westinghouse, 1923–60* (Urbana, 1983), 167.

3. Betty Friedan, *"It Changed My Life": Writings on the Women's Movement,* 1985 edition
(New York, 1976), 8–9; Fred Zeserson, telephone conversation with Daniel Horowitz, 22 June
1996. See also, Mim Kelber, telephone interview with Daniel Horowitz, 16 Sept. 1995.

4. Robert Korstad and Nelson Lichtenstein, "Opportunities Found and Lost: Labor, Radicals, and the Early Civil Rights Movement," *JAH* 75 (Dec. 1988): 786–811. See also Nelson
Lichtenstein, "From Corporatism to Collective Bargaining: Organized Labor and the Eclipse

of Social Democracy in the Postwar Era," in *The Rise and Fall of the New Deal Order, 1930–1980*, ed. Steve Fraser and Gary Gerstle (Princeton, 1989), 122–52; George Lipsitz, *Rainbow at Midnight: Labor and Culture in the 1940s* (Urbana, 1994). On the situation of unions in the war and the immediate postwar period, see Nelson Lichtenstein, *Labor's War at Home: The CIO in World War II* (New York, 1982); Gary Gerstle, "The Working Class Goes to War," in *The War in American Culture: Society and Consciousness During World War II*, ed. Lewis A. Erenberg and Susan E. Hirsch (Chicago, 1996), 105–27.

5. On the linking of the CIO and the CP, see Nelson Lichtenstein, *The Most Dangerous Man in Detroit: Walter Reuther and the Fate of American Labor* (New York, 1995), 256–57. On American anti-communism, see Richard G. Powers, *Not Without Honor: The History of American Anticommunism* (New York, 1995), and Ellen Schrecker, "The Age of McCarthyism," in *The Age of McCarthyism: A Brief History with Documents*, ed. Ellen Schrecker (Boston, 1994), 1–94. For general treatments of the history of the left in the U.S., see Michael Kazin, "The Agony and Romance of the American Left," *AHR* 100 (Dec. 1995): 1488–1512; Kevin Boyle, *The UAW and the Heyday of American Liberalism, 1945–1968* (Ithaca, 1995); Paul Buhle, *Marxism in the United States: Remapping the History of the American Left* (London, 1987). On the relationship between the Old Left of the 1930s and 1940s and the New Left of the 1960s, see Maurice Isserman, *If I Had a Hammer: The Death of the Old Left and the Birth of the New Left* (New York, 1987); James Tracy, *Direct Action: Radical Pacifism from the Union Eight to the Chicago Seven* (Chicago, 1996); Michael Honey, *Southern Labor and Black Civil Rights: Organizing Memphis Workers* (Urbana, 1993); Penina M. Glazer, "A Decade of Transition: A Study of Radical Journals of the 1940s" (Ph.D. diss., Rutgers University, 1970); Penina M. Glazer, "From the Old Left to the New: Radical Criticism in the 1940s," *AQ* 24 (Dec. 1972): 584–603. On the process by which the Mattachine Society, the path-breaking organization of homosexuals, emerged out of the Communist Party and the 1948 Progressive Party campaign, see John D'Emilio, "Dreams Deferred: The Birth and Betrayal of America's First Gay Liberation Movement," in *Making Trouble: Essays on Gay History, Politics, and the University* (New York, 1992), 17–56.

On the recent scholarly treatments of the Old Left in the 1940s and 1950s, see Michael E. Brown et al., *New Studies in the Politics and Culture of U.S. Communism* (New York, 1993); Lipsitz, *Rainbow at Midnight*; Maurice Isserman, *Which Side Were You On? The American Communist Party during the Second World War* (Middletown, Conn., 1982); Dorothy Healey and Maurice Isserman, *Dorothy Healey Remembers: A Life in the Communist Party* (New York, 1990); Fraser M. Ottanelli, *The Communist Party of the United States: From the Depression to World War II* (New Brunswick, N.J., 1991). For the older but standard study, see Joseph R. Starobin, *American Communism in Crisis, 1943–1957* (Cambridge, Mass., 1972). W. J. Rorabaugh, "Communist Biography and Autobiography," unpublished bibliographical essay, copy in author's possession, provides a useful guide to memoirs and biographies. For discussions of African Americans in the party, see Robin D. G. Kelley, *Hammer and Hoe: Alabama Communists During the Great Depression* (Chapel Hill, 1990); Nell I. Painter, *The Narrative of Hosea Hudson, His Life as a Negro Communist in the South* (Cambridge, Mass., 1979); Gerald Horne, "The Red and the Black: The Communist Party and African-Americans in Historical Perspective," in Brown et al., *New Studies*, 199–237. Among the most recent books on the relationship of the left and intellectuals is Harvey Teres, *Renewing the Left: Politics, Imagination, and the New York Intellectuals* (New York, 1996).

6. Isserman, *If I Had a Hammer*, 3–34.

7. In 1949, to cite just one example, the president of Oregon State College fired two professors because they had supported Wallace a year earlier: David Caute, *The Fellow-Travellers: Intellectual Friends of Communism*, rev. ed. (New Haven, 1988), 289. For details on the costs of McCarthyism, see Ellen Schrecker, "'A Good Deal of Trauma': The Impact of McCarthyism," *Many Are the Crimes: McCarthyism in America* (New York, 1998).

8. Adlai E. Stevenson, "Women, Husbands, and History," speech at Smith College, 6 June 1955, in *The Papers of Adlai E. Stevenson*, ed. Walter Johnson (Boston, 1974), 4: 495, 497, 498,

501, with the quotes on 495 and 501. For her commentary on the speech, see Betty Friedan, *The Feminine Mystique* (New York, 1963), 60–61.

9. Several things have kept us from seeing in the postwar period what the historian Ellen DuBois has called "left-feminism" that flourished among women in community councils, unions, and the Communist Party. Member of the National Woman's Party, who called themselves "feminists," and Popular Front activists, who had a more legitimate claim to that label, aired their disagreements. Their differences, as well as the power of McCarthyism, have made it difficult to recognize the extraordinary flowering of feminist consciousness and activity right after 1945. The phrase comes from Ellen C. DuBois, "Eleanor Flexner and the History of American Feminism," *Gender and History* 3 (spring 1991): 84; on the social bases and obscuring of this movement, see Michael Denning, *The Cultural Front: The Laboring of American Culture in the Twentieth Century* (London, 1996), 136. For her own description as a college-educated woman of her generation concerned with progressive causes, see [Betty Friedan], "Insert-left wing thought," c. 1960, 2, BF-SLRC, 16: 597. The career of Sylvia Cohen Scribner runs remarkably parallel to that of Goldstein/Friedan. A Jew from New Bedford, Massachusetts, Scribner won the Hamm Prize and graduated from Smith, Phi Beta Kappa and *summa cum laude*. She majored in labor economics and Douglas inspired her to work for the UE, which she did as an organizer and a research director from 1944 to 1958. At the UE she focused on a wide range of issues, including justice for workers, women, and African Americans. She switched to psychology in 1961, earned her Ph.D. in the discipline, and had a distinguished career in which she combined progressive social action and scientific work. See Sylvia Scribner, *Mind and Social Practice: Selected Writings of Sylvia Scribner,* ed. Ethel Tobach, Rachel J. Falmagne, Mary B. Parlee, Laura M. W. Martin, and Aggie S. Kapelman (Cambridge, U.K., 1997). On the activism of working women, see Nancy Gabin, *Feminism in the Labor Movement: Women and the United Automobile Workers, 1935–1975* (Ithaca, 1990); Dorothy Sue Cobble, *Dishing It Out: Waitresses and Their Unions in the Twentieth Century* (Urbana, 1991); Dorothy Sue Cobble, "Recapturing Working-Class Feminism: Union Women in the Postwar Era," in *Not June Cleaver: Women and Gender in Postwar America, 1945–1960,* ed. Joanne Meyerowitz (Philadelphia, 1994), 57–83. The best place to begin a more general examination of women's work is through the writings of Alice Kessler-Harris, especially *Women Have Always Worked: A Historical Overview* (Old Westbury, N.Y., 1981), *A Woman's Wage: Historical Meanings and Social Consequences* (Lexington, Ky., 1990), *Out to Work: A History of America's Wage-Earning Women in the United States* (New York, 1982).

10. Cobble, "Recapturing Working-Class Feminism," 57–83; Nancy F. Cott, *The Grounding of Modern Feminism* (New Haven, 1987); Gabin, *Feminism in the Labor Movement;* Annelise Orleck, *Common Sense and a Little Fire: Women and Working-Class Politics in the United States, 1900–1965* (Chapel Hill, 1995). On the fight over the Equal Rights Amendment, see Cynthia Harrison, *On Account of Sex: The Politics of Women's Issues, 1945–1968* (Berkeley, 1988), 3–23. On feminism and the left generally, see Mari Jo Buhle, *Women and American Socialism, 1870–1920* (Urbana, 1981); for the 1930s, see Susan Ware, *American Women in the 1930s: Holding Their Own* (Boston, 1982), 117–39; Sherna Gluck, "Socialist Feminism Between the Two World Wars: Insights from Oral History," in *Decades of Discontent: The Women's Movement, 1920–1940,* ed. Lois Scharf and Joan M. Jensen (Westport, Conn., 1983), 279–97. On the Women's Councils in the Depression, see Rosalyn Baxandall, "The Question Seldom Asked: Women and the CPUSA," in Brown et al., *New Studies,* 148–57. On the wartime experience of working women, see Sherna B. Gluck, *Rosie the Riveter Revisited: Women, the War, and Social Change* (Boston, 1987); Maureen Honey, *Creating Rosie the Riveter: Class, Gender, and Propaganda During World War II* (Amherst, 1984). For a history of American women in the 1940s, see Susan M. Hartmann, *The Home Front and Beyond: American Women in the 1940s* (Boston, 1982).

11. Eleanor Flexner to Pat King, 13 May 1983, EF-SLRC, folder 29. For additional material on which Flexner worked, see Irene Epstein, comp., *A Bibliography on the Negro Woman in the United States* (New York, c. 1953); Irene Epstein and Doxey A. Wilkerson, eds., *Questions and*

Answers on The Woman Question (New York, 1953), copy in EF-SLRC, folder 29. On the cover of *Questions,* someone, probably Flexner herself, initialed "EF." Wilkerson was an African American man involved in Old Left circles. Jacqueline Van Voris, telephone conversation with Helen L. Horowitz, 18 Oct. 1995, noted that Flexner used two pseudonyms, Betty Feldman and Irene Epstein. On Flexner's experience in the Old Left, see Eleanor Flexner, interviews by Jacqueline Van Voris, New York, N.Y. and Northampton, Mass., 8 Jan. 1977 [1–32], 15 Jan. 1977 [32–59], 16 Oct. 1982 [60–79], and 11 May 1983 [80–103], EF-SLRC, folder 6; DuBois, "Flexner," 81–90; Ellen Fitzpatrick, foreword to Eleanor Flexner and Ellen Fitzpatrick, *Century of Struggle: The Women's Rights Movement in the United States,* enlarged (Cambridge, Mass., 1996), ix–xxvii; [Eleanor Flexner], "The Woman Question," Jefferson School of Social Science, [1953–54], 1–6, EF-SLRC, folder 29. In 1982, when Flexner looked back over her life, she tended to minimize the impact of Marxism on her development: compare [Flexner], "Woman Question" with Flexner, interview, 70. On the Jefferson School, see Marvin E. Gettleman, "Jefferson School of Social Science," *Encyclopedia of the American Left,* ed. Mari Jo Buhle, Paul Buhle, and Dan Georgakas (New York, 1990), 389. The papers for the Jefferson School are in TL-NYU. For a later critique of *The Feminine Mystique* by Flexner, on the grounds that it minimized the problematic nature of work outside the home for men and women, see [Eleanor Flexner], "These days it is not fashionable . . . ," typescript of talk, probably 1970s, EF-SLRC, folder 32.

12. Amy Swerdlow, *Women Strike for Peace: Traditional Motherhood and Radical Politics in the 1960s* (Chicago, 1993), 37–38. This summary on the congress relies on Kathleen A. Weigand, "Vanguards of Women's Liberation: The Old Left and the Continuity of the Women's Movement in the United States, 1945–1970s" (Ph.D. diss., Ohio State University, 1995), 72–117; Amy Swerdlow, "The Congress of American Women: Left-Feminist Peace Politics in the Cold War," in *U.S. History as Women's History: New Feminist Essays,* ed. Linda K. Kerber, Alice Kessler-Harris, and Kathryn K. Sklar (Chapel Hill, 1995), 296–312; Amy Swerdlow, "Congress of American Women," *Encyclopedia of the American Left,* 161–62. Weigand emphasizes the continuity between Old and New Left, while Swerdlow sees in the destruction of the congress the dissolution of what she calls "the conscious connection between feminism, social reform, and peace protest" before and after the early 1950s: Swerdlow, "Left-Feminist," 312. For more information on the congress, see the papers of Women's International Democratic Federation and Congress of American Women in SSCSC. On Harriet Magil, see Swerdlow, "Left-Feminist," 312; on Goldstein's relationship, see Abe Magil to Betty Goldstein, 28 Jan. 1946, BF-SLRC, 49: 1783. For the roles of Douglas and Young, see 1949 letterhead of Congress of American Women, U.S. Congress, House of Representatives, Committee on Un-American Activities, *Report on the Congress of American Women* (Washington, D.C., 1949), 113. On Lerner, see Weigand, "Vanguards," 110, 233, 240; for her novel set in Vienna in the mid-1930s, see Gerda Lerner, *No Farewell: A Novel* (New York, 1955). On Flexner, see Flexner, interview, 67, 70. Weigand, "Vanguards," 288.

13. Swerdlow, "Left-Feminist," 306. For Flexner's attack on the ERA, see Betty Feldman, "Equal Rights Amendment Perils Women Workers," *Worker,* 16 Sept. 1951; Betty Feldman, "It Would Torpedo Laws Safeguarding Women Workers," *Worker,* 3 May 1953, clippings in EF-SLRC, folder 29.

14. Though she does not discuss Friedan's situation, the best treatment of the prominent role of women's issues in radical circles in the 1940s and 1950s is Weigand, "Vanguards," 218–65, on which this discussion of progressive feminism relies heavily. See also Gerald Zahavi, "Passionate Commitments: Race, Sex, and Communism at Schenectady General Electric, 1932–1954," *JAH* 83 (Sept. 1996): 514–48; Baxandall, "Question Seldom Asked," 141–61. For other treatments of the relationship between Communism and women's issues, see Robert Shaffer, "Women and the Communist Party, USA, 1930–1940," *Socialist Review* 45 (May 1979): 73–118; Ellen K. Trimberger, "Women in the Old and New Left: The Evolution of a Politics of Personal Life," *Feminist Studies* 5 (fall 1979): 432–61; Deborah A. Gerson, "'Is Family Devotion Now Subversive?' Familialism against McCarthyism," in Meyerowitz, *Not*

June Cleaver, 151–76; Van Gosse, "'To Organize in Every Neighborhood, in Every Home': The Gender Politics of American Communists Between the Wars," *Radical History Review* 50 (spring 1991): 109–41; Kathleen A. Brown, "Ella Reeve Bloor: Politics of the Personal in the American Communist Party" (Ph.D. diss., University of Washington, 1996); Lisa A. Kannenberg, "From World War to Cold War: Women Electrical Workers and Their Union, 1940–1955" (M.A. thesis, University of North Carolina, Charlotte, 1990); Constance Coiner, *Better Red: The Writing and Resistance of Tillie Olsen and Meridel Le Sueur* (New York, 1995); Paula Rabinowitz, *Labor and Desire: Women's Revolutionary Fiction in Depression America* (Chapel Hill, 1991); Barbara Epstein, "My Ambivalence About Feminism," unpublished paper, copy in author's possession; Kim Chernin, *In My Mother's House: A Daughter's Story* (New Haven, 1983). On another, more Bohemian strand of feminism, see Judith Schwarz, *Radical Feminists of Heterodoxy: Greenwich Village 1912–1940,* rev. ed. (Norwich, Vt., 1986). The discussion of Millard in this and the following paragraphs relies on Betty Millard, "Woman Against Myth," *New Masses* 66 (30 Dec. 1947): 7–10 and "Woman Against Myth: II," (6 Jan. 1948): 7–10. On Millard, see Weigand, "Vanguards," 108–109, 139–44; "Status of Women Commission," Congress of American Women, *Bulletin,* March–April 1948, 4. On her work in the 1950s as an anti-imperialist writer on Latin America, see Van Gosse, *Where the Boys Are: Cuba, Cold War America and the Making of a New Left* (London, 1993), 26. On the attention to women's history in the Old Left, see Weigand, "Vanguards," 235–41. For a somewhat different strand of women's activism, note the way women in the Cold War peace movement questioned traditional prescriptions of women's place: Susan Dion, "Challenges to Cold War Orthodoxy: Women and Peace, 1945–1963" (Ph.D. diss., Marquette University, 1991); Harriet H. Alonso, "Mayhem and Moderation: Women Peace Activists during the McCarthy Era," in Meyerowitz, *Not June Cleaver,* 128–50.

15. Millard, "Woman Against Myth," 30 Dec. 1947, 7; Millard, "Woman Against Myth II," 6 Jan. 1948, 7.

16. Millard, "Woman Against Myth," 30 Dec. 1947, 10.

17. Ferdinand Lundberg and Marynia F. Farnham, *Modern Woman: The Lost Sex* (New York, 1947), 166.

18. Millard, "Woman Against Myth," 30 Dec. 1947, 8; Millard, "Woman Against Myth II," 6 Jan. 1948, 10.

19. Elizabeth Hawes, *Hurry Up Please* (New York, 1946), 45, 82–83, 239. For evidence that Hawes's work was well known in circles within which Friedan moved: see J.T.M., "Every Day Is Ladies' Day With Liz," *National Guardian,* 18 Oct. 1948, 11. In addition to the books discussed here, Hawes published *It's Still Spinach* (1954), in which she argued for liberation through dress. For an illuminating discussion of Hawes, see Denning, *Cultural Front,* 148–51.

20. Bettina Berch, *Radical By Design: The Life and Style of Elizabeth Hawes* (New York, 1988), 147; Elizabeth Hawes, *Anything But Love: A Complete Digest of the Rules For Feminine Behavior From Birth to Death; Given Out In Print, On Film, and Over the Air; Read, Seen, Listened to Monthly By Some 340,000,000 American Women* (New York, 1948), 3, 7, 9, 43, 69, 107, 133, 225, 257; the quote is on 257.

21. This summary of the views of progressive feminists relies heavily on Weigand, "Vanguards." On Flynn, see Elizabeth Gurley Flynn, "Hitler's 3 K's for Woman—An American Rehash," *Political Affairs,* April 1947, reprinted in *Words on Fire: The Life and Writing of Elizabeth Gurley Flynn,* ed. Rosalyn F. Baxandall (New Brunswick, N.J., 1987), 202–8, with the quote in the title; this book, both the introduction and the reprinted essays, explores the relationship between Communism and feminism. Flynn might also have pointed to the anti-communism of Philip Wylie, author of *Generation of Vipers* (1942): see Truman F. Keefer, *Philip Wylie* (Boston, 1977). On Flexner, see Irene Epstein, "Woman Under the Double Standard," *JL* 4 (Oct. 1950): 8–12; see also letters in response to her article, "Letters from Readers," *JL* 5 (Jan. 1951): 31. For a story of anti-Semitism directed against a Jewish woman, see Edith Anderson, "Loretta," *New Masses* 64 (29 July 1947): 10–13.

22. Weigand, "Vanguards," 256; [Flexner], "Woman Question," 1–6, with the quote on 4.

This discussion relies on Weigand, "Vanguards." See also Ruth McKenney, *Love Story* (New York, 1950), in which the author chronicles her life in the Old Left in Manhattan during the 1930s, celebrates her democratic marriage in the postwar period that helped her to sustain her career as a writer, and attacks "female scabs and Benedict Arnolds" who called on women to return to the kitchen: especially 118–21, 136–37, 230–33, with the quote on 118.

23. Eve Merriam, "Occupation: Housewife," *New Masses* 62 (28 Jan. 1947): 21; Vivian Howard, "Housewives Are Simply Wonderful," *New Masses* 66 (23 Dec. 1947): 9–10. A key figure in the debate on women's issues in progressive circles, especially the nature of housework, was the California Marxist and party member Mary Inman, someone first radicalized through her involvement with the I.W.W. In 1940 she published *In Woman's Defense*, in which she used the word "feminist" positively. As Robert Shaffer has noted, what Inman wrote had strong resemblances "with feminist literature of the 1970s": Shaffer, "Women and the Communist Party," 84. Weigand, "Vanguards," 31–71, provides the most recent and fullest discussion of Inman and argues that most previous treatments of her overemphasized her exceptionalism, in good measure because they bought the story that the party had squelched her and her writings. See also Mary Inman, *In Women's Defense* (Los Angeles, 1940); Sherna B. Gluck, "Mary Inman (1895–1985)," *Encyclopedia of the American Left*, 361–62.

Drawing on the work of Jerome Davis, which Goldstein had read in Dorothy Douglas's course and which in turn relied on Elizabeth B. Schlesinger's 1933 indictment of women's magazines, Inman wrote of "The Culture of Subjugation": Inman, *In Woman's Defense*, 67, 75. See Jerome Davis, *Capitalism and Its Culture* (New York, 1935), 306–7, 536, for his reference to Elizabeth B. Schlesinger, "They Say Women Are Emancipated," *New Republic* 77 (13 Dec. 1933): 125–27. For the arguments and campaign against Inman, see Weigand, "Vanguards," 52–71; A[vram]. Landy, *Marxism and the Woman Question* (New York, 1943).

24. W.O. to *Worker*, 10 Nov. 1946, 11, quoted in Weigand, "Vanguards," 243; Baxandall, "Question Seldom Asked," 156. This discussion relies on Baxandall, "Question Seldom Asked"; Weigand, "Vanguards." Generally speaking, Weigand provides a more positive assessment of the party's consideration of women's issues, something she sees as a response to pressure from the grass roots. See Elizabeth Gurley Flynn, "The Feminine Ferment," *New Masses* 63 (13 May 1947): 6–9 for her call on progressives to pay more attention to women's issues.

25. On the story of how they met, I am relying on Zeserson, telephone conversation. For a description of the apartment, see Friedan, *Changed My Life*, 9. On Carl, see Paul Wilkes, "Mother Superior to Women's Lib," *NYTM*, 29 Nov. 1970, 141; to date the marriage, see Sondra Henry and Emily Taitz, *Betty Friedan: Fighter for Women's Rights* (Hillside, N.J., 1990), 38. The wedding announcement is in BF-SLRC, photograph box, folder 27. In 1985 Betty Friedan noted that people in her generation changed their names as "some kind of an attempt to distance yourself from that painful experience" of growing up in cities like Peoria "where you were very marginal as a Jew": Betty Friedan, "Women and Jews: The Quest for Selfhood," *Congress Monthly*, Feb.–March 1985, 8.

26. Friedan, quoted in Marcia Cohen, *The Sisterhood: The True Story of the Women Who Changed the World* (New York, 1988), 66; Goldstein, essay written at Smith College, quoted in Henry and Taitz, *Friedan*, 39; Friedan, quoted in Cohen, *Sisterhood*, 66; Friedan, quoted in Henry and Taitz, *Friedan*, 37–38.

27. "Reactionary Propaganda Exposed: Survey Discovers—Women Must Work!" *UEN*, 25 Aug. 1945; Fred Zeserson, telephone conversation. On the *National Guardian*, see Dan Georgakas, "*National Guardian* and *Guardian*," *Encyclopedia of the American Left*, 502–4.

For information on women in the UE see Zahavi, "Passionate Commitments"; Schatz, *Electrical Workers*; Ruth Milkman, *Gender at Work: The Dynamics of Job Segregation by Sex During World War II* (Urbana, 1987); Lisa Kannenberg, "The Impact of the Cold War on Women's Trade Union Activism: The UE Experience," *Labor History* 34 (spring–summer 1993): 309–23; Kannenberg, "From World War to Cold War"; Nancy B. Palmer, "Gender, Sexuality, and Work: Women and Men in the Electrical Industry, 1940–1955" (Ph.D. diss.,

Boston College, 1995). Generally speaking, Kannenberg and Schatz emphasize the genuineness of the UE's commitments, despite opposition within the union. Palmer, "Gender, Sexuality, and Work," more skeptical of women's gains in the UE, focuses on how the construction of gender in labor unions, including the UE, limited women's advances: see especially chapter 4.

Also relevant as background information on the UE, American radicalism, and women radicals are the interviews in the Oral History of the American Left at Tamiment Library, New York University, especially those of Hodee Edwards, Ruth Glassman, Louis Harrap, Rose Kryzak, Luisa [sic], Elaine Perry, Rose Podmaka, Sadie Rosenberg, Annette Rubinstein, and Ed Weise.

28. Schatz, *Electrical Workers*, xiii; Robert H. Zieger, *The CIO, 1935–1955* (Chapel Hill, 1995), 82, 240, with the quotes on 240, 254, and 376; David Montgomery, "Introduction," to K. B. Gilden [Katya Gilden and Bert Gilden], *Between the Hills and the Sea* (Ithaca, 1989). For an interview on the UE with David Montgomery, a historian who was in the UE in the 1950s, see Paul Buhle and Mark Naison, "Once Upon a Shop Floor: An Interview with David Montgomery," *Radical History Review* 23 (winter 1979–80): 37–53. Zieger, *CIO*, 253–93, assesses the role of Communists in the CIO. On the relationship between the UE and the party, see Ronald L. Filippelli and Mark McColloch, *Cold War in the Working Class: The Rise and Decline of the United Electrical Workers* (Albany, N.Y., 1995), especially 1–11, 85; Bert Cochran, *Labor and Communism: The Conflict that Shaped American Unions* (Princeton, 1977), 295; Schatz, *Electrical Workers*, 229–32.

On the relationship between the Communist Party and unions in general, see Cochran, *Labor and Communism*; Harvey A. Levenstein, *Communism, Anti-Communism, and the CIO* (Westport, Conn., 1981); Steven Rosswurm, ed. *The CIO's Left-Led Unions* (New Brunswick, N.J., 1992); Roger Keeran, "The Communist Influence on American Labor," in Brown et al., *New Studies*, 163–97. On the changing approaches to the history of the Communist Party, see Maurice Isserman, "Three Generations: Historians View American Communism," *Labor History* 26 (fall 1985): 517–45; Michael E. Brown, "The History of U.S. Communism," in Brown et al., *New Studies*, 15–44.

29. Zieger, *CIO*, 255; Zahavi, "Passionate Commitments," uses a local perspective to explore the commitment of the UE and the party to racial and gender equality. The discussion in this paragraph relies on Schatz, *Electrical Workers*, 129–30. For Goldstein's interest in the issue of seniority for African Americans, see BG-MK, "Unions Asked To Study Seniority Rights of Negroes," *FP*, 29 March 1945.

30. Schatz, *Electrical Workers*, 30, 89, 116–27, 124, 129–30; Milkman, *Gender at Work*, 77–78; Zieger, *CIO*, 87; Schatz, *Electrical Workers*, 124; Zahavi, "Passionate Commitments." For a discussion of ideas about equitable pay or comparable worth, see Kessler-Harris, *Woman's Work*, especially 98–129.

31. Friedan, *Changed My Life*, 16.

32. Flexner, interview, 62. Helen K. Chinoy, who shared a house with Friedan in the summer of 1944 or 1945, confirmed this judgment that in the 1940s party membership was not the critical issue among those on the left who identified themselves with a wide range of political positions: Helen K. Chinoy, interview by Daniel Horowitz, Northampton, Mass., 7 Oct. 1995.

33. Robert Friedman, "UE: Ten Years Strong," *New Masses* 60 (17 Sept. 1946): 3. The staff of the *UE News* shifted in composition from time to time, but this was the line-up at a crucial moment in the early 1950s. For information on Wright, the editor, see James J. Matles and James Higgins, *Them and Us: Struggles of a Rank-and-File Union* (Englewood Cliffs, N.J., 1974), 73.

34. Friedan, *Changed My Life*, 8–9; James Lerner, interview with Daniel Horowitz, Brooklyn, N.Y., 21 Aug. 1995; Milton Meltzer, *Betty Friedan: A Voice for Women's Rights* (New York, 1985), 23.

35. Meltzer, *Friedan*, 23–25; Friedan, quoted in same, 23, 25; B.G., review of Fielding

Burke, *Sons of the Stranger, UEN,* 24 Jan. 1948, 7. In 1951 she earned about one hundred dollars a week: Friedan, Application. This is roughly the same amount a woman factory worker for GE earned in the period.

36. Betty Goldstein, review of Howard Fast, *The American, UEN,* 23 Nov. 1946, 11; Betty Goldstein, "NAM Does Gleeful War Dance to Profits, Wage Cuts, Taft Law," *UEN,* 13 Dec. 1947, 4; Betty Goldstein, "A Tale of 'Sacrifice': A Story of Equality in the United States, 1951," *March of Labor,* May 1951, 16–18, BF-SLRC, 8: 334; for another of her articles in this publication, see Betty Goldstein, "Shadows Over Lawrence," *March of Labor,* March 1952, 13–15 and 27–28; Betty Goldstein, "It'll Take a Strong Union To End Winchester Tyranny," *UEN,* 7 Dec. 1946, 9; Betty Goldstein, "Fighting Together: We Will Win!" *UEN,* 31 May 1947, 5, 8; Betty Goldstein, "Labor Builds New Political Organization To Fight for a People's Congressman," *UEN,* 23 Aug. 1947, 4.

37. Betty Goldstein, "Plain People of America Organize New Political Party of Their Own," *UEN,* 31 July 1948, 6–7; B.G., review of movie "Crossfire," *UEN,* 9 Aug. 1947, 8–9; Betty Goldstein, "CIO Sold Out Fight for FEPC, T-H Repeal, Rep. Powell Reveals," *UEN,* 17 Apr. 1950, 4; B.G., review of Sinclair Lewis, *Kingsblood Royal, UEN,* 6 Sept. 1947, 7; B.G., review of movie "Gentleman's Agreement," *UEN,* 22 Nov. 1947, 11. For other progressive pieces, see Betty Goldstein, "People's Needs Forgotten: Big Business Runs Govt.," *UEN,* 12 May 1947, 5; Betty Goldstein, "In Defense of Freedom! The People Vs. the UnAmerican Committee," *UEN,* 8 Nov. 1947, 6–7; Betty Goldstein, "They Can't Shove the IBEW Down Our Throats," *UEN,* 4 Sept. 1948, 6–7; Betty Goldstein, "UnAmerican Hearing Exposed as Plot By Outsiders to Keep Grip on UE Local," *UEN,* 22 Aug. 1949, 4; Betty Goldstein, "New NAM Theme Song: Labor-Management 'Teamwork,'" *UEN,* 9 Jan. 1950, 5.

38. Goldstein, "People's Needs Forgotten"; Goldstein, "In Defense of Freedom!"; Goldstein, "Can't Shove"; Goldstein, "UnAmerican Hearing Exposed"; Goldstein, "New NAM Theme Song."

39. According to [Betty Friedan], "Curriculum Vitae of Betty Friedan," c. 1973, BF-SLRC, 1: 61, Daniel was born in 1948. Since she published few if any articles in the *UE News* between early September 1948 and late August 1949, this is the most likely period of her maternity leave. Betty Friedan, "Accomplishments," manuscript, c. 1959, 1–2, BF-SLRC, 1: 62, dates the arrival in Parkway Village in 1950. Betty Friedan, "Accomplishments (student and creative)," 2, c. 1960, BF-SLRC, 39: 1363 dates the departure from Parkway Village in 1955. If that is accurate, it is not clear where the Friedans lived in 1955–56. On the maternity leave, see Betty Friedan, interview with Daniel Horowitz, Santa Monica, Calif., 18 March 1987; Friedan, *Changed My Life,* 15.

40. On her trips to factories, see Lerner, interview. For her coverage of Latinas, see Betty Goldstein, "'It's a Union That Fights for All the Workers,'" *UEN,* [day unclear] Sept. 1951, 6–7. On what housewives paid, see Betty Goldstein, "Price Cuts Promised in Press Invisible to GE Housewives," *UEN,* 1 Feb. 1947, 7; on the inseparability of issues, see Chinoy, interview; on people's struggles, see Betty Goldstein, "Union Members Want to Know—WHO Has Too Much Money to Spend," *UEN,* 26 March 1951, 8; Dory Santos, quoted in Betty Goldstein, "Union That Fights for All the Workers," 6; Betty Goldstein, "UE Drive on Wage, Job Discrimination Wins Cheers from Women Members," *UEN,* 16 April 1951, 6.

41. [Betty Goldstein], *UE Fights for Women Workers,* UE Publication no. 232, June 1952 (New York), 5. To authenticate her authorship, I am relying on the following: Friedan, Horowitz interview; Lerner, interview; Betty Friedan, postcard to author, late August 1995, author's possession; Meltzer, *Friedan,* 25. Friedan's account of the origins of the pamphlet is that while covering a strike in New Jersey for the *UE News* in the late 1940s or early 1950s, she delineated more clearly how the workers, most of them women, were discriminated against. She wrote up an article, she remembers, and received encouragement from her superiors at the UE to turn what she had observed into a pamphlet: Friedan, Horowitz interview.

42. [Goldstein], *UE Fights,* 9–18, 26–27, 38, with the quotes on 26, 27, and 38; Kannenberg, "Impact," 318.

43. [Betty Goldstein] *Women Fight For a Better Life! UE Picture Story of Women's Role in American History* (New York, 1953), 24, 17, 20. For her statement that she believes she authored this, see Betty Friedan, postcard to author. The last piece of hers I have been able to locate in the *UE News* was Betty Goldstein, "One Out of Every Two Workers Unemployed—Victims of CIO Sellout on Speedup," *UE News*, 18 Feb. 1952.

44. On the conference, which took place in New York in early May 1953, see Kannenberg, "Impact," 318. The issues appear in "Resolution on Job Discrimination," "Resolution on Legislative Action," and "National Conference on the Problems of Working Women," mimeographed documents in BF-SLRC, 8: 336.

45. The summary in this and the following paragraph draws heavily on Palmer, "Gender, Sexuality, and Work." For a thoughtful discussion on the gendering of language in the labor movement, see Elizabeth Faue, *Community of Suffering and Struggle: Women, Men, and the Labor Movement in Minneapolis, 1915–1945* (Chapel Hill, 1991), 69–99.

46. For Friedan's continuing disappointment, see Amy Swerdlow, telephone conversation with Daniel Horowitz, 17 July 1996; on her reaction to the *Daily Worker,* see [Friedan], "Insert-left wing thought." On parallel experiences, see Ellen C. DuBois, *Feminism and Suffrage: The Emergence of an Independent Women's Movement, 1848–1869* (Ithaca, 1978); Sara Evans, *Personal Politics: The Roots of Women's Liberation in the Civil Rights Movement and the New Left* (New York, 1979).

47. Unidentified union official, quoted in Friedan, Horowitz interview.

48. [Betty Friedan], response to questionnaire for Smith College class of 1942, spring 1957, BF-SLRC, 11: 419; Betty Friedan, *The Second Stage*, rev. ed. (New York, 1986), 93; Kate Weigand to author, 10 June 1997.

49. Meltzer, *Friedan*, 29; Nathan Spero, conversation with Daniel Horowitz, New York, N.Y., 16 Jan. 1997. For additional perspectives on Friedan's departure from the *UE News*, see Kelber, interview, 16 Sept. 1995, and Lerner, interview. Lerner shared an office with Friedan during her years at the *UE News* and has noted that the union protected Friedan's position during her first pregnancy. He believes she lost her job during her second one not because she was pregnant but because the drop in the union's membership necessitated cutbacks, and the particular situation on the paper's staff presented the editor with few choices. Lerner has in his possession a document he wrote, dated March 15, 1984, that offers his perspective on Friedan's departure from the *UE News*.

50. Glazer, "Decade of Transition," especially 145–49, and Glazer, "From the Old Left to the New," 584–603, has argued, in ways that may shed light on Friedan's situation, that the isolation of radical pacifists such as A. J. Muste, Dorothy Day, and Bayard Rustin from factional debates, as well as their disillusionment with unions, enabled them to develop a radicalism in the 1940s that served as an important bridge to the radicalism of the 1960s.

51. David Montgomery, interview with Daniel Horowitz, New Haven, Conn., 17 June 1997; Kannenberg, "Impact," especially 311, 315. The precise nature of conflicts within the UE, especially as Goldstein understood them, remains unclear. In his study of Schenectady, Zahavi has emphasized that with white, male ethnic workers, once the backbone of the UE, lessening their commitments to the UE, party members in the UE increasingly appealed to women and African Americans by emphasizing the importance of sexual and racial equality. Moreover, this came at a time when party and UE activists were questioning American involvement in the Korean War, a strong commitment to many white, ethnic men. Thus by 1954, the rank-and-file voted to switch their allegiance from the UE to the IUE: Zahavi, "Passionate Commitments," 544. In addition, Frank Emspak, interview with Daniel Horowitz, Amherst, Mass., 19 July 1996; Nelson Lichtenstein, e-mail to author, 14 April 1996; and Montgomery, interview, all explore the relationship between events in the UE and Goldstein's perspective.

52. Betty Goldstein, "Vacation Time," *UEN*, 17 July 1948, 6–7; Friedan, *Changed My Life*, 16. Filippelli and McColloch, *Cold War in the Working Class*, 149, note the lack of a clear preference between the UE and the IUE among women; they add, however, that married women may have been more loyal to the UE and religious women to the IUE. For a novel

based in part on experiences in the UE in Bridgeport, Connecticut, that captures the drama of the period from World War II to 1956 and the disillusionment of two idealistic organizers, see Gilden, *Between the Hills and the Sea,* especially 102, 510.

53. Harvey Swados, "The Myth of the Happy Workers," *Nation,* 17 Aug. 1958, reprinted in Harvey Swados, *A Radical's America* (Boston, 1962), 111–20, with the quotes on 112, in the title, and on 115; C. Wright Mills, "The New Left," *New Left Review* 5 (Sept./Oct. 1960), reprinted in C. Wright Mills, *Power, Politics and People: The Collected Essays of C. Wright Mills,* ed. Irving L. Horowitz (New York, 1963), 256. On the theme of perceived middle-class orientation of the working class, see Denning, e-mail to author, 15 May 1997. Denning emphasizes how difficult it was for Popular Front radicals to give up one view of the working class and realize the centrality of the lives of African Americans who migrated from southern farms to northern factories. On Swados, see Alan M. Wald, "Harvey Swados," *Encyclopedia of the American Left,* 763–64; Michael R. Bussel, "Hard Travelling: Powers Hapgood, Harvey Swados, Bayard Rustin and the Fate of Independent Radicalism in Twentieth Century America" (Ph.D. diss., Cornell University, 1993), 206–371.

54. One of Carl's projects involved sending to labor papers publicity material that pitched certain products, such as recipes calling for a special brand: Zeserson, telephone conversation. Lyn Tornabene, "The Liberation of Betty Friedan," *McCall's,* May 1971, 138, implies that Carl's shift in career came just before Emily's birth.

55. The quotes are from Amy Swerdlow, "Left-Feminist," 312; Abe Magil to Goldstein; Epstein, "Double Standard." [Flexner], "Woman Question," refers to *UE Fights* three times and *Women Fight* once. Under a pseudonym, Friedan published two articles in *New Masses:* Lillian Stone, "Labor and the Community," *New Masses* 57 (23 Oct. 1945): 3–5; Lillian Stone, "New Day in Stamford," *New Masses* 58 (22 Jan. 1946): 3–5; in identifying Friedan as the author, I am relying on a 22 Sept. 1995 conversation with Kathy Kraft, an archivist at the Schlesinger Library; the Magil letter; Betty Goldstein, "20,000 Stamford Workers Stage Nation's First General Strike Since 1934," *FP,* 4 Jan. 1946, and on material in Betty Goldstein, "Stamford Stages General Strike," *The New World,* 3 Jan. 1946. On the possibility of Friedan's presence at meetings with Flexner, see Mim Kelber, telephone interview with Daniel Horowitz, 7 Feb. 1998.

56. Betty Friedan, "The Lady Looks Like an Angel—But She's Dynamite in the Fight for Progress," *National Guardian,* 31 Jan. 1949. On her own experience in the party, see Annette T. Rubinstein, "The Cultural World of the Communist Party: An Historical Overview," in Brown et al., *New Studies,* 239–60.

57. Susan Levine, *Degrees of Equality: The American Association of University Women and the Challenge of Twentieth-Century Feminism* (Philadelphia, 1995), 71. On the way one woman associated with the UE in the 1940s learned to be silent, see Margaret Darin Stasik, telephone conversation with Daniel Horowitz, 26 July 1996.

58. On her coverage of hearings, see, for example, Goldstein, "In Defense of Freedom!"; B.G., "The Senator Was Indiscreet," *UEN,* 6 March 1948, 11.

59. Betty Friedan, "Was Their Education UnAmerican?" unpublished article, written soon after the summer of 1952, 2–3, BF-SLRC, 11: 415; Dorothy W. Douglas, *Transitional Economic Systems: The Polish-Czech Examples* (London, 1953), 3. For Friedan's skipping over the question of whether McCarthyism affected her before 1963, see Friedan, Horowitz interview. On Douglas, see obituary for Dorothy W. Douglas, *NYT,* 11 Dec. 1968, 47; Jacquelyn D. Hall, "Open Secrets: Memory, Imagination, and the Refashioning of Southern Identity," *AQ* 50 (March 1998): 110–24; *Communist Methods of Infiltration (Education),* Hearings Before Committee on Un-American Activities, House of Representatives, 83d Cong., 1st sess. (Washington, D.C. 1953), 154–59.

60. Edward S. Reed, *James J. Gibson and the Psychology of Perception* (New Haven, 1988), 105–13. SPSSI, founded in 1936, drew activist and progressive psychologists to its ranks, including E. C. Tolman, Ralph Gundlach, James J. Gibson, and Kurt Lewin.

61. Aloise B. Heath to Betty Friedan, postcard, 1 June 1954, BF-SLRC, 7: 313; on William F. Buckley Jr., see Powers, *Not Without Honor,* 282–86; [Betty Friedan and others], draft of letter Dear Alumna, c. 1954, BF-SLRC, 22: 773; corrections to this letter appear to be in Friedan's handwriting; Ronald Reagan, *Where's The Rest of Me?* (New York, 1965), 264. On Reagan, see Schatz, *Electrical Workers,* 10–11; Powers, *Not Without Honor,* 218–21.

62. John M. Glen, *Highlander: No Ordinary School, 1932–1962* (Lexington, Ky., 1988), 136, 142, and the quote in the caption under picture following page 150.

63. On Doyle, see Healey and Isserman, *Dorothy Healey Remembers,* 134. On Gundlach, see Ellen W. Schrecker, *No Ivory Tower: McCarthyism and the Universities* (New York, 1986), 96–105, 125, 233, 284–85, 287, 311, 321–22, 336, with the quote on 101; Reed, *Gibson,* 108–10; Jane Sanders, *Cold War on the Campus: Academic Freedom at the University of Washington, 1946–64* (Seattle, 1979), 35–39, 46, 49, 55–65, 71, 74–75, 97–98, 149, 173–74, 185, 208.

64. On Tolman, see David P. Gardner, *The California Oath Controversy* (Berkeley, 1967), 163–64, 183, 207, 231, 243; Reed, *Gibson,* 111. On Sanford, see Nora Sayre, *Previous Convictions; A Journey Through the 1950s* (New Brunswick, N.J., 1995), 127; on Berkeley, see Sayre, *Previous Convictions,* 124–35; the quotes from the *Los Angeles Times* and Giannini appear in Sayre, *Previous Convictions,* 127–28.

65. Goldstein, "In Defense of Freedom!" For the impact of the bomb on discussions about women and families, see Elaine T. May, "Explosive Issues: Sex, Women and the Bomb," in *Recasting America: Culture and Politics in the Age of Cold War,* ed. Lary May (Chicago, 1989), 154–70. Friedan remained in touch with Bohm, attending his lecture when he returned to the U.S. decades after she met him: David Peat, e-mail to author, 18 July 1997. On the attack on Oppenheimer, see Peter Goodchild, *J. Robert Oppenheimer: Shatterer of Worlds* (London, 1980), 206, 217, 259–66; Caute, *Fellow-Travellers,* 295.

66. F. David Peat, *Infinite Potential: The Life and Times of David Bohm* (Reading, Mass., 1997); Schrecker, *No Ivory Tower,* 135–37, 142–44, 147, 160, 249, 296, and 306–07; Jim Holt, review of Peat, *Infinite Potential, Wall Street Journal,* 23 Jan. 1997. For my statement that Bohm was not involved in espionage, I am relying on Gregg Herken, e-mail to author, 28 Jan. 1997 and on the congressional investigations of 1949. On HUAC's investigations, see *Hearings Regarding Communist Infiltration of Radiation Laboratory and Atomic Bomb Project at the University of California, Berkeley, Calif.,* Committee on Un-American Activities, House of Representatives, 81st Cong., 1st sess. (Washington, D.C., 1949), v–vi, 319–27, 347–53. On Marxism and science, see Russell Olwell, "'Condemned to Footnotes': Marxist Scholarship in the History of Science," *Science and Society* 60 (spring 1996): 7–26. On the press coverage, see the following *NYT* articles: "Spy Inquiry Defied By Princeton Aide," 26 May 1949, 5; William S. White, "Former Atomic Aide Says a Colleague Got Him To Be Red," 11 June 1949, 1, 6; "House Unit Names Scientists as Reds," 22 July 1949, 10; "Named 'Scientist X,' He Denies Charge," 1 Oct. 1949, 1, 4.

67. [Betty Friedan], "Happy New Year, Parkway Village," typewritten poem, Dec. 1952, BF-SLRC, 10: 384; Cedric Belfrage and James Aronson, *Something To Guard: The Stormy Life of the National Guardian, 1948–1967* (New York, 1978); James Aronson, *The Press and the Cold War* (Indianapolis, 1970); Cedric Belfrage, *The American Inquisition, 1945–1960* (Indianapolis, 1973); Sayre, *Previous Convictions,* 271; Robert G. Picard, "Anticommunism in the New York Newspaper Guild," in *With Just Cause: Unionization of the American Journalist* (Lanham, Md., 1991), ed. Walter M. Brasch, 288.

68. Picard, "Anticommunism," 277–92; Daniel Leab, telephone conversation with Daniel Horowitz, 9 July 1996; Denning, *Cultural Front,* 90; Sol Jacobson, "The Fourth Estate: A Study of the American Newspaper Guild" (Ph.D. diss., New School for Social Research, 1960). To catch the flavor of the fight over the orientation of the guild, see "Police Are Blamed in Labor Rackets," *NYT,* 14 March 1947, 16; "Local Here Rebukes News Guild's Head," *NYT,* 20 March 1947, 22; "News Guild Opposes Interference of Reds," *NYT,* 27 June 1947, 4.

69. Doug Reynolds, "Federated Press," *Encyclopedia of the American Left,* 226–27.

70. U.S. Congress, *Report on the Congress of American Women,* 1, 3; Weigand, "Vanguards," 112–17; Swerdlow, "Left-Feminist," 296–312; Swerdlow, "Congress of American Women," 161–62; Swerdlow, *Women Strike for Peace,* 37–40.

71. This summary relies on Schatz, *Electrical Workers,* 167–240, with the membership figures on 217, 232; the 1946 quote is from Harry Block in Schatz, *Electrical Workers,* 181; Filippelli and McColloch, *Cold War in the Working Class,* 93; Zieger, *CIO,* 251. On the role of Richard Nixon, see, Schatz, *Electrical Workers,* 176–77. On the efforts of the Catholic Church, see [Albany] *Evangelist,* quoted in Cochran, *Labor and Communism,* 292. To coordinate its efforts, GE relied on Lemuel R. Boulware, who used his experience in the advertising and market research of home appliances to develop a concerted propaganda campaign to influence the corporation's workers and the larger public. On her coverage of hearings, Goldstein, "UnAmerican Hearing Exposed," 4–5. For the impact of the attack on UE regarding women's issues, see Kannenberg, "From World War to Cold War," 95. For a study of the competition between the UE and IUE on the local level, that includes discussion of fights over women's issues, see Mark McColloch, "The Shop-Floor Dimension of Union Rivalry: The Case of Westinghouse in the 1950s," in Rosswurm, *CIO's Left-Led Unions,* 198–99. What made the situation with the UE especially tense was that with the UE representing workers in many defense plants, anti-communists feared that the union's efforts might hinder the fighting of the Cold War or the Korean War. See, for example, Lester Velie, "Red Pipe Line Into Our Defense Plants," *Saturday Evening Post,* 18 Oct. 1952, 18–21, 106, 108, 110; without making it clear whether he meant a local or national one, Velie, "Red Pipe Line," 108, alleged that anti-communists could not make themselves heard in the union paper.

72. Zahavi, "Passionate Commitments," 529, 538–39, 544–48; Schatz, *Electrical Workers,* 229–30; Ruth Young Jandreau, interview by Ruth Milkman and Meredith Tax, 29 Aug. 1985, quoted in Zahavi, "Passionate Commitments," 545. For a uncooperative witness, see the testimony of Russell Nixon, legislative representative of the UE, author of a regular column in the *UE News,* and John F. Kennedy's economics teacher at Harvard: U.S. Congress, House of Representatives, 83d Cong., 1st sess., *Communist Methods of Infiltration (Government-Labor), Hearings Before the Committee on Un-American Activities* (Washington, D.C., 1953), 1649–83.

73. On the periodical, see David A. Hacker, "Jewish Life/Jewish Currents," *Encyclopedia of the American Left,* 390–91. For an article in which a member of the Hollywood Ten describes government investigations as under "the shadow of anti-Semitism, of ghetto segregation, concentration camps, death," see John H. Lawson, "The Politics of American Anti-Semitism," *JL* 4 (Sept. 1950): 10–13, with the quote on 11; see also Alan Wald, "Culture and Commitment: U.S. Communist Writers Reconsidered," in Brown et al., *New Studies,* 296.

74. See the following articles in *JL* by Rachel Roth: " 'We're Worse Off Every Year,' " 7 (April 1953): 11–14; "A 'Sick' Industry—But the Bosses Don't Suffer," 7 (May 1953): 10–13; "The Price of 'Collaboration,' " 7 (June 1953): 21–24. In identifying Friedan as the likely author, I am relying on the 22 Sept. 1995 conversation with Kathy Kraft. For material on the ILGWU Friedan took over from Milton Meltzer and then drew on for this article, see BF-SLRC, 10: 395. This folder contains material that parallels what appeared in the articles: see, for example, "Table 1: Women's and Misses Outerwear." The folder also contains a reprint from the IBEW's *Electrical Workers' Journal,* Feb. 1950, praising the ILGWU. For background, see Charles R. Allen Jr. and Arthur J. Dlugoff, "McCarthy and Anti-Semitism," *JL* 7 (July 1953): 4–16. On the way depictions of the Rosenbergs were highly gendered, see Virginia Carmichael, *Framing History: The Rosenberg Story and the Cold War* (Minneapolis, 1993), 103. On the responses of some Jews to the case, see Deborah D. Moore, "Reconsidering the Rosenbergs: Symbol and Substance in Second Generation American Jewish Consciousness," *Journal of American Ethnic History* 8 (fall 1988): 21–37.

75. [Betty Friedan], "Rosenberg Poem," probably late June 1953, BF-SLRC, 54: 1966. The document, written on Carl Friedan's business stationery, is in Betty Friedan's handwriting. I date this document at the time of the execution of the Rosenbergs because the prose has an immediacy that such an event would have precipitated. On Friedan's later experience with

threats to her connecting anti-feminism, Communism, and anti-Semitism in a way that might undermine her ability to speak out and to earn money, see Betty Friedan, "Anti-Semitism as a Political Tool: Its Congruence with Anti-Feminism," unpublished speech, c. late 1980s, 6–7, BF-SLRC, 86-M12 . . . 93 M146, 10: 359. For an example of other attacks on her that connected Jews, Communists, and feminists, see a crank letter in BF-SLRC, 54: 1954.

8. The Personal Is Political, 1947–63

1. Among the best books on women in the 1950s are Wini Breines, *Young, White, and Miserable: Growing Up Female in the Fifties* (Boston, 1992); Susan J. Douglas, *Where the Girls Are: Growing Up Female with the Mass Media* (New York, 1994); Elaine T. May, *Homeward Bound: American Families in the Cold War Era* (New York, 1988) and Joanne Meyerowitz, ed., *Not June Cleaver: Women and Gender in Postwar America, 1945–1960* (Philadelphia, 1994). In her own essay in the collection, "Women and Gender in Postwar America, 1945–1960," 1–16, Meyerowitz provides a thoughtful discussion of the various interpretations of women's lives in the 1950s, and rejects what she calls "the conservatism-and-constraints approach" that Friedan articulated in *The Feminine Mystique* and that others, some historians and those in control of the media, have accepted. For two recent collections of essays, one on the postwar period and one on the 1950s, see Lary May, ed., *Recasting America: Culture and Politics in the Age of Cold War* (Chicago, 1989), and Joel Foreman, ed., *The Other Fifties: Interrogating Midcentury American Icons* (Urbana, 1997).

2. Bettye Goldstein, "Through a Glass Darkly," paper written for high school class, 3 April 1938, BF-SLRC, 1: 248; Sondra Henry and Emily Taitz, *Betty Friedan: Fighter for Women's Rights* (Hillside, N.J., 1990), 37; Fred Zeserson, telephone conversation with Daniel Horowitz, 22 June 1996.

3. Myra MacPherson, and Carl Friedan quoted in same, "The Former Mr. Betty Friedan Has Scars to Prove It," probably 1971, newspaper article from unidentified source, women's liberation, biographies, individuals, box 4, folder 31, clippings on Betty Friedan, SSCSC. This paragraph also draws on Zeserson, interview; Paul Wilkes, "Mother Superior to Women's Lib," *NYTM,* 29 Nov. 1970, 141.

4. Friedan, quoted in Wilkes, "Mother Superior," 141; Henry and Taitz, *Friedan,* 40; Wilkes, "Mother Superior," 141; Lyn Tornabene, "The Liberation of Betty Friedan," *McCall's,* May 1971, 138. On violence in the marriage, see also Tornabene, "Liberation," 138; Marcia Cohen, *The Sisterhood: The True Story of the Women Who Changed the World* (New York, 1988), 17–18; MacPherson, "Former Mr. Betty Friedan." Feminists did not discuss domestic violence extensively and in public until the mid-1970s. Nineteen seventy-six was the key year: it was then that NOW established a Task Force on Battered Women and Household Violence, with Del Martin, author of *Battered Wives,* assuming a leadership role. Donald Meyer, "Betty Friedan," in *Portraits of American Women: From Settlement to the Present,* ed. G. J. Barker-Benfield and Catherine Clinton (New York, 1991), 608, notes that Betty Friedan's personal experience with the battered wife syndrome existed before it became part of the feminist agenda, though given her willingness to give as well as take, I do not think her situation fits that term.

5. For information on Parkway Village, I am relying on Morris Kaplan, "20 to 35% Rent Rise Threatens A 585-Family U.N. Community," *NYT,* 29 June, 1, 30; John McKeon, "United Nations' Uneasy Village," *Commonweal* 57 (7 Nov. 1952): 113–15; Ruth Karpf and George Barrett, "Village of All Mankind," *Collier's,* 25 Feb. 1950, 26–27, 34; and material in BF-SLRC, 10: 383. On Queens, see Sylvie Murray, "Suburban Citizens: Domesticity and Community Politics in Queens, New York, 1945–1960," manuscript, November 1995, esp. chapters 1 and 2.

6. Karpf and Barrett, "Village of All Mankind," 26–27.

7. Betty Friedan, *"It Changed My Life": Writings on the Women's Movement,* 1985 edition (New York, 1976), 13–14; Henry and Taitz, *Friedan,* 42.

8. Friedan assumed the editorship with the Feb. 1952 issue and finished with the Feb. 1954 issue: see the relevant issues of *Parkway Villager.*

9. "An International Community Fighting For Its Life—!" flier, c. Sept. 1952, BF-SLRC, 10: 382; Djalal Abdoh, quoted in "Village Profile: Djalal Abdoh," *PV,* May 1952, 2; Kaplan, "Rent Rise," 1, 30; unsigned letter to "Gentleman," at UNICC, 10 June 1956, asking for a return of their deposit: BF-SLRC, 13: 481. To follow the events, see the coverage in *NYT* during 1952: 1 July, 31; 11 July, 9; 20 July, 13; 24 July, 29; 25 July, 19; 26 July, 21; 28 July, 18; 25 Aug., 16; 27 Aug., 26; 4 Sept., 26; 23 Sept., 8; 27 Sept., 19; 28 Sept., 4; 30 Sept., 52; 1 Oct., 40; 2 Oct., 50; 16 Dec., 32; 25 Dec., 41.

10. Kaplan, "Rent Rise"; "U.N. Tells Tenants: Pay More Or Move," *NYT,* 27 Sept. 1952, 19; "Berthoud Named New PVCA Head After Election," *PV,* April 1953, 1; "PVCA Election Results," *PV,* April 1954, 1; "Villagers Mobilizing To Fight Rent Increases," *PV,* May 1952, 1; "Membership Meeting Wed.," *PV,* Feb. 1953, 4.

11. Murray, "Suburban Citizens," 146–47, 176. Contrast this with Friedan's picture of the comfortable and tame politics of suburban communities: Friedan, *Changed My Life,* 16.

12. Murray, "Suburban Citizens," 257–69; George Lipsitz, *Time Passages: Collective Memory and American Popular Culture* (Minneapolis, 1990), 39.

13. Sylvie Murray, "Suburban Citizens," 17–18, 88, 348, with the quotes on 18 and 348.

14. Murray, "Suburban Citizens," 271–76, 351–52; with the quote on 272.

15. "Rents Going Down All Over Queens—Except Here!" *PV,* May 1952, 1; "Landlord Got 100% Rentals For 5 Years," *PV,* May 1952, 1; "Village Profile: Roy Wilkins," *PV,* Feb. 1954, 2. Ralph Bunche, the African American who won the Nobel Peace Prize in 1950, had been a resident: "U.N. Tenants' Fight Gets New Support," *NYT,* 11 July 1952, 19. Eventually, still under Friedan's editorship, *Parkway Villager* returned to its chatty focus: see, for example, the issue of May 1953. BF-SLRC is missing the issues that may have appeared after May 1952 and before January 1953, at the height of the protest; I have been unable to locate copies elsewhere. Friedan, *Changed My Life,* 214 mentions the rent strike.

16. "Village Profile: Nancy Brooks," *PV,* Feb. 1952, 2; "Village Profile: Mary Albright," *PV,* Feb. 1953, 2–3. For other examples, see "Village Profile: Richard Carter," *PV,* April 1952, 2; "Village Vignette," *PV,* July–Aug. 1950, 5. In many instances the *Villager* called women by their first names rather than by Mrs., followed by that of their husbands.

17. Abdoh, quoted in "Djalal Abdoh," 2; "Village Profile: Mrs. Paz Mendez," *PV,* Oct. 1953, 2.

18. Abdoh quoted in "Djalal Abdoh," 2.

19. "Richard Carter," 2. On naming names in a different context, see Victor S. Navasky, *Naming Names* (New York, 1990). This article appeared before *On the Waterfront,* a movie with similar themes but a different political slant, directed by Elia Kazan, that many scholars believe was an anti-communist morality play.

20. "Season's Greetings," *PV,* Jan. 1953, 1–2; [Betty Friedan], "Happy New Year, Parkway Village," typewritten poem, Dec. 1952, BF-SLRC, 10: 384, and marginal comments by an unidentified colleague. Several factors lead me to conclude that Friedan wrote this poem: she was editor, there are several references to her own situation, and the original is in her papers.

21. Betty Friedan, "They Found Out 'Americans Aren't So Awful, After All!'" 2, typescript of article, c. 1955, BF-SLRC, 10: 384; Betty Friedan, "Everyday Diplomats," 3, typescript of article, c. 1956, 1, 4, BF-SLRC, 10: 384; Murray, "Suburban Citizens," 75; Friedan, "They Found Out," 6.

22. Betty Friedan, "Neuroses of Togetherness Women," two-page, handwritten notes, c. 1959, BF-SLRC, 14: 542; Friedan, *Changed My Life,* 14–16; Friedan, Horowitz interview. In Betty Friedan, draft of *The Feminine Mystique,* c. 1961, 778, BF-SLRC, 15: 575, she makes clear that this painful period began when she was pregnant with Jonathan. In her most forceful statement of these themes, she gave 1949 as the turning point because she had been asked to do a piece in 1974 on what had happened a quarter of a century earlier: Betty Friedan, interview by Daniel Horowitz, Santa Monica, Calif., 18 March 1987.

23. My guess as to the timing of the therapy relies on Wilkes, "Mother Superior," 141; Cohen, *Sisterhood,* 69. My conclusion that it was in this same period that she experienced and

overcame the feminine mystique comes from the timing of the therapy and my interpretation of her narrative inspired by her therapy.

24. This and the following paragraphs rely on Friedan, "Neuroses of Togetherness Women"; scattered material in various drafts of Friedan, *The Feminine Mystique,* c. 1961, BF-SLRC, 16: 583, 16: 584, 16: 588, 16: 589. The most focused discussion of these issues is in 15: 575, especially pages 774, 778, 779, 780, 781, 784. Internal evidence makes it possible to date this draft in 1961. The handwritten version of this typed copy is in the same folder; the relevant pages are 1790–1811. Friedan identifies the therapist as a male. My guess is that the therapist was influenced by ego psychology, a school inspired by those who sought to strengthen the ego as Jews faced survival in Europe in the 1930s and 1940s: Michael Zeitlin, "The Ego Psychologists In Lacan's Theory," *American Imago* 54 (summer 1997): 209–32; Michael Zeitlin to author, 30 July 1997, original in author's possession; Nathan G. Hale Jr., *The Rise and Crisis of Psychoanalysis in the United States: Freud and the Americans* (New York, 1995), 48–49, 232–35, 360–62; Christopher Lasch, *The Minimal Self: Psychic Survival in Troubled Times* (New York, 1984). The language of her discussion of her therapy suggests that the therapist was influenced by the "self psychology" of Heinz Kohut, which emerged fully in the 1970s but may have been available in the 1950s: see Paul H. Ornstein, "Introduction," *The Search for the Self: Selected Writings of Heinz Kohut: 1950–1978,* ed. Paul H. Ornstein (New York, 1978); Hale, *Rise and Crisis,* 372–74; Heinz Kohut, *The Restoration of the Self* (New York, 1977); see also D. W. Winnicott, *The Child and the Outside World: Studies in Developing Relationships* (London, 1957), and D. W. Winnicott, *The Child and the Family: First Relationships* (London, 1957). Many members of the psychoanalytic community exiled in the United States during the 1940s and 1950s repressed or minimized any hint of political radicalism as they gave in to pressures from ego psychologists or Neo-Freudians: see Russell Jacoby, *The Repression of Psychoanalysis: Otto Fenichel and the Political Freudians* (New York, 1983); Russell Jacoby, *Social Amnesia: A Critique of Conformist Psychology from Adler to Laing* (Boston, 1975); for a discussion of the pernicious use of psychotherapy in the Cold War, see Navasky, *Naming Names,* 128–43. For stories of conversion experience more dramatic than Friedan's, see John P. Diggins, *Up From Communism: Conservative Odysseys in American Intellectual History* (New York, 1975).

Benjamin Harris, "The Benjamin Rush Society and Marxist Psychiatry in the United States, 1944–1951," *History of Psychiatry* 6 (1995): 309–31, discusses debates within the Old Left about psychiatry. Given what Harris reveals, several things remain unclear: first, whether Friedan attended any of the classes on psychoanalytic thinking at the Jefferson School, and second, whether her deradicalization in the 1950s stemmed in part from the attack on therapy by the party that began in 1949. On the difficulty of finding out about therapists who treated members of the Old Left in the 1950s, see Benjamin Harris to author, 6 August 1997. For additional information on the connection between Marxism and psychology in Old Left circles, see Benjamin Harris, "'Don't Be Unconscious: Join Our Ranks': Psychology, Politics, and Communist Education," *Rethinking Marxism* 6 (spring 1993): 44–75.

25. For this quote, see Friedan, draft of chapter, 779.

26. The suggestive but elusive document on this subject is Betty Friedan, "statement of struggle," a two-page handwritten scenario for a play or story, c. 1962, BF-SLRC, 13: 487. The parallels between Friedan and Douglas, on the one hand, and the figures in the story, on the other, while not exact are nonetheless striking.

27. Dominick La Capra, *History and Memory after Auschwitz* (Ithaca, forthcoming), discusses how trauma causes disruption in memory.

28. Michael Ignatieff, review of Joshua Rubenstein, *Tangled Loyalties: The Life and Times of Ilya Ehrenburg,* in *New York Review of Books,* 12 June 1997, 33; Richard Crossman, ed., *The God that Failed* (New York, 1949); Friedan, *Changed My Life,* 16.

29. Betty Friedan, conversation with Daniel Horowitz, Washington, D.C., 29 March 1995; Paul Goodman and Percival Goodman, *Communitas: Means of Livelihood and Ways of Life* (Chicago, 1947). For a picture of Friedan carrying around a copy of *Communitas* years later,

see Wilkes, "Mother Superior," 27, 29. In a personal communication to the author on 13 April 1997, Taylor Stoehr, an expert on Paul Goodman's life, mentioned the names of some people known by both Goodman and Friedan in the late 1940s.

30. Henry and Taitz, *Friedan*, 45; Cohen, *Sisterhood*, 69. To date these moves, I am relying on a number of sources, including Betty Friedan to Mrs. Clifford P. Cowen, 5 Aug. 1957, BF-SLRC, 7: 313; Betty Friedan, "New York Women: Beyond the Feminine Mystique" *NYHT*, 21 Feb. 1965, SSCSC, WL, 4: 31; "Betty Friedan," *Current Biography Yearbook, 1970*, ed. Charles Moritz (New York, 1971), 146. In describing the house, I am relying on "House for Sale," a flyer in BF-SLRC, 54: 1952. For the history of the house, see Terry Talley, *Oh, What a Grand View: The Story of the Village of Grand View-on-Hudson, New York* (n.p., 1989), 75–76. For the statistics on house prices in the area, see *Rockland County Data Book* (New City, N.Y., 1957), 48.

31. Rockland County Planning Board, *Rockland County Data Book* (New City, 1959), 47; Robert Samuels, "Growing Up in Grand View," in *Kirmess Journal* (Nyack, N.Y., 1962), 48. Talley, *What a Grand View*, 29–97, tells the story of each house, including information on the residents and their occupations.

32. Lipsitz, *Time Passages*, 39–75, with the quote on 39; for an analysis of this television show in the context of changing notions of ethnicity in the 1950s, see Donald Weber, "Memory and Repression in Early Ethnic Television: The Example of Gertrude Berg and *The Goldbergs*," in *Other Fifties*, ed. Foreman, 144–67. Kenneth T. Jackson, *Crabgrass Frontier: The Suburbanization of the United States* (New York, 1985) is the standard work on the history of suburbs.

33. For information on the changes underway in the county, see *1955 Guide to Rockland County* (Suffern, N.Y., 1955); *Rockland County Data Book* (1957). I am also relying on Raymond F. Wright 2d, conversation with author, Nyack, N.Y., May 29, 1997. For her statement that Rockland was less fancy than Westchester, see Betty Friedan, "Rockland County's 'Pool of Brains,'" rough draft of article, 5, c. 1959, BF-SLRC, 9: 348.

34. A. C. Spectorsky, *The Exurbanites* (Philadelphia, 1955), 6, 7, 10, 224–30, 243–44; with the quotes on 7, 228, 229, 230, 244. See also Jhan Robbins and June Robbins, "Rockland County, We Love You!" *This Week*, probably 28 Sept. 1952, 8–9, 35, 52, copy in author's possession.

35. Robbins and Robbins, "Rockland County," 8–9, 35, 52; *Rockland County Data Book* (1957), 22, 45, 63.

36. Of the distinctiveness of Sneden's Landing, see Spectorsky, *Exurbanites*, 67. On Gutman, see Herbert Gutman, "Workers' Search for Power: Labor in the Gilded Age," in *The Gilded Age: A Reappraisal*, ed. H. Wayne Morgan (Syracuse, 1963), 38–68; Betty Goldstein, "UE Strikers Fighting for Us, Say People of Bloomfield," *FP*, 16 Jan. 1946. Leon Fink remembers meeting Paul Robeson's son at the Gutman house: e-mail to author, 29 Oct. 1996. The most relevant of C. Wright Mills's books are *The New Men of Power: America's Labor Leaders* (New York, 1948); *White Collar: The American Middle Classes* (New York, 1951); and *The Power Elite* (New York, 1956). For a derogatory comment on Friedan by Swados, see Harvey Swados, journal entry, 3 June 1963, HS-UMass. For the picture of Emily's peers in the first grade, with six out of nineteen non-whites, see photograph of Emily Friedan's first grade class, BF-SLRC, photograph box, folder 31f.

37. On the overall racial composition of the county, see *Rockland County Data Book* (1957), 44; I am also relying on Daniel Horowitz, conversation with Gloria C. Mayernik, Nyack, N.Y., 29 May 1997. This summary of race issues in the area relies on Carl Nordstrom, "Phoenician Tales: Black-White Relations in Nyack, New York and its Neighborhood, 1686–1967" (n.p., 1989), 217–324, with the Batson quote on 274. Betty Friedan did not sign the statement of support for the African American community: "What Is Brotherhood?" *Journal-News* (Nyack), 20 Feb. 1959, 7.

38. Betty Friedan, "The Intellectual Resources Pool," draft of grant proposal, 1960, 13, BF-SLRC, 9: 352.

39. Cohen, *Sisterhood*, 69–70; Tornabene, "Liberation," 138; David Halberstam, *The Fifties* (New York, 1993), 594. I believe much of what Friedan describes in *Changed My Life*, 15–16, pertains to her years in Parkway Village.

40. Zeserson, conversation; Betty Friedan, "Up From the Kitchen Floor," *NYTM*, 4 March 1973, 8; Tornabene, "Liberation," 138.

41. Tornabene, "Liberation," 138; Friedan, "New York Women," 7; Halberstam, *Fifties*, 593–94; Friedan, *Changed My Life*, 14. See also Jennifer Moses, "She's Changed Our Lives: A Profile of Betty Friedan," *Present Tense* 15 (May–June 1988): 30. On her changing story of filling out the census form and listing "Occupation: Housewife," see Rollene W. Saal, clipping from *Saturday Review*, 21 March 1964, SSCSC women's liberation, biographies, individuals, 4: 31; Harriet Walburn, "Author Boosts Careers for Wives," *Hackensack Record*, 2 May 1963, Class of 1942 folders, Betty Goldstein folder, CASC; Friedan, "Kitchen Floor," 8; Friedan, *Changed My Life*, 16. For evidence that this took place when she responded to a state census form in 1955, see Betty Friedan, "Introduction: The Togetherness Woman," 12, BF-SLRC, 16: 600; for her statement that this also took place after the move to Grand View-on-Hudson, see Friedan, *Changed My Life*, 16.

42. [Betty Friedan], response to questionnaire for class of 1942, spring 1957, BF-SLRC, 11: 419. On the income of her classmates, Betty Friedan: "Are Women Wasting Their Time in College?" unpublished article, 1957–58, 11, BF-SLRC, 12: 427. Henry and Taitz, *Friedan*, 42, discuss the child care arrangements in Parkway Village. I have identified this as Friedan's because of the handwriting and the data she offered on subjects such as the age of her children, where her husband went to college, as well as her politics, religion, and career goals.

43. [Friedan], response to questionnaire.

44. Betty Friedan to Mr. Fischer, 18 Oct. 1958, BF-SLRC, 9: 349; Betty Friedan, "Pied Pipers," rough draft, 3, 7, probably Dec. 1959, BF-SLRC, 9: 347, which dates the earliest thoughts of the program in the spring of 1957, before *Sputnik*. In this sprawling rough draft, there are often different pages with the same number. For evidence of when she began to work out the ideas for articles on the pool, see Friedan to Fischer, 18 Oct. 1958. For information on the pool, I am relying on the material in BF-SLRC, 9: 346–70 and 10: 371–76. This discussion of the pool relies on material in this section of the Friedan papers, with specific references where necessary.

45. "Plans for Saturday Seminars," Community Resources Pool, South Orangetown School District, fall 1962, BF-SLRC, 9: 361. There is some evidence of Friedan's interest during the early 1960s in education reform in urban schools: see [Betty Friedan] markings on Christoper Jencks, "Slums and Schools," *New Republic*, 10 Sept. and 17 Sept. 1962, BF-SLRC, 9: 370. For an invitation to Friedan to join those protesting the one-sided presentation by the American Legion of a movie on HUAC, see Cynthia M. Arvio to Betty Friedan, 22 April 1961, BF-SLRC, 9: 359. For Goode's belief that sexual equality was growing in importance, see Howard Brick, "Age of Contradiction: American Thought and Culture in the 1960s," 109–10, 1997 book ms., copy in author's possession.

46. On her response to the Beats, see Betty Friedan, "The Intellectual Pied Pipers of Rockland County," polished draft, 1960–61, 4, BF-SLRC, 9: 347.

47. Friedan, "Pied Pipers," rough draft, 17. The initial grant was for $13,000 a year. [Betty Friedan], "The Community Resources Pool: A Pilot Project in the Enrichment of Public Education," report for 1960–61, 103–16, BF-SLRC, 9: 358, provided interviews with thirteen students. For twelve of them, the parents' occupations are identified. Of those, five were working class, five were middle and upper-middle class, and two had fathers who did supervisory work in factories. Four of the twelve children came from homes in which the mother had paid employment—as dental technician, factory worker, and school teacher. There are two sets of numbers on this report and I have used those that appear at the top of the page.

48. Friedan, "Pied Pipers," rough draft, 12; *Advanced Study Groups & Intellectual Resources Pool*, pamphlet published by the Rockland Foundation, fall 1959, BF-SLRC, 9: 346. For Friedan's statement of a connection between the pool, the launching of *Sputnik*, and the debate

over American education, see Friedan, "Pied Pipers," rough draft, 2. On her use of common phrases, see Betty Friedan, "Committee of Intellectual Stimulation," handwritten notes, probably fall 1957, soon after *Sputnik,* in manilla folder marked "My own first notes," BF-SLRC, 10: 371.

49. Friedan, "Pied Pipers," rough draft, 12; Friedan, "Committee of Intellectual Stimulation"; Friedan, "Pied Pipers," rough draft, 2; [Friedan], "Community Resources Pool," report 1960–61, 39.

50. Betty Friedan, quoted in David Mallery, *A Community-School Venture: Top Professionals Work With School Students* (Boston, 1963), 8, BF-SLRC, 10: 376; Friedan, "Pied Pipers," rough draft, 23, 28, 49.

51. These observations rely on Friedan, "Pied Pipers," rough draft and Friedan, "Pied Pipers," polished draft.

52. Betty Friedan to Mr. Fischer, 13 Nov. 1958, 4, BF-SLRC, 9: 349. The comparison with later efforts at educational changes relies on [Friedan], "Community Resources Pool," report 1960–61, 33. For evidence of Friedan's interest in the problems professional women faced, see Alice H. Hayden to Alvin Johnson, 25 Nov. 1949, BF-SLRC, 49: 1783. Carl Nordstrom, Edgar Z. Friedenberg, and Hilary A. Gold, *Influence of Ressentiment on Student Experience in Secondary Schools* (Cooperative Research Project no. 1758, Office of Education, U.S. Department of Health, Education, and Welfare, 1965), 2; Edgar Z. Friedenberg, *The Vanishing Adolescent* (Boston, 1959), v, 9, 142–43, with the quotes on 9 and 143. Though sensitive to gendered differences among high school students, when he came to explore a group of students in depth, he focused on boys: see 26–29, 92–113. See also, Carl Nordstrom and Edgar Z. Friedenberg, *Why Successful Students in the Natural Sciences Abandon Careers in Science* (Final Report on Research Project no. 787, U.S. Office of Education, Department of Health, Education, and Welfare, 1961).

53. Edgar Z. Friedenberg, *Coming of Age in America: Growth and Acquiescence* (New York, 1965), xi, 4, 71; for a brief discussion of what he called "sex bias," see 61. Like other social critics of the mid-1960s, when he focused on a distinctive group, it was African Americans.

54. Paul Goodman, *Growing Up Absurd: Problems of Youth in the Organized System* (New York, 1960), 12, 184, 13. Articles from Goodman's book began to appear in print in February 1960, although it is possible that Friedan knew of his arguments before publication. Since Friedan began to work on the rough draft of "Pied Pipers" in late 1959, she articulated some of these issues before the publication of *Growing Up Absurd* in 1960.

55. Friedan, "Pied Pipers," rough draft, 11; *Advanced Study Groups & Intellectual Resources Pool,* fall 1959.

56. Friedan, "Committee of Intellectual Stimulation"; *Advanced Study Groups & Intellectual Resources Pool,* pamphlet published by The Rockland Foundation, fall 1958, BF-SLRC, 9: 346; *Advanced Study Groups & Intellectual Resources Pool,* fall 1959, BF-SLRC, 9: 346; "Classes Taught by Intellectuals," *NYT,* 7 Nov. 1960, 37, copy in BF-SLRC, 9: 369; Betty Friedan, "The Intellectual Resources Pool," draft of grant proposal, 1960, 2, BF-SLRC, 9: 352; [Friedan], "Community Resources Pool," report 1960–61, 3; Friedan, "Pied Pipers," rough draft, 33; [Betty Friedan], markings on Jencks, "Slums and Schools."

57. Unidentified accusers, quoted in [Friedan], "Community Resources Pool," report 1960–61, 40; [Friedan], "Community Resources Pool," report 1960–61, 41. For information on the national efforts of the John Birch Society, see Friedan's newspaper clipping at the time of the local controversy, *NYT,* 28 June 1961, BF-SLRC, 9: 358.

58. "Hartel Warns of Peril in Commie Activity," *Nyack Journal-News,* 9 June 1961, 1–2; [Friedan], "Community Resources Pool," report 1960–61, 42–43, 45, 46; unidentified mother quoted in [Friedan], "Community Resources Pool," report 1960–61, 45.

59. Richard Hofstadter, "The Pseudo-Conservative Revolt," in *The New American Right,* ed. Daniel Bell (New York, 1955), 35; Daniel Bell, "Interpretations of American Politics," in *New American Right,* ed. Bell, 22, 23.

60. Mills, *White Collar,* 54.

61. On her interest in funding from the Ford Foundation, see Friedan to Mr. Fischer, 13 Nov. 1958.

9. Free-lance Writer, 1952–63

1. As far as I can determine, the first piece Friedan wrote on a non-labor topic was "Was Their Education UnAmerican?" unpublished article, written soon after the summer of 1952, BF-SLRC, 11: 415. On her interest in a job at Time, see the letter from a *Fortune* employee in 1952, returning clippings Friedan had sent as evidence of her abilities as a writer: BF-SLRC, 53: 1932.

2. Lyn Tornabene, "The Liberation of Betty Friedan," *McCall's,* May 1971, 138, has a quote from *Redbook* editor saying Friedan wrote articles for magazines she later ended up denouncing; for Friedan's statement of her complicity in contributing to the feminine mystique in her magazine articles, see Betty Friedan, interview with Daniel Horowitz, Santa Monica, Calif., 18 March 1987. On Friedan's career as a free-lance writer, see Marcia Cohen, *The Sisterhood: The True Story of the Women Who Changed the World* (New York, 1988), 70–71, 88–93; Marilyn French, "The Emancipation of Betty Friedan," *Esquire,* December 1983, 512; David Halberstam, *The Fifties* (New York, 1993), 594–95; Sondra Henry and Emily Taitz, *Betty Friedan: Fighter for Women's Rights* (Hillside, N.J., 1990), 43–44; Milton Meltzer, *Betty Friedan: A Voice for Women's Rights* (New York, 1985), 29–30; Tornabene, "Liberation of Betty Friedan," 138; Paul Wilkes, "Mother Superior to Women's Lib," *NYTM,* 29 Nov. 1970, 141.

3. I explore these issues in Daniel Horowitz, *Vance Packard and American Social Criticism* (Chapel Hill, 1994).

4. Friedan, *The Feminine Mystique* (New York, 1963), 34, 36. Among the useful summaries of the world of popular magazines is Halberstam, *Fifties,* 590–92.

5. On her discussion of magazines, see Friedan, *Feminine Mystique,* 33–68; for her statement that in the 1950s magazines offered "only one image of woman," see Betty Friedan, "Feminism in the 1960s," speech at American University, 4 Nov. 1996, broadcast on C-SPAN. Joanne Meyerowitz, "Beyond the Feminine Mystique: A Reassessment of Postwar Mass Culture, 1946–1958," *JAH* 79 (March 1993): 1455–82, with the quotes on 1458 and 1481. For a survey of women's lives in the 1950s that emphasizes their achievements and the varied models they could emulate, see Eugenia Kaledin, *Mothers and More: American Women in the 1950s* (Boston, 1984). Kathryn Keller, *Mothers and Work in Popular American Magazines* (Westport, Conn., 1994), 13–31, emphasizes the persistence of traditional views in the 1950s. For an exploration of some of the strains in the life of a 1950s woman who combined traditional values with an emergent career, see Paul Boyer, "Minister's Wife, Widow, Reluctant Feminist: Catherine Marshall in the 1950s," *AQ* 30 (winter 1978): 703–21. For an analysis of the fiction in women's magazines in the early twentieth century that explores its contradictions, see Jennifer Scanlon, *Inarticulate Longings: The Ladies' Home Journal, Gender, and the Promises of Consumer Culture* (New York, 1995), 138–68.

6. Eva Moskowitz, " 'It's Good To Blow Your Top': Women's Magazines and a Discourse of Discontent, 1945–1965," *Journal of Women's History* 8 (fall 1996): 66–98, with the quotes on 67. For evidence that the discussion of the working mother in popular magazines in the late 1940s and 1950s was more complex (and often more positive) than Friedan claimed, see Jessica Weiss, "To Have and To Hold: Marriage and Family in the Lives of the Parents of the Baby Boom" (Ph.D. diss., University of California-Berkeley, 1994), especially 71–84.

7. Harry Kursh, "How To Make Your Spare Time Pay," draft of article, 2, BF-SLRC, 10: 380; Jhan Robbins, interview with Meg Robbins, Columbia, S.C., 22 Aug. 1996, transcript in author's possession; Jhan Robbins and June Robbins, "Why Young Mothers Feel Trapped," *Redbook,* Sept. 1960, 28–29, 84–88, and Joyce Wike quoted in same, 29; Betty Friedan, grant proposal for Intellectual Resources Pool, 1960–62, BF-SLRC, 9: 352. According to Jhan Robbins, Friedan told him the article he and his wife wrote gave her the idea for her book: Jhan Robbins, notation on copy of article, author's possession.

8. Betty Friedan, "How to Find and Develop Article Ideas," *Writer,* March 1962, 13, 15, reprinted from *Prose by Professionals,* ed. Terry Morris (Garden City, N.Y., 1961); Betty Friedan, "Accomplishments," manuscript, c. 1959, 2, BF-SLRC, 1: 62.

9. An influential book on the origins of 1960s feminism begins with a discussion of Friedan's magazine articles without seeing how they might connect parts of her career: Sara Evans, *Personal Politics: The Roots of Women's Liberation in the Civil Rights Movement and the New Left* (New York, 1979), 3.

10. On her vision of a Gestalt, see French, "Emancipation of Betty Friedan," 512; on the 1957 article, see Betty Friedan, "Day Camp in the Driveways," *Parents' Magazine,* May 1957, 36–37, 131–34.

11. Betty Friedan, "Millionaire's Wife," *Cosmopolitan,* Sept. 1956, 78–87; Friedan, *Feminine Mystique,* 53.

12. Betty Friedan, "The Gal Who Defied Dior," *Town Journal,* Oct. 1955, 33; Betty Friedan, "New Hampshire Love Story," *Family Circle,* June 1958, 40–41, 74–76.

13. Betty Friedan, "Now They're Proud of Peoria," *Reader's Digest,* Aug. 1955, 93–97; the version from which this was condensed is Betty Friedan, "'We Drove the Rackets Out of Our Town,'" *Redbook,* Aug. 1955, 36–39, 86–87. John M. Sumansky, "Peoria: The Growth and Development of a River Town," in *The Middle-Size Cities of Illinois: Their People, Politics, and Quality of Life,* ed. Daniel M. Johnson and Rebecca M. Veach (Springfield, Ill., 1980), 129, discusses reform of Peoria politics and how many nationally syndicated articles appeared on the subject. On the origins of the article, see Friedan, "How to Find," 13–14.

14. Betty Friedan, "I Went Back to Work," *Charm,* April 1955, 145, 200. This article was published seven years after the birth of the Friedan's first child and three years after the arrival of the second, of whom there was no mention in the story. Friedan's article was paired with Gladys Carter, "I Stayed Home," 144, 197, which emphasized the importance of community involvement and questioned excessive domesticity. Friedan had known Gladys Carter in Parkway Village, where they both participated in the community association and did freelance writing: "Village Profile: Richard Carter," *PV,* April 1952, 2. For a how-to article about married women with children who worked part time, see Betty Friedan, "A Part-Time Job May Solve Your Problem," draft of article, no date, BF-SLRC, 13: 471.

15. Friedan, "Was Their Education UnAmerican?" 1–7. For a reference to Dorothy Douglas and her course, without naming her, see Betty Friedan, "Free Education Made Them That Way," c. 1952, 8–9. For evidence that Friedan tried to publish this piece, see BF-SLRC, 53: 1938. For Friedan's file of articles on suburban women, dating as far back as 1953, see BF-SLRC, 2008f.

16. Julie Harris, as told to Betty Friedan, "I Was Afraid to Have a Baby," *McCall's,* Dec. 1956, 68, 72, 74; see also Julie Harris, as told to Betty Friedan, reprinted in a changed version in *Reader's Digest,* April 1957, 42–45. For Friedan's unsuccessful efforts to publish an article on a sculptor who had given up a hard-driving corporate career, gone into psychoanalysis, and then become a successful artist, see material in BF-SLRC, 13: 470; Friedan, interview with Horowitz. The draft has striking parallels to *Lady in the Dark:* Betty Friedan, "Portrait of the Artist as a Young Housewife," BF-SLRC, 13: 470. In response, a male editor at *Redbook* turned down the article, saying it was "concerned with a screamingly neurotic woman with whom our readers would have great difficulty identifying right from the start": Robert Stein to Marie Rodell, 21 Oct. 1955, BF-SLRC, 53: 1932. For a moving statement on the problems women face, see [Betty Friedan], "It is so hard . . . ," one-page document, BF-SLRC, 13: 486.

17. On her own experience with childbirth, see Friedan, "How to Find," 14.

18. Betty Friedan, "Teenage Girl in Trouble," *Coronet,* March 1958, 163–68. For a study of the discussions about problem teenagers, see James Gilbert, *A Cycle of Outrage: America's Reaction to the Juvenile Delinquent in the 1950s* (New York, 1986).

19. Marian Stone and Harold Stone [fictitious names], as told to Betty Friedan, "With Love We Live . . . ," *Coronet,* July 1957, 135–44, with quote on 144.

20. Betty Friedan, "Two Are an Island," *Mademoiselle,* July 1955, 88–89, 100–101, with quotes on 88 and 101.

21. Friedan, "How to Find," 12; Betty Friedan, "The Happy Families of Hickory Hill," *Redbook*, Feb. 1956, 39, 87–90, with quotes on 39 and 87; Betty Friedan, "'We Built a Community for Our Children,'" *Redbook*, March 1955, 42–45, 62–63. Friedan also explored the possibility of writing an article on the problematic nature of the cooperation involved in developing Usonia, a Frank Lloyd Wright–inspired community: Betty Friedan to Marie [Rodell], 21 March 1955, BF-SLRC, 11: 402.

22. Alexis de Tocqueville, quoted in Betty Friedan, "Business Problems? Call in Plato," *Rotarian*, Aug. 1960, 19, 55–58, with quote on 58.

23. Betty Friedan, "The Coming Ice Age: A True Scientific Detective Story," *Harper's Magazine*, Sept. 1958, 39–45; Friedan, "How to Find," 15; Friedan, quoted in Cohen, *Sisterhood*, 71. On the origin of this article, see Halberstam, *Fifties*, 595.

24. For the material on comprehensive health insurance plans, c. 1953 and the Harlem Child Development Clinic, c. 1954, see BF-SLRC, 13: 464 and 13: 468; on the proposed article on race in New Jersey, see handwritten note from Marie [Rodell] to Betty [Friedan] on a 3 July 1955 *NYT* article on racial integration in Teaneck; on the rejections of her article, see Marie Rodell to Betty [Friedan], 23 March 1961, BF-SLRC, 5: 1938. The pace of her writing becomes clear through an examination of her files on her free-lance work, especially when compared with the files in the same years of Vance Packard. On the process of getting articles published, see Friedan, Horowitz interview and Friedan, "How to Find," 14, in which she talked of learning not to write on speculation; for multiple rejection letters in response to her articles in the 1950s, see BF-SLRC, 53: 1938; in "Feminism in the 1960s," Friedan remarked that magazines never rejected her articles. On articles she did not complete, see the materials in BF-SLRC, 10: 385–87, 13: 471–80, and 13: 483. On the consequences of magazines ceasing publication, see, for example, Betty Friedan to Mr. and Mrs. Huntington Hartford, 30 Nov. 1955, BF-SLRC, 11: 407; *Colliers*, which went out of business in late 1956, was originally supposed to publish "The Coming Ice Age": Betty Friedan to Maurice Ewing, 27 Jan. 1957, BF-SLRC, 12: 445. On the length of time it took for an article to come out, see, for example, "New Hampshire Love Story," which appeared in print in June of 1958, even though Friedan began work on it at least as early as January 1955: Betty Friedan to [Charles] Ferguson, 24 Jan. 1955, BF-SLRC, 12: 437; Friedan began work on "Call on Plato" as early as 1956 and it appeared in print August of 1960: Betty Friedan to [Charles] Ferguson, 13 Nov. 1956, BF-SLRC, 12: 447. On projects for other media, see Betty Friedan, "Shooting Script" of story on Mr. and Mrs. Huntington Hartford, BF-SLRC, 11: 408; Betty Friedan to Mrs. [Rhoda] Clark, undated letter concerning television show or movie based on "New Hampshire Love Story," BF-SLRC, 12: 437.

25. Maurice Ewing to Betty Friedan, 24 Jan. 1957, BF-SLRC, 12: 445; Betty Friedan to Joan ———, 11 Oct. [1958], BF-SLRC, 12: 445.

26. On her interest in Fromm and May, see Betty Friedan, handwritten notes for Hickory Hill article, BF-SLRC, 11: 406; on women's skill in home repairs, see Betty Friedan, "The Big Family on Hickory Hill (outline)," 3, draft, BF-SLRC, 11: 406; on her experiments with new ways of writing, see Betty Friedan, "Our Daughter Was Promiscuous," c. 1957, BF-SLRC, 12: 451; Betty Friedan, untitled story beginning "It's been nearly a year," c. 1957, BF-SLRC, 12: 452. In Betty Friedan, "Accomplishments (student and creative)," 3, c. 1960, BF-SLRC, 39: 1363 she discussed her experimentation with writing styles.

27. On the experience with Marshall, see Friedan, *Feminine Mystique*, 36–37. On the South Norwalk community, see Betty Friedan, "To Get a House They Built a Community," draft article, c. 1955, 12–3, BF-SLRC, 10: 388, with statement from unidentified people quoted in Friedan, "To Get a House," 15; Friedan, "We Built A Community," 62. On the Clark story, see Betty Friedan, "New Hampshire Love Story: First Draft," 14, 17, 22, c. 1957, BF-SLRC, 12: 436. What Friedan initially saw as the tale of the independent Yankee spirit, a male editor convinced her to turn into a drama of how a woman achieved independence after her husband's death: James A. Skardon to Marie [Rodell], 2 May 1955, BF-SLRC, 12: 437. In the article on the clothing designer who defied Dior, the changes were subtle. From draft to

published article, Friedan toned down her discussion of the reasons McCardell took a job in a factory during the Depression, made vaguer her discussion of McCardell's family situation, and smoothed over the discussion of working conditions in the garment industry: compare Betty Friedan, "Claire McCardell: Fashion Designer for Young America," 3, 7, 27, first draft, c. 1954, BF-SLRC, 10: 393 with Friedan, "Defied Dior," 33, 97, 98.

28. Betty Friedan, "You Can Go Home Again," 3, 5, 10, 19, 22, c. 1954, BF-SLRC, 11: 397, with the quote on 3; Betty Friedan, letter to Charles Ferguson, 8 June 1954, 3, 7, BF-SLRC, 11: 397. Something similar happened with her article on how businessmen in St. Louis benefited from going back to school. Early drafts made clear what the final version only vaguely hinted at, that their reading of great books would help them counter the pressures for conformity that Sloan Wilson explored in his 1955 novel, The Man in the Gray Flannel Suit. In addition, the drafts revealed Friedan's hope that adult education would help families become more cooperative with housework and less concerned about status: Betty Friedan, "He Doesn't Have to Wear a Grey Flannel Suit," undated draft, BF-SLRC, 12: 450; Betty Friedan, "Memo," on "The Memphis Story," BF-SLRC, 12: 450.

29. Alice Barsky, quoted in Betty Friedan, "'More Than a Nosewiper': Housing Project Mothers Make a Backyard Camp for Their Kids," 2–3, 5, 7, draft of article. c. 1956, BF-SLRC, 10: 378; Harry Janoson, quoted in Friedan, "Nosewiper," 11–12; unnamed participants in the musical, quoted in Friedan, "Nosewiper," 21. Although there is not much evidence that editors were responsible for the changes I note, my knowledge of the pressures on writers for mass-circulation magazines leads me to conclude that the changes came from editors and not from Friedan's self-censorship.

30. Sylvie Murray, "Suburban Citizens: Domesticity and Community Politics in Queens, New York, 1945–1960," manuscript, November 1995, 54–84, with the quotes from Murray on 76 and 84; Friedan, "Nosewiper," 2.

31. On the tension she experienced as a writer, see Friedan, Horowitz interview.

32. On how she hoped to disprove what Lundberg and Farnham had written, see Friedan, Horowitz interview.

33. Betty Friedan, "Up From the Kitchen Floor," NYTM, 4 March 1973, 8–9, includes quote from Redbook editor; Halberstam, Fifties, 596–97. Just before her book came out, Friedan was able to publish excerpts from her forthcoming book: Betty Friedan, "Feminine Fulfillment: 'Is This All?'" Mademoiselle, May 1962, 146–47 and 205–9; "Have American Housewives Traded Brains for Brooms?" Ladies' Home Journal, Jan. 1963, 24, 26. For this piece, a friend from Smith, Neal G. [ilkyson] Stuart, was editor: Neal G. [ilkyson] Stuart to Marie Rodell, 19 July 1962, BF-SLRC, 13: 460.

34. Betty Friedan, "I say: Women are people too!" Good Housekeeping, Sept. 1960, 59–61, 161–62; Betty Goldstein Friedan, "If One Generation Can Ever Tell Another," SAQ, Feb. 1961, 68–70, with the quotes on 69, 70; Susan Ware, "American Women in the 1950s: Nonpartisan Politics and Women's Politicization," in Women, Politics, and Change, ed. Louise A. Tilly and Patricia Gurin (New York, 1990), 290.

35. Friedan, "I say," 59–61, 161–62, with the quotes on 59 and 162.

36. "Betty Friedan," Current Biography Yearbook, 1970, ed. Charles Moritz (New York, 1971), 147; Mrs. George M. Roesler, Jr., Mrs. G. W. McDonald, Jr., Mrs. Michael J. O'Neill, Irene Saylor, Joanne E. Shoestock, letters to the editor, Good Housekeeping, Nov. 1960, 19–20. For additional letters in response to this article, see BF-SLRC, 12: 455.

37. Betty Friedan to Jim Skorden, 17 Oct. 1960, BF-SLRC, 13: 487; Betty Friedan, "A Baked Potato Is Only a Baked Potato," 3, 4, sample column attached to letter to Skardon. According to a letter from him, his name was spelled Skardon: Skardon to [Rodell].

10. The Development of The Feminine Mystique, 1957–63

1. Betty Friedan, "It Changed My Life": Writings on the Women's Movement, 1985 edition (New York, 1976), 6.

2. Betty Goldstein, "UE Drive on Wage, Job Discrimination Wins Cheers from Women Members," *UEN*, 16 Apr. 1951, 6.

3. On her awareness of the relationship between her magazine articles and her book, see Betty Friedan, "Introduction: The Togetherness Woman," 8, BF-SLRC, 16: 600.

4. Justine Blau, *Betty Friedan* (New York, 1990), 49; Marcia Cohen, *The Sisterhood: The True Story of the Women Who Changed the World* (New York, 1988), 96.

5. Cohen, *Sisterhood*, 94; Betty Friedan to Scott Fletcher, 29 Sept. 1959, 1, BF-SLRC, 20a: 707; Carl Friedan, quoted in Cohen, *Sisterhood*, 96; Gloria D. Pond, "Local Author Seeks Commitment For Frustrated American Female," *Rockland Independent*, 7 Feb. 1961; Marie Rodell to George Brockway, 8 Feb. 1961, General Files, 1962, WWN-CU; Marie Rodell to Betty Friedan, 3 Dec. 1961, 86-M12-93 M146, series 6, 27: 718. In the W. W. Norton collection, the A-F files are missing for 1960. I have not found any extended correspondence that would explain how her agent and editors shaped the book. For information on the role of her editor, see Burton Beals, telephone interview by Daniel Horowitz, 9 Feb. 1998.

6. Betty Friedan, "Existentialism," reading notes, BF-SLRC, 15: 568; Betty Friedan, reading notes on Thorstein Veblen, *Theory of the Leisure Class*, BF-SLRC, 15: 568.

7. On Beauvoir, see Betty Friedan, *The Feminine Mystique* (New York, 1963), 10; Simone de Beauvoir, *The Second Sex* (New York, 1953), 698; Betty Friedan, reading notes for Simone de Beauvoir, *Second Sex*, BF-SLRC, 15: 568. In 1975 she stated that from it she learned "my own existentialism" and that eventually she built on the ways it "freed me from the rubrics of authoritative ideology and led me to whatever original analysis of women's existence I have been able to contribute": Friedan, *Changed My Life*, 304. For a comparison of the two writers, see Sandra Dijkstra, "Simone de Beauvoir and Betty Friedan: The Politics of Omission," *Feminist Studies* 6 (summer 1980): 290–303. The man who translated Beauvoir's book had taught zoology at Smith when Friedan was a student in a course (Zoology 12, in her junior year) that he may have been involved with. On his discussion of the parallels between what women and African Americans faced, as well as the employment patterns for American women, see H. M. Parshley, "Translator's Preface," to Simone de Beauvoir, *The Second Sex*, v–xi. It is possible that Friedan's awareness of the hostile reception that leading male intellectuals had given to Beauvoir's book, often cast in anti-feminist and anti-radical terms, made her cautious about acknowledging her indebtedness. On the reaction to Beauvoir, see Dwight Macdonald, "The Lady Doth Protest," *Reporter*, 14 April 1953, 36; Patrick Mullahy, review of *The Second Sex*, *Nation* 176 (21 Feb. 1953): 171–72; William Phillips, "A French Lady on the Dark Continent: Simone de Beauvoir's Impressions of America," *Commentary* 16 (July 1953): 28–29; Dijkstra, "Simone de Beauvoir and Betty Friedan," 290–92; Carol Ascher, *Simone de Beauvoir: A Life of Freedom* (Boston, 1981), 125. On Beauvoir, see the introductions to two symposia: Mary G. Dietz, "Introduction: Debating Simone de Beauvoir," *Signs* 18 (autumn 1992): 74–88; Sonia Kruks, "Introduction: A Venerable Ancestor? Re-Reading Simone de Beauvoir," *Women and Politics* 11 (1991): 53–60.

8. Friedrich Engels, "The Origin of the Family, Private Property and the State," in Karl Marx and Friedrich Engels, *Selected Work in Two Volumes* (Moscow, 1955), 2: 310; Betty Friedan, addition to reading notes on Engels's essay, BF-SLRC, 15: 568. For a similar use of this Engels quote by another Popular Front feminist, see Betty Millard, "Woman Against the Myth: II," *New Masses* 66 (6 Jan. 1948): 7–8.

9. An editor who had been a classmate and fellow journalist at Smith made clear the limited market for writing that focused only on Smith graduates: [Betty Friedan] to Neal [G. Stuart], 22 June [1961 or 1962], BF-SLRC, 20a: 708. See also, unidentified editor at *Reporter* quoted in Marie Rodell to Betty Friedan, 23 March 1962, BF-SLRC, 53: 1937; William B. Hart to Marie Rodell, 28 Feb. 1962, BF-SLRC, 53: 1937; William B. Hart to Marie Rodell, 26 Feb. 1962, BF-SLRC, 53: 1937; PHR to [Marie Rodell], 15 Aug. 1962, BF-SLRC, 53: 1937; Hiram Haydn to Marie [Rodell], 23 Aug. 1962, BF-SLRC, 53: 1937; Marshall O. Donley to Rita Alexander, 12 April 1962, BF-SLRC, 53: 1937. For some earlier correspondence, especially with Neal G. Stuart, see BF-SLRC, 53: 1938. On themes about educated women that others had articulated,

see Paula S. Fass, *Outside In: Minorities and the Transformation of American Education* (New York, 1989), 156–88.

10. Joanne Meyerowitz, "Beyond the Feminine Mystique: A Reassessment of Postwar Mass Culture, 1946–1958," *JAH* 79 (March 1993): 1418, emphasizes how rooted the book was in contemporary discussions; Eric Swenson to Pearl S. Buck, 10 Oct. 1962, Pearl S. Buck Family Trust Archives, quoted in Peter Conn, *Pearl S. Buck: A Cultural Biography* (Cambridge, U.K., 1996), 349. For additional evidence of the awareness of competing books, see Virginia Peterson to George Brockway, 4 Nov. 1962, BF-SLRC, 20a: 713; Betty Friedan, "Note to Myself," c. 1959, BF-SLRC, 15: 572; Betty Friedan, "Introduction: The Togetherness Woman," 27. Also familiar to Friedan, before she began to work on her book, were the authors of many of the studies on which she relied, including works by Erik Erikson, Mary Ann Guitar, Jean Mac-farlane, Margaret Mead, and Nevitt Sanford. Moreover, contemporaries were aware that college-educated women expected to enter the work force and that, in addition, a substantial percentage of women worked for a living. On this, see Mrs. Solon Robinson, editor, *SAQ*, to [Burton] Beals, 15 Oct. 1962, General Files, 1962, WWN-CU.

11. On the media's attention, see Friedan, *Feminine Mystique*, 22. On the response of women active in the league, see Susan Ware, "American Women in the 1950s: Nonpartisan Politics and Women's Politicization," in *Women, Politics, and Change*, ed. Louise A. Tilly and Patricia Gurin (New York, 1990), 291. On the response of some reviewers, see Gail Bederman, personal communication to author. For the response of some readers, see Eva Moskowitz, personal communication to author.

12. For a cautionary note that Friedan not construe the options women faced in either/or terms, as if the choice were between becoming a scientist or remaining a housewife, see Neal G. Stuart to Betty Friedan and Marie Rodell, 16 Oct. 1962, BF-SLRC, 13: 460. It remains unclear whether Friedan, in adopting the position on the importance of paid jobs and cooperative living, was influenced by the debate over the work of Mary Inman in the 1940s. For the quotes from the book, see Friedan, *Feminine Mystique*, 376, 49, 253. Unidentified reader, quoted in Harriet Walburn, "Author Boosts Careers for Wives," *Hackensack Record*, 2 May 1963, Bettye Goldstein folder, Class of 1942 folders, CASC. On the history of housework, which confirms Friedan's evaluation, see Ruth S. Cowen, *More Work For Mothers: The Ironies of Household Technology from the Open Hearth to the Microwave* (New York, 1983); Susan Strasser, *Never Done: A History of American Housework* (New York, 1982).

13. Friedan, *Feminine Mystique*, 366, 75, 276. On homosexuality, masculinity, and the Cold War, see John D'Emilio, "The Homosexual Menace: The Politics of Sexuality in Cold War America," in *Passion and Power: Sexuality in History*, ed. Kathy Peiss and Christina Simmons (Philadelphia, 1989), 226–40; Robert J. Corber, *Homosexuality in Cold War America: Resistance and the Crisis of Masculinity* (Durham, N.C., 1997); Van Gosse, *Where the Boys Are: Cuba, Cold War America and the Making of a New Left* (London, 1993). On the way social and behavioral scientists blamed women, see Ellen Herman, *The Romance of American Psychology: Political Culture in the Age of Experts* (Berkeley, 1995), 279.

14. On her strong political language, see, for example, the tantalizing but brief discussion of the parallel prejudices against feminists, African Americans, and union activists, Friedan, *Feminine Mystique*, 87; the discussion of the connection of the fight for the rights of African Americans and women, *Feminine Mystique*, 92; and the mention of Sojourner Truth, *Feminine Mystique*, 96. The quotes from her book are from *Feminine Mystique*, 80, 89, 90, 91, and 96. The quote from the pamphlet is from [Betty Goldstein], *Women Fight For a Better Life! UE Picture Story of Women's Role in American History* (New York, 1953). Glenna Matthews, *"Just a Housewife": The Rise and Fall of Domesticity in America* (New York, 1987), 217, which examines changing notions of domesticity, discusses the ahistorical nature of Friedan's work.

15. Friedan, *Feminine Mystique*, 34, with the quote on 148, 182; unnamed peace activist, quoted in Friedan, *Feminine Mystique*, 375. On the use of motherhood in this peace movement, see Amy Swerdlow, *Women Strike for Peace: Traditional Motherhood and Radical Politics in the 1960s* (Chicago, 1993).

16. Friedan, *Feminine Mystique*, 305–9, with the quote in the chapter title, 282; Stanley M. Elkins, *Slavery: A Problem in American Institutional and Intellectual Life* (Chicago, 1959), 81–139; Erving Goffman, *Asylums: Essays on Social Situations of Mental Patients and Other Inmates* (Garden City, N.Y., 1961). On Friedan's use of the metaphor, see Joyce Antler, *The Journey Home: Jewish Women and the American Century* (New York, 1997).

17. On her later statement of a connection between Nazi anti-Semitism and anti-feminism, as well as her emphasis on McCarthyism, see Betty Friedan, "Women and Jews: The Quest for Selfhood," *Congress Monthly*, Feb.–March 1985, 11; Betty Friedan, quoted in Amy Stone, "Friedan at 55," *Lilith*, fall 1976, 11–12, 40–41. On the relative isolation of discussions of anti-Semitism and anti-feminism, see Elinor Lerner, "American Feminism and the Jewish Question, 1890–1940," in *Anti-Semitism in American History*, ed. David A. Garber (Urbana, 1986), 305–28.

18. Friedan, *Feminine Mystique*, 319, 326–27, 333, 334–37. Friedan criticized the work of Helene Deutsch and did not discuss the more complex writings on women's psychology by Karen Horney that she had also first encountered as an undergraduate: Friedan, *Feminine Mystique*, 120.

19. On the use of psychology, see Herman, *Romance of American Psychology;* Barbara Ehrenreich, *The Hearts of Men: American Dreams and the Flight from Commitment* (New York, 1983), 88–98. For a later statement of the relationship between psychology and women's oppression, see Naomi Weisstein, " 'Kinder, Kuche, Kirche' As Scientific Law: Psychology Constructs the Female," [1968], in *Sisterhood Is Powerful: An Anthology of Writings from the Women's Liberation Movement*, ed. Robin Morgan (New York, 1970), 228–45.

20. Herman, *Romance of American Psychology*, 276–303, with the quote on 277.

21. On the importance of 1950s journalists, see Daniel Horowitz, *Vance Packard and American Social Criticism* (Chapel Hill, 1994). For the response of someone at Norton, see internal reader's report, 14 April 1959, General Files, 1962, WWN-CU. On the comparison with widely read writers, see Friedan to Fletcher, 2. For the parallel she saw between her book and Galbraith's, see Friedan, "Introduction: The Togetherness Woman," 1. For information on the contract, see Lyn Tornabene, "The Liberation of Betty Friedan," *McCall's*, May 1971, 138. For a critique of the attacks on suburban life, see Scott Donaldson, *The Suburban Myth* (New York, 1969).

22. Friedan, *Feminine Mystique*, 180; see also, 36–37, 180.

23. For my exploration of the new moralism, see Daniel Horowitz, *The Morality of Spending: Attitudes Toward the Consumer Society in America, 1875–1940* (Baltimore, 1985). On the connections with themes in the 1950s, see Betty Friedan, "The Togetherness Woman," book outline, c. 1959, BF-SLRC, 15: 571; Betty Friedan, outline for a television play on suburban conformity, c. 1959, BF-SLRC, 13: 463.

24. For critiques, see Zillah R. Eisenstein, *The Radical Future of Liberal Feminism* (New York, 1981), 177–200. At various times Friedan thought about writing the book with Mary I. Bunting of Radcliffe and a therapist named William Menaker: on Bunting, see Mary I. Bunting, Oral Memoir, Sept.–Oct. 1978, based on interviews by Jeannette B. Cheek, New Boston, N.H., and Weston, Mass., 87, SLRC; on Menaker, see [Betty Friedan], possible titles and authorship for "The Feminine Crisis," c. 1959, BF-SLRC, 13: 505.

25. For stories of the origins of *Feminine Mystique* in her reaction to her classmates' answers to the questionnaires, see Friedan, *Changed My Life*, 17–18; Betty Friedan, "Introduction to the Tenth Anniversary Edition," *Feminine Mystique* (New York, 1974), 2; Cohen, *Sisterhood*, 89–90; David Halberstam, *The Fifties* (New York, 1993), 595–98; Sondra Henry and Emily Taitz, *Betty Friedan: Fighter for Women's Rights* (Hillside, N.J., 1990), 49–51; Tornabene, "Liberation of Betty Friedan," 138; Paul Wilkes, "Mother Superior to Women's Lib," *NYTM*, 29 Nov. 1970, 141; Milton Meltzer, *Betty Friedan: A Voice for Women's Rights* (New York, 1985), 32–33; Sheila Tobias, *Faces of Feminism: An Activist's Reflections on the Women's Movement* (Boulder, 1997), 62–65. On how she saw her task, see Betty Friedan to Mrs. Clifford P. Cowen, 5 Aug. 1957, BF-SLRC, 7: 313. What worried her in 1954, for example, were the attacks on

free speech at Smith and the related questioning of the values of liberal arts education for women: Betty Friedan to editor of *SAQ,* 8 March 1954, BF-SLRC, 12: 425; Betty Friedan: "Are Women Wasting Their Time in College?" unpublished article, 1957–58, BF-SLRC, 12: 427.

26. For the remark on the mental health of her classmates, see handwritten comment by someone other than Betty Friedan, BF-SLRC, 11: 424. For the replies of her classmates, see BF-SLRC, 11: 418–9; for the summaries of the results, see BF-SLRC, 11: 421, 422, 423, 424. The fullest statement of her positive assessment is Betty Friedan, "The Key to the Trap," BF-SLRC, 18: 647. See also, Betty Friedan, draft of chapter, 1644, BF-SLRC, 16: 590. For her statement that she herself broke through the trap, see Friedan, "The Key to the Trap," 770. For additional evidence that early on she emphasized women's ability to solve the problems they faced, see Betty Friedan to Madelin, Barbara, and Bob, 26 Jan. [1959?], BF-SLRC, 20a: 707. These changes explain what Susan Ware noted about the shift in emphasis in Friedan's publications from Betty Goldstein Friedan, "If One Generation Can Ever Tell Another," *SAQ,* Feb. 1961, 68–70 to the 1963 book: Ware, "American Women in the 1950s," 290. For the section that Friedan intended to include as an entire chapter but ended up only as a few pages, see Friedan, *Feminine Mystique,* 357–59. Among the reasons that Friedan may have eliminated the chapter was that, given her strong dislike of her conventional classmates, in the book she did not want to make it appear that their lives turned out well.

27. For the comments of editors at Norton, see LM [?] to George Brockway, WWN-CU, series 2, general file, 1962, Friedan folder; Betty Friedan to Burton Beals, WWN-CU, series 2, catalogued correspondence, Betty Friedan folder; Burton Beals to Betty Friedan, WWN-CU, series 2, catalogued correspondence, Betty Friedan folder. William H. Chafe, *The American Woman: Her Changing Social, Economic, and Political Roles, 1920–1970* (New York, 1972), 199–225; see also anonymous author, "Sex, Marriage, and Divorce: Protestant Therapeutic Culture and The Feminine Mystique, 1950–1965," article submitted to *Journal of Women's History,* copy in author's possession. Especially important here was Friedan's handling of the work of the sociologist Mirra Komarovsky which she might have used to prove that female social scientists were already challenging the feminine mystique: Friedan, *Feminine Mystique,* 12, 132; Friedan, reading notes, BF-SLRC, 13: 498. Shortly after Friedan's book appeared, in October 1963 the American Academy of Arts and Sciences sponsored a conference on American women, with the papers first appearing in the spring 1964 edition of *Daedalus:* Robert J. Lifton, ed., *The Woman in America* (Boston, 1965). See especially Alice S. Rossi, "Equality Between the Sexes: An Immodest Proposal," 98–143. On the debates at Smith in the spring of 1957, see Alice Lane, "Student's Reply Challenges Claim of 'New Identity,'" *Sophia,* 25 April 1957, 2, 4, with the quote on 2. Friedan saw this statement but instead focused on evidence, on the same pages, of anti-intellectualism among Smith students: [Betty Friedan], marginal notes in response to Connie Roberts, "Letter to the Editor Urges New Identity," *Sophian,* 25 April 1957, 2, 4. See also Dorothy Rabin's editorial: D.J.R., "Freshmen Take The Lead," *Sophian,* 25 April 1957, 2. For Friedan's awareness of how some Smith students were rejecting apathy and embracing political and intellectual commitments, see [Betty Friedan], typescript notes, 15–18, BF-SLRC, 14: 527.

28. On the planned chapter, see Friedan, "Togetherness Woman," outline; see Friedan, *Feminine Mystique,* 375 for reference to "mutations," a word she used in the title of the draft chapter on exceptional women. For her negative assessment of data that seems to come from her work on the pool, see Friedan, *Feminine Mystique,* 73. On the way women successfully challenged the mystique, see, for example, Betty Friedan, draft of chapter, 1790, 1797, 1798, BF-SLRC, 15: 575; Betty Friedan, "Outline," 19, BF-SLRC, 15: 573. On what actually appeared in the book, see Friedan, *Feminine Mystique,* especially 233–57, 338–39, 358–60. For her mention of the commission, see Friedan, *Feminine Mystique,* 375.

29. For hints of her larger political vision, see Friedan, *Feminine Mystique,* 370, 374, 375. On her hopes for feminism, see Betty Friedan, book proposal that begins with "*This book," 1, c. 1959, BF-SLRC, 15: 551; for additional evidence of her hope for a revival of feminism, see

Betty Friedan, "The Togetherness Woman," 16, BF-SLRC, 15: 571. For the discussion of Aunt Toms, see handwritten note from unidentified editor, BF-SLRC, 20a: 709. On the parallels to the GI and civil rights bills, see Friedan, "Key to the Trap," 737, 756; Betty Friedan, draft of chapter, 754, 756, BF-SLRC, 15: 575; Betty Friedan, untitled essay, 1743–6, BF-SLRC, 16: 590. For her discussion of James Baldwin's *The Fire Next Time* (1963), see BF-SLRC, 14: 531. Much of Baldwin's book, which was published at the same time as Friedan's, appeared in the *New Yorker* in November 1962. She seems to have focused on the parallels after she finished her book. To gauge how white, liberal intellectuals responded to civil rights before the Greensboro sit-ins of 1960, see Walter A. Jackson, "White Liberal Intellectuals, Civil Rights and Gradualism, 1954–60," in *The Making of Martin Luther King and the Civil Rights Movement*, ed. Brian Ward and Tony Badger (New York, 1996), 96–114.

30. On the middle-class orientation, see Betty Friedan, "Togetherness Woman," BF-SLRC, 14: 527; for a muted suggestion of the class dimensions of what she was describing, see Friedan, *Feminine Mystique*, 26.

31. Fred Zeserson, telephone conversation with Daniel Horowitz, 22 June 1996. On the issue of parallels between prejudice against women, Jews, and blacks, see Betty Friedan, "The Anatomy of Prejudice," handwritten draft of chapter, date uncertain but probably between 1959 and 1964, BF-SLRC, 13: 505; Betty Friedan, "The Key to the Trap," 743 add 1. For a thoughtful discussion of the parallels between the anger women and African Americans felt against white men, see [Betty Friedan], "The Feminine Mystique, Sexual Counter-R," typescript, probably 1964, BF-SLRC, 531. To date Friedan's contact with Murray, I am relying on a bill for typing, submitted by Pauli Murray, probably 1955 or 1956, BF-SLRC, 11: 405. Friedan's agent, who was also Murray's agent, probably arranged for the typing: Rosalind Rosenberg, personal communication to author, winter 1996–97. It appears likely that Friedan and Murray did not meet until 1965: Pauli Murray, *Song in a Weary Throat: An American Pilgrimage* (New York, 1987), 365. On Murray, see Susan J. von Salis, "An Activist's Roots: The Family of Pauli Murray," *Gender and History* 8 (April 1996): 1–3.

32. On her view of women who worked for money, see, for example, Friedan, *Feminine Mystique*, 17, 54, 242; for statistics on women's participation in the work force, see Chafe, *American Woman*, especially 218. Friedan, *Feminine Mystique*, 345–47, only begins to hint at what was in the drafts on volunteer work; for earlier statements, see Friedan to Fletcher, 1; [Betty Friedan], two-page handwritten notes on volunteering, c. 1958, BF-SLRC, 13: 496; [Betty Friedan], handwritten notes on "fulfillment" and "community," c. 1959, BF-SLRC, 497.

33. [Betty Friedan], "Insert-left wing thought," c. 1960, BF-SLRC, 16: 597. For criticism of Friedan for defining women so narrowly in *The Feminine Mystique*, see, for example, bell hooks, *Feminist Theory: From Margin to Center* (Boston, 1984), 1–15.

34. Friedan, "Togetherness Woman," outline. On the death of feminism, see Friedan, *Feminine Mystique*, 15, 100. On guerilla warfare in the home, see Friedan, "*This book," 1; the early drafts of the questionnaires focused more than the final one on the question of what work husbands did around the home: compare drafts in BF-SLRC, 11: 416 with final version in BF-SLRC, 11: 418. For an editor's warning that she had to pay more attention to how husbands might respond to what she said, see note from unidentified editor, c. 1959, BF-SLRC, 15: 584. It is possible that here Friedan was also relying on the notion, common among Popular Front feminists, that capitalism, rather than male dominance, was the problem: on this issue in general, see Kathleen A. Weigand, "Vanguards of Women's Liberation: The Old Left and the Continuity of the Women's Movement in the United States, 1945–1970s" (Ph.D. diss., Ohio State University, 1995), 244.

35. Gerda Lerner to Betty Friedan, 6 Feb. 1963, 20a: 715, BF-SLRC. For information on Lerner's participation in the labor movement and the Congress of American Women, I am relying on Daniel Horowitz, phone conversation with Gerda Lerner, 18 Oct. 1995; Amy Swerdlow, "The Congress of American Women: Left-Feminist Peace Politics in the Cold War,"

in *U.S. History as Women's History: New Feminist Essays,* ed. Linda K. Kerber, Alice Kessler-Harris, and Kathryn K. Sklar (Chapel Hill, 1995), 306.

36. Friedan, *Feminine Mystique,* 205–7, 208, 211, 228. In Betty Friedan, interview by Daniel Horowitz, Santa Monica, Calif., 18 March 1987, she hinted at the connection between "The Sexual Sell" and her years as a labor journalist. Donald Meyer, "Betty Friedan," in *Portraits of American Women: From Settlement to the Present,* ed. G. J. Barker-Benfield and Catherine Clinton (New York, 1991), 604, discusses this chapter as a precursor of themes that socialist feminists would later articulate.

37. Friedan, *Feminine Mystique,* 232, 205–7.

38. Friedan, *Feminine Mystique,* 255. The discussion of male editors, which Friedan did not explicitly connect to the action of male social and behavioral scientists, college and university educators, and corporate executives, is in ibid., 51–54. According to Bunting, Oral Memoir, 87, Friedan expressed considerable anger against men as she was working on the book in the late 1950s.

39. Friedan, *Feminine Mystique,* 207.

40. Ibid., 182, 87, 37, 185. For a somewhat more dramatic use of the Nazi parallel, see Betty Friedan, "Housewife Is Not a Profession," draft of magazine article, 1, BF-SLRC, 13: 460.

41. Friedan, *Feminine Mystique,* 41, 49.

42. Ibid., 309, 333–37, 372, 374, 375, with the quotes on 333 and 100.

43. Ibid., 197, 309.

44. Ibid., 69, 70, 75, 76, 186, 187.

45. Ibid., 9.

46. Ibid., 20, 66, 70, with the quotes on 70 and 186–87.

47. On the change in representations, I am relying on George Lipsitz, *Time Passages: Collective Memory and American Popular Culture* (Minneapolis, 1990), especially 39–75 and on unpublished papers by Donald Weber and Judith Smith. On Mills, for example, see C. Wright Mills, "The New Left," in *Power, Politics and People: The Collected Essays of C. Wright Mills,* ed. Irving L. Horowitz (New York, 1963), 247–59; for the quotes, see C. Wright Mills, *White Collar* (New York, 1951), 354, xvii.

48. At one point, an editor raised questions about Friedan's attack on Margaret Mead as an anti-feminist: handwritten note from unidentified editor, BF-SLRC, 18: 649. For Friedan's critique of female writers, see *Feminine Mystique,* 56–59.

49. Without naming names, Friedan described the decision and consequences of the Smith Board of Trustees to pass over Marjorie Nicolson and instead pick Herbert Davis as president: Friedan, *Feminine Mystique,* 158–59. For a more complicated picture of the education of white women in colleges and universities than Friedan provided, see Fass, *Outside In,* 156–88.

50. Friedan, *Feminine Mystique,* 72–73; see Antler, *Journey Home,* 266–67, for a discussion of the similarities between women in *The Feminine Mystique,* Friedan's mother, and the Jewish mothers portrayed in contemporary fiction. On her guilt over not using her education, see Betty Friedan, interview by Jacqueline Van Voris, 3, New York, N.Y., 17 April 1973, CASC. For her description of the role of the therapist, see Friedan, *Feminine Mystique,* 338.

51. For evidence that Friedan realized that her interviews with women served a therapeutic need for them, see Betty Friedan, one-page handwritten paragraph that begins with "The reason," BF-SLRC, 13: 507. For her ability to convey information on women's lives in a vivid manner, see Friedan, *Feminine Mystique,* 21. On her description of her conversion, see Friedan, *Feminine Mystique,* 66. For an example of how small groups of women gained knowledge together, see Friedan, *Feminine Mystique,* 19.

52. On her strategy of providing the right ideas, see Meyer, "Friedan," 603, 605.

53. Friedan, *Feminine Mystique,* 37, 365–66.

54. Ibid., 36, 50–52, 317, 321, 364. For one origin of Friedan's emphasis on continuing education, see Betty Friedan, "Business Problems? Call in Plato," *Rotarian,* Aug. 1960, 19, 55–58.

55. Friedan, *Feminine Mystique,* 356, 375–77.

56. Friedan, *Changed My Life,* viii.

11. 1963 to the Present

1. Judith Hole and Ellen Levine, *Rebirth of Feminism* (New York, 1971); 14, 17. For biographical information, I am relying on Justine Blau, *Betty Friedan* (New York, 1990); Marcia Cohen, *The Sisterhood: The True Story of the Women Who Changed the World* (New York, 1988); Marilyn French, "The Emancipation of Betty Friedan," *Esquire*, Dec. 1983, 510; Betty Friedan, *"It Changed My Life": Writings on the Women's Movement*, 1985 edition (New York, 1976), especially 5–16; Betty Friedan, interview by Jacqueline Van Voris, New York, N.Y., 17 April 1973, CASC: Betty Friedan, interview by Daniel Horowitz, Santa Monica, Calif., 18 March 1987; Lisa Hammel, "The 'Grandmother' of Women's Lib," *NYT*, 19 Nov. 1971, 52; Sondra Henry and Emily Taitz, *Betty Friedan: Fighter for Women's Rights* (Hillside, N.J., 1990); Milton Meltzer, *Betty Friedan: A Voice for Women's Rights* (New York, 1985); Jennifer Moses, "She's Changed Our Lives: A Profile of Betty Friedan," *Present Tense*, May–June, 1988, 26–31; Lyn Tornabene, "The Liberation of Betty Friedan," *McCall's*, May 1971, 84, 136–40, 142, 146; Mary Walton, "Once More to the Ramparts," *Chicago Tribune Magazine*, 26 Oct. 1981, 16–20; Paul Wilkes, "Mother Superior to Women's Lib," *NYTM*, 29 Nov. 1970, 27–29, 140–43, 149–50, 157; Kathleen Wilson, "Betty (Naomi) Friedan," *Contemporary Authors*, New Revision Series 45 (New York, 1995): 133–36. Betty Friedan, correspondence with Curtis Brown agency, WWN-CU, 1963–74, is especially important for the international impact of book.

There is no full-scale history of NOW or of American feminism since 1963. Among the good places to begin, and on which I am relying for historical material, are Toni Carabillo, *Feminist Chronicles, 1953–1993* (Los Angeles, 1993); Cohen, *Sisterhood;* Jane S. De Hart, "The New Feminism and the Dynamics of Social Change," in *Women's America: Refocusing the Past,* ed. Linda K. Kerber and Jane S. De Hart, 4th ed. (New York, 1995), 539–60; Alice Echols, *Daring to be Bad: Radical Feminism in America, 1967–1975* (Minneapolis, 1989); Sara M. Evans, *Born for Liberty: A History of Women in America* (New York, 1989), 263–314; Jo Freeman, *The Politics of Women's Liberation: A Case Study of an Emerging Social Movement and its Relation to the Policy Process* (New York, 1975); Friedan, *Changed My Life;* Eleanor H. Haney, *A Feminist Legacy: the Ethics of Wilma Scott Heidi and Company* (Buffalo, 1985); Cynthia Harrison, *On Account of Sex: The Politics of Women's Issues, 1945–1968* (Berkeley, 1988); Susan Hartmann, *From Mainstream to Margin: American Women and Politics Since 1960* (New York, 1989); Carolyn Heilbrun, *The Education of a Woman: A Life of Gloria Steinem* (New York, 1995); Aileen Hernandez, *The First Five Years, 1966–71* (Chicago, [1971]); Hole and Levine, *Rebirth;* Blanche Linden-Ward and Carol H. Green, *American Women in the 1960s: Changing the Future* (New York, 1993); Donald G. Mathews and Jane S. De Hart, *Sex, Gender, and the Politics of the ERA* (New York, 1990); Barbara Ryan, *Feminism and the Women's Movement: Dynamics of Change in Social Movement, Ideology, and Activism* (New York, 1992); Sheila Tobias, *Faces of Feminism: An Activist's Reflections on the Women's Movement* (Boulder, 1997); Winifred D. Wandersee, *On the Move: American Women in the 1970s* (Boston, 1988). The papers of NOW, along with oral histories, are at SLRC.

2. Friedan, *Changed My Life,* 13; Betty Friedan, "New York Women: Beyond the Feminine Mystique," *NYHT*, 21 Feb. 1965, 7–15, announced her return to the city a few months earlier.

3. Myra MacPherson, and Carl Friedan quoted in same, "The Former Mr. Betty Friedan Has Scars to Prove It," probably 1971, newspaper article from unidentified source, women's liberation, biographies, individuals, box 4, folder 31, clippings on Betty Friedan, SSCSC.

4. Friedan, quoted in Blau, *Friedan,* 81; Friedan, quoted in Henry and Taitz, *Friedan,* 80; Walton, "Ramparts," 16.

5. In the late 1930s and 1940s Peterson worked in the labor union movement as an educator and lobbyist; in the 1950s she helped launch the first International School for Working Women; in the early 1960s, she assumed a series of important posts in Washington: Harrison, *On Account,* 85–86; Esther Peterson papers, SLRC; Esther Peterson, "The Reminiscences of Esther Peterson" (1983), 82–83, Oral History Collection, Columbia University. Peterson

mistakenly identified Dorothy Douglas as Emily Douglas, but correctly identified her as a professor at Smith and the first wife of Paul H. Douglas.

6. Betty Friedan, quoted in Cohen, *Sisterhood,* 132; Betty Friedan, *Changed My Life,* 83; Lisa Hammel, "They Meet in Victorian Parlor to Demand 'True Equality'—NOW," *NYT,* 22 Nov. 1966, 44. For her statement that "it might not be a bad idea to have a kind of NAACP for women," see Betty Friedan, "Working Women 1965: The False Problems and the True," *Cosmopolitan,* Jan. 1965, 48. Someone involved with this article, perhaps Friedan herself, included African American and Puerto Rican professional women in its coverage.

7. This discussion of NOW's Statement of Purpose relies on Betty Friedan, "Draft: NOW Statement of Purpose," dated 19 Oct. 1966, 9, 9 cont., 11, 22, 23, with the quote on 9 cont., BF-SLRC, 43: 1538; Betty Friedan, "Statement of Purpose," 1966, in Friedan, *Changed My Life,* 87–91. For her authorship, see Friedan, *Changed My Life,* 83. Friedan's 1967 report as president of NOW acknowledged that women in Communist nations enjoyed full equality in the economy, education, and politics, but that they also carried a tremendous burden of housework: Hole and Levine, *Rebirth,* 89.

8. Meltzer, *Friedan,* 50; letters from unidentified sources in BF-SLRC, 52: 1907; 54: 1954, BF-SLRC. On her concern over a bomb threat that connected Zionism, Communism, and feminism and might threaten her role in the women's movement and her livelihood, see Betty Friedan, "Anti-Semitism as a Political Tool: Its Congruence with Anti-Feminism," 6.

9. Unidentified reporter, quoted in Meltzer, *Friedan,* 51; unidentified colleague, quoted in ibid.; Jacqui Ceballos, quoted in Blau, *Friedan,* 61; Henry and Taitz, *Friedan,* 65; Friedan, quoted in ibid., 73.

10. Mary Anne Guitar, interview by Jacqueline Van Voris, Northampton, Mass., 8 Nov. 1973, 33; Leila J. Rupp and Verta Taylor, *Survival in the Doldrums: The American Women's Rights Movement, 1945 to the 1960s* (New York, 1987), 181–83.

11. Paula Giddings, *When and Where I Enter: The Impact of Black Women on Sex and Race in America* (New York, 1984), 308; "Aileen Hernandez," in *Notable Black American Women* (Detroit, 1992), 491–94. On the role of labor feminists in NOW, see Dennis A. Deslippe, "Organized Labor, National Politics, and Second-Wave Feminism in the United States, 1965–1975," *International Labor and Working-Class History* 49 (1996): 143–65.

12. Wandersee, *On the Move,* 44.

13. Freeman, *Politics,* 99.

14. Leaflet of December 1970, quoted in Blau, *Friedan,* 71, and Linden-Ward and Green, *American Women,* 429; Friedan quoted in Henry and Taitz, *Friedan,* 89; Betty Friedan, memorandum to NOW board members, chapter presidents, and governors, 22 Sept. 1969, cited in Hole and Levine, *Rebirth,* 221; Betty Friedan, "Critique of Sexual Politics: An Interview with Betty Friedan," *Social Policy* 1 (Nov./Dec. 1970): 38–40. Among the key texts in radical feminism are Kate Millett, *Sexual Politics* (New York, 1970); Shulamith Firestone, *The Dialectic of Sex: The Case for Feminist Revolution* (New York, 1970): Susan Brownmiller, *Against Our Will: Men, Women and Rape* (New York, 1975).

15. Blau, *Friedan,* 81.

16. Friedan quoted in Henry and Taitz, *Friedan,* 108; Walton, "Ramparts," 16.

17. Betty Friedan, "Up From the Kitchen Floor," *NYTM,* 4 March 1973, 33–34. For another discussion of infiltration by the FBI, see Betty Friedan, tape recorded interview, T97, reel 1, 97–M94, BF-SLRC.

18. Mim Kelber, letter to editor, *NYTM,* 25 March 1973, 20–21. For other reactions, see letters to the editor, as well as Friedan's own reply: *NYTM,* 25 March 1973, 16, 20, 22, 29, 108–09. On the debate over the label of feminist, see Theresa Kaminski, "'What You Call Me Doesn't Scare Me Anymore': Radical Feminists and the Construction of Feminist Identity," unpublished paper, copy in author's possession.

19. Friedan, *Changed My Life,* 187–88; Friedan, quoted in "Mother Spanks Her Offspring," *NYT,* 23 July 1972, 4: 4; Friedan, quoted in Cohen, *Sisterhood,* 350; Betty Friedan, "Betty Friedan's Notebook," *McCall's,* Aug. 1972, 82, 83, 134, 136. For the articles, see Betty Friedan,

"Betty Friedan's Notebook," *McCall's*, June 1971, 32, 34, 36; Aug. 1971, 56, 58, 59; Sept. 1972, 52, 54, 56, 134; Oct. 1971, 69, 71, 72; Nov. 1971, 50, 52, 54; Jan. 1972, 38, 119; March 1972, 58, 60, 62; May 1972, 47, 48, 52; June 1972, 24, 26, 28, 138; Aug. 1972, 82, 83, 134, 136; Nov. 1972, 74, 76, 77, 78, 172; Jan. 1973, 18, 21, 147; April 1973, 67, 108, 110. For the controversy, see Deirdre Carmody, "Feminists Scored by Betty Friedan," *NYT*, 19 July 1972, 43; Deirdre Carmody, "Feminists Rebut Friedan Charges," *NYT*, 20 July 1972, 29. For some of the McCall's columns, see Friedan, *Changed My Life*, 190–254.

20. Betty Friedan, *The Second Stage* (New York, 1981, rev. ed. 1986), 257, 327. In this discussion, I am relying on the revised edition. For a critique of this book, see Susan Faludi, *Backlash: The Undeclared War Against American Women* (New York, 1991), 318–24.

21. Friedan, *Second Stage*, 22, 203.

22. Ibid., 51, 345, 357, 323, 305, 299, 307, 313, 299–307.

23. Betty Friedan, *The Fountain of Age* (New York, 1993), 638.

24. My accounts of her stories rely on a thorough but not exhaustive examination of the published record. Though I have read and listened to some of Friedan's speeches, I do not have access to everything she has said in public settings. On her years in Peoria, Friedan has accurately told of how she developed a sense of herself as someone whose identity as a Jew, a reader, and a brainy girl made her feel freakish and lonely. Yet she has remained largely silent on the local, national, and international political issues that shaped her political consciousness during her adolescence, focusing instead on the painful dynamics of her family life and on the anti-Semitism she and her family experienced on a personal level. On her years at Smith, Friedan has suggested that her lonely life took a turn for the better. She has told the story of how Gestalt psychology and Kurt Koffka were critical in her intellectual development. Given the threat she sensed from McCarthyism after 1947, Koffka was the most convenient mentor for her to highlight. He was the most eminent and the least controversial of her major professors. Unlike Goldstein, he was very much a pro-interventionist Anglophile: on Koffka's Anglophilism, see Mitchell G. Ash, *Gestalt Psychology in German Culture, 1890–1967: Holism and the Quest for Objectivity* (Cambridge, U.K., 1995), 108. Her emphasis on her growing interest in psychology at Smith has overshadowed the few hints Friedan has offered of how as an undergraduate she was radicalized: Betty Friedan, *Feminine Mystique* (New York, 1963), 12; Betty Friedan, interview, in Jacqueline Van Voris, ed., *College: A Smith Mosaic* ([Northampton], 1975), 118–20. Though she has acknowledged how important her Smith years were in terms of the intellectual challenges they posed and the confidence they inspired, she has nonetheless insisted that her education was "divorced from the real world": Friedan, in Van Voris, *College*, 119. Friedan noted in a 1973 interview that she arrived at Smith "as very much an art for art's sake sort," and finished "with a social conscience." Yet Friedan has often been vague about how this transformation took place. In that same interview, for example, she spoke of the existence at Smith of "a tremendous commitment you get that somehow is in the air, a kind of osmosis to commit your abilities to some purpose larger than yourself": Friedan, in Van Voris, *College*, 119.

25. Friedan, Horowitz interview. This was a story, she later said, that was instrumental in "making me into a cliché," even though it was "merely an anecdote": Betty Friedan, quoted in Cohen, *Sisterhood*, 63–64.

26. Rachel C. Ledford to Daniel Horowitz, 6 Nov. 1995, author's possession, summarizes Friedan's talk that evening at the Smithsonian Institution, Washington, D.C. Yet a great deal of what Friedan has told of her life is on the mark. Moreover, the extent to which Friedan, with full consciousness and intentionality, invented aspects of her life remains an open question. In addition, she deserves credit for revealing as much as she did in a key publication in the mid-1970s, and for allowing researchers to examine her papers a dozen years later. Nor is Friedan's self-fashioning anything like what others, such as Bruno Bettelheim, have done, fabrication in order to exaggerate personal accomplishments. In contrast, Friedan decided not to reveal data that would have made her story more interesting and historically significant. Finally, what appears as Friedan's principal, but not sole, reason for distorting her past is

morally reasonable: in the early 1960s, protecting oneself from McCarthyism is an understandable and defensible act. She certainly has every right to talk about her past as she wishes. On the other hand, the historical record paints a different and more compelling picture of her life than she has offered. For other, less justifiable examples of personal reinvention, see Richard Pollak, *The Creation of Dr. B: A Biography of Bruno Bettelheim* (New York, 1997); for a self-fashioning that involved racial passing, see Henry Louis Gates Jr., "The Passing of Anatole Broyard," in *Thirteen Ways of Looking at a Black Man* (New York, 1997), 180–214. Nell I. Painter, *Sojourner Truth: A Life, a Symbol* (New York, 1996), explores the problem of separating life from myth.

27. "About Betty Friedan . . . ," biographical note accompanying Betty Friedan, "How to Find and Develop Article Ideas," *The Writer,* March 1962, 13 [originally published in Terry Morris, ed., *Prose by Professionals* (Garden City, N.Y., 1961)]; dust jacket of 1963 copy of *Feminine Mystique,* author's possession; Betty Friedan, quoted in "Betty Friedan," *Current Biography Yearbook, 1970,* ed. Charles Moritz (New York, 1971), 146; Friedan, quoted in Van Voris, *College,* 119.

28. Friedan, *Feminine Mystique,* 70; Tornabene, "Liberation," 138; Rollene W. Saal, "Author of the Month," *Saturday Review,* 21 March 1964, women's liberation, biographies, individuals, box 4, folder 31, SSCSC; *Hackensack Record,* 2 May 1963, Class of 1942 folders, Betty Goldstein folder, CASC; Friedan, "Kitchen Floor," 8. For mention of her editorial work on the Parkway Village paper, see "About Betty Friedan," 13.

29. Friedan, *Feminine Mystique,* 9, 186–87.

30. For Friedan's psychological conflicts over issues of creativity in writing and motherhood, see Julie Harris, as told to Betty Friedan, "I Was Afraid to Have a Baby," *McCall's,* Dec. 1956, 68, 72, 74. Friedan, "How to Find and Develop Article Ideas," 12–15, has some discussion of these conflicts; for a statement of the issue of pain and creativity she felt in childbirth and writing, see Betty Friedan, "Betty Friedan," one-page typewritten statement, 1956–57, BF-SLRC, 1: 62.

In the late 1950s and early 1960s, right before the story of her life took hold, Friedan had offered a narrative in which she more fully acknowledged her ambition. As a woman who worked with her at Federated Press later noted, Friedan and female college graduates she knew fully expected to have professional careers: Mim Kelber, phone conversation with Daniel Horowitz, 15 Sept. 1995. For a few years beginning in the late 1950s, Friedan admitted that besides "Occupation: Housewife," she did other things as well. She talked about how her work on the pool brought together professionals and school children. In 1957, when she wrote a letter to someone at her alma mater, she emphasized her professional roles and achievements: Betty Friedan to Mrs. Clifford P. Cowen, 5 Aug. 1957, BF-SLRC, 7: 313. A biographical note that accompanied an article she wrote in the early 1960s stated that "Betty Friedan became a free-lance writer" in the 1950s. "Since she could not see suburban housewifery as a full-time way of life, she decided to use it as a basis for free-lance writing": "About Betty Friedan," 13. Once she became famous, a different kind of story spread. "Betty," a reporter later noted of her suburban years, "was being forced into a role she detested." Only when she cut down on the housework she was doing and gave more time to her writing did she feel better and become able to stop going to the analyst. "My trips into the real world to do the interviews and visit editors in New York," Friedan herself noted years later, "was the difference between Betty Friedan in a mental institution or out": Wilkes, "Mother Superior," 141, and Friedan, quoted in same.

The impression that Friedan's suburban captivity shaped *The Feminine Mystique* took awhile to develop. Early reviews drew on the attempt by her publisher to establish Friedan's authority as a writer. W. W. Norton's initial public relations campaign mentioned neither her children nor her status as a suburban housewife. Rather, promotional material called her "eminently qualified to investigate the image of femininity that pervades our culture today," not because of personal experience but because of her training as a psychologist at Smith, her fellowship from Berkeley, her experience as a social science researcher, and the fact that she had "written extensively for leading national magazines": "The Author," *Book Find News* (New

York: Book Find Club, late 1962 or early 1963, issue no. 307, 8, BF-SLRC, 18: 668. Though they often acknowledged elements of her domestic life, a dominant note struck by reviewers of *The Feminine Mystique* was that Friedan's training as a journalist and psychologist qualified her to write the book. At the time, it was not widely acceptable for a journalist to claim she wrote out of her own experience as a frustrated suburban housewife. For early reactions to the book, see, for example, the following reviews: Marya Mannes, *NYHT Books,* 28 April 1963, 1, 11; *Economist,* 10 Aug. 1963, 519; Cynthia Seaton, *Amherst (Mass.) Journal Record,* 11 July 1963, BF-SLRC, 18: 668; transcript of review of *The Feminine Mystique,* on "Woman's Whirl," WDEF-TV Chattanooga, 5 March 1963, BF-SLRC, 18: 669; galleys of review of *The Feminine Mystique* in the *NEA Journal* (Sept. 1963), BF-SLRC, 18: 669; Friedan, quoted in review of *The Feminine Mystique, The Living Church,* 19 May 1963, BF-SLRC, 18: 669; Diane Ravich, review of *The Feminine Mystique, New Leader,* 15 April 1963, 27–29, BF-SLRC, 18: 669. After these initial responses, the story soon took hold that Friedan had written her book out of her frustrations at being a trapped housewife. This perspective obliterated the way early reviews emphasized that her authority came from her training as a psychologist and her accomplishments as a free-lance writer.

Another avenue for finding out how people understood Friedan's life is through the letters she received from readers. For an astute examination of these letters, carried out in a different context, see Elaine T. May, *Homeward Bound: American Families in the Cold War Era* (New York, 1988), 209–17.

31. This essay appears in two versions, one published in 1974 in *New York* magazine, and a second in 1976 in *Changed My Life,* 8–16; some of this summary relies on the section in which she introduced the essay. The 1974 article, which in the book was called "The Way We Were— 1949," was originally published with relatively unimportant differences, but with a more revealing title, as Betty Friedan, "In France, de Beauvoir Had Just Published 'The Second Sex,'" *New York,* 30 Dec. 1974/6 Jan. 1975, 52–55. Throughout this book I rely on the more widely read 1976 version. In Friedan, Horowitz interview, which covered mainly the years up to 1963, she discussed her move to a radical politics even as she emphasized captivity by the feminine mystique beginning in the Berkeley years.

32. Friedan, *Changed My Life,* 6, 8, 9. In 1978, Friedan talked of arguing "violently," when she returned to Peoria, with a high school friend who was a conservative Republican, "about some 'Communistic' idea like health insurance": Betty Friedan, "The E.R.A.—Does It Play in Peoria?" *NYTM,* 19 Nov. 1978, 137.

33. Friedan, *Changed My Life,* 8, 13, 16.

34. Ibid., 6, 9, 12, 16, with the quotes on 12 and 16. In the immediate postwar years, the term "feminist" usually referred to women who were Republicans, independent businesswomen, and professionals. There is at least one exception to her relative silence after 1976: in 1988, Friedan mentioned that in the 1940s, though lacking "conscious feminism," she "became involved in the antifascist left," focusing on "labor unions, working people, poor people, the oppressed": Betty Friedan, quoted in "Jewish Roots: An Interview with Betty Friedan," *Tikkun,* Jan.–Feb. 1988, 25–26. More typically, Friedan has repeated her story. In the November 1996 speech at American University, she returned to this dominant narrative she had first offered in the 1960s. Drawing on her experiences from her years at Smith through her achievements in the 1960s, Friedan talked less than she did in her 1974 article about her radical past. She denied that she learned anything of feminism at Smith, largely because the faculty included no role models other than "neurotic spinsters suffering from penis envy." She mentioned her labor journalism only in passing, never giving any hint of the issues about which she wrote. She acknowledged that she had been an anti-fascist but did not connect this with her feminism or labor activism of the 1940s. As for the postwar years, she mentioned campaigning for Adlai Stevenson but not for Henry Wallace. She minimized what she knew before 1957 about women's issues and women's history. Emphatically insisting that she was indeed a suburban housewife, she did not talk of her role in the rent protest in Parkway Village or in the pool in Rockland County. She asserted that remarkably few women combined marriage and

career in the early 1960s. Only when she discussed the founding of NOW did she mention the contributions of African American and union women. Only when she discussed the period after 1966 did she emphasize how strongly committed she was to progressive social policies and fundamental social change. At one key moment in the question and answer period, she revealed some uncertainty about her relationship to the feminine mystique. In rapid succession, she said she "really did buy it," and then remarked she "certainly was affected by it, I guess I did buy it, for a while": Betty Friedan, "Feminism in the 1960s," speech delivered at American University, 4 Nov. 1996, broadcast on C-SPAN.

35. Friedan, *Changed My Life*, 5, 6–7, 8–9, 14–16, with the quote on 16. She gave 1949 as the turning point because she had been asked to do a piece in 1974 on what had happened a quarter of a century earlier: Friedan, Horowitz interview.

36. The quotes are from "Betty (Naomi Goldstein) Friedan," *The Cambridge Dictionary of American Biography*, ed. John S. Bowman (Cambridge, U.K., 1995), 254; Donald Meyer, "Betty Friedan," in *Portraits of American Women: From Settlement to the Present*, ed. G. J. Barker-Benfield and Catherine Clinton (New York, 1991), 601. Henry and Taitz, *Friedan;* Meltzer, *Friedan;* and Blau, *Friedan,* are the only published sources that make clear that Friedan had extensive experience in the trade union movement, including on women's issues, in the 1940s and early 1950s. For versions of her life by journalists and writers in reference books, see "Friedan," *Current Biography*, 146; Wilson, "Friedan," 134; David Halberstam, *The Fifties* (New York, 1993), 593–94; French, "Emancipation," 510; Wilkes, "Mother Superior"; Tornabene, "Liberation"; Cohen, *Sisterhood*, 68–69; Murray Dubin, "The Friedan Mystique," *San Jose Mercury News*, 12 March 1996, sec. E, p. 5; "Friedan Traces Living History of Feminism," press release, American University, c. 4 Nov. 1996, copy in author's possession; Barbara McGowan, "Betty Friedan," *Handbook of American Women's History*, ed. Angela Howard Zophy (New York, 1990), 221. For historians, see Donald Meyer, *Sex and Power: The Rise of Women in America, Russia, Sweden, and Italy* (Middletown, Conn., 1987), 389; Linden-Ward and Green, *American Women*, 382; Rosalind Rosenberg, *Divided Lives: American Women in the Twentieth Century* (New York, 1992), 138–39; Miriam Schneir, "Betty Friedan: The Feminine Mystique," in *Feminism in Our Time: The Essential Writings, World War II to the Present*, ed. Miriam Schneir (New York, 1994), 48; David A. Horowitz, Peter N. Carroll, and David Lee, *On the Edge: A History of America Since World War II* (St. Paul, 1989), 214–15; Carl N. Degler, *At Odds: Women and the Family in America from the Revolution to the Present* (New York, 1980), 443; Douglas T. Miller, *Visions of America: Second World War to the Present* (St. Paul, 1988), 117, 271; Paul S. Boyer, *Promises to Keep: The United States Since World War II* (Lexington, Mass., 1995), 382; Ellen Herman, "Betty Friedan," in *A Companion to American Thought*, ed. Richard W. Fox and James T. Kloppenberg (Oxford, U.K., 1995), 253; David J. Rothman and Sheila M. Rothman, eds., *Sources of the American Social Tradition* (New York, 1975), 2: 264; Mary P. Ryan, *Womanhood in America: From Colonial Times to the Present*, 2nd ed. (New York, 1979), 223; Paul F. Boller Jr. and Ronald Story, *A More Perfect Union: Documents in U.S. History*, 4th ed. (Boston, 1996), 2: 252; Alan Brinkley, *American History: A Survey*, 9th ed. (New York, 1995), 859–62; James A. Henretta et al., *America's History*, 2nd ed. (New York, 1993), 2: 858, 909–11, 968–69; Hole and Levine, *Rebirth*, 17; David A. Hollinger and Charles Capper, eds., *The American Intellectual Tradition: A Sourcebook*, 2nd ed. (New York, 1993), 2: 344; Kerber and De Hart, *Women's America*, 512; George B. Tindall and David E. Shi, *America: A Narrative History*, brief 2nd ed. (New York, 1989), 901. On the partial use of her 1976 piece, see Henretta, *America's History*, 910. On Friedan's place in textbooks, see Van Gosse, "Consensus and Contradiction in Textbook Treatments of the Sixties," *JAH* 82 (Sept. 1995): 659.

37. On this problem, see Elizabeth V. Spelman, *Inessential Woman: Problems of Exclusion in Feminist Thought* (Boston, 1988).

38. On HUAC's investigation beginning in 1962, see Amy Swerdlow, *Women Strike for Peace: Traditional Motherhood and Radical Politics in the 1960s* (Chicago, 1993), 97–124; on the lack of historical memory of the parallel experiences of Congress of American Women and Women

Strike for Peace, see 39–40. On material in Friedan's papers on WSP, see Women's International Strike for Peace, "National Information Memo # 25," BF-SLRC, 10: 313.

39. Unidentified television show host and Friedan's response, "Hi Mom," broadcast of September 23, 1960, BF-SLRC; on "Jane Crow," see BF-SLRC, 23: 813; on her response to Baldwin, see BF-SLRC, 14: 531.

40. On how Michael Harrington consciously positioned himself and crafted *The Other America* (1961) as part of a somewhat parallel attempt to minimize Old Left connections in order to heighten the impact of his book, as well as to reflect changes in his outlook, see Michael Harrington, *Fragments of a Century* (New York, 1973), 170, 179.

41. Dorothy Dinnerstein, *The Mermaid and The Minotaur: Sexual Arrangements and Human Malaise* (New York, 1976), 258–68. I am grateful to Amy Swerdlow for suggesting that I look at Dinnerstein's book.

42. Swerdlow, *Women Strike*, 40; Friedan, *Changed My Life*, 13; Betty Friedan, *Beyond Gender: The New Politics of Work and Family*, ed. Brigid O'Farrell (Washington, D.C., 1997), 69. On the connection between Old Left and 1960s feminism in Swerdlow's own life, see Swerdlow, *Women Strike*, 5–11.

43. Friedan, "Kitchen Floor," 34. In "Feminism in the 1960s," Friedan commented that "just improbably women like myself" became historical figures in the 1960s. In the world of the CIO and the UE, the notion of entering the "mainstream" had a special meaning: for at least two decades beginning in the mid-1930s the CPUSA had told its members to avoid dual unionism and instead enter mainstream organized labor, even when this involved joining forces with anti-communists or conservatives: Ronald W. Schatz, *The Electrical Workers: A History of Labor at General Electric and Westinghouse, 1923–60* (Urbana, 1983), 230–33. For Friedan's use of "mainstream" to describe where she was during World War II, see Betty Friedan, "Feminism in the 1960s." For discussions of how women think about themselves, see Carolyn G. Heilbrun, *Writing a Woman's Life* (New York, 1988), especially 13, 17, 24, 25; Jill K. Conway, "Introduction," *Written by Herself: Autobiographies of American Women: An Anthology*, ed. Jill K. Conway (New York, 1992), x–xi; Peggy McIntosh, "Feeling Like a Fraud," *Work in Progress*, no. 18. Wellesley, Mass., Stone Center Working Paper Series, 1985; Peggy McIntosh, "Feeling Like a Fraud: Part Two," *Work in Progress*, no. 37. Wellesley, Mass., Stone Center Working Paper Series, 1989.

44. Meltzer, *Friedan*, 23, hints at the limitation that stemmed from her social position.

45. For one example of her description of her experience as a suburban wife that emphasizes domestic chores rather than professional accomplishments, see Friedan, *Second Stage*, 46.

46. Betty Friedan, "Betty Friedan's Notebook," *McCall's*, Jan. 1972, 119. On the debate in NOW over Old Left participants, see Wandersee, *On the Move*, 45.

47. De Hart, "New Feminism," 539–60; De Hart, "New Feminism," 547–48, acknowledges the presence of "a few feminist union activists"; Evans, *Born for Liberty*, 274, discusses the importance of women in the federal government with a "female reform sensibility shaped by the labor movement." Hartmann, *Margin*, 58, recognizes the importance of "labor union activists." Freeman, *Politics*, 50–51, explores the problems inherent in the application of words like reformers, radicals, rights, and liberation to the women's movement. For scholarship regarding the ways women in the 1950s struggled to resist the dominant tendencies of American society, see Eugenia Kaledin, *Mothers and More: American Women in the 1950s* (Boston, 1984); George Lipsitz, *A Life in the Struggle: Ivory Perry and the Culture of Opposition* (Philadelphia, 1988); Susan Ware, "American Women in the 1950s: Nonpartisan Politics and Women's Politicization," in *Women, Politics, and Change*, ed. Louise A. Tilly and Patricia Gurin (New York, 1990), 281–99; Kate Weigand, "The Red Menace, the Feminine Mystique, and the Ohio Un-American Activities Commission: Gender and Anti-Communism in Ohio, 1951–1954," *Journal of Women's History* 3 (winter 1992): 70–94; Swerdlow, *Women Strike*; Rupp and Taylor, *Survival in the Doldrums*.

48. Dorothy Sue Cobble, "Recapturing Working-Class Feminism: Union Women in Post-

war America," in Joanne Meyerowitz, ed., *Not June Cleaver: Women and Gender in Postwar America, 1945–1960* (Philadelphia, 1994), 57–83, especially 72–75; Harrison, *On Account of Sex*, 87. On the persistence of African American women from 1950s to 1960s, see Hartmann, *Margin*, 24–34. On African American women in a central social protest of the 1960s, see Vicki L. Crawford, Jacqueline A. Rouse, and Barbara Woods, ed., *Women in the Civil Rights Movement: Trailblazers and Torchbearers, 1941–1965* (Brooklyn, 1990). For another example of a lack of a clear break between the 1950s and the 1960s, this time for middle-class women, see Susan Levine, *Degrees of Equality: The American Association of University Women and the Challenge of Twentieth-Century Feminism* (Philadelphia, 1995).

49. George Lipsitz, *Time Passages: Collective Memory and American Popular Culture* (Minneapolis, 1990), 42. On the importance of trade unionism in the 1940s, see also George Lipsitz, *Rainbow at Midnight: Labor and Culture in the 1940s* (Urbana, 1994). On the issue of continuity, see Maurice Isserman, *If I Had a Hammer . . . : The Death of the Old Left and the Birth of the New Left* (New York, 1987); Susan Lynn, "Gender and Progressive Politics: A Bridge to Social Activism of the 1960s," in Meyerowitz, *Not June Cleaver,* 103–27; Todd Gitlin, *The Sixties: Years of Hope, Days of Rage* (New York, 1987), 11–71; Robert Korstad and Nelson Lichtenstein, "Opportunities Found and Lost: Labor, Radicals, and the Early Civil Rights Movement," *JAH* 75 (Dec. 1988): 786–811; Isserman, *If I Had A Hammer.* For some examples of this reinterpretation of the 1950s, see Wini Breines, *Young, White, and Miserable: Growing Up Female in the Fifties* (Boston, 1992); Brett Harvey, *The Fifties: A Women's Oral History* (New York, 1993); Lary May, ed., *Recasting America: Culture and Politics in the Age of Cold War* (Chicago, 1989); May, *Homeward Bound*.

We may come to see that for millions of women, the 1940s offered a situation parallel to what Robert Korstad and Nelson Lichtenstein have described for union members and radicals: what E. P. Thompson called a "window of opportunity" in the struggle for social justice. Among the forces at work, the roughly similar consequences of which they have explored for African Americans, were the war-induced economic boom that created new types and levels of economic opportunities, the wartime entry of millions of women into the work force and a smaller but significant number into CIO unions, the commitment of federal agencies to women's advancement, the organizational and ideological leadership of the Communist Party, the generation of a "rights consciousness," and the broadening of public discourse. Following the war, the returning veterans and, more significantly, an employer-led offensive closed that window by isolating Communist-influenced leaders, curbing union ambitions, and undermining the Popular Front coalition. The result, Korstad and Lichtenstein's model suggests, was that when feminism reemerged in the 1960s, "it would have a different social character and an alternative political agenda," transformed by the consequences of the lost opportunities of the 1940s. Korstad and Lichtenstein, "Opportunities," 787, 811; the Thompson quote appears on 811.

50. I am borrowing the term "left feminism" from Ellen C. DuBois, "Eleanor Flexner and the History of American Feminism," *Gender and History* 3 (spring 1991): 84. On these conversations among men, see Irving Howe, "New Styles in 'Leftism,'" [1965] Irving Howe, ed., *Beyond the New Left* (New York, 1970), 19–32, with the quote on 23. On the strains in a dialogue between women of two generations, see Ellen K. Trimberger, "Women in the Old and New Left: The Evolution of a Politics of Personal Living," *Feminist Studies* 5 (fall 1979): 432–61.

51. Kathleen A. Weigand, "Vanguards of Women's Liberation: The Old Left and the Continuity of the Women's Movement in the United States, 1945–1970s" (Ph.D. diss., Ohio State University, 1995), contains the fullest treatment of this continuity, as well as the best bibliography on the issue of women and radicalism in the postwar period. Linn Shapiro, "Red Feminism: American Communism and the Women's Rights Tradition, 1919–1956" (Ph.D. diss., American University, 1996), which came to my attention too late for me to assimilate into the text, makes a strong case for continuity on women's issues among Communists stretching back to 1919.

52. Michael Denning, *The Cultural Front: The Laboring of American Culture in the Twentieth*

Century (London, 1996), 32, notes how most Popular Front feminists, including Elizabeth Hawes, had disappeared from the public scene after the mid-1950s. On Lerner's life, especially her anti-fascism in the 1940s, see Joyce Antler, *The Journey Home: Jewish Women and the American Century* (New York, 1997), 286–91. Weigand, "Vanguards," 296, also points out that Aileen Kraditor, a historian who wrote on women's history in the 1960s, was a party member from 1947 to 1958. Weigand, "Vanguards," 297, notes that Eve Merriam and Lerner worked on a 1951 "Singing of Women," a musical that focused on women's history. On persistence in Kelber's life, see Mim Kelber, "A.F.L.-C.I.O.—for Men Only?" *Nation* 229 (17 Nov. 1979): 490–92. On Abzug, see Bella Abzug, "Bella on Bella," *Moment,* Feb. 1976, 26–29; Antler, *Journey Home,* 267–79. On Hansberry, see Judith E. Smith, "Lorraine Hansberry, *Raisin in the Sun,* and the Politics of Racial Difference," unpublished paper, copy in author's possession.

For the prominent role of Jewish women in 1960s feminism, see Howard M. Sachar, *A History of the Jews in America* (New York, 1992), 833–38. He points to Susan Brownmiller, Shulamith Firestone, and Naomi Weisstein as among NOW's founders; Karen Lipschutz De-Crow as an early official; and Muriel Fox as its executive vice president. Antler, *Journey Home,* especially 259–84, also explores the role of Jewish women in the women's movement.

53. After her graduation from Vassar in 1926, where she majored in labor economics, Katherine P. Ellickson began a career in the labor movement that included involvement in Brookwood Labor College, field work among southern textile and mine workers, and, beginning in the late 1930s, research for the CIO. In 1961 she took on the job of executive director of the President's Commission on the Status of Women. In the early 1960s, she helped create the federal Equal Employment Opportunities Commission. When she died in 1997, the writer of her obituary noted her "lifelong commitment to the women's and union movements": "K. P. Ellickson, 91, A Labor Economist," *NYT,* 13 Jan. 1997, B7. Catherine East, whom Friedan called a "prime mover" in the creation of NOW, both previously and subsequently served as a researcher and executive for federal agencies on women's issues; in the mid-1960s she became the executive director of the Citizens' Advisory Council on the Status of Women: "Catherine East, 80, Inspiration For National Women's Group," *NYT,* 20 Aug. 1996, B6; Friedan quoted in same; see also Catherine East papers, SLRC. Kathryn F. Clarenbach, whom many consider the key figure in the early years of NOW, worked on peace and anti-racism campaigns in Madison, Wisconsin in the 1940s and on the 1948 Wallace campaign: Kathryn Clarenbach interview, in "Documenting the Midwestern Origins of the Twentieth-Century Women's Movement," State Historical Society of Wisconsin, Madison, Wisc. Pauli Murray had a long and distinguished career that began with the civil rights and labor movements in the 1930s and continued with the civil rights and women's movements in the 1960s and 1970s. Worried in 1967 that NOW was focusing too much on the concerns of professional women and opposed to the ERA until 1970, she declined to play a more active role in an organization whose goals she considered too limited: Rosalind Rosenberg to author, 29 Oct. 1996, original in author's possession; Susan J. von Salis, "An Activist's Roots: The Family of Pauli Murray," *Gender and History* 8 (April 1996): 1–3; Pauli Murray, *Song in a Weary Throat: An American Pilgrimage* (New York, 1987). Dorothy Haener, active in the CIO on women's issues in the 1940s, was a founding member of NOW: Dorothy Haener, interview, in "The Twentieth Century Trade Union Woman: Vehicle for Social Change," Oral History project, Institute of Labor and Industrial Relations, University of Michigan and Wayne State University. Mary D. Keyserling was active in the National Consumer League in 1938–41, executive vice chair of the Presidential Commission on the Status of Women, and beginning in 1964 the director of the federal Women's Bureau: finding aid, Mary D. Keyserling papers, SLRC. From the 1920s until her death in 1972, Dorothy Kenyon participated in movements for women, workers, consumers, civil liberties, antifascism, civil rights, legal reform, abortion rights: Susan M. Hartmann, "Dorothy Kenyon," *Notable American Women: The Modern Period* (Cambridge, Mass., 1980), 395–97; Dorothy Kenyon papers, SSCSC. From her participation in the suffrage movement until her involvement in the women's movement in the 1970s, Florence H. Luscomb was active in the advocacy of labor, women's and civil liberties issues: Florence H. Luscomb papers, SLRC;

Ellen Cantarow, *Moving the Mountain: Women Working for Social Change* (Old Westbury, N.Y., 1980), 2–51.

The summary of Lerner's study draws on "Documenting," especially the interviews of Ruth C. Clusen, Clara Day, Mary O. Eastwood, Avronne S. Fraser, Nellie Wilson, Mary L. Munts, Mildred Jeffrey, Virginia Hart, Dorothy Haener, Kathryn F. Clarenbach. Gerda Lerner, "Midwestern Leaders of the Modern Women's Movement: An Oral History Project," *Wisconsin Academy Review*, winter 1994–95, 11–15, provides an important correction to the notion that 1960s feminism emerged spontaneously in that decade and that its leadership was mainly white, middle class.

Among the other historians who have suggested such connections, focusing mostly on women union activists and radicals, are Susan Lynn, *Progressive Women in Conservative Times: Racial Justice, Peace, and Feminism, 1945 to the 1960s* (New Brunswick, N.J., 1992); Michael E. Brown et al., *New Studies in the Politics and Culture of U.S. Communism* (New York, 1993); Lisa Kannenberg, "The Impact of the Cold War on Women's Trade Union Activism: The UE Experience," *Labor History* 34 (spring–summer 1993), 309–23; Nancy F. Gabin, *Feminism in the Labor Movement: Women and the United Auto Workers, 1935–1975* (Ithaca, 1990); Dorothy Healey and Maurice Isserman, *Dorothy Healey Remembers: A Life in the American Communist Party* (New York, 1990). Many of the contributors to Meyerowitz, *Not June Cleaver*, emphasize how the persistence of adversarial traditions in the 1940s and 1950s provided important bridges to social movements in the 1960s. The same is true of several articles in Linda K. Kerber, Alice Kessler-Harris, and Kathryn K. Sklar, ed., *U.S. History as Women's History: New Feminist Essays* (Chapel Hill, 1995), especially Joyce Antler, "Between Culture and Politics: The Emma Lazarus Federation of Jewish Women's Clubs and the Promulgation of Women's History, 1944–1989," 267–95, and Amy Swerdlow, "The Congress of American Women: Left-Feminist Peace Politics in the Cold War," 296–312. Swerdlow, *Women Strike*, explores the connection between social protests by women in the 1940s, 1950s, and 1960s. Ruth Rosen, "The Female Generation Gap: Daughters of the Fifties and the Origins of Contemporary American Feminism," 313–34, in Kerber, Kessler-Harris, and Sklar, *U.S. History as Women's History*, 313–34, explores the relationships among women in generations that span the 1950s and 1960s. Van Gosse, *Where the Boys Are: Cuba, Cold War America and the Making of a New Left* (London: 1993), 1–10, is one of the many sources that explored the origins of post-1960 social movements in the 1950s. For one of the first attempts to incorporate what I wrote in *American Quarterly*, see Tobias, *Faces of Feminism*, 71.

54. Gerald Zahavi, "Passionate Commitments: Race, Sex, and Communism at Schenectady General Electric, 1932–1954," *JAH* 83 (Sept. 1996): 514–48, discusses Helen Quirini as one example of continuity on the local level; Weigand, "Vanguards," 266–307, emphasizes continuity between old and new feminism; Weigand, "Vanguards," 283–88, discusses Eve Merriam's *After Nora Slammed the Door, American Women in the 1960s: The Unfinished Revolution* (Cleveland, 1962), an important precursor of Friedan's book and one, moreover, written by someone with a Popular Front feminist heritage; Rupp and Taylor, *Survival in the Doldrums*, 180, emphasize the contribution of union activists. On the founding of President's Commission and of NOW, see Rupp and Taylor, *Survival in the Doldrums*, 166–86.

55. Friedan, "Kitchen Floor," 28; Pauli Murray, interview, quoted in Rupp and Taylor, *Survival in the Doldrums*, 181.

56. For one of the most powerful critiques of the limited vision that Friedan and second-wave activists offered, see bell hooks, *Feminist Theory: From Margin to Center* (Boston, 1984), 1, 2; see also, Donna Franklin, quoted in Isabel Wilkerson, "Whose Side to Take: Women, Outrage And the Verdict On O. J. Simpson," *NYT*, 8 Oct. 1995, 4: 4. Not having the information on which to make a more informed judgment, hooks and Franklin, both African Americans, seem to have assumed that what shaped Friedan's writing of *The Feminine Mystique* was its author's ignorance of conditions outside affluent suburbs.

57. Wandersee, *On the Move*, 39–42, on the trickiness of political labels in late 1960s, especially given volatile political situation shaped by dramatic events; Betty Friedan, quoted

in "Friedan: Feminism Faces a Backlash," *Washington Post*, n.d. 1968, cited in Wandersee, *On the Move*, 42.

58. Friedan, quoted in *Changed My Life*, 110.

59. Friedan, "Kitchen Floor," 30. For continuity, compare "GEB Presents Union Position to Convention," *UEN*, 23 June 1952, 6–7 and many of the documents in Friedan, *Changed My Life*, 87–145.

60. Most of the books on New York intellectuals, a phrase that in many ways characterizes Friedan, do not include a consideration of her or fully explore the gendered nature of the group or their discourse: Alexander Bloom, *Prodigal Sons: The New York Intellectuals and Their World* (New York, 1986); Richard Pells, *The Liberal Mind in a Conservative Age: American Intellectuals in the 1940s and 1950s* (New York, 1985); Alan M. Wald, *The New York Intellectuals: The Rise and Decline of the Anti-Stalinist Left from the 1930s to the 1980s* (Chapel Hill, 1987); Neil Jumonville, *Critical Crossings: the New York Intellectuals in Postwar America* (Berkeley, 1991). For a thoughtful discussion of the relationship between women and New York intellectuals, see Harvey M. Teres, *Renewing the Left: Politics, Imagination, and the New York Intellectuals* (New York, 1996), 173–203. Hannah Arendt's *Eichmann in Jerusalem* and Mary McCarthy's *The Group* appeared in the same year as Friedan's *Feminine Mystique*. The standard book on neo-Conservatives is Peter Steinfels, *The Neo-Conservatives: The Men Who Are Changing America's Politics* (New York, 1979).

61. The published version of the 1996 speech, on which this summary relies, appeared as Betty Friedan, "History's Geiger Counter," in *Audacious Democracy: Labor, Intellectuals, and the Social Reconstruction of America*, ed. Steven Fraser and Joshua B. Freeman (Boston, 1997), 22–31, with quotes on 22 and 31; Friedan, *Beyond Gender*, 2. In this book, with many of the themes found in "History's Geiger Counter," Friedan reports on discussions she orchestrated in the New Paradigm Seminar at the Woodrow Wilson Center. She calls for moving beyond sexual issues such as abortion, date rape, and pornography. Instead, she makes clear her preference for a reduced work week as a way of reshaping work, family, and economic life.

Acknowledgments

In the end, I and I alone am responsible for what I write in this book. However, I could not have written it without the generous support of people and institutions who helped at every step of the way.

To begin with, I benefited from conversations with students at Smith College who listened as I told them what I had found, and responded with questions that forced me to reconsider my arguments and make clearer my conclusions. In addition, with support from the Committee on Faculty Compensation and Development, I was able to rely on the talents of research assistants. At an early stage, Rachel Ledford examined key documents. In the summer of 1995, Gina Rourke read widely in women's history and, after seeing what I was writing, vigorously pressed me to reconsider some of my conclusions. During the summer of 1996, Julia C. Brown carefully read early chapters and researched sources in the libraries at Smith College. Jennifer L. Hootman tracked down material in Peoria. Tracey Deutsch did the same at the Wisconsin State Historical Society and the University of Wisconsin-Madison. Meir Rinde checked facts and examined illustrations in the libraries of the University of California at Berkeley. With the help of the Radcliffe Research Partnership, Allison Kent responded thoughtfully to drafts, ingeniously tracked down material, and asked probing questions. As I completed my work on the book, Clair Null and Amanda Izzo checked facts and served as sounding boards.

Work on this project underscored how essential librarians are to historical research. At various points, I relied on their help at the Boston Public Library, the Oral History and Manuscripts collections of Columbia University, the Manuscripts Division of the Library of Congress, the Long Island Collection at Queens Borough Public Library, the National Archives, the

331

New York Public Library, the New School for Social Research, Manuscripts and Archives divisions at the Yale University Library. At the Tamiment Institute Library of New York University, Debra E. Bernhardt and her colleagues led me to the rich holdings in the history of American radicalism. Elaine Engst tracked down material on Bettye Goldstein in the James Gibson papers at Carl A. Kroch Library, Cornell University. Janet Wells Greene at the Robert F. Wagner Labor Archives at New York University helped me locate information in the papers of the Newspaper Guild. Jane E. Hodes of the Niebyl-Proctor Marxist Library for Social Research in Oakland responded to my questions about radicalism in Berkeley in the early 1940s. Lauren Lassleben and Bill Roberts helped me find documents at the Bancroft Library of the University of California at Berkeley. Gloria C. Mayernik, the Local History Librarian at the Nyack Library, provided material that helped me understand implications of where Betty Friedan lived beginning in 1956. Harold L. Miller at the State Historical Society of Wisconsin did the same for the Highlander Research and Education Center papers. John A. Popplestone of the Archives of the History of American Psychology at University of Akron responded to my queries about that discipline's past. David L. Rosenberg answered my questions about the UE Archives at the University of Pittsburgh. At Special Collections and Archives of the W. E. B. DuBois Library at the University of Massachusetts-Amherst, Linda Seidman helped me track down material on Friedan in the Harvey Swados papers. Mike Smith of the Archives of Labor and Urban Affairs at Wayne State University helped locate information on Federated Press and the Newspaper Guild.

As this project began and ended, the librarians at Smith College went out of their way to help me. Sika Berger, Christine G. Hannon, Robin C. Kinder, Bruce T. Sajdak, and Pamela A. Skinner, the reference librarians at William Allan Neilson Library, helped me find material in its wonderfully rich collections and elsewhere. Those at interlibrary loan, especially Naomi Sturtevant, brought to Northampton hard-to-find sources. Margery N. Sly, the College Archivist when I began my work, shared with me her seemingly unlimited knowledge of Smith history and guided me to relevant sources about the college's past. Sherrill Redmon, head of the Sophia Smith Collection, helped me discover material in this extensive collection in American women's history. Among the others who helped me with these two collections are Susan Barker, Karen Eberhart, Amy Hague, Kathleen B. Nutter, Margaret R. Jessup, and Nanci A. Young.

As an Honorary Visiting Scholar at the Schlesinger Library of Radcliffe College during 1996–97, I benefited from having an office in which to work, as well as access to the libraries of Harvard University. However, the greatest gift the Schlesinger Library had to offer was the hard work, eager audience, and good company of its staff members whose helpfulness and encouragement never ceased to amaze me. Well before I arrived, Jane S. Knowles, Kathy Kraft, Faith Adiele, Lucy Thoma, and Adelaide Kennedy had sorted the Friedan papers in order to make them accessible to scholars. Mary Maples Dunn, the Schlesinger's director, through her generosity and good humor, made not only Smith College but the Schlesinger Library a supportive environment in which to work. In addition, she gave me permission to quote from the Eleanor Flexner papers. Diane E. Hamer and Sylvia McDowell constantly arranged things so that work and intellectual exchange were pleasures. Anne Engelhart and Jane S. Knowles tracked down sources and asked probing questions. The reference librarians at the Schlesinger, Ellen Shea and Wendy Thomas, never tired of locating new material and suggesting leads. Marie-Hélène Gold and Jacalyn Blume helped me find my way through the visual materials; Kathy Herrlich, the audio; and Ruth Hill, the oral histories. Barbara Haber guided me through the Schlesinger's collection of books in American women's history. Susan von Salis helped connect me to the world via the new technologies, shared with me her knowledge of Pauli Murray, and offered significant suggestions for revision of the manuscript. Deirdre O'Neill taught me how to read Bettye Goldstein's poetry. Kathy Kraft read the manuscript with great care and pointed out things I had missed. Kate Blatt, Bert Hartry, Eva Moseley, Jessa Piaia, and Julia Soyer asked good questions, helped solve problems, and served as sounding boards for my findings. Last but not least were those who did the day-by-day work at the manuscript reading room: Christy Atler, Christine E. Burns, Cary Champlin, May Farhat, Eileen Geoghegan, Byron Jacoby, Marriah Star, Casmira Walker, and Lucy Yen.

Work on this project would not have proceeded so smoothly and quickly without the material assistance I received. The National Endowment for the Humanities awarded me a Fellowship for College Teachers that enabled me to have six months in 1995 to work without interruption. Smith College underwrote a full year sabbatical for 1996–97, without which completion of this manuscript would have taken several more years. During my time away, Robert Averitt, Barbara Day, Rick Millington, and my other colleagues in Smith's thriving American Studies Program did such a good job that I was able to keep my mind on completion of the manuscript and not on my once and future administrative responsibilities. Time and time again, the Committee on Compensation and Faculty Development at Smith College made it possible for me to make research trips and obtain materials. As deans for Academic Development, Professors Donald C. Baumer and

Susan C. Bourque, helped provide funds to pay for research trips and
photographic materials.

I chose to publish this book with the University of Massachusetts Press
because, from the beginning, the director, Bruce Wilcox, and the senior
editor, Clark Dougan, made clear how well they understood the challenges I
faced. As was true with several other people who helped me on this project,
my work with Bruce proved that it was possible for my students to become
my teachers. Long ago, colleagues who had worked with Clark told me what
a pleasure it was to have the support of such a talented historian and editor.
Mickey Rathbun helped turn a manuscript into a book. Catlin Murphy and
Ralph Kaplan lent their expertise to the promotion of the book.

As my work proceeded, I had several opportunities to discuss my findings
and benefit from the reactions of varied audiences. At Smith, I gave talks at
the Project on Women and Social Change and at two Liberal Arts Lun-
cheons. Dean John Connolly invited me to speak before members of the
Board of Trustees. Daniel Borus, Joan S. Rubin, and Robert Westbrook were
instrumental in inviting me to give a talk at the University of Rochester
under the auspices of the Verne Moore Lecture Series of the Department of
History. Robert H. Abzug arranged for me to share my findings with his
colleagues in History and American Studies at the University of Texas at
Austin. At the University of Massachusetts-Amherst, Kathy Peiss made it
possible for me to profit from the responses of students and faculty in the
history department. My talk at the Shepard Street Seminar enabled me to
gauge the reaction of an educated lay audience. Those who attended my
April 1996 talk at the Schlesinger Library responded with a wonderful mixture of proddings and support. Susan A. Crane arranged for me to speak
before her colleagues in history and women's studies at the University of
Arizona.

For help on legal issues, I relied on the advice of William F. Patry of
Cardozo Law School and Richard Kurnit and Edward H. Rosenthal of
Frankfurt, Garbus, Klein and Selz.

In addition, scores of friends, colleagues, and strangers responded to my
questions, listened to my concerns, provided leads, and shared the results of
their own research. Among them are Peter Agree, Joyce Antler, Rosalyn
Baxandall, Lissa Bell, Barton Bernstein, Robert C. Binstock, Alex Bloom,
Don Brown, Kathy Brown, Paul Buhle, Bob Bussel, Jacqui Ceballos, Lizabeth
Cohen, William C. Cooley, Travis Crosby, James E. David, Carl N. Degler,
Michael Denning, Leonard Dinnerstein, Frank Emspak, Joshua B. Freeman,
Marvin E. Gettleman, John M. Glen, Benjamin Harris, Ann Hartman, Caro-
lyn G. Heilbrun, David Hollinger, Maurice Isserman, Kenneth Jackson,

Thomas F. Jackson, Michael Kazin, Linda Kerber, Daniel Leab, Lucy Maddox, Gwendolyn Mink, Eva Moskowitz, Sylvie Murray, Abraham J. Peck, John C. Pettegrew, Meg Robbins, William Rorabaugh, Rosalind Rosenberg, Dorothy R. Ross, Edward Schapsmeier, Alice S. Rossi, Doug Rossinow, Morris Schappes, Patricia Smith, Taylor Stoehr, Amy Swerdlow, Sheila Tobias, Jacqueline Van Voris, Alan Wald, Robert Westbrook, Margaret Whitehead, Karen Winkler, Raymond F. Wright II, and Michael Zeitlin. The notes make clear my debt to the people who let me interview them.

Over the internet, Robert H. Abzug offered a tutorial on psychology in the 1950s and responses to the Holocaust; Paul Boyer, on debates over the meaning of the Bomb; Larry Friedman, on Erik Erikson; Gregg Herken, on the world of Berkeley physicists in the early 1940s; David Hollinger, on American intellectual life; Nelson Lichtenstein, on union politics of the 1930s and 1940s.

In addition to those I have already mentioned, I benefited from responses to my manuscript by a large number and wide range of readers. Each of them brought to their reading distinctive skills that together helped me strengthen the book. At the Schlesinger Library, the Honorary Visiting Scholars of 1996–97 provided sounding boards for my ideas. Yoshiko Tomishima did so as she drew on her abundant knowledge of the history of American women. Nancy Cott, Susan Ware, and Helen Lefkowitz Horowitz gave the manuscript careful readings and my questions thoughtful answers. In addition, I benefited from the cogent and critical readings of people who unstintingly gave of their time and intelligence: Robert H. Abzug, Kevin Boyle, Howard Brick, William H. Chafe, Jane S. De Hart, Rick Fantasia, Van Gosse, Jacquelyn Dowd Hall, Carolyn G. Heilbrun, Lisa Kanenberg, Judith H. Katz, Joanne Meyerowitz, Margery Sly, Ellen Schrecker, Judy Smith, Amy Swerdlow, Elizabeth von Klemperer, and Gerald Zahavi.

Several scholars deserve special mention. Chris Appy, a historian and the editor of the series in which this book appears, gave a draft an extraordinarily precise and sharp reading; moreover, at every step of the way, he gave me encouragement and helped me think through key issues. Ellen Chesler graciously allowed me to examine material she had gathered on Friedan's life in Peoria, and shared with me her perspectives on issues involved in writing Friedan's biography. Sue Cobble made it possible for me to conceive in more complicated ways the relationships between labor and women's issues. Robby Cohen helped me understand the world of college radicals in the late 1930s and early 1940s. As usual, Lynn Dumenil read multiple drafts of my work and at every step of the way listened to my concerns. As an editor, feminist, and historian, Grey Osterud brought to her consideration of my work an extraordinary range of skills that have shaped this book in numerous and profound ways. On key issues, including how Old Left women experienced McCarthyism and chauvinism, she gave me the insights and language I needed to develop my argument. Gina Rourke taught me how to understand a whole set of issues, including the implications of the class dynamics of Friedan's situation. As I was completing the final draft, Ellen C. DuBois gave it an exceptionally helpful reading. What she had to say influenced how I restated my argument at several key points.

Kate Weigand played a special and important role in the development of my thinking and research strategies. In January 1992, we first discussed her work on the connections between the Old Left and post-1963 feminism. These conversations were among the many factors that strengthened my conviction that Friedan's life recapitulated this story. When I finally got around to reading her path-breaking Ph.D. thesis, I benefited immensely from her research and arguments. Our conversations and her dissertation helped me understand the larger contexts of Friedan's life and contributions. At a later point, her reading of my manuscript influenced the final draft in myriad ways.

Finally, in more ways than usual this is a book that benefited from the personal dedication and historian's skills of Helen Lefkowitz Horowitz. This book began with talks in our kitchen in Claremont, California, in the late 1980s and ended with talks on our long walks in Northampton, Massachusetts. Colleague, best friend, scholar, writer, and wife, she made the book possible.

Index

BF stands for Betty Friedan. Page numbers in parentheses, following an endnote number, refer to the page on which the note is found.

337

anti-Communism, 91, 123–24. *See also*
McCarthyism
government investigations, 91, 110, 123–
24 (*see also* FBI)
of national unions, 114, 118, 120, 129,
149, 150
redbaiting, 40, 41, 61, 70, 77–78, 127,
137, 177–78
anti-fascism
of American Communist Party, 55
of BG, Smith College, 44, 68, 71, 77–78
and anti-war position, 58, 60–63, 73,
76, 81–82
learned in class, 42, 46, 47, 48–49, 52–
54
and unions, 71, 78
in Federated Press, 110–11
student radicals, 39–41, 47–49
Anti-Fascist Refugee Committee, 90
anti-feminism
against BF, 229
BF fears backlash, 235
of Douglas Palmer, 64–65
male chauvinism, Leftist, 128, 130
Communist Party, 130, 131, 142
at Federated Press, 104, 106, 120
of Philip Wylie, 97–98
postwar, 128, 140, 142, 149–50, 214–17,
244
in psychology, 96, 128
Antioch Review, 202
anti-Semitism. *See also* Jews; racial issues
in Federated Press, 110
among Jews, 23, 48, 73–74, 277n.12
Leftist politics, linked to, 11, 25–26, 40,
145, 151, 264n.25
in the 1930s, 25–26, 40
omitted in *The Feminine Mystique,* 205
in Peoria (IL), 23, 24, 26, 264n.25
postwar increase, 114
in redbaiting Intellectual Resources Pool,
177
at UC Berkeley, 1940s, 92, 99, 282n.10
anti-war debate, 41, 49, 55–57, 58–59, 60–
63, 67–68, 76–78, 81–82
Anything But Love (Berch), 129
Arendt, Hannah, 254
Arnold, Thurman, 84
Aronson, James, 133, 148–49
"The Aryan Myth" (Gibson), 48
Asian Americans, 90, 92, 111
athletes, female, 228

Atkinson, Ti-Grace, 231
Atomic Energy Act, 1946 (McMahon Act),
116
atomic weapons, 89, 92, 116, 122, 204–5,
243–44, 290n.32
The Authoritarian Personality (Sanford), 95,
147, 178
AYC (American Youth Congress), 40, 41, 56,
59, 112

Baby and Child Care (Spock), 161
Baldwin, James, 243, 316n.29 (211)
Barney, Nora Stanton Blatch, 126
Barsky, Alice, 192
Bartlett, Francis H., 84, 280n.43, 283n.21
(96)
Bateson, Gregory, 100
Batson, Frances, 169
Baxandall, Rosalyn, 131
Beat generation, 172, 175–76
Beauvoir, Simone de, 201, 234, 313n.7
Beecher, Katherine, 105–6, 135, 141
Behavior (Watson), 96
behavioral psychology, 54
Belfrage, Cedric, 133, 148
Bell, Daniel, 178
Berkeley (CA), 88–89. *See also* University of
California at Berkeley
Berlin-Rome axis, 25
Black Legion, 27
Blaine, Anita McCormick, 172
Blau, Justine, 30, 233
Bohm, David, 92–93, 148, 151, 290n.32
(116), 301n.65
bomb, atomic, 89, 92, 116, 122, 204–5,
243–44, 290n.32
Boulware, Lemuel R., 301n.71 (150)
Bradley College, 17
breast-feeding, 187
Brecht, Bertolt, 137
Brewster, Kingman, 56
Bridgman, Olga, 95
Bridgman, P. W., 85
Brown, Helen Gurley, 202
Brown, Warner, 95
Brownmiller, Susan, 326n.52 (251)
Bruner, Jerome, 100
Bryn Mawr Summer School for Women
Workers in Industry, 52, 226
Buck, Pearl S., 65, 98, 202
Buckley, Aloise, 146
Buckley, Priscilla, 104

Daniel Horowitz is Sylvia Dlugasch Bauman Professor of American Studies at Smith College, where he teaches courses in American studies and history. Educated at Yale, Pembroke College Cambridge, and Harvard, he has taught at Harvard University, Wellesley College, Skidmore College, Carleton College, Scripps College, and the University of Michigan. He has held fellowships from the National Endowment for the Humanities, the National Humanities Center, and the Schlesinger Library at Radcliffe College. His publications include *The Morality of Spending: Attitudes Toward the Consumer Society in America, 1875–1940* (1985), *Vance Packard and American Social Criticism* (1994) and *Suburban Life in the 1950s: Selections From Vance Packard's Status Seekers* (1995).